BMW 3- & 5-Series
Service and Repair Manual

A K Legg LAE MIMI and Larry Warren

(1948-272-5AC5)

Models covered

3-Series (E30)
316 (83 to 88), 316i (88 to 91), 318i (83 to 91), 320i (87 to 91), 325i (87 to 91).
Also Touring and Convertible versions of these models

5-Series (E28)
518 (81 to 85), 518i (85 to 88), 525i (81 to 88), 528i (81 to 88), 535i (85 to 88), M535i (85 to 88)

5-Series (E34)
518i (90 to 91), 520i (88 to 91), 525i (88 to 91), 530i (88 to 91), 535i (88 to 91)

Engines covered
1596 cc, 1766 cc, 1795 cc, 1990 cc, 2494 cc, 2788 cc, 2986 cc & 3430 cc

Does not cover Diesel, dohc or V8 engines, or four-wheel-drive models

© Haynes Publishing 1999

A book in the **Haynes Service and Repair Manual Series**

ABCDE
FGHIJ
KL

z

ISBN 1 85960 236 3

British Library Cataloguing in Publication Data
A catalogue record for this book is available from the British Library.

Printed in the USA

Haynes Publishing
Sparkford, Yeovil, Somerset BA22 7JJ, England

Haynes North America, Inc
861 Lawrence Drive, Newbury Park, California 91320, USA

Editions Haynes
4, Rue de l'Abreuvoir
92415 COURBEVOIE CEDEX, France

Haynes Publishing Nordiska AB
Box 1504, 751 45 UPPSALA, Sweden

Contents

LIVING WITH YOUR BMW

Roadside Repairs

ROUTINE MAINTENANCE

Contents

Introduction to the BMW 3- and 5-Series

The E30 3-Series range first became available in the UK in March 1983, and continued in production until April 1991, when the revised E36 3-Series range (not covered by this manual) was introduced. Convertible and Touring (Estate) models were introduced for 1988, and these models have continued in E30 form to date.

The E28 5-Series models were introduced in October 1981, and were superseded in June 1988 by the revised E34 5-Series range, Touring versions of which became available from March 1992. Throughout this manual, E28 models are also referred to as "old-shape", while E34 models are designated "new-shape".

The models covered by this manual are equipped with single overhead cam in-line four- and six-cylinder engines. Early 316 and 518 models are fitted with carburettors, but all other models are fitted with fuel injection systems. Transmissions are a five-speed manual, or three- or four-speed automatic. The transmission is mounted to the back of the engine, and power is transmitted to the fully-independent rear axle through a two-piece propeller shaft. The final drive unit is bolted solidly to a frame crossmember, and drives the rear wheels through driveshafts equipped with inner and outer constant velocity joints.

The front suspension is of MacPherson strut type, with the coil spring/shock absorber unit making up the upper suspension link. The rear suspension is made up of coil spring-over-shock absorber struts, or coil springs and conventional shock absorbers, depending on model.

The brakes are disc type at the front, with either drums or discs at the rear, depending on model. Servo assistance is standard on all models. Some later models are equipped with an Anti-lock Braking System (ABS).

All models are manufactured to fine limits, and live up to the BMW reputation of quality workmanship. Although many of the models covered by this manual appear complex at first sight, they should present no problems to the home mechanic.

Note for UK readers

The greater part of this manual was originally written in the USA. Some of the photographs used are of American-market models, but the procedures given are fully applicable to right-hand-drive models (or have been amended where necessary).

About this manual

The aim of this manual is to help you get the best value from your vehicle. It can do so in several ways. It can help you decide what work must be done (even should you choose to get it done by a garage). It will also provide information on routine maintenance and servicing, and give a logical course of action and diagnosis when random faults occur. However, it is hoped that you will use the manual by tackling the work yourself. On simpler jobs it may even be quicker than booking the car into a garage and going there twice, to leave and collect it. Perhaps most important, a lot of money can be saved by avoiding the costs a garage must charge to cover its labour and overheads.

The manual has drawings and descriptions to show the function of the various components so that their layout can be understood. Tasks are described and photographed in a clear step-by-step sequence.

References to the "left" or "right" of the vehicle are in the sense of a person in the driving seat, facing forwards.

Acknowledgements

Thanks are due to Champion Spark Plug, who supplied the illustrations showing spark plug conditions. Thanks are also due to Sykes-Pickavant Limited, who provided some of the workshop tools, and to all those people at Sparkford who helped in the production of this manual. Technical writers who contributed to this project include Robert Maddox, Mark Ryan and Mike Stubblefield.

We take great pride in the accuracy of information given in this manual, but vehicle manufacturers make alterations and design changes during the production run of a particular vehicle of which they do not inform us. No liability can be accepted by the authors or publishers for loss, damage or injury caused by any errors in, or omissions from, the information given.

Project vehicles

The main project vehicle used in the preparation of this manual for the UK market was a 1988 BMW 318i with an M40/B18 engine.

BMW 320i Saloon (E30)

BMW 325i Touring (E30)

BMW 325i Convertible (E30)

BMW 518i (E28)

BMW 535i (E34)

Working on your car can be dangerous. This page shows just some of the potential risks and hazards, with the aim of creating a safety-conscious attitude.

General hazards

Scalding

• Don't remove the radiator or expansion tank cap while the engine is hot.
• Engine oil, automatic transmission fluid or power steering fluid may also be dangerously hot if the engine has recently been running.

Burning

• Beware of burns from the exhaust system and from any part of the engine. Brake discs and drums can also be extremely hot immediately after use.

Crushing

• When working under or near a raised vehicle, always supplement the jack with axle stands, or use drive-on ramps. *Never venture under a car which is only supported by a jack.*

• Take care if loosening or tightening high-torque nuts when the vehicle is on stands. Initial loosening and final tightening should be done with the wheels on the ground.

Fire

• Fuel is highly flammable; fuel vapour is explosive.
• Don't let fuel spill onto a hot engine.
• Do not smoke or allow naked lights (including pilot lights) anywhere near a vehicle being worked on. Also beware of creating sparks (electrically or by use of tools).
• Fuel vapour is heavier than air, so don't work on the fuel system with the vehicle over an inspection pit.
• Another cause of fire is an electrical overload or short-circuit. Take care when repairing or modifying the vehicle wiring.
• Keep a fire extinguisher handy, of a type suitable for use on fuel and electrical fires.

Electric shock

• Ignition HT voltage can be dangerous, especially to people with heart problems or a pacemaker. Don't work on or near the ignition system with the engine running or the ignition switched on.

• Mains voltage is also dangerous. Make sure that any mains-operated equipment is correctly earthed. Mains power points should be protected by a residual current device (RCD) circuit breaker.

Fume or gas intoxication

• Exhaust fumes are poisonous; they often contain carbon monoxide, which is rapidly fatal if inhaled. Never run the engine in a confined space such as a garage with the doors shut.

• Fuel vapour is also poisonous, as are the vapours from some cleaning solvents and paint thinners.

Poisonous or irritant substances

• Avoid skin contact with battery acid and with any fuel, fluid or lubricant, especially antifreeze, brake hydraulic fluid and Diesel fuel. Don't syphon them by mouth. If such a substance is swallowed or gets into the eyes, seek medical advice.
• Prolonged contact with used engine oil can cause skin cancer. Wear gloves or use a barrier cream if necessary. Change out of oil-soaked clothes and do not keep oily rags in your pocket.
• Air conditioning refrigerant forms a poisonous gas if exposed to a naked flame (including a cigarette). It can also cause skin burns on contact.

Asbestos

• Asbestos dust can cause cancer if inhaled or swallowed. Asbestos may be found in gaskets and in brake and clutch linings. When dealing with such components it is safest to assume that they contain asbestos.

Special hazards

Hydrofluoric acid

• This extremely corrosive acid is formed when certain types of synthetic rubber, found in some O-rings, oil seals, fuel hoses etc, are exposed to temperatures above 400°C. The rubber changes into a charred or sticky substance containing the acid. *Once formed, the acid remains dangerous for years. If it gets onto the skin, it may be necessary to amputate the limb concerned.*
• When dealing with a vehicle which has suffered a fire, or with components salvaged from such a vehicle, wear protective gloves and discard them after use.

The battery

• Batteries contain sulphuric acid, which attacks clothing, eyes and skin. Take care when topping-up or carrying the battery.
• The hydrogen gas given off by the battery is highly explosive. Never cause a spark or allow a naked light nearby. Be careful when connecting and disconnecting battery chargers or jump leads.

Air bags

• Air bags can cause injury if they go off accidentally. Take care when removing the steering wheel and/or facia. Special storage instructions may apply.

Diesel injection equipment

• Diesel injection pumps supply fuel at very high pressure. Take care when working on the fuel injectors and fuel pipes.

⚠️ *Warning: Never expose the hands, face or any other part of the body to injector spray; the fuel can penetrate the skin with potentially fatal results.*

Remember...

DO

• Do use eye protection when using power tools, and when working under the vehicle.

• Do wear gloves or use barrier cream to protect your hands when necessary.

• Do get someone to check periodically that all is well when working alone on the vehicle.

• Do keep loose clothing and long hair well out of the way of moving mechanical parts.

• Do remove rings, wristwatch etc, before working on the vehicle – especially the electrical system.

• Do ensure that any lifting or jacking equipment has a safe working load rating adequate for the job.

DON'T

• Don't attempt to lift a heavy component which may be beyond your capability – get assistance.

• Don't rush to finish a job, or take unverified short cuts.

• Don't use ill-fitting tools which may slip and cause injury.

• Don't leave tools or parts lying around where someone can trip over them. Mop up oil and fuel spills at once.

• Don't allow children or pets to play in or near a vehicle being worked on.

Anti-theft audio system

General information

Some models are equipped with an audio system having an anti-theft feature that will render the stereo inoperative if stolen. If the power source to the stereo is cut, the stereo won't work even if the power source is immediately re-connected. If your vehicle is equipped with this anti-theft system, do not disconnect the battery or remove the stereo unless you have the individual code number for the stereo.

Refer to the owner's handbook supplied with the vehicle for more complete information on this audio system and its anti-theft feature.

Unlocking procedure

1 Turn on the radio. The word "CODE" should appear on the display.
2 Using the station preset selector buttons, enter the five-digit code. If you make a mistake when entering the code, continue the five-digit sequence anyway. If you hear a "beep," however, stop immediately and start the sequence over again. **Note:** *You have three attempts to enter the correct code. If the correct code isn't entered in three tries, you'll have to wait one hour, with the radio on, before you enter the codes again.*
5 Once the code has been entered correctly, the word "CODE" should disappear from the display, and the radio should play (you'll have to tune-in and enter your preset stations, however).
6 If you have lost your code number, contact a BMW dealer service department.

Instrument panel language display

On some later models, disconnecting the battery may cause the instrument panel display to default to the German language (this does not usually apply to UK models). If it is necessary to reset the correct language after the battery is reconnected, proceed as follows. With all the doors shut and the ignition on (engine not running), press the trip reset button until the panel displays the desired language. There are eight languages available. If you wish to bypass a particular selection, release the reset button and press again - this will cause the display to advance to the next language. Once the correct language has been selected, continue holding the reset button until the display reads "I.O. Version 2.0". Continue holding the button until it reads "H.P. Version 3.4", then release the button.

Jacking, towing and wheel changing

Jacking and wheel changing

The jack supplied with the vehicle should be used only for raising the vehicle when changing a tyre or placing axle stands under the frame.

 Warning: Never crawl under the vehicle or start the engine when this jack is being used as the only means of support.

When changing a wheel, the vehicle should be on level ground, with the handbrake firmly applied, and the wheels chocked. Select reverse gear (manual transmission) or Park (automatic transmission). Prise off the hub cap (if equipped) using the tapered end of the wheel brace. Loosen the wheel bolts half a turn, leaving them in place until the wheel is raised off the ground.

Position the head of the jack under the side of the vehicle, making sure it engages with the pocket made for this purpose (just behind the front wheel, or forward of the rear wheel). Engage the wheel brace handle and turn it clockwise until the wheel is raised off the ground. Unscrew the bolts, remove the wheel and fit the spare.

Refit the wheel bolts and tighten them finger-tight. Lower the vehicle by turning the wheel brace anti-clockwise. Remove the jack and tighten the bolts in a diagonal pattern to the torque listed in the Chapter 1 Specifications. If a torque wrench is not available, have the torque checked by a BMW dealer or tyre fitting specialist as soon as possible. Refit the hubcap.

Towing

Vehicles with manual transmission can be towed with all four wheels on the ground, if necessary. Automatic transmission-equipped vehicles can only be towed with all four wheels on the ground providing that the speed does not exceed 35 mph and the distance is not over 50 miles, otherwise transmission damage can result. For preference, regardless of transmission type, the vehicle should be towed with the driven (rear) wheels off the ground.

Proper towing equipment, specifically designed for the purpose, should be used, and should be attached to the main structural members of the vehicle, not to the bumpers or bumper brackets. Sling-type towing equipment must **not** be used on these vehicles.

Safety is a major consideration while towing. The handbrake should be released, and the transmission should be in neutral. The steering must be unlocked (ignition switch turned to position "1"). Remember that power-assisted steering (where fitted) and the brake servo will not work with the engine switched off.

Jump starting will get you out of trouble, but you must correct whatever made the battery go flat in the first place. There are three possibilities:

1 *The battery has been drained by repeated attempts to start, or by leaving the lights on.*

2 *The charging system is not working properly (alternator drivebelt slack or broken, alternator wiring fault or alternator itself faulty).*

3 *The battery itself is at fault (electrolyte low, or battery worn out).*

When jump-starting a car using a booster battery, observe the following precautions:

✔ Before connecting the booster battery, make sure that the ignition is switched off.

✔ Ensure that all electrical equipment (lights, heater, wipers, etc) is switched off.

✔ Take note of any special precautions printed on the battery case.

Jump starting

✔ Make sure that the booster battery is the same voltage as the discharged one in the vehicle.

✔ If the battery is being jump-started from the battery in another vehicle, the two vehicles MUST NOT TOUCH each other.

✔ Make sure that the transmission is in neutral (or PARK, in the case of automatic transmission).

1 Connect one end of the red jump lead to the positive (+) terminal of the flat battery

2 Connect the other end of the red lead to the positive (+) terminal of the booster battery.

3 Connect one end of the black jump lead to the negative (-) terminal of the booster battery

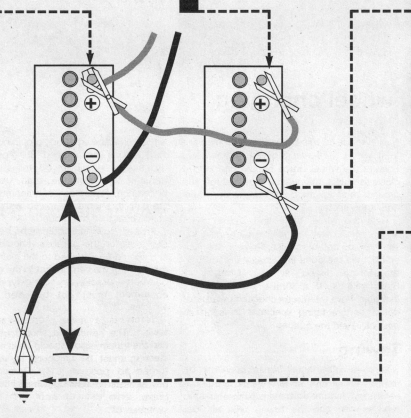

4 Connect the other end of the black jump lead to a bolt or bracket on the engine block, well away from the battery, on the vehicle to be started.

5 Make sure that the jump leads will not come into contact with the fan, drive-belts or other moving parts of the engine.

6 Start the engine using the booster battery and run it at idle speed. Switch on the lights, rear window demister and heater blower motor, then disconnect the jump leads in the reverse order of connection. Turn off the lights etc.

Identifying leaks

Puddles on the garage floor or drive, or obvious wetness under the bonnet or underneath the car, suggest a leak that needs investigating. It can sometimes be difficult to decide where the leak is coming from, especially if the engine bay is very dirty already. Leaking oil or fluid can also be blown rearwards by the passage of air under the car, giving a false impression of where the problem lies.

⚠ *Warning: Most automotive oils and fluids are poisonous. Wash them off skin, and change out of contaminated clothing, without delay.*

HAYNES HINT *The smell of a fluid leaking from the car may provide a clue to what's leaking. Some fluids are distinctively coloured. It may help to clean the car carefully and to park it over some clean paper overnight as an aid to locating the source of the leak.*
Remember that some leaks may only occur while the engine is running.

Sump oil

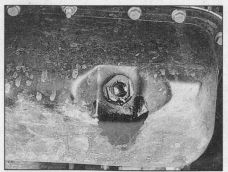

Engine oil may leak from the drain plug...

Oil from filter

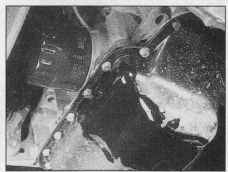

...or from the base of the oil filter.

Gearbox oil

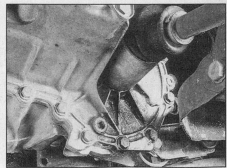

Gearbox oil can leak from the seals at the inboard ends of the driveshafts.

Antifreeze

Leaking antifreeze often leaves a crystalline deposit like this.

Brake fluid

A leak occurring at a wheel is almost certainly brake fluid.

Power steering fluid

Power steering fluid may leak from the pipe connectors on the steering rack.

Chapter 1
Routine maintenance and servicing

Contents

1

Degrees of difficulty

| Easy, suitable for novice with little experience | | Fairly easy, suitable for beginner with some experience | 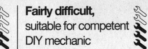 | Fairly difficult, suitable for competent DIY mechanic | | Difficult, suitable for experienced DIY mechanic | | Very difficult, suitable for expert DIY or professional | |

Specifications

Engine

Oil filter

M10 engines	Champion C121
M20 engines	Champion C160
M30 engines	
3-Series	Champion C160
5-Series	Champion X115
M40 engines	Champion X120

Valve clearances (intake and exhaust)

M10 engines	
Cold	0.20 mm
Hot	0.25 mm
M20 engines	
Cold	0.25 mm
Hot	0.30 mm
M30 engines	
Cold	0.30 mm
Hot	0.35 mm
M40 engines	Hydraulic adjusters

Cooling system

Antifreeze mixture . . . .   40% antifreeze/60% water

Fuel system

Idle speed
  3-Series, E30
    316 with M10/B18 engine . . . .   850 ± 50 rpm
    316i with M40/B16 engine . . . .   800 ± 40 rpm
    318i with M10/B18 engine (manual transmission) . . . .   850 ± 50 rpm
    318i with M10/B18 engine (automatic transmission) . . . .   750 ± 50 rpm
    318i with M40/B18 engine . . . .   800 ± 40 rpm
    320i with M20/B20 engine (L-Jetronic) . . . .   800 ± 50 rpm
    320i with M20/B20 engine (Motronic) . . . .   760 ± 40 rpm
    325i with M20/B25 engine . . . .   760 ± 40 rpm
  5-Series, E28 ("old-shape")
    518 and 518i with M10/B18 engine . . . .   800 ± 50 rpm
    All other models . . . .   850 ± 50 rpm
  5-Series, E34 ("new-shape")
    518i with M40/B18 engine . . . .   800 ± 40 rpm
    520i with M20/B20M engine . . . .   760 ± 40 rpm
    525i with M20/B25M engine . . . .   760 ± 40 rpm
    530i with M30/B30M engine . . . .   800 ± 50 rpm
    535i with M30/B35M engine . . . .   850 ± 50 rpm
CO% at 3000 rpm
  3-Series, E30
    316 with M10/B18 engine . . . .   0.5 to 1.0
    316i and 318i with M40/B16 engine . . . .   0.7 ± 0.5
    318i with M10/B18 engine . . . .   1.0 maximum
    320i with M20/B20 engine (L-Jetronic) . . . .   1.0 ± 0.5
    320i with M20/B20 engine (Motronic) . . . .   0.7 ± 0.5
    325i with M20/B25 engine . . . .   1.0 ± 0.5
  5-Series, E28 ("old-shape")
    518 and 518i with M10/B18 engine . . . .   1.0 maximum
    525i with M30/B25 engine . . . .   1.0 ± 0.5
    528i with M30/B28 engine . . . .   1.5 maximum
    535i with M30/B34 engine . . . .   0.3 to 1.5
    M535i with M30/B34 engine . . . .   0.3 to 1.5
  5-Series, E34 ("new-shape")
    All models . . . .   0.7 ± 0.5
Air filter element
  M10 engines . . . .   Champion W155 (round) or U504 (square)
  M20 engines . . . .   Champion U504 or U527
  M30 engines . . . .   Champion U504 or U527
  M40 engines . . . .   Champion U527
Fuel filter (all fuel injection engines) . . . .   Champion L206

Ignition system

Spark plug type
  M10, M20 and M30 engines . . . .   Champion N9YCC
  M40 engines
    3-Series . . . .   Champion C9YCC
    5-Series . . . .   Champion RC8DMC
Electrode gap*
  Champion N9YCC and C9YCC . . . .   0.8 mm
  Champion RC8DMC . . . .   Not adjustable
* The spark plug gap quoted is that recommended by Champion for their specified plugs listed above. If spark plugs of any other type are to be fitted, refer to their manufacturer's spark plug gap recommendations.

Brakes

Disc brake pad thickness (minimum) . . . .   2.0 mm
Drum brake shoe lining thickness (minimum) . . . .   2.0 mm

Tyre pressures (cold) - bars (psi)

	Front	Rear
3-Series, E30		
316	1.9 (28)	2.1 (30)
316i		
Saloon	2.0 (29)	2.1 (30)
Estate	2.0 (29)	2.2 (32)
318i	1.8 (26)	1.9 (28)
320i	1.9 (28)	2.0 (29)
325i	2.2 (32)	2.3 (33)
5-Series, E28 ("old-shape")		
518 and 518i	2.0 (29)	2.0 (29)
525i and 528i	2.2 (32)	2.2 (32)
535i and M535i	2.3 (33)	2.5 (36)
5-Series, E34 ("new-shape")		
518i	2.0 (29)	2.0 (29)
520i	2.1 (31)	2.1 (31)
525i, 530i and 535i	2.0 (29)	2.3 (33)

Torque wrench settings

	Nm
Automatic transmission sump bolts	
Three-speed	8 to 9
Four-speed	5 to 7
Spark plugs	
M10 engines	20 to 30
Except M10 engines	30 to 33
Oxygen sensor	30 to 33
Wheel bolts	100

Lubricants and fluids

Component or system	Lubricant type/specification
Engine	Multigrade engine oil, viscosity SAE 10W/40 to 20W/50, to API SG
Cooling system	Ethylene glycol-based antifreeze with corrosion inhibitors
Manual transmission*	Gear oil, viscosity SAE 80 to API-GL4, or single-grade mineral-based engine oil, viscosity SAE 20, 30 or 40 to API-SG
Automatic transmission	Dexron II type ATF
Final drive	BMW-approved hypoid gear oil, viscosity SAE 90**
Brake and clutch hydraulic systems	Hydraulic brake fluid to SAE J 1703 or DOT 4
Power steering	Dexron II type ATF

* E34 520i & 525i with air conditioning, E34 530i & 535i - Dexron II type ATF)
** Only available in bulk; refer to your BMW dealer

Capacities*

Engine oil
- M10 engines ... 4.0 litres
- M20 engines ... 4.3 litres
- M30 engines ... 5.8 litres
- M40 engines ... 4.0 litres

Cooling system
- M10 engines ... 7.0 litres
- M20 engines ... 10.5 litres
- M30 engines ... 12.0 litres
- M40 engines ... 7.0 litres

Fuel tank
- 3-Series, E30
  - Saloon ... 55 litres (early), 64 litres (later)
  - Estate ... 63 litres (early), 70 litres (later)
- 5-Series
  - E28 ("old-shape") ... 70 litres
  - E34 ("new-shape") ... 81 litres

Manual transmission
- ZF ... 1.2 litres
- Getrag ... 1.0 to 1.5 litres

Automatic transmission (refill)
- 3-speed ... 2.0 litres
- 4-speed ... 3.0 litres

Final drive capacity (drain and refill)
- 3-Series, E30 ... 0.9 litres
- 5-Series, E28 ("old-shape") ... 0.9 litres
- 5-Series, E34 ("new-shape") ... 1.7 litres

*All capacities approximate

Maintenance schedule

The following maintenance intervals are based on the assumption that the vehicle owner will be doing the maintenance or service work, as opposed to having a dealer service department do the work. Although the time/mileage intervals are loosely based on factory recommendations, most have been shortened to ensure, for example, that such items as lubricants and fluids are checked/changed at intervals that promote maximum engine/driveline service life. Also, subject to the preference of the individual owner interested in keeping his or her vehicle in peak condition at all times, and with the vehicle's ultimate resale in mind, many of the maintenance procedures may be performed more often than recommended in the following schedule. We encourage such owner initiative.

When the vehicle is new, it should be serviced initially by a factory-authorised dealer service department, to protect the factory warranty. In many cases, the initial maintenance check is done at no cost to the owner (check with your dealer service department for more information).

Every 250 miles or weekly, whichever comes first

☐ Check the engine oil level (Section 4)
☐ Check the engine coolant level (Section 4)
☐ Check the brake fluid level (Section 4)
☐ Check the clutch fluid level (Section 4)
☐ Check the washer fluid level (Section 4)
☐ Check the tyres and tyre pressures (Section 5)

Every 6000 miles or 6 months, whichever comes first

All items listed above, plus:

☐ Change the engine oil and oil filter (Section 6)
☐ Check the power steering fluid level (Section 7)
☐ Check the tyres, and rotate if necessary (Section 9)
☐ Check the automatic transmission fluid level (Section 8)
☐ Check the underbonnet hoses (Section 10)
☐ Check/adjust the drivebelts (Section 11)
☐ Check engine idle speed and CO (Section 12)

Every 12 000 miles or 12 months, whichever comes first

All items listed above, plus:

☐ Check/service the battery (Section 13)
☐ Check the spark plugs (Section 14)
☐ Check/renew the HT leads, distributor cap and rotor (Section 15)
☐ Check/top-up the manual transmission lubricant (Section 16)
☐ Check the differential oil level (Section 17)
☐ Check the valve clearances, and adjust if necessary - does not apply to M40 engines (Section 18)
☐ Check and lubricate the throttle linkage (Section 19)
☐ Renew the air filter (Section 20)
☐ Check the fuel system (Section 21)
☐ Inspect the cooling system (Section 22)
☐ Inspect the exhaust system (Section 23)
☐ Inspect the steering and suspension components (Section 24)
☐ Check the driveshaft gaiter(s) (Section 25)
☐ Inspect the brakes (Section 26)
☐ Inspect/renew the windscreen wiper blades (Section 27)

Every 24 000 miles or 2 years, whichever comes first

All items listed above plus:

☐ Change the automatic transmission fluid and filter (Section 28)
☐ Drain, flush and refill the cooling system (Section 29)
☐ Renew the spark plugs (Section 14)
☐ Check/renew the spark plug HT leads (Section 15)
☐ Renew the fuel filter (Section 30)
☐ Change the manual transmission lubricant (Section 31)
☐ Change the differential oil (Section 32)
☐ Check the evaporative emissions system, where applicable (Section 33)
☐ Reset the service indicator lights (Section 34)
☐ Renew brake fluid by bleeding (see Chapter 9)
☐ Check the handbrake operation (see Chapter 9)

Every 30 000 miles

☐ Renew the timing belt (Section 35)

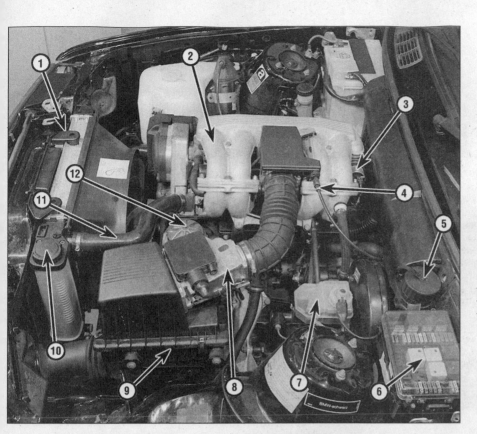

Underbonnet view (left-hand side) of a UK model 318i (1988)

1 Radiator
2 Intake manifold
3 Idle control valve
4 Accelerator cable
5 Diagnostic/service indicator resetting socket
6 Fuse/relay box
7 Brake hydraulic fluid reservoir
8 Airflow meter
9 Air cleaner unit
10 Radiator filler cap
11 Radiator top hose
12 Oil filter housing

Underbonnet view (right-hand side) of a UK model 318i (1988)

1 Oil filler cap
2 Valve cover
3 Engine oil filler dipstick
4 Viscous cooling fan
5 Distributor cap cover
6 Bottom hose
7 Windscreen washer fluid reservoir
8 Ignition coil
9 Clutch hydraulic fluid reservoir
10 Battery

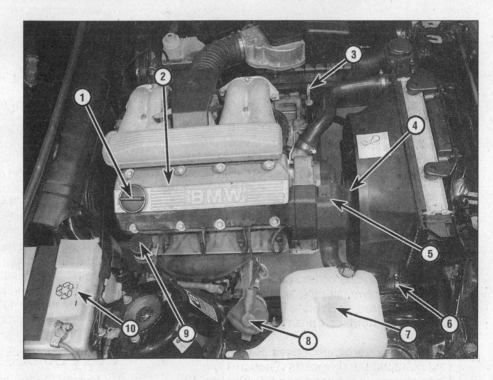

Maintenance and Servicing

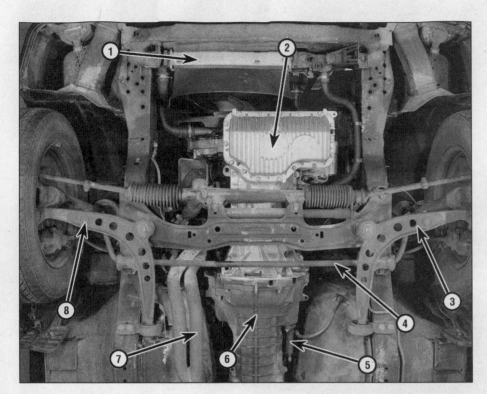

Front underbody view of a UK model 318i (1988)

1 Radiator
2 Engine oil drain plug
3 Front suspension control arm (left-hand side)
4 Front anti-roll bar
5 Clutch slave cylinder
6 Transmission
7 Exhaust downpipe
8 Front suspension control arm (right-hand side)

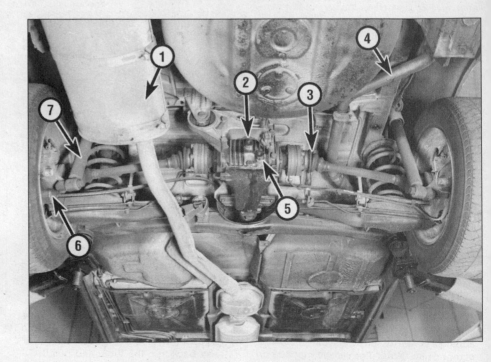

Typical rear underside components

1 Exhaust system
2 Differential fill/check plug
3 Driveshaft boot
4 Fuel tank filler tube
5 Differential drain plug
6 Rear brake
7 Rear shock absorber

1 Introduction

This Chapter is designed to help the home mechanic maintain his or her vehicle with the goals of maximum performance, economy, safety and reliability in mind. Included is a master maintenance schedule, followed by procedures dealing specifically with each item on the schedule. Visual checks, adjustments, component renewal and other helpful items are included. Refer to the accompanying illustrations of the engine compartment and the underside of the vehicle for the locations of various components. Servicing the vehicle, in accordance with the mileage/time maintenance schedule and the step-by-step procedures, will result in a planned maintenance programme that should produce a long and reliable service life. Keep in mind that it is a comprehensive plan, so maintaining some items but not others at specified intervals, will not produce the same results.

2 Routine maintenance

As you service the vehicle, you will discover that many of the procedures can - and should - be grouped together, because of the nature of the particular procedure you're performing, or because of the close proximity of two otherwise-unrelated components to one another. For example, if the vehicle is raised for chassis lubrication, you should inspect the exhaust, suspension, steering and fuel systems while you're under the vehicle. When the wheels are removed for other work, it makes good sense to check the brakes, since the wheels are already removed. Finally, let's suppose you have to borrow a torque wrench. Even if you only need it to tighten the spark plugs, you might as well check the torque of as many critical nuts and bolts as time allows.

The first step in this maintenance programme is to prepare yourself before the actual work begins. Read through all the procedures you're planning to do, then gather up all the parts and tools needed. If it looks like you might run into problems during a particular job, seek advice from a mechanic or an experienced do-it-yourselfer.

3 Engine "tune-up" - general information

The term "tune-up" is used in this manual to represent a combination of individual operations rather than one specific procedure.

If, from the time the vehicle is new, the routine maintenance schedule is followed closely, and frequent checks are made of fluid levels and high-wear items, as suggested throughout this manual, the engine will be kept in relatively good running condition, and the need for additional work will be minimised.

More likely than not, however, there will be times when the engine is running poorly due to a lack of regular maintenance. This is even more likely if a used vehicle, which has not received regular and frequent maintenance checks, is purchased. In such cases, an engine tune-up will be needed outside of the regular maintenance intervals.

The first step in any tune-up or diagnostic procedure to help correct a poor-running engine is a cylinder compression check. A compression check (see Chapter 2B) will help determine the condition of internal engine components, and should be used as a guide for tune-up and repair procedures. If, for instance, a compression check indicates serious internal engine wear, a conventional tune-up will not improve the performance of the engine, and would be a waste of time and money. Because of its importance, the compression check should be done by someone with the right equipment, and the knowledge to use it properly.

The following procedures are those most often needed to bring a generally poor-running engine back into a proper state of tune.

Minor tune-up

Check all engine-related fluids (Section 4)
Check all underbonnet hoses (Section 10)
Check and adjust the drivebelts (Section 11)
Clean, inspect and test the battery (Section 13)
Renew the spark plugs (Section 14)
Inspect the spark plug HT leads, distributor cap and rotor (Section 15)
Check the air filter (Section 20)
Check the cooling system (Section 22)

Major tune-up

All items listed under minor tune-up, plus . . .
Check the ignition system (see Chapter 5)
Check the charging system (see Chapter 5)
Check the fuel system (see Chapter 4)
Renew the spark plug HT leads, distributor cap and rotor (Section 15)

Weekly checks

4 Fluid level checks

Note: *The following are fluid level checks to be done on a 250-mile or weekly basis. Additional fluid level checks can be found in specific maintenance procedures which follow. Regardless of intervals, be alert to fluid leaks under the vehicle, which would indicate a fault to be corrected immediately.*

1 Fluids are an essential part of the lubrication, cooling, brake and windscreen washer systems. Because the fluids gradually become depleted and/or contaminated during normal operation of the vehicle, they must be periodically replenished. See *"Lubricants and fluids"* at the beginning of this Chapter before adding fluid to any of the following components. **Note:** *The vehicle must be on level ground when any fluid levels are checked.*

Engine oil

2 Engine oil is checked with a dipstick, which is located on the side of the engine (refer to the underbonnet illustrations in this Chapter for dipstick location). The dipstick extends through a metal tube down into the sump.
3 The engine oil should be checked before the vehicle has been driven, or at least 15 minutes after the engine has been shut off.

> **HAYNES HiNT** *If the oil is checked immediately after driving the vehicle, some of the oil will remain in the upper part of the engine, resulting in an inaccurate reading on the dipstick.*

4 Pull the dipstick out of the tube, and wipe all of the oil away from the end with a clean rag or paper towel. Insert the clean dipstick all the way back into the tube, and pull it out again. Note the oil at the end of the dipstick. At its highest point, the oil should be between the two notches or marks **(see illustration)**.
5 It takes one litre of oil to raise the level from the lower mark to the upper mark on the dipstick. Do not allow the level to drop below the lower mark, or oil starvation may cause

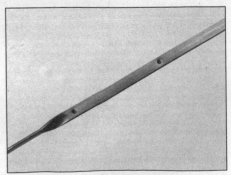

4.4 The oil level should be kept between the two marks - preferably at or near the upper one - if it isn't, add enough oil to bring the level to the upper mark

1

4.6a The threaded oil filler cap is located in the valve cover - always make sure the area around the opening is clean before unscrewing the cap

4.6b Topping-up the engine oil

4.9a On some models, the expansion tank (coolant reservoir) is mounted on the radiator - make sure the level is kept at or near the FULL mark (arrowed)

engine damage. Conversely, overfilling the engine (adding oil above the upper mark) may cause oil-fouled spark plugs, oil leaks, or oil seal failures.

6 To add oil, remove the filler cap located on the valve cover **(see illustrations)**. After adding oil, wait a few minutes to allow the level to stabilise, then pull the dipstick out and check the level again. Add more oil if required. Refit the filler cap, tightening it by hand only.

7 Checking the oil level is an important preventive maintenance step. A consistently low oil level indicates oil leakage through damaged seals or defective gaskets, or oil burning (internal leakage past worn rings or valve guides). The condition of the oil should also be noted. If the oil looks milky in colour or has water droplets in it, the cylinder head gasket may be blown, or the head or block may be cracked. The engine should be repaired immediately. Whenever you check the oil level, slide your thumb and index finger up the dipstick before wiping off the oil. If you see small dirt or metal particles clinging to the dipstick, the oil should be changed (see Section 6).

Engine coolant

⚠️ **Warning: Do not allow antifreeze to come in contact with your skin, or with the vehicle**

paintwork. Rinse off spills immediately with plenty of water. Antifreeze is highly toxic if ingested. Never leave antifreeze lying around in an open container, or in puddles on the floor; children and pets are attracted by its sweet smell, and may drink it. Check with local authorities about disposing of used antifreeze. Local collection centres may exist, to see that antifreeze is disposed of safely.

8 All vehicles covered by this manual are equipped with a pressurised coolant recovery system. On most models, a white plastic expansion tank (or coolant reservoir) located in the engine compartment is connected by a hose to the radiator. As the engine heats up during operation, the expanding coolant fills the tank. As the engine cools, the coolant is automatically drawn back into the cooling system, to maintain the correct level.

9 The coolant level in the reservoir **(see illustrations)** should be checked regularly. Add a 40%/60% mixture of ethylene glycol-based antifreeze to water **(see illustration)**.

⚠️ *Warning: Do not remove the expansion tank cap or radiator cap to check the coolant level, unless the engine is completely cold! The level in the reservoir varies with the temperature of the engine. When the engine is cold, the coolant level should be*

above the LOW mark on the reservoir. Once the engine has warmed up, the level should be at or near the FULL mark. If it isn't, allow the engine to cool, then remove the cap from the reservoir.

10 Drive the vehicle and recheck the coolant level. If only a small amount of coolant is required to bring the system up to the proper level, plain water can be used. However, repeated additions of water will dilute the antifreeze. In order to maintain the proper ratio of antifreeze and water, always top-up the coolant level with the correct mixture.

11 If the coolant level drops consistently, there must be a leak in the system. Inspect the radiator, hoses, filler cap, drain plugs and water pump (see Section 29). If no leaks are noted, have the expansion tank cap or radiator cap pressure-tested by a BMW dealer.

12 If you have to remove the cap, wait until the engine has cooled completely, then wrap a thick cloth around the cap and turn it to the first stop. If coolant or steam escapes, let the engine cool down longer, then remove the cap.

13 Check the condition of the coolant as well. It should be relatively clear. If it's brown or rust-coloured, the system should be drained, flushed and refilled. Even if the coolant appears to be normal, the corrosion

4.9b On other models, the expansion tank (coolant reservoir) is located on the side of the engine compartment - remove the cap to add coolant

4.9c On some 5-Series models, the expansion tank (coolant reservoir) is located on the bulkhead

4.9d Adding antifreeze mixture

4.15 Adding hydraulic fluid to the clutch fluid reservoir

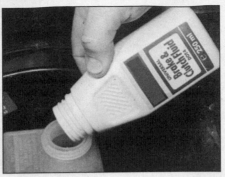

4.16 The brake fluid level should be kept above the MIN mark on the translucent reservoir - unscrew the cap to add fluid

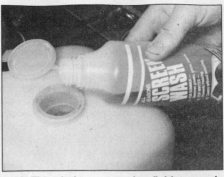

4.22 The windscreen washer fluid reservoir is located in the right front corner of the engine compartment on most models

inhibitors wear out, so it must be renewed at the specified intervals.

Brake and clutch fluid

 Warning: Brake fluid can harm your eyes and damage painted surfaces, so use extreme caution when handling or pouring it. Do not use brake fluid that has been standing open or is more than one year old. Brake fluid absorbs moisture from the air, which can cause a dangerous loss of brake effectiveness. Use only the specified type of brake fluid. Mixing different types (such as DOT 3 or 4 and DOT 5) can cause brake failure.

14 The brake master cylinder is mounted at the left rear corner of the engine compartment. The clutch fluid reservoir (manual transmission models) is mounted on the right-hand side.

15 To check the clutch fluid level, observe the level through the translucent reservoir. The level should be at or near the step moulded into the reservoir. If the level is low, remove the reservoir cap to add the specified fluid **(see illustration)**.

16 The brake fluid level is checked by looking through the plastic reservoir mounted on the master cylinder **(see illustration)**. The fluid level should be between the MAX and MIN lines on the reservoir. If the fluid level is low, first wipe the top of the reservoir and the cap with a clean rag, to prevent contamination of the system as the cap is unscrewed. Top-up with the recommended brake fluid, but do not overfill.

17 While the reservoir cap is off, check the master cylinder reservoir for contamination. If rust deposits, dirt particles or water droplets are present, the system should be drained and refilled.

18 After filling the reservoir to the proper level, make sure the cap is seated correctly, to prevent fluid leakage and/or contamination.

19 The fluid level in the master cylinder will drop slightly as the disc brake pads wear. There is no need to top up to compensate for this fall provided that the level stays above the MIN line; the level will rise again when new pads are fitted. A very low level may indicate worn brake pads. Check for wear (see Section 26).

20 If the brake fluid level drops consistently, check the entire system for leaks immediately. Examine all brake lines, hoses and connections, along with the calipers, wheel cylinders and master cylinder (see Section 26).

21 When checking the fluid level, if you discover one or both reservoirs empty or nearly empty, the brake or clutch hydraulic system should be checked for leaks and bled (see Chapters 8 and 9).

Windscreen washer fluid

22 Fluid for the windscreen washer system is stored in a plastic reservoir in the engine compartment **(see illustration)**.

23 In milder climates, plain water can be used in the reservoir, but it should be kept no more than two-thirds full, to allow for expansion if the water freezes. In colder climates, use windscreen washer system antifreeze, available at any car accessory shop, to lower the freezing point of the fluid. This comes in concentrated or pre-mixed form. If you purchase concentrated antifreeze, mix the antifreeze with water in accordance with the manufacturer's directions on the container.

 Caution: Do not use cooling system antifreeze - it will damage the vehicle's paint.

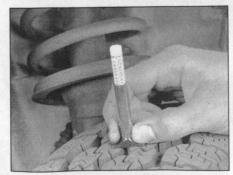

5.2 Use a tyre tread depth indicator to monitor tyre wear - they are available at car accessory shops and service stations, and cost very little

5 Tyre and tyre pressure checks

1 Periodic inspection of the tyres may save you the inconvenience of being stranded with a flat tyre. It can also provide you with vital information regarding possible problems in the steering and suspension systems before major damage occurs.

2 Tyres are equipped with bands that will appear when tread depth reaches 1.6 mm, at which time the tyres can be considered worn out. This represents the legal minimum tread depth; most authorities recommend renewing any tyre on which the tread depth is 2 mm or less. Tread wear can be monitored with a simple, inexpensive device known as a tread depth indicator **(see illustration)**.

3 Note any abnormal tyre wear **(see illustration overleaf)**. Tread pattern irregularities such as cupping, flat spots and more wear on one side than the other are indications of front end alignment and/or wheel balance problems. If any of these conditions are noted, take the vehicle to a tyre specialist to correct the problem.

4 Look closely for cuts, punctures and embedded nails or tacks. Sometimes, after a nail has embedded itself in the tread, a tyre will hold air pressure for a short time, or may

5.4a If a slow puncture is suspected, check the valve core first to make sure it's tight

1

leak down very slowly. If a slow puncture persists, check the valve stem core to make sure it is tight (see illustration). Examine the tread for an object that may have embedded itself in the tyre, or for a previous repair that may have begun to leak. If a puncture is suspected, it can be easily verified by spraying a solution of soapy water onto the puncture (see illustration). The soapy solution will bubble if there is a leak. Unless the puncture is unusually large, a tyre specialist can usually repair the tyre.

5 Carefully inspect the inner sidewall of each tyre for evidence of brake fluid leakage. If you see any, inspect the brakes immediately.

6 Correct air pressure adds miles to the life span of the tyres, improves fuel economy, and enhances overall ride quality. A tyre pressure gauge is essential.

 Keep an accurate gauge in the glove compartment. The pressure gauges attached to the nozzles of air hoses at service stations are often inaccurate.

7 Always check the tyre pressures when the tyres are cold (ie before driving the vehicle).

5.4b If the valve core is tight, raise the vehicle, and spray a soapy water solution onto the tread as the tyre is turned slowly - leaks will cause small bubbles to appear

5.8 To extend the life of the tyres, check the air pressure at least once a week with an accurate gauge (don't forget the spare!)

Checking the pressures when the tyres are warm, or hot, will result in higher readings, due to heat expansion. On no account should air be let out of the tyres in this case, or the tyres will effectively be under-inflated when cold.

8 Unscrew the valve cap protruding from the wheel or hubcap, and push the gauge firmly onto the valve stem (see illustration). Note the reading on the gauge, and compare the figure to the recommended tyre pressures shown in the Specifications listed at the beginning of this Chapter. Be sure to refit the valve cap to keep dirt and moisture out of the valve stem mechanism. Check all four tyres and, if necessary, add enough air to bring them to the recommended pressure.

9 Don't forget to keep the spare tyre inflated to the specified pressure.

Tyre tread wear patterns

Shoulder Wear

Underinflation (wear on both sides)
Under-inflation will cause overheating of the tyre, because the tyre will flex too much, and the tread will not sit correctly on the road surface. This will cause a loss of grip and excessive wear, not to mention the danger of sudden tyre failure due to heat build-up.
Check and adjust pressures
Incorrect wheel camber (wear on one side)
Repair or renew suspension parts
Hard cornering
Reduce speed!

Centre Wear

Overinflation
Over-inflation will cause rapid wear of the centre part of the tyre tread, coupled with reduced grip, harsher ride, and the danger of shock damage occurring in the tyre casing.
Check and adjust pressures

If you sometimes have to inflate your car's tyres to the higher pressures specified for maximum load or sustained high speed, don't forget to reduce the pressures to normal afterwards.

Uneven Wear

Front tyres may wear unevenly as a result of wheel misalignment. Most tyre dealers and garages can check and adjust the wheel alignment (or "tracking") for a modest charge.
Incorrect camber or castor
Repair or renew suspension parts
Malfunctioning suspension
Repair or renew suspension parts
Unbalanced wheel
Balance tyres
Incorrect toe setting
Adjust front wheel alignment
Note: *The feathered edge of the tread which typifies toe wear is best checked by feel.*

Every 6000 miles or 6 months, whichever comes first

6 Engine oil and filter change

Warning: Prolonged skin contact with used engine oil is hazardous. Use a barrier cream and wear gloves during this procedure. Change out of oil-soaked clothing immediately.

HAYNES HINT *Frequent oil changes are the most important preventive maintenance procedures that can be done by the home mechanic. As engine oil ages, it becomes diluted and contaminated, which leads to premature engine wear.*

1 Make sure that you have all the necessary tools before you begin this procedure **(see illustration)**. You should also have plenty of rags or newspapers handy for mopping up oil spills

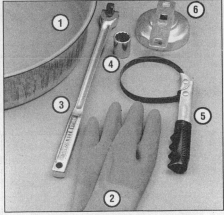

6.1 These tools are required when changing the engine oil and filter

1 **Drain pan** - It should be fairly shallow in depth, but wide enough to prevent spills
2 **Rubber gloves** - When removing the drain plug and filter, you will get oil on your hands (the gloves will prevent burns)
3 **Socket bar** - Sometimes the oil drain plug is tight, and a long bar is needed to loosen it. The correct-size ring spanner may work just as well
4 **Socket** - To be used with the bar or a ratchet (must be the correct size to fit the drain plug - six-point preferred)
5 **Filter spanner** - This is a metal band-type spanner, which requires clearance around the filter to be effective. This tool is not required on all engines.
6 **Filter spanner** - This type fits on the bottom of the filter and can be turned with a ratchet or breaker bar (different-size spanners are available for different types of filters) This tool is not required on all engines.

2 Start the engine and allow it to reach normal operating temperature - oil and sludge will flow more easily when warm. If new oil, a filter or tools are needed, use the vehicle to go and get them, thus warming up the engine oil at the same time.
3 Park on a level surface, and switch off the engine when it's warmed up. Remove the oil filler cap from the valve cover.
4 Access to the oil drain plug and filter will be improved if the vehicle can be lifted on a hoist, driven onto ramps, or supported by axle stands.

Warning: DO NOT work under a vehicle supported only by a hydraulic or scissors-type jack - always use axle stands!

5 If you haven't changed the oil on this vehicle before, get under it, and locate the drain plug and the oil filter. Note that on some engines, the oil filter is located on the top left-hand side of the engine. The exhaust components will be hot as you work, so note how they are routed to avoid touching them.
6 Being careful not to touch the hot exhaust components, position a drain pan under the plug in the bottom of the engine.
7 Clean the area around the plug, then remove the plug **(see illustration)**. It's a good idea to wear a rubber glove while unscrewing the plug the final few turns, to avoid being scalded by hot oil. Hold the drain plug against

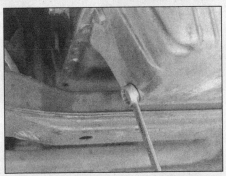

6.7 Using a ring spanner to remove the oil drain plug

6.16 Lubricate the oil filter sealing ring with clean engine oil before refitting the filter on the engine

the threads as you unscrew it, then pull it away from the drain hole suddenly. This will place your arm out of the way of the hot oil, as well as reducing the chances of dropping the drain plug into the drain pan.
8 It may be necessary to move the drain pan slightly as oil flow slows to a trickle. Inspect the old oil for the presence of metal particles, which could give early warning of engine wear.
9 After all the oil has drained, wipe off the drain plug with a clean rag. Any small metal particles clinging to the plug would immediately contaminate the new oil.
10 Refit the plug and tighten it securely. Use a new washer if necessary.
11 Move the drain pan into position under the oil filter.

Canister-type oil filter

12 Loosen the spin-off type oil filter by turning it anti-clockwise with a filter spanner. Any standard filter spanner will work.
13 Sometimes the spin-off type oil filter is screwed on so tightly that it can't be easily loosened. If it is, punch a metal bar or long screwdriver directly through it, and use it as a T-bar to turn the filter. Be prepared for oil to spurt out of the canister as it's punctured.
14 Once the filter is loose, use your hands to unscrew it from the block. Just as the filter is detached from the block, immediately tilt the open end up to prevent oil inside the filter from spilling out.
15 Using a clean rag, wipe off the mounting surface on the block. Also, make sure that none of the old sealing ring remains stuck to the mounting surface. It can be removed with a scraper if necessary.
16 Compare the old filter with the new one, to make sure they are the same type. Smear some engine oil on the rubber sealing ring of the new filter, and screw it into place **(see illustration)**. Overtightening the filter will damage the sealing ring, so don't use a filter spanner. Most filter manufacturers recommend tightening the filter by hand only. Normally, they should be tightened three-quarters of a turn after the sealing ring contacts the block, but be sure to follow the directions on the filter or container.

6.17a Unscrew the bolt . . .

1

6.17b . . . remove the cover . . .

6.17c . . . and lift out the cartridge

6.19 Renewing the rubber O-ring in the cover

Cartridge-type oil filter

17 Some models are equipped with a cartridge-type oil filter. Unscrew the bolt, remove the cover, and lift the filter out **(see illustrations)**.
18 Compare the new cartridge with the old one, to make sure they are the same type, then lower it into the housing.
19 Using a clean rag, wipe off the mounting surface of the housing and cover. If necessary, renew the rubber O-ring **(see illustration)**. Smear some clean oil on the O-ring and refit the cover and bolt. Tighten the bolt securely.

All models

20 Remove all tools and materials from under the vehicle, being careful not to spill the oil from the drain pan, then lower the vehicle.
21 Add new oil to the engine through the oil filler cap in the valve cover. Use a funnel to prevent oil from spilling onto the top of the engine. Pour the specified quantity of fresh oil into the engine. Wait a few minutes to allow the oil to drain into the sump, then check the level on the dipstick (see Section 4 if necessary). If the oil level is correct, refit the filler cap.
22 Start the engine and run it for about a minute. The oil pressure warning light may take a few seconds to go out while the new filter fills with oil; don't rev the engine while the light is on. While the engine is running, look under the vehicle, and check for leaks at the sump drain plug and around the oil filter. If

either one is leaking, stop the engine and tighten the plug or filter slightly.
23 Wait a few minutes, then recheck the level on the dipstick. Add oil as necessary.
24 During the first few days after an oil change, make it a point to check frequently for leaks and proper oil level.
25 The old oil drained from the engine cannot be re-used in its present state, and should be discarded. Oil reclamation centres and some service stations will accept the oil, which can be recycled. After the oil has cooled, it can be transferred into a container for transport to a disposal site.

OIL CARE
FOLLOW THE CODE

OIL BANK LINE
0800 66 33 66

Note: It is antisocial and illegal to dump oil down the drain. To find the location of your local oil recycling bank, call this number free.

7   Power steering fluid level check

1 Check the power steering fluid level periodically to avoid steering system problems, such as damage to the pump. Proceed as follows.

⚠ *Caution: Do not hold the steering wheel against either stop (full-left or full-right lock) for more than five seconds. If you do, the power steering pump could be damaged.*

2 On some models, the power steering fluid reservoir is located on the left side of the engine compartment, and has a twist-off cap with an integral fluid level dipstick **(see illustration)**. Other models use a hydraulic power steering and brake servo system which combines the fluid in one reservoir, located at the right rear corner of the engine compartment.
3 Park the vehicle on level ground, and apply the handbrake.
4 On models with a fluid dipstick, run the engine until it has reached normal operating temperature. With the engine at idle, turn the steering wheel back and forth several times to get any air out of the steering system. Switch off the engine, remove the cap by turning it anti-clockwise, wipe the dipstick clean, and refit the cap. Remove the cap again, and note the fluid level. It must be between the two lines **(see illustration)**.
5 On hydraulic servo models, pump the brake pedal about ten times or until the pedal is firm. Remove the nut, lift the cap off, and make sure the fluid is within 6.0 mm of the top of the reservoir.
6 Add small amounts of fluid until the level is correct **(see illustration)**.

7.2 The power steering fluid reservoir (arrowed) is located on the left side of the engine compartment

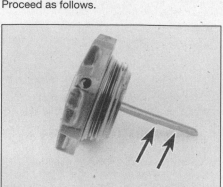

7.4 The power steering fluid level should be kept between the two arrows near the upper step on the dipstick

7.6 Adding fluid to the power steering reservoir

8.5 The automatic transmission fluid dipstick (arrowed) is located near the bulkhead on the left side of the engine compartment

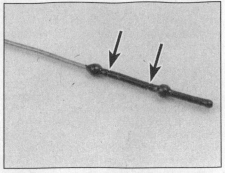

8.6 With the fluid hot, the level should be kept between the two dipstick notches, preferably near the upper one

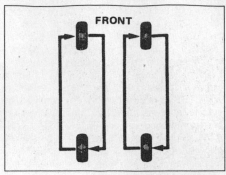

9.2 The tyre rotation pattern for these models

Caution: Do not overfill the reservoir. If too much fluid is added, remove the excess with a clean syringe. Refit the cap.

7 If frequent topping-up is needed, check the power steering hoses and connections for leaks and wear (see Section 10).

8 Check the condition and tension of the drivebelt (see Section 11).

8 Automatic transmission fluid level check

Caution: The use of transmission fluid other than the type listed in this Chapter's Specifications could result in transmission malfunctions or failure.

1 The automatic transmission fluid should be carefully maintained. Low fluid level can lead to slipping or loss of drive, while overfilling can cause foaming and loss of fluid. Either condition can cause transmission damage.

2 Since transmission fluid expands as it heats up, the fluid level should only be checked when the transmission is warm (at normal operating temperature). If the vehicle has just been driven over 20 miles (32 km), the transmission can be considered warm. You can also check the fluid level when the transmission is cold. If the vehicle has not been driven for over five hours and the fluid is about room temperature (20°C), the transmission is cold. However, the fluid level is normally checked with the transmission warm, to ensure accurate results.

Caution: If the vehicle has just been driven for a long time at high speed or in city traffic, in hot weather, or if it has been pulling a trailer, an accurate fluid level reading cannot be obtained. Allow the transmission to cool down for about 30 minutes.

3 Immediately after driving the vehicle, park it on a level surface, apply the handbrake and start the engine. While the engine is idling, depress the brake pedal and move the selector lever through all the gear ranges, beginning and ending in Park.

4 The automatic transmission dipstick tube is located in the left rear corner of the engine compartment.

5 With the engine still idling, pull the dipstick out of the tube **(see illustration)**, wipe it off with a clean rag, push it all the way back into the tube and withdraw it again, then note the fluid level.

6 The level should be between the two marks **(see illustration)**. If the level is low, add the specified automatic transmission fluid through the dipstick tube - use a clean funnel, preferably equipped with a fine mesh filter, to prevent spills.

Caution: Be careful not to introduce dirt into the transmission when topping up.

7 Add just enough of the recommended fluid to fill the transmission to the proper level. It takes about half a litre to raise the level from the low mark to the high mark when the fluid is hot, so add the fluid a little at a time, and keep checking the level until it's correct.

8 The condition of the fluid should also be checked along with the level. If the fluid is black or a dark reddish-brown colour, or if it smells burned, it should be changed (see Section 28). If you are in doubt about its condition, purchase some new fluid, and compare the two for colour and smell.

9 Tyre rotation

1 The tyres can be rotated at the specified intervals, or whenever uneven wear is noticed. However, bear in mind that if rotation succeeds in making all the tyres wear evenly, you will eventually have to renew all four at once. Since the vehicle will be raised and the wheels removed anyway, check the brakes also (see Section 26). **Note:** *Even if you don't rotate the tyres, at least check the wheel bolt tightness.*

2 It is recommended that the tyres be rotated in a specific pattern **(see illustration)** so that their direction of rotation remains the same.

3 Refer to the information in *"Jacking and towing"* at the front of this manual for the proper procedure to follow when raising the vehicle and changing a tyre.

4 The vehicle must be raised on a hoist or supported on axle stands to get all four tyres off the ground. Make sure the vehicle is safely supported!

5 After the rotation procedure is finished, check and adjust the tyre pressures as necessary, and be sure to check the wheel bolt tightness.

10 Underbonnet hose check and renewal

Warning: Renewal of air conditioning hoses must be left to a dealer service department or air conditioning specialist having the equipment to depressurise the system safely. Never disconnect air conditioning hoses or components until the system has been depressurised.

General

1 High temperatures under the bonnet can cause deterioration of the rubber and plastic hoses used for various systems. Periodic inspection should be made for cracks, loose clamps, material hardening, and leaks.

2 Information specific to the cooling system can be found in Section 22, while the braking system is covered in Section 26.

3 Most (but not all) hoses are secured with clamps. Where clamps are used, check to be sure they haven't lost their tension, allowing the hose to leak. If clamps aren't used, make sure the hose has not expanded and/or hardened where it slips over the fitting, allowing it to leak.

Vacuum hoses

4 It's quite common for vacuum hoses, especially those in the emissions system, to be colour-coded or identified by coloured stripes moulded into them. Various systems require hoses with different wall thicknesses, collapse resistance and temperature resistance. When fitting new hoses, be sure the new ones are made of the same material.

5 Often the only effective way to check a hose is to remove it completely from the vehicle. If more than one hose is removed, be sure to label the hoses and fittings to ensure correct refitting.

6 When checking vacuum hoses, be sure to include any plastic T-fittings in the check. Inspect the connections for cracks which could cause leakage.

7 A small piece of vacuum hose can be used as a stethoscope to detect vacuum leaks. Hold one end of the hose to your ear and probe around vacuum hoses and fittings, listening for the "hissing" sound characteristic of a vacuum leak.

 Warning: When probing with the vacuum hose stethoscope, be careful not to touch moving engine components such as the drivebelt, cooling fan, etc.

Fuel hoses

 Warning: There are certain precautions which must be taken when servicing or inspecting fuel system components. Work in a well-ventilated area, and do not allow open flames (cigarettes, appliance pilot lights, etc.) or bare light bulbs near the work area. Mop up any spills immediately, and do not store fuel-soaked rags where they could ignite. If you spill any fuel on your skin, rinse it off immediately with soap and water. When you perform any kind of work on the fuel system, wear safety glasses, and have a fire extinguisher on hand.

8 The fuel hoses are usually under pressure, so if any fuel hoses are to be disconnected, be prepared to catch spilled fuel.

 Warning: On vehicles equipped with fuel injection, you must depressurise the fuel system before servicing the fuel hoses. Refer to Chapter 4 for details.

9 Check all rubber fuel hoses for deterioration and chafing. Check especially for cracks in areas where the hose bends, and just before connectors, such as where a hose attaches to the fuel pump or fuel filter, for example.

10 Only high-quality fuel hose should be used. Never, under any circumstances, use unreinforced vacuum hose, clear plastic tubing or water hose for fuel hoses.

11 Band-type clamps are commonly used on fuel hoses. These clamps often lose their tension over a period of time, and can be "sprung" during removal. Renew all band-type clamps with screw clamps whenever a hose is renewed.

Metal lines

12 Sections of metal line are often used between the fuel pump and fuel injection system. Check carefully to make sure the line isn't bent, crimped or cracked.

13 If a section of metal line must be renewed, use seamless steel tubing only, since copper and aluminium tubing do not have the strength necessary to withstand the vibration caused by the engine.

14 Check the metal brake lines where they enter the master cylinder and brake proportioning or ABS unit (if used) for cracks in the lines and loose fittings. Any sign of brake fluid leakage calls for an immediate thorough inspection of the braking system.

Power steering hoses

15 Check the power steering hoses for leaks, loose connections and worn clamps. Tighten loose connections. Worn clamps or leaky hoses should be renewed.

11 Drivebelt check, adjustment and renewal

Check

1 The drivebelts, sometimes called V-belts or simply "fan" belts, are located at the front of the engine, and play an important role in the overall operation of the vehicle and its components. Due to their function and material make-up, the belts are prone to failure after a period of time, and should be inspected and adjusted periodically to prevent major engine damage.

2 The number of belts used on a particular vehicle depends on the accessories fitted. Drivebelts are used to turn the alternator, power steering pump, water pump, and air conditioning compressor. Depending on the pulley arrangement, a single belt may be used to drive more than one of these components.

3 With the engine switched off, open the bonnet and locate the various belts at the front of the engine. Using your fingers (and a torch, if necessary), move along the belts, checking for cracks and separation of the belt plies. Also check for fraying and glazing, which gives the belt a shiny appearance **(see illustration)**. Both sides of the belts should be inspected, which means you will have to twist each belt to check the underside.

4 The tension of each belt is checked by pushing firmly with your thumb and seeing how much the belt moves (deflects). Measure the deflection with a ruler **(see illustration)**. A good rule of thumb is that the belt should deflect 6 mm if the distance from pulley centre-to-pulley centre is between 180 and 280 mm. The belt should deflect 13 mm if the distance from pulley centre-to-pulley centre is between 300 and 400 mm.

Adjustment

5 If it is necessary to adjust the belt tension, either to make the belt tighter or looser, it is done by moving a belt-driven accessory on its bracket. (When the same belt drives more than one accessory, normally only one accessory is moved when making adjustment.)

6 For each component, there will be an adjusting bolt and a pivot bolt. Both bolts must be loosened slightly to enable you to move the component. On some components, the drivebelt tension can be adjusted by turning an adjusting bolt after loosening the lockbolt **(see illustration)**.

7 After the two bolts have been loosened,

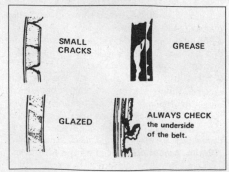

11.3 Here are some of the more common problems associated with drivebelts (check the belts very carefully to prevent an untimely breakdown)

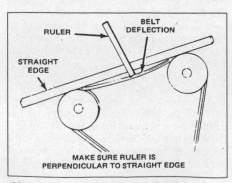

11.4 Measuring drivebelt deflection with a straightedge and ruler

11.6 Loosen the nut on the other end of the adjuster bolt (arrowed) and turn the bolt to increase or decrease tension on the drivebelt

12.3 Idle speed adjustment screw on the 2B4 carburettor (shown with the carburettor removed)

move the component away from the engine to tighten the belt, or towards the engine to loosen the belt. Hold the accessory in position, and check the belt tension. If it is correct, tighten the two bolts until just tight, then recheck the tension. If the tension is still correct, tighten the bolts.

8 It will often be necessary to use some sort of lever to move the accessory while the belt is adjusted. If this must be done to gain the proper leverage, be very careful not to damage the component being moved, or the part being prised against.

Renewal

9 To renew a belt, follow the instructions above for adjustment, but remove the belt from the pulleys.

10 In some cases, you will have to remove more than one belt, because of their arrangement on the front of the engine. Because of this, and the fact that belts will tend to fail at the same time, it is wise to renew all belts together. Mark each belt and its appropriate pulley groove, so all renewed belts can be fitted in their proper positions.

11 It is a good idea to take the old belts with you when buying new ones, in order to make a direct comparison for length, width and design.

12 Recheck the tension of new belts after a few hundred miles.

---

12 Engine idle speed and CO level check and adjustment

Note: *The engine should be at normal operating temperature, with correct ignition timing and valve clearances (where adjustable). The air filter should be in good condition, and all electrical components (including the air conditioning, where fitted) should be switched off.*

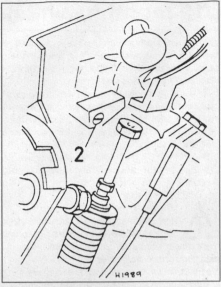

12.5 Mixture adjustment screw (2) on the 2B4 carburettor

Carburettor

1 Connect a tachometer and exhaust gas analyser (CO meter) to the engine.
2 Start the engine and allow it to idle.
3 Check that the idle speed is as given in the Specifications. Adjustment of the idle speed is only possible on the 2B4 carburettor. Turn the carburettor idle speed adjustment screw until the engine idles at the correct speed **(see illustration)**.
4 If the idle speed is low on the 2BE carburettor, and all wiring to the carburettor is in good condition, it is possible to connect a resistance into the control circuit. This should be carried out by your BMW dealer.
5 Check that the CO reading is as given in the Specifications. If not, turn the carburettor idle mixture adjustment screw until the mixture is correct **(see illustration)**.

L-Jetronic

6 Connect a tachometer and CO meter to the engine. BMW technicians use a special CO tester with a probe connected into the exhaust manifold, but the normal type of tester which locates in the exhaust tailpipe can be used instead. Note however that on models with a catalytic converter, meaningful CO readings will not be obtained at the tailpipe.
7 Start the engine and allow it to idle.
8 Check that the idle speed is as given in Specifications. If not, remove the tamperproof cap from the throttle housing, and turn the idle adjustment screw until the speed is correct.
9 Check that the CO reading is as given in the Specifications. The mixture control screw is located on the airflow meter, and a special

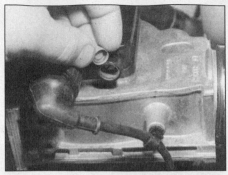

12.12a Removing the tamperproof plug from the airflow meter

tool (BMW number 13 1 060) may be required to make the adjustment.

Motronic

10 Connect a tachometer and CO meter to the engine. BMW technicians use a special CO tester with a probe connected into the exhaust manifold, but the normal type of tester which locates in the exhaust tailpipe may be used instead. Note however that on models with a catalytic converter, meaningful CO readings will not be obtained at the tailpipe.
11 It is not possible to adjust the idle speed manually, as the idle air stabiliser valve is activated by the electronic control unit. If the idle speed is not within the specified range with the engine at normal operating temperature, check for a leak in the air inlet system, and also check the operation of the idle air stabiliser valve (see Chapter 4).
12 Check that the CO reading is as given in the Specifications. If adjustment is required, prise out the tamperproof plug from the airflow meter, and turn the adjustment screw to set the CO content (on some models, an Allen key will be required). Fit a new tamperproof plug on completion **(see illustrations)**.

12.12b Adjusting the CO on the Motronic system

Every 12 000 miles or 12 months, whichever comes first

13 Battery check, maintenance and charging

Check and maintenance

Warning: Certain precautions must be followed when checking and servicing the battery. Hydrogen gas, which is highly flammable, is always present in the battery cells, so keep lighted tobacco and all other flames and sparks away from it. The electrolyte inside the battery is actually dilute sulphuric acid, which will cause injury if splashed on your skin or in your eyes. It will also ruin clothes and painted surfaces. When disconnecting the battery cables, always detach the negative cable first, and connect it last!

1 Battery maintenance is an important procedure, which will help ensure that you are not stranded because of a dead battery. Several tools are required for this procedure **(see illustration)**.

2 Before servicing the battery, always switch off the engine and all accessories, and disconnect the cable from the negative terminal of the battery.

Caution: If the radio in your vehicle is equipped with an anti-theft system, make sure you have the correct activation code before disconnecting the battery.

Note: If, after connecting the battery, the wrong language appears on the instrument panel display, refer to page 0-7 for the language resetting procedure.

3 A low-maintenance battery is standard equipment. The cell caps can be removed and distilled water can be added, if necessary. Later models may be fitted with a "maintenance-free" battery, which is sealed.

4 Remove the caps and check the electrolyte level in each of the battery cells. It must be above the plates. There's usually a split-ring indicator in each cell to indicate the correct level. If the level is low, add distilled water only, then refit the cell caps.

Caution: Overfilling the cells may cause electrolyte to spill over during periods of heavy charging, causing corrosion and damage to nearby components.

5 If the positive terminal and cable clamp on your vehicle's battery is equipped with a rubber protector, make sure that it's not torn or damaged. It should completely cover the terminal.

6 The external condition of the battery should be checked periodically. Look for damage such as a cracked case.

7 Check the tightness of the battery cable clamps to ensure good electrical connections. Check the entire length of each cable, looking for cracked or abraded insulation and frayed conductors.

8 If corrosion (visible as white, fluffy deposits) is evident, remove the cables from the terminals, clean them with a battery brush, and reconnect them **(see illustrations)**. Corrosion can be kept to a minimum by fitting specially treated washers available at car accessory shops, or by applying a layer of petroleum jelly or suitable grease to the

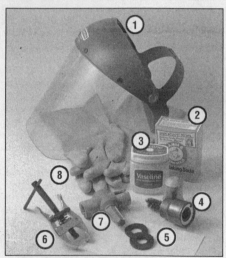

13.1 Tools and materials required for battery maintenance

1 **Face shield/safety goggles** - When removing corrosion with a brush, the acidic particles can easily fly up into your eyes
2 **Baking soda** - A solution of baking soda and water can be used to neutralise corrosion
3 **Petroleum jelly** - A layer of this on the battery posts will help prevent corrosion
4 **Battery post/cable cleaner** - This wire-brush cleaning tool will remove all traces of corrosion from the battery posts and cable clamps
5 **Treated felt washers** - Placing one of these on each post, directly under the cable clamps, will help prevent corrosion
6 **Puller** - Sometimes the cable clamps are very difficult to pull off the posts, even after the nut/bolt has been completely loosened. This tool pulls the clamp straight up and off the post without damage
7 **Battery post/cable cleaner** - Here is another cleaning tool which is a slightly different version of No 4 above, but it does the same thing
8 **Rubber gloves** - Another safety item to consider when servicing the battery; remember that's acid inside the battery!

13.8a Battery terminal corrosion usually appears as light, fluffy powder

13.8c Regardless of the type of tool used on the battery posts, a clean, shiny surface should be the result

13.8b Removing a cable from the battery post with a spanner - sometimes special battery pliers are required for this procedure, if corrosion has caused deterioration of the nut (always remove the earth cable first, and connect it last!)

13.8d When cleaning the cable clamps, all corrosion must be removed (the inside of the clamp is tapered to match the taper on the post, so don't remove too much material)

terminals and cable clamps after they are assembled.

9 Make sure that the battery carrier is in good condition, and that the hold-down clamp bolt is tight. If the battery is removed (see Chapter 5 for the removal and refitting procedure), make sure that no parts remain in the bottom of the carrier when it's refitted. When refitting the hold-down clamp, don't overtighten the bolt.

10 Corrosion on the carrier, battery case and surrounding areas can be removed with a solution of water and baking soda. Apply the mixture with a small brush, let it work, then rinse it off with plenty of clean water.

11 Any metal parts of the vehicle damaged by corrosion should be coated with a zinc-based primer, then painted.

12 Additional information on the battery and jump starting can be found in Chapter 5 and the front of this manual.

Charging

Note: *The manufacturer recommends the battery be removed from the vehicle for charging, because the gas which escapes during this procedure can damage the paint or interior, depending on the location of the battery. Fast charging with the battery cables connected can result in damage to the electrical system.*

13 Remove all of the cell caps (if applicable), and cover the holes with a clean cloth to prevent spattering electrolyte. Disconnect the

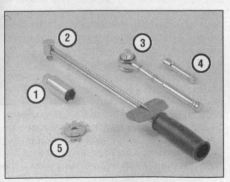

14.1 Tools required for changing spark plugs

1 *Spark plug socket* - This will have special padding inside to protect the spark plug's porcelain insulator

2 *Torque wrench* - Although not mandatory, using this tool is the best way to ensure the plugs are tightened properly

3 *Ratchet* - Standard hand tool to fit the spark plug socket

4 *Extension* - Depending on model and accessories, you may need special extensions and universal joints to reach one or more of the plugs

5 *Spark plug gap gauge* - This gauge for checking the gap comes in a variety of styles. Make sure the gap for your engine is included. Feeler blades may be used instead

battery negative cable, and connect the battery charger leads to the battery posts (positive to positive, negative to negative), then plug in the charger. Make sure it is set at 12 volts if it has a selector switch.

 Caution: If the radio in your vehicle is equipped with an anti-theft system, make sure you have the correct activation code before disconnecting the battery. Note: If, after connecting the battery, the wrong language appears on the instrument panel display, refer to page 0-7 for the language resetting procedure.

14 If you're using a charger with a rate higher than two amps, check the battery regularly during charging to make sure it doesn't overheat. If you're using a trickle charger, you can safely let the battery charge overnight after you've checked it regularly for the first couple of hours. Where a maintenance-free battery is fitted, special precautions may be necessary when charging it (for example, the charge rate is normally very low). There may be a warning label on the battery, but if not, consult a BMW dealer or auto-electrician.

15 If the battery has removable cell caps, measure the specific gravity with a hydrometer every hour during the last few hours of the charging cycle. Hydrometers are available inexpensively from car accessory shops - follow the instructions that come with the hydrometer. Consider the battery charged when there's no change in the specific gravity reading for two hours, and the electrolyte in the cells is gassing (bubbling) freely. The specific gravity reading from each cell should be very close to the others. If not, the battery probably has a bad cell(s), and a new one should be fitted.

16 Some maintenance-free (sealed) batteries have built-in hydrometers on the top, indicating the state of charge by the colour displayed in the hydrometer window. Normally, a bright-coloured hydrometer indicates a full charge, and a dark hydrometer indicates the battery still needs charging. Check the battery manufacturer's instructions to be sure you know what the colours mean.

17 If the battery is sealed and has no built-in hydrometer, you can connect a digital voltmeter across the battery terminals to check the charge. A fully-charged battery should read 12.6 volts or higher.

18 Further information on the battery and jump starting can be found in Chapter 5 and at the front of this manual.

14 Spark plug check and renewal

1 Before beginning, obtain the necessary tools, which will include a spark plug socket and a set of feeler blades. Special spark plug gap gauges can be obtained from certain spark plug manufacturers **(see illustration)**.

2 The best procedure to follow when renewing the spark plugs is to purchase the new spark plugs beforehand, adjust them to the proper gap, and then renew each plug one at a time. When buying the new spark plugs, it is important to obtain the correct plugs for your specific engine. This information can be found in the Specifications section in the front of this Chapter.

3 With the new spark plugs at hand, allow the engine to cool completely before attempting plug removal. During this time, each of the new spark plugs can be inspected for defects and the gaps can be checked.

4 The gap is checked by inserting the proper thickness gauge between the electrodes at the tip of the plug **(see illustration)**. The gap between the electrodes should be the same as that given in the Specifications. The wire should just touch each of the electrodes. If the gap is incorrect, use the notched adjuster to bend the curved side of the electrode slightly until the proper gap is achieved **(see illustration)**. **Note:** *When adjusting the gap of a new plug, bend only the base of the earth electrode, do not touch the tip. If the earth electrode is not exactly over the centre electrode, use the notched adjuster to align the two. Check for cracks in the porcelain insulator, indicating the spark plug should not be used.*

14.4a Spark plug manufacturers recommend using a wire-type gauge when checking the gap - if the wire does not slide between the electrodes with a slight drag, adjustment is required

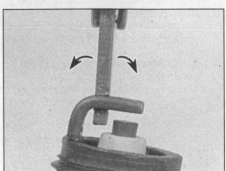

14.4b To change the gap, bend the earth electrode only, as indicated by the arrows, and be very careful not to crack or chip the porcelain insulator surrounding the centre electrode

1

14.5 When removing the spark plug HT leads, pull only on the connector

5 With the engine cool, remove the HT lead from one spark plug. Do this by grabbing the connector at the end of the wire, not the lead itself **(see illustration)**. Sometimes it is necessary to use a twisting motion while the connector and HT lead are pulled free.

6 If compressed air is available, use it to blow any dirt or foreign material away from the spark plug area. A common bicycle pump will also work. The idea here is to eliminate the possibility of debris falling into the cylinder as the spark plug is removed.

7 Place the spark plug socket over the plug, and remove it from the engine by turning it anti-clockwise **(see illustration)**.

8 Compare the spark plug with those shown in the accompanying photos to get an indication of the overall running condition of the engine.

9 Apply a little copper-based anti-seize compound to the threads of the new spark plug. Locate the plug into the head, screwing it in with your fingers until it no longer turns, then tighten it with the socket. If available, use a torque wrench to tighten the plug to ensure that it is seated correctly. The correct torque figure is included in this Chapter's Specifications.

TOOL TiP

Where there might be difficulty in inserting the spark plugs into the spark plug holes, or the possibility of cross-threading them into the head, a short piece of rubber or plastic tubing can be fitted over the end of the spark plug. The flexible tubing will act as a universal joint to help align the plug with the plug hole, and should the plug begin to cross-thread, the hose will slip on the spark plug, preventing thread damage.

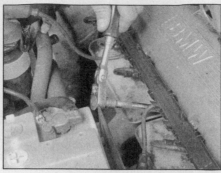

14.7 Use a socket spanner with an extension to unscrew the spark plugs

10 Before pushing the HT lead onto the end of the plug, inspect it as outlined in Section 15.

11 Attach the HT lead to the new spark plug, again using a twisting motion on the connector until it is firmly seated on the spark plug.

12 Follow the above procedure for the remaining spark plugs, renewing them one at a time to prevent mixing up the spark plug HT leads.

15 Spark plug HT leads, distributor cap and rotor - check and renewal

1 The spark plug HT leads should be checked at the recommended intervals, and whenever new spark plugs are fitted in the engine.

2 Begin this procedure by making a visual check of the spark plug HT leads while the engine is running. In a darkened garage (make sure there is ventilation) start the engine and observe each HT lead. Be careful not to come into contact with any moving engine parts. If there is a break in the wire, you will see arcing or a small spark at the damaged area. If arcing is noticed, make a note to obtain new HT leads, then allow the engine to cool.

3 Disconnect the battery negative cable.

 Caution: If the radio in your vehicle is equipped with an anti-theft system, make sure you have the correct activation code before disconnecting the battery.

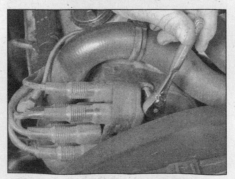

15.11a On later models, loosen the screws and detach the distributor cap up so you can inspect the inside

Note: *If, after connecting the battery, the wrong language appears on the instrument panel display, refer to page 0-7 for the language resetting procedure.*

4 The HT leads should be inspected one at a time to prevent mixing up the firing order, which is essential for proper engine operation.

5 Disconnect the HT lead from the spark plug. Do not pull on the lead itself, only on the connector.

6 Inspect inside the connector for corrosion, which will look like a white crusty powder. Push the HT lead and connector back onto the end of the spark plug. It should be a tight fit on the plug end. If it is not, remove the lead and use pliers to carefully crimp the metal terminal inside the connector until it fits securely on the end of the spark plug.

7 Using a clean rag, wipe the entire length of the HT lead to remove any built-up dirt and grease. Once the lead is clean, check for burns, cracks and other damage. Do not bend the lead excessively, since the conductor might break.

8 Disconnect the HT lead from the distributor. Again, pull only on the connector. Check for corrosion and a tight fit in the same manner as the spark plug end. Renew the HT lead in the distributor if necessary.

9 Check the remaining spark plug HT leads, making sure they are securely fastened at the distributor and spark plug when the check is complete.

10 If new spark plug HT leads are required, purchase a set for your specific engine model. Lead sets are available pre-cut, with the connectors already fitted. Remove and renew the HT leads one at a time, to avoid mix-ups in the firing order.

11 Loosen the screws or detach the clips and remove the distributor cap **(see illustration)**. Remove the screws (if applicable) and pull the rotor off the shaft **(see illustration)**. Check the distributor cap and rotor for wear. Look for cracks, carbon tracks and worn, burned or loose contacts **(see illustrations)**. Renew the cap and rotor if defects are found. It is common practice to fit a new cap and rotor whenever new spark plug HT leads are fitted. When fitting a new cap, remove the HT leads from the old cap one at a time, and attach

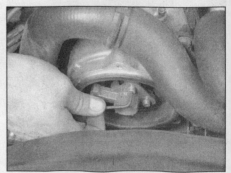

15.11b Use an Allen key to remove the screws, then lift the rotor off the shaft (later models)

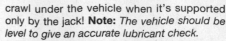

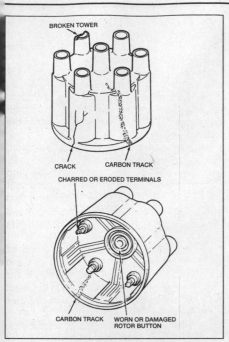

15.11c Shown here are some of the common defects to look for when inspecting the distributor cap (if in doubt about its condition, fit a new one)

them to the new cap in the exact same location - do not simultaneously remove all the HT leads, or firing order mix-ups may occur.

16 Manual transmission lubricant level check

1 The transmission has a filler/level plug which must be removed to check the lubricant level. If the vehicle is raised to gain access to the plug, be sure to support it safely - do not crawl under a vehicle which is supported only by a jack! *Note: The vehicle should be level to give an accurate lubricant check.*
2 Remove the plug from the side of the

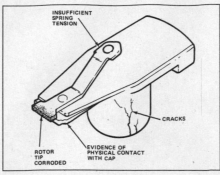

15.11d The rotor arm should be checked for wear and corrosion as indicated here (if in doubt about its condition, buy a new one)

transmission **(see illustration)** and use your little finger to reach inside the plug from the housing and feel the lubricant level. It should be at or very near the bottom of the plug hole.
3 If it isn't, add the recommended lubricant through the plug hole with a syringe or squeeze-bottle, until it just starts to run out of the hole. Refer to *"Lubricants and fluids"* at the beginning of this Chapter for the correct lubricant type. The manual transmissions on some later or high-performance models are filled with automatic transmission fluid (ATF). Such transmissions normally carry a sticker to this effect near the filler/level plug. Refer to a BMW dealer if still in doubt.
4 Refit the plug and tighten securely. Check for leaks after the first few miles of driving.
5 If regular topping-up is required, this can only be due to a leak which should be found and repaired before it becomes serious.

17 Differential lubricant level check

1 The differential has a filler/level plug which must be removed to check the lubricant level. If the vehicle is raised to gain access to the plug, be sure to support it safely - do not

crawl under the vehicle when it's supported only by the jack! **Note:** *The vehicle should be level to give an accurate lubricant check.*
2 Remove the filler/level plug from the differential **(see illustration)**. Use an Allen key to unscrew the plug.
3 Use your little finger as a dipstick to make sure the lubricant level is up to the bottom of the plug hole. If not, use a syringe or squeeze-bottle to add the recommended lubricant until it just starts to run out of the hole.
4 Refit the plug and tighten it securely.
5 If regular topping-up is required, this can only be due to a leak which should be found and repaired before it becomes serious.

18 Valve clearances - check and adjustment

Note: *This procedure does not apply to the M40 engine, which has automatic adjusters.*
1 The valve clearances can be checked with the engine hot or cold, but note that different values are specified, depending on engine temperature. If it is wished to check/adjust the valve clearances with the engine hot, if necessary start and run the engine until it reaches normal operating temperature, then shut it off.

⚠ *Caution: If the clearances are checked with the engine hot, extra care must be taken to avoid burns.*
2 Remove the valve cover from the engine (see Chapter 2A).
3 Turn the engine as necessary until No 1 piston (front) is at Top Dead Centre (TDC) on the compression stroke (see Chapter 2A).
4 Check the valve clearances for No 1 cylinder. The valve clearances can be found in the Specifications Section at the beginning of this Chapter.
5 The clearance is measured by inserting the specified size feeler gauge between the end of the valve stem and the rocker arm adjusting eccentric. You should feel a slight amount of

16.2 Use a large Allen key to remove the filler/level plug (arrowed) and check the lubricant level with your little finger. It should be level with the bottom of the hole - if it's low, add lubricant

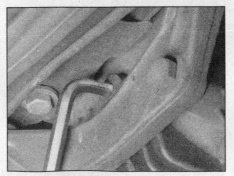

17.2 Remove the differential filler/level plug with an Allen key, and make sure the lubricant is level with the bottom of the hole

18.6 The valve clearance is adjusted by turning the eccentric with a wire hook - once the specified clearance is obtained, tighten the locknut with a spanner, then remove the feeler gauge

19.3 Check and lubricate the throttle linkage at the points shown (arrowed) - fuel injection engine shown

20.4 Detach the duct from the air cleaner housing

20.5 Use a screwdriver to detach the air cleaner cover clips

drag when the feeler gauge is moved back and forth.

6 If the gap is too large or too small, loosen the locknut, insert a hook made from large-diameter metal wire, and rotate the eccentric to obtain the correct gap (see illustration).

7 Once the gap has been set, hold the eccentric in position with the hook, and retighten the locknut securely. Recheck the clearance - sometimes it'll change slightly when the locknut is tightened. If so, re-adjust until it's correct.

8 On the M10 engine, the valves are adjusted in the firing order, which is 1-3-4-2. After adjusting No 1 cylinder valves, rotate the crankshaft half a turn (180°), then check and adjust the valves on No 3 cylinder. Repeat the procedure on the remaining cylinders.

9 On M20 and M30 engines, the valves are adjusted following the firing order, which is 1-5-3-6-2-4. After adjusting No 1 cylinder valves, rotate the crankshaft a third of a turn (120°), then check and adjust the valves on No 5 cylinder. Repeat the procedure for the remaining cylinders.

10 Refit the valve cover (use a new gasket) and tighten the mounting nuts evenly and securely.

11 Start the engine and check for oil leakage between the valve cover and the cylinder head.

19 Throttle linkage - check and lubrication

1 The throttle linkage should be checked and lubricated periodically to ensure its proper operation.

2 Check the linkage to make sure it isn't binding.

3 Inspect the linkage joints for looseness, and the connections for corrosion and damage, renewing parts as necessary (see illustration).

4 Lubricate the connections with spray lubricant or lithium-based grease.

20 Air filter renewal

Carburettor engines

1 Release the spring clips, then unscrew the centre nut and lift off the cover.

2 Remove the air filter element, and wipe clean the air cleaner body and cover

3 Fit the new air filter element, then refit the cover using a reversal of the removal procedure.

Fuel injection engines

4 Loosen the clamp on the air intake duct, and detach the duct (see illustration).

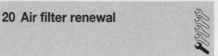

5 Release the air cleaner cover retaining clips (see illustration).

6 Rotate the cover up, lift it off and lift the element out, noting which way round it is fitted (see illustrations).

7 Wipe the inside of the air cleaner housing with a clean cloth, then fit the new element. If the element is marked TOP, be sure the marked side faces up.

8 Refit the cover and secure the clips.

9 Connect the air duct and tighten the clamp screw.

21 Fuel system check

Warning: Fuel is extremely flammable, so take extra precautions when you work on any part of the fuel system. Don't smoke, or allow open flames or bare light bulbs, near the work area. Don't work in a garage where a natural gas-type appliance (such as a water heater or clothes dryer) with a pilot light is present. Work in a well-ventilated area. If you spill any fuel on your skin, rinse it off immediately with soap and water. When you perform any kind of work on the fuel system, wear safety glasses, and have a fire extinguisher on hand. Mop up spills immediately, but do not store fuel-soaked rags where they could ignite.

1 If you smell fuel while driving or after the vehicle has been sitting in the sun, inspect the fuel system immediately.

2 Remove the fuel filler cap and inspect it for damage and corrosion. The gasket should have an unbroken sealing imprint. If the gasket is damaged or corroded, fit a new cap.

3 Inspect the fuel feed and return lines for cracks. Make sure that the connections between the fuel lines and the carburettor or fuel injection system, and between the fuel lines and the in-line fuel filter, are tight.

Warning: On fuel injection models, the fuel system must be depressurised before servicing fuel system components, as outlined in Chapter 4.

20.6a Rotate the cover upwards ...

20.6b ... and lift the air filter element out

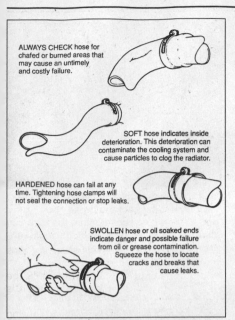

ALWAYS CHECK hose for chafed or burned areas that may cause an untimely and costly failure.

SOFT hose indicates inside deterioration. This deterioration can contaminate the cooling system and cause particles to clog the radiator.

HARDENED hose can fail at any time. Tightening hose clamps will not seal the connection or stop leaks.

SWOLLEN hose or oil soaked ends indicate danger and possible failure from oil or grease contamination. Squeeze the hose to locate cracks and breaks that cause leaks.

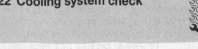

22.4 Hoses, like drivebelts, have a habit of failing at the worst possible time - to prevent the inconvenience of a blown radiator or heater hose, inspect them carefully as shown here

4 Since some components of the fuel system - the fuel tank and some of the fuel feed and return lines, for example - are underneath the vehicle, they can be inspected more easily with the vehicle raised on a hoist. If that's not possible, raise the vehicle and support it on axle stands or ramps.

5 With the vehicle raised and safely supported, inspect the fuel tank and filler neck for punctures, cracks or other damage. The connection between the filler neck and the tank is particularly critical. Sometimes a rubber filler neck will leak because of loose clamps or deteriorated rubber. Inspect all fuel tank mounting brackets and straps, to be sure the tank is securely attached to the vehicle.

⚠️ **Warning: Do not, under any circumstances, try to repair a fuel tank (except rubber components). A welding torch or any naked flame can easily cause fuel vapours inside the tank to explode.**

6 Carefully check all flexible hoses and metal lines leading away from the fuel tank. Check for loose connections, deteriorated hoses, crimped lines, and other damage. Repair or renew damaged sections as necessary (see Chapter 4).

22 Cooling system check

1 Many major engine failures can be attributed to cooling system problems. If the vehicle has automatic transmission, the engine cooling system also plays an important role in prolonging transmission life, because it cools the transmission fluid.

2 The engine should be cold for the cooling system check, so perform the following procedure before the vehicle is driven for the day, or after it has been switched off for *at least* three hours.

3 Remove the radiator cap, doing so slowly and taking adequate precautions against scalding if the engine is at all warm. Clean the cap thoroughly, inside and out, with clean water. Also clean the filler neck on the radiator. The presence of rust or corrosion in the filler neck means the coolant should be changed (see Section 29). The coolant inside the radiator should be relatively clean and clear. If it's rust-coloured, drain the system and refill with new coolant.

4 Carefully check the radiator hoses and the smaller-diameter heater hoses. Inspect each coolant hose along its entire length, renewing any hose which is cracked, swollen or deteriorated **(see illustration)**. Cracks will show up better if the hose is squeezed. Pay close attention to hose clamps that secure the hoses to cooling system components. Hose clamps can pinch and puncture hoses, resulting in coolant leaks.

5 Make sure all hose connections are tight. A leak in the cooling system will usually show up as white or rust-coloured deposits on the area adjoining the leak. If wire-type clamps are used on the hoses, it may be a good idea to replace them with screw-type clamps.

6 Clean the front of the radiator (and, where applicable, the air conditioning condenser) with compressed air if available, or a soft brush. Remove all flies, leaves, etc, embedded in the radiator fins. Be extremely careful not to damage the cooling fins or to cut your fingers on them.

7 If the coolant level has been dropping consistently and no leaks are detected, have the radiator cap and cooling system pressure-tested.

23 Exhaust system check

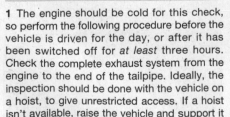

1 The engine should be cold for this check, so perform the following procedure before the vehicle is driven for the day, or after it has been switched off for *at least* three hours. Check the complete exhaust system from the engine to the end of the tailpipe. Ideally, the inspection should be done with the vehicle on a hoist, to give unrestricted access. If a hoist isn't available, raise the vehicle and support it securely on axle stands or ramps.

2 Check the exhaust pipes and connections for evidence of leaks, severe corrosion, and damage. Make sure that all brackets and mountings are in good condition, and that they are tight **(see illustration)**.

3 At the same time, inspect the underside of the body for holes, corrosion, open seams, etc. which may allow exhaust gases to enter the passenger compartment. Seal all body openings with suitable sealant.

4 Rattles and other noises can often be traced to the exhaust system, especially the mountings and heat shields. Try to move the pipes, silencers (and, where applicable, the catalytic converter). If the components can come in contact with the body or suspension parts, re-hang the exhaust system with new mountings.

5 The running condition of the engine may be checked by inspecting inside the end of the tailpipe. The exhaust deposits here are an indication of the engine's state of tune. If the pipe is black and sooty, the engine may be running too rich, indicating the need for a thorough fuel system inspection.

24 Steering and suspension check

Note: *The steering linkage and suspension components should be checked periodically. Worn or damaged suspension and steering linkage components can result in excessive and abnormal tyre wear, poor ride quality and vehicle handling, and reduced fuel economy. For detailed illustrations of the steering and suspension components, refer to Chapter 10.*

Strut/shock absorber check

1 Park the vehicle on level ground, turn the engine off and apply the handbrake. Check the tyre pressures.

2 Push down at one corner of the vehicle, then release it while noting the movement of the body. It should stop moving and come to rest in a level position with one or two bounces.

3 If the vehicle continues to move up and down, or if it fails to return to its original position, a worn or weak strut or shock absorber is probably the reason.

4 Repeat the above check at each of the three remaining corners of the vehicle.

5 Raise the vehicle and support it on axle stands.

6 Check the struts/shock absorbers for evidence of fluid leakage. A light film of fluid is

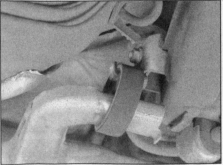

23.2 Check the exhaust system rubber mountings for cracks

1

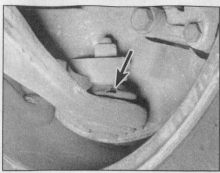

24.10 Inspect the balljoint boots for tears (arrowed)

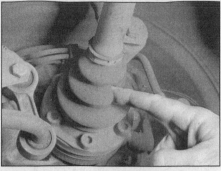

25.2 Gently probe the driveshaft boots to check for cracks

26.11 Look through the caliper inspection window to inspect the brake pads - the pad lining which rubs against the disc can also be inspected by looking through each end of the caliper

no cause for concern. Make sure that any fluid noted is from the struts/shocks, and not from any other source. If leakage is noted, renew the struts or shock absorbers in axle pairs (or as a full set).

7 Check the struts/shock absorbers to be sure that they are securely mounted and undamaged. Check the upper mountings for damage and wear. If damage or wear is noted, renew the struts or shock absorbers.

8 If the struts or shock absorbers must be renewed, refer to Chapter 10 for the procedure. Always renew both units on the same axle, or the safety of the vehicle may be compromised. If possible, renew all four as a set.

Steering and suspension check

9 Inspect the steering system components for damage and distortion. Look for leaks and damaged seals, boots and fittings.

10 Clean the lower end of the steering knuckle. Have an assistant grasp the lower edge of the tyre and move the wheel in and out, while you look for movement at the steering knuckle-to-axle arm balljoints. Inspect the balljoint boots for tears **(see illustration)**. If there is any movement, or the boots are torn or leaking, the balljoint(s) must be renewed.

11 Grasp each front tyre at the front and rear edges, push in at the front, pull out at the rear and feel for play in the steering linkage. If any free play is noted, check the steering gear mountings and the track rod balljoints for looseness. If the steering gear mountings are loose, tighten them. If the track rods are loose, the balljoints may be worn (check to make sure the nuts are tight). Additional steering and suspension system information can be found in Chapter 10.

25 Driveshaft gaiter check

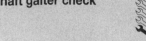

1 The driveshaft gaiters are very important because they prevent dirt, water and foreign material from entering and damaging the constant velocity (CV) joints. External oil and grease contamination can cause the gaiter

material to deteriorate prematurely, so it's a good idea to wash the gaiters with soap and water.

2 Inspect the gaiters for tears and cracks, as well as for loose clamps **(see illustration)**. If there is any evidence of cracks or leaking lubricant, the gaiter must be renewed (see Chapter 8).

26 Brake system check

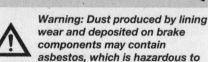

⚠️ **Warning: Dust produced by lining wear and deposited on brake components may contain asbestos, which is hazardous to your health. Do not blow it out with compressed air, and don't inhale it! Do not use petroleum-based solvents to remove the dust. Brake system cleaner or methylated spirit should be used to flush the dust into a drain pan. After the brake components are wiped with a damp rag, dispose of the contaminated rag(s) and the drain pan contents into a covered and labelled container. Try to use asbestos-free new parts whenever possible.**

Note: *In addition to the specified intervals, the brake system should be inspected each time the wheels are removed or a malfunction is indicated. Because of the obvious safety considerations, the following brake system checks are some of the most important maintenance procedures you can perform on your vehicle.*

Symptoms of brake system problems

1 The disc brakes have built-in electrical wear indicators which cause a warning light on the dash to come on when they're worn to the renewal point. When the light comes on, renew the pads immediately, or expensive damage to the brake discs could result.

2 Any of the following symptoms could indicate a potential brake system defect:

a) *Vehicle pulls to one side when the brake pedal is depressed*
b) *Brakes make squealing or dragging noises when applied*
c) *Brake pedal travel excessive*

d) *Brake pedal pulsates (normal if ABS is working)*
e) *Brake fluid leaks (usually on the inner side of the tyre or wheel)*

3 If any of these conditions are noted, inspect the brake system immediately.

Brake lines and hoses

Note: *Steel brake pipes are used throughout the brake system, with the exception of flexible, reinforced hoses at the front wheels and as connectors at the rear axle. Periodic inspection of all these lines is very important.*

4 Park the vehicle on level ground, and switch off the engine. Remove the wheel covers. Loosen, but do not remove, the bolts on all four wheels.

5 Raise the vehicle and support it securely on axle stands.

6 Remove the wheels (see "Jacking and towing" at the front of this book, or refer to your owner's handbook, if necessary).

7 Check all brake lines and hoses for cracks, chafing of the outer cover, leaks, blisters, and distortion. Check the brake hoses at front and rear of the vehicle for softening, cracks, bulging, or wear from rubbing on other components. Check all threaded fittings for leaks, and make sure the brake hose mounting bolts and clips are secure.

8 If leaks or damage are discovered, they must be repaired immediately. Refer to Chapter 9 for detailed brake system repair procedures.

Disc brakes

9 If it hasn't already been done, raise the vehicle and support it securely on axle stands. Remove the front wheels.

10 The disc brake calipers, containing the pads, are now visible. Each caliper has an outer and an inner pad - all pads should be checked.

11 Note the pad thickness by looking through the inspection hole in the caliper **(see illustration)**. If the lining material is 2.0 mm thick or less, or if it is tapered from end to end, the pads should be renewed (see Chapter 9). Keep in mind that the lining

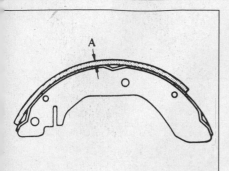

26.15 If the lining is bonded to the brake shoe, measure the lining thickness from the outer surface to the metal shoe, as shown here (A); if the lining is riveted to the shoe, measure from the lining outer surface to the rivet head

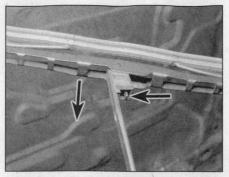

27.5 Press the retaining tab in, then slide the wiper blade assembly down and out of the hook in the end of the wiper arm

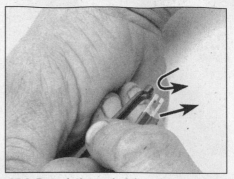

27.6 Detach the end of the wiper element from the end of the frame, then slide the element out

material is bonded to a metal plate or shoe - the metal portion is not included in this measurement. Always renew the pads on both sides of the vehicle (in axle sets), even if only one pad of the four is worn, or uneven braking may result.

12 Remove the calipers without disconnecting the brake hoses (see Chapter 9).

13 Check the condition of the brake disc. Look for score marks, deep scratches and overheated areas (they will appear blue or discoloured). If damage or wear is noted, the disc can be removed and resurfaced by an engineering workshop; otherwise, it will have to be renewed. In either case, both discs should be involved, even if only one is worn. Refer to Chapter 9 for more detailed inspection and repair procedures.

Drum brakes

14 Refer to Chapter 9 and remove the rear brake drums.

15 Note the thickness of the lining material on the rear brake shoes, and look for signs of contamination by brake fluid or grease (see Illustration). If the material is within 2.0 mm of the recessed rivets or metal shoes, renew the brake shoes. The shoes should also be renewed if they are cracked, glazed (shiny lining surfaces), or contaminated with brake fluid or grease. See Chapter 9 for the renewal procedure.

16 Check the shoe return and hold-down springs and the adjusting mechanism. Make sure all these components are fitted correctly,

and are in good condition. Deteriorated or distorted springs, if not renewed, could allow the linings to drag and wear prematurely.

17 Check the wheel cylinders for leakage by carefully peeling back the rubber boots. Slight moisture behind the boots is acceptable. If brake fluid is noted behind the boots or if it runs out of the wheel cylinder, the wheel cylinders must be overhauled or renewed (see Chapter 9).

18 Check the drums for cracks, score marks, deep scratches and high spots, which will appear as small discoloured areas. If imperfections cannot be removed with emery cloth, both drums must be resurfaced by a specialist (see Chapter 9 for more detailed information).

19 Refer to Chapter 9 and fit the brake drums.

20 Refit the wheels, but don't lower the vehicle yet.

Handbrake

21 The easiest, and perhaps most obvious, method of checking the handbrake is to park the vehicle on a steep hill with the handbrake applied and the transmission in Neutral (stay in the vehicle while performing this check). If the handbrake doesn't prevent the vehicle from rolling, refer to Chapter 9 and adjust it.

27 Wiper blades - check and renewal

1 Road film can build up on the wiper blades and affect their efficiency, so they should be

washed regularly with a mild detergent solution.

Check

2 The wiper and blade assembly should be inspected periodically. If inspection reveals hardened or cracked rubber, renew the wiper blades. If inspection reveals nothing unusual, wet the windscreen, turn the wipers on, allow them to cycle several times, then switch them off. An uneven wiper pattern across the glass, or streaks over clean glass, indicate that the blades should be renewed.

3 The operation of the wiper mechanism can loosen the retaining nuts, so they should be checked and tightened, as necessary, at the same time the wiper blades are checked (see Chapter 12 for further information regarding the wiper mechanism).

Wiper blade renewal

4 Pull the wiper/blade assembly away from the glass.

5 Press the retaining tab in, and slide the blade assembly down the wiper arm (see illustration).

6 If you wish to renew the blade rubbers separately, detach the end of the rubber from the wiper blade frame, then slide the rubber out of the frame (see illustration).

7 Compare the new rubber with the old for length, design, etc.

8 Slide the new rubber into place, and insert the end in the wiper blade frame to lock it in place.

9 Refit the blade assembly on the arm, then wet the glass and check for proper operation.

Every 24 000 miles or 2 years, whichever comes first

28 Automatic transmission fluid and filter change

1 At the specified intervals, the transmission fluid should be drained and renewed. Since the fluid will remain hot long after driving,

perform this procedure only after the engine has cooled down completely.

2 Before beginning work, purchase the specified transmission fluid (see "Lubricants and fluids" at the beginning of this Chapter) and a new filter.

3 Other tools necessary for this job include axle stands or ramps to support the vehicle in a

raised position, a drain pan capable of holding at least 4.5 litres, and newspapers and clean rags.

4 Raise the vehicle and support it securely.

5 Loosen the dipstick tube collar, then detach the dipstick tube and let the fluid drain (see illustrations).

6 Remove the transmission sump mounting bolts and brackets (see illustration).

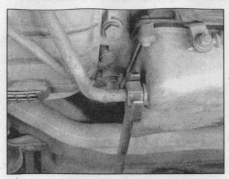

28.5a Unscrew the dipstick tube collar

28.5b Detach the tube and let the fluid drain

28.6 Use a socket and extension to remove the bolts and brackets

7 Detach the sump from the transmission and lower it, being careful not to spill the remaining fluid **(see illustration)**.
8 Carefully clean the sump-to-transmission contact surface.
9 Pour the fluid from the sump into a suitable container, then clean the sump with solvent and dry it with compressed air. Be sure to clean any metal filings from the magnet, if applicable.
10 Remove the filter from inside the transmission **(see illustrations)**.
11 Fit the O-ring and a new filter, being sure to tighten the bolts securely.
12 Make sure that the sump gasket contact surfaces are clean, then fit the new gasket. Offer the sump up to the transmission, and refit the brackets and bolts. Working around

the sump, tighten each bolt a little at a time until the torque listed in this Chapter's Specifications is reached. Don't overtighten the bolts! Connect the dipstick tube, and tighten the collar securely.
13 Lower the vehicle, and add the specified amount of fluid through the filler tube (see Section 8).
14 With the transmission in Park and the handbrake applied, run the engine at fast idle, but don't race it.
15 Move the gear selector through each position, and back to Park. Check the fluid level.
16 Check under the vehicle for leaks after the first few trips.

1 Periodically, the cooling system should be drained, flushed and refilled. This will restore the effectiveness of the antifreeze mixture and prevent formation of rust and corrosion, which can impair the performance of the cooling system and cause engine damage. When the cooling system is serviced, all hoses and the radiator cap should be checked and renewed if necessary.

Draining

2 If the vehicle has just been driven, wait several hours to allow the engine to cool down before beginning this procedure.
3 Once the engine is completely cool, remove the expansion tank cap or radiator cap. If the cap must be removed while the engine is still warm, unscrew it slowly, and take adequate precautions to avoid scalding.
4 Move a large container under the radiator to catch the coolant. Where a drain plug is fitted, unscrew it (a pair of pliers or screwdriver may be required to turn it, depending on the model) **(see illustration)**. Where there is no drain plug, it will be necessary to disconnect the bottom hose from the radiator.
5 While the coolant is draining, check the condition of the radiator hoses, heater hoses and clamps (see Section 21 if necessary).
6 Renew any damaged clamps or hoses (see Chapter 3 for detailed renewal procedures).

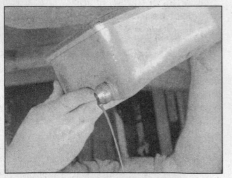

28.7 Lower the sump from the transmission

29 Cooling system - draining, flushing and refilling

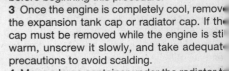

Warning: Do not allow antifreeze to come in contact with your skin, or with the painted surfaces of the vehicle. Rinse off spills immediately with plenty of water. Antifreeze is highly toxic if ingested. Never leave antifreeze lying around in an open container or in puddles on the floor; children and pets are attracted by its sweet smell, and may drink it. Check with local authorities about disposing of used antifreeze. Local collection centres may exist to see that antifreeze is disposed of safely.

28.10a Use a Torx key to remove the filter bolts . . .

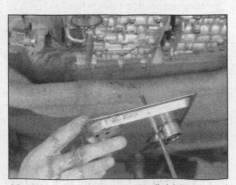

28.10b . . . then remove the fluid filter from the transmission

28.10c Remove the O-ring from the transmission. If it is in good condition, clean it and transfer it to the new fluid filter; otherwise, renew it

29.4 Radiator drain plug location (arrowed) - not fitted to all models

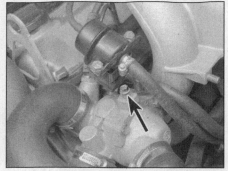

29.16 The bleed screw (arrowed) is located on the thermostat housing (six-cylinder models)

30.5 To renew the fuel filter, disconnect the hoses (A), then unscrew the nut (B) and detach the filter from the bracket (fuel injection type shown)

Flushing

7 Once the system is completely drained, flush the radiator with fresh water from a garden hose until the water runs clear at the drain or bottom hose. If the radiator is severely corroded, damaged or leaking, it should be removed (see Chapter 3) and taken to a radiator repair specialist.

8 Flushing in this way will remove sediments from the radiator, but will not remove rust and scale from the engine and cooling tube surfaces. These deposits can be removed by using a chemical cleaner. Follow the procedure outlined in the cleaner manufacturer's instructions. Remove the cylinder block drain plug before flushing the engine.

9 On models so equipped, remove the overflow hose from the coolant recovery reservoir. Drain the reservoir and flush it with clean water, then reconnect the hose.

Refilling

10 Tighten the radiator drain plug, or reconnect the radiator bottom hose. Refit and tighten the cylinder block drain plug.

Four-cylinder engines

11 Slowly add new coolant (a 40%/60% mixture of antifreeze to water) to the radiator until it is full. Add coolant to the reservoir up to the lower mark.

12 Leave the radiator cap off, and run the engine in a well-ventilated area until the thermostat opens (coolant will begin flowing through the radiator, and the upper radiator hose will become hot).

13 Turn the engine off, and let it cool. Add more coolant mixture to bring the coolant level back up to the lip on the radiator filler neck. On the M40 engine, unscrew the bleed screw from the top of the radiator, and add coolant until it comes out of the bleed screw hole. Refit and tighten the bleed screw.

14 Squeeze the upper radiator hose to expel air, then add more coolant mixture if necessary. Refit the radiator cap.

15 Start the engine, allow it to reach normal operating temperature, and check for leaks.

Six-cylinder engines

16 Loosen the bleed screw in the thermostat housing **(see illustration)**

17 Fill the radiator with a 40%/60% solution of antifreeze and water until it comes out of the bleed screw opening. Tighten the bleed screw.

18 Refit the radiator cap, and run the engine until the thermostat opens (the upper radiator hose will become hot). Slowly loosen the bleed screw until no bubbles emerge, then tighten the screw.

19 Repeat the procedure until the air is bled from the system.

30 Fuel filter renewal

⚠️ **Warning: Fuel is extremely flammable, so take extra precautions when you work on any part of the fuel system. Don't smoke, or allow open flames or bare light bulbs, near the work area. Don't work in a garage where a natural gas-type appliance (such as a water heater or clothes dryer) with a pilot light is present. If you spill any fuel on your skin, rinse it off immediately with soap and water. When you perform any kind of work on the fuel system, wear safety glasses, and have a fire extinguisher on hand.**

1 On fuel injection engines, depressurise the fuel system (see Chapter 4).

2 The fuel filter is located in the engine compartment on the bulkhead, or under the vehicle adjacent to the fuel tank.

3 Because on some models the filter is located adjacent to the starter motor, fuel could leak onto the electrical connections. For safety reasons, therefore, disconnect the battery negative cable before beginning work.

⚠️ **Caution: If the radio in your vehicle is equipped with an anti-theft system, make sure you have the correct activation code before disconnecting the battery.**

Note: *If, after connecting the battery, the wrong language appears on the instrument panel display, refer to page 0-7 for the language resetting procedure.*

4 Place a pan or rags under the fuel filter to catch any spilled fuel. If suitable hose clamps are available, clamp the inlet and outlet hoses.

5 Detach the hoses and remove the bracket screws/nuts, then remove the filter and where applicable the bracket assembly **(see illustration)**.

6 Detach the filter from the bracket.

7 Refitting is the reverse of removal. Be sure the arrow on the filter points in the direction of fuel flow.

31 Manual transmission lubricant change

1 Tools necessary for this job include axle stands to support the vehicle in a raised position, an Allen key to remove the drain plug, a drain pan, newspapers and clean rags. The correct amount of the specified lubricant should also be available (see *"Lubricants and fluids"* at the start of this Chapter).

2 The lubricant should be drained when it is hot (ie immediately after the vehicle has been driven); this will remove any contaminants better than if the lubricant were cold. Because

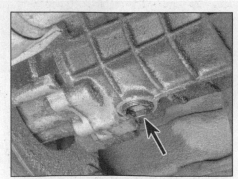

31.5 Use an Allen key to remove the drain plug (arrowed) from the bottom of the transmission

32.4 Remove the differential drain plug with an Allen key

the lubricant will be hot, it would be wise to wear rubber gloves.

3 Raise the vehicle and place it on axle stands. Make sure it is safely supported, and as level as possible.

4 Move the necessary equipment under the vehicle, being careful not to touch any of the hot exhaust components.

5 Place the drain pan under the transmission, and remove the filler/level plug from the side of the transmission. Loosen the drain plug **(see illustration)**.

6 Carefully remove the drain plug. Be careful not to burn yourself on the lubricant.

7 Allow the lubricant to drain completely. Clean the drain plug thoroughly, then refit and tighten it securely.

8 Refer to Section 16 and fill the transmission with new lubricant, then refit the filler/level plug, tightening it securely.

9 Lower the vehicle. Check for leaks at the drain plug after the first few miles of driving.

32 Differential lubricant change

1 Drive the vehicle for several miles to warm up the differential lubricant, then raise the vehicle and support it securely on axle stands.

2 Move a drain pan, rags, newspapers and an Allen key under the vehicle. Since the lubricant will be hot, wear rubber gloves to prevent burns.

3 Remove the filler/level plug from the differential; this is the upper of the two plugs.

4 With the drain pan under the differential, loosen the drain plug; this is the lower of the two plugs **(see illustration)**.

5 Carefully unscrew the drain plug until you can remove it from the case.

6 Allow all the oil to drain into the pan, then refit the drain plug and tighten it securely.

7 Refer to Section 17 and fill the differential with lubricant.

8 Refit the filler/level plug and tighten it securely.

9 Lower the vehicle. Check for leaks at the drain plug after the first few miles of driving.

33.2 Inspect the hoses (arrowed) at the top of the evaporative emissions charcoal canister for damage

33 Evaporative emissions control (EVAP) system check

1 The function of the evaporative emissions control system is to draw fuel vapours from the tank and fuel system, store them in a charcoal canister, and then burn them during normal engine operation. This system is normally only fitted to those vehicles equipped with a catalytic converter.

2 The most common symptom of a fault in the evaporative emissions system is a strong fuel odour in the engine compartment. If a fuel odour is detected, inspect the charcoal canister and system hoses for cracks. The canister is located in the front corner of the engine compartment on most models **(see illustration)**.

3 Refer to Chapter 6 for more information on the evaporative emissions system.

34 Service indicator light resetting

Service indicator lights

1 All models covered in this manual are equipped with various service indicator lights on the facia, which automatically go on when the mileage interval is reached. These lights can only be turned off by using a special tool which plugs into the service connector located in the engine compartment.

2 Although the service light resetting tool can be obtained from a dealer, reasonably-priced alternatives may also be available from aftermarket sources. When obtaining a tool, it is important to know the vehicle year and model, and whether the service connector has 15 or 20 pins **(see illustrations)**. Once the proper tool is obtained, it is a simple matter to plug it into the service connector and, following the tool manufacturer's instructions, reset the service lights. **Note:** *The brake warning light will not automatically reset if the sensor on the brake pad (or its wiring) is*

34.2a The earlier 15-pin connector (arrowed) is mounted near the front of the engine. The 20-pin connector used on later models is located in the left rear corner of the engine compartment

34.2b An aftermarket service light resetting tool such as this one can be plugged into the service connector and used to reset the service lights

damaged because it is worn through: it must be repaired first.

3 The service lights are controlled by the Service Indicator (SI) board in the instrument cluster, which is powered by rechargeable batteries. Should these batteries fail, problems will develop in the SI board. Symptoms of failed batteries include the inability to reset the service lights and malfunctions affecting the tachometer, temperature gauge and radio operation. Refer to Chapter 12 for more information on the SI board.

Every 30 000 miles

35 Engine timing belt renewal

Note: *The above renewal interval is strongly recommended as a precaution against the timing belt failing in service. If the timing belt fails while the engine is running, extensive engine damage could be caused.*

Refer to Chapter 2A, Section 10.

Chapter 2 Part A:
In-car engine repair procedures

Contents

Degrees of difficulty

2A

Easy, suitable for novice with little experience	Fairly easy, suitable for beginner with some experience	Fairly difficult, suitable for competent DIY mechanic	Difficult, suitable for experienced DIY mechanic	Very difficult, suitable for expert DIY or professional

Specifications

General

Displacement

3-series, E30 body style

316i (1988 to 1991)	1596 cc (M40/4-cylinder engine)
316 (1983 to 1988) and 318i (1983 to 1987)	1766 cc (M10/4-cylinder engine)
318i (1987 1991)	1796 cc (M40/4-cylinder engine)
320i (1987 to 1991)	1990 cc (M20/6-cylinder engine)
325i (1987 to 1991)	2494 cc (M20/6-cylinder engine)

5-series, E28 body style ("old-shape")

518 (1981 to 1985) and 518i (1985 to 1988)	1766 cc (M10/4-cylinder engine)
525i (1981 to 1988)	2494 cc (M30/6-cylinder engine)
528i (1981 to 1988)	2788 cc (M30/6-cylinder engine)
535i (1985 to 1988)	3430 cc (M30/6-cylinder engine)
M535i (1985 to 1988)	3430 cc (M30/6-cylinder engine)

5-series, E34 body style ("new-shape")

518i (1990 to 1993)	1796 cc (M40/4-cylinder engine)
520i (1988 to 1991)	1990 cc (M20/6-cylinder engine)
525i (1988 to 1991)	2494 cc (M20/6-cylinder engine)
530i (1988 to 1991)	2986 cc (M30/6-cylinder engine)
535i (1988 to 1993)	3430 cc (M30/6-cylinder engine)

Firing order

Four-cylinder engine	1-3-4-2
Six-cylinder engine	1-5-3-6-2-4

Lubrication system

Oil pressure (all engines)

At idle	0.5 to 2.0 bars
Running (for example, at 4000 rpm)	4 bars or above (typically)
Oil pump rotor clearance - M40 engine (body-to-outer rotor/outer rotor-to-inner rotor)	0.12 mm to 0.20 mm
Oil pump pressure relief valve spring length - M40 engine	84.1 mm

Torque wrench settings

	Nm
Timing chain tensioner plug	35
Timing belt tensioner bolts	22
Camshaft sprocket-to-camshaft bolt	
M10 and M30 engines	10
M20 and M40 engines	65
Flange to camshaft (M30 engine)	145
Timing chain or belt covers-to-engine	
M6 bolts	10
M8 bolts	22
M10 (bolt size) bolts	47
Crankshaft pulley bolts	22
Crankshaft hub bolt or nut	
M10 engine	190
M20 engine	410
M30 engine	440
M40 engine	310
Cylinder head bolts*	
M10 four-cylinder engine	
Stage 1	60
Stage 2 (wait 15 minutes)	Angle-tighten an additional 33°
Stage 3 (engine at normal operating temperature)	Angle-tighten an additional 25°
M20 six-cylinder engine with hex-head bolts	
Stage 1	40
Stage 2 (wait 15 minutes)	60
Stage 3 (engine at normal operating temperature)	Angle-tighten an additional 25°
M20 six-cylinder engine with Torx-head bolts	
Stage 1	30
Stage 2	Angle-tighten an additional 90°
Stage 3	Angle-tighten an additional 90°
M30 six-cylinder engine (up to and including 1987 model year)	
Stage 1	60
Stage 2 (wait 15 minutes)	Angle-tighten an additional 33°
Stage 3 (engine at normal operating temperature)	Angle-tighten an additional 33°
M30 six-cylinder engine (from 1988 model year)	
Stage 1	60
Stage 2 (wait 20 minutes)	80
Stage 3 (engine at normal operating temperature)	Angle-tighten an additional 35°
M40 four-cylinder engine	
Stage 1	30
Stage 2	Angle-tighten an additional 90°
Stage 3	Angle-tighten an additional 90°
Intake manifold-to-cylinder head bolts	
M8 bolt	22
M7 bolt	15
M6 bolt	10
Exhaust manifold-to-cylinder head nuts	
M6 nut	10
M7 nut	15
Flywheel/driveplate bolts	
Manual transmission	105
Automatic transmission	120
Intermediate shaft sprocket bolt (M20 engines)	60
Sump-to-block bolts	9 to 11
Oil pump bolts (except M40 engines)	22
Oil pump sprocket bolts (M10 and M30 engines)	10
Oil pump cover plate-to-engine front end cover (M40 engines)	9
Front end cover-to-engine bolts (M20 and M40 engines)	
M6 bolts	10
M8 bolts	22
Crankshaft rear oil seal retainer-to-block bolts	
M6 bolts	9
M8 bolts	22

* BMW recommend that the cylinder head bolts are renewed as a matter of course.

1 General information

This Part of Chapter 2 is devoted to in-vehicle engine repair procedures. All information concerning engine removal and refitting and engine block and cylinder head overhaul can be found in Chapter 2B.

The following repair procedures are based on the assumption that the engine is still fitted in the vehicle. If the engine has been removed from the vehicle and mounted on a stand, many of the steps outlined in this Part of Chapter 2 will not apply.

The Specifications included in this Part of Chapter 2 apply only to the procedures contained in this Part. Chapter 2B contains the Specifications necessary for cylinder head and engine block rebuilding.

The single overhead camshaft four- and six-cylinder engines covered in this manual are very similar in design. Where there are differences, they will be pointed out.

The means by which the overhead camshaft is driven varies according to engine type; M10 and M30 engines use a timing chain, while M20 and M40 engines have a timing belt.

2 Repair operations possible with the engine in the vehicle

Many major repair operations can be accomplished without removing the engine from the vehicle.

Clean the engine compartment and the exterior of the engine with some type of degreaser before any work is done. It will make the job easier, and help keep dirt out of the internal areas of the engine.

Depending on the components involved, it may be helpful to remove the bonnet to improve access to the engine as repairs are performed (see Chapter 11 if necessary). Cover the wings to prevent damage to the paint. Special pads are available, but an old bedspread or blanket will also work.

If vacuum, exhaust, oil or coolant leaks develop, indicating a need for gasket or seal renewal, the repairs can generally be made with the engine in the vehicle. The intake and exhaust manifold gaskets, sump gasket, crankshaft oil seals and cylinder head gasket are all accessible with the engine in place.

Exterior components, such as the intake and exhaust manifolds, the sump, the oil pump, the water pump, the starter motor, the alternator, the distributor and the fuel system components, can be removed for repair with the engine in place.

The cylinder head can be removed without removing the engine, so this procedure is covered in this Part of Chapter 2. Camshaft, rocker arm and valve component servicing is

most easily accomplished with the cylinder head removed; these procedures are covered in Part B of this Chapter. Note, however, that the camshaft on the M40 engine may be removed with the engine in the vehicle since it is retained by bearing caps.

In extreme cases caused by a lack of necessary equipment, repair or renewal of piston rings, pistons, connecting rods and big-end bearings is possible with the engine in the vehicle. However, this practice is not recommended, because of the cleaning and preparation work that must be done to the components involved.

3 Top Dead Centre (TDC) for No 1 piston - locating

Note 1: *The following procedure is based on the assumption that the distributor (if applicable) is correctly fitted. If you are trying to locate TDC to refit the distributor correctly, piston position must be determined by feeling for compression at the No 1 spark plug hole, then aligning the ignition timing marks or inserting the timing tool in the flywheel, as applicable.*
Note 2: *The No 1 cylinder is the one closest to the radiator.*

1 Top Dead Centre (TDC) is the highest point in the cylinder that each piston reaches as it travels up and down when the crankshaft turns. Each piston reaches TDC on the compression stroke and again on the exhaust stroke, but TDC generally refers to piston position on the compression stroke.

2 Positioning the piston at TDC is an essential part of many procedures, such as timing belt or chain removal and distributor removal.

3 Before beginning this procedure, be sure to place the transmission in Neutral, and apply the handbrake or chock the rear wheels. Also, disable the ignition system by detaching the coil wire from the centre terminal of the distributor cap, and earthing it on the engine block with a jumper wire. Remove the spark plugs (see Chapter 1).

4 In order to bring any piston to TDC, the crankshaft must be turned using one of the methods outlined below. When looking at the front of the engine, normal crankshaft rotation is clockwise.

(a) *The preferred method is to turn the crankshaft with a socket and ratchet attached to the bolt threaded into the front of the crankshaft.*

(b) *A remote starter switch, which may save some time, can also be used. Follow the instructions included with the switch. Once the piston is close to TDC, use a socket and ratchet as described in the previous paragraph.*

(c) *If an assistant is available to turn the ignition switch to the Start position in short bursts, you can get the piston close to TDC without a remote starter switch.*

3.8 Align the notch in the pulley with the notch on the timing plate, then check to see if the distributor rotor is pointing to the No 1 cylinder (if not, the camshaft is 180 degrees out - the crankshaft will have to be rotated 360 degrees)

Make sure your assistant is out of the vehicle, away from the ignition switch, then use a socket and ratchet as described in (a) to complete the procedure.

5 Note the position of the terminal for the No 1 spark plug lead on the distributor cap. If the terminal isn't marked, follow the plug lead from the No 1 cylinder spark plug to the cap (No 1 cylinder is nearest the radiator).

6 Use a felt-tip pen or chalk to make a mark directly below the No 1 terminal on the distributor body or timing cover.

7 Detach the distributor cap, and set it aside (see Chapter 1 if necessary).

8 Turn the crankshaft (see paragraph 4 above) until the timing marks (located at the front of the engine) are aligned **(see illustration)**. The M40 engine does not have any timing marks at the front of the engine, but instead has a timing hole in the flywheel which must be aligned with a hole in the rear flange of the cylinder block. On this engine, turn the crankshaft until the distributor rotor is approaching the No 1 TDC position, then continue to turn the crankshaft until a suitable close-fitting drill can be inserted through the hole in the cylinder block and into the flywheel.

9 Look at the distributor rotor - it should be pointing directly at the mark you made on the distributor body or timing cover.

10 If the rotor is 180 degrees out, the No 1 piston is at TDC on the exhaust stroke.

11 To get the piston to TDC on the compression stroke, turn the crankshaft one complete turn (360°) clockwise. The rotor should now be pointing at the mark on the distributor or timing cover. When the rotor is pointing at the No 1 spark plug lead terminal in the distributor cap and the ignition timing marks are aligned, the No 1 piston is at TDC on the compression stroke. **Note:** *If it's impossible to align the ignition timing marks when the rotor is pointing at the mark, the timing belt or chain may have jumped the teeth on the sprockets, or may have been fitted incorrectly.*

2A

12 After the No 1 piston has been positioned at TDC on the compression stroke, TDC for any of the remaining pistons can be located by turning the crankshaft and following the firing order. Mark the remaining spark plug lead terminal locations just like you did for the No 1 terminal, then number the marks to correspond with the cylinder numbers. As you turn the crankshaft, the rotor will also turn. When it's pointing directly at one of the marks on the distributor, the piston for that particular cylinder is at TDC on the compression stroke.

4   Valve cover - removal and refitting

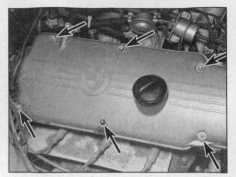

4.6a   Valve cover bolt locations (arrowed) on M10 four-cylinder engines

4.6b   Valve cover bolt locations (arrowed) on M20 six-cylinder engines

> ⚠ *Caution: If the radio in your vehicle is equipped with an anti-theft system, make sure you have the correct activation code before disconnecting the battery.*

Note: *If, after connecting the battery, the wrong language appears on the instrument panel display, refer to page 0-7 for the language resetting procedure.*

Removal

1 Disconnect the battery negative cable.
2 Detach the breather hose from the valve cover.
3 On M20 engines, unbolt and remove the intake manifold support bracket and, if applicable, the bracket for the engine sensors or idle air stabiliser (it will probably be necessary to disconnect the electrical connectors from the sensors and stabiliser).
4 On M30 engines, disconnect the electrical connector for the airflow sensor. Unclip the electrical harness, moving it out of the way.
5 Where necessary on M30 engines, remove the hoses and fittings from the intake air hose, then loosen the clamp and separate the hose from the throttle body. Unscrew the mounting nuts for the air cleaner housing, and remove the housing together with the air hose and airflow sensor.
6 Remove the valve cover retaining nuts and washers **(see illustrations)**. Where necessary, disconnect the spark plug lead clip or cover

from the stud(s), and set it aside. It will usually not be necessary to disconnect the leads from the spark plugs.
7 Remove the valve cover and gasket. Discard the old gasket. On the M40 engine, also remove the camshaft cover **(see illustrations)**. If applicable, remove the semi-circular rubber seal from the cut-out at the front of the cylinder head.

Refitting

8 Using a scraper, remove all traces of old gasket material from the sealing surfaces of the valve cover and cylinder head.

> ⚠ *Caution: Be very careful not to scratch or gouge the delicate aluminium surfaces. Gasket removal solvents are available at motor factors, and may prove helpful. After all gasket material has been removed, the gasket surfaces can be degreased by wiping them with a rag dampened with a suitable solvent.*

9 If applicable, place a new semi-circular rubber seal in the cut-out at the front of the cylinder head, then apply RTV-type gasket sealant to the joints between the seal and the mating surface for the valve cover gasket.
Note: *After the sealant is applied, you should refit the valve cover and tighten the nuts within ten minutes.*
10 Refit the camshaft cover (M40 engine), the valve cover and a new gasket. Refit the washers and nuts; tighten the nuts evenly and securely. Don't overtighten these nuts - they

should be tight enough to prevent oil from leaking past the gasket, but not so tight that they warp the valve cover.
11 The remainder of refitting is the reverse of removal.

5   Intake manifold - removal and refitting

Removal

1 Allow the engine to cool completely, then relieve the fuel pressure on fuel-injection engines (see Chapter 4).
2 Disconnect the battery negative cable.

> ⚠ *Caution: If the radio in your vehicle is equipped with an anti-theft system, make sure you have the correct activation code before disconnecting the battery.*

Note: *If, after connecting the battery, the wrong language appears on the instrument panel display, refer to page 0-7 for the language resetting procedure.*

3 Drain the engine coolant (see Chapter 1) below the level of the intake manifold. If the coolant is in good condition, it can be saved and reused.
4 On fuel injection engines, loosen the hose clamp and disconnect the large air inlet hose from the throttle body. It may also be necessary to remove the entire air cleaner/inlet hose assembly to provide enough working room (see Chapter 4).

4.7a   Removing the valve cover on the M40 engine

4.7b   Removing the camshaft cover on the M40 engine

4.7c   Removing the valve cover gasket on the M40 engine

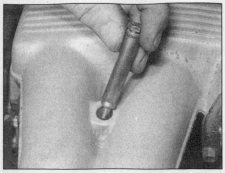

5.9a On the M40 engine, remove the nuts and special bolts . . .

5.9b . . . and remove the upper part of the intake manifold . . .

5.9c . . . and gaskets

5 On carburettor engines, remove the complete air cleaner assembly (see Chapter 4).

6 Disconnect the coolant hoses from the throttle body/intake manifold as applicable.

7 Disconnect the throttle cable and, if applicable, cruise control cable (see Chapter 4).

8 Remove the EGR valve and line where applicable (see Chapter 6).

9 At this stage on the M40 engine, the upper part of the intake manifold should be removed by unscrewing the bolts and nuts. Remove the gaskets **(see illustrations)**.

10 On fuel injection engines, disconnect the vacuum hose from the fuel pressure regulator, and disconnect the electrical connectors from the fuel injectors (see Chapter 4).

11 Disconnect the fuel lines from the fuel rail or carburettor, as applicable (see Chapter 4).

12 On the M40 engine, unbolt and remove the support bracket from the bottom of the intake manifold **(see illustration)**.

13 Disconnect all remaining hoses and wires attached between the intake manifold/throttle body assembly and the engine or chassis.

14 Remove the bolts and/or nuts that attach the manifold to the cylinder head **(see illustrations)**. Start at the ends and work toward the middle, loosening each one a little at a time until they can be removed by hand. Support the manifold while removing the fasteners so it doesn't fall. **Note:** *You can remove the manifold without removing the throttle body, injectors, vacuum/thermo*

valves, fuel pressure regulator or carburettor. If you're fitting a new manifold, transfer the components (see Chapter 4) and lines to the new manifold before it is fitted on the cylinder head.

15 Move the manifold up and down to break the gasket seal, then lift it away from the head and remove the gasket **(see illustrations)**.

Refitting

16 Remove the old gasket, then carefully scrape all traces of sealant off the head and the manifold mating surfaces. Be very careful not to nick or scratch the delicate aluminium mating surfaces. Gasket removal solvents are available at motor factors, and may prove helpful. Make sure the surfaces are perfectly clean and free of dirt and oil.

5.12 Removing the support bracket from the bottom of the intake manifold (M40 engine)

17 Check the manifold for corrosion (at the coolant passages), cracks, warping and other damage. Cracks and warping normally show up near the gasket surface, around the stud holes. If defects are found, have the manifold repaired (or renew it, as necessary).

18 When refitting the manifold, always use a new gasket. Where one side of the gasket has a graphite surface, this must face the cylinder head.

19 Refit the nuts and bolts and tighten them gradually, working from the centre out to the ends, to the torque listed in this Chapter's Specifications.

20 The remainder of refitting is the reverse of removal. On the M40 engine, renew the gaskets between the upper and lower parts of the manifold.

2A

5.14a Remove the intake manifold nuts with a socket, ratchet and long extension (M20 engine)

5.14b Removing the lower intake manifold nuts (M40 engine)

5.15a Removing the lower intake manifold (M40 engine)

5.15b Removing the lower intake manifold gasket (M40 engine)

6 Exhaust manifold - removal and refitting

Warning: Make sure the engine is completely cool before beginning work on the exhaust system.

Caution: If the radio in your vehicle is equipped with an anti-theft system, make sure you have the correct activation code before disconnecting the battery.

Note: *If, after connecting the battery, the wrong language appears on the instrument panel display, refer to page 0-7 for the language resetting procedure.*

1 Disconnect the battery negative cable.
2 On models where the air cleaner is on the exhaust manifold side of the engine, remove the air cleaner housing assembly and/or airflow sensor to provide sufficient working area (see Chapter 4, if necessary).

 HAYNES HiNT *Remove the windscreen washer reservoir from the right-hand side of the engine compartment to give more working room.*

3 Unplug the HT leads and set the spark plug lead harness aside (see Chapter 1).
4 Clearly label, then disconnect or remove, all wires, hoses, fittings, etc. that are in the way. Be sure to disconnect the oxygen sensor, where fitted.
5 Raise the vehicle, and support it securely on axle stands. Working from under the vehicle, separate the exhaust downpipe from the manifold. Use penetrating oil on the fasteners to ease removal **(see illustrations)**.
6 Remove the axle stands, and lower the vehicle. Working from the ends of the manifold toward the centre, loosen the retaining nuts gradually until they can be removed. Again, penetrating oil may prove helpful.
7 Pull the manifold off the head, then remove the old gaskets **(see illustrations)**. **Note:** *Be very careful not to damage the oxygen sensor, where fitted.*

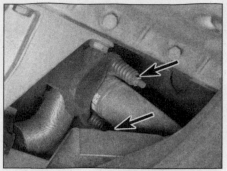

6.5a Remove the exhaust manifold nuts (arrowed) from the exhaust pipe (M20 engine) - soaking the nuts with penetrating oil should make them easier to remove

8 Clean the gasket mating surfaces of the head and manifold, and make sure the threads on the exhaust manifold studs are in good condition.
9 Check for corrosion, warping, cracks, and other damage. Repair or renew the manifold as necessary.
10 When refitting the manifold, use new gaskets. Tighten the manifold-to-head retaining nuts gradually, starting at the centre and working out to the ends, to the torque listed in this Chapter's Specifications. Also tighten the downpipe-to-manifold nuts.
11 The remaining steps are simply a reversal of the removal procedure.

7 Timing chain covers - removal and refitting

Note 1: *This procedure applies to M10 and M30 engines.*
Note 2: *The upper timing chain cover can be removed separately. If you need to remove both the upper and lower covers, special tools are required. Read paragraphs 8 and 9 before beginning work.*

Removal

1 Disconnect the battery negative cable.

6.5b Exhaust manifold-to-downpipe flange (M40 engine)

Caution: If the radio in your vehicle is equipped with an anti-theft system, make sure you have the correct activation code before disconnecting the battery.

Note: *If, after connecting the battery, the wrong language appears on the instrument panel display, refer to page 0-7 for the language resetting procedure.*

2 If you're removing the lower timing chain cover (the upper cover can be removed separately), remove the cooling fan and fan shroud, the radiator and the fan drivebelt pulley (see Chapter 3).
3 On the M10 engine only, remove the water pump (see Chapter 3).
4 On engines where the distributor cap is mounted directly to the timing chain cover, remove the cap, rotor and the black plastic cover beneath the rotor (see Chapter 1).
5 On the M30 engine fitted with the L-Jetronic fuel system, remove the distributor from the upper timing cover (see Chapter 5).
6 Remove the valve cover (see Section 4).
7 If you'll be removing the lower timing chain cover on the M30 engine, remove the crankshaft pulley from the vibration damper/hub. Hold the pulley stationary with a socket on the centre bolt, and remove the pulley bolts with another socket **(see illustration)**.
8 If you'll be removing the lower timing chain

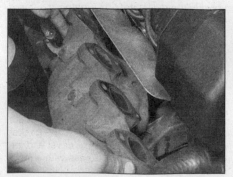

6.7a Removing the exhaust manifold (M40 engine)

6.7b Removing the exhaust manifold gasket (M40 engine)

6.7c Removing the exhaust manifold-to-downpipe gasket (M40 engine)

7.7 Place a socket and ratchet on the centre bolt to keep the pulley stationary, and use another socket and ratchet to remove the smaller bolts attaching the pulley to the vibration damper

7.10 Unscrew the plug from the timing chain cover, and remove the tensioner spring and plunger

7.14 From underneath the vehicle, remove the three bolts (arrowed) that connect the cover and the sump

cover, remove the vibration damper/hub by locking the crankshaft in position and loosening the large centre bolt. Since the bolt is on very tight, you'll need to use an extension bar and socket to break it loose. On M30 engines, BMW recommends using a 3/4-inch drive socket and extension bar, since the bolt is extremely tight on these engines. To lock the crankshaft in place while the bolt is being loosened, use BMW special tool No. 11 2 100 (or equivalent).

9 On the M10 engine, if the special tool listed in the previous paragraph is not available, you may try locking the crankshaft by removing the flywheel/driveplate inspection cover and jamming a wide-bladed screwdriver into the ring gear teeth. On the M30 engine, since the bolt is so extremely tight, we don't recommend substitute methods. Use the correct tool. On the M10 engine, after the centre bolt is removed, it will probably be necessary to use a jaw-type puller to pull the vibration damper off the crankshaft. Position the jaws behind the inner pulley groove, and tighten the puller centre bolt very slowly, checking the pulley to make sure it does not get bent or otherwise damaged by the puller.

 HAYNES HINT *If the pulley seems to be sticking on the crankshaft, it may help to spray the hub area with some penetrating oil, and to gently tap on the hub area with a hammer.*

10 Unscrew the plug and remove the timing chain tensioner spring **(see illustration)**. The tensioner plunger may come out with the spring. If not, reach down into the hole where the tensioner spring was, and remove the plunger. To check the plunger for proper operation, see Section 8.

⚠️ *Caution: The spring is under tension, and this could cause the plug to be ejected from its hole with considerable force. Hold the tensioner plug securely as it's being*

unscrewed, and release the spring tension slowly.

11 On the M30 engine, if you're removing the upper timing cover, unbolt the thermostat cover and remove the thermostat (see Chapter 3).
12 On the M30 engine, if you're removing the lower timing cover, loosen the alternator mounting bolts, and swing the alternator to one side. Remove the front lower mounting bracket bolt, and loosen the other bolts. Also unbolt the power steering pump mounting bracket, and move it to one side.
13 Remove the bolts and nuts securing the upper timing chain cover to the engine block, and remove the cover. Draw a simple diagram showing the location of the bolts, so they can be returned to the same holes from which they're removed. Remove the upper timing chain cover. If it sticks to the engine block, tap it gently with a rubber mallet, or place a piece of wood against the cover and hit the wood with a hammer. On the M30 engine fitted with the L-Jetronic fuel system, remove the distributor driveshaft.
14 Remove the bolts and nuts attaching the lower timing chain cover to the engine block. Be sure to remove the three bolts from underneath that connect the front of the sump to the bottom of the front cover **(see illustration)**. Loosen the remaining sump bolts.
15 Run a sharp, thin knife between the sump gasket and lower timing chain cover, cutting the cover free from the gasket. Be very careful not to damage or dirty the gasket, so you can re-use it.
16 Break the lower timing chain cover-to-block gasket seal by tapping the cover with a rubber mallet, or with a hammer and block of wood. Do not prise between the cover and the engine block, as damage to the gasket sealing surfaces will result.
17 Using a scraper, remove all traces of old gasket material from the sealing surfaces of the covers and engine block.

⚠️ *Caution: Be very careful not to scratch or gouge the delicate aluminium surfaces. Also, do not damage the sump gasket, and keep it clean. Gasket removal solvents are available at motor factors, and may prove helpful. After all gasket material has been*

removed, the gasket surfaces can be degreased by wiping them with a rag dampened with a suitable solvent.

Refitting

18 Renew the front oil seals (see Section 11). It's not wise to take a chance on an old seal, since renewal with the covers removed is very easy. Be sure to apply a little oil to the front oil seal lips.
19 Apply a film of RTV-type gasket sealant to the surface of the sump gasket that mates with the lower timing chain cover. Apply extra beads of RTV sealant to the edges where the gasket meets the engine block. **Note:** *If the sump gasket is damaged, instead of fitting a whole new gasket, you might try trimming the front portion of the gasket off at the point where it meets the engine block, then trim off the front portion of a new sump gasket so it's exactly the same size. Cover the exposed inside area of the sump with a rag, then clean all traces of old gasket material off the area where the gasket was removed. Attach the new gasket piece to the sump with contact-cement-type gasket adhesive, then apply RTV-type sealant as described at the beginning of this paragraph.*
20 Coat both sides of the new gasket with RTV-type gasket sealant, then attach the lower timing chain cover to the front of the engine. Refit the bolts, and tighten them evenly to the torque listed in this Chapter's Specifications. Work from bolt-to-bolt in a criss-cross pattern to be sure they're tightened evenly. **Note 1:** *Tighten the lower cover-to-block bolts first, then tighten the sump-to-cover bolts. If the gasket protrudes above the cover-to-block joint, or bunches up at the cover-to-sump joint, trim the gasket so it fits correctly.* **Note 2:** *After applying RTV-type sealant, reassembly must be completed in about 10 minutes so the RTV won't prematurely harden.*
21 Refit the upper timing chain cover in the same way as the lower cover. If the gasket protrudes beyond the top of the cover and the engine block, trim off the excess with a razor blade.
22 Refitting is otherwise the reverse of removal.

2A

8 Timing chain and sprockets - removal, inspection and refitting

Note: *This procedure applies to M10 and M30 engines.*

⚠️ **Caution: Once the engine is set at TDC, do not rotate the camshaft or crankshaft until the timing chain is reinstalled. If the crankshaft or camshaft is rotated with the timing chain removed, the valves could hit the pistons, causing expensive internal engine damage.**

Removal

1 Position the No 1 cylinder at Top Dead Centre (TDC) on the compression stroke (see Section 3).
2 Remove the valve cover (see Section 4). Double-check that the No 1 cylinder is at TDC on the compression stroke by making sure the No 1 cylinder rocker arms are loose (not compressing their valve springs).
3 Remove the upper timing chain cover (see Section 7). Note the location of the camshaft timing marks, which should now be aligned. On four-cylinder (M10) engines, there's usually a stamped line on the camshaft flange that aligns with a cast mark on the top of the cylinder head; also, the camshaft sprocket dowel pin hole will be at its lowest point. On six-cylinder (M30) engines, a line drawn through two of the camshaft sprocket bolts opposite each other would be exactly vertical, while a line drawn through the other two bolts would be horizontal. Additionally, the locating pin should be in the lower left corner (between the 7 and 8 o'clock positions). Be sure you've identified the correct camshaft TDC position before dismantling, because correct valve timing depends on you aligning them exactly on reassembly. **Note:** *As the engine is mounted in the engine compartment at an angle, all references to horizontal and vertical whilst timing the camshafts are in relation to the crankshaft, and not the ground.*
4 Hold the crankshaft stationary with a socket and ratchet on the vibration damper centre bolt, then loosen (but don't unscrew completely) the four bolts attaching the camshaft sprocket to the camshaft. Be very careful not to rotate the camshaft or crankshaft. **Note:** *Some earlier models may have locking tabs for the camshaft sprocket bolts. Bend the tabs down before loosening the bolts. The tabs are no longer available from the manufacturer, and do not have to be used on refitting.*
5 Remove the lower timing chain cover (see Section 7).
6 Unscrew and remove the four camshaft sprocket bolts, then disengage the chain from the crankshaft sprocket and carefully remove the chain and camshaft sprocket from the engine. It may be necessary to gently prise the camshaft sprocket loose from the camshaft with a screwdriver.

Inspection

Timing sprockets

7 Examine the teeth on both the crankshaft sprocket and the camshaft sprocket for wear. Each tooth forms an inverted V. If worn, the side of each tooth under tension will be slightly concave in shape when compared with the other side of the tooth (i.e. one side of the inverted V will be concave when compared with the other, giving the teeth a hooked appearance). If the teeth appear to be worn, the sprockets must be renewed. **Note:** *The crankshaft sprocket is a press fit on the crankshaft, and can be removed with a jaw-type puller after the Woodruff key and oil pump are removed (see Section 14). However, BMW recommends the new sprocket be pressed onto the crankshaft after being heated to 80° C (175° F) on the M10 engine, or to 200° C (390° F) on the M30 engine. For this reason, if the crankshaft sprocket requires renewal, we recommend removing the crankshaft (see Part B of this Chapter) and taking it to an engineering works to have the old sprocket pressed off and a new one pressed on.*

Timing chain

8 The chain should be renewed if the sprockets are worn or if the chain is loose (indicated by excessive noise in operation). It's a good idea to renew the chain anyway if the engine is stripped down for overhaul. The rollers on a very badly worn chain may be slightly grooved. To avoid future problems, if there's any doubt at all about the chain's condition, renew it.

Chain rail and tensioner

9 Inspect the chain guide rail and tensioner rail for deep grooves caused by chain contact. Renew them if they are excessively worn. The rails can be renewed after removing the circlips with a pointed tool or needle-nose pliers (see illustration).

10 Shake the tensioner plunger, and listen for a rattling sound from the check ball. If you can't hear the ball rattling, renew the plunger.
11 To further check the tensioner plunger, blow through it first from the closed end, then from the slotted (guide) end. No air should flow through the plunger when you blow through the closed end, and air should flow through it freely when you blow through the slotted end. If the tensioner fails either test, renew it.

Refitting

12 Refit the tensioner rail and chain guide rail, if removed.
13 Temporarily refit the lower timing chain cover and vibration damper, so you can check the crankshaft timing marks. Once you've verified the TDC marks are aligned, remove the damper and cover.
14 Loop the timing chain over the crankshaft sprocket, then loop it over the camshaft sprocket and, guiding the chain between the chain guide and tensioner rail, refit the camshaft sprocket on the camshaft. Make sure the camshaft timing marks are aligned.
15 The remainder of refitting is the reverse of removal. Be sure to tighten the fasteners to the correct torques (see this Chapter's Specifications).

9 Timing belt covers - removal and refitting

Note: *This procedure applies to M20 and M40 engines.*

⚠️ **Caution: If the radio in your vehicle is equipped with an anti-theft system, make sure you have the correct activation code before disconnecting the battery.**

Note: *If, after connecting the battery, the wrong language appears on the instrument panel display, refer to page 0-7 for the language resetting procedure.*

1 Disconnect the battery negative cable.
2 Remove the fan clutch and fan shroud (see Chapter 3).
3 On the M20 engine, remove the radiator (see Chapter 3).
4 Remove the fan drivebelt pulley.

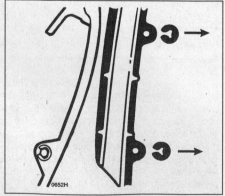

8.9 To remove the tensioner or chain guide rail, remove the circlips with a pointed tool or needle-nose pliers - the circlips tend to fly off when they're released, so make sure you catch them or they'll get lost (or, worse, wind up in the engine!)

9.6a Unbolt the distributor cap (M40 engine) . . .

9.6b ... then unbolt the rotor ...

9.6c ... and remove the black plastic cover

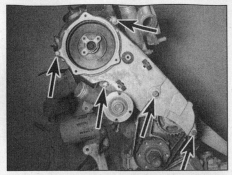
9.8 Remove all the nuts/ bolts (arrowed) that attach the upper and lower covers (M20 engine - removed for clarity)

9.9a Remove the upper timing belt cover first, then the lower cover (M20 engine)

1 Upper timing belt cover
2 Lower timing belt cover

5 If applicable, disconnect the reference sensor wiring harness which runs across the front of the timing belt cover, and set it aside.
6 If the distributor cap is mounted directly to the upper timing belt cover, remove the cap, rotor and the black plastic cover beneath the rotor (see illustrations).
7 Remove the lower fan drivebelt pulley and vibration damper. Secure the crankshaft pulley centre bolt while you loosen the outer pulley/damper bolts (see illustration 7.7).
8 Remove the bolts/nuts attaching the timing belt covers to the engine (see illustration).
9 Remove the upper cover first, then the lower cover (see illustrations). Note: The upper cover has two alignment sleeves in the top bolt positions. Be sure these are in place upon reassembly.
10 Refitting is the reverse of the removal procedure. Tighten the cover bolts securely.

10 Timing belt and sprockets - removal, inspection and refitting

Note 1: This procedure applies to M20 and M40 engines.
Note 2: Before removing the camshaft sprocket on the M40 engine, it is necessary to obtain a tool to hold the camshaft for the refitting procedure (see paragraph 10).

9.9b Removing the upper timing belt cover on the M40 engine

⚠ Caution: If the radio in your vehicle is equipped with an anti-theft system, make sure you have the correct activation code before disconnecting the battery.
Note: If, after connecting the battery, the wrong language appears on the instrument panel display, refer to page 0-7 for the language resetting procedure.

Removal

1 Disconnect the negative cable from the battery.
2 Remove the timing belt covers (see Section 9).
3 On the M40 engine, drain the cooling system (see Chapter 1), then disconnect the

10.5a Align the groove in the hub on the end of the crankshaft with the notch in the front inner cover (arrowed) and mark them for assembly reference later on

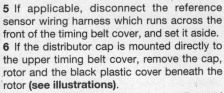
9.9c Removing the lower timing belt cover on the M40 engine

hose, unbolt the thermostat housing and remove the thermostat (see Chapter 3).
4 Set the No 1 piston at TDC (see Section 3).

⚠ Caution: Once the engine is set at TDC, do not rotate the camshaft or crankshaft until the timing belt is refitted. If the crankshaft or camshaft is rotated with the timing belt removed, the valves could hit the pistons, causing expensive internal engine damage.

5 On the M20 engine, the crankshaft mark should be aligned with the mark on the inner cover (see illustration). The mark on the camshaft sprocket should be aligned with the stamped line on the cylinder head (see illustration). On the M40 engine, make an

10.5b Align the mark on the camshaft sprocket with the mark on the cylinder head (arrowed)

2A

10.6 Loosen the idler pulley bolts (arrowed) to relieve the tension on the timing belt so it can be removed

10.9b Removing the timing belt from the camshaft sprocket on the M40 engine

10.10 Removing the camshaft sprocket on the M40 engine

10.11a The BMW tool for holding the camshaft in the TDC position on M40 engines

10.9a When removing the timing belt on models with a two-piece crankshaft hub, it's a tight fit to remove it around the hub, but it's a lot easier than removing the crankshaft hub assembly, which is secured by a very tight bolt

alignment mark on the camshaft sprocket and rear timing cover to ensure correct refitting.

6 On the M20 engine, loosen the two tensioner roller retaining bolts a little, and push the tensioner towards the water pump (see illustration). With the timing belt tension relieved, re-tighten the retaining bolt.

7 On the M40 engine, loosen the tensioner retaining nut, and use an Allen key to rotate the tensioner clockwise. This will relieve the tension of the timing belt. Tighten the retaining nut to hold the tensioner in its free position.

8 If the same belt is to be refitted, mark it with an arrow indicating direction of rotation.

⚠ **Caution: It is not advisable to refit a timing belt which has been removed unless it is virtually new. On the M40 engine, BMW recommend that the timing belt is renewed every time the tensioner roller is released.**

9 Remove the timing belt by slipping it off the roller(s) and the other sprockets (see illustrations).

10 If it's necessary to remove the camshaft or the intermediate shaft sprocket, remove the sprocket bolt while holding the sprocket to prevent it from moving. To hold the sprocket, wrap it with a piece of an old timing belt (toothed side engaging the sprocket teeth) or

10.11b The BMW camshaft-holding tool in position on the M40 engine

a piece of leather, then hold the sprocket using a strap spanner. If a strap spanner is not available, clamp the ends of the piece of belt or leather tightly together with a pair of grips. Before loosening the bolt, make sure you have the necessary tool for positioning the camshaft as described in the following paragraph (see illustration).

⚠ **Caution: Do not use the timing belt you're planning to refit to hold the sprocket. Also, be sure to hold the camshaft sprocket very steady, because if it moves more than a few degrees, the valves could hit the pistons.**

Note: *On the M40 engine, the sprocket is not directly located on the camshaft with a key, as the groove in the end of the camshaft allows the sprocket to move several degrees in either direction. The retaining bolt locks the sprocket onto a taper after positioning the camshaft with a special tool.*

11 The BMW tool for positioning the camshaft on the M40 engine consists of a metal plate which locates over the square lug near the No 1 cylinder lobes on the camshaft - the valve cover must be removed first (see illustrations). If the BMW tool cannot be obtained, a home-made tool should be fabricated out of metal plate. The tool must be made to hold the square lug on the camshaft at right-angles to the upper face of the cylinder head (ie the contact face of the valve cover).

12 If it's necessary to remove the crankshaft sprocket, remove the crankshaft hub centre bolt while holding the crankshaft steady. Note: *The removal of the crankshaft hub mounting bolt requires a heavy-duty holding device because of the high torque used to tighten the bolt. BMW has a special tool, numbered 112150 (M20 engines) or 112170 (M40 engines), for this purpose. If this tool cannot be bought or borrowed, check with a tool dealer or motor factors for a tool capable of doing the job. Note that the tool number 112170 bolts on the rear of the cylinder head and engages with the flywheel ring gear, so it will only be possible to use this tool if the gearbox has been removed, or if the engine is out of the vehicle (see illustrations). On*

10.12a Home-made tool for holding the crankshaft stationary while the crankshaft pulley bolt is being loosened (engine removed for clarity)

models with a two-piece hub, after removing the outer hub piece, you'll then need to remove the sprocket with a bolt-type puller (available at most motor factors). When using the puller, thread the crankshaft centre bolt in approximately three turns, and use this as a bearing point for the puller's centre bolt.

Inspection

13 Check for a cracked, worn or damaged belt. Renew it if any of these conditions are found (see illustrations). Also look at the sprockets for any signs of irregular wear or damage, indicating the need for renewal. Note: If any parts are to be renewed, check with your local BMW dealer parts department to be sure compatible parts are used. On M20 engines, later sprockets, tensioner rollers and timing belts are marked "Z 127". Renewal of the timing belt on M20 engines will mean that the later belt tensioner should also be fitted, if not already done.

14 Inspect the idler roller and, on M20 engines, the tension spring. Rotate the tensioner roller to be sure it rotates freely, with no noise or play. Note: When fitting a new timing belt, it is recommended that a new tensioner be fitted also.

Refitting

15 On the M20 engine, refit the idler/tensioner/spring so that the timing belt can be fitted loosely.

16 Refit the sprockets using a reversal of the removal procedure; tighten the retaining bolts to the specified torque. On the M40 engine, turn the camshaft sprocket clockwise as far as possible within the location groove, then tighten the retaining bolt to an initial torque of 1 to 3 Nm at this stage.

17 If you are refitting the old belt, make sure the mark made to indicate belt direction of rotation is pointing the right way (the belt should rotate in a clockwise direction as you face the front of the engine).

18 Refit the timing belt, placing the belt under the crankshaft sprocket first to get by

10.21 On the M20 engine, after the belt has been installed correctly around all sprockets and the tensioner pulley, lightly apply pressure to the tensioner, to be sure the tensioner isn't stuck and has full movement against the timing belt

10.12b Removing the crankshaft pulley bolt (M40 engine)

the housing. Guide the belt around the other sprocket(s).

19 Finally, place the belt over the idler/tensioner rollers.

20 On the M20 engine, loosen the tensioner bolts and allow the spring tension to be applied to the belt.

21 On the M20 engine, lightly apply pressure behind the tensioner to be sure spring pressure is being applied to the belt (see illustration). Don't tighten the bolts while applying pressure; lightly tighten the bolts only after releasing the tensioner.

22 On the M40 engine, unbolt and remove the valve cover, then use the special tool to hold the camshaft in the TDC position (see paragraph 11).

23 On the M40 engine, loosen the tensioner roller retaining nut, and use an Allen key to rotate the roller anti-clockwise until the timing belt is tensioned correctly. The 90°-twist method of checking the tension of the timing belt is not accurate enough for this engine, and it is strongly recommended that the special BMW tensioning tool is obtained if at all possible (apply 32 ±2 graduations on the tool) (see illustration). A reasonably accurate alternative can be made using an Allen key and a spring balance (see illustration). Make sure that the spring balance is positioned as shown, since the tensioner roller is on an eccentric, and different readings will be obtained otherwise. The spring balance should be connected 85 mm along the Allen key, and a force of 2.0 kg (4.4 lb) should be

10.23a Using the special BMW tool to check the tension of the timing belt on the M40 engine

10.12c Removing the crankshaft sprocket from the front of the crankshaft

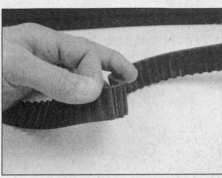

10.13a Inspect the timing belt carefully for cracking, as shown here...

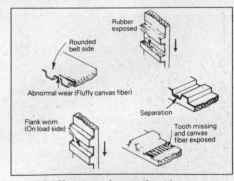

10.13b ...and any other damage

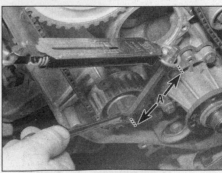

10.23b Using a spring balance and Allen key to adjust the tension of the timing belt on the M40 engine

Dimension A = 85 mm

2A

applied. Tighten the retaining nut to the specified torque to hold the tensioner in its correct position. **Note:** *It is important that the timing belt is tensioned correctly. If the belt is over-tightened, it will howl, and there is the possibility of it being damaged. If the belt is too slack, it may jump on the sprockets.*

24 Check to make sure the camshaft and crankshaft timing marks are still aligned **(see illustrations 10.5a and 10.5b).**

25 Turn the crankshaft clockwise through two complete revolutions. (Remove the camshaft positioning tool from the M40 engine first.)

⚠️ *Caution: This is necessary to stretch the new belt. If not done, the belt tensioner will be too loose, and damage could result.*

26 On the M20 engine, loosen the tensioner roller bolts, then tighten them to the torque listed in this Chapter's Specifications.

27 On the M40 engine, loosen the tensioner roller retaining nut, and re-adjust the tension of the timing belt as described in paragraph 23. On completion, tighten the tensioner roller retaining nut, then fully tighten the camshaft sprocket bolt if previously loosened **(see illustration).**

28 Verify that the timing marks are still perfectly aligned. If not, remove and refit the timing belt.

29 The remainder of refitting is the reverse of removal.

11 Front oil seals - renewal

Note: *Oil seals are fitted with their sealing lips facing inwards (towards the engine).*

M10 and M30 (timing chain) engines

Camshaft front seal (M30 engines only)

1 Remove the upper timing chain cover only (see Section 7).

2 Support the cover on two blocks of wood, and drive out the seal from behind with a hammer and screwdriver. Be very careful not to damage the seal bore in the process.

3 Coat the outside diameter and lip of the new seal with multi-purpose grease, and drive the seal into the cover with a hammer and a socket slightly smaller in diameter than the outside diameter of the seal.

4 The remainder of refitting is the reverse of removal.

Crankshaft front seal (M10 and M30 engines)

5 Remove the crankshaft pulley and vibration damper (see Section 7).

6 Carefully prise the old seal out of the cover with a large screwdriver. Be very careful not to damage the seal bore or the crankshaft with the tool. Wrap the tip of the screwdriver with a piece of tape to prevent damage.

7 Clean the bore in the cover, and coat the outer edge of the new seal with engine oil or multi-purpose grease. Also lubricate the lips of the seal with multi-purpose grease. Using a socket with an outside diameter slightly smaller than the outside diameter of the seal, carefully drive the new seal into place with a hammer **(see illustration).** If a socket isn't available, a short section of large-diameter pipe will work. Check the seal after refitting to be sure the spring around the inside of the seal lip didn't pop out of place.

8 The remainder of refitting is the reverse of removal.

M20 and M40 (timing belt) engines

Camshaft front seal (M20 and M40 engines)

9 Remove the timing belt and camshaft sprocket (see Section 10).

10 On the M20 engine only, remove the two screws, and separate the camshaft seal housing from the cylinder head by pulling it as you rotate it back and forth.

11 On the M20 engine only, support the housing on two blocks of wood, and drive the seal out of the housing from behind using a

hammer and screwdriver. Be very careful not to damage the seal housing.

12 On the M40 engine, prise the seal out from the cylinder head using a screwdriver, being careful not to damage the camshaft surface or the seal bore.

13 Coat the lip and outside diameter of the new seal with multi-purpose grease.

14 On the M40 engine, wrap some adhesive tape around the end of the camshaft to protect the new seal from the location groove as it is being fitted **(see illustration).**

15 Carefully locate the new seal in position and press it in by hand initially so that it enters the bore. Drive the new seal into the housing or cylinder head (as applicable) using a hammer and a socket with a diameter slightly smaller than the outside diameter of the seal. On the M40 engine, remove the adhesive tape from the end of the camshaft.

16 On the M20 engine, renew the O-ring on the back of the seal housing, and work the lip of the seal over the end of the camshaft. Refit the screws and tighten them securely.

17 The remainder of refitting is the reverse of removal.

Crankshaft and intermediate shaft front seals (M20 engines)

18 Remove the timing belt and crankshaft and intermediate shaft pulleys as applicable (see Section 10). **Note:** *We recommend the timing belt be renewed any time it is removed.*

19 Remove the bolts and nuts securing the front cover to the engine block. Be sure to remove the three bolts from underneath that connect the front of the sump to the bottom of the front cover **(see illustration 7.14).**

20 Run a sharp, thin knife between the sump gasket and the front cover, cutting the cover free from the gasket. Be very careful not to damage the gasket, and keep it clean so you can re-use it.

21 Break the front cover-to-block gasket seal by tapping the cover with a rubber mallet or block of wood and hammer. Do not prise between the cover and the engine block, as damage to the gasket sealing surfaces will result.

10.27 Tightening the camshaft sprocket retaining bolt on the M40 engine

11.7 The crankshaft front oil seal is pressed into the front of the lower timing chain cover (cover removed from the engine for clarity)

11.14 Fitting a new camshaft oil seal on the M40 engine (note the adhesive tape around the end of the camshaft to protect the seal)

22 Using a scraper, remove all traces of old gasket material from the sealing surfaces of the covers and engine block.

 Caution: Be very careful not to scratch or gouge the delicate aluminium surfaces. Also, do not damage the sump gasket, and keep it clean. Gasket removal solvents are available at motor factors, and may prove helpful. After all gasket material has been removed, the gasket surfaces can be degreased by wiping them with a rag dampened with a suitable solvent.

23 Support the cover on two blocks of wood, and drive out the seals from behind with a hammer and screwdriver. Be very careful not to damage the seal bores in the process.
24 Coat the outside diameters and lips of the new seals with multi-purpose grease, and drive the seals into the cover with a hammer and a socket slightly smaller in diameter than the outside diameter of the seal.
25 Apply a film of RTV-type gasket sealant to the surface of the sump gasket that mates with the front cover. Apply extra beads of RTV sealant to the edges where the gasket meets the engine block. **Note:** *If the sump gasket is damaged, instead of fitting a whole new gasket, you might try trimming the front portion of the gasket off at the point where it meets the engine block, then trim off the front portion of a new sump gasket so it's exactly the same size. Cover the exposed inside area of the sump with a rag, then clean all traces of old gasket material off the area where the gasket was removed. Attach the new gasket piece to the sump with contact-cement-type gasket adhesive, then apply RTV-type sealant as described at the beginning of this paragraph.*
26 Coat both sides of the new gasket with RTV-type gasket sealant, then attach the front cover to the front of the engine, carefully working the seals over the crankshaft and intermediate shaft. Refit the bolts and tighten them evenly to the torque listed in this Chapter's Specifications. Work from bolt-to-bolt in a criss-cross pattern, to be sure they're tightened evenly. **Note 1:** *Tighten the front cover-to-block bolts first, then tighten the sump-to-cover bolts.* **Note 2:** *After applying RTV-type sealant, reassembly must be completed in about 10 minutes so the RTV won't prematurely harden.*
27 The remainder of refitting is the reverse of removal.

Crankshaft front seal (M40 engines)

28 Remove the timing belt and crankshaft sprocket (see Section 10).
29 Remove the Woodruff key from the groove in the end of the crankshaft.
30 Note the fitted position of the oil seal, then prise it out from the front cover using a screwdriver, but take care not to damage the bore of the cover or the surface of the crankshaft. If the seal is tight, drill two small holes in the metal end of the seal, and use two self-tapping screws to pull out the seal. Make sure all remains of swarf are removed.
31 Coat the outside diameter and lip of the new seal with multi-purpose grease, then drive it into the cover with a hammer and a socket slightly smaller in diameter than the outside diameter of the seal. Make sure the seal enters squarely.
32 The remainder of refitting is the reverse of removal. Note that it is recommended that the timing belt be renewed - see Section 10.

---

12 Cylinder head - removal and refitting

Removal

1 Relieve the fuel pressure on all fuel injection engines (see Chapter 4).
2 Disconnect the negative cable from the battery. Where the battery is located in the engine compartment, the battery may be removed completely (see Chapter 5).

 Caution: If the radio in your vehicle is equipped with an anti-theft system, make sure you have the correct activation code before disconnecting the battery.
Note: *If, after connecting the battery, the wrong language appears on the instrument panel display, refer to page 0-7 for the language resetting procedure.*

3 Remove the air cleaner assembly (see Chapter 4).
4 Disconnect the wiring from the distributor (mark all wiring for position first, if necessary), and the HT lead from the coil (see Chapter 5).
5 Disconnect the lead from the coolant temperature sender unit (see Chapter 3).
6 Disconnect the fuel lines from the fuel rail or carburettor as applicable (see Chapter 4).
7 Drain the cooling system (see Chapter 3).
8 Clearly label then disconnect all other hoses from the throttle body, intake manifold, carburettor and cylinder head, as applicable.
9 Disconnect the throttle cable from the throttle linkage or carburettor (see Chapter 4).
10 Disconnect the exhaust manifold from the cylinder head (see Section 6). Depending on the engine type, It may not be necessary to disconnect the manifold from the exhaust pipe; however, on right-hand-drive models, the steering column intermediate shaft may not allow the manifold to clear the studs on the cylinder head.
11 Remove or disconnect any remaining hoses or lines from the intake manifold, including the ignition advance vacuum line(s), and the coolant and heater hoses.
12 On early carburettor models, disconnect the wiring from the alternator and starter motor.

13 Remove the intake manifold (see Section 5). Do not dismantle or remove any fuel injection system components unless it is absolutely necessary.
14 Remove the fan drivebelt and fan (see Chapter 3).
15 Remove the valve cover and gasket (see Section 4). Remove the semi-circular rubber seal from the front of the cylinder head, where this is not incorporated in the valve cover gasket.
16 Set No 1 piston at Top Dead Centre on the compression stroke (see Section 3).
17 Remove the timing chain or belt (see Section 8 or 10). **Note:** *If you want to save time by not removing and refitting the timing belt or chain and re-timing the engine, you can unfasten the camshaft sprocket and suspend it out of the way - with the belt or chain still attached - by a piece of rope. Be sure the rope keeps firm tension on the belt or chain, so it won't become disengaged from any of the sprockets.*
18 Loosen the cylinder head bolts a quarter-turn at a time each, in the reverse of the tightening sequence shown **(see illustrations 12.30a, 12.30b, 12.30c or 12.30d). Do not** dismantle or remove the rocker arm assembly at this time on M10, M20 and M30 engines.
19 Remove the cylinder head by lifting it straight up and off the engine block. Do not prise between the cylinder head and the engine block, as damage to the gasket sealing surfaces may result. Instead, use a blunt bar positioned in an intake port to gently prise the head loose.
20 Remove any remaining external components from the head to allow for thorough cleaning and inspection. See Chapter 2B for cylinder head servicing procedures. On the M40 engine, remove the rubber O-ring from the groove in the top of the oil pump/front end cover housing.

Refitting

21 The mating surfaces of the cylinder head and block must be perfectly clean when the head is refitted.
22 Use a gasket scraper to remove all traces of carbon and old gasket material, then clean the mating surfaces with a suitable solvent. If there's oil on the mating surfaces when the head is refitted, the gasket may not seal correctly, and leaks could develop. When working on the block, stuff the cylinders with clean rags to keep out debris. Use a vacuum cleaner to remove material that falls into the cylinders.
23 Check the block and head mating surfaces for nicks, deep scratches and other damage. If the damage is slight, it can be removed with a file; if it's excessive, machining may be the only alternative.
24 Use a tap of the correct size to chase the threads in the head bolt holes, then clean the holes with compressed air - make sure that

2A

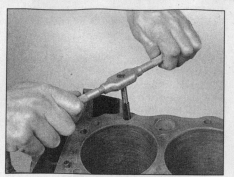

12.24 The cylinder head bolt holes should be cleaned and restored with a tap (be sure to remove debris from the holes after this is done)

12.25 A die should be used to remove sealant and corrosion from the head bolt threads prior to installation

12.26 Fitting a new rubber O-ring in the groove in the top of the oil pump/front end cover on the M40 engine

nothing (including oil, water, etc) remains in the holes **(see illustration)**.

25 BMW recommend head bolts are renewed, but if the old ones are re-used, mount each bolt in a vice, and run a die down the threads to remove corrosion and restore the threads. Dirt, corrosion, sealant and damaged threads will affect torque readings **(see illustration)**. If the bolts or their threads are damaged, do not re-use the bolts - fit a new set.

26 Refit any components removed from the head prior to cleaning and inspection. On the M40 engine, locate a new rubber O-ring in the groove in the top of the oil pump/front end cover housing **(see illustration)**.

27 Make sure the gasket sealing surfaces of the engine block and cylinder head are clean and oil-free. Lay the head gasket in place on the block, with the manufacturer's stamped mark facing up (it usually says "UP," "OBEN" or something similar). Use the dowel pins in the top of the block to properly locate the gasket.

28 Carefully set the cylinder head in place on the block. Use the dowel pins to properly align it. Where the engine is tilted slightly (ie M40 engine) you may find it helpful to fit guide studs to ensure correct positioning of the cylinder head on the block. Use two old head bolts, one screwed into each end of the block. Cut the heads off the bolts, and use a hacksaw to cut slots in the tops of the bolts so they can be removed once the cylinder head is in position **(see illustration)**.

29 Fit the cylinder head bolts **(see illustration)**.

30 Tighten the cylinder head bolts, in the sequence shown, to the torque listed in this Chapter's Specifications **(see illustrations)**. Note that on some engines the final stage of tightening takes place after the engine has been run.

31 The remainder of refitting is the reverse of removal. Set the valve clearances on M10, M20 and M30 engines (see Chapter 1) before refitting the valve cover (check them again after the engine is warmed-up). Run the engine and check for leaks.

12.28 Lowering the cylinder head onto the block (M40 engine)

12.29 Inserting a cylinder head bolt (M40 engine)

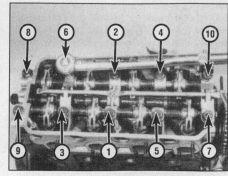

12.30a Cylinder head bolt TIGHTENING sequence for M10 (four-cylinder) engines

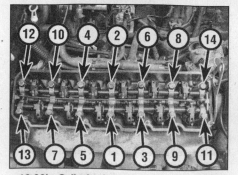

12.30b Cylinder head bolt TIGHTENING sequence for M20 (six-cylinder) engines

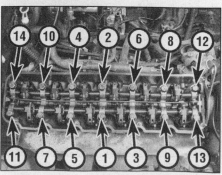

12.30c Cylinder head bolt TIGHTENING sequence for M30 (six-cylinder) engines

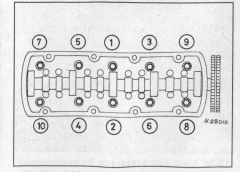

12.30d Cylinder head bolt TIGHTENING sequence for M40 (four-cylinder) engines

12.30e Angle-tightening the cylinder head bolts (M40 engine)

13 Sump - removal and refitting

1 Drain the engine oil (see Chapter 1).
2 Raise the front of the vehicle and place it securely on axle stands.
3 Remove the splash shields from under the engine.
4 Where applicable, disconnect the hoses attached to the sump, and move them to one side **(see illustration)**.
5 Where applicable, disconnect the oil level sensor electrical connector **(see illustration)**.
6 Where applicable, remove the cast-aluminium inspection cover that covers the rear of the sump **(see illustrations)**.
7 On models with the M40 engine, unbolt and remove the lower sump section and remove the gasket (this is necessary for access to the front mounting bolts). Unscrew the mounting bolt, and pull the oil dipstick tube from the sump **(see illustrations)**. Check the condition of the O-ring, and renew it if necessary.
8 On models with the M40 engine, unscrew the engine mounting nuts on both sides, then attach a suitable hoist and lift the engine sufficiently to allow the sump to be removed. As a safety precaution, position axle stands or blocks of wood beneath the engine.
9 Remove the bolts securing the sump to the

13.4 If applicable, remove the nut securing the power steering lines to the sump, and move the lines to one side to allow you to get at the sump bolts

engine block and front/rear covers **(see illustration)**.
10 Tap on the sump with a soft-faced hammer to break the gasket seal, and lower the sump from the engine.
11 Using a gasket scraper, scrape off all traces of the old gasket from the engine block, the timing chain cover, the rear main oil seal housing, and the sump. Be especially careful not to nick or gouge the gasket sealing surfaces of the timing chain cover and the oil seal housing (they are made of aluminium, and are quite soft).
12 Clean the sump with solvent, and dry it thoroughly. Check the gasket sealing surfaces for distortion. Clean any residue from the

13.6a Remove the four inspection cover bolts (arrowed) and . . .

13.5 If applicable, disconnect the oil level sensor connector at the left side of the engine, down near the power steering pump mounting bracket

gasket sealing surfaces on the sump and engine with a rag dampened with a suitable solvent.
13 Before refitting the sump, apply a little RTV-type gasket sealant to the area where the front and rear covers join the cylinder block. Lay a new sump gasket in place on the block. If necessary, apply more sealant to hold the gasket in place.
14 Carefully position the sump in place (do not disturb the gasket) and refit the bolts. Start with the bolts closest to the centre of the sump, and tighten them to the torque listed in this Chapter's Specifications, using a criss-cross pattern. Do not overtighten them, or leakage may occur.

2A

13.6b . . . remove the cover to get to all the sump bolts

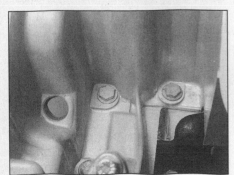

13.7a Main sump retaining bolts accessed after removal of the lower sump section on the M40 engine (engine on bench for clarity)

13.7b Removing the oil dipstick tube bracket mounting bolt

13.9 Remove the bolts holding the sump to the engine block and front cover, as shown here on a six-cylinder engine

15 The remainder of refitting is the reverse of removal. Fit a new gasket to the lower sump section on models with the M40 engine.

16 On completion refill the engine with oil (Chapter 1). Run the engine and check that there are no oil leaks from the sump gasket or other disturbed components.

14 Oil pump - removal, inspection and refitting

Removal

1 Remove the sump (see Section 13).

M10, M20 and M30 engines

2 On M10 and M30 engines, remove the three bolts that attach the gear to the front of the pump **(see illustration)**. **Note:** *Some models have a single centre nut attaching the gear to the oil pump.*

3 Unbolt the oil pump from the engine block **(see illustrations)** and remove it.

4 On the M20 engine, the intermediate shaft drives the oil pump driveshaft, which drives the oil pump. To remove the driveshaft, remove the hold-down plate from the block, and lift out the plug. Check the condition of the O-ring, and renew it if necessary. Lift the driveshaft out and check both gears for wear, renewing them if worn or damaged **(see illustration)**.

5 If the gear on the intermediate shaft is worn, or the intermediate shaft bearing is worn or damaged, the intermediate shaft must be removed. Remove the engine (see Chapter 2B), then remove the timing belt, crankshaft and intermediate shaft sprockets (see Section 10) and the engine front cover (see Section 11). The intermediate shaft can be slid out the front of the engine.

M40 engines

6 Remove the timing belt as described in Section 10.

7 Remove the cylinder head as described in Section 12.

8 Unscrew the nut and remove the timing belt tensioner from the front end cover **(see illustration)**. If necessary, unscrew the stud from the cylinder block.

14.2 On M10 and M30 engines, remove the three bolts that hold the driven gear to the oil pump, and remove the gear

14.3b On M10 and M30 engines, the oil pump is bolted to the front and centre of the engine block

9 Unscrew and remove the crankshaft hub bolt while holding the crankshaft stationary. The bolt is tightened to a very high torque, and it will be necessary to prevent the crankshaft turning. Ideally, a metal bar should be bolted to the sprocket, or the starter motor may be removed and the flywheel held using a wide-bladed screwdriver. Beware of possible damage to surrounding components if it is necessary to improvise some method of immobilising the crankshaft.

10 Remove the sprocket and spacer, noting that the shoulder on the spacer faces inwards.

11 Unscrew the bolts and remove the stabilising and guide rollers from the front end cover **(see illustrations)**.

14.3a On M20 engines, the oil pump is bolted across the engine block from side to side, towards the front of the engine

14.4 If necessary on the M20 engine, remove the plug and oil pump driveshaft from the engine. Inspect the driveshaft gear, as well as this intermediate shaft gear in the engine block (arrowed)

12 Using a small screwdriver or similar instrument, remove the key from the groove in the nose of the crankshaft **(see illustration)**.

13 Pull the spacer ring off the crankshaft **(see illustration)**.

14 Unscrew the remaining bolts, and remove the front end cover and oil pump from the cylinder block. Note the locations of the front cover bolts, as they are of different sizes. With the cover removed, extract the rubber O-ring from the groove in the nose of the crankshaft **(see illustrations)**.

15 Note the fitted location of the oil seal, then prise it out of the housing.

14.8 Removing the timing belt tensioner (M40 engine)

14.11a Removing the stabilising roller from the front end cover (M40 engine)

14.11b Removing the guide roller from the front end cover (M40 engine)

14.12 Removing the key from the groove in the nose of the crankshaft (M40 engine)

14.13 Removing the spacer ring from the front of the crankshaft

14.14a Front end cover and oil pump in position on the front of the M40 engine

14.14b Extract the rubber O-ring from the groove in the nose of the crankshaft (M40 engine)

14.21a Unscrew the bolts . . .

14.21b . . . and remove the oil pump cover (M40 engine)

2A

Inspection

Note: *Considering that a malfunctioning oil pump can easily cause major engine damage, we recommend that the oil pump should always be renewed during engine overhaul, unless it's in as-new condition.*

M10, M20 and M30 engines

16 Remove the cover and check the pump body, gears or rotors and cover for cracks and wear (especially in the gear or rotor contact areas).

17 Check the strainer to make sure it is not clogged or damaged.

18 Lubricate the gears with clean engine oil, then attach the pump cover to the body and tighten the bolts evenly and securely.

19 Before refitting the pump - new, rebuilt or original - on the engine, check it for proper operation. Fill a clean container to a depth of one inch with fresh engine oil of the recommended viscosity.

20 Immerse the oil pump inlet in the oil, and turn the driveshaft anti-clockwise by hand. As the shaft is turned, oil should be discharged from the pump outlet.

M40 engines

21 With the front end cover on the bench, unscrew the bolts and remove the cover plate to expose the oil pump rotors **(see illustrations)**.

22 Identify the rotors for position, then remove them from the housing **(see illustrations)**.

23 Clean the housing and the rotors thoroughly, then refit the rotors, making sure that they are in their previously-noted positions. The inner rotor must be fitted with the guide facing the body.

24 Using feeler blades, measure the clearance between the oil pump body and the outer rotor, then check the clearance between the outer and inner rotors **(see illustrations)**.

25 If the clearance is not as given in the Specifications, the complete oil pump and front end cover should be renewed. If the clearance is within tolerance, remove the rotors, then pour a little engine oil into the housing. Refit the rotors and turn them to spread the oil around.

14.22a Removing the inner rotor . . .

14.22b . . . and outer rotor from the oil pump (M40 engine)

14.24a Measuring the clearance between the oil pump body and the outer rotor (M40 engine)

14.24b Measuring the clearance between the oil pump outer and inner rotors (M40 engine)

14.27a Extract the circlip from the oil pump (M40 engine) . . .

14.27b . . . and remove the sleeve . . .

26 Refit the cover plate and tighten the bolts to the specified torque.

27 To check the pressure relief valve, extract the circlip and remove the sleeve, spring and piston. Check that the length of the spring is as given in the Specifications (see illustrations). Reassemble the pressure relief valve using a reversal of the dismantling procedure.

Refitting

M10, M20 and M30 engines

28 Make sure the mounting surfaces are clean, then insert the pump into the engine block recess. Refit the bolts and tighten them to the torque specified at the beginning of this Chapter.

29 Refitting is the reverse of removal.

M40 engines

30 Clean the mating surfaces, then refit the front end cover and oil pump to the cylinder block, together with a new gasket (see illustration). Tighten the bolts to the specified torque. Note that there are two sizes of bolts, and they have different torque settings.

31 Fit the spacer ring on the front of the crankshaft.

32 Apply engine oil to the lips of the new oil seal, then press it into the housing to its previously-noted position. To ensure the oil seal enters the housing squarely, use a large socket and the crankshaft pulley bolt to pull it into position (see illustration).

33 Refit the key to the groove in the nose of the crankshaft.

34 Refit the stabilising roller to the front end cover, and tighten the bolt.

35 Refit the sprocket, spacer and crankshaft pulley bolt. Tighten the bolt to the specified torque while holding the crankshaft stationary using one of the methods previously described.

36 Refit the timing belt tensioning roller, but do not tighten the bolt at this stage.

37 Refit the cylinder head as described in Section 12.

38 Refit the timing belt as described in Section 10.

39 Refit the sump (see Section 13).

15 Flywheel/driveplate - removal and refitting

1 Remove the transmission (on vehicles with manual transmission, see Chapter 7A; on vehicles with automatic transmission, see Chapter 7B).

2 On vehicles with manual transmission, remove the clutch (see Chapter 8).

3 Where necessary, mark the relationship of the flywheel/driveplate to the crankshaft, so it can be refitted the same way.

4 The flywheel/driveplate is attached to the rear of the crankshaft with eight bolts. Loosen and remove the bolts, then separate it from

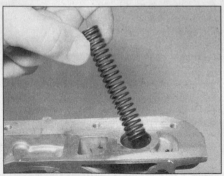

14.27c . . . spring . . .

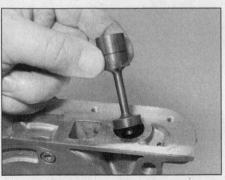

14.27d . . . and piston

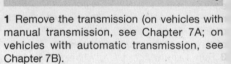

14.27e Checking the length of the pressure relief valve spring (M40 engine)

14.30 Locating a new gasket on the front of the cylinder block (M40 engine)

14.32 Using a large socket and the crankshaft pulley bolt to pull the oil seal into the housing (M40 engine)

15.4 Using a socket and ratchet, remove the eight bolts that hold the flywheel/ driveplate to the crankshaft flange - prevent the flywheel/driveplate from turning by locking the ring gear with a lever

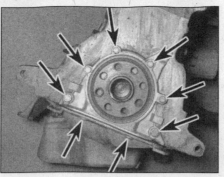

16.2 Remove the six bolts from the rear of the block and the two from underneath at the sump

16.6 After removing the retainer from the block, support it on two wood blocks, and drive out the old seal with a punch and hammer

the crankshaft flange **(see illustration)**. Be careful - the flywheel is heavy.
5 To refit the flywheel/driveplate on the crankshaft, use a liquid thread-locking compound on the bolts, and tighten them gradually, using a criss-cross pattern, to the torque listed in this Chapter's Specifications.
6 The remainder of refitting is the reverse of removal.

16 Crankshaft rear oil seal - renewal

1 Remove the flywheel or driveplate (see Section 15).
2 Remove the bolts and/or nuts attaching the seal retainer to the engine block. Be sure to remove the two bolts (from underneath) connecting the rear of the sump to the bottom of the seal retainer **(see illustration)**.
3 Run a sharp, thin knife between the sump gasket and the seal retainer, cutting the retainer free from the gasket. Be very careful not to damage the gasket, and keep it clean so you can re-use it.
4 Break the seal retainer-to-block gasket seal by tapping the retainer with a plastic mallet or block of wood and hammer. Do not prise between the retainer and the engine block, as damage to the gasket sealing surfaces will result.
5 Using a scraper, remove all traces of old gasket material from the sealing surfaces of the retainer and engine block. Gasket removal solvents are available at car accessory shops, and may prove helpful. After all gasket material has been removed, the gasket surfaces can be degreased by wiping them with a rag dampened with a suitable solvent.

 Caution: Be very careful not to scratch or gouge the delicate aluminium surfaces. Also, do not damage the sump gasket, and keep it clean.

6 Support the retainer on two blocks of wood, and drive out the seal from behind with a hammer and screwdriver **(see illustration)**.

Be very careful not to damage the seal bore in the process.
7 Coat the outside diameter and lip of the new seal with multi-purpose grease, and drive the seal into the retainer with a hammer and a block of wood **(see illustration)**.
8 Apply a film of RTV-type gasket sealant to the surface of the sump gasket that mates with the seal retainer. Apply extra beads of RTV sealant to the edges where the gasket meets the engine block. **Note:** *If the sump gasket is damaged, instead of fitting a whole new gasket, you might try trimming the rear portion of the gasket off at the point where it meets the engine block, then trim off the rear portion of a new sump gasket so it's exactly the same size. Cover the exposed inside area of the sump with a rag, then clean all traces of old gasket material off the area where the gasket was removed. Attach the new gasket piece to the sump with contact-cement-type gasket adhesive, then apply RTV-type sealant as described at the beginning of this paragraph.*
9 Coat both sides of the new retainer gasket with RTV-type gasket sealant, then attach the gasket to the seal retainer. Fit the seal retainer to the rear of the engine, then refit the bolts and tighten them evenly to the torque listed in this Chapter's Specifications. Work from bolt-to-bolt in a criss-cross pattern to be sure they're tightened evenly. **Note 1:** *Tighten the retainer-to-block bolts first, then tighten the sump-to-retainer bolts.* **Note 2:** *After applying RTV-type sealant, reassembly must be*

16.7 Drive the new seal into the retainer with a block of wood, or a section of pipe, if you have one large enough - make sure the seal enters the retainer bore squarely

completed in about 10 minutes so the RTV won't prematurely harden.
10 Refit the flywheel/driveplate (see Section 15).
11 Refit the transmission (on vehicles with manual transmission, see Chapter 7A; on vehicles with automatic transmission, see Chapter 7B).

17 Engine mountings - check and renewal

1 Engine mountings seldom require attention, but broken or deteriorated mountings should be renewed immediately, or the added strain placed on the driveline components may cause damage or wear.

Check

2 During the check, the engine must be raised slightly to remove its weight from the mounts.
3 Raise the vehicle and support it securely on axle stands, then position a jack under the engine sump. Place a large block of wood between the jack head and the sump, then carefully raise the engine just enough to take its weight off the mounts.

 Warning: DO NOT place any part of your body under the engine when it's supported only by a jack!

17.4 As engine mountings wear or age, they should be inspected for cracking or separation from their metal plates

2A

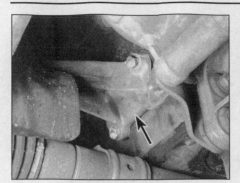

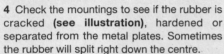

17.5 Lever gently between the block and the engine mounting attachment point (arrowed) - if there is movement, tighten the bolts

17.6 Engine mounting and damper on the M40 engine

17.10 To remove an engine mounting, first remove the stud nut (arrowed) - M30 engine shown, others similar

4 Check the mountings to see if the rubber is cracked **(see illustration)**, hardened or separated from the metal plates. Sometimes the rubber will split right down the centre.

5 Check for relative movement between the mounting plates and the engine or frame (use a large screwdriver or lever to attempt to move the mountings). If movement is noted, lower the engine and tighten the mounting nuts or bolts **(see illustration)**. Rubber preservative should be applied to the mountings, to slow deterioration.

6 On models with the M40 engine, check the condition of the dampers on each mounting by disconnecting them and attempting to compress and expand them **(see illustration)**. If there is very little resistance to movement, the dampers should be renewed.

Renewal

7 If the dampers on the M40 engine are to be renewed, simply unscrew the bolts, then fit the new dampers and tighten the bolts.

8 To renew the mountings, disconnect the battery negative cable, then raise the vehicle and support it securely on axle stands if you haven't already done so.

 Caution: If the radio in your vehicle is equipped with an anti-theft system, make sure you have the correct activation code

before disconnecting the battery.

Note: *If, after connecting the battery, the wrong language appears on the instrument panel display, refer to page 0-7 for the language resetting procedure.*

9 Support the engine as described in paragraph 3.

10 Remove the large bracket-to-mounting nut **(see illustration)**. Raise the engine slightly, then remove the lower mounting-to-frame bolts/nuts and detach the mounting

11 Refitting of the mountings is the reverse of removal. Use thread-locking compound on the mounting bolts/nuts, and be sure to tighten them securely.

Chapter 2 Part B:
General engine overhaul procedures

Contents

Degrees of difficulty

Easy, suitable for novice with little experience	**Fairly easy,** suitable for beginner with some experience	**Fairly difficult,** suitable for competent DIY mechanic	**Difficult,** suitable for experienced DIY mechanic	**Very difficult,** suitable for expert DIY or professional

Specifications

General

Cylinder compression pressure (all engines)	10 to 11 bars
Oil pressure (all engines)	
At idle	0.5 to 2.0 bars
Running (for example, at 4000 rpm)	4 bars or above (typically)
Cylinder head warpage limit	
Except M40 engine	0.10 mm
M40 engine	0.03 mm
Minimum cylinder head thickness (do not resurface the head to a thickness less than listed)	
M10 and M30 engines	128.6 mm
M20 engines	124.7 mm
M40 engine	140.55 mm

Valves

Valve stem diameter (standard)	
M10 and M30 engines	8.0 mm
M20 engine	7.0 mm
M40 engine	
Intake	6.975 mm
Exhaust	6.960 mm
Minimum valve margin width	
Intake	1.191 mm
Exhaust	1.98 mm
Valve stem maximum lateral movement (see text)	0.787 mm
Valve face angle	
Intake	45°
Exhaust	45°

Camshaft and rocker arms

Camshaft bearing oil clearance	0.033 to 0.076 mm
Camshaft endfloat	
M10 engine	0.02 to 0.13 mm
M20 engine	0.2 mm maximum
M30 engine	0.03 to 0.18 mm
M40 engine	0.065 to 0.150 mm
Rocker arm radial clearance	0.015 to 0.051 mm

Crankshaft

Endfloat	
M10 and M30 engines	0.085 to 0.174 mm
M20 and M40 engines	0.080 to 0.163 mm
Main bearing journal diameter (standard)	
M10 engines	
Red classification	54.98 to 54.99 mm
Blue classification	54.97 to 54.98 mm
M20 engines	
Red classification	59.98 to 59.99 mm
Blue classification	59.97 to 59.98 mm
M30 and M40 engines	
Yellow classification	59.984 to 59.990 mm
Green classification	59.977 to 59.983 mm
White classification	59.971 to 59.976 mm
Main bearing journal diameter undersizes	
1st undersize	0.25 mm
2nd undersize	0.50 mm
3rd undersize (where applicable)	0.75 mm
Main bearing oil clearance	
M10 and M20 engines	0.030 to 0.070 mm
M30 and M40 engines	0.020 to 0.046 mm
Connecting rod journal diameter (standard)	
M10 and M30 engines	47.975 to 47.991 mm
M20 and M40 engines	44.975 to 44.991 mm
Connecting rod journal diameter undersizes	
1st undersize	0.25 mm
2nd undersize	0.50 mm
3rd undersize (where applicable)	0.75 mm

Connecting rods

Connecting rod side play (all engines)	0.041 mm
Connecting big-end bearing oil clearance	
M10 engines	0.030 to 0.070 mm
M20 and M30 engines	0.020 to 0.055 mm
M40 engines	0.010 to 0.052 mm

Engine block

Cylinder bore - diameter (standard)	
M10/B18 engine	89.00 to 89.01 mm
M20/B20 engine	80.00 to 80.01 mm
M20/B25 engine	84.00 to 84.01 mm
M30/B25 engine	86.00 to 86.01 mm
M30/B28 engine	86.00 to 86.01 mm
M30/B30M engine	89.00 to 89.01 mm
M30/B34 engine	92.00 to 92.01 mm
M30/B35M engine	92.00 to 92.01 mm
M40/B16 engine	84.000 to 84.014 mm
M40/B18 engine	84.000 to 84.014 mm
Cylinder out-of-round limit (maximum)	
M20/B20 engine	0.02 mm
M20/B25 engine	0.03 mm
All other engines	0.01 mm
Cylinder taper (maximum)	
M20/B20 and M20/B25 engines	0.02 mm
All other engines	0.01 mm

Pistons and piston rings

Piston diameter (standard)	
M10 engines	88.97 mm
M20 engines	
B20	79.98 mm
B25	83.98 mm
M30 engines	
B30M	
Alcan	88.970 mm
KS	88.980 mm
B35M	
Alcan	91.972 mm
Mahle	91.980 mm
M40 engines	
Factory stage 0	83.985 mm
Factory stage 00	84.065 mm
Piston-to-cylinder wall clearance	
New	
M10 and M30 engines	0.02 to 0.05 mm
M20 and M40 engines	0.01 to 0.04 mm
Service limit	
Except B25 engine	0.15 mm
B25 engine	0.12 mm
Piston ring end gap	
M10 engine	
Top compression ring	0.30 to 0.70 mm
Second compression ring	0.20 to 0.40 mm
Oil ring	0.25 to 0.50 mm
M20 engine	
All rings	0.20 to 0.50 mm
M30 engine	
Top compression ring	0.20 to 0.45 mm
Second compression ring	0.40 to 0.65 mm
Oil ring	0.30 to 0.60 mm
M40 engine	
Top compression ring	0.20 to 1.00 mm
Second compression ring	0.20 to 1.00 mm
Oil ring	
B16 engine	0.20 to 1.00 mm
B18 engine	0.40 to 1.40 mm
Piston ring side clearance	
M10 engine	
Top compression ring	0.06 to 0.09 mm
Second compression ring	0.03 to 0.072 mm
Oil ring	0.02 to 0.06 mm
M20 engine	
Top compression ring	0.04 to 0.08 mm
Second compression ring	0.03 to 0.07 mm
Oil ring	0.02 to 0.05 mm
M30 engine	
Top compression ring	0.04 to 0.072 mm
Second compression ring	0.03 to 0.062 mm
Oil ring	0.02 to 0.055 mm
M40 engine	
Top compression ring	0.02 to 0.20 mm
Second compression ring	0.02 to 0.10 mm
Oil ring	
B16 engine	0.02 to 0.10 mm
B18 engine	Not measured

Torque wrench settings

	Nm
Main bearing cap-to-engine block bolts*	
M10, M20 and M30 engines	60
M40 engines	
Stage 1	20
Stage 2	Angle-tighten an additional 50°

2B

Torque wrench settings (continued)

	Nm
Connecting rod cap bolts/nuts	
M10 and M30 engines	55
M20 and M40 engines	
Stage 1	20
Stage 2	Angle-tighten an additional 70°
Camshaft bearing caps (M40 engine)	10
Intermediate shaft sprocket-to-shaft bolt (M20 engine)	60
Oil supply tube bolt(s)	
M6 (normal) and M8 (banjo)	10
M5	5

* BMW recommend that the main bearing bolts are renewed as a matter of course.

1 General information

Included in this Part of Chapter 2 are the general overhaul procedures for the cylinder head and engine internal components.

The information ranges from advice concerning preparation for an overhaul and the purchase of new parts to detailed, paragraph-by-paragraph procedures covering removal and refitting of internal components and the inspection of parts.

The following Sections have been written based on the assumption that the engine has been removed from the vehicle. For information concerning in-vehicle engine repair, as well as removal and refitting of the external components necessary for the overhaul, see Chapter 2A, and Section 7 of this Part.

The Specifications included in this Part are only those necessary for the inspection and overhaul procedures which follow. Refer to Part A for additional Specifications.

2 Engine overhaul - general information

It's not always easy to determine when, or if, an engine should be completely overhauled, as a number of factors must be considered.

High mileage is not necessarily an indication that an overhaul is needed, while low mileage doesn't preclude the need for an overhaul. Frequency of servicing is probably the most important consideration. An engine that's had regular and frequent oil and filter changes, as well as other required maintenance, will most likely give many thousands of miles of reliable service. Conversely, a neglected engine may require an overhaul very early in its life.

Excessive oil consumption is an indication that piston rings, valve seals and/or valve guides are in need of attention. Make sure that oil leaks aren't responsible before deciding that the rings and/or guides are worn. Perform a cylinder compression check to determine the extent of the work required (see Section 3).

Check the oil pressure: Unscrew the oil pressure sender unit, and connect an oil pressure gauge in its place. Measure the oil pressure with the engine at its normal operating temperature. Compare your readings to the oil pressures listed in this Chapter's Specifications. If the readings are significantly below these (and if the oil and oil filter are in good condition), the crankshaft bearings and/or the oil pump are probably worn out. On M10 and M30 engines, the oil pressure sender unit is located high on the left rear of the cylinder head. On M20 engines, the sender unit is threaded into the side of the engine block, below the oil filter. On M40 engines, the sender unit is threaded into the rear of the oil filter housing.

Loss of power, rough running, knocking or metallic engine noises, excessive valve train noise and high fuel consumption may also point to the need for an overhaul, especially if they're all present at the same time. If a complete tune-up doesn't remedy the situation, major mechanical work is the only solution.

An engine overhaul involves restoring the internal parts to the specifications of a new engine. During an overhaul, new piston rings are fitted and the cylinder walls are reconditioned (rebored and/or honed). If a rebore is done by an engineering works, new oversize pistons will also be fitted. The main bearings and connecting big-end bearings are generally renewed and, if necessary, the crankshaft may be reground to restore the journals. Generally, the valves are serviced as well, since they're usually in less-than-perfect condition at this point. While the engine is being overhauled, other components, such as the distributor, starter and alternator, can be rebuilt as well. The end result should be a like-new engine that will give many thousands of trouble-free miles. **Note:** *Critical cooling system components such as the hoses, drivebelts, thermostat and water pump MUST be renewed when an engine is overhauled. The radiator should be checked carefully, to ensure that it isn't clogged or leaking (see Chapters 1 or 3). Also, we don't recommend overhauling the oil pump - always fit a new one when an engine is rebuilt.*

Before beginning the engine overhaul, read through the entire procedure to familiarise yourself with the scope and requirements of the job. Overhauling an engine isn't difficult if you follow all of the instructions carefully, have the necessary tools and equipment and pay close attention to all specifications; however, it is time consuming. Plan on the vehicle being tied up for a minimum of two weeks, especially if parts must be taken to an automotive machine shop for repair or reconditioning. Check on availability of parts and make sure that any necessary special tools and equipment are obtained in advance. Most work can be done with typical hand tools, although a number of precision measuring tools are required for inspecting parts to determine if they must be replaced. Often an automotive machine shop will handle the inspection of parts and offer advice concerning reconditioning and renewal. **Note:** *Always wait until the engine has been completely disassembled and all components, especially the engine block, have been inspected before deciding what service and repair operations must be performed by an automotive machine shop. Since the block's condition will be the major factor to consider when determining whether to overhaul the original engine or buy a rebuilt one, never purchase parts or have machine work done on other components until the block has been thoroughly inspected. As a general rule, time is the primary cost of an overhaul, so it doesn't pay to refit worn or substandard parts.*

As a final note, to ensure maximum life and minimum trouble from a rebuilt engine, everything must be assembled with care, in a spotlessly-clean environment.

3 Compression check

1 A compression check will tell you what mechanical condition the upper end (pistons, rings, valves, head gaskets) of your engine is in. Specifically, it can tell you if the compression is down due to leakage caused by worn piston rings, defective valves and seats, or a blown head gasket. **Note:** *The engine must be at normal operating temperature, and the battery must be fully-charged, for this check.*

2 Begin by cleaning the area around the spark plugs before you remove them (compressed air should be used, if available,

3.5 As a safety precaution, before performing a compression check, remove the cover and the main relay (arrowed) from the left side of the engine compartment to disable the fuel and ignition systems (525i model shown, other models similar)

otherwise a small brush or even a bicycle tyre pump will work). The idea is to prevent dirt from getting into the cylinders as the compression check is being done.

3 Remove all the spark plugs from the engine (see Chapter 1).

4 Block the throttle wide open, or have an assistant hold the throttle pedal down.

5 On carburettor models, disconnect the LT lead from the coil. On fuel injection models, disable the fuel pump and ignition circuit by removing the main relay **(see illustration)**. This is to avoid the possibility of a fire from fuel being sprayed in the engine compartment. The location of the main relay is generally near the fuse panel area under the bonnet, but refer to Chapter 12 for the specific location on your model.

6 Fit the compression gauge in the No 1 spark plug hole (No 1 cylinder is nearest the radiator).

7 Turn the engine on the starter motor over at least seven compression strokes, and watch the gauge. The compression should build up quickly in a healthy engine. Low compression on the first stroke, followed by gradually-increasing pressure on successive strokes, indicates worn piston rings. A low compression reading on the first stroke, which doesn't build up during successive strokes, indicates leaking valves or a blown head gasket (a cracked head could also be the cause). Deposits on the undersides of the valve heads can also cause low compression. Record the highest gauge reading obtained.

8 Repeat the procedure for the remaining cylinders, and compare the results to the compression listed in this Chapter's Specifications.

9 If compression was low, add some engine oil (about three squirts from a plunger-type oil can) to each cylinder, through the spark plug hole, and repeat the test.

10 If the compression increases after the oil is added, the piston rings are definitely worn. If the compression doesn't increase

significantly, the leakage is occurring at the valves or head gasket. Leakage past the valves may be caused by burned valve seats and/or faces or warped, cracked or bent valves.

11 If two adjacent cylinders have equally low compression, there's a strong possibility that the head gasket between them is blown. The appearance of coolant in the combustion chambers or the crankcase would verify this condition.

12 If one cylinder is 20 percent lower than the others, and the engine has a slightly rough idle, a worn exhaust lobe on the camshaft could be the cause.

13 If the compression is unusually high, the combustion chambers are probably coated with carbon deposits. If that's the case, the cylinder head should be removed and decarbonised.

14 If compression is way down, or varies greatly between cylinders, it would be a good idea to have a leak-down test performed by a garage. This test will pinpoint exactly where the leakage is occurring and how severe it is.

 4 Engine removal - methods and precautions

If you've decided that an engine must be removed for overhaul or major repair work, several preliminary steps should be taken.

Locating a suitable place to work is extremely important. Adequate work space, along with storage space for the vehicle, will be needed. If a workshop or garage isn't available, at the very least a flat, level, clean work surface made of concrete or asphalt is required.

Cleaning the engine compartment and engine before beginning the removal procedure will help keep tools clean and organised.

An engine hoist or A-frame will also be necessary. Make sure the equipment is rated in excess of the combined weight of the engine and accessories. Safety is of primary importance, considering the potential hazards involved in lifting the engine out of the vehicle.

If the engine is being removed by a novice, a helper should be available. Advice and aid from someone more experienced would also be helpful. There are many instances when one person cannot simultaneously perform all of the operations required when lifting the engine out of the vehicle.

Plan the operation ahead of time. Arrange for or obtain all the tools and equipment you'll need prior to beginning the job. Some of the equipment necessary to perform engine removal and refitting safely and with relative ease are (in addition to an engine hoist) a heavy-duty trolley jack, complete sets of spanners and sockets as described in the

front of this manual, wooden blocks, and plenty of rags and cleaning solvent for mopping up spilled oil, coolant and fuel. If the hoist must be hired, make sure that you arrange for it in advance, and perform all of the operations possible without it beforehand. This will save you money and time.

Plan for the vehicle to be out of use for quite a while. A machine shop will be required to perform some of the work which the do-it-yourselfer can't accomplish without special equipment. These establishments often have a busy schedule, so it would be a good idea to consult them before removing the engine, in order to accurately estimate the amount of time required to rebuild or repair components that may need work.

Always be extremely careful when removing and refitting the engine. Serious injury can result from careless actions. Plan ahead, take your time and a job of this nature, although major, can be accomplished successfully.

⚠️ *Warning: The air conditioning system is under high pressure. Do not loosen any fittings or remove any components until after the system has been discharged by a qualified engineer. Always wear eye protection when disconnecting air conditioning system fittings.*

⚠️ *Caution: If removing the M40 engine, it is important not to turn the engine upside-down for longer than 10 minutes since it is possible for the oil to drain out of the hydraulic tappets. This would render the tappets unserviceable, and damage could possibly occur to the engine when it is next started up.*

 5 Engine - removal and refitting

⚠️ *Caution: If the radio in your vehicle is equipped with an anti-theft system, make sure you have the correct activation code before disconnecting the battery.*
Note: *If, after connecting the battery, the wrong language appears on the instrument panel display, refer to page 0-7 for the language resetting procedure.*

Removal

1 Relieve the fuel system pressure (see Chapter 4), then disconnect the negative cable from the battery.
2 Cover the wings and front panel, and remove the bonnet (see Chapter 11). Special pads are available to protect the wings, but an old bedspread or blanket will also work.
3 Remove the air cleaner housing and intake ducts (see Chapter 4).
4 Drain the cooling system (see Chapter 1).
5 Label the vacuum lines, emissions system hoses, wiring connectors, earth straps and fuel lines, to ensure correct refitting, then

2B

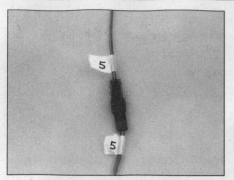

5.5 Label each wire before unplugging the connector

5.26 Removing the engine rear plate - M40 engine

detach them. Pieces of masking tape with numbers or letters written on them work well **(see illustration)**.

> **HAYNES HiNT** *If there's any possibility of confusion, make a sketch of the engine compartment and clearly label the lines, hoses and wires.*

6 Label and detach all coolant hoses from the engine (see Chapter 3).
7 Remove the cooling fan, shroud and radiator (see Chapter 3). **Note:** *On the M40 engine, it is only necessary to remove the cooling fan and shroud; however, prevent damage to the radiator by covering it with a piece of wood or cardboard.*
8 Remove the drivebelts (see Chapter 1).
9 Disconnect the fuel lines from the fuel rail (see Chapter 4).

> ⚠ **Warning: Fuel is extremely flammable, so take extra precautions when you work on any part of the fuel system. Don't smoke, or allow open flames or bare light bulbs, near the work area, and don't work in a garage where a natural gas-type appliance (such as a water heater or clothes dryer) with a pilot light is present. If you spill any fuel on your skin, rinse it off immediately with soap and water. When you perform any kind of work on the fuel system, wear safety glasses, and have a fire extinguisher on hand.**

10 Disconnect the accelerator cable (see Chapter 4) and kickdown linkage/speed control cable (see Chapter 7B), if applicable, from the engine.
11 Where fitted, unbolt the power steering pump (see Chapter 10). Leave the lines/hoses attached, and make sure the pump is kept in an upright position in the engine compartment (use wire or rope to restrain it out of the way).
12 On air-conditioned models, unbolt the compressor (see Chapter 3) and set it aside, or tie it up out of the way. **Do not** disconnect the hoses.
13 Drain the engine oil (see Chapter 1) and remove the filter. Remove the engine splash guard from under the engine.
14 Remove the starter motor (see Chapter 5).

15 Remove the alternator (see Chapter 5). This is not essential on all models, but it is a good idea in any case to avoid accidental damage.
16 Unbolt the exhaust system from the engine (see Chapter 4).
17 If you're working on a vehicle with an automatic transmission, remove the torque converter-to-driveplate fasteners (see Chapter 7B). On the M40 engine, unbolt the automatic transmission fluid coolant pipes from the sump.
18 Support the transmission with a jack. Position a block of wood between them, to prevent damage to the transmission. Special transmission jacks with safety chains are available - use one if possible.
19 Attach an engine sling or a length of chain to the lifting brackets on the engine. If the brackets have been removed, the chain can be bolted directly to the intake manifold studs, but place a flat washer between the chain and the nut, and tighten the nut all the way up to the chain, to avoid the possibility of the studs bending.
20 Roll the hoist into position and connect the sling to it. Take up the slack in the sling or chain, but don't lift the engine.

> ⚠ **Warning: DO NOT place any part of your body under the engine when it's supported only by a hoist or other lifting device.**

21 On M10, M20 and M30 engines, remove the transmission rear crossmember, and slightly lower the rear of the transmission.
22 Remove the transmission-to-engine block bolts using a Torx socket. **Note:** *The bolts holding the bellhousing to the engine block will require a swivel at the socket, and a very long extension going back towards the transmission.*
23 Remove the engine mounting-to-frame bracket nuts. On the M40 engine, unbolt the dampers from the mountings.
24 Recheck to be sure nothing is still connecting the engine to the transmission or vehicle. Disconnect anything still remaining.
25 Raise the engine slightly. Carefully work it forwards to separate it from the transmission. If you're working on a vehicle with an automatic transmission, you may find the torque converter comes forward with the

engine. If it stays with the transmission, leave it, but you may find it easier to let it come forward until it can be grasped easier and be pulled from the crankshaft. **Note:** *When refitting the torque converter to the transmission before the engine is refitted, be sure to renew the transmission front pump seal, which will probably be damaged when the converter comes out with the engine. Either method is acceptable, but be prepared for some fluid to leak from the torque converter if it comes out of the transmission. If you're working on a vehicle with a manual transmission, draw the engine forwards until the input shaft is completely disengaged from the clutch. Slowly raise the engine out of the engine compartment. Check carefully to make sure everything is disconnected.*
26 Remove the flywheel/driveplate (and where applicable, the engine rear plate), and mount the engine on an engine stand **(see illustration)**. Do not turn the M40 engine upside-down (see **Caution** in Section 4).

Refitting

27 Check the engine and transmission mountings. If they're worn or damaged, renew them.
28 Refit the flywheel or driveplate (see Chapter 2A). If you're working on a manual transmission vehicle, refit the clutch and pressure plate (see Chapter 7A). Now is a good time to fit a new clutch.
29 If the torque converter came out with the engine during removal, carefully refit the converter into the transmission before the engine is lowered into the vehicle.
30 Carefully lower the engine into the engine compartment - make sure the engine mountings line up.
31 If you're working on an automatic transmission vehicle, guide the torque converter onto the crankshaft following the procedure outlined in Chapter 7B.
32 If you're working on a manual transmission vehicle, apply a dab of high-melting-point grease to the input shaft, and guide it into the clutch and crankshaft pilot bearing until the bellhousing is flush with the engine block.. Do not allow the weight of the engine to hang on the input shaft.

> **HAYNES HiNT** *It may be necessary to rock the engine slightly, or to turn the crankshaft, to allow the input shaft splines to mate with the clutch plate*

33 Refit the transmission-to-engine bolts, and tighten them securely.

> ⚠ **Caution: DO NOT use the bolts to force the transmission and engine together.**

34 Refit the remaining components in the reverse order of removal.
35 Add coolant, oil, power steering and transmission fluid as needed.

36 Run the engine and check for leaks and proper operation of all accessories, then refit the bonnet and test drive the vehicle.
37 Where necessary, have the air conditioning system recharged and leak-tested.

6 Engine overhaul - alternatives

The do-it-yourselfer is faced with a number of options when performing an engine overhaul. The decision to renew the engine block, piston/connecting rod assemblies and crankshaft depends on a number of factors, with the number one consideration being the condition of the block. Other considerations are cost, access to machine shop facilities, parts availability, time required to complete the project, and the extent of prior mechanical experience on the part of the do-it-yourselfer.

Some of the alternatives include:

Individual parts - If the inspection procedures reveal that the engine block and most engine components are in re-usable condition, purchasing individual parts may be the most economical alternative. The block, crankshaft and piston/connecting rod assemblies should all be inspected carefully. Even if the block shows little wear, the cylinder bores should be surface-honed.

Crankshaft kit - A crankshaft kit (where available) consists of a reground crankshaft with matched undersize new main and connecting big-end bearings. Sometimes, reconditioned connecting rods and new pistons and rings are included with the kit (such a kit is sometimes called an "engine kit"). If the block is in good condition, but the crankshaft journals are scored or worn, a crankshaft kit and other individual parts may be the most economical alternative.

Short block - A short block consists of an engine block with a crankshaft and piston/connecting rod assemblies already fitted. New bearings are fitted, and all clearances will be correct. The existing camshaft, valve train components, cylinder head and external parts can be bolted to the short block with little or no machine shop work necessary.

Full block - A "full" or "complete" block consists of a short block plus an oil pump, sump, cylinder head, valve cover, camshaft and valve train components, timing sprockets and chain (or belt) and timing cover. All components are fitted with new bearings, seals and gaskets used throughout. The refitting of manifolds and external parts is all that's necessary.

Give careful thought to which alternative is best for you, and discuss the situation with local machine shops, parts dealers and experienced rebuilders before ordering or purchasing new parts.

7 Engine overhaul - dismantling sequence

1 It's much easier to dismantle and work on the engine if it's mounted on a portable engine stand. A stand can often be hired quite cheaply from a tool hire shop. Before the engine is mounted on a stand, the flywheel/driveplate should be removed from the engine.
2 If a stand isn't available, it's possible to dismantle the engine with it blocked up on the floor. Be extra-careful not to tip or drop the engine when working without a stand.
3 If you're going to obtain a rebuilt engine, all the external components listed below must come off first, to be transferred to the new engine if applicable. This is also the case if you're doing a complete engine overhaul yourself. **Note:** *When removing the external components from the engine, pay close attention to details that may be helpful or important during refitting. Note the fitted position of gaskets, seals, spacers, pins, brackets, washers, bolts and other small items.*

Alternator and brackets
Emissions control components
Distributor, HT leads and spark plugs
Thermostat and housing cover
Water pump
Fuel injection/carburettor and fuel system components
Intake and exhaust manifolds
Oil filter and oil pressure sending unit
Engine mounting brackets **(see illustration)**
Clutch and flywheel/driveplate
Engine rear plate (where applicable)

4 If you're obtaining a short block, which consists of the engine block, crankshaft, pistons and connecting rods all assembled, then the cylinder head, sump and oil pump will have to be removed as well. See Section 6 for additional information regarding the different possibilities to be considered.
5 If you're planning a complete overhaul, the engine must be dismantled and the internal components removed in the following general order:

Valve cover
Intake and exhaust manifolds
Timing belt or chain covers
Timing chain/belt
Water pump
Cylinder head
Sump
Oil pump
Piston/connecting rod assemblies
Crankshaft and main bearings
Camshaft
Rocker shafts and rocker arms (M10, M20 and M30 engines)
Cam followers and hydraulic tappets (M40 engine)
Valve spring retainers and springs
Valves

6 Before beginning the dismantling and

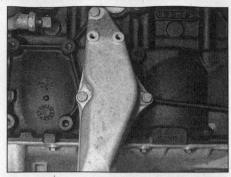

7.3 Engine left-hand mounting bracket - M40 engine

overhaul procedures, make sure the following items are available. Also, refer to Section 21 for a list of tools and materials needed for engine reassembly.

Common hand tools
Small cardboard boxes or plastic bags for storing parts
Compartment-type metal box for storing the hydraulic tappets (M40 engine)
Gasket scraper
Ridge reamer
Vibration damper puller
Micrometers
Telescoping gauges
Dial indicator set
Valve spring compressor
Cylinder surfacing hone
Piston ring groove cleaning tool
Electric drill motor
Tap and die set
Wire brushes
Oil gallery brushes
Cleaning solvent

8 Cylinder head - dismantling

1 Remove the cylinder head (see Chapter 2A).
2 Remove the oil supply tube from its mounting on top of the cylinder head **(see illustrations)**. **Note:** *It's important to renew the seals under the tube mounting bolts.*

8.2a Remove the oil tube from the top of the cylinder head (M10 engine). Be sure to note the location of all gaskets and washers for reassembly

8.2b Removing the oil tube from the camshaft bearing caps on the top of the cylinder head (M40 engine)

M10, M20 and M30 engines

3 Adjust all valves to their maximum clearance by rotating the eccentric on the valve end of the rocker arm towards the centre of the head (see Chapter 1, if necessary).

4 Before removing the thrustplate, measure the camshaft endfloat by mounting a dial indicator to the front end of the cylinder head, with the probe resting on the camshaft (see illustration). Prise the camshaft back-and-forth in the cylinder head. The reading is the camshaft endfloat. Compare the reading to this Chapter's Specifications.

5 Unbolt and remove the camshaft thrustplate. **Note:** *There are two different locations for the thrustplate. On M10 and M30 engines, it is attached on the front of the cylinder head, behind the timing gear flange. On M20 and M40 engines, the thrustplate is located inside the head, by the rocker shafts, at the forward end of the cylinder head.*

6 Remove the rear cover plate from the back of the cylinder head (see illustration).

7 Remove the retaining clips from each of the rocker arms. **Note:** *There is more than one style of clip. The wire-type clips (see illustration) are fitted one each side of the rocker arm; the spring-steel-type goes over the rocker arm, and clips onto either side of it.*

8 Before removing the rocker arm shafts, measure the rocker arm radial clearance, using a dial indicator, and compare your measurement to the Specifications at the

8.7 Remove the retaining clips from the rocker arms - the wire-type clip is shown here

8.4 To check camshaft endfloat, mount a dial indicator so that its stem is in-line with the camshaft and just touching the camshaft at the front

beginning of this Chapter. Without sliding the rocker arm along the shaft, try to rotate the rocker arm against the shaft in each direction (see illustration). The total movement measured at the camshaft end of the rocker arm is the radial clearance. If the clearance is excessive, either the rocker arm bush, rocker arm shaft, or both, will need to be renewed.

9 Remove the rubber retaining plugs, or the threaded plugs, at the front of the cylinder head, as applicable. There is a plug in front of each rocker shaft.

 Caution: If your engine has welded-in retaining plugs at the front of the rocker shafts, take the cylinder head to a machine shop for plug removal, to avoid possible damage to the cylinder head or the rocker arm shafts.

10 Rotate the camshaft until the most rocker arms possible are loose (not compressing their associated valve springs).

11 For the remaining rocker arms that are still compressing their valve springs, BMW recommends using a special forked tool to compress the rocker arms against the valve springs (and therefore take the valve spring tension off the camshaft lobe). If the tool is not available, insert a standard screwdriver into the gap above the adjuster eccentric at the valve-end tip of each rocker arm. Using the

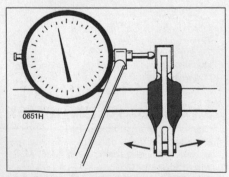

8.8 Check the rocker arm-to-shaft radial clearance by setting up a dial indicator as shown, and trying to rotate the rocker arm against the shaft - DO NOT slide the rocker arm along the shaft

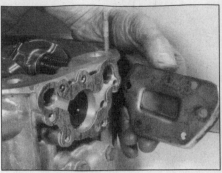

8.6 Remove the cover from the rear of the cylinder head - be sure to note the locations of any washers, gaskets and seals while you are removing the cover

screwdrivers, prise the rocker arms against the valve springs, and hold them in place as the camshaft is removed (see the next paragraph). At least one assistant will be necessary for this operation, since three or four valve springs usually need compressing. If no assistance is available, you could try retaining the screwdrivers that are compressing the valve springs to the bench with lengths of sturdy wire.

 Warning: Be sure the wire is securely attached to the bench and screwdrivers, or the screwdrivers could fly off the cylinder head, possibly causing injury.

12 When all the rocker arms are no longer contacting the camshaft lobes, slowly and carefully pull the camshaft out the front of the cylinder head. It may be necessary to rotate the camshaft as it is removed.

 Caution: Be very careful not to scratch the camshaft bearing journals in the cylinder head as the camshaft is withdrawn.

13 After removing the camshaft, carefully remove the rocker arm shafts. On models without threaded holes at the front of the shafts, drive them out from the rear of the cylinder head with a hammer and hardwood dowel that is slightly smaller in diameter than the rocker arm shaft (see illustration). For

8.13 Removing a rocker arm shaft from the front of the cylinder head - the shaft must be either driven out from the rear of the head with a hardwood dowel or, on models where the rocker shaft is threaded at the front, pulled out from the front with a slide-hammer-type puller

8.17a Removing the camshaft bearing caps . . .

8.17b . . . and camshaft - M40 engine

8.19 Compartmentalised box to hold the hydraulic tappets (M40 engine)

rocker shafts with a threaded front hole, screw in a slide hammer to pull the shaft from the head.

14 As each rocker arm shaft is slid out of the cylinder head, the rocker arms will be released, one by one.

15 Drop each rocker arm into a labelled bag, so they can be returned to their original locations on reassembly. While you're removing the rocker arm shafts, note their orientation. The guide plate notches and the small oil holes face in; the large oil holes face down, toward the valve guides. Also, label the rocker shafts so they can be returned to their original locations in the cylinder head.

M40 engines

 Caution: Keep the cylinder head upright until all of the hydraulic tappets have been removed. If this precaution is not taken, the oil may drain out of the tappets and render them unserviceable.

16 Check that the camshaft bearing caps are numbered or identified for location.

17 Progressively unscrew and remove the camshaft bearing cap retaining bolts, then remove the caps (see illustrations).

18 Lift the camshaft from the top of the cylinder head, and remove the oil seal from the timing end.

19 Have ready a compartmentalised box filled with engine oil to receive the hydraulic tappets so that they are kept identified for their correct location (see illustration). Also have a further box ready to receive the cam followers.

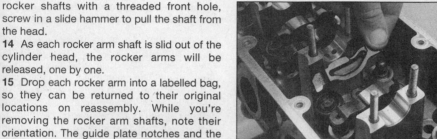

8.20a Remove the cam followers . . .

8.20b . . . and thrust discs . . .

20 Remove the cam followers and thrust discs, then lift out the hydraulic tappets from their bores in the cylinder head (see illustrations).

All engines

21 Before the valves are removed, arrange to label and store them, along with their related components, so they can be kept separate and reinstalled in the same valve guides from which they're removed (see illustration).

22 Compress the springs on the first valve with a spring compressor, and remove the collets (see illustration). Carefully release the valve spring compressor, and remove the retainer, the spring and the spring seat (if used).

23 Pull the valve out of the head, then remove the oil seal from the guide.

TOOL TiP

If the valve binds in the guide (won't pull through), push it back into the head, and deburr the area around the collet groove with a fine file or whetstone.

8.20c . . . then lift out the hydraulic tappets

8.21 A small plastic bag, with an appropriate label, can be used to store the valve components so they can be kept together and refitted in the original position

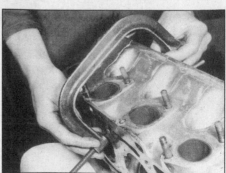

8.22 Using a valve spring compressor to compress a valve spring

2B

24 Repeat the procedure for the remaining valves. Remember to keep all the parts for each valve together, so they can be refitted in the same locations.

25 Once the valves and related components have been removed and stored in an organised manner, the head should be thoroughly cleaned and inspected. If a complete engine overhaul is being done, finish the engine dismantling procedures before beginning the cylinder head cleaning and inspection process.

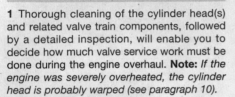

9 Cylinder head and components - cleaning and inspection

1 Thorough cleaning of the cylinder head(s) and related valve train components, followed by a detailed inspection, will enable you to decide how much valve service work must be done during the engine overhaul. **Note:** *If the engine was severely overheated, the cylinder head is probably warped (see paragraph 10).*

Cleaning

2 Scrape all traces of old gasket material and sealing compound off the cylinder head, intake manifold and exhaust manifold sealing surfaces. Be very careful not to gouge the cylinder head. Special gasket removal solvents are available at motor factors.

3 Remove all built-up scale from the coolant passages.

4 Run a stiff brush through the various holes to remove deposits that may have formed in them.

5 Run an appropriate-size tap into each of the threaded holes, to remove corrosion and thread sealant that may be present. If compressed air is available, use it to clear the holes of debris produced by this operation.

 Warning: Wear eye protection when using compressed air!

6 Clean the cylinder head with solvent, and dry it thoroughly. Compressed air will speed the drying process, and ensure that all holes

9.12 A dial indicator can be used to determine the valve stem-to-guide clearance (move the valve as indicated by the arrows)

and recessed areas are clean. **Note:** *Decarbonising chemicals are available, and may prove very useful when cleaning cylinder heads and valve train components. They are very caustic, however, and should be used with caution. Be sure to follow the instructions on the container.*

7 Clean all the rocker shafts/arms/followers, springs, valve springs, spring seats, keepers and retainers with solvent, and dry them thoroughly. Clean the components from one valve at a time, to avoid mixing up the parts.

 Caution: DO NOT clean the hydraulic tappets of the M40 engine; leave them completely immersed in oil.

8 Scrape off any heavy deposits that may have formed on the valves, then use a motorised wire brush to remove deposits from the valve heads and stems. Again, make sure the valves don't get mixed up.

Inspection

Note: *Be sure to perform all of the following inspection procedures before concluding that machine shop work is required. Make a list of the items that need attention.*

Cylinder head

9 Inspect the head very carefully for cracks, evidence of coolant leakage, and other damage. If cracks are found, check with an machine shop concerning repair. If repair isn't possible, a new cylinder head should be obtained.

10 Using a straightedge and feeler gauge, check the head gasket mating surface for warpage **(see illustration)**. If the warpage exceeds the limit listed in this Chapter's Specifications, it may be possible to have it resurfaced at a machine shop, providing the head is not reduced to less than the specified minimum thickness.

11 Examine the valve seats in each of the combustion chambers. If they're badly pitted, cracked or burned, the head will require servicing that's beyond the scope of the home mechanic.

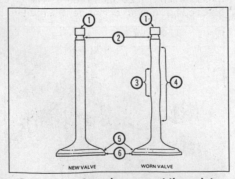

9.13 Check for valve wear at the points shown here

1 Valve tip
2 Collet groove
3 Stem (least-worn area)
4 Stem (most-worn area)
5 Valve face
6 Margin

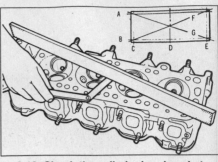

9.10 Check the cylinder head gasket surface for warpage by trying to slip a feeler gauge under the straightedge (see this Chapter's Specifications for the maximum warpage allowed, and use a feeler gauge of that thickness)

12 Check the valve stem-to-guide clearance by measuring the lateral movement of the valve stem with a dial indicator **(see illustration)**. The valve must be in the guide and approximately 2.0 mm off the seat. The total valve stem movement indicated by the gauge needle must be divided by two, to obtain the actual clearance. After this is done, if there's still some doubt regarding the condition of the valve guides, they should be checked by a machine shop (the cost should be minimal).

Valves

13 Carefully inspect each valve face for uneven wear, deformation, cracks, pits and burned areas **(see illustration)**. Check the valve stem for scuffing and the neck for cracks. Rotate the valve, and check for any obvious indication that it's bent. Look for pits and excessive wear on the end of the stem. The presence of any of these conditions indicates the need for valve service as described in the next Section.

14 Measure the margin width on each valve **(see illustration)**. Any valve with a margin narrower than specified will have to be replaced with a new one.

Valve components

15 Check each valve spring for wear on the ends. The tension of all springs should be checked with a special fixture before deciding

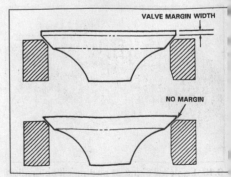

9.14 The margin width on each valve must be as specified (if no margin exists, the valve cannot be reused)

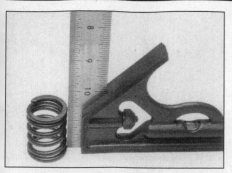

9.16 Check each valve spring for squareness

that they're suitable for use in a rebuilt engine (take the springs to a machine shop for this check).

16 Stand each spring on a flat surface, and check it for squareness **(see illustration)**. If any of the springs are distorted or sagged, or possibly have a broken coil, fit new parts.

17 Check the spring retainers and keepers for obvious wear and cracks. Any questionable parts should be renewed, as extensive damage will occur if they fail during engine operation.

Rocker arms (M10, M20 and M30 engines)

Note: The rocker arms for the exhaust valves are the most subject to wear, and should be checked with particular care.

18 Inspect all the rocker arms for excessive wear on the tips that contact the valve stem and camshaft **(see illustration)**.

19 Check the rocker arm radial clearance (see Section 8). If it's excessive, either the rocker arm bush or the shaft (or both) is excessively worn. To determine which is more worn, slide the rocker arm onto an unworn portion of the rocker arm shaft, and check the radial clearance again. If it's now within specifications, the shaft is probably the most-worn component. If it's not within specifications, the rocker arm bushes should be renewed.

Rocker arm shafts (M10, M20 and M30 engines)

20 Check the shafts for scoring, excessive wear and other damage. The areas where the

9.18 Look for signs of pitting, discoloration or excessive wear on the ends of the rocker arms where they contact the camshaft and the valve stem tip

rocker arms contact the shafts should be smooth. If there is a visible ridge at the edge of where the rocker arm rides, the shaft is probably worn excessively.

Cam followers and hydraulic tappets (M40 engines)

21 Check the cam followers where they contact the valve stems and pivot posts for wear, scoring and pitting. If there is excessive wear on both the followers and camshaft, then a new camshaft, complete with cam followers, must be obtained.

22 Similarly check the hydraulic tappets where they contact the bores in the cylinder head for wear, scoring and pitting. Occasionally, a hydraulic tappet may be noisy and require renewal, and this will have been noticed when the engine was running. It is not easy to check a tappet for internal damage or wear once it has been removed; if there is any doubt, a complete set of new tappets should be fitted.

Camshaft

23 Inspect the camshaft journals (the round bearing areas) and lobes for scoring, pitting, flaking and excessive wear. Using a micrometer, measure the height of each exhaust and intake lobe. Compare the heights of all the exhaust lobes and intake lobes. If the readings among the exhaust valve lobes or intake valve lobes vary more than about 0.08 mm, or if the camshaft is exhibiting any signs of wear, renew the camshaft.

24 Inspect the camshaft bearing surfaces in the cylinder head for scoring and other damage. If the bearing surfaces are scored or damaged, you'll normally have to renew the cylinder head, since the bearings are simply a machined surface in the cylinder head. **Note:** *A machine shop (particularly one that specialises in BMWs) or dealer service department may be able to provide an alternative to fitting a new cylinder head, if the only problem with the head is mildly-scored camshaft bearing surfaces.*

25 Using a micrometer, measure the journals on the camshaft, and record the measurements **(see illustration)**. Using a telescoping gauge or inside micrometer,

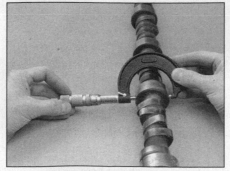

9.25 Measure each camshaft bearing journal and its corresponding bearing diameter in the cylinder head, then subtract the journal diameter from the bearing inside diameter to obtain the oil clearance

measure the camshaft bearing diameters in the cylinder head (on the M40 engine, refit the bearing caps first). Subtract the camshaft journal measurement from its corresponding bearing inside diameter to obtain the oil clearance. Compare the oil clearance to what's listed in this Chapter's Specifications. If it's not within tolerance, a new camshaft and/or cylinder head will be required. **Note:** *Before fitting a new cylinder head, check with a machine shop (particularly one that specialises in BMWs). They may be able to repair the head.*

10 Valves - servicing

1 Examine the valves as described in Section 9, paragraphs 13 and 14. Renew any valve that shows signs of wear or damage.

2 If the valve appears satisfactory at this stage, measure the valve stem diameter at several points using a micrometer **(see illustration 9.13)**. Any significant difference in the readings obtained indicates wear of the valve stem. Should any of these conditions be apparent, the valve(s) must be renewed.

3 If the valves are in satisfactory condition they should be ground (lapped) into their respective seats to ensure a gas-tight seal. If the seat is only lightly pitted, or if it has been re-cut, fine grinding compound should be used to produce the required finish. Coarse valve-grinding compound should not normally be used, unless a seat is badly burned or deeply pitted. If this is the case, the cylinder head and valves should be inspected by an expert, to decide whether seat re-cutting or even the renewal of the valve or seat insert is required.

4 Valve grinding is carried out as follows. Place the cylinder head upside-down on a bench, with a block of wood at each end to give clearance for the valve stems.

5 Smear a trace of the appropriate grade of valve-grinding compound on the seat face, and press a suction grinding tool onto the valve head. With a semi-rotary action, grind the valve head to its seat, lifting the valve occasionally to redistribute the grinding compound **(see illustration)**.

2B

10.5 Grinding-in a valve - do not grind-in the valves any more than absolutely necessary, or their seats will be prematurely sunk into the cylinder head

11.4a Lubricate the valve guide seal, and place it on the guide (the valve should be in place too) . . .

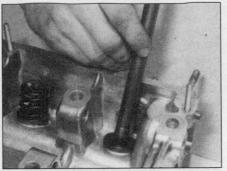

11.4b . . .then lightly drive on the seal with a socket or piece of tubing

11.6 With the retainer fitted, compress the valve spring and refit the collets as shown

HAYNES HiNT *A light spring placed under the valve head will greatly ease the valve grinding operation.*

6 If coarse grinding compound is being used, work only until a dull, matt even surface is produced on both the valve seat and the valve, then wipe off the used compound and repeat the process with fine compound. When a smooth, unbroken ring of light grey matt finish is produced on both the valve and seat, the grinding operation is complete. **Do not** grind in the valves any further than absolutely necessary.

7 When all the valves have been ground-in, carefully wash off **all** traces of grinding compound using paraffin or a suitable solvent before reassembly of the cylinder head.

11 Cylinder head - reassembly

1 Make sure the cylinder head is spotlessly-clean before beginning reassembly.
2 If the head was sent out for valve servicing, the valves and related components will already be in place. Begin the reassembly procedure with paragraph 8.
3 Starting at one end of the head, apply

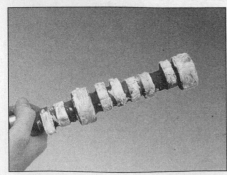

11.9 Lubricate the camshaft bearing journals and lobes with engine assembly paste or molybdenum disulphide ("moly") grease

molybdenum disulphide ("moly") grease or clean engine oil to each valve stem, and refit the first valve.
4 Lubricate the lip of the valve guide seal, carefully slide it over the tip of the valve, then slide it all the way down the stem to the guide. Using a hammer and a deep socket or seal-fitting tool, gently tap the seal into place until it's completely seated on the guide **(see illustrations)**. Don't twist or distort a seal during fitting, or it won't seal properly against the valve stem. **Note:** *On some engines, the seals for intake and exhaust valves are different - don't mix them up.*
5 Drop the spring seat or shim(s) over the valve guide, and set the valve spring and retainer in place.
6 Compress the spring with a valve spring compressor and carefully refit the collets in the upper groove, then slowly release the compressor and make sure the collets seat properly **(see illustration)**.

TOOL TiP

Apply a small dab of grease to each collet to hold it in place, if necessary.

7 Repeat paragraphs 3 to 6 for each of the valves. Be sure to return the components to their original locations - don't mix them up!

M10, M20 and M30 engines

8 Refit the rocker arms and shafts by reversing the dismantling sequence. Be sure to refit the rocker shafts in the correct orientation. The guide plate notches and the small oil holes face inwards; the large oil holes face down, toward the valve guides.
9 Lubricate the camshaft journals and lobes

(see illustration), then carefully insert it into the cylinder head, rotating it as you go so the camshaft lobes will clear the rocker arms. It will also be necessary to compress the rocker arms against the valve springs, as described in Section 8, so they'll clear the camshaft lobes. Be very careful not to scratch or gouge the camshaft bearing surfaces in the cylinder head.

M40 engines

10 Lubricate the bores for the hydraulic tappets in the cylinder head, then insert the tappets in their original positions.
11 Locate the thrust discs and cam followers on the valves and pivot posts in their original positions.
12 Lubricate the bearing surfaces of the camshaft in the cylinder head.
13 Locate the camshaft in the cylinder head so that the valves of No 1 cylinder are both closed, and the valves of No 4 cylinder are "rocking" (exhaust closing and inlet opening). No 1 cylinder is at the timing belt end.
14 Lubricate the bearing surfaces in the bearing caps, then locate them in their correct positions and insert the retaining bolts. Progressively tighten the bolts to the specified torque.
15 Fit a new oil seal to the camshaft front bearing cap (see Chapter 2A, Section 11).

All engines

16 Refit the oil supply tube to the top of the cylinder head together with new seals, then tighten the bolts to the specified torque.
17 The cylinder head may now be refitted (see Chapter 2A).

12 Pistons/connecting rods - removal

Note: *Before removing the piston/connecting rod assemblies, remove the cylinder head and the sump. On M10, M20 and M30 engines only, remove the oil pump. Refer to the appropriate Sections in Chapter 2A.*
1 Use your fingernail to feel if a ridge has formed at the upper limit of ring travel (about 6 mm down from the top of each cylinder). If

12.1 A ridge reamer is required to remove the ridge from the top of each cylinder - do this before removing the pistons!

12.3 Check the connecting rod side play with a feeler gauge as shown

12.4 Mark the big-end bearing caps in order from the front of the engine to the rear (one mark for the front cap, two for the second one and so on)

carbon deposits or cylinder wear have produced ridges, they must be completely removed with a special tool called a ridge reamer **(see illustration)**. Follow the manufacturer's instructions provided with the tool. Failure to remove the ridges before attempting to remove the piston/connecting rod assemblies may result in piston ring breakage.

2 After the cylinder ridges have been removed, turn the engine upside-down so the crankshaft is facing up.

3 Before the connecting rods are removed, check the side play with feeler gauges. Slide them between the first connecting rod and crankshaft web until no play is apparent **(see illustration)**. The side play is equal to the thickness of the feeler gauge(s). If the side play exceeds the service limit, new connecting rods will be required. If new rods (or a new crankshaft) are fitted, ensure that some side play is retained (if not, the rods will have to be machined to restore it - consult a machine shop for advice if necessary). Repeat the procedure for the remaining connecting rods.

4 Check the connecting rods and caps for identification marks. If they aren't plainly marked, use a small centre-punch to make the appropriate number of indentations **(see illustration)** on each rod and cap (1, 2, 3, etc., depending on the cylinder they're associated with).

5 Loosen each of the connecting rod cap nuts/bolts a half-turn at a time until they can be removed by hand. Remove the No 1 connecting rod cap and bearing shell. Don't drop the bearing shell out of the cap.

6 Where applicable, slip a short length of plastic or rubber hose over each connecting rod cap stud to protect the crankshaft journal and cylinder wall as the piston is removed **(see illustration)**.

7 Remove the bearing shell, and push the connecting rod/piston assembly out through the top of the engine. Use a wooden hammer handle to push on the upper bearing surface in the connecting rod. If resistance is felt, double-check to make sure that all of the ridge was removed from the cylinder.

8 Repeat the procedure for the remaining cylinders.

9 After removal, reassemble the connecting rod caps and bearing shells in their respective connecting rods, and refit the cap nuts/bolts finger-tight. Leaving the old bearing shells in place until reassembly will help prevent the connecting big-end bearing surfaces from being accidentally nicked or gouged.

10 Don't separate the pistons from the connecting rods (see Section 18).

13 Crankshaft - removal

Note: *The crankshaft can be removed only after the engine has been removed from the vehicle. It's assumed that the flywheel or driveplate, vibration damper, timing chain or belt, sump, oil pump and piston/connecting rod assemblies have already been removed. The rear main oil seal housing must be unbolted and separated from the block before proceeding with crankshaft removal.*

1 Before the crankshaft is removed, check the endfloat. Mount a dial indicator with the stem in line with the crankshaft and touching the nose of the crankshaft, or one of its webs **(see illustration)**.

2 Push the crankshaft all the way to the rear,

12.6 To prevent damage to the crankshaft journals and cylinder walls, slip sections of rubber or plastic hose over the rod bolts before removing the pistons

and zero the dial indicator. Next, prise the crankshaft to the front as far as possible, and check the reading on the dial indicator. The distance that it moves is the endfloat. If it's greater than the maximum endfloat listed in this Chapter's Specifications, check the crankshaft thrust surfaces for wear. If no wear is evident, new main bearings should correct the endfloat.

3 If a dial indicator isn't available, feeler gauges can be used. Identify the main bearing with the thrust flanges either side of it - this is referred to as the "thrust" main bearing (see Section 24, paragraph 6). Gently prise or push the crankshaft all the way to the front of the engine. Slip feeler gauges between the crankshaft and the front face of the thrust main bearing to determine the clearance.

4 Check the main bearing caps to see if they're marked to indicate their locations. They should be numbered consecutively from the front of the engine to the rear. If they aren't, mark them with number-stamping dies or a centre-punch **(see illustration)**. Main bearing caps generally have a cast-in arrow, which points to the front of the engine. Loosen the main bearing cap bolts a quarter-turn at a time each, working from the outer ends towards the centre, until they can be removed by hand. Note if any stud bolts are used, and make sure they're returned to their original locations when the crankshaft is refitted.

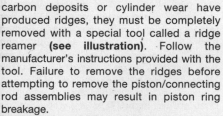

 2B

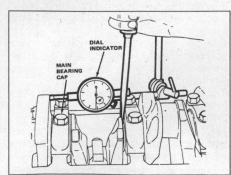

13.1 Checking crankshaft endfloat with a dial indicator

5 Gently tap the caps with a soft-faced hammer, then separate them from the engine block. If necessary, use the bolts as levers to remove the caps. Try not to drop the bearing shells if they come out with the caps.

6 Carefully lift the crankshaft out of the engine. It may be a good idea to have an assistant available, since the crankshaft is quite heavy **(see illustration)**. With the bearing shells in place in the engine block and main bearing caps, return the caps to their respective locations on the engine block, and tighten the bolts finger-tight.

14 Intermediate shaft - removal and inspection

Note: *The intermediate shaft is used on the M20 engine only. The shaft rotates in the engine block parallel to the crankshaft. It is driven by the timing belt, and its only purpose is to drive the oil pump.*

1 Remove the timing belt (see Chapter 2A).

2 With the belt removed, unbolt the gear from the intermediate shaft and unbolt the front cover.

3 Remove the oil pump driveshaft (see Chapter 2A).

4 The shaft is held in the cylinder block by a retaining plate with two bolts. Remove the bolts, and pull the shaft forwards and out of the block.

5 Look for any signs of abnormal wear on the bearing surfaces or the gear at the back end of the shaft, which drives the oil pump shaft. If the bearing surfaces in the engine block show wear, they'll have to be attended to by a machine shop.

15 Engine block - cleaning

Caution: The core plugs may be difficult or impossible to retrieve if they're driven into the block coolant passages.

1 Remove the core plugs from the engine block. To do this, knock one side of each plug into the block with a hammer and punch, grasp the other side by its edge with large pliers, and pull it out.

2 Using a gasket scraper, remove all traces of gasket material from the engine block. Be very careful not to nick or gouge the gasket sealing surfaces.

3 Remove the main bearing caps, and separate the bearing shells from the caps and the engine block. Tag the bearings, indicating which cylinder they were removed from and whether they were in the cap or the block, then set them aside.

4 Remove all of the threaded oil gallery plugs from the block. The plugs are usually very tight - they may have to be drilled out and the

13.4 Use a centre-punch or number-stamping dies to mark the main bearing caps to ensure refitting in their original locations on the block (make the punch marks near one of the bolt heads)

holes retapped. Use new plugs when the engine is reassembled.

5 If the engine is extremely dirty, it should be taken to a machine shop to be steam-cleaned.

6 After the block is returned, clean all oil holes and oil galleries one more time. Brushes specifically designed for this purpose are available at most motor factors. Flush the passages with warm water until the water runs clear, dry the block thoroughly, and wipe all machined surfaces with a light, rust-preventive oil. If you have access to compressed air, use it to speed the drying process and to blow out all the oil holes and galleries.

Warning: Wear eye protection when using compressed air!

7 If the block isn't extremely dirty or sludged up, you can do an adequate cleaning job with hot soapy water and a stiff brush. Take plenty of time, and do a thorough job. Regardless of the cleaning method used, be sure to clean all oil holes and galleries very thoroughly, dry the block completely, and coat all machined surfaces with light oil.

8 The threaded holes in the block must be clean to ensure accurate torque readings

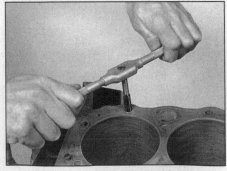

15.8 All bolt holes in the block - particularly the main bearing cap and head bolt holes - should be cleaned and restored with a tap (be sure to remove debris from the holes after this is done)

13.6 Remove the crankshaft by lifting straight up. Be very careful when removing the crankshaft - it is very heavy

during reassembly. Run the proper-size tap into each of the holes to remove rust, corrosion, thread sealant or sludge, and to restore damaged threads **(see illustration)**. If possible, use compressed air to clear the holes of debris produced by this operation. Be sure also that the holes are **dry** - any oil or other fluid present could cause the block to be cracked by hydraulic pressure when the bolts are tightened. Now is a good time to clean the threads on all bolts. Note that BMW recommend that the cylinder head bolts and main bearing bolts are renewed as a matter of course.

9 Refit the main bearing caps, and tighten the bolts finger-tight.

10 After coating the sealing surfaces of the new core plugs with a suitable sealant, refit them in the engine block **(see illustration)**. Make sure they're driven in straight and seated properly, or leakage could result. Special tools are available for this purpose, but a large socket, with an outside diameter that will just slip into the core plug, a 1/2-inch drive extension, and a hammer, will work just as well.

11 Apply non-hardening sealant to the new oil gallery plugs, and thread them into the holes in the block. Make sure they're tightened securely.

12 If the engine isn't going to be reassembled right away, cover it with a large plastic bag to keep it clean.

15.10 A large socket on an extension can be used to drive the new core plugs into the block

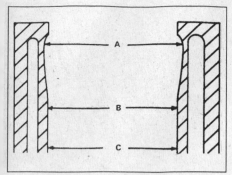

16.4a Measure the diameter of each cylinder just under the wear ridge (A), at the centre (B) and at the bottom (C)

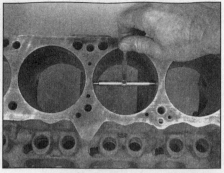

16.4b The ability to "feel" when the telescoping gauge is at the correct point will be developed over time, so work slowly, and repeat the check until you're satisfied the bore measurement is accurate

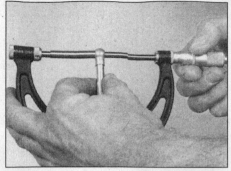

16.4c The gauge is then measured with a micrometer to determine the bore size

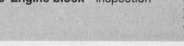

16 Engine block - inspection

1 Before the block is inspected, it should be cleaned (see Section 15).

2 Visually check the block for cracks, rust and corrosion. Look for stripped threads in the threaded holes. It's also a good idea to have the block checked for hidden cracks by a machine shop that has the special equipment to do this type of work. If defects are found, have the block repaired, if possible; otherwise, a new block will be required.

3 Check the cylinder bores for scuffing and scoring.

4 Measure the diameter of each cylinder at the top (just under the wear ridge area), centre and bottom of the cylinder bore, parallel to the crankshaft axis (see illustrations).

5 Next, measure each cylinder's diameter at the same three locations across the crankshaft axis. Compare the results to this Chapter's Specifications.

6 If the required precision measuring tools aren't available, the piston-to-cylinder clearances can be obtained, though not quite as accurately, using feeler gauges.

7 To check the clearance, select a feeler gauge, and slip it into the cylinder along with the matching piston. The piston must be positioned exactly as it normally would be. The feeler gauge must be between the piston and cylinder on one of the thrust faces (90° to the gudgeon pin bore).

8 The piston should slip through the cylinder (with the feeler gauge in place) with moderate pressure.

9 If it falls through or slides through easily, the clearance is excessive, and a new piston will be required. If the piston binds at the lower end of the cylinder and is loose toward the top, the cylinder is tapered. If tight spots are encountered as the piston/feeler gauge is rotated in the cylinder, the cylinder is out-of-round.

10 Repeat the procedure for the remaining pistons and cylinders.

11 If the cylinder walls are badly scuffed or scored, or if they're out-of-round or tapered beyond the limits given in this Chapter's Specifications, have the engine block rebored and honed at a machine shop. If a rebore is done, oversize pistons and rings will be required.

12 If the cylinders are in reasonably good condition and not worn to the outside of the limits, and if the piston-to-cylinder clearances can be maintained properly, then they don't have to be rebored. Honing (see Section 17) and a new set of piston rings is all that's necessary.

17 Cylinder honing

1 Prior to engine reassembly, the cylinder bores must be honed so the new piston rings will seat correctly and provide the best possible combustion chamber seal. **Note:** *If you don't have the tools, or don't want to tackle the honing operation, most machine shops will do it for a reasonable fee.*

2 Before honing the cylinders, refit the main bearing caps, and tighten the bolts to the torque listed in this Chapter's Specifications.

3 Two types of cylinder hones are commonly available - the flex hone or "bottle brush"

type, and the more traditional surfacing hone with spring-loaded stones. Both will do the job, but for the less-experienced mechanic, the "bottle brush" hone will probably be easier to use. You'll also need some paraffin or honing oil, rags and an electric drill. Proceed as follows.

4 Mount the hone in the drill, compress the stones, and slip it into the first cylinder **(see illustration)**. Be sure to wear safety goggles or a face shield!

5 Lubricate the cylinder with plenty of honing oil, turn on the drill, and move the hone up and down in the cylinder at a pace that will produce a fine crosshatch pattern on the cylinder walls. Ideally, the crosshatch lines should intersect at approximately a 60° angle **(see illustration)**. Be sure to use plenty of lubricant, and don't take off any more material than is absolutely necessary to produce the desired finish. **Note:** *Piston ring manufacturers may specify a smaller crosshatch angle than the traditional 60° - read and follow any instructions included with the new rings.*

6 Don't withdraw the hone from the cylinder while it's running. Instead, shut off the drill and continue moving the hone up and down in the cylinder until it comes to a complete stop, then compress the stones and withdraw the hone. If you're using a "bottle brush" type hone, stop the drill, then turn the chuck in the normal direction of rotation while withdrawing the hone from the cylinder.

2B

17.4 A "bottle brush" hone will produce better results if you've never honed cylinders before

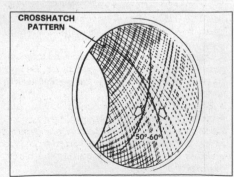

17.5 The cylinder hone should leave a smooth, crosshatch pattern, with the lines intersecting at approximately a 60° angle

18.2 Removing the compression rings with a ring expander - note the mark (arrowed) facing up

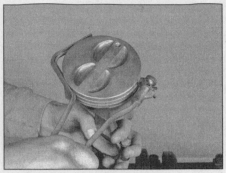

18.4 The piston ring grooves can be cleaned with a special tool, as shown here

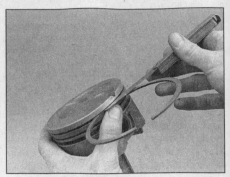

18.10 Check the ring side clearance with a feeler gauge at several points around the groove

7 Wipe the oil out of the cylinder, and repeat the procedure for the remaining cylinders.

8 After the honing job is complete, chamfer the top edges of the cylinder bores with a small file, so the rings won't catch when the pistons are refitted. Be very careful not to nick the cylinder walls with the end of the file.

9 The entire engine block must be washed again very thoroughly with warm, soapy water, to remove all traces of the abrasive grit produced during the honing operation. **Note:** *The bores can be considered clean when a lint-free white cloth - dampened with clean engine oil - used to wipe them out doesn't pick up any more honing residue, which will show up as grey areas on the cloth.* Be sure to run a brush through all oil holes and galleries, and flush them with running water.

10 After rinsing, dry the block, and apply a coat of light rust-preventive oil to all machined surfaces. Wrap the block in a plastic bag to keep it clean, and set it aside until reassembly.

18 Pistons/connecting rods - inspection

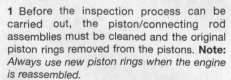

1 Before the inspection process can be carried out, the piston/connecting rod assemblies must be cleaned and the original piston rings removed from the pistons. **Note:** *Always use new piston rings when the engine is reassembled.*

2 Using a piston ring refitting tool, carefully remove the rings from the pistons. Be careful not to nick or gouge the pistons in the process **(see illustration)**.

3 Scrape all traces of carbon from the top of the piston. A hand-held wire brush or a piece of fine emery cloth can be used once the majority of the deposits have been scraped away. Do not, under any circumstances, use a wire brush mounted in a drill motor to remove deposits from the pistons. The piston material is soft, and may be damaged by the wire brush.

4 Use a piston ring groove cleaning tool to remove carbon deposits from the ring grooves. Be very careful to remove only the

carbon deposits - don't remove any metal, and do not nick or scratch the sides of the ring grooves **(see illustration)**.

TOOL TIP

If a groove cleaning tool isn't available, a piece broken off the old ring will do the job, but protect your hands - piston rings can be sharp

5 Once the deposits have been removed, clean the piston/rod assemblies with solvent, and dry them with compressed air (if available). Make sure the oil return holes in the back sides of the ring grooves are clear.

6 If the pistons and cylinder walls aren't damaged or worn excessively, and if the engine block is not rebored, new pistons won't be necessary. Normal piston wear appears as even vertical wear on the piston thrust surfaces (90° to the gudgeon pin bore), and slight looseness of the top ring in its groove. New piston rings, however, should always be used when an engine is rebuilt.

7 Carefully inspect each piston for cracks around the skirt, at the pin bosses, and at the ring lands.

8 Look for scoring and scuffing on the thrust faces of the skirt, holes in the piston crown, and burned areas at the edge of the crown. If the skirt is scored or scuffed, the engine may have been suffering from overheating and/or abnormal combustion, which caused excessively high operating temperatures. The cooling and lubrication systems should be checked thoroughly. A hole in the piston crown is an indication that abnormal combustion (pre-ignition) was occurring. Burned areas at the edge of the piston crown are usually evidence of spark knock (detonation). If any of the above

problems exist, the causes must be corrected, or the damage will occur again. The causes may include intake air leaks, incorrect fuel/air mixture, or incorrect ignition timing. On later vehicles with high levels of exhaust emission control, including catalytic converters, the problem may be with the EGR (exhaust gas recirculation) system, where applicable.

9 Corrosion of the piston, in the form of small pits, indicates that coolant is leaking into the combustion chamber and/or the crankcase. Again, the cause must be corrected or the problem may persist in the rebuilt engine.

10 Measure the piston ring side clearance by laying a new piston ring in each ring groove and slipping a feeler gauge in beside it **(see illustration)**. Check the clearance at three or four locations around each groove. Be sure to use the correct ring for each groove - they are different. If the side clearance is greater than the figure listed in this Chapter's Specifications, new pistons will have to be used.

11 Check the piston-to-bore clearance by measuring the bore (see Section 16) and the piston diameter. Make sure the pistons and bores are correctly matched. Measure the piston across the skirt, at 90° to, and in line with, the gudgeon pin **(see illustration)**. (Any difference between these two measurements indicates that the piston is no longer perfectly round.) Subtract the piston diameter from the bore diameter to obtain the clearance. If it's greater than specified, the block will have to be rebored, and new pistons and rings fitted.

18.11 Measure the piston diameter at a 90-degree angle to the gudgeon pin, at the same height as the gudgeon pin

19.1 The oil holes should be chamfered so sharp edges don't gouge or scratch the new bearings

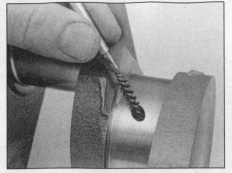

19.2 Use a wire or stiff plastic bristle brush to clean the oil passages in the crankshaft

19.4 Rubbing a penny lengthways on each journal will reveal its condition - if copper rubs off and is embedded in the crankshaft, the journals should be reground

12 Check the piston-to-rod clearance by twisting the piston and rod in opposite directions. Any noticeable play indicates excessive wear, which must be corrected. The piston/connecting rod assemblies should be taken to a machine shop for attention.

13 If the pistons must be removed from the connecting rods for any reason, they should be taken to a machine shop. When this is done, have the connecting rods checked for bend and twist, since most machine shops have special equipment for this purpose. **Note:** *Unless new pistons and/or connecting rods must be fitted, do not dismantle the pistons and connecting rods.*

14 Check the connecting rods for cracks and other damage. Temporarily remove the rod caps, lift out the old bearing shells, wipe the rod and cap bearing surfaces clean, and inspect them for nicks, gouges and scratches. After checking the rods, fit new bearing shells, slip the caps into place, and tighten the nuts finger-tight.

19 Crankshaft - inspection

1 Remove all burrs from the crankshaft oil holes with a stone, file or scraper **(see illustration)**.

2 Clean the crankshaft with solvent, and dry it with compressed air (if available). Be sure to clean the oil holes with a stiff brush **(see illustration)**, and flush them with solvent.
3 Check the main and connecting big-end bearing journals for uneven wear, scoring, pits and cracks.
4 Rub a copper coin across each journal several times **(see illustration)**. If a journal picks up copper from the coin, it's too rough and must be reground.
5 Check the rest of the crankshaft for cracks and other damage. If necessary, have a machine shop inspect the crankshaft.
6 Using a micrometer, measure the diameter of the main and connecting rod journals, and compare the results to this Chapter's Specifi-cations **(see illustration)**. By measuring the diameter at a number of points around each journal's circumference, you'll be able to determine whether or not the journal is out-of-round. Take the measurement at each end of the journal, near the crank webs, to determine if the journal is tapered.
7 If the crankshaft journals are damaged, tapered, out-of-round or worn beyond the limits given in the Specifications, have the crankshaft reground by a machine shop. Be sure to use the correct-size bearing shells if the crankshaft is reconditioned.
8 Check the oil seal journals at each end of

the crankshaft for wear and damage. If the seal has worn a groove in the journal, or if it's nicked or scratched **(see illustration)**, the new seal may leak when the engine is reassembled. In some cases, a machine shop may be able to repair the journal by pressing on a thin sleeve. If repair isn't feasible, a new or different crankshaft should be fitted.
9 Examine the main and big-end bearing shells (see Section 20).

20 Main and connecting big-end bearings - inspection

1 Even though the main and connecting big-end bearings should be renewed during the engine overhaul, the old bearings should be retained for close examination, as they may reveal valuable information about the condition of the engine **(see illustration)**.
2 Bearing failure occurs because of lack of lubrication, the presence of dirt or other foreign particles, overloading the engine, and corrosion. Regardless of the cause of bearing failure, it must be corrected before the engine is reassembled, to prevent it from happening again.

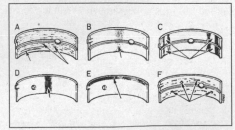

20.1 Typical bearing failures

A *Scratched by dirt: debris embedded into bearing material*
B *Lack of oil: overlay wiped out*
C *Improper seating: bright (polished) sections*
D *Tapered journal: overlay gone from entire surface*
E *Radius ride*
F *Fatigue failure: craters or pockets*

2B

19.6 Measure the diameter of each crankshaft journal at several points to detect taper and out-of-round conditions

19.8 If the seals have worn grooves in the crankshaft journals, or if the seal contact surfaces are nicked or scratched, the new seals will leak

3 When examining the bearings, remove them from the engine block, the main bearing caps, the connecting rods and the rod caps, and lay them out on a clean surface in the same general position as their location in the engine. This will enable you to match any bearing problems with the corresponding crankshaft journal.

4 Dirt and other foreign particles get into the engine in a variety of ways. It may be left in the engine during assembly, or it may pass through filters or the crankcase ventilation (PCV) system. It may get into the oil, and from there into the bearings. Metal chips from machining operations and normal engine wear are often present. Abrasives are sometimes left in engine components after reconditioning, especially when parts are not thoroughly cleaned using the proper cleaning methods. Whatever the source, these foreign objects often end up embedded in the soft bearing material, and are easily recognised. Large particles will not embed in the bearing, and will score or gouge the bearing and journal. The best prevention for this cause of bearing failure is to clean all parts thoroughly, and to keep everything spotlessly-clean during engine assembly. Frequent and regular engine oil and filter changes are also recommended.

5 Lack of lubrication (or lubrication breakdown) has a number of interrelated causes. Excessive heat (which thins the oil), overloading (which squeezes the oil from the bearing face) and oil "leakage" or "throw off" (from excessive bearing clearances, worn oil pump, or high engine speeds) all contribute to lubrication breakdown. Blocked oil passages, which usually are the result of misaligned oil holes in a bearing shell, will also oil-starve a bearing and destroy it. When lack of lubrication is the cause of bearing failure, the bearing material is wiped or extruded from the steel backing of the bearing. Temperatures may increase to the point where the steel backing turns blue from overheating.

6 Driving habits can have a definite effect on bearing life. Full-throttle, low-speed operation (labouring the engine) puts very high loads on

bearings, which tends to squeeze out the oil film. These loads cause the bearings to flex, which produces fine cracks in the bearing face (fatigue failure). Eventually, the bearing material will loosen in places, and tear away from the steel backing. Short-trip driving leads to corrosion of bearings, because insufficient engine heat is produced to drive off the condensation and corrosive gases. These products collect in the engine oil, forming acid and sludge. As the oil is carried to the engine bearings, the acid attacks and corrodes the bearing material.

7 Incorrect bearing refitting during engine assembly will lead to bearing failure as well. Tight-fitting bearings leave insufficient bearing oil clearance, and will result in oil starvation. Dirt or foreign particles trapped behind a bearing shell result in high spots on the bearing, which will lead to failure.

21 Engine overhaul - reassembly sequence

1 Before beginning engine reassembly, make sure you have all the necessary new parts, gaskets and seals, as well as the following items on hand:

Common hand tools
A torque wrench
Piston ring refitting tool
Piston ring compressor
Vibration damper refitting tool
Short lengths of rubber or plastic hose to fit over connecting rod bolts (where applicable)
Plastigage
Feeler gauges
A fine-tooth file
New engine oil
Engine assembly oil or molybdenum disulphide ("moly") grease
Gasket sealant
Thread-locking compound

2 In order to save time and avoid problems, engine reassembly should be done in the following general order:

Piston rings
Crankshaft and main bearings
Piston/connecting rod assemblies
Oil pump
Sump
Cylinder head assembly
Timing belt or chain and tensioner assemblies
Water pump
Timing belt or chain covers
Intake and exhaust manifolds
Valve cover
Engine rear plate
Flywheel/driveplate

22 Piston rings - refitting

1 Before fitting the new piston rings, the ring end gaps must be checked. It's assumed that the piston ring side clearance has been checked and verified (see Section 18).

2 Lay out the piston/connecting rod assemblies and the new ring sets, so that the ring sets will be matched with the same piston and cylinder during the end gap measurement and engine assembly.

3 Insert the top ring into the first cylinder, and square it up with the cylinder walls by pushing it in with the top of the piston **(see illustration)**. The ring should be near the bottom of the cylinder, at the lower limit of ring travel.

4 To measure the end gap, slip feeler gauges between the ends of the ring until a gauge equal to the gap width is found **(see illustration)**. The feeler gauge should slide between the ring ends with a slight amount of drag. Compare the measurement to this Chapter's Specifications. If the gap is larger or smaller than specified, double-check to make sure you have the correct rings before proceeding.

5 If the gap is too small, it must be enlarged, or the ring ends may come in contact with each other during engine operation, which can cause serious damage to the engine. The end gap can be increased by filing the ring ends very carefully with a fine file. Mount the

22.3 When checking piston ring end gap, the ring must be square in the cylinder bore (this is done by pushing the ring down with the top of a piston as shown)

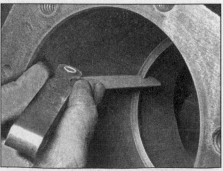

22.4 With the ring square in the cylinder, measure the end gap with a feeler gauge

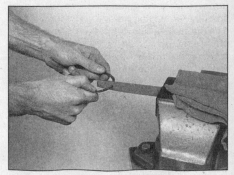

22.5 If the end gap is too small, clamp a file in a vice, and file the ring ends (from the outside in only) to enlarge the gap slightly

22.9a Refitting the spacer/expander in the oil control ring groove

22.9b DO NOT use a piston ring refitting tool when refitting the oil ring side rails

file in a vice equipped with soft jaws, slip the ring over the file, with the ends contacting the file face, and slowly move the ring to remove material from the ends. When performing this operation, file only from the outside in **(see illustration)**.

6 Excess end gap isn't critical unless it's greater than 1.0 mm. Again, double-check to make sure you have the correct rings for your engine.

7 Repeat the procedure for each ring that will be fitted in the first cylinder and for each ring in the remaining cylinders. Remember to keep rings, pistons and cylinders matched up.

8 Once the ring end gaps have been checked/corrected, the rings can be fitted on the pistons.

9 The oil control ring (lowest one on the piston) is usually fitted first. It's normally composed of three separate components. Slip the spacer/expander into the groove **(see illustration)**. If an anti-rotation tang is used, make sure it's inserted into the drilled hole in the ring groove. Next, refit the lower side rail. Don't use a piston ring refitting tool on the oil ring side rails, as they may be damaged. Instead, place one end of the side rail into the groove between the spacer/expander and the ring land, hold it firmly in place, and slide a finger around the piston while pushing the rail into the groove **(see illustration)**. Next, refit the upper side rail in the same manner.

10 After the three oil ring components have been fitted, check to make sure that both the upper and lower side rails can be turned smoothly in the ring groove.

11 The middle ring is fitted next. It's usually stamped with a mark which must face up, towards the top of the piston. **Note:** *Always follow the instructions printed on the ring package or box - different manufacturers may require different approaches. Do not mix up the top and middle rings, as they have different cross-sections.*

12 Make sure the identification mark is facing the top of the piston, then slip the ring into the middle groove on the piston **(see illustration 18.2)**. Don't expand the ring any more than necessary to slide it over the piston. Use a proper ring-fitting tool if available; with care, old feeler gauges can be used to prevent the rings dropping into empty grooves.

13 Refit the top ring in the same manner. Make sure the mark is facing upwards. Be careful not to confuse the top and middle rings.

14 Repeat the procedure for the remaining pistons and rings.

23 Intermediate shaft - refitting

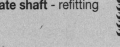

1 Clean the intermediate shaft bearing surfaces and the pressed-in bearing sleeves in the cylinder block.

2 Lubricate the shaft, and slide it into the block.

3 Refit the two bolts that hold the retaining plate to the block.

4 The remainder of the parts are fitted in the reverse order of removal.

24 Crankshaft - refitting and main bearing oil clearance check

1 Crankshaft refitting is the first major step in engine reassembly. It's assumed at this point that the engine block and crankshaft have been cleaned, inspected, and repaired or reconditioned.

2 Position the block upside-down.

3 Remove the main bearing cap bolts, and lift

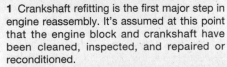

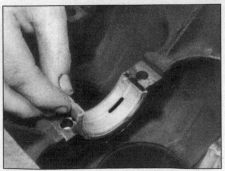

24.6 Refitting a thrust main bearing (note the flanges) in the engine block bearing saddle

out the caps. Lay them out in the proper order to ensure correct refitting.

4 If they're still in place, remove the original bearing shells from the block and the main bearing caps. Wipe the bearing surfaces of the block and caps with a clean, lint-free cloth. They must be kept spotlessly-clean.

Main bearing oil clearance check

5 Clean the back sides of the new main bearing shells, and lay one in each main bearing saddle in the block. If one of the bearing shells from each set has a large groove in it, make sure the grooved shell is fitted in the block. Lay the other bearing from each set in the corresponding main bearing cap. Make sure the tab on the bearing shell fits into the recess in the block or cap.

⚠️ **Caution: The oil holes in the block must line up with the oil holes in the bearing shell. Do not hammer the bearing into place, and don't nick or gouge the bearing faces. No lubrication should be used at this time.**

6 The flanged thrust bearing must be fitted in the No 3 bearing cap and saddle in the M10 engine, in the No 6 bearing cap and saddle in the M20 engine **(see illustration)**, in the No 4 bearing cap and saddle in the M30 engine, and in the No 4 bearing saddle only in the M40 engine.

7 Clean the faces of the bearings in the block and the crankshaft main bearing journals with a clean, lint-free cloth.

8 Check or clean the oil holes in the crankshaft, as any dirt here can go only one way - straight through the new bearings.

9 Once you're certain the crankshaft is clean, carefully lay it in position in the main bearings.

10 Before the crankshaft can be permanently fitted, the main bearing oil clearance must be checked.

11 Cut several pieces of the appropriate-size Plastigage (they must be slightly shorter than the width of the main bearings), and place one piece on each crankshaft main bearing journal, parallel with the crankshaft centreline **(see illustration)**.

12 Clean the faces of the bearings in the caps, and refit the caps in their respective

24.11 Lay the Plastigage strips on the main bearing journals, parallel to the crankshaft centreline

24.15 Compare the width of the crushed Plastigage to the scale on the envelope to determine the main bearing oil clearance (always take the measurement at the widest point of the Plastigage); be sure to use the correct scale - standard and metric ones are included

positions (don't mix them up) with the arrows pointing towards the front of the engine. Don't disturb the Plastigage.

13 Starting with the centre main bearing and working out toward the ends, progressively tighten the main bearing cap bolts to the torque listed in this Chapter's Specifications. On M10, M20 and M30 engines, tighten the bolts in three stages. On the M40 engine, tighten all the bolts initially to the Stage 1 torque, then angle-tighten them by the angle given in the Specifications. Carry out the angle-tightening on each bolt in one controlled movement. Don't rotate the crankshaft at any time during the tightening operation.

14 Remove the bolts and carefully lift off the main bearing caps. Keep them in order. Don't disturb the Plastigage or rotate the crankshaft. If any of the main bearing caps are difficult to remove, tap them gently from side-to-side with a soft-face hammer to loosen them.

15 Compare the width of the crushed Plastigage on each journal to the scale printed on the Plastigage envelope to obtain the main bearing oil clearance **(see illustration)**. Check the Specifications to make sure it's correct.

16 If the clearance is not as specified, the

bearing shells may be the wrong size (which means different ones will be required). Before deciding that different shells are needed, make sure that no dirt or oil was between the bearing shells and the caps or block when the clearance was measured. If the Plastigage was wider at one end than the other, the journal may be tapered (see Section 19).

17 Carefully scrape all traces of the Plastigage material off the main bearing journals and/or the bearing faces. Use your fingernail or the edge of a credit card - don't nick or scratch the bearing faces.

Final crankshaft refitting

18 Carefully lift the crankshaft out of the engine.

19 Clean the bearing faces in the block, then apply a thin, uniform layer of molybdenum disulphide ("moly") grease or engine oil to each of the bearing surfaces. Be sure to coat the thrust faces as well as the journal face of the thrust bearing.

20 Make sure the crankshaft journals are clean, then lay the crankshaft back in place in the block.

21 Clean the faces of the bearings in the caps, then apply engine oil to them.

22 Refit the caps in their respective positions, with the arrows pointing towards the front of the engine.

23 Refit the bolts finger-tight.

24 Lightly tap the ends of the crankshaft forward and backward with a lead or brass hammer, to line up the main bearing and crankshaft thrust surfaces.

25 Tighten the bearing cap bolts to the specified torque, working from the centre outwards. On M10, M20 and M30 engines, tighten the bolts in three stages to the final torque, leaving out the thrust bearing cap bolts at this stage. On M40 engines, tighten all of the bolts in the two stages given in the Specifications.

26 On M10, M20 and M30 engines, tighten the thrust bearing cap bolts to the torque listed in this Chapter's Specifications.

27 On manual transmission models, fit a new pilot bearing in the end of the crankshaft (see Chapter 8).

28 Rotate the crankshaft a number of times by hand to check for any obvious binding.

29 The final step is to check the crankshaft endfloat with a feeler gauge or a dial indicator as described in Section 13. The endfloat should be correct, providing the crankshaft thrust faces aren't worn or damaged, and new bearings have been fitted.

30 Fit the new seal, then bolt the housing to the block (see Section 25).

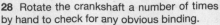

25 Crankshaft rear oil seal - refitting

1 The crankshaft must be fitted first, and the main bearing caps bolted in place. The new seal should then be fitted in the retainer, and the retainer bolted to the block.

2 Before refitting the crankshaft, check the seal contact surface very carefully for scratches and nicks that could damage the new seal lip and cause oil leaks. If the crankshaft is damaged, the only alternative is a new or different crankshaft, unless a machine shop can suggest a means of repair.

3 The old seal can be removed from the housing with a hammer and punch by driving it out from the back side **(see illustration)**. Be sure to note how far it's recessed into the housing bore before removing it; the new seal will have to be recessed an equal amount. Be very careful not to scratch or otherwise damage the bore in the housing, or oil leaks could develop.

4 Make sure the retainer is clean, then apply a thin coat of engine oil to the outer edge of the new seal. The seal must be pressed squarely into the housing bore, so hammering it into place is not recommended. At the very least, use a block of wood as shown, or a section of large-diameter pipe **(see illustration)**. If you don't have access to a press, sandwich the housing and seal between two smooth pieces of wood, and press the seal into place with the jaws of a large vice. The pieces of wood must be thick enough to distribute the force evenly around the entire circumference of the seal. Work

25.3 After removing the retainer from the block, support it on two wooden blocks, and drive out the old seal with a punch and hammer

25.4 Drive the new seal into the retainer with a wooden block or a section of pipe, if you have one large enough - make sure the seal enters the retainer bore squarely

25.5 Lubricate the lip of the seal, and bolt the retainer to the rear of the engine block

slowly, and make sure the seal enters the bore squarely.

5 The seal lips must be lubricated with multi-purpose grease or clean engine oil before the seal/retainer is slipped over the crankshaft and bolted to the block **(see illustration)**. Use a new gasket - no sealant is required - and make sure the dowel pins are in place before refitting the retainer.

6 Tighten the retainer nuts/screws a little at a time until they're all snug, then tighten them to the torque listed in the Specifications in Chapter 2A.

26 Pistons/connecting rods - refitting and big-end bearing oil clearance check

1 Before refitting the piston/connecting rod assemblies, the cylinder walls must be perfectly clean, the top edge of each cylinder must be chamfered, and the crankshaft must be in place.

2 Remove the cap from the end of No 1 connecting rod (refer to the marks made during removal). Remove the original bearing shells, and wipe the bearing surfaces of the connecting rod and cap with a clean, lint-free cloth. They must be kept spotlessly-clean.

Connecting rod big-end bearing oil clearance check

3 Clean the back side of the new upper bearing shell, then lay it in place in the connecting rod. Make sure the tab on the bearing fits into the recess in the rod. Don't hammer the bearing shell into place, and be very careful not to nick or gouge the bearing face. Don't lubricate the bearing at this time.

4 Clean the back side of the other bearing shell, and refit it in the rod cap. Again, make sure the tab on the bearing fits into the recess in the cap, and don't apply any lubricant. It's critically important that the mating surfaces of the bearing and connecting rod are perfectly

clean and oil-free when they're assembled for this check.

5 Position the piston ring gaps so they're staggered 120° from each other.

6 Where applicable, slip a section of plastic or rubber hose over each connecting rod cap bolt.

7 Lubricate the piston and rings with clean engine oil, and attach a piston ring compressor to the piston. Leave the skirt protruding about 6 or 7 mm to guide the piston into the cylinder. The rings must be compressed until they're flush with the piston.

8 Rotate the crankshaft until the No 1 connecting rod journal is at BDC (bottom dead centre). Apply a coat of engine oil to the cylinder walls.

9 With the mark or notch on top of the piston facing the front of the engine, gently insert the piston/connecting rod assembly into the No 1 cylinder bore, and rest the bottom edge of the ring compressor on the engine block.

10 Tap the top edge of the ring compressor to make sure it's contacting the block around its entire circumference.

11 Gently tap on the top of the piston with the end of a wooden hammer handle **(see illustration)** while guiding the end of the connecting rod into place on the crankshaft journal. Work slowly, and if any resistance is felt as the piston enters the cylinder, stop immediately. Find out what's catching, and fix it before proceeding. Do not, for any reason, force the piston into the cylinder - you might break a ring and/or the piston.

> **HAYNES HINT** *The piston rings may try to pop out of the ring compressor just before entering the cylinder bore, so keep some downward pressure on the ring compressor*

12 Once the piston/connecting rod assembly is fitted, the connecting rod big-end bearing oil clearance must be checked before the rod cap is permanently bolted in place.

13 Cut a piece of the appropriate-size Plastigage slightly shorter than the width of the connecting rod big-end bearing, and lay it in place on the No 1 connecting rod journal, parallel with the crankshaft centre-line.

14 Clean the connecting rod cap bearing face, remove the protective hoses from the connecting rod bolts, and refit the rod cap. Make sure the mating mark on the cap is on the same side as the mark on the connecting rod.

15 Refit the nuts/bolts, and tighten them to the torque listed in this Chapter's Specifications. On M10 and M30 engines, work up to the final torque in three stages. **Note:** *Use a thin-wall socket, to avoid erroneous torque readings that can result if the socket is wedged between the rod cap and nut. If the socket tends to wedge itself between the nut and the cap, lift up on it slightly until it no longer contacts the cap.* Do not rotate the crankshaft at any time during this operation.

16 Undo the nuts and remove the rod cap, being very careful not to disturb the Plastigage.

17 Compare the width of the crushed Plastigage to the scale printed on the Plastigage envelope to obtain the oil clearance **(see illustration)**. Compare it to the Specifications to make sure the clearance is correct.

18 If the clearance is not as specified, the bearing shells may be the wrong size (which means different ones will be required). Before deciding that different shells are needed, make sure that no dirt or oil was between the bearing shells and the connecting rod or cap when the clearance was measured. Also, recheck the journal diameter. If the Plastigage was wider at one end than the other, the journal may be tapered (see Section 19).

Final connecting rod refitting

19 Carefully scrape all traces of the Plastigage material off the rod journal and/or bearing face. Be very careful not to scratch

26.11 Drive the piston gently into the cylinder bore with the end of a wooden or plastic hammer handle

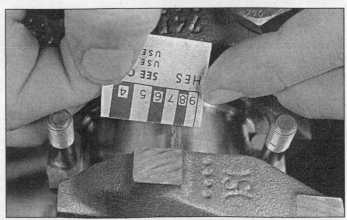

26.17 Measuring the width of the crushed Plastigage to determine the big-end bearing oil clearance (be sure to use the correct scale - standard and metric ones are included)

2B

the bearing - use your fingernail or the edge of a credit card.

20 Make sure the bearing faces are perfectly clean, then apply a uniform layer of molybdenum disulphide ("moly") grease or engine assembly oil to both of them. You'll have to push the piston into the cylinder to expose the face of the bearing shell in the connecting rod - be sure to slip the protective hoses over the rod bolts first, where applicable.

21 Slide the connecting rod back into place on the journal, and remove the protective hoses from the rod cap bolts. Refit the rod cap, and tighten the nuts/bolts to the specified torque.

22 Repeat the entire procedure for the remaining pistons/connecting rods.

23 The important points to remember are:

a) *Keep the back sides of the bearing shells and the insides of the connecting rods and caps perfectly clean when assembling them.*

b) *Make sure you have the correct piston/rod assembly for each cylinder.*

c) *The notch or mark on the piston must face the front of the engine.*

d) *Lubricate the cylinder walls with clean oil.*

e) *Lubricate the bearing faces when refitting the rod caps after the oil clearance has been checked.*

24 After all the piston/connecting rod assemblies have been properly fitted, rotate the crankshaft a number of times by hand to check for any obvious binding.

25 Check the connecting rod side play (see Section 13).

26 Compare the measured side play to the Specifications to make sure it's correct. If it was correct before dismantling, and the original crankshaft and rods were refitted, it should still be right. If new rods or a new crankshaft were fitted, the side play may be incorrect. If so, the rods will have to be removed and taken to a machine shop for attention.

27 Initial start-up and running-in after overhaul

⚠️ *Warning:* **Have a fire extinguisher handy when starting the engine for the first time.**

1 Once the engine has been refitted in the vehicle, double-check the engine oil and coolant levels.

2 With the spark plugs removed and the ignition system disabled (see Section 3), crank the engine until oil pressure registers on the gauge, or until the oil pressure warning light goes out.

3 Refit the spark plugs, connect the HT leads, and restore the ignition system functions (see Section 3).

4 Start the engine. It may take a few moments for the fuel system to build up pressure, but the engine should start without a great deal of effort. **Note:** *If backfiring occurs through the throttle body or carburettor, check the valve timing (check that the timing chain/belt has been correctly fitted), the firing order (check the fitted order of the spark plug HT leads), and the ignition timing.*

5 After the engine starts, it should be allowed to warm up to normal operating temperature. While the engine is warming up, make a thorough check for fuel, oil and coolant leaks.

6 Shut the engine off and recheck the engine oil and coolant levels.

7 Drive the vehicle to an area with minimum traffic, accelerate at full throttle from 30 to 50 mph, then lift off the throttle completely, and allow the vehicle to slow to 30 mph with the throttle closed. Repeat the procedure 10 or 12 times. This will load the piston rings, and cause them to seat properly against the cylinder walls. Check again for oil and coolant leaks.

8 Drive the vehicle gently for the first 500 miles (no sustained high speeds) and keep a constant check on the oil level. It is not unusual for an engine to use oil during the running-in period.

9 At approximately 500 to 600 miles, change the oil and filter.

10 For the next few hundred miles, drive the vehicle normally - don't nurse it, but don't abuse it, either.

11 After 2000 miles, change the oil and filter again. The engine may now be considered to be fully run-in.

Chapter 3
Cooling, heating and air conditioning systems

Contents

Degrees of difficulty

| Easy, suitable for novice with little experience | Fairly easy, suitable for beginner with some experience | Fairly difficult, suitable for competent DIY mechanic | Difficult, suitable for experienced DIY mechanic | Very difficult, suitable for expert DIY or professional |

Specifications

General

Coolant capacity .... See Chapter 1
Thermostat rating
  Opening temperature .... 80°C (176°F)
  Fully open at .... 100°C (212°F)
Cooling fan thermo-switch - switching temperatures
  Low-speed .... 91°C (196°F)
  High-speed .... 99°C (210°F)

Torque wrench settings   Nm

Mechanical cooling fan clutch-to-water pump securing
  nut (left-hand thread) 40
Mechanical cooling fan-to-clutch bolts 10
Water pump bolts
  Small bolts (M6) 10
  Large bolts (M8) 22
Thermostat housing bolts 10

1 General information

Engine cooling system

All vehicles covered by this manual employ a pressurised engine cooling system, with thermostatically-controlled coolant circulation.

An impeller-type water pump mounted on the front of the block pumps coolant through the engine. The coolant flows around each cylinder, and towards the rear of the engine. Cast-in coolant passages direct coolant around the intake and exhaust ports, near the spark plug areas, and in close proximity to the exhaust valve guides.

A wax-pellet-type thermostat is located in-line in the bottom hose on M10 engines, in a housing near the front of the engine on M20 and M30 engines, or behind an elbow under the timing belt upper cover (on the front of the cylinder head) on M40 engines. During warm-up, the closed thermostat prevents coolant from circulating through the radiator. As the engine nears normal operating temperature, the thermostat opens and allows hot coolant to travel through the radiator, where it's cooled before returning to the engine.

The pressure in the system raises the boiling point of the coolant, and increases the cooling efficiency of the radiator. The cooling system is sealed by a pressure-type cap. If the system pressure exceeds the cap pressure relief value, the excess pressure in the system forces the spring-loaded valve inside the cap off its seat, and allows the coolant to escape through the overflow tube.

The pressure cap on four-cylinder models is on the top of the radiator; on six-cylinder models, it's on top of a translucent plastic expansion tank. The cap pressure rating is moulded into the top of the cap. The pressure rating is either 1.0 bar (14 psi) or 1.2 bars (17 psi).

Warning: *Do not remove the pressure cap from the radiator or expansion tank until the engine has cooled completely and there's no pressure remaining in the cooling system. Removing the cap from a hot engine risks personal injury by scalding.*

Heating system

The heating system consists of a blower fan and heater matrix located in the heater box, with hoses connecting the heater matrix to the engine cooling system, and the heater/air conditioning control head on the dashboard. Hot engine coolant is circulated through the heater matrix passages all the time the engine is running. Switching the heater on opens a flap door to direct air through the heater matrix, and the warmed air enters the passenger compartment. A fan switch on the control head activates the blower motor, which forces more air through the heater matrix, giving additional heater output for demisting, etc.

Air conditioning system

The air conditioning system consists of a condenser mounted in front of the radiator, an evaporator mounted adjacent to the heater matrix, a compressor mounted on the engine, a filter-drier (receiver-drier) which contains a high-pressure relief valve, and the plumbing connecting all of the above components.

A blower fan forces the warmer air of the passenger compartment through the evaporator matrix (a radiator-in-reverse), transferring the heat from the air to the refrigerant. The liquid refrigerant boils off into low-pressure vapour, taking the heat with it when it leaves the evaporator.

Note: *Refer to the precautions at the start of Section 12 concerning the potential dangers associated with the air conditioning system.*

2 Antifreeze -
general information

 Warning: *Do not allow antifreeze to come in contact with your skin or painted surfaces of the vehicle. Rinse off spills immediately with plenty of water. If consumed, antifreeze can be fatal; children and pets are attracted by its sweet taste, so wipe up garage floor and drip pan coolant spills immediately. Keep antifreeze containers covered, and repair leaks in your cooling system as soon as they are noticed.*

The cooling system should be filled with a 60/40% water/ethylene-glycol-based anti-freeze solution, which will prevent freezing down to approximately -27°C (-17°F). The antifreeze also raises the boiling point of the coolant, and (if of good quality) provides protection against corrosion.

The cooling system should be drained, flushed and refilled at the specified intervals (see Chapter 1). Old or contaminated antifreeze solutions are likely to cause damage, and encourage the formation of rust and scale in the system. Use distilled water with the antifreeze, if available, or clean rainwater. Tap water will do, but not if the water in your area is at all "hard".

Before adding antifreeze, check all hose connections, because antifreeze tends to search out and leak through very minute openings. Engines don't normally consume coolant, so if the level goes down, find the cause and correct it.

The antifreeze mixture should be maintained at its correct proportions; adding too much antifreeze reduces the efficiency of the cooling system. If necessary, consult the mixture ratio chart on the antifreeze container before adding coolant. Hydrometers are available at most car accessory shops to test the coolant. Use antifreeze which meets the vehicle manufacturer's specifications.

3 Thermostat -
check and renewal

 Warning: *Do not remove the radiator cap, drain the coolant, or renew the thermostat until the engine has cooled completely.*

Check

1 Before assuming the thermostat is to blame for a cooling system problem, check the coolant level, drivebelt tension (see Chapter 1) and temperature gauge (or warning light) operation.

2 If the engine seems to be taking a long time to warm up (based on heater output or temperature gauge operation), the thermostat is probably stuck open. Renew the thermostat.

3 If the engine runs hot, use your hand to check the temperature of the upper radiator hose. If the hose isn't hot, but the engine is, the thermostat is probably stuck closed,

3.8 On the M10 (four-cylinder) engine, the thermostat (arrowed) is connected in-line in the radiator hose

preventing the coolant inside the engine from circulating to the radiator. Renew the thermostat.

 Caution: *Don't drive the vehicle without a thermostat. The engine will be very slow to warm-up in cold conditions, resulting in poor fuel economy and driveability. A new thermostat is normally an inexpensive component anyway.*

4 If the upper radiator hose is hot, it means that the coolant is flowing and the thermostat is at least partly open. Consult the *"Fault finding"* Section at the rear of this manual for cooling system diagnosis.

Renewal
All models

5 Disconnect the negative cable from the battery.

 Caution: *If the radio in your vehicle is equipped with an anti-theft system, make sure you have the correct activation code before disconnecting the battery.*

Note: *If, after connecting the battery, the wrong language appears on the instrument panel display, refer to page 0-7 for the language resetting procedure.*

6 Drain the cooling system (see Chapter 1). If the coolant is relatively new or in good condition, save it and re-use it.

M10 engines

7 The thermostat is located in the bottom hose. First remove the cooling fan.

8 Note the fitted position of the thermostat, then unscrew the hose clamps and withdraw the thermostat from the hose connections **(see illustration)**.

9 Refit the thermostat-to-hose connections, and tighten the hose clamps.

10 Refit the cooling fan.

M20 and M30 engines

11 Loosen the hose clamp **(see illustration)**, then detach the hose(s) from the thermostat cover.

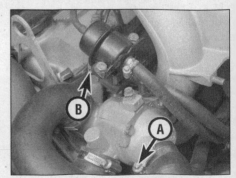

3.11 On M20 and M30 engine models, loosen the hose clamp (A) and disconnect the hose from the thermostat housing cover - note that the coolant temperature sender unit (barely visible behind the fuel pressure regulator) is located at the top of the thermostat housing (B)

3.15 On M20 and M30 engine models, after the housing and thermostat have been removed, take the O-ring out of the housing and clean the recess in the housing to be sure of a good seal upon reassembly

3.20a Removing the elbow from the cylinder head (M40 engine)

3.20b Removing the thermostat (M40 engine)

12 If the outer surface of the fitting that mates with the hose is deteriorated (corroded, pitted, etc.), it may be damaged further by hose removal. If it is, a new thermostat housing cover will be required.

13 Remove the bolts and detach the housing cover. If the cover is stuck, tap it with a soft-faced hammer to jar it loose. Be prepared for some coolant to spill as the gasket seal is broken.

14 Note how it's fitted, then remove the thermostat.

15 Stuff a rag into the engine opening, then remove all traces of old gasket material (if the gasket is paper type). Otherwise, remove the rubber O-ring **(see illustration)** and sealant from the housing and cover with a gasket scraper. Remove the rag from the opening and clean the gasket mating surfaces.

16 Fit the new thermostat and gasket in the housing. Make sure the correct end faces out - the spring end is normally directed towards the engine.

17 Refit the cover and bolts. Tighten the bolts to the torque listed in this Chapter's Specifications.

M40 engines

18 Remove the cooling fan and timing belt upper cover.

19 Unscrew the hose clamp and detach the

bottom hose from the elbow on the front of the cylinder head.

20 Unbolt the elbow from the cylinder head. Note the fitted position of the thermostat, then remove it **(see illustrations)**. Remove the rubber O-ring; a new one will be needed for reassembly.

21 Locate the thermostat in the cylinder head in the same position as noted during removal (arrow pointing upwards).

22 Press a new O-ring in the groove, and locate the elbow on the cylinder head. Tighten the bolts.

23 Connect the bottom hose to the elbow, and tighten the hose clamp.

24 Refit the upper timing belt cover and cooling fan.

All models

25 Refill the cooling system (see Chapter 1).

26 Connect the battery negative cable.

27 Start the engine and allow it to reach normal operating temperature, then check for leaks and proper thermostat operation (as described earlier in this Section).

---

4 Radiator -
removal and refitting

⚠ *Warning: Wait until the engine is completely cool before beginning this procedure.*

Note: *If the radiator is being removed because it is leaking, note that minor leaks can often be repaired without removing the radiator, using a radiator sealant.*

⚠ ***Caution: If the radio in your vehicle is equipped with an anti-theft system, make sure you have the correct activation code before disconnecting the battery.***

Note: *If, after connecting the battery, the wrong language appears on the instrument panel display, refer to page 0-7 for the language resetting procedure.*

Removal

1 Disconnect the battery negative cable.

2 Drain the cooling system (see Chapter 1). If the coolant is relatively new, or in good condition, save it and re-use it.

3 Loosen the hose clamps, then detach the hoses from the radiator **(see illustrations)**. If they're stuck, grasp each hose near the end with a pair of water pump pliers, twist gently to break the seal, then pull off - be careful not to distort or break the radiator outlets! If the hoses are old or deteriorated, cut them off and refit new ones.

4 On M20 and M30 engines, disconnect the reservoir hose from the radiator filler neck.

5 Remove the screws or plastic fasteners that attach the shroud to the radiator, and slide the shroud towards the engine **(see illustration)**. On some engines it is possible to completely remove the shroud.

6 If the vehicle has automatic transmission,

4.3a Disconnecting the top hose from the radiator

4.3b Bottom hose connection to the radiator

4.5 Plastic fastener retaining the radiator shroud on some engines

3

4.7 Sensors that control the high- and low-speed operation of the auxiliary cooling fan are located in various places in the radiator tanks

4.8 The radiator is bolted to the front panel at either the sides or the top of the radiator

disconnect the fluid cooler lines from the radiator. Use a drip tray to catch spilled fluid. Plug the fluid cooler lines and fittings.

7 Disconnect the coolant sensors located on the radiator **(see illustration)**. The thermostatically-controlled switches for high- and low-speed operation of the auxiliary fan are located in the radiator tanks, in various locations depending on engine and model.

8 Remove the radiator mounting bolt(s). The mountings are either on the top or sides of the radiator **(see illustration)**.

9 Carefully lift out the radiator from the bottom mountings, taking care not to damage the cooling fins. Don't spill coolant on the vehicle, or scratch the paint.

10 With the radiator removed, it can be inspected for leaks and damage. If it needs repair, have a specialist perform the work, as special techniques are required.

11 Flies and dirt can be removed from the radiator with compressed air and a soft brush. Don't bend the cooling fins as this is done.

12 Check the radiator mountings for deterioration, and renew if necessary **(see illustration)**.

Refitting

13 Refitting is the reverse of the removal procedure.

14 After refitting, fill the cooling system with the proper mixture of antifreeze and water. Refer to Chapter 1 if necessary.

4.12 When the radiator is out, the radiator mountings can be inspected - check for signs of deterioration, and renew them, if needed

15 Start the engine and check for leaks. Allow the engine to reach normal operating temperature, indicated by the upper radiator hose becoming hot. Recheck the coolant level, and add more if required.

16 If you're working on an automatic transmission model, check and add transmission fluid as needed.

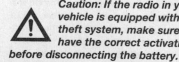

5 Engine cooling fan(s) and clutch - check, removal and refitting

Warning: To avoid possible injury or damage, DO NOT operate the engine with a damaged fan. Do not attempt to repair fan blades - fit a new fan. Also, the electric auxiliary fan in front of the radiator or air conditioning condenser can come on without the engine running or ignition being on. It is controlled by the coolant temperature of the thermo-switches located in the radiator.

Check

Electric auxiliary fan

Note : *This fan on most models is controlled by two thermo-switches placed in the radiator: one for low-speed/low-temperature operation, and one for high-speed/high-temperature operation. Each switch comes on at a different coolant temperature (refer to the Specifications at the beginning of this Chapter).*

1 The thermostatically-controlled switches for high- and low-speed operation of the auxiliary fan are fitted in various locations in the radiator **(see illustration 4.7)**, depending on engine or model. Two single switches, or one dual switch, may be fitted.

2 Insert a small screwdriver into the connector to lift the lock tab, and unplug the fan wire harness.

3 To test the fan motor, unplug the electrical connector at the motor, and use jumper wires to connect the fan directly to the battery. If the fan doesn't work when connected directly to the battery, the motor is proved faulty, and must be renewed. If the fan works, there's a

good chance the switch is malfunctioning. To more accurately diagnose the problem, follow the steps that apply to your model. **Note**: *Spin the auxiliary fan motor by hand, to check that the motor or fan isn't binding. Make sure, however, that the engine is sufficiently cool that there is no danger of the fan cutting-in on its own when this is done.*

4 To test the low-speed and high-speed circuits, disconnect the electrical connector from one of the fan switches, and bridge the terminals of the switch's electrical connector with a short piece of wire. The fan should run at low or high speed, depending on which switch has been disconnected. On some models the ignition must be on before the fan will run.

5 Repeat the test at the other switch so that both high and low speeds are tested.

6 If the low-speed and high-speed circuits are OK, but there has been a problem with the fan not operating correctly in service, renew the switch (or switches). To remove a switch, drain the coolant below the level of the switch (see Chapter 1), then unscrew the switch and screw in the new one. Refill the system with coolant.

7 If the switches are satisfactory, but the motor still does not operate, the problem lies in the fuse, the relay, the wiring which connects the components (or the fan motor itself). Carefully check the fuse, relay, all wiring and connections. See Chapter 12 for more information on how to carry out these checks.

Mechanical fan with viscous clutch

8 Disconnect the battery negative cable, and rock the fan back and forth by hand to check for excessive bearing play.

Caution: If the radio in your vehicle is equipped with an anti-theft system, make sure you have the correct activation code before disconnecting the battery.

Note: *If, after connecting the battery, the wrong language appears on the instrument panel display, refer to page 0-7 for the language resetting procedure.*

9 With the engine cold, turn the fan blades by hand. The fan should turn with slight resistance.

10 Visually inspect for substantial fluid leakage from the fan clutch assembly. If problems are noted, renew the fan clutch assembly.

11 With the engine completely warmed up, turn off the ignition switch and disconnect the battery negative cable. Turn the fan by hand. Heavier resistance should be evident. If the fan turns easily, a new fan clutch may be needed.

Removal and refitting

Electric auxiliary fan

12 Disconnect the battery negative cable.

13 To remove the auxiliary fan follow the procedure that applies to your vehicle.

5.27a The cooling fan on the water pump is attached to the shaft by a left-hand-threaded nut located directly behind the fan . . .

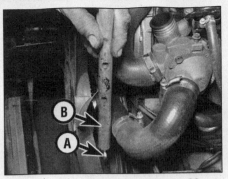

5.27b . . . to loosen the nut, place a 32 mm open-ended spanner on the nut, and sharply strike the spanner (A) with a metal drift (B) and hammer; this will loosen the nut and allow it to be turned easily so the fan can be removed

5.29 Removing the water pump pulley (M40 engine)

3-Series models

14 Remove the radiator grille assembly (see Chapter 11).
15 Unbolt and remove the fan bracket and shroud assembly from the radiator (see Section 5).
16 Remove the radiator (see Section 4).
17 Unbolt the air conditioning condenser mounting bolts, where applicable. Do not remove the condenser or disconnect any refrigerant lines from the condenser.
18 Carefully pull the condenser back towards the engine, slightly, to gain access to lift the auxiliary fan.
19 Disconnect the fan motor electrical connection and remove the auxiliary fan.
20 Refitting is the reverse of removal.

5-Series models

21 Remove the screws and trim panel in front of the radiator.
22 Unbolt the fan assembly from the condenser mounting points.
23 Disconnect the fan electrical connector.
24 Remove the fan and housing from the car, being careful not to damage the air conditioning condenser (when applicable) while removing the fan.
25 Refitting is the reverse of removal.

Mechanical fan with viscous clutch

26 Disconnect the battery negative cable. Remove the fan shroud mounting screws or plastic fasteners, and detach the shroud (see Section 4).
27 Use a 32 mm open-ended spanner to remove the fan/clutch assembly. Place the spanner on the large nut ahead of the pulley **(see illustrations)**, and tap the end of the spanner to loosen the nut.

 Caution: The nut has left-handed threads, so it loosens by being turned clockwise, as viewed from the front of the vehicle.

28 Lift the fan/clutch assembly (and shroud, if necessary) out of the engine compartment.
29 If necessary, remove the four bolts attaching the pulley to the water pump hub. The pulley can then be removed after removing the drivebelt(s) **(see illustration)**.

30 Carefully inspect the fan blades for damage and defects. Renew it if necessary.
31 At this point, the fan may be unbolted from the clutch, if necessary. If the fan clutch is stored, position it with the radiator side facing down.
32 Refitting is the reverse of removal.

6 Water pump - check

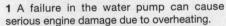

1 A failure in the water pump can cause serious engine damage due to overheating.
2 There are two ways to check the operation of the water pump while it's fitted on the engine. If either of the following checks suggest that the pump is defective, a new one should be fitted.
3 Water pumps are equipped with "weep" or "vent" holes. If a failure occurs in the pump seal, coolant will leak from the hole. In most cases, you'll need a torch to find the hole on the water pump from underneath to check for leaks.
4 If the water pump shaft bearings fail, there may be a howling sound at the front of the engine while it's running. Shaft wear can be felt if the water pump pulley is rocked up and down (with the drivebelt removed). Don't mistake drivebelt slippage, which causes a squealing sound, for water pump bearing failure. Alternator bearing failure can also cause a howling sound, but after removing the drivebelt(s) it should be easy enough to tell which component is responsible.

7 Water pump - removal and refitting

 Warning: Wait until the engine is completely cool before beginning this procedure.

 Caution: If the radio in your vehicle is equipped with an anti-theft system, make sure you have the correct activation code before disconnecting the battery.

Note: *If, after connecting the battery, the wrong language appears on the instrument panel display, refer to page 0-7 for the language resetting procedure.*

Removal

1 Disconnect the battery negative cable.
2 Drain the cooling system (see Chapter 1). If the coolant is relatively new, or in good condition, save it and re-use it.
3 Remove the cooling fan shroud (see Section 5).
4 Remove the drivebelts (see Chapter 1).
5 Where applicable, loosen the clamps and detach the hoses from the water pump. If they're stuck, grasp each hose near the end with a pair of water pump pliers and gently twist it to break the seal, then pull it off. If the hoses are deteriorated, cut them off and refit new ones.
6 Remove the fan and clutch assembly and the pulley at the end of the water pump shaft (see Section 5).
7 To remove the water pump, follow the specific steps that apply to your engine.

M10 engine

8 Unscrew the mounting bolts and remove the water pump **(see illustration)**.

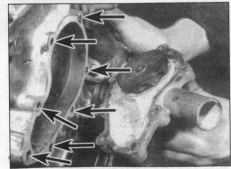

7.8 On M10 engines, there are seven bolts (locations arrowed) that hold the water pump to the block

7.12 Water pump bolt locations on the M20 engine

7.18a With the water pump mounting bolts removed, screw two bolts into the special lugs (one top and one bottom) . . .

7.18b . . . and remove the water pump (M40 engine)

M20 engine

9 Remove the distributor cap and HT leads, ignition rotor and dust shield (see Chapter 1).
10 Where applicable, remove the timing sensor (see Chapter 5).
11 Remove the timing belt upper cover (see Chapter 2A).
12 Loosen all three water pump mounting bolts. Remove the top and right-hand side bolts, but DON'T remove the lower bolt (see illustration).
13 Rotate the pump downwards, and remove the drivebelt tensioner spring and pin.
14 Remove the final water pump bolt, and remove the pump.

 Caution: Leave the tensioner bolt tight. Be careful to not move the camshaft gear, as damage can occur if the valves are moved.

M30 engine

15 Remove the engine lifting bracket.
16 Remove the bolts that mount the water pump to the engine block.
17 Remove the water pump, and recover the gasket.

M40 engine

18 Unscrew the mounting bolts and remove the water pump. If the pump is tight in the cylinder head, insert two bolts in the special lugs at the top and bottom of the pump, and tighten them evenly to press the pump out of the head (see illustrations).

Refitting

19 Clean the bolt threads and the threaded holes in the engine to remove corrosion and sealant.
20 Compare the new pump to the old one, to make sure they're identical.
21 Remove all traces of old gasket material from the engine with a gasket scraper.
22 Clean the water pump mating surfaces.
23 On the M40 engine, locate a new O-ring on the pump (see illustration).
24 Locate the gasket on the pump, and offer the pump up to the engine (see illustration). Slip a couple of bolts through the pump mounting holes to hold the gasket in place.
25 Carefully attach the pump and gasket to the engine, threading the bolts into the holes finger-tight. Note: On the M20 engine, refit the lower bolt finger-tight, then rotate the water pump into position with the drivebelt tensioner spring and pin in position.
26 Refit the remaining bolts (if they also hold an accessory bracket in place, be sure to reposition the bracket at this time). Tighten them to the torque listed in this Chapter's Specifications, in quarter-turn increments. Don't overtighten them, or the pump may be distorted.
27 Refit all parts removed for access to the pump.
28 Refill the cooling system and check the drivebelt tension (see Chapter 1). Run the engine and check for leaks.

8 Coolant temperature sender unit - check and renewal

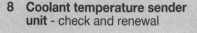

 Warning: Wait until the engine is completely cool before beginning this procedure.

1 The coolant temperature indicator system is composed of a temperature gauge mounted in the instrument panel, and a coolant temperature sender unit that's normally mounted on the thermostat housing (see illustration 3.11). Some vehicles have more than one sender unit, but only one is used for the temperature gauge. On the M40 engine, the sender unit is mounted on the left-hand side of the cylinder head, towards the rear.
2 If the gauge reading is suspect, first check the coolant level in the system. Make sure the wiring between the gauge and the sending unit is secure, and that all fuses are intact. (If the fuel gauge reading is suspect as well, the problem is almost certainly in the instrument panel or its wiring.)
3 Before testing the circuit, refer to the relevant wiring diagrams (see Chapter 12). Where the sender unit simply earths out the circuit, test by earthing the wire connected to the sending unit while the ignition is on (but without the engine running, for safety). If the gauge now deflects to the end of the scale, renew the sender unit. If the gauge does not respond satisfactorily, the gauge, or the wiring to the gauge, is faulty. Where the sender unit has two terminals, test the circuit by checking the resistance of the unit. No figures were available at the time of writing, but typically readings of several hundred or several thousand ohms (depending on temperature) would be expected. A reading of zero (short-circuit) or infinity (open-circuit) would indicate a faulty sender unit.

 Caution: Do not earth the wire for more than a second or two, or damage to the gauge could occur.

7.23 Fit a new O-ring on the M40 engine water pump

7.24 New outer gasket on the M40 engine water pump

4 If a new sender unit is to be fitted, make sure the engine is completely cool. There will be some coolant loss when the unit is unscrewed, so be prepared to catch it, or have the new unit ready to fit immediately the old one is removed. Disconnect the wiring, then unscrew the old unit from the engine, and fit the new one. Use sealant on the threads. Reconnect the wiring, and check the coolant level on completion.

9 Heater and air conditioning blower motor - removal, testing and refitting

Removal

Note: *The 3-Series models covered by this manual have always used a single blower motor for ventilation, heating and air conditioning. "Old-shape" (E28) 5-Series models use two separate blower motors: one for ventilation and heating, and another for air conditioning. "New-shape" (E34) 5-Series models have a single blower motor, like the 3-Series. The removal and refitting of the single blower motor, and the old-shape 5-Series vent/heat motor, is described below. The removal and refitting of the old-shape 5-Series air conditioning blower motor is described in Section 14 of this Chapter.*

⚠️ **Caution: If the radio in your vehicle is equipped with an anti-theft system, make sure you have the correct activation code before disconnecting the battery.**

Note: *If, after connecting the battery, the wrong language appears on the instrument panel display, refer to page 0-7 for the language resetting procedure.*

1 Disconnect the battery negative cable.
2 The blower motor is located behind the bulkhead, under an access panel. Remove the panel securing screws **(see illustrations)**.
3 Disconnect or cut the plastic ties holding the wiring harness to the panel, and move the wiring out of the way.
4 Remove the panel.
5 Unclip the blower housing retaining clip, and the clip securing the blower motor **(see illustrations)**.

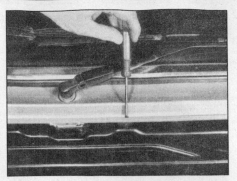

9.2a To get to the heater blower motor, the access panel must be removed - a fastener from the front and . . .

6 Disconnect the wiring and remove the blower motor **(see illustration)**.

Testing

7 You can test the blower motor by applying battery voltage to the blower motor's terminals with fused jumper wires (be sure the fan blades won't hit anything when they rotate). If the blower motor spins the fan blades rapidly (this test simulates high-speed operation), the blower motor is OK. If the blower motor does not operate, or operates slowly or noisily, renew it.
Note: *If the fan blade assemblies need to be removed, mark their relationship to the shaft. The assemblies are balanced during production, and excessive noise or shortened bearing life could result if they are not refitted in exactly the same position in relation to the shaft.*

Refitting

8 Refitting is the reverse of removal. **Note:** *The blower motor may have to be rotated to allow the retaining clip to line up correctly.*

10 Heater and air conditioner control assembly - removal and refitting

Removal

1 Disconnect the battery negative cable.

9.2b . . . a fastener from the top secure the panel

⚠️ **Caution: If the radio in your vehicle is equipped with an anti-theft system, make sure you have the correct activation code before disconnecting the battery.**

Note: *If, after connecting the battery, the wrong language appears on the instrument panel display, refer to page 0-7 for the language resetting procedure.*

3-Series models

2 Remove the centre console and side trim pieces.
3 Remove the radio (see Chapter 12), then pull the knobs off the heater/air conditioning control levers.
4 Remove the heater trim panel to gain access to the control cables.
5 Disconnect the cables, marking them for accurate refitting.
6 Disconnect the electrical connector.
7 Remove the lever assembly.
8 Each lever assembly can be removed separately.

5-Series models

9 Remove the centre console (see Chapter 11).
10 Remove the radio (see Chapter 12), then pull the knobs off the heater/air conditioning control levers.

9.5a Unclip the retaining strap to remove the blower housing . . .

9.5b . . . and unclip the centre strap that secures the blower motor assembly

9.6 Lift out the assembly, and disconnect the electrical connection from the blower motor

11.3a Pull out the glovebox support strap pins . . .

11.3b . . . and where applicable, remove the torch socket from the glovebox

11.4a Release the fasteners (arrowed) from the trim panel next to the glovebox location . . .

11 Remove the trim bezel, and pull the control unit from the dash. This will allow you to disconnect the control cables from the lever assembly.

12 Disconnect the cables from the clips securing them to the lever assembly, marking them for accurate refitting.

13 Disconnect the electrical connection from the control assembly.

14 Remove the screws attaching the bezel to the control assembly, and remove the control assembly.

Refitting

15 Refitting is the reverse of the removal procedure.

11 Heater matrix - removal and refitting

⚠️ **Caution: If the radio in your vehicle is equipped with an anti-theft system, make sure you have the correct activation code before disconnecting the battery.**

Note: *If, after connecting the battery, the wrong language appears on the instrument panel display, refer to page 0-7 for the language resetting procedure.*

1 Drain the cooling system, as described in Chapter 1.

2 Remove the centre console, as described in Chapter 11.

3-series
Removal

3 Open and support the glovebox from below, then pull out the support strap pins **(see illustration)**. Close the glovebox on the catch, then remove the three hinge screws from underneath. Release the glovebox catch and lower the glovebox out of position. Where applicable, release the torch wiring socket **(see illustration)**, and detach the wiring from the clips on the side of the glovebox.

4 Working in the passenger front footwell, remove the trim panel next to the glovebox location by removing the top screw and by turning the two plastic fasteners through 90° **(see illustrations)**.

5 Remove the corrugated ventilation duct between the heater housing and the floor on the passenger side **(see illustration)**.

6 Remove the vent nozzle from the passenger side of the heater housing, after removing the Torx screw **(see illustrations)**.

7 On right-hand-drive models, the brake pedal cross-shaft pivot assembly prevents removal of the heater matrix, and this assembly must now be disconnected and removed.

8 For improved access, remove the passenger side under-dash panel, by removing the top screw and by turning the plastic fastener on the left-hand side of the panel through 90° **(see illustration)**.

11.4b . . . and remove the trim panel

11.5 Removing the floor ventilation duct

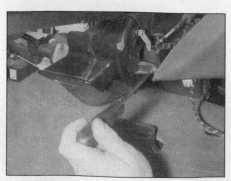

11.6a Remove the Torx securing screw . . .

11.6b . . . and remove the vent nozzle from the passenger side of the heater housing

11.8 Remove the screw and the plastic fastener, and remove the passenger side under-dash trim panel

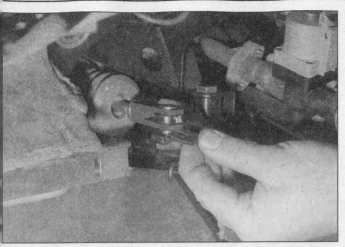

11.9a Slide out the spring clip . . .

11.9b . . . and withdraw the clevis pin from the servo pushrod-to-pivot connection

9 Slide out the spring clip, and remove the clevis pin from the brake servo pushrod-to-pivot connection (see illustrations).

10 Similarly remove the clip and clevis pin from the pivot connection to the brake pedal cross-shaft (see illustration). As the pin is removed, the pivot assembly spring will release - this is not a violent action, but be prepared for the pivot to swing outwards.

11 When both clevis pins have been removed and the linkages detached, mark the fitted position of each part of the linkage in relation

to the threaded adjusters, to preserve the settings. Either use a drop of paint to mark it, or tape each link to the threaded rod.

12 The four nuts securing the vacuum servo unit to the bulkhead must now be removed, from inside the car (see illustration). The servo unit should be supported, using cable-ties or a suitable block of wood, before the nuts are completely removed, although the servo does not have to be moved further.

13 Unscrew and remove the four bolts

securing the cross-shaft/servo pivot bracket, and remove the bracket from the car (see illustrations).

14 Working in the engine compartment, unscrew the hose clips and disconnect the two heater hoses from the connections on the bulkhead (see illustration).

15 Returning to the passenger footwell, remove the screws and disconnect the hose extension(s) (which pass through the bulkhead) from the stub(s) on the heater matrix. Do not use excessive force in

3

11.10 Removing the spring clip from the brake pedal cross-shaft connection

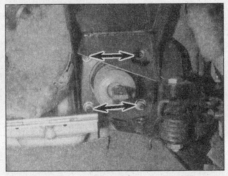

11.12 Brake vacuum servo mounting nuts (arrowed)

11.13a Unscrew and remove the two pivot bracket bolts from the top . . .

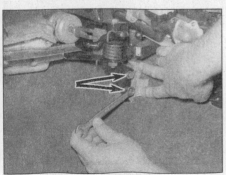

11.13b . . . and from the bottom (arrowed) . . .

11.13c . . . and remove the pivot bracket from the car

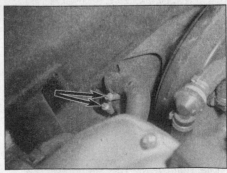

11.14 Heater hose clips (arrowed) at the engine compartment bulkhead

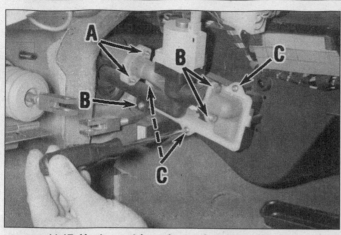

11.17 Heater matrix and associated attachments

A Hose extension screws
B Electronic heater valve screws
C Heater matrix screws (one hidden)

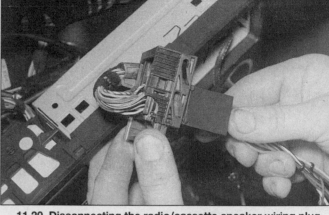

11.20 Disconnecting the radio/cassette speaker wiring plug

disconnecting the pipes from the matrix, or the pipes may fracture. Recover the sealing O-ring from the end of each pipe.

16 Where applicable, disconnect the electronically-controlled heater valve (black plastic assembly) from the end of the matrix. Recover the O-rings, where fitted.

17 Remove the three securing screws from the end of the matrix (see illustration), and slide the matrix out of the heater housing into the footwell. Take precautions against the spillage of coolant, but try to keep the open ends of the matrix stubs tilted slightly upwards, to prevent unnecessary spillage.

Refitting

18 Refitting is a reversal of removal, noting the following points:

a) Use new O-ring seals on the heater matrix pipe connections.
b) When refitting the brake pedal cross-shaft, ensure that the linkage adjustments have not been disturbed. Tension the pivot spring slightly as the clevis pins are refitted. Refit the clevis pins from the top, and secure with the spring clips.
c) When refitting the glovebox, check for satisfactory closure and adjust the catch position if necessary.

d) Refill the cooling system as described in Chapter 1, and check for leaks before proceeding.
e) Refit the centre console as described in Chapter 11.

5-series

Removal

19 To gain access to the heater matrix, the heater control panel must be removed. Remove the two screws either side of the control panel which were temporarily refitted during centre console removal. Support the control panel as the screws are removed.

20 Remove the radio/cassette unit from the heater/ventilation control panel. Exact details will vary according to the unit fitted, but typically, the unit will be released by depressing two spring-loaded retaining catches and pulling the unit forwards out of the panel. Disconnect the aerial lead, power supply/earth leads and speaker wiring from the rear of the unit, labelling the wires if necessary to avoid confusion on refitting (see illustration).

21 The wiring plugs and heater control cables must now be released from the rear of the heater/ventilation control panel. Note the

positions of all components carefully before proceeding.

22 Depress the retaining tabs and disconnect the wiring plug(s) from the switch(es) at the left-hand end of the control panel (see illustration). If wished, the switch(es) can be pressed out of the control panel.

23 The three heater control cables with the red, blue and green colour-coded end fittings are all disconnected in the same way. Before proceeding, however, note the order of fitting for use on reassembly. From the top cable down, the sequence of colours is red-blue-green.

24 Squeeze together the tabs on the cable outer, and release the cable from the rear of the control panel. Pull the cable towards the facia panel at an angle of approximately 45° to release the cable inner from the control lever (see illustrations). Repeat this procedure for the remaining control cables.

25 The uppermost control cable (where fitted) is colour-coded yellow. The cable end fitting is released from its control lever in the same way as for the other cables previously described. The cable is released from the heater control panel by squeezing together the retaining tabs top and bottom, and pulling the cable out of its retaining collar.

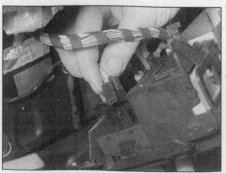

11.22 Switch wiring plug removal from the heater control panel

11.24a Squeeze together the cable outer retaining tabs . . .

11.24b . . . then release the cable inner from the control lever

11.26 Press the wiring plug retaining 'handle' to one side to disconnect the plug

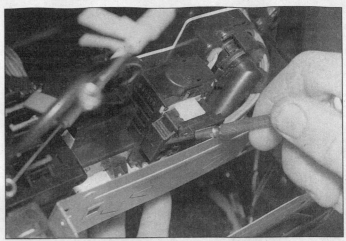

11.27a Pull back the retaining catch . . .

11.27b . . . and pull off the blower fan switch wiring plug

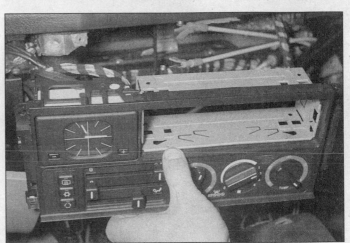

11.28 Withdrawing the heater control panel

3

26 Press the retaining 'handle' to one side, and pull off the temperature control multi-plug **(see illustration)**.
27 Pull back the retaining catch, and pull off the blower fan switch multi-plug **(see illustrations)**.
28 Pull the heater control panel forwards, and move it to one side **(see illustration)**. If wished, the clock can be released from the

panel using the removal lever provided. Push out the clock as far as possible using the plastic lever, then pull the clock forwards off its multi-plug connector. The heater control panel may now be completely removed.
29 Unplug the cabin temperature sensor wiring plug on the left-hand side of the matrix cover panel, and unclip the wiring. Pull the temperature sensor from the cover panel for

safekeeping **(see illustrations)**. Where applicable, repeat this procedure and remove the sensor from the right-hand side of the panel.
30 Where applicable, release the heater control cable from the top of the matrix cover panel **(see illustration)**, and disconnect the cable end fitting from the heater flap door.

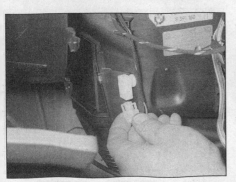

11.29a Disconnect the wiring plug from the cabin temperature sensor . . .

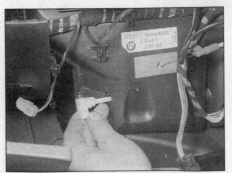

11.29b . . . and remove the sensor from the matrix cover panel

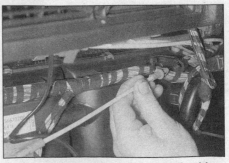

11.30 Release the heater control cable from the retaining collar on top of the matrix cover panel

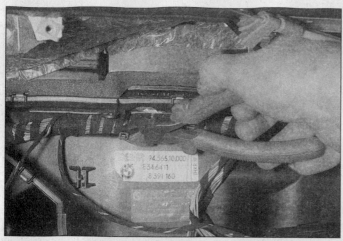

11.31 Cut the plastic cable-ties securing the wiring harness to the cover panel

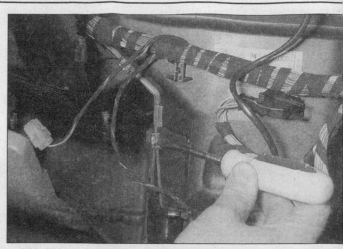

11.32 Using a suitable screwdriver, prise off the cover retaining clips

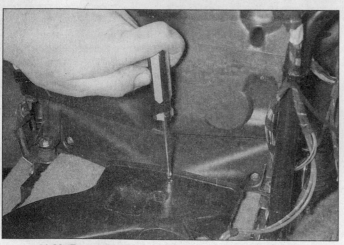

11.33 Removing the ventilation duct securing screw

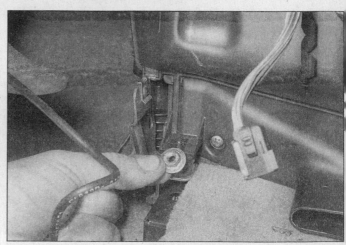

11.34a Remove the cover panel-to-mounting bracket nut . . .

31 Carefully cut the plastic cable-ties securing the wiring harness to the matrix cover panel, and move the wiring out of the way **(see illustration)**.
32 Using a small flat-bladed screwdriver, release all the spring clips around the edge of the matrix cover panel **(see illustration)**.

33 Where applicable, remove the top screw securing the ventilation duct to the rear passenger air vent, and move the duct to one side **(see illustration)**. Two more spring clips will now be exposed - release these using a small flat-bladed screwdriver.
34 At the base of the matrix cover panel, remove the nuts and bolts securing the

console and cover panel mounting brackets, and remove the brackets from the car **(see illustrations)**.
35 Where applicable, remove the two screws at the base of the matrix cover panel securing the ventilation cowl to the facia **(see illustration)**.
36 Loosen and remove the bolt securing the

11.34b . . . the bolt securing the console mounting bracket to the floor . . .

11.34c . . . and the matrix cover panel floor bracket

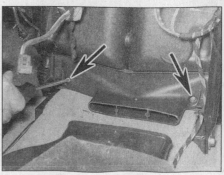

11.35 Remove the screws (arrowed) securing the ventilation cowl

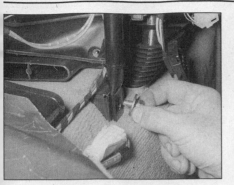

11.36 Remove the steering column support bar bolt

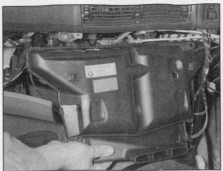

11.37 Removing the matrix cover panel

11.38 General view of the heater matrix, showing the flap door control linkage (arrowed)

bottom of the steering column support bar to the vehicle floor **(see illustration)**.

37 The matrix cover panel may now be removed by pulling it to the left past the steering column support bar, and swinging it upwards away from the facia **(see illustration)**. Pull the steering column support bar aside to ease removal of the panel.

38 Where applicable, release each end of the heater flap door linkage which runs across the front of the heater matrix **(see illustration)**, and remove it out of the way.

39 Before disconnecting the pipes to the heater matrix, take suitable precautions against the spillage of coolant.

40 Unscrew the bolt securing each heater pipe to the heater matrix **(see illustrations)**. Do not use excessive force in disconnecting the pipes from the matrix, or the pipes may fracture. Recover the sealing O-ring from the end of each pipe.

41 Slide the matrix to the rear to release its retaining lug at the top, then lift it out of its housing.

Refitting

42 Refitting is a reversal of removal, noting the following points:

a) Use new O-ring seals on the heater matrix pipe connections, and tighten the pipe securing bolts securely.
b) Refill the cooling system as described in Chapter 1, and check for leaks before proceeding.
c) Take great care that no wiring is trapped behind the matrix cover panel as it is refitted.
d) Secure the wiring harness to the matrix cover panel using new cable-ties.
e) Refit the centre console as described in Chapter 11.

12 Air conditioning system - precautions and maintenance

Precautions

⚠️ *Warning: The air conditioning system is under high pressure. DO NOT loosen any hose or line fittings, or remove any components, until after the system has been discharged. Air conditioning refrigerant should be properly discharged*

by a qualified refrigeration engineer. The refrigerant used in the system must not be allowed into contact with your skin or eyes, or there is a risk of frostbite. Should the refrigerant come into contact with a naked flame, a poisonous gas will be produced. Smoking in the presence of refrigerant is therefore highly dangerous, particularly if refrigerant vapour is inhaled through a lighted cigarette. The refrigerant is heavier than air, and it may cause suffocation if discharged in an enclosed space such as a domestic garage. Finally, uncontrolled release of the refrigerant causes environmental damage, by contributing to the "greenhouse effect".

Maintenance

1 The following maintenance checks should be performed on a regular basis to ensure the air conditioner continues to operate at peak efficiency:

a) Check the drivebelt. If it's worn or deteriorated, renew it (see Chapter 1).
b) Check the system hoses. Look for cracks, bubbles, hard spots and deterioration. Inspect the hoses and all fittings for oil

3

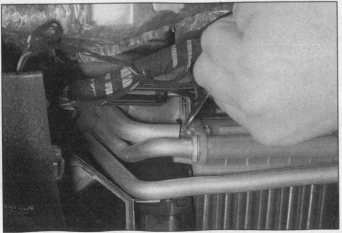

11.40a Remove the heater matrix pipe securing bolts at the side . . .

11.40b . . . and at the front of the matrix

bubbles and seepage. If there's any evidence of wear, damage or leaks, have new hose(s) fitted.

c) Inspect the condenser fins for leaves, flies and other debris. Use a "fin comb" or compressed air to clean the condenser.

d) Make sure the system has the correct refrigerant charge, as described below.

2 It's a good idea to operate the system for about 10 minutes at least once a month, particularly during the winter. Long-term non-use can cause hardening, and subsequent failure, of the seals.

3 Because of the complexity of the air conditioning system and the special equipment necessary to service it, in-depth fault diagnosis and repair procedures are not included in this manual. However, simple checks and component renewal procedures are provided in this Chapter.

4 The most common cause of poor cooling is simply a low system refrigerant charge. If a noticeable loss of cool air output occurs, the following quick check may help you determine if the refrigerant level is low.

5 Warm the engine up to normal operating temperature.

6 Set the air conditioning temperature selector at the coldest setting, and put the blower at the highest setting. Open the doors (to make sure the air conditioning system doesn't switch off as soon as it cools the passenger compartment).

7 With the compressor engaged - the compressor clutch will make an audible click, and the centre of the clutch will rotate - feel the tube located adjacent to the right front frame rail, near the radiator.

8 If a significant temperature drop is noticed, the refrigerant level is probably OK.

9 If the inlet line has frost accumulation, or feels cooler than the receiver-drier surface, the refrigerant charge is low. Recharging the system should be carried out by a qualified refrigeration engineer.

13 Air conditioning compressor - removal and refitting

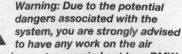

 Warning: Due to the potential dangers associated with the system, you are strongly advised to have any work on the air conditioning system carried out by a BMW dealer or air conditioning specialist. At the very least, DO NOT dismantle any part of the system (hoses, compressor, line fittings, etc.) until after the system has been discharged by a qualified engineer. Refer to the precautions given at the start of Section 12.

Note: If a new compressor is fitted, the receiver-drier (see Section 16) should also be renewed.

Removal

1 Have the air conditioning system discharged (see Warning above).

2 Disconnect the battery negative cable.

 Caution: If the radio in your vehicle is equipped with an anti-theft system, make sure you have the correct activation code before disconnecting the battery.

Note: If, after connecting the battery, the wrong language appears on the instrument panel display, refer to page 0-7 for the language resetting procedure.

3 Disconnect the compressor clutch wiring harness.

4 Remove the drivebelt (see Chapter 1).

5 Disconnect the refrigerant lines from the rear of the compressor. Plug the open fittings to prevent entry of dirt and moisture.

6 Unbolt the compressor from the mounting brackets, and lift it up and out of the vehicle (see illustration).

Refitting

7 If a new compressor is being fitted, follow any instructions supplied with the compressor regarding the draining of excess oil prior to fitting.

8 The clutch may have to be transferred to the new compressor.

9 Refitting is the reverse of removal. All O-rings should be replaced with new ones specifically made for use in air conditioning systems. Lubricate them with refrigerant oil when fitting.

10 Have the system evacuated, recharged and leak-tested by the qualified engineer who discharged it.

14 Air conditioning blower motor (E28/"old-shape" 5-series models) - removal and refitting

Note: Refer to Section 9 for information on "new-shape" (E34) 5-Series models.

 Caution: If the radio in your vehicle is equipped with an anti-theft system, make sure you have the correct activation code before disconnecting the battery.

Note: If, after connecting the battery, the wrong language appears on the instrument panel display, refer to page 0-7 for the language resetting procedure.

Removal

1 Disconnect the battery negative cable.

2 Remove the centre console (see Chapter 11).

3 Disconnect the blower motor electrical connector from the motor.

4 Unbolt the blower motor mountings from the main case.

5 Remove the air conditioning blower motor

13.6 From under the vehicle, remove the bolt from the lower air conditioning compressor mounting

assembly. You can check the motor by following the procedure described in Section 9.

Refitting

6 Refitting is the reverse of removal.

15 Air conditioning condenser - removal and refitting

 Warning: Due to the potential dangers associated with the system, you are strongly advised to have any work on the air conditioning system carried out by a BMW dealer or air conditioning specialist. At the very least, DO NOT dismantle any part of the system (hoses, compressor, line fittings, etc.) until after the system has been discharged by a qualified engineer. Refer to the precautions given at the start of Section 12.

Note: If a new condenser is fitted, the receiver-drier (see Section 16) should also be renewed.

Removal

1 Have the air conditioning system discharged (see Warning above).

2 Remove the radiator (see Section 4) except on "new-shape" (E34) 5-series models. On the latter, remove the front bumper (see Chapter 11).

3 Remove the radiator grille (see Chapter 11).

4 Unbolt the auxiliary fan from the air conditioning condenser mounting brackets.

5 Disconnect the refrigerant lines from the condenser.

6 Remove the mounting bolts from the condenser brackets.

7 Lift the condenser out of the vehicle, and plug the lines to keep dirt and moisture out.

8 If the original condenser is being refitted, store it with the line fittings uppermost, to prevent oil from draining out.

Refitting

9 Refit the components in the reverse order

of removal. Be sure the rubber pads are in place under the condenser.

10 Have the system evacuated, recharged and leak-tested by the qualified engineer who discharged it.

16 Air conditioner receiver-drier - removal and refitting

 Warning: Due to the potential dangers associated with the system, you are strongly advised to have any work on the air conditioning system carried out by a BMW dealer or air conditioning specialist. At the very least, DO NOT dismantle any part of the system (hoses, compressor, line fittings, etc.) until after the system has been discharged by a qualified engineer. Refer to the precautions given at the start of Section 12.

Removal

1 Have the system discharged (see Warning above).

2 Disconnect the battery negative cable.

Caution: If the radio in your vehicle is equipped with an anti-theft system, make sure you have the correct activation code before disconnecting the battery.

Note: *If, after connecting the battery, the wrong language appears on the instrument panel display, refer to page 0-7 for the language resetting procedure.*

3 Remove the windscreen washer fluid reservoir.

4 Disconnect the electrical connector(s) from the receiver-drier - note that not all models have both the high- and low-pressure switches **(see illustration)**.

5 Disconnect the refrigerant lines from the receiver-drier.

6 Plug the open line fittings, to prevent the entry of dirt and moisture.

7 Remove the mounting screws and remove the receiver-drier.

Refitting

8 If a new receiver-drier is being fitted, it may be necessary to add a quantity of refrigerant oil - follow the instructions supplied with the new unit.

9 Remove the old refrigerant line O-rings, and fit new ones. This should be done regardless of whether a new receiver-drier is being fitted.

10 If a new receiver-drier is being fitted, unscrew the pressure switches and transfer them to the new unit before fitting **(see illustration 16.4)**. Not all models have both the high- and low-pressure switches.

11 Lubricate the O-rings with refrigerant oil before assembly.

Refitting

12 Refitting is the reverse of removal, but be

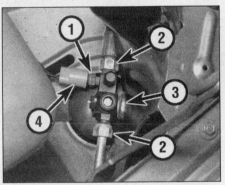

16.4 All models have the receiver-drier located behind the right headlight, although the configuration of lines and switches may vary

1 High-pressure switch
2 Refrigerant lines
3 Low-pressure switch
4 Electrical connector

sure to lubricate the O-rings with refrigerant oil before connecting the fittings.

13 Have the system evacuated, recharged and leak-tested by the qualified engineer who discharged it.

17 Evaporator matrix - removal and refitting

 Warning: Due to the potential dangers associated with the system, you are strongly advised to have any work on the air conditioning system carried out by a BMW dealer or air conditioning specialist. At the very least, DO NOT dismantle any part of the system (hoses, compressor, line fittings, etc.) until after the system has been discharged by a qualified engineer. Refer to the pre-cautions given at the start of Section 12.

Removal

1 Have the air conditioning system discharged (see **Warning** above).

2 Remove the trim panel on the sides of the centre console (see Chapter 11)

3 Disconnect the electrical lead and remove the evaporator sensor.

4 Remove the evaporator cover, exposing the refrigerant lines.

5 Disconnect the refrigerant lines from the evaporator matrix.

6 Remove the evaporator matrix from the case.

Refitting

7 Refitting is the reverse procedure of the removal.

8 Have the system evacuated, recharged and leak-tested by the qualified engineer who discharged it.

3

Notes

Chapter 4 Fuel and exhaust systems

Contents

4

Degrees of difficulty

Easy, suitable for novice with little experience	**Fairly easy,** suitable for beginner with some experience	**Fairly difficult,** suitable for competent DIY mechanic 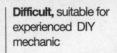	**Difficult,** suitable for experienced DIY mechanic	**Very difficult,** suitable for expert DIY or professional

Specifications

Carburettor (Solex 2B4)

Main jet
    Stage 1 . . . . X120
    Stage 2 . . . . X90
Air correction jet
    Stage 1 135
    Stage 2 75
Venturi diameter
    Stage 1 . . . . 24 mm
    Stage 2 . . . . 28 mm
Idle/air jet
    Stage 1 . . . . 50/120
    Stage 2 . . . . 40/125
Float needle valve diameter . . . . 2.0 mm
Choke gap (pulldown) . . . . 4.0 to 5.5 mm
Throttle positioner spring preload . . . . 22.0 to 24.0 mm
Float level
    Stage 1 float chamber . . . . 27.0 to 29.0 mm
    Stage 2 float chamber . . . . 29.0 to 31.0 mm

Carburettor (Solex 2BE)

Main jet	
Stage 1	X120
Stage 2	X110
Air correction jet	
Stage 1	140
Stage 2	70
Venturi diameter	
Stage 1	24 mm
Stage 2	28 mm
Idle fuel jet	
Stage 1	47.5 mm
Idle air jet	
Stage 2	180
Float needle valve diameter	2.0 mm
Throttle positioner coil resistance	0.97 to 1.63 ohms
Intake air temperature resistance	
-10° C	8200 to 10 500 ohms
20° C	2200 to 2700 ohms
80° C	300 to 360 ohms
Float level	
Stage 1 float chamber	27.0 to 29.0 mm
Stage 2 float chamber	29.0 to 31.0 mm

Fuel pressure checks (carburettor engines)

Fuel pump delivery pressure (engine idling)	0.1 to 0.3 bars

Fuel pressure checks (fuel injection engines)

Fuel system pressure (relative to intake manifold pressure)	
3-Series (E30)	
316i with M40/B16 engine	3.0 ± 0.06 bars
318i with M10/B18 engine	2.5 to 3.0 bars
318i with M40/B18 engine	3.0 ± 0.06 bars
320i with M20/B20 engine (L-Jetronic)	2.5 to 3.0 bars
320i with M20/B20 engine (Motronic)	2.5 ± 0.05 bars
325i with M20/B25 engine	3.0 ± 0.05 bars
5-Series (E28/"old-shape")	
All models	2.5 to 3.0 bars
5-Series (E34/"new-shape")	
518i with M40/B18 engine	3.0 ± 0.06 bars
All other models	2.5 to 3.0 bars
Fuel system hold pressure	2.1 bars
Fuel pump maximum pressure	6.3 to 6.9 bars
Fuel pump hold pressure	5.5 bars
Transfer pump pressure	0.28 to 0.35 bars

Injectors

Injector resistance	14.5 to 17.5 ohms

Accelerator cable free play
1.0 mm

Torque wrench settings

	Nm
Carburettor mountings	10
Fuel pump to cylinder head	12
Throttle body nuts/bolts	19 to 26

1 General information

With the exception of early models (316 and 518 models) all engines are equipped with electronic fuel injection.

Early 316 and 518 models are equipped with Solex carburettors. The carburettor fitted is either a Solex 2B4 (early models) or 2BE (later models). The mechanical fuel pump is driven by an eccentric lobe on the camshaft.

Fuel injection models are equipped with either the L-Jetronic or the Motronic fuel injection system. From 1988, fuel injection models are equipped with an updated version of the Motronic system - this system is easily distinguished from the earlier system by the absence of a cold start injector. The electric fuel pump is located beneath the rear of the vehicle, or inside the fuel tank. The fuel pump relay on Motronic systems is activated from a earth signal from the Motronic control unit (ECU). The fuel pump operates for a few seconds when the ignition is first switched on, and it continues to operate only when the engine is actually running.

Air intake system

The air intake system consists of the air filter housing, the airflow meter and throttle body (fuel injection models), and the intake manifold. All components except the intake manifold are covered in this Chapter; for information on removing and refitting the intake manifold, refer to Chapter 2A.

The throttle valve inside the throttle body or carburettor is actuated by the accelerator cable. When you depress the accelerator pedal, the throttle plate opens and airflow through the intake system increases.

On fuel injection systems, a flap inside the airflow meter opens wider as the airflow increases. A throttle position switch attached to the pivot shaft of the flap detects the angle of the flap (how much it's open) and converts this to a voltage signal, which it sends to the computer.

Fuel system

On carburettor models, the fuel pump supplies fuel under pressure to the carburettor. A needle valve in the float chamber maintains the fuel at a constant level. A fuel return system channels excess fuel back to the fuel tank.

On fuel injection models, an electric fuel pump supplies fuel under constant pressure to the fuel rail, which distributes fuel to the injectors. The electric fuel pump is located inside the fuel tank on later models, or beside the fuel tank on early models. Early models also have a transfer pump located in the fuel tank. The transfer pump acts as an aid to the larger main pump for delivering the necessary pressure. A fuel pressure regulator controls the pressure in the fuel system. The fuel system also has a fuel pulsation damper located near the fuel filter. The damper reduces the pressure pulsations caused by fuel pump operation, and the opening and closing of the injectors. The amount of fuel injected into the intake ports is precisely controlled by an Electronic Control Unit (ECU or computer). Some later 5-Series models have a fuel cooler in the return line.

Electronic control system (fuel injection system)

Besides altering the injector opening duration as described above, the electronic control unit performs a number of other tasks related to fuel and emissions control. It accomplishes these tasks by using data relayed to it by a wide array of information sensors located throughout the engine compartment, comparing this information to its stored map, and altering engine operation by controlling a number of different actuators. Since special equipment is required, most fault diagnosis and repair of the electronic control system is beyond the scope of the home mechanic. Additional information and testing procedures for the emissions system components (oxygen sensor, coolant temperature sensor, EVAP system, etc.) is contained in Chapter 6.

2 Fuel injection system - depressurising

Warning: Fuel is extremely *flammable, so take extra precautions when you work on any part of the fuel system. Don't smoke or allow open flames or bare light bulbs near the work area. Also, don't work in a garage where a natural gas-type appliance with a pilot light is present.*

1 Remove the fuel pump fuse from the main fuse panel **(see illustrations)**. Note: *Consult your owner's handbook for the exact location of the fuel pump fuse, if the information is not stamped onto the fusebox cover.*

2 Start the engine, and wait for it to stall. Switch off the ignition.

3 Remove the fuel filler cap to relieve the fuel tank pressure.

4 The fuel system is now depressurised. Note: *Place a rag around fuel lines before disconnecting, to prevent any residual fuel from spilling onto the engine* **(see illustration)**.

5 Disconnect the battery negative cable before working on any part of the system.

Caution: If the radio in your vehicle is equipped with an anti-theft system, make sure you have the correct activation code before disconnecting the battery. Refer to the information on page 0-7 at the front of this manual before detaching the cable.
Note: *If, after connecting the battery, the wrong language appears on the instrument panel display, refer to page 0-7 for the language resetting procedure.*

3 Fuel pump/fuel pressure - check

Warning: Fuel is extremely flammable, so take extra precautions when you work on any part of the fuel system. Don't smoke, or allow open flames or bare light bulbs, near the work area. Also, don't work in a garage where a natural gas-type appliance with a pilot light is present.

Carburettor engines

1 To test the fuel pump, it will be necessary to connect a suitable pressure gauge between the fuel pump outlet, and the carburettor supply pipe. For this particular test, the fuel return valve, which is normally connected in the fuel line from the fuel pump to the carburettor, *must* be bypassed.

2 With the engine running at idle speed, the pump pressure should be between 0.1 and 0.3 bars.

3 Should a pressure gauge not be available, a simpler (but less accurate) method of testing the fuel pump is as follows.

4 Disconnect the outlet hose from the fuel pump.

5 Disconnect the LT lead from the coil, to prevent the engine firing, then turn the engine over on the starter. Well-defined spurts of fuel should be ejected from the outlet hose.

Fuel injection engines

Note 1: *The electric fuel pump is located inside the fuel tank on later models, or beside the fuel tank on early models. Early models are also equipped with a transfer pump located in the fuel tank. The transfer pump feeds the main pump, but can't generate the high pressure required by the system.*
Note 2: *The fuel pump relay on Motronic systems is activated by an earth signal from the Motronic control unit (ECU). The fuel pump operates for a few seconds when the ignition is first switched on, and then continues to operate only when the engine is actually running.*

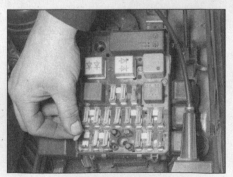

2.1a Removing the fuel pump fuse on 3-Series models

2.1b Removing the fuel pump fuse on 5-Series models

2.4 Be sure to place a rag under and around any fuel line when disconnecting

3.6a On L-Jetronic systems, use a jumper wire to bridge the terminals on the connector that correspond to the fuel pump relay pins 30 and 87b

3.6b On Motronic systems, use a jumper wire to bridge the terminals on the , connector that correspond to the fuel pump relay pins 30 and 87

3.6c On all 1989 and later models, remove the four bolts and the protective cover to gain access to the fuel pump relay and ECU . . .

Note 3: *The following checks assume the fuel filter is in good condition. If you doubt the condition of your fuel filter, renew it (see Chapter 1).*

Note 4: *In order to get accurate test results, it is recommended that the fuel pressure be checked from both the main fuel pump and transfer pump where applicable.*

Fuel pump/transfer pump operational check

6 Bridge the connector terminals that correspond to the fuel pump relay pins 30 and 87b (L-Jetronic systems) or 30 and 87 (Motronic systems) with a suitable jumper wire **(see illustrations)**.

7 Have an assistant switch the ignition on while you listen at the fuel tank. You should hear a whirring sound for a couple of seconds. **Note:** *This test applies to the transfer pump also. If there is no whirring sound, there is a problem in the fuel pump circuit. Check the fuel pump main fuse and relay first (see Chapter 12). If the main relay is OK, test the fuel pump relay.*

Fuel system pressure check

8 Depressurise the fuel system (see Section 2).
9 Detach the battery negative cable.

 Caution: If the radio in your vehicle is equipped with an anti-theft system, make sure you have the correct activation code

before disconnecting the battery. Refer to the information on page 0-7 at the front of this manual before detaching the cable.
Note: *If, after connecting the battery, the wrong language appears on the instrument panel display, refer to page 0-7 for the language resetting procedure.*

10 Detach the fuel feed line from the fuel rail on L-Jetronic **(see illustration)** and early Motronic systems, or from the fuel filter to the main fuel line on later Motronic systems.
11 Using a tee-piece (three-way fitting), a short section of high-pressure fuel hose and clamps, attach a fuel pressure gauge without disturbing normal fuel flow **(see illustration)**.

 Warning: Do not use a plastic tee fitting for this test. It won't be able to withstand the fuel system pressure.

12 Reconnect the battery.
13 Bridge the terminals of the fuel pump relay using a jumper wire.
14 Turn the ignition switch on.
15 Note the fuel pressure, and compare it with the pressure listed in this Chapter's Specifications.
16 If the system fuel pressure is less than specified:
a) Check the system for fuel leaks. Repair any leaks found, and recheck the fuel pressure.

b) If there are no leaks, fit a new fuel filter and recheck the fuel pressure.
c) If the pressure is still low, check the fuel pump pressure (see below) and the fuel pressure regulator (see Section 18).
17 If the pressure is higher than specified, check the fuel return line for an obstruction. If the line is not obstructed, renew the fuel pressure regulator.
18 Turn the ignition off, wait five minutes and look at the gauge. Compare the reading with the system hold pressure listed in this Chapter's Specifications. If the hold pressure is less than specified:
a) Check the system for fuel leaks. Repair any leaks found, and recheck the fuel pressure.
b) Check the fuel pump pressure (see below).
c) Check the fuel pressure regulator (see Section 18).
d) Check the injectors (see Section 20).

Fuel pump pressure check

 Warning: For this test, a fuel pressure gauge with a bleed valve will be needed, in order to relieve the high fuel pressure safely. After the test is completed, the normal procedure for depressurising will not work, because the gauge is connected directly to the fuel pump.

3.6d . . . then, use a jumper wire to bridge the terminals on the connector that correspond to fuel pump relay pins 30 and 87

3.10 Disconnect the fuel feed line (arrowed) from the fuel rail (L-Jetronic system shown) . . .

3.11 . . . and connect the gauge between the fuel feed line and the fuel rail using a tee-piece fitting

19 Depressurise the fuel system (see Section 2).

20 Detach the battery negative cable.

Caution: If the radio in your vehicle is equipped with an anti-theft system, make sure you have the correct activation code before disconnecting the battery. Refer to the information on page 0-7 at the front of this manual before detaching the cable.

Note: *If, after connecting the battery, the wrong language appears on the instrument panel display, refer to page 0-7 for the language resetting procedure.*

21 Detach the fuel feed hose from the fuel rail, and attach a fuel pressure gauge directly to the hose. **Note:** *If the tee fitting is still connected to the gauge, be sure to plug the open end.*

22 Reconnect the battery.

23 Using a jumper wire, bridge the terminals of the fuel pump relay.

24 Turn the ignition switch on to operate the fuel pump.

25 Note the pressure reading on the gauge, and compare the reading to the fuel pump pressure listed in this Chapter's Specifications.

26 If the indicated pressure is less than specified, inspect the fuel line for leaks between the pump and gauge. If no leaks are found, renew the fuel pump.

27 Turn the ignition off and wait five minutes. Note the reading on the gauge, and compare it to the fuel pump hold pressure listed in this Chapter's Specifications. If the hold pressure is less than specified, check the fuel lines between the pump and gauge for leaks. If no leaks are found, renew the fuel pump.

28 Remove the jumper wire. Relieve the fuel pressure by opening the bleed valve on the gauge and directing the fuel into a suitable container. Remove the gauge and reconnect the fuel line.

Transfer pump pressure check

29 Depressurise the fuel system (see Section 2).

30 Detach the battery negative cable.

Caution: If the radio in your vehicle is equipped with an anti-theft system, make sure you have the correct activation code before disconnecting the battery. Refer to the information on page 0-7 at the front of this manual before detaching the cable.

Note: *If, after connecting the battery, the wrong language appears on the instrument panel display, refer to page 0-7 for the language resetting procedure.*

31 Remove the transfer pump access plate (on some models, it's located under the rear seat cushion - on others, it's located under the carpet in the luggage compartment). Disconnect the output hose from the transfer pump, and connect a fuel pressure gauge to the outlet pipe.

32 Reconnect the battery.

33 Using a jumper wire, bridge the terminals of the fuel pump relay.

34 Turn the ignition switch on to operate the fuel pump.

35 Note the pressure reading on the gauge, and compare to the value listed in this Chapter's Specifications.

36 If the indicated pressure is less than specified, renew the transfer pump.

Fuel pump relay check

37 Switch on the ignition.

38 Using a voltmeter, probe the following terminals from the back of the relay electrical connector. Check for battery voltage at terminal 30 (M20 and M30 engines) or terminal 15 (M10 and M40 engines). **Note:** *If there is no voltage on models with luggage compartment-mounted batteries, check for a faulty fusible link. The 50-amp link is about 6 inches from the battery, in a black wire.*

39 Turn the ignition off, and disconnect the relay from the electrical connector. Using a voltmeter, probe the connector terminals that correspond to fuel pump relay pins 85 (-) and 86(+) on M20 and M30 engines, or terminal 50 and earth on M10 and M40 engines. Have an assistant turn the engine over on the starter, and observe the voltage reading. Battery voltage should be indicated.

40 If there is no voltage, check the fuse(s) and the wiring circuit for the fuel pump relay. If the voltage readings are correct, and the fuel pump only runs with the jumper wire in place, then renew the relay.

41 If the fuel pump still does not run, check for the proper voltage at the fuel pump terminals (see Section 4). If necessary, renew the fuel pump.

---

4 Fuel pump, transfer pump and fuel level sender unit - removal and refitting

Warning: Fuel is extremely flammable, so take extra precautions when you work on any part of the fuel system. Don't smoke, or allow open flames or bare light bulbs, near the work area. Also, don't work in a garage where a natural gas-type appliance with a pilot light is present.

Fuel pump (carburettor engines)

1 Disconnect the battery negative cable. Disconnect both hoses from the pump, and unscrew and remove the two securing nuts **(see illustration).**

2 Carefully withdraw the pump from the cylinder head. If it's stuck, a slight downward tap on the thick insulating distance piece with a piece of wood, should free it.

3 Remove the two thin gaskets.

4 The fuel pump is a sealed unit, and it is not possible to renew any of the internal components. Should an internal fault occur, it must be renewed complete.

4.1 Fuel pump on carburettor engines

5 Refitting is a reversal of the removal procedure, but renew the thin gaskets each side of the insulating distance piece, and tighten the fuel pump down evenly to the torque stated in the Specifications. On no account alter the thickness of the distance piece, or the correct operation of the fuel pump will be upset.

Fuel pump (fuel injection engines)

Note 1: *The electric fuel pump is located inside the fuel tank on later models with the Motronic system, or adjacent to the fuel tank on the L-Jetronic system. The early models are also equipped with a transfer pump located in the fuel tank. The transfer pump feeds the larger main pump, which delivers the high pressure required for proper fuel system operation.*

Note 2: *The fuel level sender unit is located in the fuel tank with the transfer pump on early models, or with the main fuel pump on later models.*

6 Depressurise the fuel system (see Section 2) and remove the fuel tank filler cap to relieve pressure in the tank.

7 Disconnect the battery negative cable.

Caution: If the radio in your vehicle is equipped with an anti-theft system, make sure you have the correct activation code before disconnecting the battery. Refer to the information on page 0-7 at the front of this manual before detaching the cable.

Note: *If, after connecting the battery, the wrong language appears on the instrument panel display, refer to page 0-7 for the language resetting procedure.*

Externally-mounted fuel pump

8 Raise and support the vehicle.

9 Remove the two rubber boots that protect the fuel pump connectors, and disconnect the wires from the pump **(see illustration).**

10 Using hose clamps, pinch shut the fuel hoses on each side of the fuel pump. If you don't have any hose clamps, wrap the hoses with rags, and clamp them shut with self-locking pliers, tightened just enough to prevent fuel from flowing out.

11 Disconnect the hoses from the pump.

12 Remove the fuel pump mounting screws

4

4.9 Lift up the rubber boots (arrowed) and detach the electrical connectors from the fuel pump

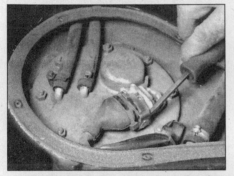

4.17b To unplug the connector, prise the bracket until the notch aligns with the slot on the retaining clip, and release the connector from the assembly

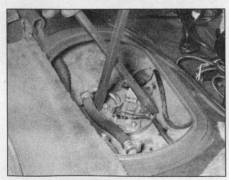

4.18a On models with locking lugs, use two screwdrivers to rotate the assembly out of the notches

4.18c On later Motronic systems, first remove the fuel level sender unit . . .

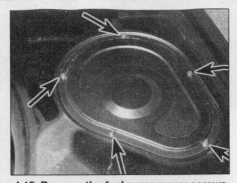

4.15 Remove the fuel pump cover screws (arrowed) and lift the cover off the floor of the vehicle (on some models, the fuel pump cover is located under the rear seat - on other models it's located in the luggage compartment)

and clamps, and remove the fuel pump from the under the vehicle.

13 Refitting is the reverse of removal.

In-tank fuel pump or transfer pump

14 On some models, access to the fuel pump is gained by removing the rear seat cushion. On other models, access is gained by removing the carpet from the luggage compartment.

15 Remove the screws from the fuel pump access cover **(see illustration)**.

16 Remove the cover.

17 Locate the fuel pump and sender unit electrical connectors **(see illustrations)** and

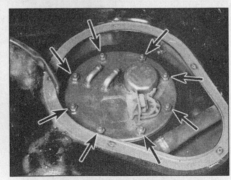

4.18b On models with mounting nuts, remove the nuts (arrowed) to release the assembly from the fuel tank

4.18d . . . then pull the fuel pump straight up and out of the turret at the bottom of the fuel tank (keep all the fuel lines intact)

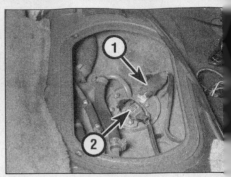

4.17a Transfer pump (1) and fuel level sender unit (2) electrical connectors on an early Motronic system

unplug them. Also, disconnect the fuel inlet and return lines.

18 On some models, the assembly must be rotated anti-clockwise to disengage the locking lugs from the fuel tank **(see illustration)**. On other models, the assembly is secured to the tank with nuts **(see illustration)**. Carefully lift the assembly from the fuel tank **(see illustrations)**. It may be necessary to twist the assembly slightly, to get the float to clear the opening.

19 On early models, remove the transfer pump mounting screws and clamps, and separate the transfer pump from the assembly.

20 Refitting is the reverse of removal. If the gasket between the fuel pump and fuel tank is dried, cracked or damaged, renew it.

Fuel level sender unit - check and renewal

21 Remove the main fuel pump or transfer pump (as described previously) along with the fuel level sender unit.

22 Connect an ohmmeter across the designated terminals, and check for the

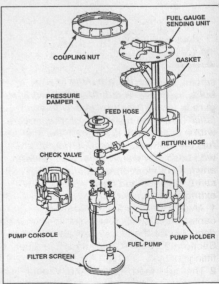

4.18e Exploded view of the fuel pump assembly on later Motronic systems

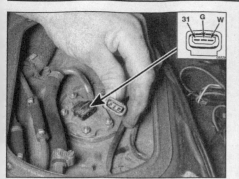

4.22a Fuel level sender unit terminal designations on L-Jetronic and early Motronic systems

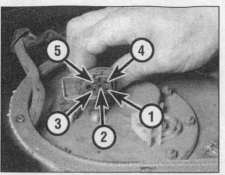

4.22b Fuel level sender unit terminal designations on later Motronic systems - check the sender unit resistance across terminals 1 and 3 of the connector

1 Fuel level sender unit earth
2 Warning light
3 Sender unit
4 Fuel pump earth
5 Fuel pump

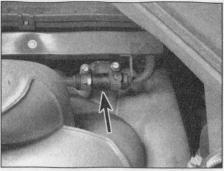

5.2 When checking the fuel lines, don't overlook these short sections of fuel hose attached to the main fuel rail - they're a common source of fuel leaks

correct resistance. On L-Jetronic and early Motronic systems, follow the table below. On later Motronic systems, connect the ohmmeter probes onto the fuel level sender unit terminals that correspond to pins 1 and 3 on the electrical connector (see illustrations). The resistance should decrease as the plunger rises.

L-Jetronic and early Motronic systems

Terminals	Float position	Resistance
G and 31	Slowly moving from the EMPTY position to the FULL position	Resistance slowly decreases
	EMPTY	71.7 ± 2.3 ohms
	FULL	3.2 ± 0.7 ohms
W and 31	EMPTY (low fuel warning)	Continuity

23 If the resistance readings are incorrect, renew the sender unit.
24 Refitting is the reverse of removal.

5 Fuel lines and fittings - repair and renewal

Warning: Fuel is extremely flammable, so take extra precautions when you work on any part of the fuel system. Don't smoke, or allow open flames or bare light bulbs, near the work area. Don't work in a garage where a natural gas-type appliance (such as a water heater or clothes dryer) with a pilot light is present. If you spill any fuel on your skin, rinse it off immediately with soap and water. When you perform any kind of work on the fuel system, wear safety glasses, and have a fire extinguisher on hand.

1 Always disconnect the battery negative cable, and (on fuel injection models) depressurise the fuel system as described in Section 2, before servicing fuel lines or fittings.
2 The fuel feed, return and vapour lines extend from the fuel tank to the engine compartment. The lines are secured to the underbody with clip and screw assemblies.

These lines must be occasionally inspected for leaks, kinks and dents (see illustration).
3 If evidence of dirt is found in the system or fuel filter during dismantling, the lines should be disconnected and blown out. On fuel injection models, check the fuel strainer on the in-tank fuel pump for damage and deterioration.
4 Because fuel lines used on fuel injection vehicles are under high pressure, they require special consideration. If renewal of a rigid fuel line or emission line is called for, use welded steel tubing meeting BMW specification or its equivalent. Don't use plastic, copper or aluminium tubing to renew steel tubing. These materials cannot withstand normal vehicle vibration.
5 When renewing fuel hoses, be sure to use only hoses of original-equipment standard.

6 Fuel tank - removal and refitting

Warning: Fuel is extremely flammable, so take extra precautions when you work on any part of the fuel system. Don't smoke, or allow open flames or bare light bulbs, near the work area. Also, don't work in a garage where a natural gas-type appliance with a pilot light is present. When you perform any kind of work on the fuel system, wear safety glasses, and have a fire extinguisher on hand. If you spill any fuel on your skin, clean it off immediately with soap and water.

Note: To avoid draining large amounts of fuel, make sure the fuel tank is nearly empty (if possible) before beginning this procedure.

1 Remove the fuel tank filler cap to relieve fuel tank pressure.

2 On fuel injection models, depressurise the fuel system (see Section 2).
3 Detach the battery negative cable.

Caution: If the radio in your vehicle is equipped with an anti-theft system, make sure you have the correct activation code before disconnecting the battery. Refer to the information on page 0-7 at the front of this manual before detaching the cable.
Note: If, after connecting the battery, the wrong language appears on the instrument panel display, refer to page 0-7 for the language resetting procedure.

4 Remove the tank drain plug (see illustration) and drain the fuel into an approved fuel container. If no drain plug is fitted, it should be possible to syphon the fuel out (not by mouth), otherwise the fuel will have to be drained during the removal operation.
5 Unplug the fuel pump/sender unit electrical connector (as applicable) and detach the fuel feed, return and vapour hoses (see Section 4). Where applicable, remove the rear seat cushion for access.
6 Remove the fuel tank shield (see illustration).
7 Detach the fuel filler neck and breather hoses.
8 Raise and support the vehicle. On some models, it will also be necessary to remove the exhaust system and propeller shaft.
9 Support the tank with a trolley jack.

6.4 Remove the tank drain plug (arrowed) and drain the fuel into a suitable container

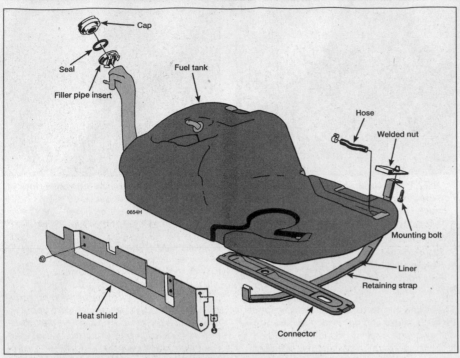

6.6 Exploded view of the fuel tank assembly on later 5-Series models

- Cap
- Seal
- Filler pipe insert
- Fuel tank
- Hose
- Welded nut
- Mounting bolt
- Liner
- Retaining strap
- Connector
- Heat shield

Position a block of wood between the jack head and the fuel tank to protect the tank.

10 Remove the mounting bolts at the corners of the fuel tank, and unbolt the retaining straps (see illustrations). Pivot the straps down until they're hanging out of the way.

11 Lower the tank just enough so you can see the top, and make sure you have detached everything. Finish lowering the tank, and remove it from the vehicle.

12 Refitting is the reverse of removal.

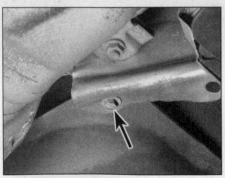

6.10a Remove the fuel tank mounting bolts (one arrowed)

6.10b Remove the retaining strap bolts (one arrowed) and lower the fuel tank

8.2a Release the air cleaner cover spring clips . . .

8.2b . . . then remove the air cleaner cover centre nut, and lift off the cover

7 Fuel tank cleaning and repair - general information

1 All repairs to the fuel tank or filler neck should be carried out by a professional who has experience in this critical and potentially dangerous work. Even after cleaning and flushing of the fuel system, explosive fumes can remain and ignite during repair of the tank.

2 If the fuel tank is removed from the vehicle, it should not be placed in an area where sparks or open flames could ignite the fumes coming out of the tank. Be especially careful inside garages where a natural gas-type appliance is located, because the pilot light could cause an explosion.

8 Air cleaner assembly - removal and refitting

1 Detach the battery negative cable. Caution: If the radio in your vehicle is equipped with an anti-theft system, make sure you have the correct activation code before disconnecting the battery. Refer to the information on page 0-7 at the front of this manual before detaching the cable. Note: If, after connecting the battery, the wrong language appears on the instrument panel display, refer to page 0-7 for the language resetting procedure.

Carburettor engines

2 Release the spring clips, then unscrew the centre nut and lift off the cover (see illustrations).

3 Remove the air filter element, and wipe clean the air cleaner body and cover (see illustration).

4 To remove the body, first disconnect the inlet duct and warm-air hose (see illustration).

5 Disconnect the vacuum line at the carburettor.

8.3 Remove the air cleaner element, and wipe clean the body and cover

8.4 Air cleaner inlet duct (1) and warm-air hose (2)

8.6a Unscrew the four air cleaner-to-carburettor nuts . . .

8.6b . . . and remove the metal ring

8.7 Air cleaner mounting bracket nut (arrowed)

8.8 Disconnecting the crankcase ventilation hose from the air cleaner

8.9 Align the air cleaner cover arrows when refitting

6 Unscrew the four nuts retaining the air cleaner to the carburettor, and remove the metal ring **(see illustrations)**.
7 Unscrew the nut from the mounting bracket **(see illustration)**.
8 Lift the air cleaner from the carburettor, and disconnect the crankcase ventilation hose **(see illustration)**. If necessary, prise the sealing ring from the bottom of the air cleaner.
9 Refitting is a reversal of removal, but align the arrow on the cover with the arrow on the inlet tube **(see illustration)**.

Fuel injection engines

10 Detach the air intake duct from the front side of the air cleaner.

8.14 Remove the two nuts (arrowed) from the air cleaner assembly (Motronic system shown), and lift it off its mountings

11 Detach the duct between the air cleaner and the throttle body.
12 Remove the air filter (see Chapter 1).
13 Unplug the electrical connector from the airflow meter (see Section 12).
14 Remove the air cleaner mounting bolts **(see illustration)** and lift the air cleaner assembly from the engine compartment.
15 Refitting is the reverse of removal. Ensure that all ducts are securely refitted, or air leaks will result.

9 **Accelerator cable** - check, adjustment and renewal

Check

1 Separate the air intake duct from the throttle body (fuel injection models) or remove the air cleaner (carburettor models).
2 Have an assistant depress the accelerator pedal to the floor while you watch the throttle valve. It should move to the fully-open position.
3 Release the accelerator pedal, and make sure the throttle valve returns smoothly to the fully-closed position. The throttle valve should not contact the body at any time during its movement; if it does, the unit must be renewed.

Adjustment

4 Warm the engine to normal operating temperature, then switch it off. Depress the

accelerator pedal to the floor twice, then check the cable free play at the carburettor/throttle body. Compare it to the value listed in this Chapter's Specifications.
5 If the free play isn't as specified, adjust it by turning the adjustment nut **(see illustration)**.
6 Have an assistant help you verify the throttle valve is fully open when the accelerator pedal is depressed to the floor.

Renewal

Note: *The following paragraphs describe the procedure for fuel injection engines - the procedure is similar on carburettor engines*
7 Disconnect the battery negative cable.

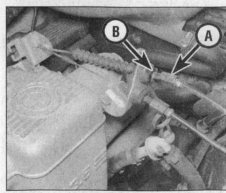

9.5 To adjust the accelerator cable free play, hold nut B stationary and turn nut A (fuel injection engine shown)

4

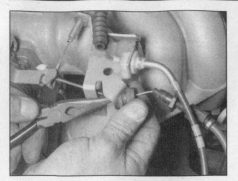

9.8 Push the rubber grommet from the rear, and separate the cable from the bracket

⚠️ *Caution: If the radio in your vehicle is equipped with an anti-theft system, make sure you have the correct activation code before disconnecting the battery. Refer to the information on page 0-7 at the front of this manual before detaching the cable.*

Note: *If, after connecting the battery, the wrong language appears on the instrument panel display, refer to page 0-7 for the language resetting procedure.*

8 Loosen the cable adjuster locknuts, and detach the cable from its support bracket located on the intake manifold **(see illustration)**.

9 Pinch the plastic retainer with a pair of needle-nose pliers, and push it out of the bracket **(see illustration)**.

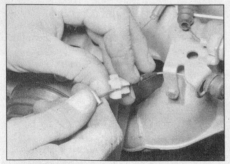

9.10b After the cable is off the throttle valve assembly, remove the plastic retainer from the cable

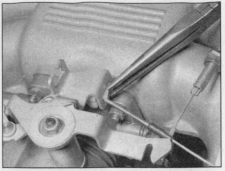

9.9 Pinch the plastic retainer, and push it through the bracket recess on the throttle valve

10 Pull the cable down through the slot and away from the bracket **(see illustrations)**.
11 Working from underneath the driver's side of the facia, reach up and detach the accelerator cable from the top of the pedal.
12 Pull the cable through the bulkhead, from the engine compartment side.
13 Refitting is the reverse of removal. Adjust the cable as described earlier.

10 Carburettor - general information

1 Early models are fitted with a Solex 2B4 carburettor, and later models are fitted with a Solex 2BE carburettor. Both carburettors are of downdraught, two-stage type. The first stage is operated mechanically by the accelerator pedal, and the second stage by vacuum control.
2 Each stage has its own float chamber, float assembly and needle valve, designed to reduce the effects of braking and centrifugal forces.
3 On the 2B4 version, the primary stage choke valve is operated by an automatic choke (a bi-metal spring which is electrically heated) during the warm-up period. Warm-up enrichment is also provided by a coolant-operated thermal valve and air temperature-controlled flow valve.
4 On the 2BE version, an electronic control

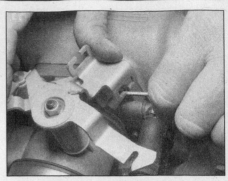

9.10a Rotate the throttle valve and remove the cable end from the slotted portion of the valve

unit is used to automatically adjust the carburettor settings during warm-up and normal temperature operation. The control unit is located beneath the right-hand side of the facia.

11 Carburettor - removal and refitting

Removal

1 Remove the air cleaner as described in Section 8.
2 Disconnect the accelerator cable from the carburettor with reference to Section 9.
3 On automatic transmission models, disconnect the kickdown cable.
4 Disconnect the wiring from the carburettor, noting the location of each wire.
5 Remove the screw, and disconnect the earth cable from the throttle positioner bracket **(see illustration)**.
6 Disconnect the vacuum hoses, noting that the hose with the white tracer is located on the white plastic 'T' piece, and the distributor vacuum hoses are located on the side of the carburettor **(see illustration)**.
7 On the 2B4 carburettor, disconnect and plug the coolant hoses from the TM (thermal starter) valve.
8 Disconnect the fuel supply hose **(see illustration)**.

11.5 Remove the screw, and disconnect the carburettor earth cable (arrowed)

11.6 Note the locations of the carburettor vacuum hoses (arrowed) before disconnecting them

11.8 Disconnect the fuel supply hose (arrowed)

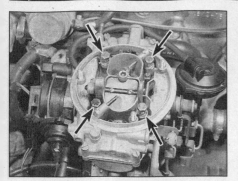

11.9 Unscrew the four bolts (arrowed) and lift the carburettor from the intake manifold

11.10 Carburettor insulating flange on the intake manifold can be removed if necessary

12.3 Using a screwdriver to disconnect the accelerator pump linkage (arrowed)

9 Unscrew the four bolts, and lift the carburettor from the insulating flange on the intake manifold **(see illustration)**.
10 If necessary, unscrew the nuts and remove the insulating flange from the intake manifold **(see illustration)**.

Refitting

11 Refitting is a reversal of removal, but clean the mating faces thoroughly. The insulating flange may be re-used, if it's in good condition. Adjust the accelerator cable with reference to Section 9, and the kickdown cable (where applicable) with reference to Chapter 7B.

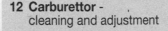

12 Carburettor - cleaning and adjustment

Note: *This Section describes the procedure for the 2B4 carburettor. The procedure for the 2BE carburettor is similar.*

Cleaning

1 Obtain a complete set of gaskets and seals for the carburettor.
2 Wash clean the exterior surfaces of the carburettor.

3 Using a screwdriver, prise the accelerator pump linkage from the primary throttle arm **(see illustration)**.
4 Unscrew the bolts securing the cover to the main body. An Allen key is necessary to remove the centre bolt **(see illustration)**.
5 Prise the link from the choke valve plastic lever **(see illustration)**.
6 Lift the cover from the main body, and remove the gasket **(see illustrations)**.
7 Remove the screw securing the throttle positioner bracket to the throttle housing **(see illustration)**.
8 Disconnect the vacuum unit pullrod from the secondary throttle lever **(see illustration)**.

12.4 Using an Allen key to remove the carburettor cover centre bolt

12.5 Prise the link (arrowed) from the choke valve plastic lever

12.6a Lifting the cover from the carburettor main body

12.6b View of the underside of the cover

12.6c View of the carburettor main body with the cover removed

12.7 Throttle positioner bracket-to-throttle housing screw (arrowed)

 4

12.8 Disconnecting the vacuum unit pullrod

12.9 Throttle housing-to-main body securing screws (arrowed)

12.10 Primary throttle lever securing nut - if removed, take care not to disturb the return spring

12.11a Throttle housing removed from the carburettor

12.11b Underside of the main body with throttle housing removed - note gasket

12.12a Tap out the float pivot pins, and remove the floats . . .

12.12b . . . then lift out the needle valves, keeping all components identified side for side

12.13a Unscrew the bypass jet from the secondary float chamber

12.13b Secondary main jet (1) and TM (thermal starter) fuel jet (2)

12.13c Secondary main jet (left) and TM fuel jet (right) tightened in the cover

12.13d Secondary bypass air jet (1), TM air jet (2), and air correction jet (3)

12.13e The jet positions in the cover (arrowed)

12.15a Choke linkage arm located in the automatic choke lever

12.15b To check the float level, measure the distance between the contact face and the top of the float

12.15c Accelerator pump seal (arrowed)

9 Remove the screws securing the throttle housing to the main body **(see illustration)**.
10 Prise out the intermediate throttle link. If this proves difficult, unscrew the nut and disconnect the lever from the primary throttle spindle, taking care not to disturb the return spring **(see illustration)**.
11 Separate the throttle housing from the main body, and remove the gasket **(see illustrations)**.
12 With the cover inverted, tap out the float pivot pins, remove the floats, and lift out the two needle valves - keeping all the components identified side for side **(see illustrations)**.
13 Unscrew the bypass fuel jet from the secondary float chamber, then similarly remove the jets from the cover - keeping them all identified for location **(see illustrations)**.
14 Clean all the components, and blow all the internal channels clear using low air pressure.
15 Reassembly is a reversal of dismantling, but note the following points:
a) Fit the new gaskets and seals supplied in the repair kit.
b) Before refitting the cover, check that the choke linkage arm is correctly located in the lever **(see illustration)**.
c) Check and if necessary adjust the float settings. Invert the cover, and check the

distance from the contact face (without gasket) to the top of the float, making sure that the needle valve spring-tensioned ball is not depressed **(see illustration)**. Note that the dimension is different for the primary and secondary floats (see Specifications). If adjustment is necessary, bend the float arm as required.
d) Make sure that the seal is fitted to the top of the accelerator pump **(see illustration)**.

Adjustment

Note: *Idle speed and mixture adjustments are covered in Chapter 1.*

Automatic choke (2B4)

16 Check that the automatic choke cover and housing alignment marks are clearly visible; if not, make new marks.
17 Remove the three screws and withdraw the metal ring **(see illustration)**.
18 Remove the plastic cover, at the same time disengaging the bi-metal spring from the control lever **(see illustration)**.
19 Fit a rubber band to the bottom of the control lever. Push the pulldown lever to the right and use a 4.2 mm diameter drill to check the distance between the lower edge of the choke valve and the wall of the carburettor

12.17 Remove the three screws and withdraw the metal ring

(see illustration). Alternatively apply vacuum to the pulldown unit to move the lever.
20 If adjustment is necessary, turn the screw on the end of the pulldown unit **(see illustration)**.
21 Refit the cover in reverse order, making sure that the alignment marks are in line.

Throttle positioner (2B4)

22 With the throttle in the idle position, check that the length of the spring on the throttle positioner is 23.0 ± 1.0 mm. If not, adjust the nut as required.
23 With no vacuum applied (engine stopped) check that the control travel, measured between the stop screw and lever, is 5.0 ± 0.5 mm. If necessary, loosen the locknut and turn the diaphragm rod as required. Tighten the locknut on completion.

12.18 Remove the automatic choke cover, at the same time disengaging the bi-metal spring from the control lever

12.19 Fit a rubber band (2) to the bottom of the control lever, then push the pulldown lever to the right, and use a 4.2 mm diameter drill (1) to check the distance between the lower edge of the choke valve and the wall of the carburettor

12.20 If adjustment is necessary, turn the screw (arrowed) on the end of the pulldown unit

Throttle positioner (2BE)

24 Special tools are required to carry out a comprehensive adjustment on the 2BE carburettor. This work should therefore be left to a BMW dealer.

13 Fuel injection - general information

The fuel injection system is composed of three basic sub-systems: fuel system, air intake system and electronic control system.

Fuel system

An electric fuel pump, located inside the fuel tank or beside the fuel tank, supplies fuel under constant pressure to the fuel rail, which distributes fuel evenly to all injectors. From the fuel rail, fuel is injected into the intake ports, just above the intake valves, by the fuel injectors. The amount of fuel supplied by the injectors is precisely controlled by an Electronic Control Unit (ECU). An additional injector, known as the cold start injector (L-Jetronic and early Motronic systems only), supplies extra fuel into the intake manifold for starting. A pressure regulator controls system pressure in relation to intake manifold vacuum. A fuel filter between the fuel pump and the fuel rail filters the fuel, to protect the components of the system.

Air intake system

The air intake system consists of an air filter housing, an airflow meter, a throttle body, the intake manifold, and the associated ducting. The airflow meter is an information-gathering device for the ECU. These models are equipped with the vane-type airflow meter. A potentiometer measures intake airflow, and a temperature sensor measures intake air temperature. This information helps the ECU determine the amount of fuel to be injected by the injectors (injection duration). The throttle plate inside the throttle body is controlled by the driver. As the throttle plate opens, the amount of air that can pass through the system increases, so the potentiometer opens further and the ECU signals the injectors to increase the amount of fuel delivered to the intake ports.

Electronic control system

The computer control system controls the fuel system and other systems by means of an Electronic Control Unit (ECU). The ECU receives signals from a number of information sensors which monitor such variables as intake air volume, intake air temperature, coolant temperature, engine rpm, acceleration/deceleration, and exhaust oxygen content. These signals help the ECU determine the injection duration necessary for the optimum air/fuel ratio. These sensors and their corresponding ECU-controlled output

actuators are located throughout the engine compartment. For further information regarding the ECU and its relationship to the engine electrical systems and ignition system, refer to Chapters 5 and 6.

Either an L-Jetronic system or a Motronic system is fitted. Later models have an updated version of the original Motronic system.

14 Fuel injection systems

L-Jetronic fuel injection system

The Bosch L-Jetronic fuel injection system is used on most 3-Series models up to 1987, and on most E28 ("old-shape") 5-Series models. It is an electronically-controlled fuel injection system that utilises one solenoid-operated fuel injector per cylinder. The system is governed by an Electronic Control Unit (ECU) which processes information sent by various sensors, and in turn precisely meters the fuel to the cylinders by adjusting the amount of time that the injectors are open.

An electric fuel pump delivers fuel under high pressure to the injectors, through the fuel feed line and an in-line filter. A pressure regulator keeps fuel available at an optimum pressure, allowing pressure to rise or fall depending on engine speed and load. Any excess fuel is returned to the fuel tank by a separate line.

A sensor in the air intake duct constantly measures the mass of the incoming air, and the ECU adjusts the fuel mixture to provide an optimum air/fuel ratio.

Other components incorporated in the system are the throttle valve (which controls airflow to the engine), the coolant temperature sensor, the throttle position switch, idle stabiliser valve (which bypasses air around the throttle plate to control idle speed) and associated relays and fuses.

Motronic fuel injection system

The Motronic system combines the fuel control of the L-Jetronic fuel injection system with the control of ignition timing, idle speed and emissions into one control unit.

The fuel injection and idle speed control functions are similar to those used on the L-Jetronic system described above. For more information on the Motronic system, see Chapter 6.

An oxygen sensor is mounted in the exhaust system on later models with a catalytic converter. This sensor continually reads the oxygen content of the exhaust gas. The information is used by the ECU to adjust the duration of injection, making it possible to adjust the fuel mixture for optimum converter efficiency and minimum emissions.

15 Fuel injection system - check

⚠ **Warning: Fuel is extremely flammable, so take extra precautions when you work on any part of the fuel system. Don't smoke, or allow open flames or bare light bulbs, near the work area. Don't work in a garage where a natural gas-type appliance (such as a water heater or clothes dryer) with a pilot light is present. If you spill any fuel on your skin, rinse it off immediately with soap and water. When you perform any kind of work on the fuel system, wear safety glasses, and have a fire extinguisher on hand.**

1 Check the earth wire connections. Check all wiring harness connectors that are related to the system. Loose connectors and poor earths can cause many problems that resemble more serious malfunctions.

2 Make sure the battery is fully charged, as the control unit and sensors depend on an accurate supply voltage in order to properly meter the fuel.

3 Check the air filter element - a dirty or partially-blocked filter will severely impede performance and economy (see Chapter 1).

4 If a blown fuse is found, renew it and see if it blows again. If it does, search for an earthed wire in the harness related to the system.

5 Check the air intake duct from the airflow meter to the intake manifold for leaks. Intake air leaks can cause a variety of problems. Also check the condition of the vacuum hoses connected to the intake manifold.

6 Remove the air intake duct from the throttle body, and check for dirt, carbon and other residue build-up. If it's dirty, clean it with carburettor cleaner and a toothbrush.

7 With the engine running, place a screwdriver or a stethoscope against each injector, one at a time, and listen for a clicking sound, indicating operation **(see illustration)**.

15.7 Use a stethoscope or screwdriver to determine if the injectors are working properly - they should make a steady clicking sound that rises and falls with engine speed changes

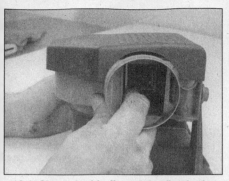

16.1 Check for binding of the flap in the airflow meter as it nears closing position or wide-open position. Any hesitation or binding will cause erratic idle conditions, rich fuel mixture or poor acceleration and throttle response (airflow meter removed for clarity)

8 Check the fuel system pressure (see Section 3).

9 If these checks do not locate the problem, take the vehicle to a BMW dealer, who will be able to read the fault codes stored in the ECU, using special equipment.

16 Airflow meter - check, removal and refitting

Check (L-Jetronic systems)

1 Remove the duct from the intake end of the airflow meter. Carefully open and close the sensor flap **(see illustration)**, and check for binding. The flap can bend during a backfire, and cause incorrect resistance readings. The flap will bind and stick in a partially-open position, causing the engine to run rich, and stall when it returns to idle.

2 Disconnect the electrical connector from the airflow meter.

3 Using an ohmmeter, check the resistance

16.3 Connect an ohmmeter to terminals 7 and 8 of the airflow meter, and check for a smooth change in resistance as the vane door of the airflow meter is slowly opened and closed

between terminals 7 and 8 **(see illustration)**. The resistance should increase steadily (without any "flat spots") as the sensor flap is slowly moved from the fully-closed position to the fully-open position.

4 Also, check the intake air temperature sensor (inside the airflow meter). Using an ohmmeter, probe terminals 8 and 9 **(see illustration 16.3)** and check for the proper resistance. The resistance should be 2200 to 2700 ohms at 20° C.

5 If the resistance readings are correct, check the wiring harness (see Chapter 12). Plug in the connector to the airflow meter. Ensure that the ignition is switched off. Disconnect the electrical connector from the ECU (located under the right-hand side of the facia) and probe terminals 7 and 8 **(see illustration)** with an ohmmeter. Carefully move the door of the airflow meter, and observe the change in resistance as it moves from closed to fully-open. The test results should be the same as paragraph 3. If there are any differences in the test results, there may be a shorted-out or broken wire in the harness.

Check (Motronic systems)

6 Ensure that the ignition is switched off.

16.5 The ECU is located under the right-hand side of the facia. Unplug the electrical connector, and check the resistance between terminals 7 and 8 as in paragraph 3. The test results should be the same.

Remove the ECU access cover (see Chapter 6) and disconnect the harness connector **(see illustration)**.

7 Using an ohmmeter, probe the designated terminals of the ECU electrical connector **(see illustrations)** and check for the proper change in resistance while moving the sensor flap. On early Motronic systems, probe terminals 7 and 9. On later Motronic systems, probe terminals 7 and 12. The resistance should increase steadily (without any "flat spots") as the sensor flap is slowly moved from the fully-closed position to the fully-open position. **Note:** *Early Motronic systems are distinguishable by the 35-pin ECU electrical connector; later Motronic systems use a 55-pin connector.*

8 If the resistance readings are incorrect, check the wiring harness.

Removal and refitting (all systems)

9 Disconnect the electrical connector from the airflow meter.

10 Remove the air cleaner assembly (see Section 8).

11 Remove the nuts **(see illustrations)**, and lift the airflow meter from the engine compartment or from the air cleaner assembly.

12 Refitting is the reverse of removal.

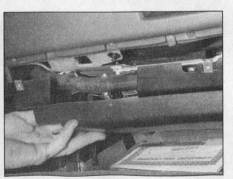

16.6 Remove the under-facia panel to gain access to the ECU on Motronic systems (left-hand-drive model shown)

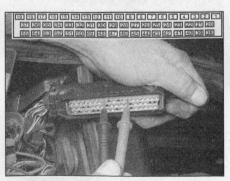

16.7a Connect the ohmmeter probes to terminals 7 and 12 (later Motronic systems) of the ECU connector and check for a smooth change in resistance as the door on the airflow meter is slowly opened and closed

16.7b Unplug the connector, connect the ohmmeter probes to terminals 7 and 9 (early Motronic systems) and check for a smooth change in resistance as the door on the airflow meter is slowly opened and closed

4

16.11a Push the tab and remove the air duct from inside the air cleaner assembly

16.11b Remove the nuts (arrowed) from the air cleaner housing, and detach the airflow meter

17.11 Remove the nuts (arrowed) and lift the throttle body from the intake manifold (the two lower bolts are hidden from view)

17 Throttle body - check, removal and refitting

Check

1 Detach the air intake duct from the throttle body (see Section 8) and move the duct out of the way.
2 Have an assistant depress the throttle pedal while you watch the throttle valve. Check that the throttle valve moves smoothly when the throttle is moved from closed (idle position) to fully-open (wide-open throttle).
3 If the throttle valve is not working properly, renew the throttle body unit.

⚠️ *Warning: Wait until the engine is completely cool before beginning this procedure.*

⚠️ *Caution: If the radio in your vehicle is equipped with an anti-theft system, make sure you have the correct activation code before disconnecting the battery. Refer to the information on page 0-7 at the front of this manual before detaching the cable.*
Note: *If, after connecting the battery, the wrong language appears on the instrument panel display, refer to page 0-7 for the language resetting procedure.*

Removal and refitting

4 Detach the battery negative cable.
5 Detach the air intake duct from the throttle body, and place to one side.
6 Detach the accelerator cable from the throttle body (see Section 9).
7 Detach the cruise control cable, if applicable.
8 Clearly label all electrical connectors (throttle position sensor, cold start injector, idle air stabiliser, etc), then unplug them.
9 Clearly label all vacuum hoses, then detach them.
10 Unscrew the radiator or expansion tank cap to relieve any residual pressure in the cooling system, then refit it. Clamp shut the coolant hoses, then loosen the hose clamps and detach the hoses. Be prepared for some coolant leakage.

11 Remove the throttle body mounting nuts (upper) and bolts (lower), and detach the throttle body from the air intake plenum **(see illustration)**.
12 Cover the air intake plenum opening with a clean cloth, to prevent dust or dirt from entering while the throttle body is removed.
13 Refitting is the reverse of removal. Be sure to tighten the throttle body mounting nuts to the torque listed in this Chapter's Specifications, and adjust the throttle cable (see Section 9) on completion.

18 Fuel pressure regulator - check and renewal

⚠️ *Warning: Fuel is extremely flammable, so take extra precautions when you work on any part of the fuel system. Don't smoke, or allow open flames or bare light bulbs, near the work area. Don't work in a garage where a natural gas-type appliance (such as a water heater or clothes dryer) with a pilot light is present. If you spill any fuel on your skin, rinse it off immediately with soap and water. When you perform any kind of work on the fuel system, wear safety glasses, and have a fire extinguisher on hand.*

⚠️ *Caution: If the radio in your vehicle is equipped with an anti-theft system, make sure you have the correct activation code before disconnecting the battery. Refer to the information on page 0-7 at the front of this manual before detaching the cable.*
Note: *If, after connecting the battery, the wrong language appears on the instrument panel display, refer to page 0-7 for the language resetting procedure.*

Check

1 Depressurise the fuel system (see Section 2).
2 Detach the battery negative cable.
3 Disconnect the fuel line and connect a fuel pressure gauge (see Section 3). Reconnect the battery.

4 Pressurise the fuel system (refit the fuel pump fuse and switch on the ignition), and check for leakage around the gauge connections.
5 Connect a vacuum pump to the fuel pressure regulator **(see illustration)**.
6 Run the fuel pump (see Section 3). Read the fuel pressure gauge with vacuum applied to the pressure regulator, and also with no vacuum applied. The fuel pressure should decrease as vacuum increases.
7 Stop the fuel pump and reconnect the vacuum hose to the regulator. Start the engine and check the fuel system pressure at idle, comparing your reading with the value listed in this Chapter's Specifications. Disconnect the vacuum hose and watch the gauge - the pressure should jump up to maximum as soon as the hose is disconnected.
8 If the fuel pressure is low, pinch the fuel return line shut and watch the gauge. If the pressure doesn't rise, the fuel pump is defective, or there is a restriction in the fuel feed line. If the pressure now rises sharply, renew the pressure regulator.
9 If the indicated fuel pressure is too high, stop the engine, disconnect the fuel return line and blow through it to check for a blockage. If there is no blockage, renew the fuel pressure regulator.
10 If the pressure doesn't fluctuate as described in paragraph 7, connect a vacuum

18.5 Carefully watch the fuel pressure gauge as vacuum is applied (fuel pressure should decrease as vacuum increases)

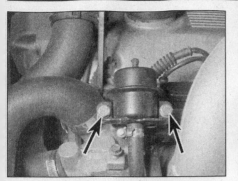

18.15 Remove the two bolts (arrowed) and remove the fuel pressure regulator from the fuel rail

19.1 Cold start injector electrical connector (arrowed) on the M10 engine. Most cold start injectors are mounted in the intake manifold

19.2 Watch for a steady, conical-shaped spray of fuel when the starter motor is operated

gauge to the pressure regulator vacuum hose, and check for vacuum (engine idling).

11 If there is vacuum present, renew the fuel pressure regulator.

12 If there isn't any reading on the gauge, check the hose and its port for a leak or a restriction.

Renewal

13 Depressurise the fuel system (see Section 2).

14 Detach the battery negative cable.

⚠️ *Caution: If the radio in your vehicle is equipped with an anti-theft system, make sure you have the correct activation code before disconnecting the battery. Refer to the information on page 0-7 at the front of this manual before detaching the cable.*
Note: *If, after connecting the battery, the wrong language appears on the instrument panel display, refer to page 0-7 for the language resetting procedure.*

15 Detach the vacuum hose and fuel return hose from the pressure regulator, then unscrew the mounting bolts **(see illustration)**.

16 Remove the pressure regulator.

17 Refitting is the reverse of removal. Be sure to use a new O-ring. Coat the O-ring with a light film of engine oil prior to refitting.

18 Check for fuel leaks after refitting the pressure regulator.

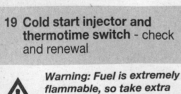

19 Cold start injector and thermotime switch - check and renewal

⚠️ *Warning: Fuel is extremely flammable, so take extra precautions when you work on any part of the fuel system. Don't smoke, or allow open flames or bare light bulbs, near the work area. Don't work in a garage where a natural gas-type appliance (such as a water heater or clothes dryer) with a pilot light is present. If you spill any fuel on your skin, rinse it off immediately with soap and water. When you perform*

any kind of work on the fuel system, wear safety glasses, and have a fire extinguisher on hand.

Check

Cold start injector

1 The engine coolant should be below 30°C for this check. Preferably, the engine should have been switched off for several hours. Disconnect the electrical connector from the cold start injector **(see illustration)** and move it aside, away from the work area - there will be fuel vapour present. Remove the two screws holding the injector to the air intake plenum, and take the injector out. The fuel line must be left connected. Wipe the injector nozzle. Disable the ignition system by detaching the coil wire from the centre terminal of the distributor cap, and earthing it on the engine block with a jumper wire. Run the fuel pump for 1 minute by bridging the appropriate relay terminals (see Section 3). There must be no fuel dripping from the nozzle. If there is, the injector is faulty and must be renewed. Switch off the ignition and remake the original fuel pump relay connections.

2 Now direct the nozzle of the injector into a can or jar. Reconnect the electrical connector to the injector. Have an assistant switch on the ignition and operate the starter. The injector should squirt a conical-shaped spray

into the jar **(see illustration)**. If the spray pattern is good, the injector is working properly. If the spray pattern is irregular, the injector is fouled or damaged, and should be cleaned or renewed.

3 If the cold start injector does not spray any fuel, check for a voltage signal at the electrical connector for the cold start injector when the starter motor is operated **(see illustration)**. If there is no voltage, check the thermotime switch.

Thermotime switch

4 The thermotime switch detects the temperature of the engine, and controls the action of the cold start injector. It is usually located up front, near the coolant temperature sensor. The engine coolant should be below 30°C for this check. Preferably, the engine should have been switched off for several hours. Disable the ignition system by detaching the coil wire from the centre terminal of the distributor cap, and earthing it on the engine block with a jumper wire. Pull back the rubber boot from the thermotime switch **(see illustration)** and probe the black/yellow wire connector terminal with a voltmeter.

5 Have an assistant switch on the ignition and operate the starter. The voltmeter should register a voltage signal the moment the starter engages. This signal should last approximately 6 to 10 seconds, depending on the temperature of the engine.

19.3 Check for a voltage signal (about 12 volts) at the cold start injector connector when the starter motor is operated

19.4 Check for a voltage signal on the black/yellow wire of the thermotime switch when the ignition is on

4

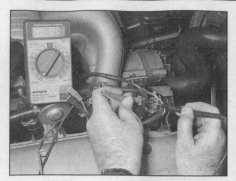

19.6 Check the resistance of the thermotime switch with the engine coolant temperature below 30° C. There should be continuity

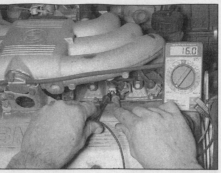

20.5 Check the resistance of each of the fuel injectors

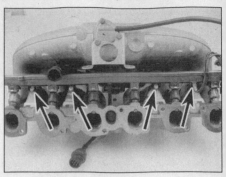

20.8 Remove the bolts (arrowed) and separate the fuel rail and injectors from the intake manifold

6 If the voltage is correct, unplug the electrical connector and, using an ohmmeter, check for continuity between the terminals of the thermotime switch **(see illustration)**. Continuity should exist.

7 Reconnect the coil lead, start the engine and warm it up above 41°C. When the engine is warm, there should be no continuity between the terminals. If there is, the switch is faulty and must be renewed. **Note:** *On 5-Series models, there are several types of thermotime switch. Each one is stamped with an opening temperature and maximum duration.*

Renewal

Cold start injector

8 Depressurise the fuel system (see Section 2).

9 Disconnect the electrical connector from the cold start injector.

10 Where applicable, using a ring spanner or deep socket, remove the fuel line fitting connected to the cold start injector. On other models, simply loosen the hose clamp and detach the hose from the injector.

11 Remove the cold start injector securing bolts, and remove the injector.

12 Refitting is the reverse of removal. Clean the mating surfaces, and use a new gasket.

Thermotime switch

⚠ *Warning: Wait until the engine is completely cool before beginning this procedure. Also, remove the cap from the expansion tank or radiator to relieve any residual pressure in the cooling system.*

13 Prepare the new thermotime switch for fitting by applying a light coat of thread sealant to the threads.

14 Disconnect the electrical connector from the old thermotime switch.

15 Using a deep socket, or a ring spanner, unscrew the switch. Once the switch is removed coolant will start to leak out, so insert the new switch as quickly as possible. Tighten the switch securely, and plug in the electrical connector.

20 Fuel injectors - check and renewal

⚠ *Warning: Fuel is extremely flammable, so take extra precautions when you work on any part of the fuel system. Don't smoke, or allow open flames or bare light bulbs, near the work area. Don't work in a garage where a natural gas-type appliance (such as a water heater or clothes dryer) with a pilot light is present. If you spill any fuel on your skin, rinse it off immediately with soap and water. When you perform any kind of work on the fuel system, wear safety glasses, and have a fire extinguisher on hand.*

Check

In-vehicle check

1 Using a mechanic's stethoscope (available at most car accessory shops), check for a clicking sound at each of the injectors while the engine is idling **(see illustration 15.7)**.

 HAYNES HINT *If you don't have a mechanic's stethoscope, a screwdriver can be used to check for a clicking sound at the injectors. Place the tip of the screwdriver against the injector, and press your ear against the handle.*

2 The injectors should make a steady clicking sound if they are operating properly.

3 Increase the engine speed above 3500 rpm. The frequency of the clicking sound should rise with engine speed.

4 If an injector isn't functioning (not clicking), purchase a special injector test light (a car accessory shop or fuel injection specialist may be able to help) and connect it to the injector electrical connector. Start the engine and make sure the light flashes. If it does, the injector is receiving the proper voltage, so the injector itself must be faulty.

5 Unplug each injector connector, and check

the resistance of the injector **(see illustration)**. Check your readings with the values listed in this Chapter's Specifications. Renew any that do not give the correct resistance reading.

Volume test

6 Because a special injection checker is required to test injector volume, this procedure is beyond the scope of the home mechanic. Have the injector volume test performed by a BMW dealer or other specialist.

Renewal

7 Unplug the main electrical connector for the fuel injector wiring harness. Remove the intake manifold (see Chapter 2A).

8 Detach the fuel hoses from the fuel rail, and remove the fuel rail mounting bolts **(see illustration)**.

9 Lift the fuel rail/injector assembly from the intake manifold.

10 Unplug the electrical connectors from the fuel injectors. Detach the injectors from the fuel rail.

11 Refitting is the reverse of removal. Be sure to renew all O-rings. Coat the O-rings with a light film of engine oil to prevent damage during refitting. Pressurise the fuel system (refit the fuel pump fuse and switch on the ignition) and check for leaks before starting the engine.

21 Idle air stabiliser valve - check, adjustment and renewal

1 The idle air stabiliser system works to maintain engine idle speed within a 200 rpm range, regardless of varying engine loads at idle. An electrically-operated valve allows a small amount of air to bypass the throttle plate, to raise the idle speed whenever the idle speed drops below approximately 750 rpm. If the idle speed rises above approximately 950 rpm, the idle air stabiliser valve closes and stops extra air from bypassing the throttle plate, reducing the idle speed.

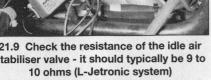

21.9 Check the resistance of the idle air stabiliser valve - it should typically be 9 to 10 ohms (L-Jetronic system)

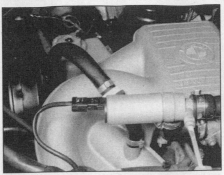

21.19 Location of the adjustment screw on the metal-type idle air stabiliser valve (L-Jetronic system)

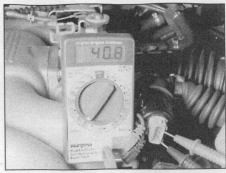

21.21 Check the idle air stabiliser valve resistance on the two outer terminals on later Motronic systems - it should be about 40 ohms

2 L-Jetronic systems are equipped with a separate idle speed control unit (computer) located under the facia. The idle air stabiliser valve has an adjusting screw. Early models are equipped with plastic valves, but they still can be adjusted by removing the hose and inserting a very thin screwdriver inside.

3 Early Motronic systems are also equipped with a separate idle speed control unit (computer) located under the facia. The idle air stabiliser valve has an adjusting screw.

4 On later Motronic systems, the idle air stabiliser valve is ECU-controlled, and no provision is made for adjustment.

Preliminary check

5 Before performing any checks on the idle air stabiliser valve, make sure these criteria are met:

a) *The engine must be at operating temperature (60ºC)*
b) *Turn off all electrical accessories (air conditioning, heater controls, headlights, auxiliary cooling fan, etc)*
c) *The throttle position sensor must be operating correctly (see Chapter 6)*
d) *There must not be any exhaust leaks*
e) *There must not be any vacuum leaks*
f) *Where fitted, the oxygen sensor must be operating properly (see Chapter 6)*

6 Connect a tachometer in accordance with the manufacturer's instructions.

 Caution: The ignition must be switched off before making any electrical connections.

7 The idle air stabiliser valve operates continuously when the ignition is on. Start the engine and make sure the valve is vibrating and humming slightly.

L-Jetronic system

Check

8 With the engine running, disconnect the electrical connector from the valve. The idle speed should increase to about 2,000 rpm.

9 If the idle speed does not increase, turn the engine off. Using an ohmmeter, check the resistance across the terminals of the valve

(see illustration). It should be 9 to 10 ohms with the ambient air temperature at about 20° C.

10 Using a pair of jumper wires, apply battery voltage to the valve, and confirm that the valve closes tightly. When the voltage is removed, the valve should re-open.

11 If the idle air stabiliser valve fails any of the tests, renew it.

12 If the idle air stabiliser valve passes the tests, check the control current.

13 Unplug the electrical connector from the valve. Using a jumper wire, connect one terminal of the electrical connector to one of the terminals on the valve, Connect an ammeter (0 to 1000 mA range) between the other terminal on the electrical connector and the remaining terminal on the valve. Start the engine and allow it to idle. With the engine running, the current reading should be between 400 and 500 mA. Adjust the valve if the current reading is not as specified (see paragraph 15). **Note**: *The idle air stabiliser current will fluctuate between 400 and 1100 mA if the engine is too cold, if the coolant temperature sensor is faulty, if the idle speed needs to be adjusted, if there is an engine vacuum leak or if electrical accessories are on.*

14 If there is no current reading, have the idle speed control unit diagnosed by a BMW dealer or other specialist. **Note**: *The idle air stabiliser control unit (located under the facia) can develop an electrical connector problem that intermittently turns the valve on and off. Check the connector very carefully before fitting any new parts. Sometimes, a new control unit will only fix the problem temporarily.*

Adjustment

15 With the ignition switched off, connect a tachometer in accordance with the equipment manufacturer's instructions.

16 Make sure the ignition timing is correct (see Chapter 5).

17 Connect an ammeter to the valve (see paragraph 13).

18 With the engine running, the current reading should be 450 to 470 mA at 850 to

900 rpm (manual transmission), or 460 to 480 mA at 850 to 900 rpm (automatic transmission).

19 If the control current is not correct, turn the adjusting screw until it is within the correct range **(see illustration)**. **Note**: *On metal-type valves, the adjusting screw is mounted externally. On plastic-type valves, the adjustment screw is inside, and can be reached by removing the hose at the end of the valve.*

Motronic systems

Check

Note: *There are two types of idle air stabiliser valve on these systems; early models usually have a two-wire valve, while later models are equipped with a three-wire valve.*

20 With the engine running, disconnect the electrical connector from the valve. The idle speed should increase to about 2000 rpm.

21 If the idle speed does not increase:

a) *Two-wire valve - Using a pair of jumper wires, apply battery voltage to the valve, and confirm that the valve closes tightly. When the voltage is removed, the valve should re-open. Also, check the resistance of the valve (see illustration 21.9). The resistance should be about 9 or 10 ohms.*
b) *Three-wire valve - Turn the engine off and unplug the electrical connector from the valve. Using an ohmmeter, check the resistance on the two outer terminals of the valve. (see illustration). It should be about 40 ohms. Check the resistance on the centre and outside terminals of the valve. They should both be about 20 ohms.*

22 If the idle air stabiliser valve fails any of the tests, renew it.

23 If the idle air stabiliser valve tests are all correct, check the control current (two-wire valve) or the voltage (three-wire valve) as follows.

24 On two-wire valves, connect an ammeter (0 to 1000 mA range) as described in paragraph 13. Start the engine, and allow it to idle. With the engine running, the current

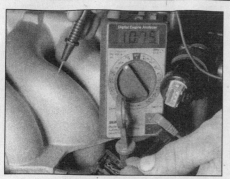

21.26 Check for battery voltage on the centre terminal

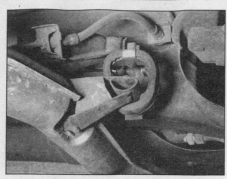

22.1 A typical exhaust system rubber mounting

reading should be between 400 and 500 mA. Adjust the valve if the current reading is not as specified. **Note**: *The idle air stabiliser current will fluctuate between 400 and 1100 mA if the engine is too cold, if the coolant temperature sensor is faulty, if there is an engine vacuum leak, or if electrical accessories are on.*

25 If there is no current reading, have the idle speed control unit (under the facia) checked by a BMW dealer or other specialist.

26 On three-wire valves, check for voltage at the electrical connector. With the ignition on, there should be battery voltage present at the centre terminal **(see illustration)**. There should be about 10 volts between the centre terminal and each of the outer terminals.

27 If there is no voltage reading, have the idle speed control unit (early models) or the ECU (later models) checked by a dealer service department or other specialist.

Adjustment (early models only)

28 With the ignition switched off, connect a tachometer in accordance with the equipment manufacturer's instructions.

29 Make sure the ignition timing is correct (see Chapter 5).

30 Connect an ammeter to the valve as described in paragraph 13.

31 With the engine running, the current draw should be 450 to 470 mA at 700 to 750 rpm.

32 If the control current is not correct, turn the adjusting screw until it is within the specified range. **Note**: *Turn the idle air bypass screw clockwise to increase the current, or anti-clockwise to decrease the current.*

Renewal

33 Remove the electrical connector and the bracket from the idle air stabiliser valve. Remove the valve, disconnecting the hoses.

34 Refitting is the reverse of removal.

22 Exhaust system servicing - general information

 Warning: Inspect or repair exhaust system components only when the system is completely cool. When working under the vehicle, make sure it is securely supported.

Silencer and pipes

1 The exhaust system consists of the exhaust manifold, catalytic converter, silencers, and all connecting pipes, brackets, mountings **(see illustration)** and clamps. The exhaust system is attached to the body with brackets and rubber mountings. If any of the parts are improperly fitted, excessive noise and vibration may be transmitted to the body.

2 Inspect the exhaust system regularly. Look for any damaged or bent parts, open seams, holes, loose connections, excessive corrosion, or other defects which could allow exhaust fumes to enter the vehicle. Generally, deteriorated exhaust system components cannot be satisfactorily repaired; they should be renewed.

3 If the exhaust system components are extremely corroded or rusted together, it may be necessary to cut off the old components with a hacksaw. Be sure to wear safety goggles to protect your eyes from metal chips, and wear work gloves to protect your hands.

4 Here are some simple guidelines to follow when repairing the exhaust system:

a) *Work from the back to the front of the vehicle when removing exhaust system components.*

b) *Apply penetrating oil to the exhaust system nuts and bolts to make them easier to remove.*

c) *Use new gaskets, mountings and clamps when fitting exhaust system components.*

d) *Apply anti-seize compound to the threads of all exhaust system nuts and bolts during reassembly.*

e) *Be sure to allow sufficient clearance between newly-fitted parts and all points on the underbody, to avoid overheating the floorpan, and possibly damaging the interior carpet and insulation. Pay particularly close attention to the catalytic converters and heat shields. Also, make sure that the exhaust will not come into contact with suspension parts, etc.*

Catalytic converter

5 Although the catalytic converter is an emissions-related component, it is discussed here because, physically, it's an integral part of the exhaust system. Always check the converter whenever you raise the vehicle to inspect or service the exhaust system.

6 Raise and support the vehicle.

7 Inspect the catalytic converter for cracks or damage.

8 Check the converter connections for tightness.

9 Check the insulation covers welded onto the catalytic converter for damage or a loose fit.

 Caution: If an insulation cover is dented so that it touches the converter housing inside, excessive heat may be transferred to the floor.

10 Start the engine and run it at idle speed. Check all converter connections for exhaust gas leakage.

Fuel injection system - fault finding

L-Jetronic fuel injection system

Engine difficult to start, or fails to start (when cold)

Probable cause	Corrective action
Cold start injector or thermotime switch faulty	Test cold start injector and thermotime switch. Renew faulty components (see Section 19)
Fuel pump inoperative	Check fuel pump fuse and fuel pump relay (see Sections 3 and 4)
Airflow meter flap (door) binding or stuck in open position	Inspect the airflow meter for damage (see Section 16)
Fuel pressure incorrect	Test system pressure (see Section 3). Test fuel pressure regulator (Section 18)
Intake air leaks	Inspect all vacuum lines, air ducts, and oil filler and dipstick seals
Fuel injectors clogged or not operating	Check fuel injectors (see Section 20) and wiring harness
Coolant temperature sensor faulty or wiring problem	Test coolant temperature sensor (see Chapter 6, Section 4)
Throttle position sensor (TPS) incorrectly adjusted	Check TPS adjustment (see Chapter 6, Section 4)
Incorrect ignition timing	Check ignition timing (see Chapter 5). Check vacuum advance system
Dirt or other contaminants in fuel	Check the fuel and drain the tank if necessary
Faulty ECU	Have the ECU tested at a dealer service department or other specialist

Engine difficult to start, or fails to start (when warm)

Probable cause	Corrective action
Cold start injector leaking or operating continuously	Test cold start injector and thermotime switch (see Section 19)
Fuel pressure incorrect	Test fuel pump(s). Renew if necessary (see Section 3)
Insufficient residual fuel pressure	Test residual fuel pressure. Renew fuel pump or fuel accumulator as necessary (see Section 18)
Fuel leak(s)	Inspect fuel lines and fuel injectors for leaks. Correct leaks as required (see Chapter 4)
Coolant temperature sensor faulty or wiring problem	Test coolant temperature sensor (see Chapter 6, Section 4)
Vapour lock (warm weather)	Check fuel pressure (see Section 3)
EVAP system faulty (where applicable)	Check EVAP system (see Chapter 6, Section 6)
Incorrect ignition timing	Check ignition timing (see Chapter 5). Check vacuum advance system
Faulty ECU	Have the ECU tested at a dealer service department or other specialist
Idle speed control system faulty	Test the idle air stabiliser valve (see Section 21)

Engine misses and hesitates under load

Probable cause	Corrective action
Fuel injector clogged or faulty	Test fuel injectors. Check for clogged injector lines. Renew faulty injectors (see Section 20)
Fuel pressure incorrect	Test fuel system pressure (see Section 3). Test fuel pressure regulator (see Section 18)
Fuel leak(s)	Inspect fuel lines and fuel injectors for leaks (see Chapter 4)
Engine maintenance	Tune-up engine (see Chapter 1). Check the distributor cap, rotor, HT leads and spark plugs, and renew any faulty components
Airflow meter flap (door) binding, or stuck in open position	Inspect the airflow meter for damage (see Section 16)
Intake air leaks	Inspect all vacuum lines, air ducts and oil filler and dipstick seals

Engine has erratic idle speed

Probable cause	Corrective action
Idle air stabiliser valve faulty	Check the idle air stabiliser valve (see Section 21)
No power to the idle air stabiliser valve	Check the idle air stabiliser relay and wiring circuit (see Chapter 12)
Vacuum advance system faulty	Check vacuum advance system and electronic vacuum advance relay
Idle speed control unit faulty	Have the idle speed control unit checked by a dealer

Motronic fuel injection system

Note: *With this system, when faults occur, the ECU stores a fault code in its memory. These codes can only be read by a BMW dealer, as specialised equipment is required. It may save time to have at least the initial fault diagnosis carried out by a dealer.*

Lack of power

Probable cause	Corrective action
Coolant temperature sensor faulty, or wire to sensor broken	Test coolant temperature sensor and wiring. Repair wiring or renew sensor if faulty (see Chapter 6)
Fuel pressure incorrect	Check fuel pressure from main pump and transfer pump, as applicable (see Section 3)
Throttle plate not opening fully	Check accelerator cable adjustment to make sure throttle is opening fully. Adjust cable if necessary (see Section 9)

4

Engine difficult to start, or fails to start (when cold)

Probable cause	Corrective action
Cold start injector or thermotime switch faulty (early Motronic system only)	Test cold start injector and thermotime switch. Renew faulty components (see Section 19)
Fuel pump not running	Check fuel pump fuse and fuel pump relay (see Sections 2 and 3)
Airflow meter flap (door) binding, or stuck in open position	Inspect the airflow meter for damage (see Section 16)
Fuel pressure incorrect	Test system pressure (see Section 3)
Intake air leaks	Inspect all vacuum lines, air ducts and oil filler and dipstick seals
Fuel injectors clogged or not operating	Check fuel injectors (see Section 20) and wiring harness
Coolant temperature sensor faulty or wiring problem	Test coolant temperature sensor (see Chapter 6, Section 4)
TPS (throttle position sensor) incorrectly adjusted	Check TPS adjustment (see Chapter 6, Section 4)
Dirt or other contaminants in fuel	Check the fuel and drain the tank if necessary
Faulty ECU	Have the ECU tested at a dealer service department or other specialist
Crankshaft position signal missing	Faulty position sensor or flywheel, or reference pin missing (see Chapter 5)

Engine difficult to start, or fails to start (when warm)

Probable cause	Corrective action
Cold start injector leaking or operating continuously (early Motronic system only)	Test cold start injector and thermotime switch (see Section 19)
Fuel pressure incorrect	Test fuel pressure (see Section 3)
Insufficient residual fuel pressure	Test fuel system hold pressure (see Section 3)
Fuel leak(s)	Inspect fuel lines and fuel injectors for leaks. Correct leaks as necessary
Coolant temperature sensor faulty or wiring problem	Test coolant temperature sensor (see Chapter 6, Section 4)
Vapour lock (in warm weather)	Check fuel pressure (see Section 3)
EVAP system faulty	Check EVAP system (see Chapter 6, Section 6)
Faulty ECU	Have the ECU tested at a dealer service department or other specialist
Idle speed control system faulty	Test the idle air stabiliser valve (see Section 21)
Oxygen sensor faulty (where applicable)	Check the oxygen sensor (see Chapter 6, Section 4)

Engine misses and hesitates under load

Probable cause	Corrective action
Fuel injector clogged	Test fuel injectors. Check for clogged injector lines. Renew faulty injectors (see Section 20)
Fuel pressure incorrect	Test fuel system pressure (see Section 3). Test fuel pressure regulator (see Section 18)
Fuel leak(s)	Inspect fuel lines and fuel injectors for leaks (see Chapter 4)
Engine maintenance	Tune-up engine (see Chapter 1). Check the distributor cap, rotor, HT leads and spark plugs, and renew any faulty components
Airflow meter flap (door) binding, or stuck in open position	Inspect the airflow meter for damage (see Section 16)
Intake air leaks	Inspect all vacuum lines, air ducts, and oil filler and dipstick seals
Throttle position sensor (TPS) incorrectly adjusted	Check TPS adjustment (see Chapter 6)

Engine idles too fast

Probable cause	Corrective action
Accelerator pedal, cable or throttle valve binding	Check for worn or broken components, kinked cable, or other damage. Renew faulty components
Air leaking past throttle valve	Inspect throttle valve, and adjust or renew as required

Engine has erratic idle speed

Probable cause	Corrective action
Idle air stabiliser valve faulty	Check the idle air stabiliser valve (see Section 21)
No power to the idle air stabiliser valve	Check the idle air stabiliser relay and wiring circuit (see Chapter 12)
Idle speed control unit faulty	Have the idle speed control unit checked by a dealer

Poor fuel economy

Probable cause	Corrective action
Cold start injector leaking (early Motronic system only)	Test and, if necessary, renew cold start injector (see Section 19)
Oxygen sensor faulty (where applicable)	Test the oxygen sensor (see Chapter 6, Section 4))
Sticking handbrake/binding brakes	Check the handbrake/braking system (see Chapter 9)
Tyre pressures low	Check tyre pressures (Chapter 1)

Chapter 5 Engine electrical systems

Contents

Degrees of difficulty

Easy, suitable for novice with little experience	Fairly easy, suitable for beginner with some experience	Fairly difficult, suitable for competent DIY mechanic	Difficult, suitable for experienced DIY mechanic	Very difficult, suitable for expert DIY or professional

Specifications

General
Application
  Models with carburettor or L-Jetronic fuel injection .... Transistorised Coil Ignition (TCI) system
  Models with Motronic fuel injection .... Ignition functions controlled by Motronic system

Ignition coil
Primary resistance
  TCI system .... 0.82 ohms
  Motronic system .... 0.50 ohms
Secondary resistance
  TCI system .... 8250 ohms
  Motronic system .... 5000 to 6000 ohms

Distributor (models with TCI system)
Air gap .... 0.3 mm to 0.7 mm
Pick-up coil/impulse generator resistance .... 900 to 1200 ohms

Ignition timing (models with TCI system)
(Vacuum line disconnected at distributor)
316 with M10/B18 engine .... 25° BTDC at 2500 rpm (2900 rpm from 9/83)
318i with M10/B18 engine .... 30° BTDC at 3000 rpm
320i with M20/B20 engine .... 23° BTDC at 5000 ±50 rpm
518 with M10/B18 engine .... 25° BTDC at 2900 ±50 rpm
518i with M10/B18 engine .... 30° BTDC at 3000 ±50 rpm
520i with M20/B20 engine .... 23° BTDC at 5000 rpm
525i with M30/B25 engine (except distributor
  237 302 033) .... 22° BTDC at 1800 ±50 rpm
525i with M30/B25 engine (distributor 237 302 033) .... 22° BTDC at 2150 ±50 rpm
528i with M30/B28 engine .... 22° BTDC at 2150 ±50 rpm

5

1 General information

The engine electrical systems include all ignition, charging and starting components. Because of their engine-related functions, these components are discussed separately from body-related electrical devices such as the lights, the instruments, etc. (which are included in Chapter 12).

Always observe the following precautions when working on the electrical systems:

a) *Be extremely careful when servicing engine electrical components. They are easily damaged if improperly checked, connected or handled.*

b) *Never leave the ignition switched on for long periods of time with the engine off.*

c) *Don't disconnect the battery cables while the engine is running.*

d) *Observe the rules when jump-starting your vehicle. Read the precautions at the front of this manual.*

e) *Always disconnect the battery negative cable first, and connect it last, to reduce the risk of accidental short-circuits.*

f) *Don't charge the battery with the cables connected to the terminals.*

It's also a good idea to review the safety-related information regarding the engine electrical systems in the *"Safety first"* section near the front of this manual before beginning any operation included in this Chapter.

⚠ **Caution: If the radio in your vehicle is equipped with an anti-theft system, make sure you have the correct activation code before disconnecting the battery. Refer to the information on page 0-7 at the front of this manual before detaching the cable.**
Note: *If, after connecting the battery, the wrong language appears on the instrument panel display, refer to page 0-7 for the language resetting procedure.*

2 Battery - emergency jump starting

Refer to the *"Jump starting"* procedure at the front of this manual.

3 Battery - removal and refitting

Note: *Depending on the model, the battery may be located in the engine compartment, in the rear luggage compartment, or under the rear seat. Consult your owners handbook for the location of the battery, if not already known to you.*

⚠ **Caution: If the radio in your vehicle is equipped with an anti-theft system, make sure you have the correct activation code before disconnecting the battery. Refer to the information on page 0-7 at the front of this manual before detaching the cable.**
Note: *If, after connecting the battery, the wrong language appears on the instrument panel display, refer to page 0-7 for the language resetting procedure.*

1 Disconnect the battery negative cable.
2 Detach the cable from the positive terminal.
3 Remove the battery hold-down bracket **(see illustrations)** and lift out the battery. Be careful - it's heavy. Do not tilt the battery to any extent while it is being removed, and store it upright.
4 While the battery is out, inspect the carrier (tray) for corrosion (see Chapter 1).
5 If you are renewing the battery, make sure that you get one that's identical, with the same dimensions, amperage rating, cold cranking rating, etc.
6 Refitting is the reverse of removal.

4 Battery cables - check and renewal

Check

1 Periodically inspect the entire length of each battery cable for damage, cracked or burned insulation, and corrosion. Poor battery cable connections can cause starting problems and decreased engine performance.

⚠ **Caution: If the radio in your vehicle is equipped with an anti-theft system, make sure you have the correct activation code before disconnecting the battery. Refer to the information on page 0-7 at the front of this manual before detaching the cable.**
Note: *If, after connecting the battery, the wrong language appears on the instrument panel display, refer to page 0-7 for the language resetting procedure.*

3.3a Always detach the cable from the battery negative terminal first, then detach the positive cable – to remove the hold-down assembly, remove the nuts (arrowed) or single bolt

2 Check the cable-to-terminal connections at the ends of the cables for cracks, loose wire strands, and corrosion. The presence of white, fluffy deposits under the insulation at the cable terminal connection is a sign that the cable is corroded, and should be cleaned or renewed. Check the terminals for distortion, missing mounting bolts, and corrosion.

Renewal

3 When removing the cables, always disconnect the negative cable first and connect it up last. This reduces the risk of accidental short-circuits. Even if only a new positive cable is being fitted, be sure to disconnect the negative cable from the battery first (see Chapter 1 for further information regarding battery cable removal).
4 Disconnect the old cables from the battery, then trace each of them to their opposite ends and detach them from the starter solenoid and earth terminals. Note the routing of each cable to ensure correct refitting.
5 If the old cables are to be renewed, take them with you when buying new cables. It is vitally important that you renew the cables with identical parts. Cables have characteristics that make them easy to identify: positive cables are usually red, larger in cross-section, and have a larger-diameter battery post clamp; earth cables are usually black, smaller in cross-section, and have a slightly smaller diameter clamp for the negative post.
6 Clean the threads of the solenoid or earth connection with a wire brush to remove rust and corrosion.

> **HAYNES HiNT** *Apply a light coat of battery terminal corrosion inhibitor, or petroleum jelly, to the terminal threads, to prevent future corrosion.*

7 Attach the cable to the solenoid or earth connection, and tighten the mounting nut/bolt securely.
8 Before connecting a new cable to the battery, make sure that it reaches the battery post without having to be stretched.
9 Connect the positive cable first, followed by the negative cable.

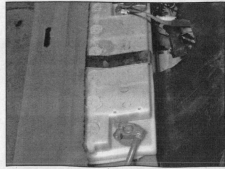

3.3b The battery is mounted under the rear seat on some models

5 Ignition system - general information and precautions

The ignition system includes the ignition switch, the battery, the distributor, the primary (low-voltage/low-tension or LT) and secondary (high-voltage/high-tension or HT) wiring circuits, the spark plugs and the spark plug leads. Models fitted with a carburettor or L-Jetronic fuel injection are equipped with a Transistorised Coil Ignition (TCI) system. Models fitted with the Motronic fuel injection system have the ignition system incorporated within the Motronic system (Digital Motor Electronics or DME).

Transistorised Coil Ignition (TCI) system

This system is has four major components; the impulse generator, the ignition control unit, the coil, and the spark plugs. The impulse generator provides a timing signal for the ignition system. Equivalent to cam-actuated breaker points in a standard distributor, the impulse generator creates an A/C voltage signal every time the trigger wheel tabs pass the impulse generator tabs. When the ignition control unit (capacitive discharge unit) receives the voltage signal, it triggers a spark discharge from the coil by interrupting the primary coil circuit. The ignition dwell (coil charging time) is adjusted by the ignition control unit for the most intense spark. **Note:** *The air gap (distance between the impulse generator and trigger wheel tabs) can be adjusted (see Section 11).*

Ignition timing is mechanically adjusted (see Section 7). A centrifugal advance unit that consists of spring-loaded rotating weights advances ignition timing as engine speed increases. The vacuum advance adjusts ignition timing to compensate for changes in engine load.

Motronic ignition system

This system, also known as Digital Motor Electronics (DME), incorporates all ignition and fuel injection functions into one central control unit or ECU (computer). The ignition timing is based on inputs the ECU receives for engine load, engine speed, coolant temperature and intake air temperature. The only function the distributor performs is the distribution of the high voltage signal to the individual spark plugs. The distributor is attached directly to the cylinder head. There is no mechanical spark advance system used on these systems.

Ignition timing is electronically-controlled, and is not adjustable on Motronic systems. During starting, a crankshaft position sensor (reference sensor) relays the crankshaft position to the ECU, and an initial baseline ignition point is determined. Once the engine

is running, the ignition timing is continually changing, based on the various input signals to the ECU. Engine speed is signalled by a speed sensor. Early Motronic systems have the position reference sensor and the speed sensor mounted on the bellhousing over the flywheel on the left-hand side. Later Motronic systems have a single sensor (pulse sensor) mounted over the crankshaft pulley. This sensor functions as a speed sensor as well as a position reference sensor. Refer to Section 12 for checking and renewing the ignition sensors. **Note:** *Some models are equipped with a TDC sensor mounted on the front of the engine. This sensor is strictly for the BMW service test unit, and it is not part of the Motronic ignition system.*

Precautions

Certain precautions must be observed when working on a transistorised ignition system.
a) *Do not disconnect the battery cables when the engine is running*
b) *Make sure the ignition control unit (TCI ignition system) is always well earthed (see Section 10).*
c) *Keep water away from the distributor and HT leads.*
d) *If a tachometer is to be connected to the engine, always connect the tachometer positive (+) lead to the ignition coil negative terminal (-) and never to the distributor.*
e) *Do not allow the coil terminals to be earthed, as the impulse generator or coil could be damaged.*
f) *Do not leave the ignition switch on for more than ten minutes with the engine off, or if the engine will not start.*

6 Ignition system - check

Warning: Because of the high voltage generated by the ignition system, extreme care should be taken whenever an operation is performed involving ignition components. This not only includes the impulse generator (electronic ignition), coil, distributor and spark plug HT leads, but related components such as spark plug connectors, tachometer and other test equipment.

1 If the engine turns over but will not start, disconnect the spark plug HT lead from any spark plug, and attach it to a calibrated spark tester (available at most car accessory shops).
Note: *There are two different types of spark testers. Be sure to specify electronic (breakerless) ignition. Connect the clip on the*

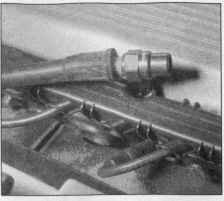

6.1 To use a spark tester, simply disconnect a spark plug HT lead, clip the tester to a convenient earth (like a valve cover bolt or nut) and operate the starter – if there is enough power to fire the plug, sparks will be visible between the electrode tip and the tester body

tester to an earth point such as a metal bracket **(see illustration).**
2 If you are unable to obtain a calibrated spark tester, remove the spark plug HT lead from one of the spark plugs. Using an insulated tool, hold the lead about a quarter-inch from the engine block - make sure the gap is not more than a quarter-inch, or damage may be caused to the electronic components.
3 Crank the engine, and observe the tip of the tester or spark plug HT lead to see if a spark occurs. If bright-blue, well-defined sparks occur, sufficient voltage is reaching the plugs to fire the engine. However, the plugs themselves may be fouled, so remove and check them as described in Chapter 1.
4 If there's no spark, check another HT lead in the same manner. A few sparks followed by no spark is the same condition as no spark at all.
5 If no spark occurs, remove the distributor cap, and check the cap and rotor as described in Chapter 1. If moisture is present, use a water-dispersant aerosol (or something similar) to dry out the cap and rotor, then refit the cap and repeat the spark test.
6 If there's still no spark, disconnect the coil HT lead from the distributor cap, and test this lead as described for the spark plug leads.
7 If no spark occurs, check the primary wire connections at the coil to make sure they're clean and tight. Make any necessary repairs, then repeat the check.
8 If sparks do occur from the coil HT lead, the distributor cap, rotor, plug HT lead(s) or spark plug(s) may be defective. If there's still no spark, the coil-to-cap HT lead may be defective. If a substitute lead doesn't make any difference, check the ignition coil (see Section 9). **Note:** *Refer to Sections 10 and 11 for more test procedures on the distributors fitted with the TCI ignition system.*

5

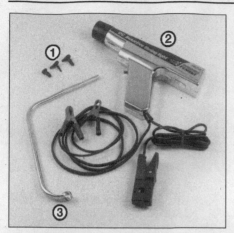

7.1 Tools for checking and adjusting the ignition timing

1 **Vacuum plugs** - *Vacuum hoses will, in most cases, have to be disconnected and plugged. Moulded plugs in various shapes and sizes can be used for this, if wished*

2 **Inductive pick-up timing light** - *Flashes a bright, concentrated beam of light when No 1 spark plug fires. Connect the leads according to the instructions supplied with the light*

3 **Distributor spanner** - *On some models, the hold-down bolt for the distributor is difficult to reach and turn with conventional spanners or sockets. A special spanner like this must be used*

7 Ignition timing (TCI system) - check and adjustment

⚠ **Warning: Keep hands, equipment and wires well clear of the viscous cooling fan during adjustment of the ignition timing.**

Note: *This Section describes the procedure for checking and adjusting the ignition timing on engines fitted with the TCI system. On engines fitted with the Motronic engine management system, the ignition timing is controlled by the electronic control unit, and no adjustment is possible. The timing can be checked using the following procedure, but no ignition timing values were available at the time of writing. If the timing is thought to be incorrect, refer to a BMW dealer.*

1 Some special tools are required for this procedure **(see illustration)**. The engine must be at normal operating temperature, and the air conditioning (where fitted) must be switched off. Make sure the idle speed is correct.

2 Apply the handbrake, and chock the wheels to prevent movement of the vehicle. The transmission must be in neutral (manual) or Park (automatic).

3 The timing marks are located on the engine flywheel (viewed through the timing check

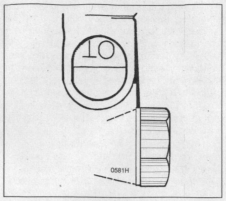

7.9a Flywheel "OT" timing mark

hole in the bellhousing) and/or on the vibration damper on the front of the engine.

4 Where applicable, disconnect the vacuum hose from the distributor vacuum advance unit.

5 Connect a tachometer and timing light according to the equipment manufacturer's instructions (an inductive pick-up timing light is preferred). Generally, the power leads for the timing light are attached to the battery terminals, and the pick-up lead is attached to the No 1 spark plug HT lead. The No 1 spark plug is the one at the front of the engine.

⚠ **Caution: If an inductive pick-up timing light isn't available, don't puncture the spark plug HT lead to attach the timing light pick-up lead. Instead, use an adapter between the spark plug and HT lead. If the insulation on the HT lead is damaged, the secondary voltage will jump to earth at the damaged point, and the engine will misfire.**

Note: *On some models, a TDC transmitter is fitted for checking the ignition system. However, a special BMW tester must be connected to the diagnostic socket to use it, so unless the special tester is available, a conventional timing light should be used. The ignition timing mark may be on the vibration damper, but if not, normally the TDC mark will be. If the timing light is of the adjustable delay type, then the ignition timing may be determined by zeroing the adjustment, then turning the adjustment until the TDC marks are aligned, and then reading off the amount of advance from the timing light. If a standard timing light is being used, make a mark on the vibration damper in accordance with the specified advance, using the following formula to calculate the distance from the TDC mark to the timing mark:*

$$\text{Distance} = \frac{2Pr \times advance}{360}$$

where $P = 3.142$

   r = radius of vibration damper
   advance = specified advance
                BTDC in degrees

6 With the ignition off, loosen the distributor clamp nut just enough to allow the distributor to pivot without any slipping.

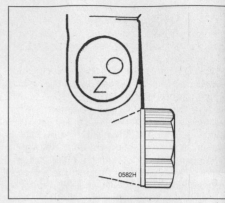

7.9b Flywheel "OZ" timing mark

7 Make sure the timing light wires are routed away from the drivebelts and fan, then start the engine.

8 Raise the engine rpm to the specified speed, and then point the flashing timing light at the timing marks - be very careful of moving engine components.

9 The mark on the flywheel or vibration damper will appear stationary. If it's aligned with the specified point on the bellhousing or engine front cover, the ignition timing is correct **(see illustrations)**.

10 If the marks aren't aligned, adjustment is required. Turn the distributor very slowly until the marks are aligned, taking care not to touch the HT leads.

11 Tighten the nut on the distributor clamp, and recheck the timing.

12 Switch off the engine, and remove the timing light and tachometer. Reconnect the vacuum hose where applicable.

8 Distributor - removal and refitting

TCI system

Removal

1 After carefully marking them for position, remove the coil HT lead and spark plug HT leads from the distributor cap (see Chapter 1).

2 Remove No 1 spark plug (the one nearest you when you are standing in front of the engine).

3 Manually rotate the engine to Top Dead Centre (TDC) on the compression stroke for No 1 piston (see Chapter 2A)

4 Carefully mark the vacuum hoses, if more than one is present on your distributor.

5 Disconnect the vacuum hose(s).

6 Disconnect the primary circuit wires from the distributor.

7 Mark the relationship of the rotor tip to the distributor housing **(see illustration)**. Also mark the relationship of the distributor housing to the engine.

8.7 Mark the relationship of the rotor to the distributor housing (arrowed)

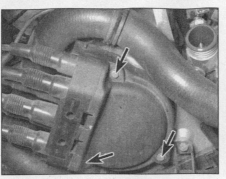

8.18 Remove the three bolts (arrowed) from the distributor cap

8.19 Remove the rotor screws (arrowed) with an Allen key, and pull the rotor off the shaft

8 Remove the hold-down nut or bolt and clamp.

9 Remove the distributor. **Note:** *Do not rotate the engine with the distributor out.*

Refitting

10 Before refitting the distributor, make certain No 1 piston is still at TDC on the compression stroke.

11 Insert the distributor into the engine, with the adjusting clamp centred over the hold-down hole. Make allowance for the gear to turn as the distributor is inserted.

12 Refit the hold-down nut or bolt. The marks previously made on the distributor housing, and on the rotor and engine, should line up before the nut or bolt is tightened.

13 Refit the distributor cap.

14 Connect the wiring for the distributor.

15 Reconnect the spark plug HT leads.

16 Reconnect the vacuum hoses as previously marked.

17 Check the ignition timing (see Section 7).

Motronic system

Removal

18 Remove the cover from the distributor **(see illustration)** and remove the distributor cap (see Chapter 1).

19 Using a small Allen key, remove the three screws from the rotor **(see illustration)**.

20 Remove the rotor.

Refitting

21 Refitting is the reverse of removal.

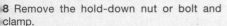

9 Ignition coil - check and renewal

Caution: Do not earth the coil, as the coil and/or impulse generator could be damaged.

Note: *On models equipped with the Motronic system, a faulty ECU can cause the ignition coil to become damaged. Be sure to test the ignition coil if the engine will not start and an ECU fault is suspected.*

1 Mark the wires and terminals for position, then remove the primary circuit wires and the HT lead from the coil.

9.4a Using an ohmmeter, measure the resistance between the primary terminals of the ignition coil (TCI system shown)

2 Remove the coil assembly from its mounting, then clean the outer casing and check it for cracks and other damage.

3 Inspect the coil primary terminals and the coil tower terminal for corrosion. Clean them with a wire brush if any corrosion is found.

4 Check the coil primary resistance by attaching an ohmmeter to the primary terminals **(see illustrations)**. Compare the measured resistance to the Specifications listed in this Chapter.

5 Check the coil secondary resistance by connecting one of the ohmmeter leads to one of the primary terminals, and the other ohmmeter lead to the coil high-tension terminal **(see illustrations)**. On TCI systems,

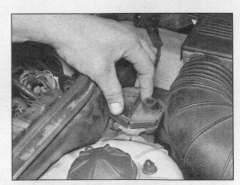

9.4b Some Motronic systems use a different type of coil. First, remove the coil cover and . . .

9.4c . . . using an ohmmeter, measure the resistance between the primary terminals of the coil

9.5a Using an ohmmeter, measure the secondary resistance of the coil (TCI system)

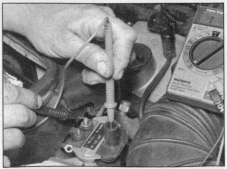

9.5b Using an ohmmeter, measure the secondary resistance of the coil (later Motronic system)

5

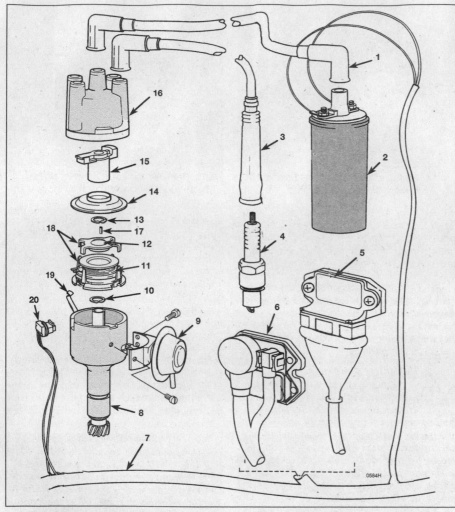

10.1 Schematic of the ignition components used on engines with the TCI system

1 Coil HT lead	8 Distributor housing with	15 Ignition rotor
2 Ignition coil	centrifugal advance	16 Distributor
3 Spark plug HT lead	counterweights	17 Roll pin
4 Spark plug	9 Vacuum diaphragm	18 Trigger wheel and impulse
5 Ignition control unit (Bosch)	10 Circlip	generator tabs
6 Ignition control unit	11 Impulse generator	19 Cap retaining clip
(Siemens/Telefunken)	12 Trigger wheel	20 Impulse generator
7 Wiring harness	13 Circlip	connector
	14 Dust shield	

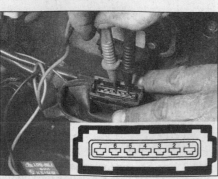

10.2a Check for voltage at terminals 2 and 4 on the control unit electrical connector (Bosch system shown)

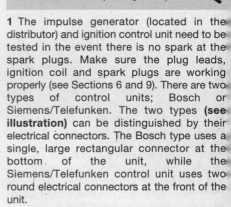

10.2b Check for voltage at terminals 6 and 3 on the control unit electrical connector (Siemens/Telefunken system shown)

connect the ohmmeter to coil terminal 1 (-) and the centre tower. On Motronic systems, connect the ohmmeter to coil terminal 15 (+) and the centre tower. Compare the measured resistance with the values given in the Specifications in this Chapter.

6 If the measured resistances are not close to those specified, the coil is defective and should be renewed. Note that the measured resistance will vary according to the temperature of the coil, so don't rush to condemn the coil if the resistance is only a little way out.

7 It is essential for proper ignition system operation that all coil terminals and wire leads be kept clean and dry.

8 Refit the coil in its mounting, and reconnect the wiring. Refitting is the reverse of removal.

10 Impulse generator and ignition control unit - check and renewal (TCI system)

1 The impulse generator (located in the distributor) and ignition control unit need to be tested in the event there is no spark at the spark plugs. Make sure the plug leads, ignition coil and spark plugs are working properly (see Sections 6 and 9). There are two types of control units; Bosch or Siemens/Telefunken. The two types (see illustration) can be distinguished by their electrical connectors. The Bosch type uses a single, large rectangular connector at the bottom of the unit, while the Siemens/Telefunken control unit uses two round electrical connectors at the front of the unit.

Check
Voltage supply and earth to ignition control unit

2 With the ignition off, remove the harness connectors from the ignition control unit (see illustrations). Connect a voltmeter between connector terminals 2 and 4 on Bosch systems, or between terminals 6 and 3 on Siemens/Telefunken systems.

3 Turn the ignition on. There should be battery voltage on the designated terminals. If there is no voltage, check the wiring harness for an open-circuit (see Chapter 12).

4 Using an ohmmeter, check for continuity between connector terminal 2 (Bosch) or 6 (Siemens/Telefunken) and the earth to the vehicle body. Continuity should exist.

5 Using an ohmmeter, check for continuity between connector terminal 4 (Bosch) or 3 (Siemens/Telefunken) and terminal 15 of the ignition coil. Continuity should exist.

6 If the readings are incorrect, repair the wiring harness.

Impulse generator signal

7 If the ignition control unit is receiving battery voltage, check the A/C signal voltage coming from the impulse generator to the control unit.

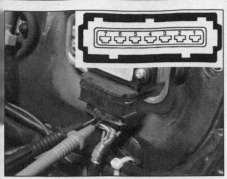

10.8 Back-probe the ignition control unit connector, and check for signal voltage on terminals 5 and 6 (Bosch system shown). It is very helpful to use angled probes

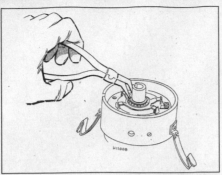

10.18 Use circlip pliers and remove the circlip from the distributor shaft

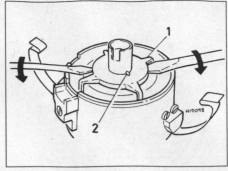

10.19 Carefully prise the trigger wheel off the distributor shaft

8 Use a digital voltmeter for the following tests:

a) On Bosch systems, connect the positive probe to connector terminal 5, and the negative probe to terminal 6 **(see illustration)**.

b) On Siemens/Telefunken systems, connect the positive probe to terminal (+) of the smaller connector, and the negative probe to terminal (-).

9 Have an assistant crank the engine over, and check that there is 1 to 2 volts A/C present. If there is no voltage, check the wiring harness between the impulse generator (in the distributor) and the control unit. If the harness is OK, check the impulse generator resistance.

> ⚠ **Warning: Do not crank the engine over for an excessive length of time. If necessary, disconnect the cold start injector electrical connector (see Chapter 4) to stop the flow of fuel into the engine.**

10 To check the resistance in the impulse generator, proceed as described for your system below:

a) On Bosch units, measure the resistance between connector terminals 5 and 6 **(see illustration 10.8)**. The reading should be 1000 to 1200 ohms.

b) On Siemens/Telefunken units, measure the resistance between the terminals of the smaller connector. The reading should be 1000 to 1200 ohms.

11 If the resistance readings are incorrect, renew the impulse generator. If the resistance readings for the impulse generator are correct and the control unit voltages (supply voltage [paragraphs 1 to 6] and signal voltage [paragraphs 7 to 9]) are incorrect, renew the control unit.

Renewal
Ignition control unit

12 Make sure the ignition is switched off.
13 Disconnect the electrical connector(s) from the control unit.
14 Remove the mounting screws from the control unit, and lift it from the engine compartment.

15 Refitting is the reverse of removal. **Note:** On Bosch control units, a special dielectric grease is used between the heat sink and the back of the control unit. In the event the two are separated (renewal or testing) the old grease must be removed, and the heat sink cleaned off using 180-grit sandpaper. Apply Curil K2 (Bosch part number 81 22 9 243). A silicon dielectric compound can be used as a substitute. This treatment is very important for the long life of these expensive ignition parts.

Impulse generator

> ⚠ **Caution: If the radio in your vehicle is equipped with an anti-theft system, make sure you have the correct activation code before disconnecting the battery. Refer to the information on page 0-7 at the front of this manual before detaching the cable.**
> **Note:** If, after connecting the battery, the wrong language appears on the instrument panel display, refer to page 0-7 for the language resetting procedure.

16 Disconnect the battery negative cable.
17 Remove the distributor from the engine (see Section 8).
18 Using a pair of circlip pliers, remove the circlip retaining the trigger wheel **(see illustration)**.
19 Use two flat-bladed screwdrivers positioned at opposite sides of the trigger wheel, and carefully prise it up **(see illustration)**. **Note:** Push the screwdrivers in as far as possible without bending the trigger wheel. Prise only on the strongest, centre portion of the trigger wheel. In the event the trigger wheel is bent, it must be replaced with a new one. **Note:** Be sure not to lose the roll pin when lifting out the trigger wheel.
20 Remove the mounting screws from the impulse generator electrical connector, the vacuum diaphragm and the baseplate.
21 Remove the two screws from the vacuum advance unit, and separate it from the distributor by moving the assembly down while unhooking it from the baseplate pin.
22 Use circlip pliers to remove the circlip that retains the impulse generator and the baseplate assembly.
23 Carefully remove the impulse generator and the baseplate assembly as a single unit.

24 Remove the three screws, and separate the baseplate assembly from the impulse generator.
25 Refitting is the reverse of removal. **Note:** Be sure to position the insulating ring between the generator coil and the baseplate. It must be centred before tightening the mounting screws. Also, it will be necessary to check/adjust the air gap if the trigger wheel has been removed, or tampered with to the point that the clearance is incorrect (see Section 11).

11 Air gap (TCI system) - check and adjustment

> ⚠ **Caution: If the radio in your vehicle is equipped with an anti-theft system, make sure you have the correct activation code before disconnecting the battery. Refer to the information on page 0-7 at the front of this manual before detaching the cable.**
> **Note:** If, after connecting the battery, the wrong language appears on the instrument panel display, refer to page 0-7 for the language resetting procedure.

1 Disconnect the battery negative cable.
2 Insert a brass feeler gauge between the trigger wheel tab and the impulse generator **(see illustration)**. Slide the feeler gauge up

11.2 Use a brass feeler gauge to check the air gap (be sure the gauge rubs lightly against the trigger wheel as well as the locating pin for the correct adjustment)

5

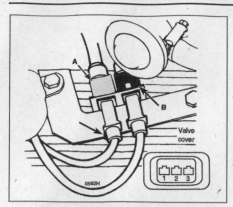

12.1a Location of the position sensor (grey connector) (A) and the speed sensor (black connector) (B) on Motronic systems (early models)

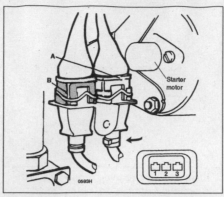

12.1b Location of the position sensor (grey connector) (A) and the speed sensor (black connector) (B) on Motronic systems (later models)

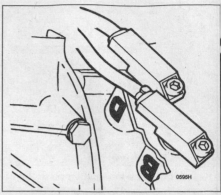

12.5 Location of the position sensor (B) and speed sensor (D) on the bellhousing on all Motronic systems – do not interchange the sensors, or the engine will not start

and down - you should feel a slight drag on the feeler gauge as it is moved if the gap is correct. The gap must be as given in this Chapter's Specifications.

3 To adjust the gap, it is necessary to remove the impulse generator and the baseplate assembly from the distributor **(see illustration 10.1).**

4 Follow paragraphs 17 to 24 in Section 10 and loosen the screws that retain the impulse generator to the baseplate assembly.

5 Carefully insert the feeler gauge and tighten the screws.

6 Refit the assembly back into the distributor and recheck the adjustment.

12.7a On later 3-Series models, the pulse sensor connector (arrowed) is located next to the 20-pin diagnostic connector

12 Ignition sensors (Motronic system) - check and renewal

Note: *Some models are equipped with a TDC sensor mounted on the front of the engine. This sensor is strictly for the BMW service test unit, and is not part of the Motronic ignition system.*

Speed and position sensors
Check

1 Locate the two electrical connectors for the sensors **(see illustrations).** The grey connector is for the position sensor, and the white connector is for the speed sensor.

2 Using an ohmmeter, check the resistance between terminal 1 (yellow wire) and terminal 2 (black wire) on the sensor side of each connector. The resistance should be 860 to 1,060 ohms.

3 Also check the resistance between terminal 3 and either terminal 1 or terminal 2. The resistance should be approximately 100 000 ohms.

4 If the reading(s) are incorrect, renew the sensor(s).

Renewal

5 Remove the sensor mounting screw(s),

using an Allen key where necessary, and pull the sensor(s) from the sockets. Disconnect the wiring from one sensor at a time - be sure the connectors are not interchanged when fitting new sensors. The bellhousing is marked with a B for the position sensor (grey connector) and D for the speed sensor (black connector) **(see illustration). Note:** *It is a good idea to check the condition of the raised pin on the flywheel while the sensors are out of the sockets. Turn the engine by hand as necessary to bring the pin into view.*

6 Tighten the sensor mounting screw(s) securely, but be careful not to overtighten.

Pulse sensor (later models)

Check

7 Locate the two electrical connectors for the sensor **(see illustrations).** Disconnect the electrical connector from the front.

8 Using an ohmmeter, check resistance between terminal 1 (yellow wire) and terminal 2 (black wire) on the sensor side of each connector **(see illustration).** The resistance should be 500 to 600 ohms.

9 If the reading is incorrect, renew the sensor.

Renewal

10 Remove the pulse sensor mounting bolt using a 5 mm hex spanner **(see illustration).**

12.7b On later 5-Series models, the pulse sensor connector (arrowed) is located next to the valve cover

12.8 The resistance of the pulse sensor should be 500 to 600 ohms (later models)

12.10 The pulse sensor itself (arrowed) is located on the timing belt cover, to one side of the pulley (later models)

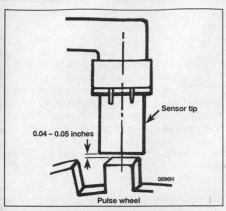

12.11 The sensor tip should be set at 1.0 ± 0.3 mm from the pulse wheel

Withdraw the sensor from its bracket and remove it.
11 When fitting the new sensor, use a brass feeler gauge to position the tip of the sensor the correct distance from the pulse wheel **(see illustration)**.
12 Tighten the mounting bolt, but be careful not to overtighten it.

13 Charging system - general information and precautions

There are two different types of alternator fitted on these models; Bosch and Motorola. Also, there are three different amperage ratings available; 65A, 80A or 90A. A stamped serial number on the rear of the alternator will identify the type and amperage rating. Perform the charging system checks (see Section 14) to diagnose any problems with the alternator.

The voltage regulator and the alternator brushes are mounted as a single assembly. On Bosch alternators, this unit can be removed from the alternator (see Section 16) and the components serviced individually.

The alternator on all models is mounted on the left front of the engine, and utilises a V-belt and pulley drive system. Drivebelt tension and battery servicing are the two primary maintenance requirements for these systems. See Chapter 1 for the procedures regarding engine drivebelt checking and battery servicing.

The ignition/no-charge warning light should come on when the ignition key is turned to Start, then go off immediately the engine starts. If it remains on, there is a malfunction in the charging system (see Section 14). Some vehicles are also equipped with a voltmeter. If the voltmeter indicates abnormally high or low voltage, check the charging system (see Section 14). **Note:** On models up to 1986, a blown ignition/no-charge warning light will prevent the alternator from charging. After 1987, a resistor is wired in parallel with the warning light in order to allow current to bypass the light in the event of a broken circuit (blown warning light).

Precautions

Be very careful when making electrical circuit connections to the alternator, and note the following:
a) When reconnecting wires to the alternator from the battery, be sure to note the polarity.
b) Before using arc-welding equipment to repair any part of the vehicle, disconnect the wires from the battery terminals and from the alternator.
⚠ **Caution: If the radio in your vehicle is equipped with an anti-theft system, make sure you have the correct activation code before disconnecting the battery. Refer to the information on page 0-7 at the front of this manual before detaching the cable.**
Note: If, after connecting the battery, the wrong language appears on the instrument panel display, refer to page 0-7 for the language resetting procedure.
c) Never start the engine with a battery charger connected. Always disconnect both battery cables before using a battery charger.
d) Never disconnect cables from the battery or from the alternator while the engine is running.
e) The alternator is turned by an engine drivebelt. Serious injury could result if your hands, hair or clothes become entangled in the belt with the engine running.
f) Because the alternator is connected directly to the battery, take care not to short out the main terminal to earth.
g) Wrap a plastic bag over the alternator, and secure it with rubber bands, before steam-cleaning the engine.

14 Charging system - check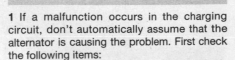

1 If a malfunction occurs in the charging circuit, don't automatically assume that the alternator is causing the problem. First check the following items:
a) Check the drivebelt tension and condition (see Chapter 1). Renew the drivebelt if it's worn or deteriorated.
b) Make sure the alternator mounting and adjustment bolts are tight.
c) Inspect the alternator wiring harness and the connectors at the alternator and voltage regulator. They must be in good condition and tight.
d) Check the fuses.
e) Start the engine and check the alternator for abnormal noises (a shrieking or squealing sound indicates a worn bearing, but could also be due to a slipping drivebelt - see a) above).

f) Check the specific gravity of the battery electrolyte. If it's low, charge the battery (doesn't apply to maintenance-free batteries).
g) Make sure the battery is fully-charged (one bad cell in a battery can cause overcharging by the alternator).
h) Disconnect the battery cables (negative first, then positive). Inspect the battery posts and the cable clamps for corrosion. Clean them thoroughly if necessary (see Chapter 1).

⚠ **Caution: If the radio in your vehicle is equipped with an anti-theft system, make sure you have the correct activation code before disconnecting the battery. Refer to the information on page 0-7 at the front of this manual before detaching the cable.**
Note: If, after connecting the battery, the wrong language appears on the instrument panel display, refer to page 0-7 for the language resetting procedure.

2 With the ignition off, connect a 12 volt test light between the battery negative post and the disconnected negative cable clamp. If the test light does not come on, refit the cable and proceed to paragraph 4. If the test light comes on, there is a short (drain) in the electrical system of the vehicle. The short must be repaired before the charging system can be checked. **Note:** Accessories which are always on (such as the clock or the radio station memory) must be disconnected before performing this check.
3 Disconnect the alternator wiring harness. If the test light now goes out, the alternator is faulty. If the light stays on, remove each fuse in turn until the light goes out (this will tell you which component is shorting out).
4 Using a voltmeter, check the battery voltage with the engine off. It should be approximately 12 volts.
5 Start the engine and check the battery voltage again. It should now be approximately 14 to 15 volts.
6 Turn on the headlights. The voltage should drop, and then come back up, if the charging system is working properly.
7 If the voltage reading is more than the specified charging voltage, renew the voltage regulator (refer to Section 16). If the voltage is less, the alternator diode(s), stator or rotor may be faulty, or the voltage regulator may be malfunctioning.
8 If there is no short-circuit causing battery drain but the battery is constantly discharging, then either the battery itself is defective, the alternator drivebelt is loose (see Chapter 1), the alternator brushes are worn, dirty or disconnected (see Section 17), the voltage regulator is malfunctioning (see Section 16) or the diodes, stator coil or rotor coil are defective. Repairing or renewing the diodes, stator coil or rotor coil is beyond the scope of the home mechanic. Either renew

5

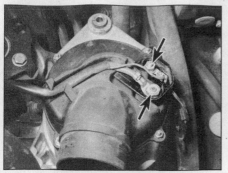

15.2 Depending on how many accessories the vehicle has, sometimes it's easier to remove the alternator from the brackets first, and then turn it sideways to gain access to the connections (arrowed) on the rear of the alternator body

the alternator complete, or take it to an automotive electrician, who may be able to overhaul it. **Note:** *On models up to 1986, a blown ignition/no-charge warning light bulb will prevent the alternator from charging. After 1987, a resistor is wired in parallel with the warning light, in order to allow current to bypass the light in the event of a broken circuit (blown warning light).*

15 Alternator - removal and refitting

Caution: If the radio in your vehicle is equipped with an anti-theft system, make sure you have the correct activation code before disconnecting the battery. Refer to the information on page 0-7 at the front of this manual before detaching the cable. **Note:** *If, after connecting the battery, the wrong language appears on the instrument panel display, refer to page 0-7 for the language resetting procedure.*

Removal

1 Detach the battery negative cable.

2 Detach the electrical connectors from the alternator, noting their locations for refitting **(see illustration). Note:** *On some models, it may be necessary to remove the air cleaner assembly and airflow meter to gain access to the alternator.*
3 Loosen the alternator adjustment and pivot bolts, and slip off the drivebelt (see Chapter 1).
4 Remove the adjustment and pivot bolts, and separate the alternator from the engine.

Refitting

5 If you are renewing the alternator, take the old one with you when purchasing a new or reconditioned unit. Make sure the new unit looks identical to the old alternator. Look at the terminals - they should be the same in number, size and location as the terminals on the old alternator. Finally, look at the identification numbers - they will be stamped into the housing, or printed on a tag attached to the housing. Make sure the numbers are the same on both alternators.
6 Many new alternators do not come with a pulley fitted, so you may have to transfer the pulley from the old unit to the new one.
7 Refitting is the reverse of removal.
8 After the alternator is fitted, adjust the drivebelt tension (see Chapter 1).
9 Check the charging voltage to verify proper operation of the alternator (see Section 14).

16 Voltage regulator - renewal

1 The voltage regulator controls the charging system voltage by limiting the alternator output. The regulator is a sealed unit, and isn't adjustable.
2 If the voltmeter indicates that the alternator is not charging (or if the ignition/no-charge warning light comes on) and the alternator, battery, drivebelt tension and electrical connections seem to be fine, have the

regulator checked by a dealer service department or electrical specialist.
3 Disconnect the battery negative cable.

Caution: If the radio in your vehicle is equipped with an anti-theft system, make sure you have the correct activation code before disconnecting the battery. Refer to the information on page 0-7 at the front of this manual before detaching the cable. **Note:** *If, after connecting the battery, the wrong language appears on the instrument panel display, refer to page 0-7 for the language resetting procedure.*

Bosch alternator

4 The voltage regulator is mounted externally on the alternator housing. To renew the regulator, remove the mounting screws **(see illustration)** and lift it off the alternator **(see illustration). Note:** *Some Bosch alternators have an integral voltage regulator which is part of the brush assembly.*
5 Refitting is the reverse of removal. **Note:** *Before refitting the regulator, check the condition of the slip rings* **(see illustration).** *Use a torch and check for any scoring or deep wear grooves. Renew the alternator if necessary.*

Motorola alternator

6 Remove the alternator from the engine compartment (see Section 15).
7 Remove the rear cover and diode carrier, remove the voltage regulator mounting screws **(see illustration)** and lift the regulator off the alternator body.
8 Refitting is the reverse of removal.

17 Alternator brushes - check and renewal

Caution: If the radio in your vehicle is equipped with an anti-theft system, make sure you have the correct activation code before disconnecting the battery.

16.4a Remove the nuts and lift off the small terminal protector from the alternator cover, then remove the nuts and the cover

16.4b The regulator can be withdrawn easily on Bosch alternators. This type of regulator is integral with the brush assembly

16.5 Use a torch to check the slip rings for scoring or deep grooves

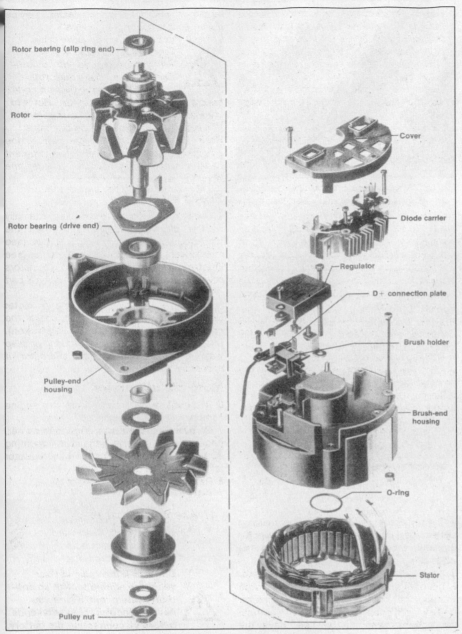

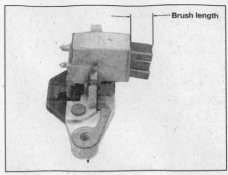

17.3 Check the brush length in the normal rest position (spring uncoiled)

16.7 Exploded view of the Motorola alternator

8 Reconnect the battery negative cable.

Motorola alternator

9 Remove the alternator.
10 The brushes are mounted under the regulator on the rear of the alternator (see illustration 16.7).
11 Remove the mounting screws and insulating washers, and separate the voltage regulator and brush holder from the brush end housing.
12 Measure the length of the brushes (see illustration 17.3). If any brush is less then 6.0 mm long, renew them all as a set.
13 Make sure the brushes move smoothly in the holder.
14 Refit the brush holder/regulator. Tighten the screws securely. Make sure the brushes aren't earthed.
15 Refitting is the reverse of removal.

18 Starting system - general information and precautions

The sole function of the starting system is to turn over the engine quickly enough to allow it to start.

The starting system consists of the battery, the starter motor, the starter solenoid, the ignition switch, and the wires connecting them. The solenoid is mounted directly on the starter motor. The starter/solenoid motor assembly is fitted on the lower part of the engine, next to the transmission bellhousing.

When the ignition key is turned to the Start position, the starter solenoid is actuated through the starter control circuit. The starter solenoid then connects the battery to the starter, and moves the starter pinion into mesh with the flywheel ring gear. The battery supplies the electrical energy to the starter motor, which does the actual work of cranking the engine.

The starter motor on some manual transmission vehicles can only be operated when the clutch pedal is depressed. On a vehicle equipped with automatic transmission, the starter can only be operated

Refer to the information on page 0-7 at the front of this manual before detaching the cable.
Note: *If, after connecting the battery, the wrong language appears on the instrument panel display, refer to page 0-7 for the language resetting procedure.*

1 Disconnect the battery negative cable.

Bosch alternator

2 Remove the voltage regulator from the back of the alternator (see Section 16).
3 Measure the length of the brushes (see illustration). They should not be less than 6.0 mm. If any are worn past this point, renew them all as a set.

4 Also check for excessively worn slip rings (see illustration 16.5).
5 The brushes are retained either by set screws or by solder. If you are not skilled at soldering, it may be best to have an auto electrician fit the new brushes. **Note:** *Be careful not to apply heat to the solder joint for more than 5 seconds. If necessary, use a heat sink to capture the excess heat. This can be accomplished by clamping a pair of needle-nose pliers next to the solder joint.*
6 On the screw type, hold the assembly in place and refit the screws. Tighten them evenly, a little at a time, so the holder isn't distorted.
7 Refit the regulator assembly to the alternator.

5

when the transmission selector lever is in Park or Neutral.

Always detach the battery negative cable before working on the starting system.

19 Starter motor - in-vehicle check

Note: *Before diagnosing starter problems, make sure the battery is fully charged.*

1 If the starter motor does not turn at all when the switch is operated, make sure that the gear lever is in Neutral or Park (automatic transmission) or, where applicable, that the clutch pedal is depressed (manual transmission).

2 Make sure that the battery is charged, and that all cables, both at the battery and starter solenoid terminals, are clean and secure.

3 If the starter motor spins but the engine is not cranking, the overrun clutch in the starter motor is slipping, and the starter motor must be renewed.

4 If, when the switch is actuated, the starter motor does not operate at all but the solenoid clicks, then the problem lies either in the battery, the main solenoid contacts, or the starter motor itself (or the engine is seized).

5 If the solenoid plunger cannot be heard when the switch is actuated, the battery is faulty, the switch is defective, the fusible link is burned-out (the circuit is open), or the solenoid itself is defective.

6 To check the solenoid, connect a jumper lead between the battery (+) and the ignition switch wire terminal (the small terminal) on the solenoid. If the starter motor now operates, the solenoid is OK and the problem is in the ignition switch, starter inhibitor switch (automatic transmission models), clutch switch (some manual transmission models), or the wiring.

7 If the starter motor still does not operate, remove the starter/solenoid assembly for dismantling, testing and repair.

8 If the starter motor cranks the engine at an abnormally-slow speed, first make sure that the battery is charged, and that all terminal connections are tight. If the engine is partially-seized, or has the wrong viscosity oil in it, it will crank slowly.

9 Run the engine until normal operating temperature is reached, then disconnect the coil HT lead from the distributor cap and earth it on the engine.

10 Connect a voltmeter positive lead to the battery positive post, and connect the negative lead to the negative post.

20.4a Working under the vehicle, remove the starter lower mounting bolt and nut (arrowed)

11 Crank the engine, and take the voltmeter readings as soon as a steady figure is indicated. Do not allow the starter motor to turn for more than 10 seconds at a time. A reading of 9 volts or more, with the starter motor turning at normal cranking speed, is normal. If the reading is 9 volts or more but the cranking speed is slow, the solenoid contacts are burned, there is a bad connection, or the starter motor itself is faulty. If the reading is less than 9 volts and the cranking speed is slow, the starter motor is faulty or the battery is responsible (defective or discharged).

20 Starter motor - removal and refitting

Note: *If the starter motor is defective, it should be renewed, or taken to an auto electrical specialist for repair. Overhaul of the starter motor is unlikely to be a practical proposition for the home mechanic, even if spare parts are available. However, the solenoid can be renewed separately (see Section 21).*

Removal

⚠️ **Caution: If the radio in your vehicle is equipped with an anti-theft system, make sure you have the correct activation code before disconnecting the battery. Refer to the information on page 0-7 at the front of this manual before detaching the cable.**
Note: *If, after connecting the battery, the wrong language appears on the instrument panel display, refer to page 0-7 for the language resetting procedure.*

1 Detach the battery negative cable.

2 Raise the vehicle and support it securely on axle stands.

3 Clearly label the wires from the terminals on

20.4b Withdrawing the starter motor from the M40 engine

the starter motor and solenoid, then disconnect them. **Note:** *On some models, it may be necessary to remove the air cleaner (see Chapter 4), coolant expansion tank (see Chapter 3) and the heater hoses to gain access to the top of the starter. Carefully label any hoses or components that need to be removed from the engine compartment, to avoid confusion when reassembling.*

4 Unscrew the mounting bolts and detach the starter **(see illustrations)**.

Refitting

5 Refitting is the reverse of removal.

21 Starter solenoid - removal and refitting

Removal

⚠️ **Caution: If the radio in your vehicle is equipped with an anti-theft system, make sure you have the correct activation code before disconnecting the battery. Refer to the information on page 0-7 at the front of this manual before detaching the cable.**
Note: *If, after connecting the battery, the wrong language appears on the instrument panel display, refer to page 0-7 for the language resetting procedure.*

1 Disconnect the battery negative cable.

2 Remove the starter motor (see Section 20).

3 Disconnect the cable from the solenoid to the starter motor terminal.

4 Remove the screws which secure the solenoid to the starter motor.

5 Detach the solenoid from the starter body.

6 Remove the plunger and plunger spring.

Refitting

7 Refitting is the reverse of removal.

Chapter 6
Engine management and emission control systems

Contents

Degrees of difficulty

Easy, suitable for novice with little experience	**Fairly easy,** suitable for beginner with some experience	**Fairly difficult,** suitable for competent DIY mechanic	**Difficult,** suitable for experienced DIY mechanic	**Very difficult,** suitable for expert DIY or professional

1 General information

To prevent pollution of the atmosphere from incomplete combustion or evaporation of the fuel, and to maintain good driveability and fuel economy, a number of emission control systems are used on these vehicles. Not all of these systems are fitted to all models, but they include the following:

Catalytic converter
Evaporative emission control (EVAP) system
Positive crankcase ventilation (PCV) system
Electronic engine management

The Sections in this Chapter include general descriptions and checking procedures within the scope of the home mechanic, as well as component renewal procedures (when possible) for each of the systems listed above.

Before assuming that an emissions control system is malfunctioning, check the fuel and ignition systems carefully. The diagnosis of some emission control devices requires specialised tools, equipment and training. If checking and servicing become too difficult, or if a procedure is beyond your ability, consult a dealer service department or other specialist.

 The most frequent cause of emission system problems is simply a leaking vacuum hose or loose wire, so always check the hose and wiring connections first.

This doesn't mean, however, that emission control systems are particularly difficult to maintain and repair. You can quickly and easily perform many checks, and do most of the regular maintenance at home with common tune-up and hand tools.

Pay close attention to any special precautions outlined in this Chapter. It should be noted that the illustrations of the various systems may not exactly match the system fitted on your vehicle because of changes made by the manufacturer during production.

2 Motronic engine management system self-diagnosis - general information

The Motronic engine management system control unit (computer) has a built-in self-diagnosis system, which detects malfunctions in the system sensors and stores them as fault codes in its memory. It is not possible without dedicated test equipment to extract these fault codes from the control unit. However, the procedures given in Chapters 4 and 5 may be used to check individual components and sensors of the Motronic system. If this fails to pinpoint a fault, then the vehicle should be taken to a BMW dealer, who will have the necessary diagnostic equipment to call up the fault codes from the control unit. You will then have the option to repair the fault yourself, or alternatively have the fault repaired by the BMW dealer.

3 Electronic control unit (ECU) - removal and refitting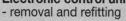

Removal

1 The Electronic Control Unit (ECU) is located either inside the passenger compartment under the right-hand side of the facia panel on 3-Series models, or in the engine compartment on the right-hand side on 5-Series models (see Chapter 4).
2 Disconnect the battery negative cable.

 Caution: If the radio in your vehicle is equipped with an anti-theft system, make sure you have the correct activation code before disconnecting the battery. Refer to the information on page 0-7 at the front of this manual before detaching the cable.
Note: *If, after connecting the battery, the wrong language appears on the instrument panel display, refer to page 0-7 for the language resetting procedure.*
3 First remove the access cover on models with the ECU on the right-hand side of the engine compartment (see Chapter 4).
4 If the ECU is located inside the vehicle, remove the access cover on the right-hand side.
5 Unplug the electrical connectors from the ECU.
6 Remove the retaining bolts from the ECU bracket.
7 Carefully remove the ECU. **Note**: *Avoid static electricity damage to the ECU by wearing rubber gloves, and do not touch the connector pins.*

Refitting

8 Refitting is a reversal of removal.

6

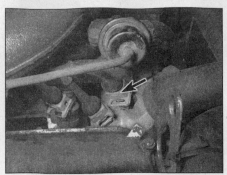

4.1 The coolant temperature sensor (arrowed) is usually located next to the temperature sender unit, near the fuel pressure regulator

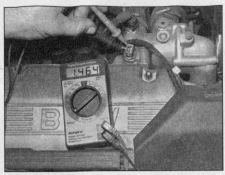

4.2 Check the resistance of the coolant temperature sensor at different temperatures

4.6 The oxygen sensor (arrowed) is usually located in the exhaust pipe, downstream from the exhaust manifold

4 Information sensors

Note: *Refer to Chapters 4 and 5 for additional information on the location and diagnosis of the information sensors that are not covered in this Section.*

Coolant temperature sensor

General description

1 The coolant temperature sensor **(see illustration)** is a thermistor (a resistor which varies its resistance value in accordance with temperature changes). The change in the resistance value regulates the amount of voltage that can pass through the sensor. At low temperatures, the sensor's resistance is high. As the sensor temperature increases, its resistance will decrease. Any failure in this sensor circuit will in most cases be due to a loose or shorted-out wire; if no wiring problems are evident, check the sensor as described below.

Check

2 To check the sensor, first check its resistance **(see illustration)** when it is completely cold (typically 2100 to 2900 ohms). Next, start the engine and warm it up until it reaches operating temperature. The resistance should be lower (typically 270 to 400 ohms). **Note**: *If restricted access to the coolant temperature sensor makes it difficult to attach electrical probes to the terminals, remove the sensor as described below, and perform the tests in a container of heated water to simulate the conditions.*

 Warning: Wait until the engine is completely cool before beginning this procedure.

Renewal

3 To remove the sensor, depress the spring lock, unplug the electrical connector, then carefully unscrew the sensor. Be prepared for some coolant spillage; to reduce this, have the new sensor ready for fitting as quickly as possible.

Caution: Handle the coolant sensor with care. Damage to this sensor will affect the operation of the entire fuel injection system.
Note: *It may be necessary to drain a small amount of coolant from the radiator before removing the sensor.*
4 Before the sensor is fitted, ensure its threads are clean, and apply a little sealant to them.
5 Refitting is the reverse of removal.

Oxygen sensor

General description

Note: *Oxygen sensors are normally only fitted to those vehicles equipped with a catalytic converter. Most oxygen sensors are located in the exhaust pipe, downstream from the exhaust manifold. On 535 models, the oxygen sensor is mounted in the catalytic converter. The sensor's electrical connector is located near the bulkhead (left side) for easy access.*
6 The oxygen sensor, which is located in the exhaust system **(see illustration)**, monitors the oxygen content of the exhaust gas. The oxygen content in the exhaust reacts with the oxygen sensor, to produce a voltage output which varies from 0.1 volts (high oxygen, lean mixture) to 0.9 volts (low oxygen, rich mixture). The ECU constantly monitors this variable voltage output to determine the ratio of oxygen to fuel in the mixture. The ECU alters the air/fuel mixture ratio by controlling the pulse width (open time) of the fuel injectors. A mixture ratio of 14.7 parts air to 1 part fuel is the ideal mixture ratio for minimising exhaust emissions, thus allowing the catalytic converter to operate at maximum efficiency. It is this ratio of 14.7 to 1 which the ECU and the oxygen sensor attempt to maintain at all times.
7 The oxygen sensor produces no voltage when it is below its normal operating temperature of about 320° C. During this initial period before warm-up, the ECU operates in "open-loop" mode (ie without the information from the sensor).
8 If the engine reaches normal operating temperature and/or has been running for two or more minutes, and if the oxygen sensor is producing a steady signal voltage below

0.45 volts at 1500 rpm or greater, the ECU fault code memory will be activated.
9 When there is a problem with the oxygen sensor or its circuit, the ECU operates in the "open-loop" mode - that is, it controls fuel delivery in accordance with a programmed default value instead of with feedback information from the oxygen sensor.
10 The proper operation of the oxygen sensor depends on four conditions:
a) *Electrical - The low voltages generated by the sensor depend upon good, clean connections, which should be checked whenever a malfunction of the sensor is suspected or indicated.*
b) *Outside air supply - The sensor is designed to allow air circulation to the internal portion of the sensor. Whenever the sensor is disturbed, make sure the air passages are not restricted.*
c) *Proper operating temperature - The ECU will not react to the sensor signal until the sensor reaches approximately 320° C. This factor must be taken into consideration when evaluating the performance of the sensor.*
d) *Unleaded fuel - The use of unleaded fuel is essential for proper operation of the sensor. Make sure the fuel you are using is of this type.*
11 In addition to observing the above conditions, special care must be taken whenever the sensor is serviced.
a) *The oxygen sensor has a permanently-attached pigtail and electrical connector, which should not be removed from the sensor. Damage or removal of the pigtail or electrical connector can adversely affect operation of the sensor.*
b) *Grease, dirt and other contaminants should be kept away from the electrical connector and the louvered end of the sensor.*
c) *Do not use cleaning solvents of any kind on the oxygen sensor.*
d) *Do not drop or roughly handle the sensor.*
e) *The silicone boot must be fitted in the correct position, to prevent the boot from being melted and to allow the sensor to operate properly.*

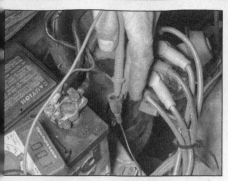

4.12a The oxygen sensor, once it is warmed up (320° C), puts out a very small voltage signal. To verify it is working, check for voltage with a digital voltmeter (the voltage signals usually range from 0.1 to 1.0 volt)

Check

12 Warm up the engine, and let it run at idle. Disconnect the oxygen sensor electrical connector, and connect the positive probe of a voltmeter to the oxygen sensor output connector terminal (refer to the following table) and the negative probe to earth **(see illustrations)**.
Note: *Most oxygen sensor electrical connectors are located at the rear of the engine, near the bulkhead. Look for a large rubber boot attached to a thick wire harness. On early 535i models, the connector for the oxygen sensor heater circuit is under the vehicle. Look for a small protective cover. These models should have the updated oxygen sensor fitted, to make access similar to other models. Consult your dealer service department for additional information.*
13 Increase and then decrease the engine speed, and monitor the voltage.
14 When the speed is increased, the voltage should increase to 0.5 to 1.0 volts. When the speed is decreased, the voltage should fall to about 0 to 0.4 volts.
15 Also where applicable, inspect the oxygen sensor heater (models with multi-wire sensors). With the ignition on, disconnect the oxygen sensor electrical connector, and connect a voltmeter across the terminals designated in the chart (see below). There should be battery voltage (approximately 12 volts).
16 If the reading is not correct, check the oxygen sensor heater relay (see Chapter 12). If the information is not available, check the owner's handbook for the exact location of the oxygen sensor heater relay. The relay should receive battery voltage.
17 If the oxygen sensor fails any of these tests, renew it.

Renewal

Note: *Because it is fitted in the exhaust manifold, converter or pipe, which contracts when cool, the oxygen sensor may be very difficult to loosen when the engine is cold. Rather than risk damage to the sensor*

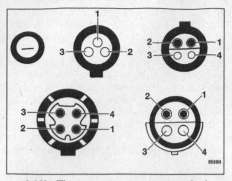

4.12b These oxygen sensor terminal designations are for the harness side only. Use the corresponding terminals on the sensor side for the testing procedures (there are three different four-wire oxygen sensor connectors available - don't get them mixed up)

(assuming you are planning to re-use it in another manifold or pipe), start and run the engine for a minute or two, then switch it off. Be careful not to burn yourself during the following procedure.
18 Disconnect the battery negative cable.

⚠️ *Caution: If the radio in your vehicle is equipped with an anti-theft system, make sure you have the correct activation code before disconnecting the battery. Refer to the information on page 0-7 at the front of this manual before detaching the cable.*
Note: *If, after connecting the battery, the wrong language appears on the instrument panel display, refer to page 0-7 for the language resetting procedure.*
19 Raise and support the vehicle.
20 Disconnect the electrical connector from the sensor.
21 Carefully unscrew the sensor.

⚠️ *Caution: Excessive force may damage the threads.*

22 A high-temperature anti-seize compound must be used on the threads of the sensor, to facilitate future removal. The threads of new sensors will already be coated with this compound, but if an old sensor is removed and refitted, recoat the threads.

4.28a The TPS on L-Jetronic systems is located under the intake manifold (terminals arrowed)

23 Refit the sensor and tighten it securely.
24 Reconnect the electrical connector of the pigtail lead to the main engine wiring harness.
25 Lower the vehicle, and reconnect the battery.

Oxygen sensor type	Sensor output signal	Heated power supply (12V)
Unheated (single-wire)	black wire (+)	Not applicable
Heated (three-wire)	terminal 1 (+)	terminals 3 (+) and 2 (-)
Heated (four-wire)	terminal 2 (+)	terminals 4 (+) and 3 (-)

Throttle Position Sensor (TPS)
General description

26 The Throttle Position Sensor (TPS) is located on the end of the throttle shaft on the throttle body. By monitoring the output voltage from the TPS, the ECU can determine fuel delivery based on throttle valve angle (driver demand). In this system, the TPS acts as a switch rather than a potentiometer. One set of throttle valve switch contacts is closed (continuity) only at idle. A second set of contacts closes as the engine approaches full-throttle. Both sets of contacts are open (no continuity) between these positions. A broken or loose TPS can cause intermittent bursts of fuel from the injector and an unstable idle, because the ECU thinks the throttle is moving.
27 All models (except for early 535i models with automatic transmission) combine the idle and full-throttle switch; a separate idle position switch indicates the closed-throttle position, while the TPS is used for the full-throttle position. On 535i models with automatic transmission, the TPS is connected directly to the automatic transmission control unit. With the throttle fully open, the transmission control unit sends the full-throttle signal to the Motronic control unit.

All models except early 535i with automatic transmission
Check
28 Remove the electrical connector from the TPS, and connect an ohmmeter to terminals 2 and 18 **(see illustrations)**. Open the throttle

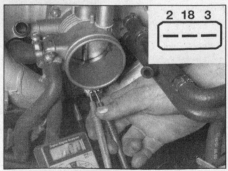

4.28b First check for continuity between terminals 2 and 18 with the throttle closed (later Motronic system shown) . . .

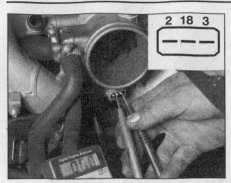

4.28c . . . then check for continuity between terminals 3 and 18 as the throttle is opened

slightly by hand. Release the throttle slowly until it reaches 0.2 to 0.6 mm from the throttle stop. There should be continuity.

29 Check the resistance between terminals 3 and 18 as the throttle is opened. There should be continuity when the throttle switch is within 8 to 12 degrees of fully-open. If the readings are incorrect, adjust the TPS.

30 If all the resistance readings are correct and the TPS is properly adjusted, check for power (5 volts) at the sensor, and if necessary trace any wiring circuit problems between the sensor and ECU (see Chapter 12).

Adjustment

31 If the adjustment is not as specified (paragraphs 28 to 30), loosen the screws on the TPS, and rotate the sensor into the correct adjustment. Follow the procedure for checking the TPS given above, and tighten the screws when the setting is correct.

32 Recheck the TPS once more; if the readings are correct, reconnect the TPS harness connector.

Early 535i models with automatic transmission

Check

33 First test the continuity of the TPS. Follow paragraphs 28 to 30 and check for continuity.

34 Next, test the idle position switch **(see illustration)**. Unplug the electrical connector in the idle position switch harness, and

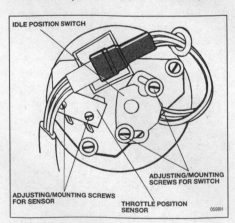

4.34 Idle position switch and TPS on early 535i models with automatic transmission

connect an ohmmeter to terminals 1 and 2. There should be continuity. Open the throttle slightly, and measure the resistance. There should now be no continuity.

35 Check for the correct voltage signals from the TPS, with the throttle closed and the ignition on. Probe the back of the TPS connector with a voltmeter, and check for voltage at terminal 3 (black wire) and earth. There should be 5 volts present. Also, probe terminal 3 (black wire) and terminal 1 (brown wire). There should be 5 volts present here also.

36 Check for voltage at terminal 2 (yellow wire) and terminal 1 (brown wire), and slowly open the throttle. The voltage should increase steadily from 0.7 volts (throttle closed) to 4.8 volts (throttle fully-open).

Adjustment

37 First measure the stabilised voltage. With the ignition on and the throttle closed, measure the voltage between terminal 3 (black wire) and terminal 1 (brown wire). It should be about 5 volts.

38 Next, loosen the sensor mounting screws, and connect the voltmeter to terminal 2 (yellow wire) and terminal 3 (black wire). With the throttle fully open, rotate the switch until there is 0.20 to 0.24 volts less than the stabilised voltage. **Note:** *You will need a digital voltmeter to measure these small changes in voltage.*

39 Recheck the TPS once more; if the readings are correct, reconnect the TPS electrical connector. It is a good idea to lock the TPS screws with paint or thread-locking compound.

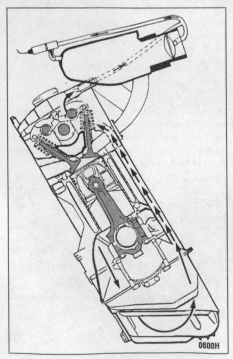

5.1 Diagram of the PCV system on the M20 engine (others similar)

Airflow meter

General description

40 The airflow meter is located on the air intake duct. The airflow meter measures the amount of air entering the engine. The ECU uses this information to control fuel delivery. A large volume of air indicates acceleration, while a small volume of air indicates deceleration or idle. Refer to Chapter 4 for all the diagnostic checks and renewal procedures for the airflow meter.

Ignition timing sensors

41 Ignition timing is electronically-controlled on Motronic systems, and is not adjustable. During starting, a crankshaft position sensor relays the crankshaft position to the ECU, and an initial baseline ignition point is determined. Once the engine is running, the ignition point is continually changing based on the various input signals to the ECU. Engine speed is signalled by a speed sensor. Early Motronic systems have the reference sensor and the speed sensor mounted on the bellhousing over the flywheel. Later Motronic systems have a single sensor (pulse sensor) mounted over the crankshaft pulley. This sensor functions as a speed sensor as well as a position sensor. Refer to Chapter 5 for more information. **Note**: *Some models are equipped with a TDC sensor mounted on the front of the engine. This sensor is strictly for the BMW service test unit, and it is not part of the Motronic ignition system.*

---

5 Positive crankcase ventilation (PCV) system

1 The Positive Crankcase Ventilation (PCV) system **(see illustration)** reduces hydrocarbon emissions by scavenging crankcase vapours. It does this by circulating blow-by gases and then re-routing them to the intake manifold by way of the air cleaner.

2 This PCV system is a sealed system. The crankcase blow-by vapours are routed directly to the air cleaner or air collector with crankcase pressure behind them. The vapour is not purged with fresh air on most models or

5.2 PCV hose being removed from the valve cover

5.3 It's a good idea to check for excess residue from the crankcase vapours circulating in the hoses and ports - this can eventually clog the system, and cause a pressure increase in the engine block

filtered with a flame trap like most conventional systems. There are no conventional PCV valves fitted on these systems - just a hose **(see illustration)**.

3 The main components of the PCV system are the hoses that connect the valve cover to the throttle body or air cleaner. If abnormal operating conditions (such as piston ring problems) arise, the system is designed to allow excessive amounts of blow-by gases to

flow back through the crankcase vent tube into the intake system, to be consumed by normal combustion. **Note**: *Since these models don't use a filtering element, it's a good idea to check the PCV system passageways for clogging from sludge and combustion residue* **(see illustration)**.

6 Evaporative emissions control (EVAP) system

General description

Note: *This system is normally only fitted to those vehicles equipped with a catalytic converter.*

1 When the engine isn't running, the fuel in the fuel tank evaporates to some extent, creating fuel vapour. The evaporative emissions control system **(see illustration)** stores these fuel vapours in a charcoal canister. When the engine is cruising, the purge control valve is opened slightly, and a small amount of fuel vapour is drawn into the intake manifold and burned. When the engine is starting cold or idling, the purge valve prevents any vapours from entering the intake manifold and causing excessively-rich fuel mixture.

2 Two types of purge valve are used; electrically-operated or vacuum-operated. To find out which type is on your vehicle, follow the hose from the charcoal canister until you locate the purge valve. Some are located on the intake manifold, and others near the charcoal canister. Look for either an electrical connector, or vacuum lines, to the purge valve.

3 A faulty EVAP system will only affect engine driveability when the engine is warm. The EVAP system is not usually the cause of difficult cold starting or any other cold-running problems.

Check
Vacuum-operated purge valve

4 Remove the vacuum lines from the purge valve, and blow into the larger valve port. It should be closed, and not pass any air. **Note:** *Some models have a thermo-vacuum valve that delays canister purging until the coolant temperature reaches approximately 46° C. Check this valve to make sure that vacuum is controlled at the proper temperatures. The valve is usually located in the intake manifold, near the thermo-time switch and the coolant temperature sensor.*

5 Disconnect the small vacuum hose from the purge valve, and apply vacuum with a hand-

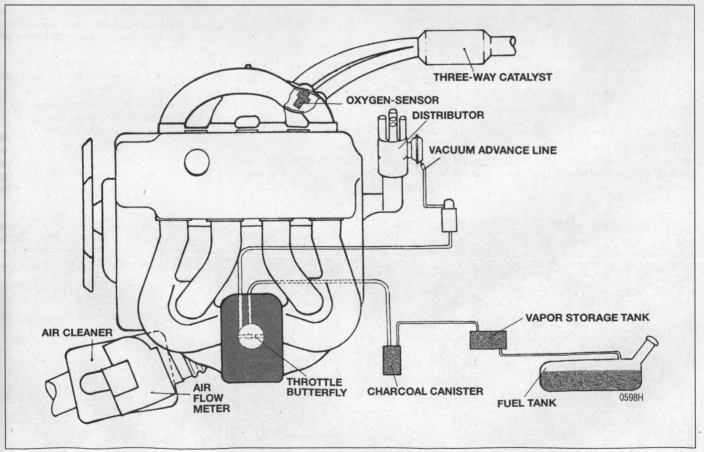

6.1 Diagram of the EVAP system on the M10 engine (others similar)

6.8 When the ignition is switched on, there should be a distinct "click" from the purge valve

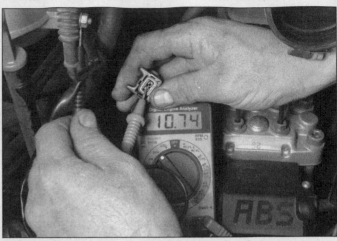

6.9 Check for battery voltage at the electrical connector to the purge valve

held vacuum pump. The purge valve should be open, and air should be able to pass through.

6 If the test results are unsatisfactory, renew the purge valve.

Electrically-operated purge valve

7 Disconnect any lines from the purge valve, and (without disconnecting the electrical connector) place it in a convenient spot for testing.

8 Check that the valve makes a "click" sound as the ignition is switched on (see illustration).

9 If the valve does not "click", disconnect the valve connector, and check for power to the valve using a test light or a voltmeter (see illustration).

10 If battery voltage is present, but the valve does not work, renew it. If there is no voltage present, check the Motronic control unit and the wiring.

Canister

11 Mark all the hoses for position, then detach them from the canister.

12 Slide the canister out of its mounting clip. On some models, it will be necessary to release the retaining clip (see illustration).

13 Visually examine the canister for leakage or damage.

14 Renew the canister if you find evidence of damage or leakage.

---

7 Catalytic converter

General description

1 To reduce emissions of unburnt hydrocarbons (HC), carbon monoxide (CO) and oxides of nitrogen (NOx), the later vehicles covered by this manual are equipped with a catalytic converter (see illustration). The converter contains a ceramic honeycomb coated with precious metals, which speed up the reaction between the pollutants listed previously and the oxygen in the exhaust gas. The pollutants are oxidised to produce water (H_2O), nitrogen and carbon dioxide (CO_2).

Check

2 Visually examine the converter(s) for cracks or damage. Make sure all nuts and bolts are tight.

3 Inspect the insulation cover (if applicable) welded onto the converter - it should not be loose.

⚠ *Caution: If an insulation cover is dented so that it touches the converter housing inside, excessive heat may be transferred to the floor.*

4 Start the engine and run it at idle speed.

5 Check for exhaust gas leakage from the

6.12 EVAP system charcoal canister viewed from under the vehicle (316i model)

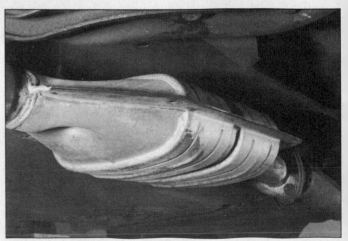

7.1 Typical catalytic converter (M10 engine type shown, others similar)

converter flanges. Check the body of each converter for holes.

Component renewal

6 See Chapter 4 for removal and refitting procedures.

Precautions

7 The catalytic converter is a reliable and simple device, which needs no maintenance in itself, but there are some facts of which an owner should be aware, if the converter is to function properly for its full service life.

(a) *DO NOT use leaded (eg UK "4-star") petrol in a car equipped with a catalytic converter - the lead will coat the precious metals, reducing their converting efficiency, and will eventually destroy the converter.*

(b) *Always keep the ignition and fuel systems well-maintained in accordance with the manufacturer's schedule, as given in Chapter 1. In particular, ensure that the air cleaner filter element, the fuel filter (where fitted) and the spark plugs are renewed at the correct interval. If the intake air/fuel mixture is allowed to become too rich due to neglect, unburned fuel will enter the catalytic converter, overheating the element and eventually destroying the converter.*

(c) *If the engine develops a misfire, do not drive the car at all (or at least as little as possible) until the fault is cured - the misfire will allow unburned fuel to enter the converter, which will result in its overheating, as noted above.*

(d) *DO NOT push- or tow-start the car - this will soak the catalytic converter in unburned fuel, causing it to overheat when the engine does start - see (b) or (c) above.*

(e) *DO NOT switch off the ignition at high engine speeds - ie do not "blip" the throttle immediately before switching off the engine. If the ignition is switched off at anything above idle speed, unburned fuel will enter the (very hot) catalytic converter, with the possible risk of its igniting on the element and damaging the converter.*

(f) *DO NOT use fuel or engine oil additives - these may contain substances harmful to the catalytic converter.*

(g) *DO NOT continue to use the car if the engine burns oil to the extent of leaving a visible trail of blue smoke - the unburned carbon deposits will clog the converter passages, and reduce its efficiency; in severe cases, the element will overheat.*

(h) *Remember that the catalytic converter operates at very high temperatures - hence the heat shields on the car's underbody - and the casing will become hot enough to ignite combustible materials which brush against it. DO NOT, therefore, park the car in dry undergrowth, or over long grass or piles of dead leaves.*

(i) *Remember that the catalytic converter is FRAGILE - do not strike it with tools during servicing work, and take great care when working on the exhaust system. Ensure that the converter is well clear of any jacks or other lifting gear used to raise the car, and do not drive the car over rough ground, road humps, etc, in such a way as to "ground" the exhaust system.*

(j) *In some cases, particularly when the car is new and/or is used for stop/start driving, a sulphurous smell (like that of rotten eggs) may be noticed from the exhaust. This is common to many catalytic converter-equipped cars, and seems to be due to the small amount of sulphur found in some petrols reacting with hydrogen in the exhaust, to produce hydrogen sulphide (H_2S) gas; while this gas is toxic, it is not produced in sufficient amounts to be a problem. Once the car has covered a few thousand miles, the problem should disappear - in the meanwhile, a change of driving style, or of the brand of petrol used, may effect a solution.*

(k) *The catalytic converter, used on a well-maintained and well-driven car, should last for 50 000 to 100 000 miles - from this point on, the CO level should be carefully checked regularly, to ensure that the converter is still operating efficiently. If the converter is no longer effective, it must be renewed.*

6

Notes

Chapter 7 Part A: Manual transmission

Contents

Degrees of difficulty

Easy, suitable for novice with little experience		**Fairly easy,** suitable for beginner with some experience		**Fairly difficult,** suitable for competent DIY mechanic		**Difficult,** suitable for experienced DIY mechanic		**Very difficult,** suitable for expert DIY or professional	

Specifications

Torque wrench settings	Nm
Output shaft flange nut	
ZF transmission (use thread-locking compound)	100
Getrag transmission	
First stage	170
Second stage	Loosen completely
Third stage	120
Transmission-to-engine hex-head bolts	
M8	22 to 27
M10	47 to 51
M12	66 to 82
Transmission-to-engine Torx-head bolts	
M8	20 to 24
M10	38 to 47
M12	64 to 80
Transmission rear support nut	22 to 24
Rubber mountings (to transmission or crossmember)	43 to 48
Transmission drain plug/filler plug	40 to 60

1 General information

The manual transmission used in the vehicles covered by this manual is a five-speed unit, of Getrag or ZF manufacture. To identify a transmission, look for the manufacturer's stamp and code numbers and letters. The manufacturer's stamp is on the case, just in front of the mounting for the clutch slave cylinder; the identification code and letters are located on top of the bellhousing.

2 Gear lever - removal and refitting

Removal

1 Put the transmission in reverse. Raise and support the front of the vehicle. Be sure to chock the rear wheels to keep the vehicle from rolling.

2 Pull the gear lever knob up and off the gear lever.

3 Remove the gaiter and the sound-deadening material beneath.

4 Remove the rubber dust cover. On models with an aluminium gearchange housing, unplug the connector for the reversing light switch before removing the dust cover.

5 Working from under the vehicle, disconnect the gear lever from the gearchange rod by removing the retaining clip (see illustration).

6 On models with a pressed steel gearchange housing, remove the circlip from the top of the gear lever bearing (see illustration) and lift out the gear lever.

7 On models with an aluminium gearchange housing, use two screwdrivers to engage the slots of the bearing retaining ring from below the gear lever lower bearing. To unlock the

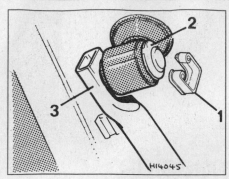

2.5 Working from under the vehicle, remove the retaining clip (1) to disconnect the gear lever (2) from the gearchange rod (3)

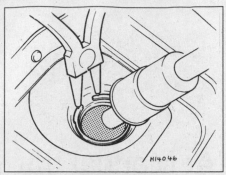

2.6 On models with a pressed steel gearchange housing, remove the circlip from the top of the gear lever bearing, and lift out the gear lever

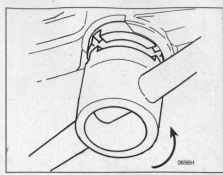

2.7 On models with an aluminium gearchange housing, turn the bearing retaining ring a quarter-turn anti-clockwise, and lift out the gear lever (special tool shown here, but two screwdrivers, with tips engaged in opposite slots, can be used)

ring, turn it a quarter-turn anti-clockwise **(see illustration)** and lift out the gear lever.

Refitting

8 Refitting is the reverse of the removal procedure.

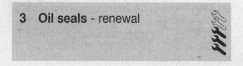

3 Oil seals - renewal

1 Worn or damaged transmission oil seals will cause leaks. Insufficient lubricant in the transmission can cause difficult gear changing, jumping out of gear, and transmission noise. Ultimately, this loss of lubricant will lead to increased wear, and component failure.
2 All three transmission seals can be renewed without dismantling the transmission; two of them can be renewed without even removing the transmission.
3 If you suspect a leaking seal, get underneath the transmission and inspect the seals closely. Raise and support the front of the vehicle. Be sure to chock the rear wheels to keep the vehicle from rolling.
4 Do not confuse engine oil leaks with those from the transmission - hypoid gear oil has a unique smell, for example, and can thus readily be distinguished from engine oil. If the oil is coating the front of the propeller shaft, either the selector shaft or the output shaft seal is leaking. If you find oil in the bottom of the bellhousing, the input shaft seal may be leaking (of course, the crankshaft rear oil seal could also cause engine oil to collect in the bottom of the bellhousing). Whenever you decide to renew a seal, always check the vent on top of the transmission housing first. A clogged or damaged vent can cause pressure inside the transmission to rise enough to pump lubricant past the seals. If you simply renew a seal without cleaning out a clogged vent, the new seal will quickly fail.

Output shaft oil seal

5 Raise and support the front of the vehicle. Be sure to chock the rear wheels to keep the vehicle from rolling.
6 Where necessary for access, remove the exhaust system (see Chapter 4).
7 Remove the propeller shaft (see Chapter 8). Alternatively, if care is taken not to strain the universal joints, the propeller shaft may remain connected to the final drive.
8 Bend the lockplate tabs out of their respective grooves, and remove the lockplate. Hold the flange stationary (if necessary, bolt a long bar to it) and remove the flange nut with a 30 mm thin-walled socket. Remove the flange from the output shaft. Use a puller, if necessary.
9 Using a seal removal tool or a small screwdriver, carefully prise out the old oil seal **(see illustration)**. Make sure you don't damage the seal bore when you prise out the seal.
10 Apply a light coat of lubricant to the lip of the new seal, and clean off the end of the output shaft. Slide the seal onto the shaft, and carefully drive it into place using a short section of pipe with an outside diameter slightly smaller than the outside diameter of the seal.
11 Refit the flange. Coat the side of the nut that faces toward the flange with sealant, to prevent leaks. Tighten the flange nut to the torque listed in this Chapter's Specifications. Note that the nut must be tightened in three stages on Getrag transmissions. Thread-locking compound should be applied to its threads on ZF transmissions. Fit a new lockplate, and bend the tabs into their respective grooves.
12 The remainder of refitting is the reverse of removal.

Selector shaft oil seal

13 Follow paragraphs 5 to 8 above.
14 To disconnect the gearchange rod from the selector shaft on early models, remove the bush lockring, then use a small drift to drive out the pin.

15 To disconnect the gearchange rod from the selector shaft on later models, put the transmission in 3rd gear, pull back on the spring sleeve, and drive out the pin.
16 Prise out the selector shaft seal **(see illustration 3.9)** with a seal removal tool or a small screwdriver. Make sure you don't damage the seal bore while prising out the seal.
17 Coat the new seal lip with lubricant, then slide the seal onto the end of the selector shaft. Drive the seal into place with a socket or piece of pipe of suitable dimensions.
18 Reconnect the gearchange rod to the selector shaft.
19 Refit the flange (see paragraph 11 above). The remainder of refitting is the reverse of removal.

Input shaft seal

20 Remove the transmission (see Section 5).
21 Remove the clutch release bearing and release lever (see Chapter 8).

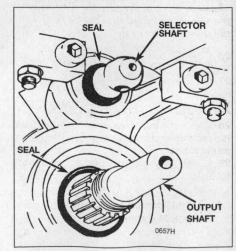

3.9 Using a seal removal tool or a small screwdriver, carefully prise out the old output shaft oil seal or selector shaft seal

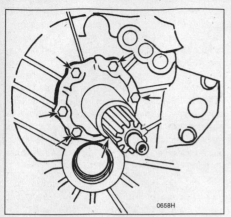

3.22a Locations of the guide sleeve bolts (arrowed) on a 3-Series model (Getrag 240 transmission shown)

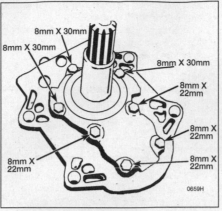

3.22b Locations of the guide sleeve bolts (arrowed) on a 5-Series model (Getrag 265 transmission shown)

4.1 To check a transmission mounting for wear, insert a large screwdriver or lever over the crossmember and under the end of the transmission, and try to prise the transmission upwards - if the transmission lifts easily, renew the mounting(s)

22 Remove the bolts for the clutch release guide sleeve (see illustrations). The bolts are not all the same size on some models, so be sure to note where each bolt goes. Remove the sleeve and any spacers behind it.

23 Using a seal removal tool or a screwdriver, prise out the old seal. Make sure you don't damage the seal bore.

24 Lubricate the lip of the new seal with lubricant, and drive it into place with a section of pipe of suitable dimensions. Where applicable, renew the O-ring in the guide sleeve groove.

25 Clean the mounting bolts and sealing surfaces of the guide sleeve, and the bolt threads in the case. On 3-Series models with ZF transmissions, use a new gasket without sealant. On Getrag transmissions without an O-ring, apply suitable sealant to the guide sleeve sealing surface. Refit the guide sleeve and spacer(s).

⚠ *Caution: On Getrag transmissions (3-Series models only), make sure the groove in the sleeve is aligned with the oil bore in the transmission case.*

26 Coat the bolt shoulders with sealant, refit the bolts and tighten them.

27 The remainder of refitting is the reverse of removal.

All seals

28 Check the transmission oil level, and add the recommended lubricant (see Chapter 1) as necessary.

29 Lower the vehicle, test-drive it and check for leaks.

4 Transmission mountings - check and renewal

1 Raise and support the vehicle. Insert a large screwdriver or lever over the crossmember and under the rear of the transmission housing (see illustration). Try to prise the transmission up slightly.

2 The transmission should move very little. If it moves easily, the mount is probably cracked or torn. Renew it.

3 To renew the mounting, first support the weight of the transmission with a trolley jack. Remove the nuts and bolts securing the mounting to the crossmember and to the transmission, then raise the transmission slightly and remove the mounting.

4 Refitting is the reverse of removal.

5 Transmission - removal and refitting

⚠ *Caution: If the radio in your vehicle is equipped with an anti-theft system, make sure you have the correct activation code before disconnecting the battery. Refer to the information on page 0-7 at the front of this manual before detaching the cable.*
Note: *If, after connecting the battery, the wrong language appears on the instrument panel display, refer to page 0-7 for the language resetting procedure.*

Removal

1 Disconnect the battery negative cable.

2 Remove the exhaust system (see Chapter 4).

3 Remove the propeller shaft (see Chapter 8).

4 Disconnect the gearchange linkage (see Section 2).

5 Unbolt and remove the gearchange housing mounting brackets. Before proceeding, ensure that the gearchange linkage is completely disconnected.

6 Disconnect or remove the TDC sensor, speed/position sensors and reversing light switch, as applicable, from the transmission (see Chapter 5).

7 Remove the clutch slave cylinder (see Chapter 8). Do not disconnect the clutch hydraulic fluid hose. Suspend the slave cylinder with a piece of wire.

⚠ *Caution: Do NOT operate the clutch while the slave cylinder is removed from the transmission. The slave cylinder could be damaged if the pushrod is forced out of the cylinder.*

8 Support the transmission with a transmission jack or a trolley jack, and remove the transmission support mounting nuts.

9 Carefully lower the transmission/engine assembly until it's resting on the front crossmember.

⚠ *Caution: Never allow the weight of the transmission to hang unsupported on the transmission input shaft. Such a load will damage the clutch and the transmission components.*

10 Remove the bolts that attach the transmission to the engine. Some bolts may have a Torx head; you'll need to use a special Torx socket for these bolts.

11 Carefully separate the transmission from the engine. Make sure you don't place any strain on the transmission input shaft. Lower the jack until there's enough clearance to pull the transmission out from under the vehicle.

Refitting

12 Refitting is basically the reverse of removal. Be sure to lightly lubricate the input shaft splines with Microlube GL 261 or its equivalent, then carefully position the transmission on the engine.

7A

HAYNES HiNT *The splines of the input shaft and the splines of the clutch disc may not quite line up; if they don't, turn the crankshaft pulley with a spanner to rotate the crankshaft slightly.*

Caution: BMW recommends using only Microlube GL 261 on the clutch disc and transmission input shaft splines. Otherwise, the clutch disc could bind on the input shaft and cause difficult gearchanging. Microlube GL 261 is available at BMW dealers (BMW Part No 81 22 9 407 436).

Note: *If any of the transmission bolts are the Torx-head type, be sure to use washers when refitting the bolts; refitting bolts without washers can cause the bolts to seal so tightly*

against the transmission housing that they're extremely difficult to loosen.

13 If the transmission was drained, be sure to refill it with the correct lubricant once refitting is complete (see Chapter 1).

6 Transmission overhaul - general information

The overhaul of a manual transmission is a somewhat difficult job for the home mechanic. It involves the dismantling and reassembly of many small parts. Numerous clearances must be precisely measured and, if necessary, adjusted with selective-fit spacers and circlips. For this reason, we strongly recommend the home mechanic not to attempt any more than the operations already described in this Chapter, leaving overhaul to a transmission specialist. Exchange transmissions are available at reasonable prices, and the cost involved in overhauling the transmission at home is almost sure to exceed the cost of a rebuilt unit, to say nothing of the time required to do so.

Chapter 7 Part B: Automatic transmission

Contents

Degrees of difficulty

| Easy, suitable for novice with little experience | | Fairly easy, suitable for beginner with some experience | | Fairly difficult, suitable for competent DIY mechanic | | Difficult, suitable for experienced DIY mechanic | | Very difficult, suitable for expert DIY or professional | |

Specifications

Kickdown cable adjustment
Distance between cable stop and end of cable sleeve
 At idle .... 0.50 ± 0.25 mm
 With accelerator pedal in kickdown position .... 44.0 mm (minimum)

Torque wrench settings
Nm

Transmission-to-engine hex-head bolts
 M8 24
 M10 45
 M12 82
Transmission-to-engine Torx-head bolts
 M8 21
 M10 42
 M12 63
Transmission rear support-to-body 21
Torque converter-to-driveplate
 M8 26
 M10 49
Transmission reinforcement plate 23
Output shaft flange nut 100
Fluid cooler lines
 3-Series
  Cooler lines-to-transmission case 35
 5-Series
  Cooler line coupling nuts 18
  Cooler line hollow bolt 35
  Cooler line adapter coupling 35
Fluid filler tube-to-transmission sump
 3 HP 22 .... 100 to 110
 4 HP 22 H/EH 98
Transmission sump drain plug 16

7B

1 General information

Early models use a three-speed ZF 3 HP 22 automatic transmission. Later models use a four-speed ZF 4 HP 22 automatic transmission, or a ZF 4 HP EH automatic transmission with electronic shifting control.

Because of the complexity of the clutch mechanisms and the hydraulic control systems, and because of the special tools and expertise needed to overhaul an automatic transmission, this work is usually beyond the scope of the home mechanic. The procedures in this Chapter are therefore limited to general diagnosis, routine maintenance, adjustments, and transmission removal and refitting.

Should the transmission require major repair work, take it to a dealer service department or an automatic transmission specialist. You can at least save the expense of removing and refitting the transmission by doing that yourself, but note that most fault diagnosis tests require the transmission to be in the vehicle.

If you decide to fit a new or reconditioned transmission unit, make sure you purchase the right unit. The transmission identification plate is located on the left side of the housing, just behind the transmission selector lever **(see illustration)**.

2 Fault finding - general

Note: *Automatic transmission problems may be attributable to five general areas: poor engine performance, incorrect adjustment, hydraulic or mechanical malfunctions, or malfunctions in the computer or its signal network. Diagnosis of these problems should always begin with a check of the easily-repaired items: fluid level and fluid condition (see Chapter 1), selector linkage adjustment and throttle linkage adjustment. Next, perform a road test to determine if the problem has*

1.4 The automatic transmission identification plate is located on the left side of the transmission housing, just behind the manual selector lever

been corrected, or if more diagnosis is necessary. If the problem persists after the preliminary tests and corrections are completed, additional diagnosis should be done by a dealer service department or automatic transmission specialist. Refer to the "Fault finding" section at the rear of this manual for information on symptoms of transmission problems.

Preliminary checks

1 Drive the vehicle to warm the transmission to normal operating temperature.
2 Check the fluid level as described in Chapter 1:
a) *If the fluid level is unusually low, add enough fluid to bring the level within the designated area of the dipstick, then check for external leaks (see below).*
b) *If the fluid level is abnormally high, drain off the excess, then check the drained fluid for contamination by coolant. The presence of engine coolant in the automatic transmission fluid indicates that a failure has occurred in the internal radiator walls that separate the coolant from the transmission fluid (see Chapter 3).*
c) *If the fluid is foaming, drain it and refill the transmission, and check for coolant in the fluid.*
d) *Check the condition of the fluid on the dipstick. The fluid is normally dark red. If it is brown, or has a "burned" smell, drain and refill the transmission. If the fluid appears to be in poor condition, this either indicates lack of regular maintenance, or the presence of an internal fault in the transmission.*

3 Check the engine idle speed. **Note:** *If the engine is obviously not running well, do not proceed with the preliminary transmission checks until it has been repaired and runs normally.*
4 Check the kickdown cable for freedom of movement. Adjust it if necessary (see Section 3). **Note:** *The kickdown cable may function properly when the engine is stopped and cold, only to give problems once the engine is hot. Check it cold and at normal engine operating temperature.*
5 Inspect the selector control linkage (see Section 5). Make sure that it's properly adjusted, and that the linkage operates smoothly.

Checking for fluid leaks

6 Most fluid leaks are easy to locate visually. Repair usually consists of renewing a seal or gasket. If a leak is difficult to find, the following may help.
7 Identify the fluid. Make sure it's transmission fluid, and not engine oil or brake fluid (automatic transmission fluid is a dark red colour).
8 Try to pinpoint the source of the leak. Drive the vehicle several miles, then park it over a large sheet of clean cardboard or newspaper.

After a minute or two, you should be able to locate the leak by determining the source of the dripping fluid.
9 Make a careful visual inspection of the suspected component and the area immediately around it. Pay particular attention to gasket mating surfaces. A mirror is often helpful for finding leaks in areas that are hard to see.
10 If the leak still cannot be found, clean the suspected area thoroughly with a degreaser or solvent, then dry it.
11 When the car is moving, airflow can sometimes blow leaking oil or fluid onto other components, making pinpointing the source of the leak more difficult. Having cleaned the suspected area, either drive the vehicle at low speed (so reducing the airflow) or allow the vehicle to warm up while stationary (apply the handbrake firmly if this is done). Run the engine at different speeds, and shift the transmission through all positions several times. Afterwards, inspect the suspected component again.
12 Once the leak has been located, the cause must be determined before it can be properly repaired. If a new gasket is fitted but the sealing flange is bent, the new gasket will not stop the leak. The bent flange must be straightened.
13 Before attempting to repair a leak, check that the conditions listed under the relevant headings below are corrected, or they may cause another leak. **Note:** *Some of the following conditions cannot be fixed without highly-specialised tools and expertise. Such problems must be referred to an automatic transmission specialist or a dealer service department.*

Gasket leaks

14 Check the transmission sump periodically. Make sure that the bolts are all present and that they are tight, and that the sump is undamaged (dents in the sump may have resulted in damage to the valve body inside).
15 If the sump gasket is leaking, the fluid level may be too high, the vent may be blocked, the sump bolts may be too tight, the sump sealing flange may be warped, the sealing surface of the transmission housing may be damaged, or the gasket itself is damaged. If sealant is used between the sump and the transmission housing, it may be the wrong sealant. The leak may even be due to a cracked or porous transmission casting.

Seal leaks

16 If a transmission seal is leaking, the fluid level or pressure may be too high, the vent may be blocked, the seal bore may be damaged, the seal itself may be damaged or improperly fitted, the surface of the shaft protruding through the seal may be damaged, or a loose bearing may be causing excessive shaft movement.
17 Make sure the dipstick/filler tube nut is tight. Periodically check the area around the

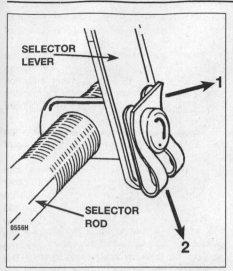

3.2 To disconnect the selector rod from the lower selector lever on the 3 HP 22 transmission, pull the top of the clip out (1), then slide the clip off the pin (2)

speedometer gear or sensor for leakage. If transmission fluid is evident, check the O-ring for damage.

Case leaks

18 If the case itself appears to be leaking, the casting is porous and will have to be repaired or renewed.
19 Make sure the fluid cooler hose fittings are tight and in good condition.

Fluid comes out of vent pipe or filler tube

20 If this condition occurs, the transmission is overfilled, there is coolant in the fluid, the dipstick is incorrect, the vent is blocked, or the drain-back holes are blocked.

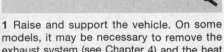

3 Selector lever linkage - adjustment

1 Raise and support the vehicle. On some models, it may be necessary to remove the exhaust system (see Chapter 4) and the heat shield to reach the lower end of the selector lever.

3 HP 22 transmission

2 Remove the retaining clip (see illustration) from the selector rod pin. Pull out the pin and disconnect the selector rod from the bottom of the selector lever.
3 Pull the selector lever on the transmission back as far as it will go, then push it forward two clicks. The transmission should now be in Neutral.
4 Working from inside the vehicle, place the selector lever in the Neutral (N) position.
5 Have an assistant push the selector lever forwards against the Neutral position stop in the selector gate. Working under the vehicle, turn the selector pin on the selector rod until

3.8 To adjust the selector linkage on the 4 HP 22 transmission, loosen this nut (arrowed), push the transmission selector lever forwards (towards the engine), pull the selector cable rod back and tighten the nut securely. Note: *The linkage shown here (on a later-model 5-Series) is typical; however, the lever on some older units may face up instead of down, and utilise a clevis arrangement between the rod and the lever instead of a nut).*

the pin lines up with the hole on the lower end of the selector lever. Shorten the linkage by turning the pin an extra one or two turns in a clockwise direction.
6 Refit the selector rod pin. Verify that the linkage is correctly adjusted by starting the engine, applying the brakes firmly and moving the selector lever though all selector positions.

4 HP 22 transmissions

7 Inside the vehicle, place the selector lever in the Park (P) position.
8 Loosen the nut (see illustration) which attaches the cable to the selector lever on the transmission.
9 Push the selector lever on the transmission forwards (towards the engine) and pull the selector cable rod backwards.
10 Reconnect the cable rod at the transmission selector lever, and tighten the nut securely.
11 Verify that the linkage is correctly adjusted by starting the engine, applying the brakes firmly and moving the selector lever though all selector positions.

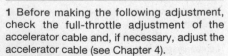

4 Kickdown cable - adjustment

1 Before making the following adjustment, check the full-throttle adjustment of the accelerator cable and, if necessary, adjust the accelerator cable (see Chapter 4).
2 With the accelerator pedal released, use a feeler gauge to check the distance between the cable stop and the end of the cable threaded sleeve (see illustration), and compare your measurement with the adjustment dimensions listed in this Chapter's Specifications. If the distance is incorrect,

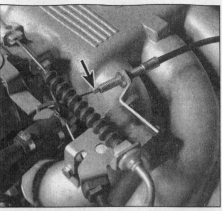

4.2 With the throttle at the idle position, check the distance between the cable stop (arrowed) and the end of the cable threaded sleeve (the correct dimensions are listed in this Chapter's Specifications); if the distance is incorrect, loosen the locknuts, adjust the position of the cable sleeve, and tighten the nuts

loosen the locknuts, adjust the position of the cable sleeve, and tighten the nuts.
3 Loosen the kickdown switch locknut under the accelerator pedal (see illustration) and screw the switch in as far as possible.
4 Depress the accelerator pedal to the point at which you can feel resistance, and hold the pedal in this position; unscrew the kickdown switch so that it now just contacts the pedal, and tighten the locknut.
5 Check your adjustment by depressing the accelerator pedal to the kickdown position and noting the position of the cable stop (see paragraph 2 above). Compare the measurement with the dimension given in this Chapter's Specifications. If the cable can't be adjusted to the correct specifications, recheck, and if necessary readjust, the full-throttle adjustment of the accelerator cable. When the accelerator cable adjustment is correct, try adjusting the kickdown cable again.

7B

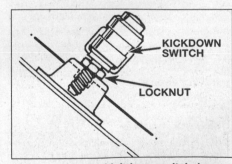

4.3 To adjust the kickdown switch, loosen the locknut, and screw the switch in as far as possible. Depress the accelerator pedal to the point at which you can feel resistance, and hold the pedal in this position; unscrew the kickdown switch so that it now just contacts the pedal, and tighten the locknut

5.2 Prise out the trim panel around the base of the selector lever (on some 5-Series models, you'll also need to remove the trim bezel screws and the trim bezel)

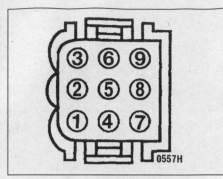

5.4 Inhibitor switch wiring connector on early 5-Series models

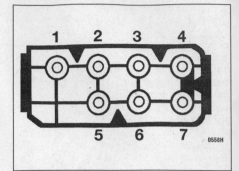

5.5 Inhibitor switch wiring connector on later 5-Series models

5 Starter inhibitor/reversing light switch - check and renewal

1 If the engine can be started with the selector lever in positions other than Park or Neutral, or if the reversing lights do not come on when the lever is moved to Reverse, check the starter inhibitor switch.
2 Remove the selector lever knob retaining screw, and pull off the selector lever knob. Prise out the trim panel around the base of the selector lever (see illustration). Remove the trim bezel screws and the trim bezel if necessary.

3-Series models

3 Place the selector lever in Neutral, detach the wiring connector to the switch, then connect an ohmmeter between the terminals for the blue/white wire and the green/black wire, and verify that there's continuity. Put the selector lever in Park, and try the same test again. There should still be continuity. Place the selector lever in Drive, 1 and 2, and verify there's no continuity when you connect the ohmmeter between the blue/white wire and the green/yellow wire terminals AND when you put the ohmmeter probes between the terminals for the blue/white wire and the green/black wire. Finally, put the selector lever in Reverse, and verify that there's continuity between the terminals for blue/white wire and the green/yellow wire.

5-Series models

Note: If the connector terminal pattern for the inhibitor switch on your vehicle doesn't match either of the two types shown here, special checking procedures may be required to determine if the switch is operating properly. Have the switch checked by a dealer service department or specialist.
4 On early 5-Series models, unplug the connector(s) (see illustration), then check for continuity between the following terminals:

Selector position	Terminals
Park	3 and 4
Reverse	3 and 5
Neutral	3 and 6
Drive	3 and 7
3	3 and 1
2	3 and 8
1	3 and 9

5 On later 5-Series models, unplug the connector (see illustration) and check for continuity between the following terminals:

Selector position	Terminals
Park	1 and 3 and 7
Reverse	1 and 4 and 7; 5 and 6
Neutral	1 and 2 and 3
Drive	1 and 4
3	1 and 2
2	1 and 7
1	1 and 2 and 7

6 Automatic transmission - removal and refitting

⚠ **Caution: If the radio in your vehicle is equipped with an anti-theft system, make sure you have the correct activation code before disconnecting the battery. Refer to the information on page 0-7 at the front of this manual before detaching the cable.**
Note: If, after connecting the battery, the wrong language appears on the instrument panel display, refer to page 0-7 for the language resetting procedure.

Removal

1 Disconnect the battery negative cable.
2 Disconnect the kickdown cable, and detach it from the bracket on the intake manifold (see Chapter 4).
3 On the M10 engine, remove the distributor cap to prevent damage when the engine tilts back during transmission removal.
4 Raise and support the vehicle.
5 Remove the exhaust system (see Chapter 4).
6 Disconnect the selector rod or cable (see Section 3).
7 Remove the propeller shaft (see Chapter 8).

8 Drain the transmission (see Chapter 1). Detach the filler tube, and disconnect the fluid cooler lines (see illustration). Plug the lines, to prevent contaminants from entering the transmission.
9 On the 3 HP 22 transmission, remove the transmission cover at the bottom of the bellhousing. On other units, remove the reinforcement plate and the transmission bump stop at the bottom of the bellhousing.
10 Reach through the opening in the bellhousing and remove the bolts that attach the torque converter to the driveplate. On 3 HP 22 transmissions, there are four bolts; on 4 HP 22 units, there are three. Turn the engine as necessary to bring each bolt into view.
11 On vehicles with a Motronic fuel injection system, remove the engine speed and position sensors mounted in the bellhousing (see Chapter 5).
12 On vehicles with the 4 HP 22 EH transmission, unplug the control unit electrical connector from the left side of the transmission, just above the transmission sump.
13 Support the transmission from underneath with a transmission jack or a trolley jack. If you use a trolley jack, place a block of wood between the jack head and the transmission sump to protect the sump. Remove the transmission rear support and, if applicable, the reinforcement bar by removing the bolts that hold them to the body. Lower the engine and transmission onto the front axle carrier.

6.8 Fluid filler tube union and fluid cooler lines (arrowed)

Caution: *Do NOT allow the torque converter shaft to support the weight of the transmission, or you will damage the torque converter or transmission.*

14 Remove the bolts that attach the transmission bellhousing to the engine.

15 To gain access to the torque converter, remove the inspection grille from the side of the bellhousing. Using a lever to ensure that the torque converter stays firmly mounted to the transmission, separate the transmission from the engine.

16 If you're fitting a new/rebuilt transmission, remove the torque converter and transfer it to the new/rebuilt unit. To get the torque converter off the old transmission, refit two long bolts halfway into the converter mounting holes, and pull evenly on both bolts. To refit the converter, see Section 7, paragraph 7.

Refitting

17 Refitting is basically the reverse of removal, but note the following:
a) *Tighten the torque converter bolts to the torque listed in this Chapter's Specifications.*
b) *Before reconnecting the fluid cooler lines and cooler, blow them out with compressed air, then flush them with clean fluid, to remove any friction lining particles that could clog the new or rebuilt transmission.*
c) *Use a new gasket on the transmission sump drain plug, and a new O-ring on the fluid filler tube connection to the sump.*
d) *When you plug in the control unit connector on 4 HP 22 EH transmissions, make sure the markings are aligned.*
e) *Refill the transmission with clean fluid (see Chapter 1).*
f) *Adjust the selector lever linkage and the kickdown cable (see Sections 3 and 4).*

7 Fluid seals - renewal

1 There are three seals in the automatic transmission - the torque converter seal, the transmission selector lever shaft seal, and the transmission output shaft seal - that can cause fluid leaks. If the torque converter seal is leaking, you'll find fluid in the bottom of the bellhousing. If the transmission selector lever shaft seal leaks, you'll see fluid on the side of the transmission case and the sump. If the output shaft seal leaks, you'll find fluid on the extension housing and the front of the propeller shaft.

2 You can renew all of these seals without dismantling the transmission, although

7.5 Using a hooked seal removal tool or a large screwdriver, carefully prise the old torque converter seal out of the transmission

renewing the torque converter seal requires removal of the transmission and the torque converter .

Torque converter seal

3 Remove the transmission and the torque converter (see Section 6).

4 Inspect the bush in the torque converter hub. If it's worn, the new seal will soon leak. Try removing any sharp edges or burrs with fine emery cloth. If the hub is too deeply scored to smooth out, a new torque converter should be fitted.

5 Using a hooked seal removal tool or a screwdriver, prise the old seal out of transmission case **(see illustration)**. Make sure you don't gouge the surface of the seal bore when prising out the old seal.

6 Lubricate the lip of the new seal with fluid, and carefully drive it into place with a socket or a section of pipe with an outside diameter slightly smaller than the outside diameter of the seal.

7 Refit the converter, making sure it is completely engaged with the front pump (to do this, turn the converter as you push it into place - continue turning and pushing until you're sure it's fully seated). Refit the transmission/converter assembly (see Section 6).

Transmission selector lever shaft seal

8 Raise and support the vehicle.

9 Remove the transmission selector lever **(see illustration 3.8)** from its shaft on the side of the transmission. Do not disconnect the linkage from the lever, or you'll have to readjust it.

10 Prise out the old seal with a small hooked seal removal tool or a small screwdriver. Make sure you don't gouge the surface of the seal bore when prising out the old seal.

11 Lubricate the lip of the new seal with fluid,

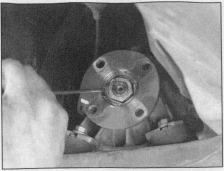

7.16 Bend back the tab on the locking plate, hold the flange stationary, and remove the flange nut with a 30 mm socket. Remove the flange from the output shaft, using a puller if necessary

and carefully drive it into place with a socket or a section of pipe with an outside diameter slightly smaller than the outside diameter of the seal.

12 Refit the transmission selector lever and tighten the nut. If you didn't disconnect the linkage, it should not be necessary to readjust it.

Output shaft seal

13 Raise and support the rear of the vehicle. Be sure to chock the front wheels to keep the vehicle from rolling.

14 Where necessary for access, remove the exhaust system (see Chapter 4).

15 Remove the propeller shaft (see Chapter 8).

16 Bend back the tab on the locking plate **(see illustration)**, hold the flange stationary and remove the flange nut with a 30 mm socket. Remove the flange from the output shaft. Use a puller, if necessary.

17 Using a seal removal tool or a small screwdriver, carefully prise out the old seal. Make sure you don't damage the seal bore when you prise out the seal.

18 Apply a light coating of fluid to the lip of the new seal, then clean off the end of the output shaft. Slide the seal onto the shaft, and carefully drive it into place using a short section of pipe with an outside diameter slightly smaller than the outside diameter of the seal.

19 Refit the flange. Coat the side of the nut that faces toward the flange with sealant, to prevent leaks. Tighten the flange nut to the torque listed in this Chapter's Specifications. Fit a new lockplate, and bend the tab into the slot.

20 The remainder of refitting is the reverse of removal.

All seals

21 Check the transmission fluid level and top up if necessary (Chapter 1).

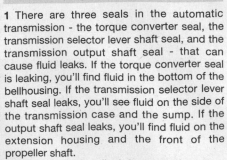

7B

Notes

Chapter 8 Clutch and driveline

Contents

Degrees of difficulty

Easy, suitable for novice with little experience	**Fairly easy,** suitable for beginner with some experience	**Fairly difficult,** suitable for competent DIY mechanic	**Difficult,** suitable for experienced DIY mechanic	**Very difficult,** suitable for expert DIY or professional

Specifications

General

Clutch pedal-to-bulkhead distance (dimension "A")	
3-Series	235 + 10 mm
5-Series	245 + 10 mm
Maximum allowable clutch disc run-out	0.5 mm
Minimum allowable clutch disc thickness	7.5 mm

Torque wrench settings

	Nm
Clutch master cylinder mounting bolts	22
Clutch slave cylinder bolts	22
Pressure plate-to-flywheel bolts	24
Propeller shaft	
Centre universal joint yoke mounting bolt	97
Centre bearing mounting bolts	21
Splined section clamping sleeve	10
Rear universal joint-to-final drive flange	
Nut with nylon insert ("squeeze-nut")	64
Ribbed nut	90
Flexible coupling-to-transmission flange	
M10 (Grade 8.8) bolts	48
M10 (Grade 10.9) bolts	64
M12 (Grade 8.8) bolts	81
M12 (Grade 10.9) bolts	100
Driveshafts	
M10 bolts without locking teeth	83
M10 bolts with locking teeth	
Allen-type	96
Torx-type	100
M8 bolts with locking teeth	64
M12 bolts	110
Driveshaft nut (3-Series)	200
Pinion shaft flange nut	
M20 bolts	185 (maximum), or until marks line up (see text)
M22 bolts	210 (maximum), or until marks line up (see text)

1 General information

Clutch

Models with manual transmissions are equipped with a hydraulically-actuated diaphragm-type clutch. The clutch disc is clamped by spring pressure between the diaphragm-type pressure plate assembly and the engine flywheel. The splined hub of the clutch disc rides on the transmission input shaft; the pressure plate cover is bolted to the engine flywheel.

When the clutch pedal is depressed, the master cylinder generates hydraulic pressure, which forces a pushrod out of the clutch slave (release) cylinder, moving the release lever and release bearing. As the release bearing pushes against the pressure plate release tangs, clamping pressure on the clutch disc is eased, disconnecting the engine from the transmission.

Two different types of clutch discs are used on the models covered by this manual, depending on the type of flywheel. On models with a conventional plate-type flywheel, the clutch disc has integral cushion springs and dampening springs. The cushion springs - located between the friction surfaces of the disc - help reduce the shock when the clutch is engaged; the dampening springs - visible in the centre of the hub - help absorb the rotating power pulses of the engine. On models with dual-mass flywheels, the dampening springs are integrated into the flywheel itself.

Propeller shaft

Power is transmitted from the transmission to the rear axle by a two-piece propeller shaft, joined behind the centre bearing by a "slip joint," a sliding, splined coupling. The slip joint allows slight fore-and-aft movement of the propeller shaft. The forward end of the propeller shaft is attached to the output flange of the transmission by a flexible rubber coupling. This coupling, sometimes referred to as a "Guibo" coupling or a "flex-disc," isolates the propeller shaft and differential from the sudden torque forces of the engine. On some models, a vibration damper is mounted between the transmission output flange and the flexible coupling. The middle of the propeller shaft is supported by the centre bearing, which is rubber-mounted to isolate propeller shaft vibrations. The bearing housing is bolted to the vehicle body. The forward end of the propeller shaft is aligned with the transmission by a centring guide recessed into the propeller shaft; the centring guide engages a centring pin on the transmission output flange. Universal joints are located at the centre bearing and at the rear end of the propeller shaft, to compensate for movement of the transmission and differential on their mountings and for any flexing of the chassis.

Differential (final drive) assembly

The rear-mounted differential assembly includes the drive pinion, the ring gear, the differential and the output flanges. The drive pinion, which drives the ring gear, is also known as the differential input shaft. It's connected to the propeller shaft via an input flange. The differential is bolted to the ring gear and drives the rear wheels through a pair of output flanges bolted to driveshafts with constant velocity (CV) joints at either end. The differential allows the wheels to turn at different speeds when cornering (the outside wheel must travel further - and therefore faster - than the inside wheel in the same period of time). The differential assembly is bolted to the rear axle carrier, and is attached to the body by flexible rubber bushings.

Major repair work on the differential assembly components (drive pinion, ring-and-pinion, and differential) requires many special tools and a high degree of expertise, and therefore should not be attempted by the home mechanic. If major repairs become necessary, we recommend that they be performed by a dealer service department or other garage.

Driveshafts and CV joints

The driveshafts deliver power from the differential output flanges to the rear wheels. The driveshafts are equipped with Constant Velocity (CV) joints at each end. A CV joint is similar in function to a standard universal joint, but can accept more radical driveshaft angles than the universal joint. CV joints allow the driveshafts to deliver power to the rear wheels while moving up and down with the rear suspension, even though the differential assembly, the driveshafts and the wheels are never in perfect alignment.

The inner CV joints on all models are bolted to the differential flanges. The outer CV joints on 3-Series models engage the splines of the wheel hubs, and are secured by an axle nut. The outer joints on 5-Series models are identical to the inner joints. Each joint is packed with a special CV joint lubricant, and sealed by a rubber boot. Inspect the boots regularly, to make sure they're in good condition. A ripped or torn boot will allow dirt to contaminate the CV joint. The CV joints on the vehicles covered by this manual cannot be overhauled, but they can be dismantled for cleaning during boot renewal (except for the outer joint on 3-Series models). The inner CV joint can be renewed separately on all models, as well as the outer joint on 5-Series models. On 3-Series models, the outer CV joint and the driveshaft must be renewed as a complete assembly.

2 Clutch - description and checking

Description

1 Manual transmission models feature a single dry plate, diaphragm spring-type clutch (see illustration). The actuation is through a hydraulic system.

2 When the clutch pedal is depressed, hydraulic fluid (under pressure from the clutch master cylinder) transfers force to the slave cylinder. Because the slave cylinder is connected to the clutch release fork, the fork moves the release bearing into contact with the clutch cover/pressure plate release fingers (tangs), disengaging the clutch disc.

3 The hydraulic system adjusts the clutch automatically, so no adjustment of the linkage or pedal is required, unless you renew the clutch master cylinder and/or pushrod.

4 Terminology can be a problem regarding clutch components because manufacturers, parts departments and the automotive aftermarket use different names for the same parts. For example, the driven plate is also called the clutch plate or friction disc, the slave cylinder is sometimes called the operating cylinder, the pressure plate is also called a clutch cover, etc.

Checking

5 Components with obvious damage must be renewed, but there are some preliminary checks you can make to diagnose a clutch system failure caused by less obvious problems.

6 The first check should be of the fluid level in the clutch master cylinder. If the fluid level is low, add fluid as necessary, and re-test. If the master cylinder runs dry, or if any of the hydraulic components are serviced, bleed the hydraulic system (see Section 7). If frequent topping-up is required, this can only be due to a leak.

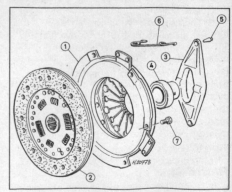

2.1 An exploded view of a typical clutch assembly

1 Pressure plate
2 Clutch disc
3 Release lever
4 Release bearing
5 Ball stud
6 Lever retaining spring
7 Bolt

7 To check "clutch spin-down time," run the engine at normal idle speed with the transmission in neutral (clutch pedal up). Disengage the clutch (pedal down), wait nine seconds, then select reverse gear. You should hear no grinding noises. A grinding noise indicates component failure, probably in the clutch cover assembly or the clutch disc.

8 To check for complete clutch release, run the engine (with the brake on to prevent movement) and hold the clutch pedal approximately 1/2-inch from the floor mat. Shift from first gear to reverse several times. If the gearchange is not smooth, component failure is indicated.

9 Visually inspect the clutch pedal bush at the top of the clutch pedal to make sure there is no sticking or excessive wear.

3 Clutch master cylinder - removal and refitting

> **Warning: Hydraulic fluid is poisonous. It is also an effective paint stripper. Take care not to get fluid onto the skin or in your eyes. Have some rags handy to catch any spillages, and wash any splashes off paintwork immediately with plenty of cold water.**

Removal

1 Remove the brake fluid reservoir cap (left-hand-drive models) or clutch fluid reservoir cap (right-hand-drive models) and remove the fluid in the reservoir with a syringe. On left-hand-drive models, fluid level should be below the brake line connection for the master cylinder.

2 On right-hand-drive models, disconnect the fluid hose from the bottom of the reservoir, and drain any remaining fluid.

3 Unscrew the union nut, and disconnect the threaded fitting for the clutch hydraulic line from the front of the master cylinder.

4 Working under the dash, remove the lower trim panel from the driver's side (see Chapter 11). Remove the bolt that secures the clutch master cylinder pushrod to the clutch pedal **(see illustration)**.

5 Remove the two bolts that hold the master cylinder to the clutch pedal bracket, detach the fluid hose from the top of the master cylinder, and remove the master cylinder. Have a rag handy to wipe up any spilled fluid.

Refitting

6 Refitting is basically the reverse of removal. Where applicable, make sure that the over-centre helper spring is engaged correctly in its guide. Be sure to tighten the clutch master cylinder mounting bolts to the torque listed in this Chapter's Specifications. Tighten the union nut for the clutch fluid line securely.

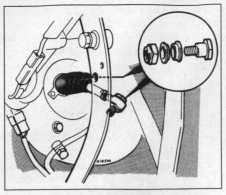

3.4 Typical clutch master cylinder pushrod-to-clutch pedal fitting

7 Check the clutch pedal adjustment (see Section 4). When applicable, also check the clutch start switch adjustment (see Section 5).

8 Fill the fluid reservoir with fresh hydraulic fluid, and bleed the clutch system (see Section 7).

4 Clutch pedal - adjustment

Note: *Hydraulic clutch systems are self-adjusting, so a correctly-adjusted clutch pedal should never get out of adjustment. However, clutch pedal height should be checked when fitting a new clutch master cylinder, to ensure correct initial adjustment.*

1 Measure the distance from the lower rear edge of the pedal footpad to the bulkhead **(see illustration)**, and compare your measurement to the dimension listed in this Chapter's Specifications.

2 If the distance is incorrect, loosen the pushrod nut and bolt. The bolt is eccentric; rotating it changes the distance from the pedal to the bulkhead. When the distance is correct, tighten the nut and bolt. Where the eccentric bolt has a dot marked on it, the dot should be positioned opposite the master cylinder as a starting point.

3 Some models also have an adjustable clutch master cylinder pushrod. If the pedal can't be adjusted by rotating the eccentric bolt, loosen the pushrod locknut, and turn the pushrod until the distance from the pedal to the bulkhead is correct, then tighten the locknut securely.

> **Caution: Don't screw the pushrod all the way in. This could cause the locknut to jam against the clutch pedal during operation, which could break the pushrod. If you do change the pushrod length, make sure you check the locknut clearance before operating the clutch pedal. Also, don't overtighten the pushrod locknut. If the threads are stripped, the master cylinder may jam, causing clutch failure.**

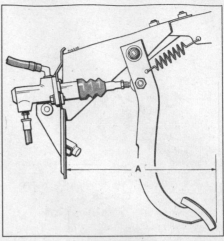

4.1 To check the clutch pedal adjustment, measure the distance from the lower rear edge of the pedal footpad to the bulkhead (dimension A)

5 Clutch start switch (where fitted) - check and renewal

1 The clutch start switch, located at the top of the clutch pedal, prevents the engine from being started unless the clutch pedal is depressed. The switch, which is part of the starting circuit, is normally open. When the clutch pedal is depressed, it depresses a small pushrod in the switch, closing the circuit and allowing the starter to operate.

2 If the vehicle starts without the clutch being depressed, either the switch is malfunctioning, or is incorrectly adjusted. To check its operation, unplug the electrical connector and connect an ohmmeter across the connector terminals. There should be no continuity when the pedal is released (pedal up), and continuity when the pedal is depressed. If the switch doesn't operate as described, try adjusting it. If it still doesn't operate correctly, renew it.

6 Clutch slave cylinder - removal and refitting

> **Warning: Hydraulic fluid is poisonous. It is also an effective paint stripper. Take care not to get fluid onto the skin or in your eyes. Have some rags handy to catch any spillages, and wash any splashes off paintwork immediately with plenty of cold water.**

Removal

Note: *Before beginning this procedure, contact local parts stores and dealers concerning the purchase of an overhaul kit or a new slave cylinder. Availability and cost of the necessary parts may dictate whether the*

8

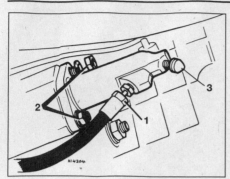

6.4 A typical hydraulic clutch slave cylinder

1 Hydraulic line   3 Bleed screw
2 Mounting nuts

cylinder is overhauled or renewed. If you decide to overhaul the cylinder, follow the instructions contained in the overhaul kit.

1 Remove the brake fluid reservoir cap (left-hand-drive models) or clutch fluid reservoir cap (right-hand-drive models) and remove the fluid in the reservoir with a syringe. On left-hand-drive models, the fluid level should be below the clutch line connection for the master cylinder.

2 Raise the vehicle and support it securely on axle stands.

3 Wipe the area around the threaded fitting for the hydraulic fluid line, and disconnect the fluid line from the slave cylinder. If available, use a split ring spanner to avoid damaging the fitting. Have a rag handy to mop up any spilled fluid. Plug or tape the end of the line, to contain the remaining fluid in the line, and to keep dirt out. On models where the slave cylinder is not easily accessed, it may be better to unbolt the slave cylinder before disconnecting the fitting.

4 Remove the slave cylinder mounting nuts (see illustration) and remove the cylinder from the transmission.

5 Inspect the plastic tip of the pushrod and the release lever for wear. The pushrod should only be worn on the tip. The release lever should show wear only in the recess for the pushrod. Wear on the sides of the pushrod tip, or wear on the release lever anywhere besides the recess, indicates that the pushrod is misaligned.

6 Inspect the slave cylinder for leaks. If the pushrod seal is leaking, renew the slave cylinder. If you have to renew the slave cylinder, make sure you obtain the correct unit. Models with a conventional flywheel use a slave cylinder with a diameter of 20.64 mm; models with a dual-mass flywheel use a slave cylinder with a 22.2 mm diameter.

Refitting

7 Refitting is the reverse of removal. Be sure to apply a light coat of molybdenum disulphide ("moly") grease to the plastic pushrod tip, and make sure the tip engages the recess in the release lever properly. Tighten the slave cylinder mounting nuts to

the torque listed in this Chapter's Specifications.

8 Refill the fluid reservoir, and bleed the clutch hydraulic system (see Section 7).

7 Clutch hydraulic system - bleeding

> **Warning: Hydraulic fluid is poisonous. It is also an effective paint stripper. Take care not to get fluid onto the skin or in your eyes. Have some rags handy to catch any spillages, and wash any splashes off paintwork immediately with plenty of cold water.**

1 If air gets into the clutch hydraulic system, the clutch may not release completely when the pedal is depressed. Air can enter the system whenever any part of it is dismantled, or if the fluid level in the master cylinder reservoir runs low. Air can also leak into the system through holes too small to allow fluid to leak out. In this case, it indicates that a general overhaul of the system is required.

2 To bleed the air out, you will need an assistant to pump the clutch pedal, a clear plastic container, and a section of clear flexible plastic tubing which will fit over the bleed screw. Alternatively, a "one-man" bleeding kit can be used. A "one-man" kit usually contains a tube or bottle with a one-way valve incorporated - in this way, the pedal can be pumped as normal, but air is not drawn back into the system when the pedal is released. If a one-man kit is used, follow the instructions provided with it. In either case, you will also need a supply of new brake fluid of the recommended type, and a spanner for the bleed screw.

3 Check the fluid level in the reservoir. Add fluid, if necessary, to bring the level up to the "full" or "MAX" mark. Use only the recommended brake fluid, and do not mix different types. Never use fluid from a container that has been standing uncapped, as it will have absorbed moisture from the air, rendering it unfit for use. You will have to check the fluid level in the reservoir often during the bleeding procedure. If the level drops too far, air will enter the system.

4 Apply the handbrake. Raise the front of the vehicle, and support it securely on axle stands.

5 Remove the bleed screw cap from the bleed screw on the slave cylinder (see illustration 6.4).

6 Attach one end of the plastic tube to the bleed screw fitting. Fill the container about one-third full with clean fluid, then submerge the other end of the tube in this.

7 Loosen the bleed screw slightly, then tighten it to the point where it is snug yet easily loosened.

8 Have your assistant pump the clutch pedal

several times, and hold it in the fully-depressed position.

9 With pressure on the pedal, open the bleed screw approximately a half-turn. As the fluid stops flowing through the tube and into the container, tighten the bleed screw. Again, pump the pedal, hold it in the fully-depressed position and loosen the bleed screw momentarily. Do not allow the pedal to be released with the bleed screw in the open position.

10 Repeat the procedure until no air bubbles are visible in the fluid flowing through the tube. Be sure to check the fluid level in the reservoir while performing the bleeding operation.

11 Tighten the bleed screw completely, remove the tube, and refit the bleed screw cap.

12 Check the fluid level in the reservoir to make sure it is up to the maximum mark, then test drive the vehicle and check for proper clutch operation.

8 Clutch components - removal, inspection and refitting

Removal

1 Access to the clutch components is normally accomplished by removing the transmission, leaving the engine in the vehicle. If the engine is being removed for major overhaul, then the opportunity should always be taken to check the clutch for wear, renewing worn components as necessary. The following procedures assume that the engine is in place.

2 Referring to Chapter 7A, remove the transmission from the vehicle.

3 To support the clutch disc during removal, fit a clutch alignment tool or an old transmission input shaft through the middle of the clutch (see illustration).

4 Carefully inspect the flywheel and pressure plate for indexing marks. If no marks are visible, use a centre-punch, scriber or paint to mark the pressure plate and flywheel, so they

8.3 Use a clutch alignment tool to support the clutch disc during pressure plate removal, and to centre the disc during refitting

8.4 Be sure to mark the pressure plate and flywheel to ensure proper alignment during refitting (this is only necessary if the same pressure plate will be re-used)

8.5 Loosen the pressure plate bolts (arrowed) a little at a time until the spring tension is released

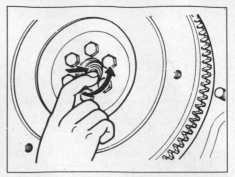

8.8 Turn the pilot bearing by hand while pressing on it - if it's rough or noisy, fit a new one

can be refitted in the same relative positions **(see illustration)**.

5 Turning each bolt only a little at a time, loosen the pressure plate-to-flywheel bolts. Work in a criss-cross pattern, until all spring pressure is relieved **(see illustration)**. Grasp the pressure plate and completely remove the bolts, then separate the pressure plate and clutch disc from the flywheel. Note which way round the clutch disc is fitted.

Inspection

6 Ordinarily, when a problem develops in the clutch, it can be attributed to wear of the clutch driven plate assembly (clutch disc). However, all components should be inspected at this time.

7 Inspect the flywheel (see Chapter 2A).

8 Check the pilot bearing in the end of the crankshaft. Make sure that it turns smoothly and quietly **(see illustration)**. If the transmission input shaft contact surface on the bearing is worn or damaged, fit a new bearing.

9 Use a puller to remove the pilot bearing **(see illustration)**. Fit a new bearing with a socket and hammer **(see illustration)**.

10 Inspect the lining on the clutch disc **(see illustration)**. Look for oil contamination and

8.9a You'll need a slide hammer puller with a special attachment to extract the pilot bearing

8.9b Using a hammer and a socket, carefully drive the new bearing into place

general wear. If the disc lining looks contaminated or worn, renew the disc. Check the thickness and run-out of the clutch disc, and compare your measurements to the figures listed in this Chapter's Specifications. If the clutch is too thin or is warped, renew it. Check for loose rivets, distortion, cracks, broken springs, and any other obvious damage. As mentioned above, the clutch disc is normally renewed each time it is removed, so if there is any doubt about its condition, fit a new one.

11 Ordinarily, the release bearing is renewed at the same time as the clutch disc. Remove the bearing from the input shaft **(see illustration)**. It's also a good idea to pop

loose the return spring, remove the release arm, and inspect the recess for the tip of the slave cylinder pushrod. Refitting the release arm and bearing is simply the reverse of this step.

12 Check the machined surface of the pressure plate. If it's cracked, grooved, scored, discoloured by heat or oil contamination, or otherwise damaged, it must be renewed. Lay a straightedge across the

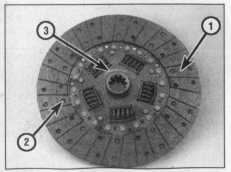

8.10 The clutch plate

1 *Lining* - This will wear down in use
2 *Rivets* - These secure the lining, and will damage the flywheel or pressure plate if allowed to contact the surfaces
3 *Markings*- "Flywheel side" or something similar

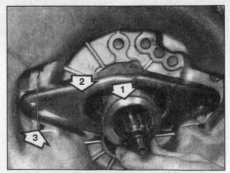

8.11 To remove the release bearing (1), simply slide it off the input shaft; to remove the release arm (2), pop off the return spring (3)

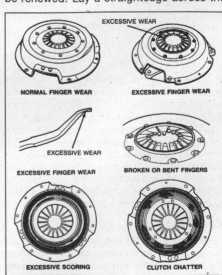

8.12 Renew the pressure plate if any of these conditions is present

surface, and verify that it's flat. Look for loose rivets and bent or misaligned release fingers (see illustration). If the pressure plate shows any signs of wear, renew it. It is good practice to renew the clutch components as a set (clutch disc, pressure plate and release bearing) at time of major overhaul, or if the old components have covered a high mileage.

Refitting

13 Before refitting, carefully clean the flywheel and pressure plate machined surfaces. Handle the parts only with clean hands. DO NOT get oil or grease on the clutch friction surfaces.

14 Position the clutch disc and pressure plate on the flywheel, with the clutch disc held in place with the alignment tool. Make sure the disc is fitted properly (new discs are usually marked with "flywheel side" or some similar identification). If the same pressure plate is being re-used, make sure the previously-applied marks are in alignment.

15 Tighten the pressure plate-to-flywheel bolts finger-tight only, working around the pressure plate.

16 If not already done, insert an alignment tool through the middle of the clutch disc (see illustration 8.3). Move the disc until it is exactly in the centre, so the transmission input shaft will pass easily through the disc and into the pilot bearing. If the disc is not correctly aligned, it will be impossible to refit the transmission.

17 Tighten the pressure plate-to-flywheel bolts a little at a time, working in a diagonal pattern to prevent distorting the pressure plate, to the torque listed in this Chapter's Specifications.

18 Using high-temperature grease, lubricate the entire inner surface of the release bearing. Make sure the groove inside is completely filled. Also place grease on the ball socket and the fork fingers.

19 Refit the transmission, slave cylinder and all components removed previously.

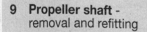

9 Propeller shaft - removal and refitting

Removal

1 Chock the front wheels, then raise the rear of the vehicle, and support it securely on axle stands.

2 On 3-Series models, remove the rear reinforcement bar and, if applicable, the exhaust and fuel tank heat shields. **Note:** *On some models, the holder for the oxygen sensor plug is attached to the body by one of the reinforcement bar bolts. On these models, make sure you don't damage the sensor leads during removal of the bar. On later models with the 4 HP 22 automatic transmission, it will be necessary to support the transmission with a trolley jack.*

9.6a To ensure that the driveshaft is refitted in the same position, paint or scribe alignment marks across the transmission output flange and front universal joint flange, as shown on this 5-Series model (most other models use a flexible coupling; a few 5-Series models use a CV joint) . . .

9.10 Support the weight of the driveshaft at the centre bearing, and remove the bolts (arrowed) from the centre bearing assembly

3 Remove the exhaust system (see Chapter 4).

4 On 5-Series models, remove the exhaust heat shield.

5 At the sliding coupling (slip joint), loosen the clamping sleeve (if applicable) several turns, but don't remove it. **Note:** *Later 5-Series models don't have a clamping sleeve.*

6 Using paint, a punch or a scribe, make alignment marks across the transmission output flange and flexible coupling (or front universal joint, on some models), and across the rear universal joint and differential input flange, to ensure that the transmission is refitted in the same position (see illustrations).

7 Remove the nuts and bolts which attach the flexible coupling (see illustration 10.3) or universal joint (see illustration 9.6a) to the transmission output flange. Don't separate the propeller shaft from the flange yet.

8 On (some 5-Series) models with a front CV joint, first use a suitable jack to support the transmission. Loosen the transmission rear support mounting nuts and bolts (see Chapter 7), then slide the mounting towards the rear and remove the six CV joint-to-transmission mounting nuts and bolts.

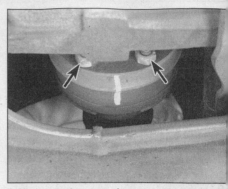

9.6b . . . and across the rear universal joint and differential input flange

9.11 Bend the propeller shaft down at the centre bearing, then slide it off the centring pin on the transmission output flange - slide the splined coupling together to make enough room if you have to, but do NOT pull the two driveshaft sections apart

9 Remove the nuts and bolts from the propeller shaft rear flange (see illustration 9.6b).

10 Support the propeller shaft at the centre, and remove the centre bearing bolts (see illustration).

11 Bend the propeller shaft down at the centre bearing, then slide it off the centring pin on the transmission output flange (see illustration). You may have to slide the splined coupling together to make enough room. Do NOT pull the two propeller shaft sections apart. **Note:** *On models with a vibration damper, rotate the damper assembly 60 degrees before pulling it off the centring pin on the transmission output flange.*

12 If you're planning to clean the splined coupling, or renew the rubber bush, mark the two sections of the propeller shaft before pulling the coupling apart. After cleaning the splines, lubricate them with molybdenum disulphide ("moly") grease before reassembly. If you pull the two sections apart without marking them, reassemble the splined coupling so that the universal joints are on the same plane. If the propeller shaft vibrates after refitting, the two sections are 180 degrees out of balance. You'll have to remove the propeller

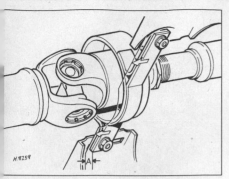

9.18 Preload the centre bearing by sliding it forward from its unloaded position, and tighten the bolts to the torque listed in this Chapter's Specifications

shaft and separate the two sections at the splined coupling, then rotate one section 180 degrees before refitting it.

Refitting

13 Refitting is basically the reverse of removal. However, the following points should be noted.

14 Apply a light coat of molybdenum disulphide ("moly") grease to the centring pin on the transmission output flange.

15 Position the propeller shaft against the differential input flange first, slide it onto the centring pin at the transmission output flange, then position the centre bearing up against the pin and loosely refit the mounting bolts, but don't tighten them yet. Where CV joints are fitted, make sure that the gaskets are still serviceable, and renew if necessary.

16 Align the marks you made across the rear universal joint flange and the differential input flange prior to removal. Refit the rear propeller shaft section to the differential input flange with NEW self-locking nuts, and tighten the nuts to the torque listed in this Chapter's Specifications.

⚠️ **Caution: Don't re-use old self-locking nuts.**

17 Align the marks you made at the front end of the propeller shaft prior to removal, and reconnect the flexible coupling, universal joint, or CV joint, to the transmission output shaft

with new self-locking nuts. Tighten the bolts to the torque listed in this Chapter's Specifications. **Note 1:** *Several grades of bolts are used, and the different grades must be tightened to different torques; you'll find the bolt grade stamped on the bolt head.* **Note 2:** *To avoid stressing the flexible coupling when tightening the bolts, hold the bolt with a spanner, and tighten the nut on the flange side.* **Note 3:** *On flexible couplings, it's easier to refit the bolts if you place a large hose clamp around the coupling and tighten it slightly to compress the coupling.*

18 Preload the centre bearing by sliding it forward 4 to 6 mm (propeller shafts with sliding centre member), or 2 to 4 mm (propeller shafts without sliding centre member) from its unloaded position **(see illustration)**, then tighten the mounting bolts to the torque listed in this Chapter's Specifications.

19 On (5-Series) models with CV joints, slide the transmission rear bracket forwards, and tighten the mounting bolts. Remove the jack from the transmission.

20 Tighten the clamping sleeve on the splined coupling.

21 The remainder of refitting is the reverse of removal.

10 Flexible coupling - check and renewal

Check

1 Although BMW specifies no maintenance interval for checking the flexible coupling between the front section of the propeller shaft and the transmission, you should inspect it whenever you're working under the vehicle. The coupling is made of rubber, so it's vulnerable to road grit, heat generated by the exhaust system, and the twisting torque of the propeller shaft. Inspect the coupling for cracks, tears, missing pieces, and distortion. If it's cracked or generally worn, renew it as follows.

Renewal

2 Remove the propeller shaft (see Section 9).
3 Remove the flexible coupling nuts and bolts **(see illustration)** and remove the coupling from

the propeller shaft. **Note:** *To facilitate removal and refitting of the bolts, place a large hose clamp around the flexible coupling, and tighten the clamp slightly to compress the coupling.*

4 Fit the new coupling with NEW self-locking nuts. If the coupling has directional arrows on it, the arrows must face toward the flange arms, NOT toward the bolt heads **(see illustration)**. Tighten the nuts to the torque listed in this Chapter's Specifications.

5 Refit the propeller shaft (see Section 9).

11 Centre bearing - check and renewal

Check

1 The centre bearing consists of a ball-bearing assembly encircled by a rubber mounting. The bearing assembly is pressed onto the rear end of the front section of the propeller shaft, and is secured by a circlip. The centre bearing is protected by dust caps on either side, but water and dirt can still enter the bearing and ruin it. Propeller shaft vibration can also lead to bearing failure. To inspect the centre bearing properly, you'll need to remove the propeller shaft (see Section 9). Conversely, whenever the propeller shaft is removed for any reason, always use the opportunity to inspect the bearing. Rotate the bearing and note whether it turns smoothly; if it's difficult to turn, or if it has a gritty feeling, renew it. Also inspect the rubber portion. If it's cracked or deteriorated, renew it.

Renewal

2 Make alignment marks on the front and rear sections of the propeller shaft.
3 Unscrew and remove the clamping sleeve, then pull the two sections of the propeller shaft apart. Remove the rubber bush, washer and clamping sleeve from the front section of the propeller shaft.
4 Inspect the condition of the rubber bush for the splined coupling. If it's torn or cracked, renew it.
5 Remove the centre bearing circlip and dust guard **(see illustration)**.

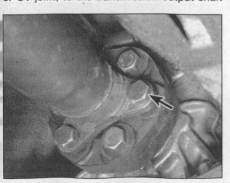

10.3 Remove the flexible coupling nuts and bolts

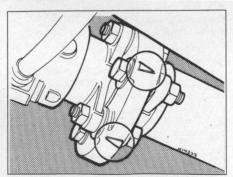

10.4 If the coupling has directional arrows on it, the arrows must face toward the flange arms, not toward the bolt heads

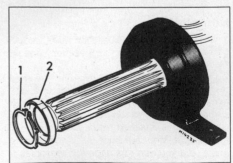

11.5 Remove the centre bearing circlip and dust guard

1 Circlip   2 Dust guard

8

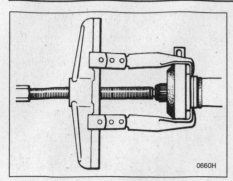

11.6 When you fit a puller to remove the centre bearing assembly, make sure it's pulling on the hub; pulling on the outer ring of the mounting may tear the rubber, necessitating the renewal of the entire bearing/mounting assembly

6 Using a puller, remove the bearing mounting **(see illustration)**.

 Caution: Fit the puller so that it's pulling on the bearing hub. Pulling on the outer ring of the mounting may tear the rubber, necessitating the renewal of the entire bearing/mounting assembly.

7 If a new bearing or mounting is required, take the assembly to a garage, as a press is required to separate and reassemble the bearing and mounting.

8 Make sure the dust guard is still on the propeller shaft, then press the centre mounting assembly onto the propeller shaft so that it's flush with the dust guard.

9 On models with a splined-section propeller shaft, refit the clamping sleeve, washer and rubber bush on the front propeller shaft section. Lubricate the splines with molybdenum disulphide ("moly") grease, then reassemble the propeller shaft. Make sure the matching marks align. Don't retighten the clamping sleeve until the propeller shaft is refitted.

10 Refit the propeller shaft (see Section 9).

11 On models without a splined-section propeller shaft, apply thread-locking fluid to the propeller shaft yoke mounting bolt, then tighten it to the torque listed in this Chapter's Specifications.

12 On models with a splined-section propeller shaft, tighten the clamping sleeve to the torque listed in this Chapter's Specifications.

12 Universal joints - check and renewal

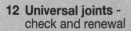

Check

1 Wear in the universal joints is characterised by vibration in the transmission, noise during acceleration, and metallic squeaking and grating sounds as the bearings disintegrate.

2 It's easy to check the universal joints for

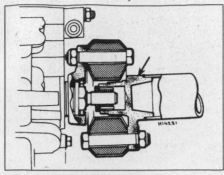

13.1 Cutaway view of the centring guide (arrowed)

wear with the propeller shaft still fitted. To check the rear universal joint, try to turn the propeller shaft while holding the differential input flange. To check the front universal joint, try to turn the propeller shaft while holding the transmission output flange. Free play between the propeller shaft and the front or rear flanges indicates excessive wear.

3 If the propeller shaft is already removed, you can check the universal joints by holding the shaft in one hand and turning the yoke or flange with the other. If the axial movement is excessive, renew the propeller shaft.

Renewal

4 The universal joints cannot be overhauled by the home mechanic. Therefore, when the joints become worn, the propeller shaft and universal joints must be replaced as a single unit. It may be possible to obtain a reconditioned shaft on an exchange basis; consult an automotive engineering specialist.

5 Removal and refitting of the propeller shaft is covered in Section 9.

13 Front centring guide - check and renewal

Check

1 The front centring guide **(see illustration)** positions the propeller shaft precisely in relation to the transmission output flange. The guide, which is press-fitted into a cavity in the front of the propeller shaft, engages a guide pin on the transmission output flange. A worn centring guide will allow the front of the propeller shaft to wobble and vibrate.

2 To check the centring guide, remove the nuts and bolts that attach the flexible coupling to the transmission output flange, grasp the front end of the propeller shaft, and try to move it up and down and side to side. It should fit snugly over the pin on the transmission output flange. If there's excessive free play, renew the guide. **Note:** *Some propeller shafts have a dust cover on the front end, over the centring guide. This cover is sometimes bent or distorted during removal of the propeller shaft. Damage to this*

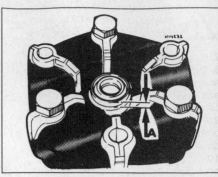

13.5 Make sure the sealing lip of the new centring guide protrudes 4.5 mm (dimension A) from the front of the driveshaft

cover shouldn't affect the operation of the centring guide, and shouldn't be confused with guide wear.

Renewal

3 Remove the propeller shaft (see Section 9).

4 Pack the cavity behind the centring guide with a heavy grease until the grease is flush with the lower edge of the guide. Insert a close-fitting metal rod into the guide (approximately 14 mm diameter), cover the guide with a rag, and strike the bar with a hammer (don't try to use a rod that's too small - it won't work; the grease will escape around the sides). The pressure of the rod against the grease should push the centring guide out of the propeller shaft.

5 Lubricate the new centring guide with molybdenum disulphide ("moly") grease, and drive it into the propeller shaft. Make sure the sealing lip of the guide faces outwards, and protrudes from the face of the propeller shaft by about 4.5 mm **(see illustration)**.

6 Refit the propeller shaft (see Section 9).

14 Propeller shaft constant velocity (CV) joint - renewal

1 The constant velocity (CV) joint on the front of the propeller shaft on some models bolts directly to the transmission output flange. Renewing it requires removal of the propeller shaft. Make sure you renew the clamps, circlips, boots, gaskets and covers.

2 Remove the propeller shaft (see Section 9).

3 Remove the boot clamp from the back of the CV joint.

4 At the front of the joint, remove the circlip that attaches the CV joint to the shaft. Pull the joint off the shaft with a suitable puller (the joint is cemented to the shaft with a thread-locking agent, and you can't easily break it free without a puller).

5 Remove the mounting bolts from the CV joint. The bolt shoulders are knurled, so you'll have to drive them out of the CV joint.

6 Pack the new CV joint with 80 grams of CV joint grease. Work the grease down into the cage.

Caution: Do NOT swivel the CV joint inner race while packing it. The balls can fall out of the cage.

7 Refit a new gasket and dust cover.

8 Tap the bolts and retainers through the joint holes. Clean the splines on the propeller shaft, and apply a small amount of thread-locking compound to the splines.

9 Place the boot on the shaft. Refit the joint onto the shaft, and tap it on with a wooden dowel.

10 Fit a new circlip on the shaft, and a new boot clamp on the boot.

11 Refit the propeller shaft (see Section 9).

15 Driveshafts - removal and refitting

Removal

1 Apply the handbrake firmly. On 3-Series models, lever off the dust cap in the centre of the wheel hub, lift out the lockplate around the driveshaft nut, and loosen - but don't yet remove - the nut. This nut is very tight.

2 Loosen the rear wheel bolts, but don't remove them yet.

3 Raise the rear of the vehicle, and support it securely with axle stands. Remove the wheel(s).

4 Wipe off the inner and outer CV joints to prevent dirt from contaminating them when they're opened.

5 Remove the six Allen-head bolts **(see illustration)** from the inner CV joint, and detach it from the inner flange.

6 On 5-Series models, remove the six Allen-head bolts from the outer CV joint **(see illustration)**, and detach it from the outer flange.

7 On 3-Series models, remove the driveshaft nut, and press the stub axle out of the wheel hub with a puller. If necessary, prevent the hub from turning by refitting two wheel bolts, and wedging a large screwdriver or lever between them.

8 Remove the driveshaft.

15.5 On all models, remove the Allen-head bolts from the inner CV joint, and detach the joint from the differential flange (5-Series model shown, 3-Series models similar)

Refitting

9 Refitting is the reverse of removal. Be sure to tighten the CV joint Allen bolts, and (on 3-Series models) the driveshaft nut, to the torques listed in this Chapter's Specifications.

16 Constant velocity (CV) joints and boots - check and renewal

Note 1: *Some motor factors carry "split" type renewal boots, which can be fitted without removing the driveshaft from the vehicle (these effectively wrap around the joint, once the old boot has been cut free). This is a convenient alternative; however, we recommend that the driveshaft be removed, the CV joint cleaned to ensure that it's free from moisture and dirt (which will accelerate CV joint wear), and a new one-piece boot fitted.*

Note 2: *If the outer boot on 3-Series models requires renewal, you'll have to remove the inner CV joint first.*

Note 3: *If the CV joints exhibit signs of wear (usually caused initially by torn boots), they must be renewed. On 3-Series models, the inner CV joint can be renewed separately; if the outer CV joint is damaged, you must renew the driveshaft as well - they can't be*

15.6 On 5-Series models, remove the Allen-head bolts from the outer CV joint, and detach the joint from the drive flange

separated. On 5-Series models, both joints can be renewed separately.

Note 4: *Complete rebuilt driveshafts are available on an exchange basis, which eliminates much time and work. Whichever route you choose to take, check on the cost and availability of parts before dismantling your vehicle.*

Check

1 The CV joints and boots should be inspected periodically, and whenever the vehicle is raised.

2 Raise the vehicle, and support it securely on axle stands. Inspect the CV joint boots for cracks, leaks and broken retaining bands. If lubricant leaks out through a hole or crack in a boot, the CV joint will wear prematurely and require renewal. Renew any damaged boots immediately.

3 Grasping each driveshaft in turn, rotate it in both directions, and move it in and out, to check for excessive movement, indicating worn splines or loose CV joints.

CV joint and boot renewal

Note: *To renew the outer driveshaft boot on a 3-Series model, the inner CV joint and boot must be removed first.*

4 Remove the driveshaft (see Section 15).

5 Prise open and remove the boot clamps **(see illustrations)** and discard them.

6 Remove the protective cap from the CV joint **(see illustration)**.

8

16.5a Prise open the large boot clamp . . .

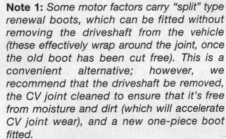

16.5b . . . and the smaller boot clamp, and discard both of them

16.6 Tap off the protective cap from the CV joint with a hammer and chisel

16.7 Remove the large circlip with a pair of circlip pliers

16.8 Using a soft-faced hammer, carefully tap on the end of the driveshaft (NOT the CV races) and separate the shaft from the joint

16.13 Cover the splines on the end of the driveshaft with tape to protect the new boot(s) from damage during refitting

7 Remove the large circlip that retains the CV joint on the driveshaft **(see illustration)**.

8 Carefully tap on the end of the driveshaft (NOT the CV races) and separate the shaft from the joint **(see illustration)**.

9 Pull the old boot off the driveshaft.

10 If you're working on a 3-Series model and are also renewing the outer boot, cut the inner and outer boot clamps, and pull that boot off too.

11 Thoroughly clean the CV joint(s) with solvent. Wash out all the old grease, and blow the solvent out with compressed air, if available.

 Warning: Wear safety goggles when using compressed air.

12 Inspect the CV joint(s) for scoring, pitting or other signs of excessive wear. If a CV joint is damaged, renew it. **Note:** *If the outer CV joint on a 3-Series model is damaged, the driveshaft and outer CV joint must be renewed as an assembly.*

13 Wrap the splines on the end of the driveshaft with tape to protect the boot(s) from damage **(see illustration)**. Fit the new boot(s), then remove the tape.

14 Carefully tap the CV joint onto the driveshaft **(see illustration)**. Be extremely careful not to damage the races. Use a brass or rubber hammer. Refit the circlip.

15 Fill the cavity in the back of the joint with

CV joint grease, and work it into the joint **(see illustrations)**.

16 Seat the boot into the groove on the driveshaft, and refit the small boot clamp **(see illustrations)**.

17 Fill the rest of the CV joint with CV joint grease **(see illustrations 16.15a and 16.15b)**. Work it into the joint, and then refit the protective end cover.

18 Refit the large boot clamp and tighten it **(see illustrations 16.16a and 16.16b)**.

19 Refit the driveshaft (see Section 15).

17 Differential housing side seals - renewal

1 Raise the rear of the vehicle, and support it on axle stands.

2 Drain the differential lubricant (see Chapter 1).

3 Separate the driveshaft from the differential (see Section 15) and suspend it out of the way with a piece of wire. Do not let it hang down unsupported, or it may be damaged.

4 Using a suitable lever or a big screwdriver, remove the differential flange from the differential **(see illustration)**. Be ready to catch the flange as it comes out.

5 Remove the flange circlip **(see illustration)**.

6 Inspect the flange shaft. If there's a groove

16.14 Carefully tap the CV joint onto the driveshaft - use a soft-faced hammer so you don't damage the races

16.15a Fill the cavity in the back of the joint with CV joint grease . . .

16.15b . . . and work it into the joint

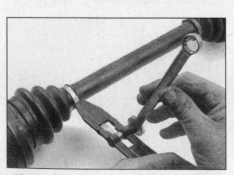

16.16a Slide the boot into place, refit the smaller boot clamp, and tighten it with a band-tightening tool (available at most motor factors)

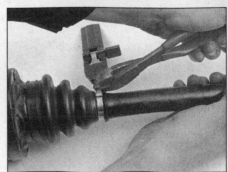

16.16b Bend the end of the clamp back, and cut off the excess

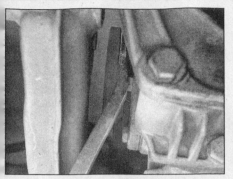

17.4 Using a suitable lever or a big screwdriver, remove the differential flange from the differential - be ready to catch the flange as it comes out

worn in the shaft where it contacts the oil seal, renew the flange.

7 Extract the old seal with a seal removal tool or a large screwdriver **(see illustration)**. Make sure you don't nick or gouge the seal bore in the differential housing.

8 Coat the new seal with differential lubricant, then use a large socket or section of pipe and a hammer to fit the seal **(see illustration)**. Make sure the seal is the right way round (lips inwards).

9 Fit a new circlip in the groove. Make sure both ends of the circlip are fully seated in the groove.

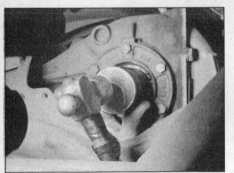

17.8 Coat the new seal with differential lubricant, then use a large socket or section of pipe and a hammer to fit the seal

18.6b On 5-Series models, remove the two differential rear mounting bolts (arrowed) on the top of the rear axle carrier (left side shown)

17.5 Remove the flange circlip with a small screwdriver

10 Coat the lip of the seal with grease, then refit the differential flange. Push the flange in until you feel the circlip engage.

11 The rest of refitting is the reverse of removal.

18 Differential housing - removal and refitting

Removal

1 Raise the rear of the vehicle, and place it securely on axle stands. Drain the differential lubricant (see Chapter 1).

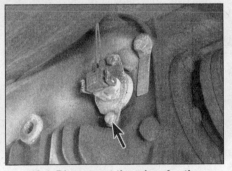

18.4 Disconnect the wires for the speedometer pulse sender, remove the two sender securing bolts (one arrowed) and remove it (3-Series model shown, 5-Series models similar)

18.7a On 3-Series models, support the differential with a trolley jack, then remove the front mounting bolts (arrowed) - right-hand side shown

17.7 Extract the old seal with a seal removal tool (shown) or a large screwdriver

2 Disconnect the propeller shaft from the pinion flange (see Section 9). Support the end of the propeller shaft with a piece of wire so the centre bearing isn't damaged.

3 Unbolt the inner ends of the driveshafts from the differential flanges (see Section 15). Support the driveshafts with pieces of wire to avoid damaging the CV joints.

4 Unplug the electrical connector from the speedometer pulse sender **(see illustration)**. Remove the two sender securing bolts and remove the sender.

5 Support the differential with a trolley jack.

6 On 3-Series models, remove the differential rear mounting bolt **(see illustration)**; on 5-Series models, remove the two differential rear mounting bolts on the top of the rear axle carrier **(see illustration)**.

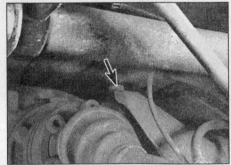

18.6a On 3-Series models, remove the differential rear mounting bolt (arrowed)

18.7b On 5-Series models, remove the differential front mounting bolt (arrowed)

8

18.8 On 3-Series models, remove the nut and bolt (arrowed) for the rubber mounting bush

7 Remove the two front mounting bolts (3-Series models) or the single front mounting bolt (5-Series models) **(see illustrations)**.

8 On 3-Series models, remove the nut and bolt for the rubber mounting bush **(see illustration)**.

9 Lower the differential and remove it from under the vehicle.

Refitting

10 Position the differential housing in place against its mountings and loosely refit the bolts (don't tighten any of them until they are all fitted), then tighten all of the fasteners securely.

11 The remainder of refitting is the reverse of removal.

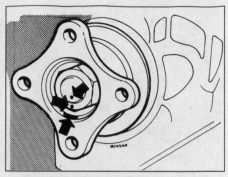

19.3 Scribe or paint alignment marks (arrowed) on the flange, the pinion shaft and the pinion shaft nut to ensure proper reassembly

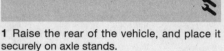

19 Pinion oil seal - renewal

1 Raise the rear of the vehicle, and place it securely on axle stands.

2 Remove the differential housing (see Section 18).

3 Make alignment marks on the pinion shaft, the flange nut and the flange **(see illustration)**.

4 Remove the lockplate, then hold the input flange stationary and remove the flange nut.

5 Using a puller, remove the input flange. **Note:** *If the pinion shaft is grooved where the old oil seal was in contact with it, consult a dealer service department or other qualified garage. A new pinion shaft sleeve may also be required (see paragraph 8).*

6 Extract the old seal with a seal removal tool or a screwdriver. Make sure you don't nick or gouge the seal bore.

7 Dip the new seal in differential lubricant. Drive it into position, lips inwards, with a large socket or a section of pipe.

8 Lightly lubricate the input shaft, and press the input flange back on, but don't try to press it right home. Refit the flange nut and, using a torque wrench, slowly tighten the nut, noting the torque at which the marks line up - it should be near the torque value listed in this Chapter's Specifications. If the torque required to align the marks is some way short of the specified torque, the pinion shaft sleeve probably needs to be renewed. Due to the special tools required and the critical nature of the job, renewal of the pinion shaft sleeve should be left to a dealer service department or other qualified garage.

9 If the specified torque is reached *before* the alignment marks line up, don't continue to turn the nut until they do.

⚠ *Caution: Don't tighten the nut past the alignment marks and then back it off, as this could over-compress the pinion shaft sleeve.*

Chapter 9 Braking system

Contents

Degrees of difficulty

| Easy, suitable for novice with little experience | Fairly easy, suitable for beginner with some experience | Fairly difficult, suitable for competent DIY mechanic 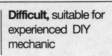 | Difficult, suitable for experienced DIY mechanic | Very difficult, suitable for expert DIY or professional |

Specifications

General
Brake fluid type .... See Chapter 1

Disc brakes
Minimum brake pad thickness .... See Chapter 1
Brake disc minimum permissible thickness (wear limit)*

Front
  3-Series
    Solid discs .... 10.7 mm
    Ventilated discs .... 20.0 mm
  5-Series
    Solid discs .... 10.0 mm
    Ventilated discs .... 20.0 mm
Rear .... 8.0 mm

Brake disc minimum thickness after machining
Front
  3-Series
    Solid discs .... 11.1 mm
    Ventilated discs .... 20.4 mm
  5-Series
    Solid discs .... 10.4 mm
    Ventilated discs .... 20.4 mm
Rear .... 8.4 mm
Parallelism (difference between any two measurements) .... 0.02 mm
Maximum disc run-out .... 0.2 mm

*Refer to marks cast into the disc (they supersede information printed here)

Brake pedal adjustments
Brake pedal/servo pushrod adjustment (A) (3-Series) .... 125 mm
Brake pedal height (pedal-to-bulkhead distance)
  3-Series
    Left-hand-drive .... 235 mm
    Right-hand-drive .... 273 mm
  5-Series .... 245 mm
Stop-light switch adjustment (dimension A - see text) .... 5.0 mm to 6.0 mm

Handbrake
Handbrake shoe lining minimum thickness .... 1.5 mm
Handbrake lever travel .... 5 to 8 clicks

Torque wrench settings

	Nm
Front disc brake caliper	
Caliper guide (mounting) bolts	30 to 35
Caliper bracket-to-strut housing bolts	
3-Series, E30	123
5-Series, E28 ("old-shape")	123
5-Series, E34 ("new-shape")	110
Rear disc brake caliper	
Caliper guide (mounting) bolts	30 to 35
Carrier-to-trailing arm bolts	67
Brake hose-to-caliper fitting	14 to 17
Master cylinder-to-brake servo nuts	
3-Series	24
5-Series	25 to 29
Brake servo mounting nuts	22 to 24
Hydraulic line-to-hydraulic brake servo threaded fittings - 5-Series, E28 ("old-shape")	31
Wheel bolts	See Chapter 1

1 General information

All 3-Series models, and 5-Series E28 ("old-shape") models, are equipped with front disc brakes and either rear drum or rear disc brakes. 5-Series E34 ("new-shape") models have disc brakes front and rear. Front and rear brakes are self-adjusting on all models. Some later models are equipped with an Anti-lock Braking System (ABS); this is described in Section 2.

Hydraulic system

The hydraulic system consists of two separate circuits. The master cylinder has separate reservoirs for the two circuits; in the event of a leak or failure in one hydraulic circuit, the other circuit will remain operative.

Brake servo

The vacuum brake servo, utilising engine manifold vacuum and atmospheric pressure to provide assistance to the hydraulically operated brakes, is mounted on the bulkhead in the engine compartment.

A hydraulic brake servo system is used on 5-Series E28 models. This system uses hydraulic pressure from the power steering pump to assist braking.

Handbrake

The handbrake operates the rear brakes, and is cable-operated via a lever mounted in the centre console. The handbrake assembly on rear drum brake models is part of the rear drum brake assembly, and is self-adjusting. On rear disc brake models, the handbrake uses a pair of brake shoes located inside the centre portion of the rear brake disc, and is manually-adjusted.

Brake pad wear warning system

The brake pad wear warning system is linked to a red warning light in the instrument cluster, which comes on when the brake pads have worn down to the point at which they require renewal. DO NOT ignore this reminder. If you don't renew the pads shortly after the brake pad wear warning light comes on, the brake discs will be damaged.

On some models, the brake pad wear warning system also includes an early warning light that comes on only when the brake pedal is depressed, letting you know in advance that the pads need to be renewed.

The wear sensor is attached to the brake pads. The sensor is located at the left front wheel; on some models, there is another sensor at the right rear wheel. The wear sensor is part of a closed circuit. Once the pads wear down to the point at which they're flush with the sensor, the disc grinds away the side of the sensor facing the disc. Thus, the wire inside the sensor is broken, and the red light on the instrument panel comes on.

Always check the sensor(s) when renewing the pads. If you change the pads before the warning light comes on, the sensor(s) may still be good; once the light has come on, renew the sensor.

Service

After completing any operation involving dismantling of any part of the brake system, always test drive the vehicle to check for proper braking performance before resuming normal driving. When testing the brakes, try to select a clean, dry, road with no camber (ie as flat as possible) and with no other traffic. Conditions other than these can lead to inaccurate test results.

Test the brakes at various speeds with both light and heavy pedal pressure. The vehicle should stop evenly, without pulling to one side or the other. Avoid locking the brakes, because this slides the tyres and diminishes braking efficiency and control of the vehicle.

Tyres, vehicle load and wheel alignment are factors which also affect braking performance.

2 Anti-lock Braking system (ABS) - general information

The Anti-lock Braking System is designed to maintain vehicle control, directional stability and optimum deceleration under severe braking conditions on most road surfaces. It does so by monitoring the rotational speed of each wheel and controlling the brake line pressure to each wheel during braking. This prevents the wheels from locking up.

The ABS system has three main components - the wheel speed sensors, the electronic control unit, and the hydraulic control unit. The sensors - one at each wheel since 1985, but at both front wheels and one at the rear differential on earlier models - send a variable voltage signal to the control unit, which monitors these signals, compares them to its program information, and determines whether a wheel is about to lock up. When a wheel is about to lock up, the control unit signals the hydraulic unit to reduce hydraulic pressure (or not increase it further) at that wheel's brake caliper. Pressure modulation is handled by electrically-operated solenoid valves.

If a problem develops within the system, an "ABS" warning light will glow on the dashboard. Sometimes, a visual inspection of the ABS system can help you locate the problem. Carefully inspect the ABS wiring harness. Pay particularly close attention to the harness and connections near each wheel. Look for signs of chafing and other damage caused by incorrectly-routed wires. If a wheel sensor harness is damaged, the sensor should be renewed (the harness and sensor are integral).

⚠️ **Warning: DO NOT try to repair an ABS wiring harness. The ABS system is sensitive to even the smallest changes in resistance. Repairing the harness could alter resistance values** and cause the system to malfunction. If the ABS wiring harness is damaged in any way, it must be renewed.

⚠ **Caution: Make sure the ignition is turned off before unplugging or re-making any electrical connections.**

Diagnosis and repair

If the dashboard warning light comes on and stays on while the vehicle is in operation, the ABS system requires attention. Although special electronic ABS diagnostic testing tools are necessary to properly diagnose the system, you can perform a few preliminary checks before taking the vehicle to a dealer service department.

a) Check the brake fluid level in the reservoir.
b) Verify that the electronic control unit connectors are securely connected.
c) Check the electrical connectors at the hydraulic control unit.
d) Check the fuses.
e) Follow the wiring harness to each front and rear wheel, and verify that all connections are secure and that the wiring is undamaged.

If the above preliminary checks do not rectify the problem, the vehicle should be diagnosed by a dealer service department. Due to the complex nature of this system, all actual repair work must be done by a dealer service department.

3 Disc brake pads - renewal

⚠ **Warning: Disc brake pads must be renewed on both front wheels or both rear wheels at the same time - NEVER renew the pads on only one wheel. Also, the dust created by the brake system may contain asbestos, which is harmful to your health. Never blow it out with compressed air, and don't inhale any of it. An approved filtering mask should be worn when working on the brakes. Do not, under any circumstances, use petroleum-based solvents to clean brake parts. Use brake system cleaner only! When servicing the disc brakes, use only original-equipment or high-quality brand-name pads.**

⚠ **Warning: Brake fluid is poisonous. It is also an effective paint stripper. Refer to the warning at the start of Section 16.**

Note: This procedure applies to both the front and rear disc brakes.

1 Remove the cap(s) from the brake fluid reservoir, and syphon off about two-thirds of the fluid from the reservoir. Failing to do this could result in the reservoir overflowing when the caliper pistons are pressed back into their bores.

2 Loosen the wheel bolts, raise the front or rear of the vehicle and support it securely on axle stands.

3 Remove the front or rear wheels, as applicable. Work on one brake assembly at a time, using the assembled brake for reference if necessary.

4 Inspect the brake disc carefully as outlined in Section 5. If machining is necessary, follow the information in that Section to remove the disc, at which time the pads can be removed from the calipers as well.

5 Follow the accompanying photos, beginning with illustration 3.5a, for the pad removal procedure. Be sure to stay in order, and read the caption under each illustration.

Note 1: Different types of front calipers are used on 3 and 5-Series models. Illustrations 3.5a to 3.5e are for the front calipers on 3-Series models. Illustrations 3.5f to 3.5m are for the front calipers on 5-Series models. There's no photo sequence for rear calipers; although slightly different in size, they're identical in design to the front brake calipers used on 5-Series models. **Note 2:** Some models may have different numbers and types of anti-squeal shims and other hardware than what is shown in this Chapter. It's best to note how the hardware is fitted on the vehicle before dismantling, so you can duplicate it on reassembly.

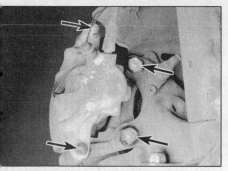

3.5a On 3-Series models, unscrew the caliper mounting bolts (left arrows); right arrows point to the caliper bracket bolts, which should only be removed if you're removing the brake disc

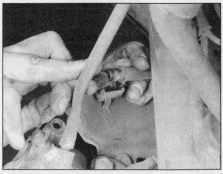

3.5b Unplug the electrical connector for the brake pad wear sensor (3-Series)

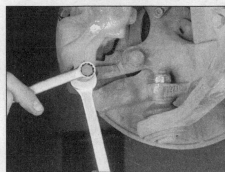

3.5c Hold the guide pins while loosening the caliper mounting bolts (3-Series)

3.5d Remove the caliper, brake pad wear sensor and inner pad all at the same time (3-Series), then refit the inner pad on the piston and press the piston fully into the bore with a C-clamp

3.5e Remove the outer brake pad (3-Series) - to fit the new pads, reverse the removal procedure

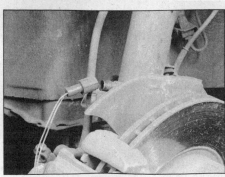

3.5f On 5-Series models, unplug the electrical connector for the brake pad wear sensor

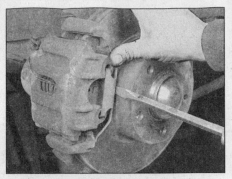

3.5g Remove the plugs for the brake caliper mounting bolts, then remove the bolts (5-Series)

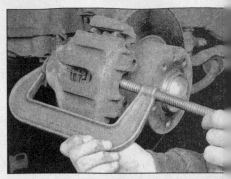

3.5h Prise off the anti-rattle spring (5-Series)

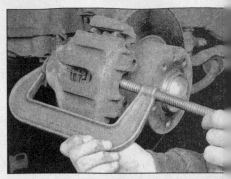

3.5i Depress the piston with a C-clamp (5-Series)

3.5j Remove the caliper and inner brake pad (5-Series)

3.5k Unclip the inner brake pad from the piston (5-Series)

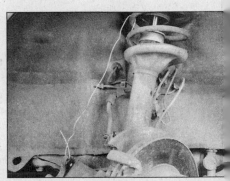

3.5l Hang the caliper out of the way with a piece of wire

3.5m Remove the outer brake pad - to fit the new pads, reverse the removal procedure

6 Be sure to inspect the wear sensor(s) (left front wheel only, or left front and right rear wheel). If they're OK, transfer them from the old pads to the new ones; if they're worn by abrasion, fit new sensors on the new pads.
7 To fit the new pads, reverse the removal procedure. When refitting the caliper, be sure to tighten the mounting bolts to the torque listed in this Chapter's Specifications.

⚠ Warning: Check and if necessary renew the mounting bolts on 3-Series models whenever they are removed. If in doubt, use new bolts.

8 After the job is completed, firmly depress the brake pedal a few times, to bring the pads into contact with the discs. The pedal should

be at normal height above the floor, and firm. Check the level of the brake fluid, adding some if necessary. Check carefully for leaks, and check the operation of the brakes before returning the vehicle to normal service.
9 Avoid heavy braking as far as possible for the first hundred miles or so until the new pads have bedded in.

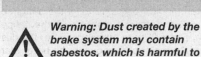

4 Disc brake caliper - removal, overhaul and refitting

⚠ Warning: Dust created by the brake system may contain asbestos, which is harmful to your health. Never blow it out with compressed air, and don't inhale any of it. An approved filtering mask should be worn when working on the brakes. Do not, under any circumstances, use petroleum-based solvents to clean brake parts. Use brake system cleaner only!

⚠ Warning: Brake fluid is poisonous. It is also an effective paint stripper. Refer to the warning at the start of Section 16.

Note: If an overhaul is indicated (usually because of fluid leakage), explore all options before beginning the job. Overhauled calipers may be available on an exchange basis, which makes this job quite easy. If you decide to overhaul the calipers, make sure that an

overhaul kit is available before proceeding. Always overhaul the calipers in pairs - never overhaul just one of them.

Removal

1 Loosen the wheel bolts, raise the front or rear of the vehicle, and place it securely on axle stands. Remove the wheel.
2 If you're just removing the caliper for access to other components, it isn't necessary to detach the brake line. If you're removing the caliper for overhaul, disconnect the brake line from the caliper, for preference using a split ring ("brake") spanner to protect the fitting. Plug the line, to keep contaminants out of the brake system and to prevent losing brake fluid unnecessarily.
3 Refer to Section 3 for the front or rear caliper removal procedure - it's part of the brake pad renewal procedure. Note: The rear caliper is similar in design to the front caliper on 5-series models.

Overhaul

4 On all calipers except the front calipers on 3-Series models, remove the circlip for the dust seal (see illustration), then remove the dust boot (see illustration). Before you remove the piston, place a block of wood between the piston and caliper to prevent damage as it is removed.
5 To remove the piston from the caliper, apply compressed air to the brake fluid hose connection on the caliper body (see

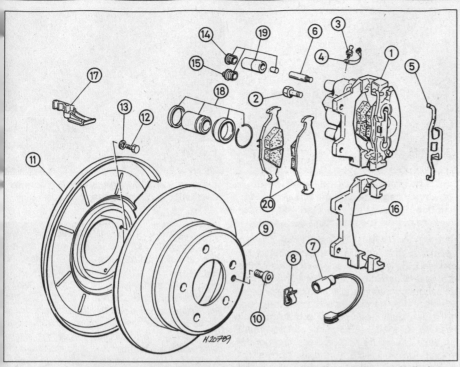

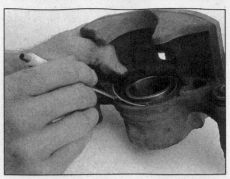

4.4b Remove the circlip for the dust seal

4.5 With the caliper padded to catch the piston, use low pressure compressed air to force the piston out of its bore - make sure your fingers are not between the piston and the caliper

4.4a An exploded view of a typical rear caliper assembly (front calipers similar)

1 Caliper assembly	8 Cable clamp	15 Plug
2 Bracket mounting bolt	9 Brake disc	16 Caliper bracket
3 Bleed screw	10 Allen bolt	17 Cable clamp
4 Dust cap	11 Shield	18 Piston seal, piston, dust
5 Anti-rattle spring	12 Bolt	boot and circlip
6 Guide bolt	13 Washer	19 Guide bush repair kit
7 Brake pad wear warning	14 Plug	20 Brake pads
light wire		

16 If the hose was disconnected from the caliper, bleed the brake system (see Section 16).

5 Brake disc - inspection, removal and refitting

Note: *This procedure applies to both the front and rear brake discs. Brake discs should always be renewed or refinished in pairs (both front or both rear discs) even if only one is damaged or defective.*

4.7 Remove the piston seal from the caliper bore using a wooden or plastic tool (metal tools may damage the cylinder bore)

illustration). Use only low pressure, such as that produced by a foot pump, to ease the piston out of its bore.

> ⚠ **Warning: Be careful not to place your fingers between the piston and the caliper, as the piston may come out with some force. If you're working on a front caliper of a 3-Series model, remove the dust boot.**

6 Inspect the mating surfaces of the piston and caliper bore wall. If there is any scoring, rust, pitting or bright areas, renew the complete caliper unit.

7 If these components are in good condition, remove the piston seal from the caliper bore using a wooden or plastic tool **(see illustration)**. Metal tools may damage the cylinder bore.

8 Remove the caliper guide pins or bolts and remove the rubber dust boots.

9 Wash all the components using methylated spirit or brake system cleaner.

10 Using the correct overhaul kit for your vehicle, reassemble the caliper as follows.

11 Dip the new rubber seal in clean brake fluid, and refit it in the lower groove in the caliper bore, making sure it isn't twisted.

12 On all calipers except the front calipers of 3-Series models, coat the walls of the caliper

bore and the piston with clean brake fluid, and refit the piston at this time. Do not force the piston into the bore, but make sure that it is squarely in place, then apply firm (but not excessive) pressure to refit it. Fit the new rubber dust boot and the retaining ring.

13 On the front calipers of 3-Series models, coat the piston with clean brake fluid, and stretch the new dust boot over the bottom of the piston. Hold the piston over the caliper bore, and insert the rubber flange of the dust boot into the upper groove in the bore. Start with the furthest side from you, and work your way around towards the front until it is completely seated. Push the piston into the caliper bore until it is bottomed in the bore, then seat the top of the dust boot in the groove in the piston.

14 Lubricate the sliding surfaces of the guide pins or bolts with silicone-based grease (usually supplied in the kit), and push them into the caliper. Refit the dust boots.

Refitting

15 Refit the caliper by reversing the removal procedure (see Section 3).

> ⚠ **Warning: Check and if necessary renew the mounting bolts on 3-Series models whenever they are removed. If in doubt, use new bolts.**

9

5.2 Remove the caliper mounting bracket bolts (arrowed) and remove the bracket

5.3 The brake pads on this vehicle were obviously neglected, as the backing plate cut deep grooves into the disc - wear this severe means the disc must be renewed

5.4a To check disc run-out, mount a dial indicator as shown, and rotate the disc

Inspection

1 Loosen the wheel bolts, raise the vehicle and support it securely on axle stands. Remove the wheel, and refit three bolts to hold the disc in place. If the rear brake disc is being worked on, release the handbrake.

2 Remove the brake caliper as outlined in Section 4. It is not necessary to disconnect the brake hose. After removing the caliper, suspend it out of the way with a piece of wire. Remove the caliper mounting bracket **(see illustration)**.

3 Inspect the disc surface for scoring, cracks or other damage. Light scratches and shallow grooves are normal after use, and are not usually detrimental to brake operation, but deep scoring requires disc removal and

renewal, or (if possible) refinishing by a specialist. If a disc is cracked it must be renewed. Be sure to check both sides of the disc **(see illustration)**. If severe vibration has been noticed during application of the brakes, the discs may be warped (excessive run-out). If the vehicle is equipped with the Anti-lock Braking System (ABS), do not confuse vibration caused by warped discs with normal operation of the ABS. It is quite normal for some vibration to be felt through the pedal when the system is working.

4 To check disc run-out, place a dial indicator at a point about 13 mm from the outer edge of the disc **(see illustration)**. Set the indicator to zero, and rotate the disc. The indicator reading should not exceed the specified

allowable run-out limit. If it does (and if the run-out is not due to wheel bearing wear), the disc should be renewed or (if possible) refinished by a specialist. **Note:** *It is recommended that the discs be resurfaced regardless of the dial indicator reading, as this will impart a smooth finish and ensure a perfectly flat surface, eliminating any vibration felt through the brake pedal or other undesirable symptoms related to questionable discs. At the very least, if you elect not to have the discs resurfaced, remove the glazing from the surface with emery cloth or sandpaper, using a swirling motion* **(see illustration)**.

5 It is absolutely critical that the disc not be machined to a thickness less than that specified. The minimum wear (or discard) thickness is stamped into the hub of the disc. The disc thickness can be checked with a micrometer **(see illustration)**.

Removal

6 Remove the disc retaining screw **(see illustration)** and remove the disc from the hub **(see illustration)**. If the disc is stuck to the hub, spray a generous amount of penetrating oil onto the area between the hub and the disc **(see illustration)** and allow a few minutes for it to loosen the rust between the two components. If a rear disc still sticks, insert a thin, flat-bladed screwdriver through the hub flange, rotate the starwheel on the handbrake

5.4b Using a swirling motion, remove the glaze from the disc surface with sandpaper or emery cloth

5.5 The disc thickness can be checked with a micrometer

5.6a Remove the disc retaining screw . . .

5.6b . . . and remove the disc from the hub

5.6c If the disc is stuck to the hub, spray some penetrating oil onto the area between the hub and the disc, and give the oil a few minutes to separate the two parts

5.6d If a rear disc still sticks to the hub, insert a thin, flat-bladed screwdriver through the hub flange, rotate the starwheel on the handbrake adjusting screw, and contract the handbrake shoes (disc removed for clarity)

adjusting screw and contract the handbrake shoes **(see illustration)**.

HAYNES HINT *If the front disc is stuck, on some discs it is possible to thread two or three bolts into the holes provided and tighten them. Alternate between the bolts, turning them a couple of turns at a time, until the disc is free.*

Refitting

7 Ensure that the disc is completely clean before refitting. If penetrating oil was used to remove the disc, make sure that no trace of this is present. Place the disc on the hub, and refit the disc retaining screw. Tighten the screw securely.
8 Refit the caliper mounting bracket (if removed), brake pads and caliper (see Sections 3 and 4). Tighten all fasteners to the torques listed in this Chapter's Specifications.
9 Refit the wheel, then lower the vehicle to the ground. Depress the brake pedal a few times to bring the brake pads into contact with the disc.
10 Adjust the handbrake shoes, if necessary (Section 11).
11 Check the operation of the brakes carefully before returning the vehicle to normal service.

6 Drum brake shoes - renewal

Warning: Brake shoes must be renewed on both wheels at the same time - never renew the shoes on only one wheel. Also, the dust created by the brake system may contain asbestos, which is harmful to your health. Never blow it out with compressed air, and don't inhale any of it. Always wear an approved filtering mask when servicing the brake system. Do not, under any

circumstances, use petroleum-based solvents to clean brake parts. Use brake system cleaner only.

  Caution: Whenever the brake shoes are renewed, new return and hold-down springs and new automatic adjuster thermo-clips should also be fitted. Due to the continuous heating/cooling cycle to which the springs are subjected, they may lose their tension over a period of time, allowing the shoes to drag on the drum, and wear at a much faster rate than normal. When fitting new brake shoes, use only original-equipment or high-quality brand name parts.

Note 1: *All four rear brake shoes must be renewed at the same time, but to avoid mixing up parts, work on only one brake assembly at a time. Some rear brake components are different for left and right-hand sides, so don't mix them up.*
Note 2: *If the wheel cylinder is found to be leaking or otherwise defective, renew it after removing the brake shoes. This is simply a matter of disconnecting the hydraulic line and unbolting the cylinder from the backplate. Attempting to overhaul a leaking cylinder is unlikely to be satisfactory, even if spare parts are available.*

1 Chock the front wheels, then loosen the rear wheel bolts, raise the rear of the vehicle and place it securely on axle stands. Remove the rear wheels and release the handbrake.
2 Remove the drum retaining screw **(see illustration)** and remove the drum. If the drum is stuck to the hub, spray the area between the hub and the drum with penetrating oil **(see illustration)**. If the drum still won't come off, the shoes have probably worn ridges into the drum, and will have to be retracted. Insert a narrow flat-bladed screwdriver through one of the holes in the hub flange **(see illustration)** and back off the adjuster wheel until the drum can be removed.
3 Inspect the drum for cracks, score marks, deep scratches and hard spots, which will appear as small discoloured areas. If the hard spots can't be removed with emery cloth or if any of the other conditions exist, the drum must be taken to a specialist to have the drum resurfaced. **Note:** *Professionals recommend*

6.2a Removing the drum retaining screw

6.2b If the drum is stuck to the hub, apply penetrating oil around the hub/drum area, and give it a few minutes to loosen up any rust

6.2c If the brake shoes have worn a groove in the drum and it won't come off, insert a thin flat-bladed screwdriver through one of the wheel bolt holes in the flange, and loosen the automatic adjuster mechanism (for the sake of clarity, the drum has already been removed in this photo, and the screwdriver is being inserted underneath the flange instead of though a wheel bolt hole)

resurfacing the drums whenever a brake job is done. Resurfacing will eliminate the possibility of out-of-round drums. If the drums are worn so much that they can't be resurfaced without exceeding the maximum allowable diameter (which is cast into the drum) **(see illustration)**, then new ones will be required. At the very least, if you elect not to have the drums resurfaced, remove the glazing from the surface with emery cloth or sandpaper, using a swirling motion.

6.3 The maximum allowable inside diameter of the drum is cast into the drum

  9

6.4a Unhook the lower return spring from the front shoe . . .

6.4b . . . then unhook it from the rear shoe and remove it

6.5a Unhook the upper return spring from the front shoe . . .

6.5b . . . then unhook it from the rear shoe and remove it

6.6a Remove the front shoe hold-down spring . . .

6.6b . . . and the rear shoe hold-down spring

6.7 Remove the front shoe, automatic adjuster lever and spring as an assembly, then remove the lever and spring, and set them aside for attachment to the new shoe

4 Unhook and remove the lower return spring (see illustrations).
5 Unhook and remove the upper return spring (see illustrations).
6 Remove the front and rear brake shoe hold-down springs (see illustrations).
7 Remove the front shoe (see illustration).
8 Remove the adjuster assembly (see illustration). Clean the adjuster and make sure that the adjuster wheel moves freely on the threads. It is recommended that the thermo-clip (the spring clip next to the adjuster wheel) be renewed whenever new shoes are fitted. Turn the adjuster wheel so that the assembly is at its shortest position ready for refitting.
9 Disconnect the handbrake cable from the handbrake lever, and remove the rear shoe (see illustration).
10 Refitting is basically the reverse of removal, but note the following points.
11 Apply a smear of high-temperature brake grease to the backing plate (see illustration). Be careful not to get grease onto the

6.8 Remove the automatic adjuster assembly

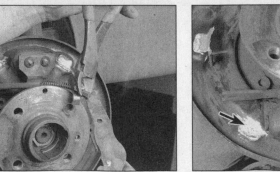

6.9 To disconnect the handbrake cable from the handbrake lever, pull on the plug at the end of the cable, and detach the cable from the bracket on the upper end of the lever (diagonal cutting pliers are being used here because they grip the cable well, but care must be taken not to nick the cable)

6.11 Before you fit the new shoes, apply some high-temperature brake grease to the friction surfaces where the inner edge of the shoe slides on the brake backing plate - when you refit the automatic adjuster mechanism, make sure each end engages properly with its respective notch in the brake shoe

6.13a Refit the automatic adjuster lever first - make sure it's properly engaged with the notch in the front end of the adjuster mechanism . . .

6.13b . . . then hook the lower end of the spring onto the lever as shown; stretch the spring, and hook the upper end into its hole in the handbrake shoe

6.14 When you get everything back together, this is how it should look!

friction surfaces of the brake shoes or drums.

12 Make sure the adjuster assembly is properly engaged with its respective notch in the handbrake lever.

13 When refitting the automatic adjustment mechanism, fit the lever on the shoe first **(see illustration)**, then hook the lower end of the spring onto the lever and the upper end into its hole in the front shoe **(see illustration)**.

14 When you're done, the brake assembly should look like this **(see illustration)**. Now proceed to the other brake.

15 When you're done with both brakes, refit the brake drums.

16 If the wheel cylinder was renewed (see Note 2), bleed the hydraulic system as described in Section 16.

17 Depress the brake pedal repeatedly to actuate the self-adjusting mechanism. A clicking sound will be heard from the brake drums as the adjusters take up the slack.

18 Check the handbrake adjustment (Section 11).

19 Refit the wheels and bolts. Lower the vehicle to the ground, and tighten the wheel bolts to the torque listed in the Chapter 1 Specifications. Check the operation of the brakes carefully before driving the vehicle in traffic.

---

7 Master cylinder - removal and refitting

 Warning: Brake fluid is poisonous. It is also an effective paint stripper. Refer to the warning at the start of Section 16.

Note: *Although master cylinder parts and overhaul kits are available for most models, we recommend fitting a new or overhauled master cylinder complete. It will take you more time to overhaul the master cylinder than to renew it, and you can't even determine whether the master cylinder is in good enough condition to overhaul it until you have dismantled it. You may very well find that it*

can't be overhauled because of its internal condition.

Removal

1 The master cylinder is connected to the brake vacuum servo, and both are attached to the bulkhead, located on the left-hand side of the engine compartment **(see illustration)**.

2 Remove as much fluid as you can from the reservoir with a syringe.

3 Place rags under the line fittings, and prepare caps or plastic bags to cover the ends of the lines once they are disconnected.

 Caution: Brake fluid will damage paint. Cover all body parts, and be careful not to spill fluid during this procedure.

4 Loosen the union nuts at the ends of the brake lines where they enter the master cylinder. To prevent rounding off the flats on these nuts, a split ring ("brake") spanner, which wraps around the nut, should be used.

5 Pull the brake lines away from the master cylinder slightly, and plug the ends to prevent dirt contamination and further fluid loss.

6 Disconnect any electrical connectors at the master cylinder, then remove the nuts

7.1 To remove the master cylinder, unplug the electrical connector (top arrow), disconnect the brake fluid hydraulic line fittings (lower right arrow, other fitting not visible in this photo) and remove the two master cylinder mounting nuts (lower left arrow, other nut not visible in this photo) - 5-Series master cylinder shown, 3-Series similar

attaching the master cylinder to the brake servo. Pull the master cylinder off the studs, and lift it out of the engine compartment. Again, be careful not to spill fluid as this is done. Discard the old O-ring **(see illustration)** between the master cylinder and the servo unit.

 Warning: The O-ring should always be renewed. A faulty O-ring can cause a vacuum leak, which can reduce braking performance and cause an erratic idle.

Bleeding procedure

7 Before fitting a new or overhauled master cylinder, it should be bled on the bench. Because it will be necessary to apply pressure to the master cylinder piston and, at the same time, control flow from the brake line outlets, it is recommended that the master cylinder be mounted in a vice. Use a vice with protected jaws, and don't clamp the vice too tightly, or the master cylinder body might crack.

8 Insert threaded plugs into the brake line outlet holes. Tighten them down so that there will be no air leakage past them, but not so tight that they cannot be easily loosened.

9 Fill the reservoir with brake fluid of the recommended type (see *"Lubricants, fluids and capacities"* in Chapter 1).

10 Remove one plug, and push the piston assembly into the master cylinder bore to

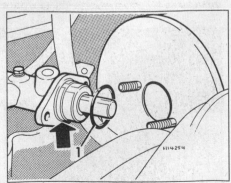

7.6 Always renew the O-ring (1) - groove arrowed - between the master cylinder and the brake servo

9

expel the air from the master cylinder. A large Phillips screwdriver can be used to push on the piston assembly.

11 To prevent air from being drawn back into the master cylinder, the plug must be refitted and tightened down before releasing the pressure on the piston assembly.

12 Repeat the procedure until brake fluid free of air bubbles is expelled from the brake line outlet hole. Repeat the procedure with the other outlet hole and plug. Be sure to keep the master cylinder reservoir filled with brake fluid, to prevent the introduction of air into the system.

13 High pressure is not involved in the bench bleeding procedure, so the plugs described above need not be refitted each time the piston is released, if wished. Instead, before releasing the piston, simply put your finger tightly over the hole to keep air from being drawn back into the master cylinder. Wait several seconds for brake fluid to be drawn from the reservoir into the piston bore, then depress the piston again, removing your finger as brake fluid is expelled. Be sure to put your finger back over the hole each time before releasing the piston, and when the bleeding procedure is complete for that outlet, refit the plug and tighten it up before going on to the other port.

Refitting

14 Refit the master cylinder (together with a new O-ring) over the studs on the brake servo, and tighten the mounting nuts only finger-tight at this time.

15 Thread the brake line fittings into the master cylinder. Since the master cylinder is still a bit loose, it can be moved slightly in order for the fittings to thread in easily. Do not strip the threads as the fittings are tightened.

16 Tighten the brake fittings securely, and the mounting nuts to the torque listed in this Chapter's Specifications.

17 Fill the master cylinder reservoir with fluid, then bleed the master cylinder (only if the cylinder has not already been bled) and the brake system as described in Section 16.

18 To bleed the cylinder on the vehicle, have an assistant pump the brake pedal several

times and then hold the pedal to the floor. Loosen the fitting nut to allow air and fluid to escape, then tighten the nut. Repeat this procedure on both fittings until the fluid is clear of air bubbles. Test the operation of the brake system carefully before returning the vehicle to normal service.

8 Brake vacuum servo - check, removal and refitting

Operating check

1 Depress the brake pedal several times with the engine off, until there is no change in the pedal travel.

2 Depress and hold the pedal, then start the engine. If the pedal goes down slightly, operation is normal.

Airtightness check

3 Start the engine, and turn it off after one or two minutes. Depress the brake pedal several times slowly. If the pedal goes down further the first time but gradually rises after the second or third depression, the servo is airtight.

4 Depress the brake pedal while the engine is running, then stop the engine with the pedal depressed. If there is no change in the pedal travel after holding the pedal for 30 seconds, the servo is airtight.

Removal and refitting

5 Dismantling the vacuum servo requires special tools, and cannot be performed by the home mechanic. If a problem develops, it is recommended that a new unit be fitted.

6 Remove the master cylinder as described in Section 7.

7 Disconnect the vacuum hose from the brake servo.

8 Working in the passenger compartment, remove the glovebox and lower left-hand trim panels.

9 Remove the clip and clevis pin to disconnect the pushrod from the cross-shaft lever (right-hand-drive models) or brake pedal

8.9 Disconnect the brake pedal return spring, then remove the clip and clevis pin (arrows) to disconnect the pushrod from the brake pedal (left-hand-drive models)

(left-hand-drive models) **(see illustration)**. On left-hand-drive models, also disconnect the brake pedal return spring.

10 Remove the four mounting nuts **(see illustration)** and withdraw the servo unit from the engine compartment.

11 Inspect the small foam filter **(see illustration)** inside the rubber boot on the pushrod. If the filter is clogged, it may affect the servo's performance. To clean the filter, wash it in a mild soapy solution. If it's still dirty, renew it.

12 Refitting is the reverse of the removal procedure. Tighten the brake servo mounting nuts to the torque listed in this Chapter's Specifications. Before you slide the boot into place over the servo pushrod air filter, make sure the notches in the filter offset the notches in the damper by 180 degrees.

13 On 3-Series models, adjust the basic setting of the pushrod's threaded clevis until the dimension is correct **(see illustration)**. When the basic setting is correct, tighten the locknut, then adjust the brake pedal travel and

8.10 Remove the four mounting nuts (arrows) and withdraw the servo unit from the engine compartment (left-hand-drive model shown)

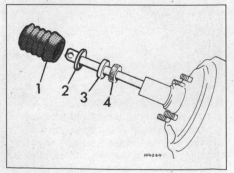

8.11 An exploded view of a typical servo pushrod assembly

1 Boot   2 Holder   3 Damper   4 Air filter

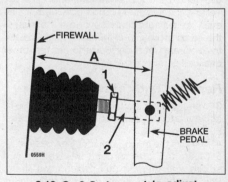

8.13 On 3-Series models, adjust dimension A (the distance between the middle of the brake lever and the bulkhead/"firewall") by loosening the locknut (1) at the pushrod clevis (2) and turning the threaded part of the pushrod until dimension A matches the dimension listed in this Chapter's Specifications. When the basic setting is correct, tighten the locknut, then adjust the brake pedal height and the stop-light switch

the stop-light switch (see Section 13). **Note:** *On right-hand-drive models, the brake pedal in on the right-hand side of the vehicle, and is connected to the left-hand side by a cross-shaft. The adjustment is carried out on the pushrod at the left-hand side, but the dimension is measured at the pedal on the right-hand side.*

14 On 5-Series models, adjust the brake pedal height and the stop-light switch (see Section 13).

15 Refit the master cylinder (see Section 7) and attach the vacuum hose.

16 Carefully test the operation of the brakes before returning the vehicle to normal use

9 Hydraulic brake servo - description, removal and refitting

Warning: Brake fluid is poisonous. It is also an effective paint stripper. Refer to the warning at the start of Section 16.

Description

1 On 5-Series E28 ("old-shape") models, a hydraulic brake servo system is fitted. The servo unit, located between the brake pedal (left-hand-drive) or cross-shaft lever (right-hand-drive) and the master cylinder, is operated by hydraulic pressure generated by the power steering pump. When the engine is running, the power steering pump supplies hydraulic pressure to a power flow regulator/accumulator. The regulator/accumulator stores and regulates the pressure to the hydraulic brake servo. When you press the brake pedal, the pressure in the servo helps actuate the master cylinder, reducing pedal effort.

2 The hydraulic brake servo cannot be overhauled; if it fails, a new one must be fitted. Testing the system requires special tools, so even fault diagnosis is beyond the scope of the home mechanic. If the system fails, take it to a dealer service department or other qualified garage for repairs.

Removal and refitting

3 With the engine off, discharge the hydraulic accumulator by depressing the brake pedal 20 times or more.

4 Remove the master cylinder (see Section 7).

5 Clean the area around the return and supply line fittings, then disconnect them. Plug the lines, to prevent dirt from entering the system, and to prevent further fluid loss.

Caution: Even a particle of dirt can damage the servo, so be extremely careful to prevent dirt from entering the system while the lines are disconnected.

6 Working from inside the passenger compartment, remove the lower left trim panels above the brake pedal (left-hand-drive models) or glovebox and trim (right-hand-

drive models). On left-hand-drive models, also disconnect the pedal return spring.

7 Prise off the retaining clip, and disconnect the pushrod from the brake pedal **(see illustration 8.9)** or cross-shaft lever.

8 Remove the four mounting nuts and remove the brake servo **(see illustration 8.10)**.

9 Refitting is the reverse of removal. Tighten the hydraulic lines to the torque listed in this Chapter's Specifications. **Note:** *Don't try to tighten these fittings without a torque wrench. If they're loose, they can leak, which can affect system operation; if they're tight, they can be damaged, and they'll also leak. You'll need a crowfoot-type split ring ("brake") attachment for your torque wrench to tighten the fittings properly.*

10 When you're done, bleed the brake hydraulic system (Section 16) and adjust the brake pedal travel and the stop-light switch (see Section 13).

10 Handbrake cable(s) - renewal

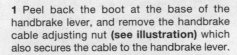

1 Peel back the boot at the base of the handbrake lever, and remove the handbrake cable adjusting nut **(see illustration)** which also secures the cable to the handbrake lever.

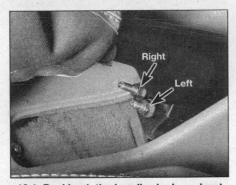

10.1 Peel back the handbrake lever boot and remove the relevant handbrake cable adjusting nut (both arrowed)

10.4b . . . then remove the pin securing the cable to the inner cam, and remove the inner cam

There are two cables - one for each rear wheel - and a nut for each cable. On some models, it may be necessary to remove the centre console completely for access.

2 Raise the vehicle and support it securely on axle stands.

3 Remove the rear brake drum (see Section 6) or rear brake disc (see Section 5).

4 On rear drum models, unhook the handbrake cable from the lever on the rear brake shoe (see Section 6). On rear disc models, remove the handbrake shoes and the actuator (see Section 12) and unhook the handbrake cable from the actuator **(see illustrations)**.

5 On rear drum models, pull the cable and cable conduit (tube) out of the back of the brake backplate, then detach the cable conduit from the cable clips on the back of the trailing arm (it's easier to pull out the old cable, and fit the new cable, with the conduit straight instead of curved). On rear disc models, it's unnecessary to detach the cable conduit from the brake backplate, but it's a good idea to detach the conduit from the clips and guides securing it to the trailing arm, to take some of the bend out of the conduit.

6 Working from the wheel end of the cable conduit, pull the cable out of the conduit **(see illustration)**.

7 Lubricate the new cable with multi-purpose grease, then insert it into the cable conduit

10.4a To detach the handbrake cable from the handbrake actuator on models with rear disc brakes, pull on the outer cam and disconnect it from the inner cam . . .

10.6 Pull the cable out of its conduit; before you refit the new cable, be sure to lubricate it with multi-purpose grease

9

and push it through until the forward end comes out at the handbrake lever.

8 Insert the cable conduit through the backplate, and attach the rear end of the cable to the handbrake lever (rear drum models) or the actuator (rear disc models). Make sure you don't kink the cable while connecting it.

9 Refit the cable conduit to the clips on the back of the trailing arm.

10 On rear drum models, refit the brake shoes and drum (see Section 6). On rear disc models, refit the handbrake shoes and actuator (see Section 12) and the rear brake disc (see Section 5).

11 Lower the vehicle, and refit the adjusting nut at the handbrake lever. Adjust the handbrake cable (see Section 11) and refit the handbrake lever boot.

11 Handbrake - adjustment

Rear drum brake models

Note: *Adjustment of the handbrake cable(s) on models with rear drum brakes should only be necessary when you renew a cable or detach if from the rear brake assembly for some reason. Failure of the handbrake system to hold the vehicle usually indicates worn brake shoes or a faulty self-adjusting mechanism.*

1 Raise the rear of the vehicle, and place it securely on axle stands.

2 Fully release the handbrake lever, then apply the brakes firmly several times with the footbrake pedal.

3 Pull the handbrake lever up five clicks.

4 Tighten or loosen the adjusting nuts by equal amounts until the rear brake shoes just begin to drag on the brake drum. You should feel the same amount of resistance at both wheels when you rotate them.

5 Release the handbrake lever, and verify that the wheels rotate freely. If they don't, re-adjust them.

Rear disc brake models

Note: *The handbrake system is not self-adjusting on models with rear disc brakes. The handbrake therefore requires periodic adjustment to compensate for wear. It should also be adjusted anytime either cable, brake disc or handbrake assembly is renewed or removed for some reason.*

6 Slowly apply the handbrake, and count the number of clicks at the lever. If the lever can be pulled up further than the eighth click, adjust the handbrake cable as follows.

7 Peel back the handbrake lever boot, and loosen the cable adjusting nut **(see illustration 10.1).** On some models, it may be necessary to remove the centre console completely for access.

8 Loosen a single bolt in each rear wheel.

Raise the vehicle and place it securely on axle stands.

9 Remove the bolt you loosened in each rear wheel. Turn the wheel until, using a torch, you can see the adjuster starwheel through the bolt hole.

10 Turn the adjuster - clockwise to expand the shoes, anti-clockwise to retract them - until the brake shoes just contact the brake drum **(see illustration 5.6d).** Back off the brake shoes so the wheel spins freely (three to four teeth on the adjuster). **Note:** *If the adjuster starwheel is hard to turn, remove the wheel and brake disc, lubricate the adjuster wheel, and try again.*

11 With the disc fitted, apply the handbrake three times to stretch and seat the cables, then slowly pull up on the handbrake lever to the fifth click. Tighten the cable adjusting nuts by equal amounts until the rear brake shoes just touch the brake drum. Verify that both wheels have the same amount of resistance.

12 Release the handbrake, and verify that both rear wheels rotate freely.

13 Tighten the wheel bolts to the torque listed in Chapter 1 Specifications.

12 Handbrake assembly - check, removal and refitting

⚠️ **Warning: The handbrake linings on rear disc brake models may be manufactured of asbestos-based material. Refer to the warning at the start of Section 6. When servicing these components, do not create dust by grinding or sanding the linings.**

1 The handbrake system should be checked regularly. With the vehicle parked on a hill, apply the handbrake, select neutral, and check that the handbrake alone will hold the vehicle when the footbrake is released (be sure to stay in the vehicle during this check). However, every 2 years (or whenever a fault is suspected), the assembly itself should be inspected.

2 With the vehicle raised and supported on

axle stands, remove the rear wheels.

3 On rear brake drum models, refer to Chapter 1; checking the thickness of the brake shoes is a routine maintenance procedure.

4 On rear disc brake models, remove the rear discs as outlined in Section 5. Support the caliper assemblies with a coat hanger or heavy wire; do not disconnect the brake line from the caliper.

5 With the disc removed, the handbrake components are visible, and can be inspected for wear and damage. The linings should last the life of the vehicle. However, they can wear down if the handbrake system has been improperly adjusted, or if the handbrake is regularly used to stop the vehicle. There is no minimum thickness specification for the handbrake shoes, but as a rule of thumb, if the shoe material is less than 1.5 mm thick, you should renew them. Also check the springs and adjuster mechanism and inspect the drum for deep scratches and other damage.

Removal and refitting

Note: *The following procedure applies only to models with rear disc brakes. The handbrake system on models with rear drum brakes is an integral part of the rear brake assembly (see Section 6).*

6 Loosen the rear wheel bolts, raise the rear of the vehicle and place it securely on axle stands. Remove the rear wheels. Remove the brake discs (see Section 5). Work on only one side at a time, so you can use the other side as a reference during reassembly, and to avoid mixing up parts.

7 Remove the shoe return and hold-down springs **(see illustrations).**

8 Remove the shoes **(see illustration).**

9 Refitting is the reverse of removal. When you're done, the actuator should be properly seated between the two shoes as shown **(see illustration).**

10 After refitting the brake disc, adjust the handbrake shoes. Temporarily refit two wheel bolts, turn the adjuster **(see illustration 5.6d)** and expand the shoes until the disc locks,

12.7a Remove the lower shoe return spring (diagonal cutting pliers are being used here because they grip the spring well, but care must be taken not to cut or nick the spring)

12.7b Remove the upper shoe return spring

12.7c Remove the shoe hold-down springs

12.8 Remove the shoes

12.9 When you're done, the actuator should be properly seated between the two shoes as shown (hub removed for clarity)

then back off the adjuster until the shoes don't drag (see Section 11). Refit the wheel bolts, and tighten them to the torque given in Chapter 1 Specifications.

13 Brake pedal - adjustment

Note: *You should always adjust brake pedal height after the master cylinder or brake servo has been removed or renewed. You should also adjust the stop-light switch (see Section 14).*

1 Measure the distance between the lower edge of the brake pedal footpad (ie the edge furthest from the bulkhead) and the bulkhead **(see illustration)**, and compare your measurement with the dimension listed in this Chapter's Specifications. If it's not as listed, loosen the locknut on the pushrod, and rotate

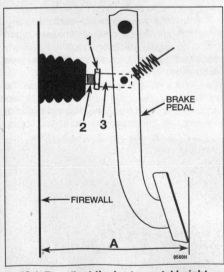

13.1 To adjust the brake pedal height, loosen the locknut (1) and turn the pushrod (2) while holding the clevis (3) until dimension A (the distance between the lower edge of the brake pedal and the bulkhead/"firewall") is within the range listed in this Chapter's Specifications (left-hand-drive shown, right-hand-drive similar)

the pushrod while holding the clevis stationary until the distance is correct. **Note:** *On right-hand-drive models, the adjustment is carried out at the left-hand side of the cross-shaft, after removing the glovebox, but the dimension is still measured at the pedal.*

14 Stop-light switch - check and adjustment

Note: *The stop-light switch should be checked and, if necessary, adjusted after the master cylinder or brake servo has been removed or renewed.*

1 The stop-light switch is located on a bracket at the top of the brake pedal. The switch activates the brake lights whenever the pedal is depressed.
2 With the brake pedal in the rest position, measure the distance between the switch contact point on the brake pedal and the switch housing **(see illustration)** and compare your measurement with dimension A listed in this Chapter's Specifications.
3 If your measurement is outside the

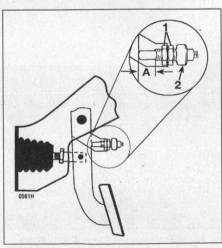

14.2 To adjust the stop-light switch, loosen the locknuts (1) and screw the switch (2) in or out until dimension A is correct

indicated dimension, disconnect the wires from the switch. Loosen the locknuts, screw the switch in or out until the plunger dimension is correct, and retighten the locknuts. Reconnect the wires and check for correct operation.

15 Brake hoses and lines - inspection and renewal

⚠ **Warning: Brake fluid is poisonous. It is also an effective paint stripper. Refer to the warning at the start of Section 16.**

Inspection

1 At the intervals specified in Chapter 1, the brake hoses and lines should be inspected. With the vehicle raised and placed securely on axle stands, the flexible hoses should be checked for cracks, chafing of the outer cover, leaks, blisters and other damage. These are important and vulnerable parts of the brake system, and inspection should be thorough. The metal pipes should be checked for excessive pitting and corrosion. If a hose or pipe exhibits any of the conditions described, renew it.

> **HAYNES HINT** *A torch and mirror will prove helpful for a complete hose and line check.*

Flexible hose renewal

2 Clean all dirt away from the ends of the hose. Have ready a suitable container to catch spilled brake fluid when the hose is disconnected.
3 To disconnect the hose at the chassis end, use a spanner to hold the hex-shaped fitting on the end of the flexible hose, and loosen the nut on the metal brake line **(see illustration)**. If the nut is stuck, soak it with penetrating oil. After the hose is disconnected from the metal line, remove the spring clip from the bracket and detach the hose from the bracket.
4 To detach the flexible hose from the caliper,

9

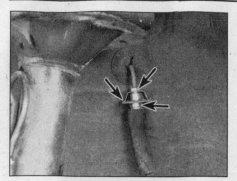

15.3 A typical brake line-to-brake hose connection: To disconnect it, use one spanner to hold the hex-shaped fitting on the end of the flexible hose (lower right arrow) and loosen the threaded fitting on the metal line with a split ring ("brake") spanner (upper right arrow), then remove the spring clip (left arrow)

simply unscrew it. Plug the open fitting in the caliper if the hose is removed for any length of time, to prevent dirt ingress.

5 Refitting is the reverse of the removal procedure. Make sure the brackets are in good condition and the locknuts are securely tightened. Renew the spring clips if they don't fit tightly.

6 Carefully check to make sure the suspension and steering components do not make contact with the hoses. Have an assistant turn the steering wheel from lock-to-lock during inspection.

7 Bleed the brake system as described in Section 16.

Metal brake line renewal

8 When renewing brake lines, use genuine parts only - preferably from a BMW dealer.

9 Genuine BMW brake lines are supplied straight. You'll need a pipe-bending tool to bend them to the proper shape.

10 First, remove the line you intend to renew, lay it on a clean workbench and measure it carefully. Obtain a new line of the same length, and bend it to match the pattern of the old line.

> ⚠ **Warning: Do not crimp or damage the line. No bend should have a smaller radius than 14 mm. Make sure the protective coating on the new line is undamaged at the bends.**

11 When fitting the new line, make sure it's well supported by the brackets, that the routing matches the original, and that there's plenty of clearance between movable components or those components which will become hot.

12 After refitting, check the master cylinder fluid level, and add fluid as necessary. Bleed the brake system as outlined in Section 16, and test the brakes carefully before driving the vehicle. Be sure there are no leaks.

16 Brake hydraulic system - bleeding

> ⚠ **Warning: Wear eye protection when bleeding the brake system. If the fluid comes in contact with your eyes, immediately rinse them with water, and seek medical attention. Most types of brake fluid are highly flammable, and may ignite if spilled onto hot engine components, for example. In this respect, brake fluid should be treated with as much care as if it were petrol. When topping-up or renewing the fluid, always use the recommended type, and ensure that it comes from a freshly-opened sealed container. Never re-use old brake fluid bled from the system, and don't top-up with fluid which has been standing open for a long time, as it is potentially dangerous to do so.**

> **HAYNES HiNT** *Brake fluid is an effective paint stripper, and will attack plastics; if any is spilt, wash it off immediately with copious amounts of water.*

Note: *Bleeding the hydraulic system is necessary to remove any air which has entered the system during removal and refitting of a hose, line, caliper or master cylinder.*

1 It will probably be necessary to bleed the system at all four brakes if air has entered the system due to low fluid level, or if the brake lines have been disconnected at the master cylinder.

2 If a brake line was disconnected at only one wheel, then only that caliper or wheel cylinder need be bled.

3 If a brake line is disconnected at a fitting located between the master cylinder and any of the brakes, that part of the system served by the disconnected line must be bled.

4 Bleed the right rear, the left rear, the right front and the left front brake, in that order, when the entire system is involved.

5 Remove any residual vacuum from the brake servo by applying the brakes about 30 times with the engine off. This will also relieve any pressure in the anti-lock brake system (where applicable).

6 Remove the master cylinder reservoir cover, and fill the reservoir with brake fluid. Refit the cover. **Note:** *Check the fluid level often during the bleeding operation, and add fluid as necessary to prevent the fluid level from falling low enough to allow air into the master cylinder.*

7 Have an assistant on hand, an empty clear plastic container, and a length of clear plastic or vinyl tubing to fit over the bleed screws. Alternatively, a "one-man" bleeding kit can be used. A "one-man" kit usually contains a tube

or bottle with a one-way valve incorporated - in this way, the pedal can be pumped as normal, but air is not drawn back into the system when the pedal is released. If a one-man kit is used, follow the instructions provided with it; similarly with pressure bleeding kits. In any case, you will also need a supply of new brake fluid of the recommended type, and a spanner for the bleed screw.

8 Beginning at the right rear wheel, loosen the bleed screw slightly, then tighten it to a point where it is tight but can still be loosened quickly and easily.

9 Place one end of the tubing over the bleed nipple, and submerge the other end in brake fluid in the container (**see illustration**).

10 Have the assistant pump the brakes a few times, then hold the pedal firmly depressed. **Note:** *If the vehicle is equipped with ABS, have the assistant pump the pedal at least 12 times.*

11 While the pedal is held depressed, open the bleed screw just enough to allow a flow of fluid to leave the caliper or wheel cylinder. Your assistant should press the brake pedal smoothly to the floor, and hold it there. Watch for air bubbles coming out of the submerged end of the tube. When the fluid flow slows after a couple of seconds, close the screw and have your assistant release the pedal.

12 Repeat paragraphs 10 and 11 until no more air is seen leaving the tube, then tighten the bleed screw and proceed to the left rear wheel, the right front wheel and the left front wheel, in that order, and perform the same procedure. Be sure to check the fluid in the master cylinder reservoir frequently.

> ⚠ **Warning: Never re-use old brake fluid. It absorbs moisture from the atmosphere, which can allow the fluid to boil and render the brakes inoperative.**

13 Refill the master cylinder with fluid at the end of the operation.

14 Check the operation of the brakes. The pedal should feel solid when depressed, with no sponginess. If necessary, repeat the entire process. *Do not operate the vehicle if you are in doubt about the effectiveness of the brake system.*

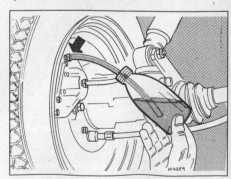

16.9 Place one end of the tubing over the bleed screw, and submerge the other end in brake fluid in the container

Chapter 10 Suspension and steering systems

Contents

Degrees of difficulty

Easy, suitable for novice with little experience	**Fairly easy,** suitable for beginner with some experience	**Fairly difficult,** suitable for competent DIY mechanic	**Difficult,** suitable for experienced DIY mechanic	**Very difficult,** suitable for expert DIY or professional

Specifications

General

Power steering fluid type .... See Chapter 1

Tyres

Tyre sizes

3-Series, E30

316	175/70x14
316i	175/70x14, 195/65x14
318i	175/70x14
320i	195/65x14
325i	195/65x14, 200/60x356, 205/55x15

5-Series, E28 ("old-shape")

518	175x14
518i	175x14
525i	175x14, 195/70x14
528i	195/70x14
535i and M535i	220/55x390

5-Series, E34 ("new-shape")

518i	195/65x15
520i	195/65x15, 225/60x15
525i	195/65x15, 205/65x15, 225/65x15
530i	205/65x15, 225/60x15
535i	225/60x15, 240/45x415

Tyre pressures .... See Chapter 1 Specifications

Torque wrench settings

Front suspension

	Nm
Strut damper rod nut	
Rod with external hexagon	65
Rod with internal hexagon	44
Strut cartridge threaded collar	130
Strut upper mounting nuts	22
Front control arm (3-Series)	
Control arm-to-steering knuckle balljoint nut	64
Control arm-to-subframe balljoint nut	83
Control arm bush bracket bolts	41
Lower control arm (5-Series)	
Control arm-to-steering arm balljoint stud nut	85
Control arm pivot bolt	77
Thrust arm (5-Series)	
Thrust arm-to-steering arm balljoint stud nut	85
Thrust arm through-bolt	130
Front hub (wheel bearing) nut	290
Steering arm-to-strut bolts (5-Series)	65
Anti-roll bar (3-Series)	
Anti-roll bar-to-connecting link bolt	41
Anti-roll bar mounting brackets-to-subframe	22
Connecting link-to-bracket	22
Connecting link bracket-to-control arm	41
Anti-roll bar (5-Series)	
Anti-roll bar mounting brackets	22
Anti-roll bar link-to-strut housing locknut	
Yellow chrome	20
White chrome	33
Yellow	58

Torque wrench settings

Rear suspension

	Nm
Rear shock absorber (3-Series)	
Shock absorber-to-upper mounting bracket	12 to 15
Shock absorber-to-trailing arm	71 to 85
Rear shock absorber (5-Series)	
Lower mounting bolt	125 to 142
Upper mounting nut	22 to 24
Upper spring mounting-to-shock absorber locknut	22 to 24
Trailing arms (3-Series)	
Trailing arm-to-lower mounting	71 to 85
Trailing arm-to-anti-roll bar	22 to 23
Trailing arms (5-Series)	
Trailing arm-to-rear axle carrier (rubber bush through-bolt and nut)	66
Trailing arm-to-axle carrier connecting link (1983-on)	126
Rear wheel bearing drive flange axle nut (5-Series)	
M22	175 to 210
M27	235 to 260

Steering system

	Nm
Steering wheel retaining nut	79
Steering column universal joint pinch-bolt	22
Steering gear-to-subframe mounting bolts (3-Series)	41
Steering box-to-front suspension subframe bolts (5-Series)	42
Track rod end-to-steering arm nut	37
Track rod end clamping bolt	14
Pitman arm-to-steering box (5-Series)	140
Steering linkage balljoints (all)	37

1 General information

Warning: Whenever any of the suspension or steering fasteners are loosened or removed, they must be inspected and if necessary, new ones fitted, of the same part number or of original-equipment quality and design. Torque specifications must be followed for proper reassembly and component retention. Never attempt to heat, straighten or weld any suspension or steering component. Any bent or damaged parts must be renewed.

The front suspension (see illustrations) is a MacPherson strut design. The struts are secured at the upper ends to reinforced areas at the top of the wheel arches, and at the lower ends to the steering arms/control arms. An anti-roll bar is attached to the control arms via connecting links, and to the suspension subframe (3-Series models) or the underbody (5-Series models).

The independent rear suspension system on 3-Series models (see illustration) features coil springs and telescopic shock absorbers. The upper ends of the shock absorbers are attached to the body; the lower ends are connected to trailing arms. An anti-roll bar is attached to the trailing arms via links, and to the body with clamps.

The independent rear suspension system on 5-Series models (see illustration) uses coil-over shock absorber units instead of separate shock absorbers and coil springs. The upper ends are attached to the body; the lower ends are connected to the trailing arms. The rear suspension of 5-Series models is otherwise similar to that of 3-Series models: two trailing arms connected by an anti-roll bar.

The steering system consists of the steering wheel, a steering column, a universal joint shaft, the steering gear, the power steering pump (where fitted) and the steering linkage, which connects the steering gear to the steering arms. On 3-Series models, a rack-and-pinion steering gear is attached directly to the steering arms via the track rods and track rod ends. On 5-Series models, a recirculating-ball steering box is connected to the steering arms via a Pitman arm, a centre track rod, the outer track rods and the track rod ends.

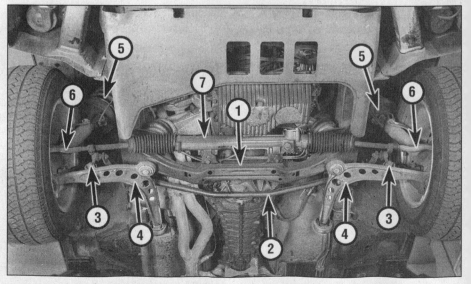

1.1a Front suspension and steering components (3-Series models)

1 Subframe	3 Anti-roll bar link	5 Strut
2 Anti-roll bar	4 Control arm	6 Track rod end
		7 Steering gear

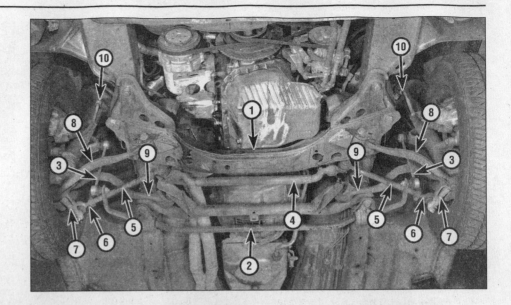

1.1b Front suspension and steering components (5-Series models - left-hand-drive shown)

1 Subframe
2 Anti-roll bar
3 Anti-roll bar link
4 Centre track rod
5 Outer track rod
6 Track rod end
7 Steering arm
8 Control arm
9 Thrust arm
10 Strut

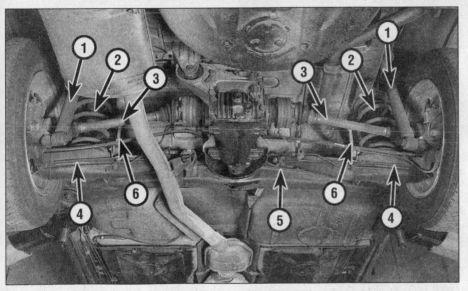

1.2 Rear suspension components (3-Series models)

1 Shock absorber
2 Coil spring
3 Driveshaft
4 Trailing arm
5 Rear axle carrier
6 Anti-roll bar link

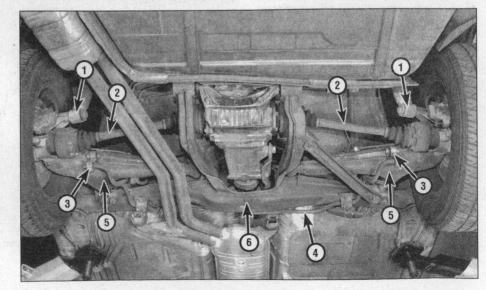

1.3 Rear suspension components (5-Series models - left-hand-drive shown)

1 Shock absorber/coil spring assembly
2 Driveshaft
3 Anti-roll bar link
4 Anti-roll bar
5 Trailing arm
6 Rear axle carrier

10

2.2a On 3-Series models, remove the nut (upper arrow) securing the anti-roll bar to the upper end of the connecting link (left side shown, right side similar). If a new control arm is being fitted, remove the lower nut (lower arrow) and disconnect the link assembly and bracket from the arm

2.2b On 5-Series models, remove the nut (arrowed) securing the anti-roll bar to the connecting link (left side shown, right side similar)

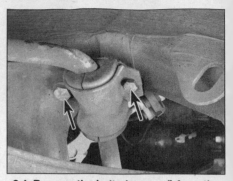

2.4 Remove the bolts (arrowed) from the anti-roll bar brackets to detach the anti-roll bar from the subframe (3-Series model shown, 5-series similar)

2 Front anti-roll bar - removal and refitting

Removal

1 Raise the front of the vehicle, and support it securely on axle stands.

2 If you're removing or renewing the anti-roll bar itself, or disconnecting the bar to renew the strut assembly on a 3-Series model, disconnect it from the anti-roll bar links **(see illustrations)**. If you're renewing the strut assembly on a 5-Series model, disconnect the anti-roll bar link from the strut housing.

3 On 3-Series models, disconnect the left control arm rubber bush from the underbody (see Section 3).

4 Remove the bolts from the anti-roll bar brackets which attach the anti-roll bar to the subframe **(see illustration)**.

5 Remove the anti-roll bar from the vehicle. Where necessary, separate the anti-roll bar from the strut bar bracket.

Refitting

6 Refitting is the reverse of the removal procedure. Be sure to tighten all nuts and bolts to the torques listed in this Chapter's Specifications.

3.4 Remove the two bolts (arrowed) securing the bush bracket to the underbody

3 Control arm (3-Series) - inspection, removal and refitting, and bush renewal

Inspection

1 Raise the front end of the vehicle, and support it securely on axle stands.

2 Grip the top and bottom of each balljoint with a large pair of water pump ("parrot jaw") pliers, and squeeze to check for free play. Alternatively, insert a lever or large screwdriver between the control arm and the subframe or strut housing. If there's any free play, renew the control arm (the balljoints can't be renewed separately).

3 Inspect the rubber bush. If it's cracked, dry, torn or otherwise deteriorated, renew it (see below).

Bush renewal

Note: *Rubber bushes should always be renewed in pairs. Make sure both new bushes have the same markings (indicating they're manufactured by the same firm).*

4 Remove the two bolts **(see illustration)** which attach the bush bracket to the underbody.

5 Using a puller, remove the bracket and

3.12 Remove the self-locking nut from the balljoint stud protruding through the top of the subframe (not shown in this photo, but it's directly above the balljoint) and separate the balljoint from the subframe. Try not to damage the dust boot

bush from the end of the control arm. If the puller slips on the end of the control arm, centre-punch the control arm to give the puller bolt a place to seat.

6 Note the orientation of the old bush. This is exactly how the new bush should be orientated when it's fitted. Press the old rubber bush out of the bracket, or have it pressed out by an engineering works.

7 Coat the end of the control arm with BMW's special lubricant (Part No. 81 22 9 407 284), and press the new bush and bracket onto the arm - or have it pressed on at an engineering works - all the way to the stop.

 Caution: Don't try to use any other type of lubricant; 30 minutes after it's applied, this lubricant loses its properties and the bush is permanently located in its proper position. Make sure the new bush is pressed on so it's orientated exactly the same way as the old bush.

8 Refit the bracket bolts and tighten them to the torque listed in this Chapter's Specifications.

9 Lower the vehicle, and leave it at rest for at least 30 minutes (this will give the special lubricant time to dry).

Control arm removal and refitting

Note: *If either balljoint is worn or damaged, the only way to renew it is to renew the control arm. If you're fitting a new control arm, a new bush must also be fitted. The old bush can't be removed from the old control arm and re-used in the new control arm.*

10 Loosen but do not remove the wheel bolts, raise the front of the vehicle and support it on axle stands. Remove the wheel bolts and the front wheel.

11 Remove the two bolts which attach the rubber bush bracket to the underbody **(see illustration 3.4)**.

12 Remove the nut which secures the control arm balljoint to the subframe, and remove the balljoint stud from the subframe. **Note:** *It may be necessary to use a balljoint separator to separate the balljoint from the subframe* **(see illustration)**, *but take care not to damage the*

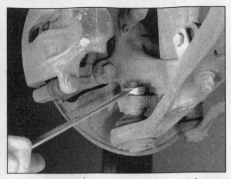

3.13a Remove the self-locking nut from the balljoint stud which attaches the outer end of the control arm to the steering knuckle. If you don't have a balljoint separator tool . . .

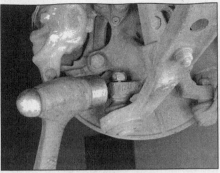

3.13b . . . give the steering knuckle a few sharp knocks with a hammer to release the balljoint stud from the strut housing, and remove the control arm

dust boot. If the boot does become damaged (and you're refitting the same control arm and balljoint), be sure to fit a new boot.

13 Unscrew the nut which secures the outer control arm balljoint to the steering knuckle **(see illustration)** and detach the balljoint stud from the knuckle **(see illustration)**. Ideally you should use a purpose-made balljoint separator tool for this job. Using a hammer is OK if you're going to fit new parts anyway, but is not recommended if you're planning to re-use parts.

14 Remove the control arm.

15 If you're renewing the control arm, you'll have to fit a new bush (see above). The old bush can't be removed re-used in another control arm.

16 Refitting is the reverse of removal. Be sure to use new self-locking nuts on the balljoint studs and tighten them, and the bush bracket bolts, to the torques listed in this Chapter's Specifications.

17 When you're finished, have the front wheel alignment checked by a dealer service department or qualified garage.

4 Control and thrust arms (5-Series) - inspection, removal and refitting and bush renewal

Inspection

1 Inspect the thrust arm rubber bush **(see illustration 4.6b)**. If the bush is cracked, torn or otherwise deteriorated, renew it. The control arm bush can't be inspected until the control arm is removed.

2 Raise the vehicle and place it securely on axle stands.

3 To inspect the control arm and thrust arm balljoints for wear, grip the top and bottom of each balljoint with a large pair of water pump ("parrot jaw") pliers, and try to squeeze them. Alternatively, use a lever or large screwdriver to move them up and down. If there's any free play, renew the control arm or thrust arm. The balljoints can't be renewed separately.

Removal

Note: If a balljoint is worn or damaged, the only way to renew it is to renew the control arm or thrust arm. If you're fitting a new control arm or thrust arm, a new bush must also be fitted. The old bush can't be removed from the old control arm or thrust arm and re-used in the new arm.

4 Loosen the wheel bolts, raise the vehicle and support it securely on axle stands. Remove the wheel.

5 If you're removing the control arm, remove the three bolts from the steering arm **(see illustration)** and separate the strut assembly from the arm.

6 Remove the nut and the through-bolt that secure the control arm or thrust arm rear mounting **(see illustrations)**.

7 Remove the nut from the balljoint **(see illustration)**. Support the steering arm and separate the balljoint from the steering arm **(see illustrations)**. Ideally you should use a purpose-made balljoint separator tool for this job. Using a hammer is OK if you're going to fit new parts anyway, but is not recommended if you're planning to re-use parts.

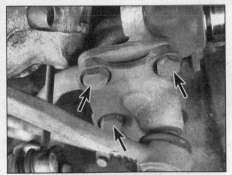

4.5 If you're removing the control arm, remove the three bolts (arrowed) from the steering arm, and separate the strut assembly from the arm

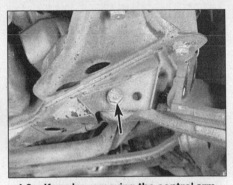

4.6a If you're removing the control arm, remove the self-locking nut and the through-bolt (arrowed) that attach the inner end of the arm to the vehicle

4.6b If you're removing the thrust arm, remove the nut and bolt (arrowed) that secure the rear end of the arm

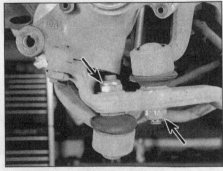

4.7a Remove the self-locking nut (control arm nut, left arrow; thrust arm nut, right arrow) from the balljoint, then support the steering arm, and press or knock the balljoint out of the steering arm

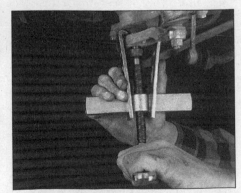

4.7b You can separate the thrust arm balljoint from the steering arm with a puller . . .

10

4.7c ... but you may have to use a hammer to knock the control arm balljoint stud loose from the steering arm, because there's no room to use a puller. A purpose-made balljoint separator tool would be better

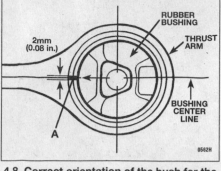

4.8 Correct orientation of the bush for the 5-Series thrust arm. The arrow on the rubber bush is aligned with the mark on the arm, and the centre of the bush is concentric with the bore

Bush inspection and renewal

8 If the bush is cracked, torn or otherwise deteriorated, take the arm to a BMW dealer service department or an engineering works, and have it pressed out and a new bush pressed in. Bushes should always be renewed in pairs (a new bush should be fitted in each arm, and both bushes should have the same manufacturer markings). If you're fitting a new thrust arm bush, make sure it's correctly orientated (see illustration).

Refitting

9 Refitting is the reverse of removal. Be sure to use new self-locking nuts on the balljoint stud nut and the through-bolt. Don't forget to refit the washers on both sides of the through-bolt. If you're refitting the control arm, be sure to use thread-locking compound on the steering arm mounting bolts. Don't tighten the through-bolt to the final torque yet. **Note**: *Thrust arms are marked "L" for the left side, and "R" for the right side. Be sure to check the marking before fitting a new arm.*

10 Support the control arm with a trolley jack, and raise it to simulate normal ride height, then tighten the through-bolt to the torque listed in this Chapter's Specifications.

Refit the wheel and tighten the wheel bolts to the torque listed in the Chapter 1 Specifications.

11 Have the front end alignment checked at a dealer service department or qualified garage.

---

5 Front strut assembly - removal and refitting

Removal

Note: *Although strut assemblies don't always fail or wear out simultaneously, renew both left and right struts at the same time, to prevent handling peculiarities or abnormal ride quality.*

1 Loosen but do not remove the front wheel bolts.

2 Raise the front of the vehicle and support it on axle stands.

3 Remove the front wheel.

4 Detach all brake hoses and electrical wires attached to the strut housing.

5 Disconnect the electrical connections for the ABS system, if applicable.

6 If you're removing the left strut, disconnect

the electrical connector for the brake pad wear sensor.

7 Remove the bolt securing the ABS wheel sensor, if applicable. Remove the brake disc (see Chapter 9).

8 Remove the brake splash shield (see illustration).

9 On 3-Series models, disconnect the anti-roll bar from its connecting link (see Section 2). On 5-Series models, disconnect the anti-roll bar link from the strut housing (see Section 2).

10 On 3-Series models, disconnect the control arm balljoint from the steering knuckle (see Section 3) and the track rod end from the steering arm (see Section 17).

11 On 5-Series models, disconnect the bolts that attach the steering arm to the strut housing (see illustration 4.5).

12 Pull out the lower end of the strut housing far enough to clear the end of the control arm (3-Series) or the steering arm (5-Series).

13 Support the weight of the strut and remove the three mounting nuts at the top of the strut, located inside the engine compartment (see illustration) and remove the strut.

14 Remove the strut assembly. If a new shock absorber (strut cartridge) is being fitted, see Section 6.

Refitting

15 Refitting is the reverse of removal. On 3-Series models, be sure to use new self-locking nuts on the control arm balljoint, the track rod end balljoint and the strut upper mountings. On 5-Series models, make sure the tang in the steering arm is mated with the notch in the strut housing (see illustration). BMW recommends using a thread-locking compound on the steering arm mounting bolts. On all models, tighten the fasteners to the torques listed in this Chapter's Specifications.

16 When you're done, drive the vehicle to a dealer service department or qualified garage and have the wheel alignment checked, and if necessary, adjusted.

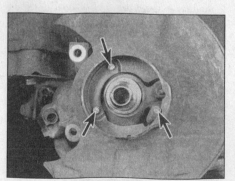

5.8 To remove the brake splash shield, remove these three bolts (arrowed)

5.13 Support the weight of the strut and remove the three mounting nuts (arrowed) at the top of the strut (5-Series shown, 3-Series similar)

5.15 On 5-Series models, make sure the tang in the steering arm is mated with the notch in the strut housing (arrowed)

6 Strut or shock absorber/coil spring - renewal

Note: *This section applies to all front strut assemblies and, on 5-Series models, the rear coil-over shock absorber assemblies.*

1 If the struts, shock absorbers or coil springs exhibit the telltale signs of wear (leaking fluid, loss of damping capability, chipped, sagging or cracked coil springs) explore all options before beginning any work. Strut or shock absorber assemblies complete with springs may be available on an exchange basis, which eliminates much time and work. Whichever route you choose to take, check on the cost and availability of parts before dismantling the vehicle.

⚠️ *Warning: Dismantling a strut or coil-over shock absorber assembly is a potentially dangerous undertaking, and utmost attention must be directed to the job, or serious injury may result. Use only a high-quality spring compressor, and carefully follow the manufacturer's instructions supplied with the tool. After removing the coil spring from the strut assembly, set it aside in a safe, isolated area.*

2 Remove the strut or shock absorber assembly (see Section 5 or 11). Mount the assembly in a vice. Line the vice jaws with wood or rags to prevent damage to the unit, and don't tighten the vice excessively.

3 Following the tool manufacturer's instructions, fit the spring compressor (these can be obtained at most car accessory shops, or it may be possible to hire one) on the spring, and compress it sufficiently to relieve all pressure from the suspension support **(see illustration)**. This can be verified by wiggling the spring.

4 Prise the protective cap off the damper rod self-locking nut. Loosen the nut **(see illustration)** with a spanner while holding the

6.9 Loosen and remove the threaded collar, and pull the old strut cartridge from the strut housing - on all struts except gas-charged units, pour the old oil from the strut housing. (Spring should have been removed first!)

6.3 Following the tool manufacturer's instructions, fit the spring compressor to the spring, and compress it sufficiently to relieve all pressure from the suspension support

damper rod stationary with another spanner or an Allen key.

5 Remove the nut, the strut bearing, the insulator and the large washer. Check the bearing for smooth operation. If it doesn't turn smoothly, renew it. Check the rubber insulator for cracking and general deterioration. If there is any separation of the rubber, renew the insulator.

6 Lift off the spring retainer and the rubber ring at the top of the spring. Check the rubber ring for cracking and hardness. Renew it if necessary.

7 Carefully lift the compressed spring from the assembly and set it in a safe place, such as a steel cabinet.

⚠️ *Warning: Never place your head near the end of the spring!*

8 Slide the protective tube and rubber bumper off the damper rod. If either is damaged or worn, renew it.

9 If you're working on a front strut, loosen and remove the threaded collar **(see illustration)** and pull the old strut cartridge from the strut housing. Pour the old oil from the strut housing.

10 On all struts except gas-charged units, fill the strut housing with 20 to 25 cc (3-Series), 42 to 47 cc (518i and 520i 5-Series models) or 20 to 25 cc (all other 5-Series models) of

6.11 Make sure you align the end of the coil spring with the shoulder of the rubber ring, and with the spring retainer

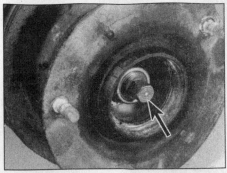

6.4 Prise the protective cap off the damper rod nut, and remove the large nut (arrowed) - to prevent the damper rod from turning, place an Allen key in the end of the shaft

engine oil (the oil helps cool the shock absorber by transferring heat to the strut housing). **Note:** *It doesn't matter what viscosity or grade of engine oil is used.*

11 Refitting is otherwise the reverse of removal. Tighten the threaded collar to the torque listed in this Chapter's Specifications. Make sure you align the end of the coil spring with the shoulder of the rubber ring and with the spring retainer **(see illustration)**. Tighten the damper rod nut to the torque listed in this Chapter's Specifications.

12 Refit the strut or shock absorber assembly (see Section 5 or 11).

7 Balljoints - check and renewal

Check

Note: *On 3-Series models, there are two balljoints on each control arm - one between the middle of the arm and the subframe, and the other between the outer end of the arm and the steering knuckle. On 5-Series models, there are balljoints on the outer ends of the control arm and the thrust arm.*

1 Raise the vehicle and support it securely on axle stands.

2 Visually inspect the rubber boot between the balljoint and the subframe or steering knuckle, etc for cuts, tears or leaking grease. If you note any of these conditions, renew the control arm or thrust arm - the balljoints are not available separately.

3 Place a large lever under the balljoint, and try to push the balljoint up. Next, position the lever between the arm and the subframe or between the arm and steering knuckle. If you can see or feel any movement during either check, a worn balljoint is indicated.

4 Have an assistant grasp the tyre at the top and bottom, and shake the top of the tyre with an in-and-out motion. Touch the balljoint stud nut. If any looseness is felt, suspect a worn balljoint stud or a widened hole in the subframe or steering knuckle. If the latter

10

8.2 Using a hammer and chisel, knock out the dust cap in the centre of the hub

8.3 Using a chisel, knock out the staked portion of the hub nut

8.8a If the hub sticks, knock it loose with a hammer

problem exists, a new subframe or steering arm (5-Series) or steering knuckle (3-Series), which is integral with the strut housing, should be fitted as well as the new balljoint.

Renewal

Note: *None of these balljoints can be serviced or renewed individually. If one of them is worn, a complete new arm must be fitted.*

8 Front hub and wheel bearing assembly - removal and refitting

Note: *Removing the front hub/bearing assembly renders it unfit for re-use. A new assembly will be required for refitting.*

Removal

1 Loosen the wheel bolts, then raise the front of the vehicle, and support it securely on axle stands. Remove the wheel bolts and the wheel.
2 Using a hammer and chisel, remove the dust cap from the centre of the wheel hub **(see illustration)**.
3 Unstake the hub nut **(see illustration)**.
4 Refit the wheel and lower the vehicle to the ground. Loosen, but do not remove, the hub nut.

 Warning: Always loosen and tighten the hub nut with the vehicle on the ground. The

leverage needed to loosen the nut (which is very tight) could topple the vehicle off a lift or an axle stand.
5 Raise the front of the vehicle, support it securely on axle stands, and remove the front wheel again.
6 Remove the front brake caliper and mounting bracket (see Chapter 9). There is no need to disconnect the brake hose. Hang the caliper out of the way with a piece of wire.
7 Remove the brake disc (see Chapter 9).
8 Remove the hub nut, and pull the hub and bearing assembly off the stub axle. You may have to tap it off if it's stuck **(see illustration)**. If the inner race of the bearing remains on the stub axle (it probably will), remove the dust shield (rubber boot) behind the bearing, and use a puller to remove the inner race **(see illustration)**.

Refitting

9 Fit a new dust shield.
10 Push the new hub and bearing onto the stub axle. If it's necessary to use force, press or drive only against the bearing inner race **(see illustration)**.
11 Fit a new hub nut, and tighten it finger-tight at this stage.
12 Refit the brake disc, its countersunk retaining screw, and the brake caliper (see Chapter 9).
13 Refit the wheel, and lower the vehicle to the ground.
14 Tighten the hub nut to the torque listed in

this Chapter's Specifications. Again, make sure you do this with the vehicle on the ground, not up on axle stands.
15 Raise the front of the vehicle and place it securely on axle stands. Remove the wheel.
16 Stake the collar of the nut into the groove of the spindle.
17 Apply suitable sealant to a new grease cap, and fit the cap by driving it into place with a soft-faced mallet.
18 Refit the wheel and wheel bolts. Lower the vehicle to the ground, and tighten the wheel bolts to the torque listed in the Chapter 1 Specifications.

9 Rear shock absorbers (3-Series) - removal and refitting

Removal

Note: *Although shock absorbers don't always wear out simultaneously, renew both left and right shock absorbers at the same time, to prevent handling peculiarities or abnormal ride quality.*
1 Chock the front wheels.
2 Raise the rear of the vehicle, and support it securely on axle stands. Support the trailing arm with a trolley jack. Place a block of wood on the jack head to serve as a cushion.
3 Remove the shock absorber lower mounting bolt **(see illustration)**.

8.8b If the inner race of the bearing sticks to the stub axle, use a puller to get it off

8.10 Use a large socket or a suitable piece of pipe to drive against the inner race of the new bearing

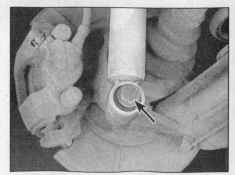

9.3 Remove the shock absorber lower mounting bolt (arrowed)

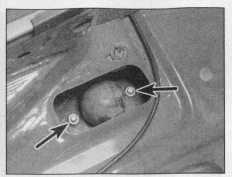

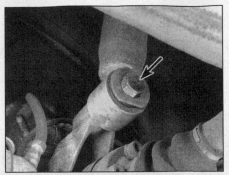

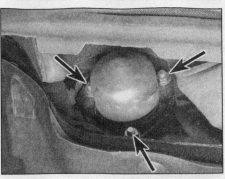

9.4 Shock absorber upper mounting nuts (arrowed) - late-model convertible shown. On other early models, upper nuts are accessible from the luggage compartment; on later models, they're behind the back of the rear seat, up under the parcel shelf

11.2 Remove the shock absorber lower mounting bolt (arrowed)

11.3 Shock absorber upper mounting nuts (arrowed) on a later (E34) 5-Series model

4 On some models, working inside the boot, you can remove the trim to access the upper mounting nuts; on later models, you'll have to remove the rear seat back to get at the upper mounting nuts. On Touring (Estate) models, remove the side backrest and rear seat belt reels, and unscrew the centring shell on the wheel arch. On Convertibles, simply remove the top from the recessed well behind the passenger compartment, and remove the small rubber access cover. As you remove the mounting nuts **(see illustration)**, have an assistant support the shock absorber from below so it doesn't fall out.

5 Look for oil leaking past the seal in the top of the shock absorber body. Inspect the rubber bushings in the shock absorber eye. If they're cracked, dried or torn, renew them. To test the shock absorber, grasp the shock absorber body firmly with one hand, and push the damper rod in and out with the other. The strokes should be smooth and firm. If the rod goes in and out too easily, or unevenly, the shock absorber is defective and must be renewed.

Refitting

6 Fit the shock absorbers in the reverse order of removal, but don't tighten the mounting bolts and nuts yet.

7 Bounce the rear of the vehicle a couple of times to settle the bushings, then tighten the nuts and bolts to the torque values listed in this Chapter's Specifications.

10 Rear coil springs (3-Series) - removal and refitting

Note: *Although coil springs don't always wear out simultaneously, renew both left and right springs at the same time, to prevent handling peculiarities or abnormal ride quality.*

Removal

1 Loosen the wheel bolts. Chock the front wheels, then raise the rear of the vehicle and

support it securely on axle stands. Make sure the stands don't interfere with the rear suspension when it's lowered and raised during this procedure. Remove the wheels.

2 Disconnect the mountings and brackets which support the rear portion of the exhaust system, and temporarily lower the exhaust system (see Chapter 4). Lower the exhaust system only enough to lower the suspension and remove the springs. Suspend the exhaust with a piece of wire.

3 Support the differential with a trolley jack, then remove the differential rear mounting bolt. Push the differential down, and wedge it into this lowered position with a block of wood. This reduces the drive angle, preventing damage to the CV joints when the trailing arms are lowered to remove the springs.

4 Place a trolley jack under the trailing arm.

5 If the vehicle has a rear anti-roll bar, disconnect the bar from its connecting links, or disconnect the links from the trailing arms (see Section 12).

6 Loop a chain through the coil spring, and bolt the chain together, to prevent the coil spring from popping out when the trailing arm is lowered. Be sure to leave enough slack in the chain to allow the spring to extend completely.

7 Disconnect the shock absorber lower mounting bolt (see Section 9), carefully lower the trailing arm and remove the coil spring.

Refitting

8 Refitting is the reverse of removal. As the trailing arm is raised back up, make sure the spring seats properly.

11 Rear shock absorber/coil spring assembly (5-Series) - removal and refitting

Removal

Note: *Although shock absorbers don't always wear out simultaneously, renew both left and right shock absorbers at the same time, to prevent handling peculiarities or abnormal ride quality.*

1 Loosen the wheel bolts, then chock the front wheels. Raise the vehicle and support it securely on axle stands. Remove the wheels.

2 Remove the shock absorber lower mounting bolt **(see illustration)**.

3 On early models, peel back the trim inside the luggage compartment far enough to access the upper mounting nuts. To get at the upper mounting nuts on later models, first remove the rear seat cushion (see Chapter 11), then remove the two bolts holding the rear seat backrest, and remove the backrest. Support the trailing arm with a jack, and remove the upper mounting nuts **(see illustration)**. Lower the jack, and remove the shock absorber and the gasket. To separate the shock absorber and spring, refer to Section 6.

Refitting

4 Refitting is the reverse of removal. Don't forget to fit the gasket between the upper end of the shock absorber and the body. Tighten the upper nuts to the torque listed in this Chapter's Specifications. Don't tighten the lower bolt until the vehicle is lowered.

5 Lower the vehicle, and with it sitting at the normal ride height, tighten the lower bolt to the torque listed in this Chapter's Specifications.

12 Rear anti-roll bar - removal and refitting

Removal

Note: *The rear anti-roll bar is mounted basically the same way on all models. Follow these general removal and refitting procedures, keeping in mind any variations.*

1 Chock the front wheels, then raise the rear of the vehicle and support it securely on axle stands.

2 Remove the anti-roll bar bracket bolts or nuts **(see illustration)**.

3 Disconnect the anti-roll bar from the link at each end of the bar **(see illustrations)** and detach the anti-roll bar.

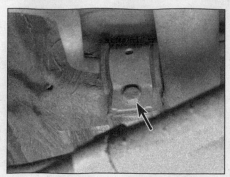

12.2 Rear anti-roll bar bracket bolt (arrowed) (3-Series)

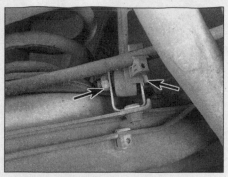

12.3a A nut and bolt (arrowed) connect each rear anti-roll bar link to the rear trailing arms (3-Series)

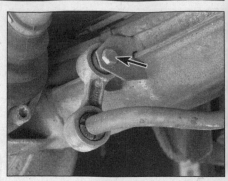

12.3b Bolt (arrowed) connecting rear anti-roll bar link to trailing arm (5-Series)

4 Inspect and, if necessary, renew any worn or defective bolts, washers, bushes or links.

Refitting

5 Refitting is the reverse of removal. Tighten all fasteners securely.

13 Rear trailing arms (3-Series) - removal and refitting

Removal

1 Loosen the wheel bolts, then chock the front wheels. Raise the rear of the vehicle, and support it securely on axle stands. Remove the wheel(s).
2 Remove the driveshaft (see Chapter 8), or disconnect it from the final drive output flange.
3 Disconnect the rear brake hose from the metal brake line at the bracket on the trailing arm **(see illustration)**. **Note**: *For information on disconnecting brake hose-to-metal line connections, see Chapter 9. Plug the line and hose, to prevent dirt ingress and loss of brake fluid.*
4 Disconnect the handbrake cable (see Chapter 9).
5 Disconnect the lower end of the shock

absorber from the trailing arm (see Section 9), and lower the trailing arm.
6 Remove the trailing arm pivot bolts **(see illustration)** and remove the trailing arm.
7 Inspect the pivot bolt bushes. If they're cracked, dried out or torn, take the trailing arm to an engineering works and have them new ones fitted. Each bush has a larger diameter shoulder on one end. Make sure this larger diameter shoulder on each bush faces away from the trailing arm, ie the inner bush shoulder faces the centre of the vehicle, and the outer bush shoulder faces away from the vehicle.

Refitting

8 Refitting is the reverse of removal. Support the trailing arm with a trolley jack, and raise it to simulate normal ride height, then tighten the nuts and bolts to the torque listed in this Chapter's Specifications. Be sure to bleed the brakes as described in Chapter 9.

14 Rear trailing arms (5-Series) - removal and refitting

Removal

1 Loosen the wheel bolts, then chock the front wheels. Raise the rear of the vehicle and support it securely on axle stands. Remove the wheel(s).

2 Remove the driveshaft (see Chapter 8).
3 Disconnect the rear brake hose from the metal brake line at the bracket on the trailing arm **(see illustration)**. **Note**: *For information on disconnecting brake hose-to-metal line connections, see Chapter 9. Plug the line and hose, to prevent dirt ingress and loss of brake fluid.*
4 Disconnect the handbrake cable from the handbrake actuator, and unclip the handbrake cable from the trailing arm (see Chapter 9).
5 Remove the ABS wheel sensor (if applicable) from the trailing arm, and unclip the sensor wire harness from the arm. Position the sensor aside so it won't be damaged during removal of the trailing arm.
6 If you're removing the right trailing arm, unplug the connector for the brake pad wear sensor, if applicable.
7 Disconnect the rear anti-roll bar from the trailing arm (see Section 12).
8 On 1983 and later models, remove one of the rear axle carrier bolts **(see illustration)**.
9 Disconnect the shock absorber lower mounting bolt (see Section 11).
10 Remove the two trailing arm pivot bolts and nuts, and remove the trailing arm from the vehicle.
11 Inspect the pivot bolt bushes. If they're cracked, dried out or torn, take the trailing arm to an engineering works, and have new ones fitted. The bush inner sleeve is longer on one side. Make sure the bushes are fitted with

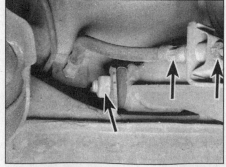

13.3 Disconnect the rear brake hose (middle arrow) from the metal brake line fitting (right arrow) at this bracket on the trailing arm, then plug the line and hose immediately; the other arrow points to the nut for the inner pivot bolt

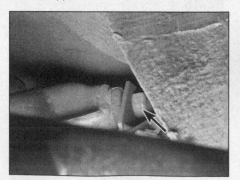

13.6 Nut (arrowed) for the outer pivot bolt

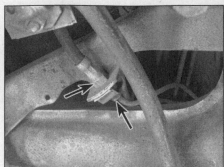

14.3 Disconnect the brake hose (left arrow) from the fitting on the metal brake line (right arrow) at this bracket

14.8 On 1983 and later models, remove one of these trailing arm-to-axle carrier bolts (it doesn't matter which one you remove - one attaches the link to the trailing arm, and the other attaches the link to the axle carrier)

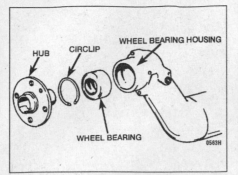

15.4 An exploded view of the 3-Series rear wheel bearing assembly

15.7 Prise out the lockplate that secures the drive flange nut - once you've prised out an edge of the lockplate, pull it out with a pair of needle-nose pliers

the longer side of the sleeve facing towards the centre of the vehicle.

Refitting

12 Refitting is the reverse of removal. Refit the inner pivot bolt first. Don't fully tighten the nuts on the pivot bolts or the shock absorber yet.
13 Bleed the brakes as described in Chapter 9.
14 Support the trailing arm with a trolley jack, and raise it to simulate normal ride height. Tighten the bolts and nuts to the torques listed in this Chapter's Specifications.

15 Rear wheel bearings - renewal

3-Series models

1 Loosen the driveshaft nut and the rear wheel bolts, then chock the front wheels. Raise the rear of the vehicle and place it securely on axle stands. Remove the rear wheel. **Note:** *Depending on the type of rear wheel, it may be necessary to remove the wheel first, remove the hubcap, then refit the wheel and loosen the driveshaft nut.*
2 Remove the driveshaft (see Chapter 8).

3 On models with rear brake drums, remove the drum. On models with rear disc brakes, remove the brake caliper and mounting bracket. Don't disconnect the hose. Hang the caliper out of the way with a piece of wire. Remove the brake disc (see Chapter 9). Working from behind, drive the wheel hub out of the wheel bearing with a large socket or a piece of pipe.

> **HAYNES HiNT** *If the bearing inner race sticks to the hub (it probably will), use a puller to remove the race from the hub.*

4 Remove the large circlip **(see illustration)** that holds the wheel bearing in the wheel bearing housing, then drive out the bearing with a large socket or piece of pipe.
5 Refitting is basically the reverse of removal, bearing in mind the following points:
a) *Be extremely careful where you place the socket or piece of pipe when you drive the new bearing into the housing. It should be butted up against the outer race of the bearing. Driving in the new bearing using the inner race will ruin the bearing.*
b) *Refit the wheel and lower the vehicle to the ground before attempting to tighten the driveshaft nut to the torque listed in the Chapter 8 Specifications.*

5-Series models

6 Chock the front wheels, then raise the rear of the vehicle and support it securely on axle stands. Disconnect the outer CV joint from the drive flange (see Chapter 8). Support the outer end of the driveshaft with a piece of wire - don't let it hang, as this could damage the inner CV joint.
7 Prise out the lockplate that secures the drive flange nut **(see illustration)**. Once you've prised out an edge of the lockplate, pull it out with a pair of needle-nose pliers.
8 Lower the vehicle and unscrew the drive flange nut, but don't remove it yet. You'll need a long bar **(see illustration)**.

> ⚠ **Warning: Don't attempt to loosen this nut with the vehicle on axle stands. The force required to loosen the nut could topple the vehicle from the stands.**

9 Loosen the rear wheel bolts, raise the rear of the vehicle again, place it securely on axle stands and remove the wheel.
10 Remove the brake caliper and the brake disc (see Chapter 9). Hang the caliper out of the way with a piece of wire.
11 Remove the drive flange nut. Using a suitable puller, remove the drive flange **(see illustration)**.
12 Using a soft-faced hammer, drive the stub axle out of the bearing **(see illustration)**. If the bearing inner race comes off with the stub

15.8 Lower the vehicle and loosen the drive flange nut

15.11 Remove the drive flange with a puller

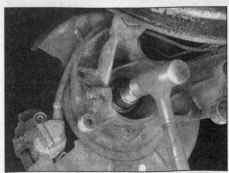

15.12 Using a soft-faced hammer, drive the stub axle out of the bearing

10

15.13a Remove the large circlip that retains the bearing in the housing . . .

15.13b . . . then drive the bearing out of the housing with a large socket or a suitable piece of pipe

15.14a To refit the new bearing, use a large socket or a piece of pipe with an outside diameter the same diameter as the outer race of the bearing - don't apply force to the inner race - and make sure the bearing is fully seated against the back of its bore

axle (it probably will), use a puller to remove the race from the stub axle. If you can't get the race off with a puller, take the stub axle to an engineering works and have it pressed off.

13 Remove the large circlip that retains the bearing in the bearing housing **(see illustration)**, then drive the bearing out of the bearing housing with a large socket or a suitable piece of pipe **(see illustration)**.

14 Refitting is basically a reversal of removal, bearing in mind the following points:

a) *Fit the new bearing using a large socket or a suitable piece of pipe, with an outside diameter the same diameter as the outer race **(see illustration)**. Don't apply force to the inner race. Make sure the bearing is fully seated against the back of the bore. Refit the circlip, making sure it's fully seated into its groove.*

b) *BMW dealers use special tools (Part Nos. 23 1 1300, 33 4 080 and 33 4 020) to pull the stub axle into the bearing, because the smooth portion between the splined portion of the stub axle and the flange is a press-fit, and knocks out the wheel bearing inner race during refitting of the stub axle. However, you can refit the stub axle without these tools, using the old inner race and a piece of pipe 13 mm long by 38 mm inside diameter **(see***

illustration). *First, insert the stub axle through the new bearing until the threaded portion protrudes from the inner race. Refit the nut and tighten it until the splined portion of the stub axle shaft bottoms against the nut. You'll need to hold the stub axle flange with a lever or a large screwdriver while tightening the nut **(see illustration)**. Remove the nut, refit your piece of pipe, centred on the inner race and refit the nut **(see illustration)**. Tighten the nut again until it bottoms against the splines. Remove the nut, refit the old inner race, refit the nut and tighten it once more until it bottoms against the splines. Remove the nut, remove the old inner race, refit your piece of pipe, refit the old inner race, refit the nut and tighten it until it bottoms against the splines. Remove the nut, the old race and the pipe. Refit the drive flange, refit the nut and tighten it securely, but don't attempt to tighten it to the final torque until the vehicle is lowered to the ground.*

c) *Refit the wheel and lower the vehicle to the ground before tightening the stub axle nut to the torque listed in this Chapter's Specifications.*

15 The remainder of refitting is the reverse of removal.

16 Steering system - general information

On 3-Series models, the steering wheel and steering column are connected to a rack-and-pinion steering gear (power-assisted where applicable) via a short universal joint shaft. When the steering wheel is turned, the steering column and universal joint turn a pinion gear shaft on top of the rack. The pinion gear teeth mesh with the gear teeth of the rack, so the rack moves right or left in the housing when the pinion is turned. The movement of the rack is transmitted through the track rods and track rod ends to the steering arms, which are an integral part of the strut housings.

On 5-Series models, the upper part of the steering system is identical to a 3-Series. Instead of a rack-and-pinion set-up, however, these models use a power-assisted recirculating ball steering box which steers the front wheels via a steering linkage consisting of a Pitman arm, an idler arm, a centre track rod, a pair of inner track rods, and two track rod ends.

15.14b You can fabricate your own spacer tool from a piece of 13 mm long, 38 mm inside diameter pipe (left); you'll also need to use the old inner race (right)

15.14c Hold the stub axle flange with a large lever while tightening the nut

15.14d When you refit the spacer, make sure it's centred on the inner race of the bearing before tightening the nut

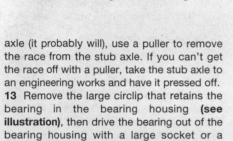

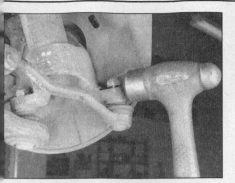

17.2 Loosen the nut on the track rod balljoint stud. For preference use a balljoint separator; otherwise, give the steering arm a few light blows with a hammer to release the balljoint stud. Remove the nut, and separate the balljoint stud from the steering arm

17.3 Loosen the clamp bolt (arrowed) that locks the track rod end to the inner track rod. Paint an alignment mark on the threads, to ensure the track rod end is refitted in the same position, and unscrew the track rod end from the inner track rod

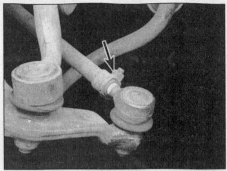

17.6 Measure the length of the track rod and record your measurement, or paint an alignment mark on the threads to ensure the track rod end is refitted in the same position, then loosen the clamp bolt (arrowed)

Where power-assistance is fitted, hydraulic pressure (provided by an engine-driven pump) delivers power steering fluid to the rack-and-pinion steering gear or the recirculating-ball steering box - this enhances steering response and reduces steering effort.

Aside from maintaining the proper level of power steering fluid in the system and checking the tension of the drivebelt (see Chapter 1, where applicable), the steering system requires no maintenance. However, on high-mileage vehicles, the track rod end balljoints, the universal joints on either end of the universal joint shaft, and the rubber coupling between the steering column and the universal joint shaft will wear, develop excessive play, and cause the steering to feel somewhat loose. At this point, you'll have to renew these items; they can't be serviced.

Before you conclude that the steering system needs work, however, always check the tyres (see Section 25) and tyre pressures (see Chapter 1). Also inspect the bearings in the strut upper mounts (see Section 5), the front hub bearings (see Section 8) and other suspension parts, which may also be contributing to an imprecise steering feel.

17 Track rod ends - removal and refitting

1 Loosen but do not remove the wheel bolts, then raise the front of the vehicle and secure it on axle stands. Remove the front wheel.

3-Series models

2 Loosen the nut on the track rod balljoint stud, and free the balljoint stud from the steering arm using a balljoint separator. In the absence of a separator tool, try giving the steering arm a few light blows with a hammer **(see illustration)**. Remove the nut, and separate the balljoint stud from the steering arm.

3 Loosen the clamp bolt that locks the track rod end to the inner track rod. Measure the length of the track rod end, or paint an alignment mark on the threads to ensure the track rod end is refitted in the same position **(see illustration)**. Unscrew the track rod end from the inner track rod.
4 Refitting is the reverse of removal. Make sure the mark you made on the threads of the track rod end is aligned correctly, if applicable. If you measured the track rod end, make sure it is refitted to the same distance.
5 Have the toe-in checked and, if necessary, adjusted at a dealer service department or qualified garage.

5-Series models

6 Measure the length of the track rod and record your measurement, or paint an alignment mark on the threads to ensure the track rod end is refitted in the same position **(see illustration)**. Loosen the clamp bolt.
7 Use a balljoint separator or a puller to separate the track rod end from the steering arm **(see illustration)**.
8 Unscrew the track rod end.
9 Refitting is the reverse of removal. Make sure you align the paint mark made on the threads of the track rod end, if applicable. If you measured the track rod end, make sure it is refitted to the same distance.
10 Have the toe-in checked and, if necessary, adjusted at a dealer service department or qualified garage.

18 Steering gear boots (3-Series) - renewal

1 Remove the track rod ends (see Section 17).
2 Cut the boot clamps at both ends of the old boots, and slide off the boots.
3 While the boots are removed, inspect the seals in the end of the steering gear. If they're

17.7 Using a puller to separate the track rod end from the steering arm

leaking, renew the steering gear (see Section 19).
4 Slide the new boots into place and fit new boot clamps.
5 Refit the track rod ends (see Section 17).

19 Rack-and-pinion steering gear (3-Series) - removal and refitting

Removal

1 Loosen but do not remove the wheel bolts, raise the vehicle and support it securely on axle stands. Remove the front wheels.
2 Mark the lower universal joint on the steering shaft and the pinion shaft, to ensure proper alignment when they're reassembled. Remove the nut and bolt that attach the lower end of the universal joint shaft to the steering gear pinion shaft. Loosen the bolt and nut at the upper end of the universal joint shaft. Slide the universal joint shaft up a little, disengage it from the pinion shaft, and remove it. Inspect the universal joints and the rubber coupling for wear. If any of them are worn or defective, renew the universal joint shaft.
3 On power steering models, using a large

19.6 Rack-and-pinion steering gear mounting bolts (arrowed) - 3-Series models - (self-locking nuts not visible in this photo)

syringe or hand pump, empty the power steering fluid reservoir.

4 On power steering models, remove the banjo bolts and disconnect the power steering pressure and return lines from the steering gear. Place a container under the lines to catch spilled fluid. Plug the lines to prevent excessive fluid loss and contamination. Discard the sealing washers (new ones should be used when reassembling).

5 Disconnect the track rod ends from the steering arms (see Section 17).

6 Remove the nuts and bolts from the steering gear mounting brackets **(see illustration)**. Discard the old nuts.

7 Withdraw the assembly from beneath the vehicle. Take care not to damage the steering gear boots.

Refitting

8 Refitting is the reverse of removal. Make sure the marks you made on the lower universal joint and the pinion shaft are aligned before you tighten the clamping bolts for the upper and lower universal joints. Use new self-locking nuts on the steering rack

20.4 To remove an outer track rod, remove this nut (arrowed) from the end of the centre track rod, and use a balljoint separator to separate the balljoint stud from the centre track rod (if you're renewing the inner track rod end, mark the threads with paint before loosening the clamp bolt and nut)

mounting bolts, and new sealing washers on the hydraulic line fittings. Tighten the mounting bolts, the track rod end nuts and the universal joint shaft clamping bolts to the torque values listed in this Chapter's Specifications.

9 Lower the vehicle to the ground.

10 On power steering models, fill the reservoir with the recommended fluid (see Chapter 1) and bleed the power steering system (see Section 23).

11 It's a good idea to have the front wheel alignment checked by a dealer service department or qualified garage.

20 Steering linkage (5-Series) - inspection, removal and refitting

Inspection

1 Raise the vehicle and place it securely on axle stands.

2 Firmly grasp each front tyre at the top and bottom, then at the front and rear, and check for play in the steering linkage by rocking the tyre back and forth. There should be little or no play in any of the linkage balljoints. Inspect the Pitman arm, the idler arm, the centre track rod, the inner track rods, the track rod ends and the steering arms for any obvious damage. Try forcing the linkage parts in opposite directions from one another. There should be no play between any of them. If any of the parts are bent or damaged in any way, or if any of the balljoints are worn, renew the parts concerned.

Removal

3 Before dismantling the steering linkage, obtain a suitable balljoint separator. A two-jaw puller or a wedge-type tool will work (although the wedge-type tends to tear the balljoint boots). Sometimes, you can also jar a balljoint taper pin free from its eye by striking opposite sides of the eye simultaneously with two large hammers, but the space available to do this is limited, and the balljoint stud sometimes

20.7 To unbolt the idler arm from the subframe crossmember, remove this nut (arrowed)

sticks to the eye because of rust and dirt. There is also a risk of damaging the component being struck.

4 To remove the outer track rods, disconnect the track rod ends from the steering arms (see Section 17). Remove the nut that attaches the balljoint on the inner end of each outer track rod to the centre track rod **(see illustration)**. Using a balljoint separator, disconnect the outer track rods from the centre track rod. If you're renewing the balljoint at either end of the outer track rods, paint or scribe alignment marks on the threads to mark their respective positions as a guide to adjustment during reassembly **(see illustration 17.3)**.

5 To remove the centre track rod, remove the nuts that attach the centre track rod balljoints to the Pitman arm and the idler arm, and use a balljoint separator to disconnect the balljoints from the two arms.

6 To remove the Pitman arm, you'll have to remove the steering box first (see Section 21). Look for match marks between the sector shaft and arm. If there aren't any, scribe a mark across the bottom face of both parts. Remove the Pitman arm pinch-bolt and nut, then remove the arm with a puller.

7 To unbolt the idler arm, first remove the small cover bolted to the top of the subframe crossmember. Put a spanner on the bolt, and remove the nut recessed into the underside of the subframe crossmember **(see illustration)**. Check the idler arm rubber bush for wear. If it's damaged or worn, renew it.

8 Check each balljoint for excessive play or stiffness, and for split or deteriorated rubber dust boots. Renew all worn or damaged balljoints. The inner and outer track rod ends on the outer track rods can be renewed individually; if either balljoint on the centre track rod is damaged or worn, you must renew the centre track rod.

Refitting

9 Refitting is the reverse of the removal procedure, but observe the following points:

a) Realign the match marks on the Pitman arm and the steering box sector shaft when reassembling them.

b) If you're fitting new inner or outer track rod ends on the outer track rods, position them so that the match marks made during dismantling are aligned, and make sure they are equally spaced on each side.

c) Position the track rod end balljoint studs on the outer track rods at an angle of 90° to each other.

d) Make sure the left and right outer track rods are equal in length when they are fitted.

e) Tighten all retaining bolts to the torque values listed in this Chapter's Specifications.

f) When reassembly of the linkage is complete, have the front wheel alignment checked, and if necessary, adjusted.

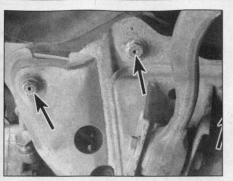

21.7 Subframe crossmember bolts (arrowed)

21.9 Disconnect the power steering pressure line fitting (right arrow) and the return line fitting (left arrow). Note that the return line fitting banjo bolt is larger than the bolt for the pressure line fitting (left-hand-drive shown)

21.10a This bolt (arrowed) secures the steering box to the subframe crossmember. The nut, not visible in this photo, is accessed through a hole in the crossmember (engine removed for clarity, left-hand-drive shown)

21 Steering box (5-Series) - removal and refitting

Removal

Note: *If you find that the steering box is defective, it is not recommended that you overhaul it. Because of the special tools needed to do the job, it is best to let your dealer service department overhaul it for you (otherwise, fit a new unit). Removal and refitting the steering box is outlined here.*

1 On 5-Series E28 ("old-shape") models, discharge the hydraulic system by depressing the brake pedal about 20 times.
2 Using a large syringe or hand pump, empty the power steering fluid reservoir (see Chapter 1).
3 Raise the front of the vehicle and support it securely on axle stands.
4 Support the front of the engine with a trolley jack. Place a block of wood between the jack head and the sump to protect the sump from damage.
5 Remove the pivot bolts from the inner ends of the front control arms (see Section 4).
6 Remove the nuts from the left and right engine mountings (see Chapter 2).
7 Remove the mounting bolts (two on each side on earlier models, three on each side on later models) from the subframe crossmember **(see illustration)** and remove the subframe.
8 Remove the nuts and bolts that secure the universal joint shaft to the steering box worm shaft. Slide the universal joint shaft up and off the worm shaft. Inspect the universal joint shaft for wear. If it's stiff or worn, renew it.
9 Remove the banjo bolts, and disconnect the hydraulic pressure line and the return line from the box **(see illustration)**. Plug the ends of the lines to prevent fluid loss and contamination. Discard the sealing washers - new ones should be used when reassembling.
10 Remove the steering box retaining bolts **(see illustrations)** and remove the steering box.
11 If it's necessary to detach the Pitman arm from the box sector shaft (to have the box serviced or to switch the arm to a new or

rebuilt unit), make a match mark across the two for correct reassembly. Remove the Pitman arm retaining nut and washer. Use a puller to withdraw the arm if necessary.

Refitting

12 Refit the Pitman arm by aligning the match marks made during removal, then tighten the nut to the torque listed in this Chapter's Specifications.
13 When fitted the Pitman arm must not have any measurable endfloat within 100° from the neutral position. If play exists, have the following parts checked:
a) *Sector shaft and bearings (for wear)*
b) *Thrust washer and adjuster bolt head (for wear)*
c) *Ball nut and worm shaft (for wear)*
14 Refit the steering box. Align the mark on the pinion gear shaft with the mark on the universal joint shaft, and tighten the steering box bolts to the torque listed in this Chapter's Specifications.
15 The remainder of refitting is the reverse of removal. Be sure to use new self-locking nuts on the universal joint shaft, the centre track rod, the steering box and the crossmember. Also, use new sealing washers on the hydraulic line fittings.
16 Refer to Chapter 1 and fill the power

steering reservoir with the recommended fluid, then bleed the system as described in Section 23. Check for leakage from the lines and connections.

22 Power steering pump - removal and refitting

Removal

1 Raise the vehicle and support it securely on axle stands. Remove the engine undertray.
2 On 5-Series E28 ("old-shape") models, discharge the hydraulic system by depressing the brake pedal about 20 times before loosening the hydraulic line fittings.
3 Disconnect the fluid return hose, and drain the power steering fluid from the reservoir into a clean container. Disconnect the pressure line from the pump.
4 If you need to remove the pulley from the pump, push on the power steering pump drivebelt by hand to increase the tension, and unscrew the pulley nuts or bolts.
5 Loosen the power steering pump drivebelt tensioner bolt, and remove the drivebelt (see Chapter 1).
6 Remove the mounting bolts **(see illustrations)** and detach the power steering pump.

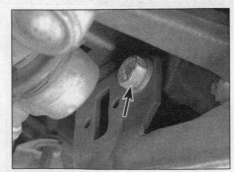

21.10b This bolt (arrowed) attaches the steering box to the body (the nut, not visible in this photo, is on the front side of the steering box)

22.6a Typical 3-Series power steering pump adjusting bolt (arrowed) . . .

10

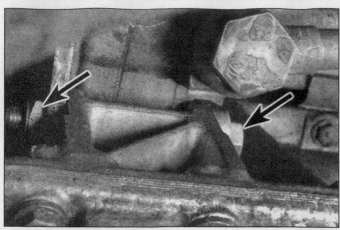

22.6b . . . and mounting nut and bolt (arrowed)

22.6c Typical 5-Series power steering pump mounting bolts (arrowed)

Refitting

7 Refitting is the reverse of removal. Tighten the nuts and bolts securely. Adjust the drivebelt tension (see Chapter 1).
8 Top-up the fluid level in the reservoir (see Chapter 1) and bleed the system (see Section 23).

23 Power steering system - bleeding

1 To bleed the power steering system, begin by checking the power steering fluid level and adding fluid if necessary (see Chapter 1).
2 Raise and support the front of the vehicle on axle stands.
3 Turn the steering wheel from lock-to-lock several times. Recheck the fluid level and top up if necessary.
4 Start the engine and run it at 1000 rpm or less. Turn the steering wheel from lock-to-lock again (three or four times) and recheck the fluid level one more time. **Note:** On 5-

24.3 After removing the steering wheel nut, mark the relationship of the steering wheel to the steering shaft (arrowed) to ensure proper alignment during reassembly

Series E28 ("old-shape") models, pump the brake pedal five or six times before turning the steering wheel. Once the fluid level remains constant, continue turning the wheel back and forth until no more bubbles appear in the fluid in the reservoir.
5 Lower the vehicle to the ground. Run the engine and again turn the wheels from lock-to-lock several more times. Recheck the fluid level. Position the wheels straight-ahead.

24 Steering wheel - removal and refitting

Warning: If the vehicle is equipped with an airbag, do not attempt this procedure. Have it performed by a dealer service department or other qualified specialist, as there is a risk of injury if the airbag is accidentally triggered.

Caution: If the radio in your vehicle is equipped with an anti-theft system, make sure you have the correct activation code before disconnecting the battery.

Note: If, after connecting the battery, the wrong language appears on the instrument panel display, refer to page 0-7 for the language resetting procedure.

Removal

1 Disconnect the battery negative cable.
2 Using a small screwdriver, prise off the BMW emblem in the centre of the steering wheel.
3 Remove the steering wheel nut, and mark the relationship of the steering wheel hub to the shaft **(see illustration)**.
4 On all 3-Series models, and on 1986 and later 5-Series models, turn the ignition key to the first position to unlock the ignition lock.
5 Remove the steering wheel from the

steering shaft. If the wheel is difficult to remove from the shaft, use a steering wheel puller to remove it - don't hammer on the shaft.

Refitting

6 Refitting is the reverse of removal. Be sure to align the match marks you made on the steering wheel and the shaft. Tighten the steering wheel nut to the torque listed in this Chapter's Specifications.

25 Wheels and tyres - general information

Note: For more information on care and maintenance of tyres, refer to Chapter 1.
1 All vehicles covered by this manual are equipped with steel-belted radial tyres as original equipment. Use of other types or sizes of tyres may affect the ride and handling of the vehicle. Don't mix different types or sizes of tyres, as the handling and braking may be seriously affected. It's recommended that tyres be renewed in pairs on the same axle; if only one new tyre is being fitted, be sure it's the same size, structure and tread design as the other.
2 Because tyre pressure has a substantial effect on handling and wear, the pressure on all tyres should be checked at least once a month or before any extended trips (see Chapter 1).
3 Wheels must be renewed if they are bent, heavily dented, leak air, or are otherwise damaged.
4 Tyre and wheel balance is important in the overall handling, braking and performance of the vehicle. Unbalanced wheels can adversely affect handling and ride characteristics, as well as tyre life. Whenever a new tyre is fitted, the tyre and wheel should be balanced.

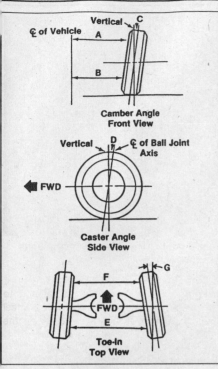

26.1 Wheel alignment details

1 *A minus B = C (degrees camber)*
2 *E minus F = toe-in*
  (expressed in inches or mm)
3 *G = toe-in (expressed in degrees)*

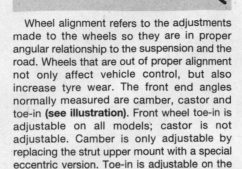

26 Wheel alignment -
general information

Wheel alignment refers to the adjustments made to the wheels so they are in proper angular relationship to the suspension and the road. Wheels that are out of proper alignment not only affect vehicle control, but also increase tyre wear. The front end angles normally measured are camber, castor and toe-in **(see illustration)**. Front wheel toe-in is adjustable on all models; castor is not adjustable. Camber is only adjustable by replacing the strut upper mount with a special eccentric version. Toe-in is adjustable on the rear wheels, but only by replacing the trailing arm outer bushings with special eccentric bushings.

Setting the proper wheel alignment is a very exacting process, one in which complicated and expensive equipment is necessary to perform the job properly. Because of this, you should have a technician with the proper equipment perform these tasks. We will, however, use this space to give you a basic idea of what is involved with wheel alignment so you can better understand the process.

Toe-in is the "turning in" of the wheels. The purpose of a toe specification is to ensure parallel rolling of the wheels. In a vehicle with zero toe-in, the distance between the front edges of the wheels will be the same as the distance between the rear edges of the wheels. The actual amount of toe-in is normally very small. On the front end, toe-in is controlled by the track rod end position on the track rod. On the rear end, toe-in can only be adjusted by fitting special eccentric bushings in the trailing arm outer mounting. Incorrect toe-in will cause the tyres to wear improperly by making them scrub against the road surface.

Camber is the "tilting" of the wheels from vertical, when viewed from one end of the vehicle. When the wheels tilt out at the top, the camber is said to be positive (+). When the wheels tilt in at the top the camber is negative (-). The amount of tilt is measured in degrees from vertical, and this measurement is called the camber angle. This angle affects the amount of tyre tread which contacts the road, and compensates for changes in the suspension geometry when the vehicle is cornering or travelling over an undulating surface.

Castor is the "tilting" of the front steering axis from the vertical. A tilt toward the rear at the top is positive castor; a tilt toward the front is negative castor. Castor is not adjustable on the vehicles covered by this manual.

Notes

Chapter 11 Bodywork and fittings

Contents

Degrees of difficulty

Easy, suitable for novice with little experience	**Fairly easy,** suitable for beginner with some experience	**Fairly difficult,** suitable for competent DIY mechanic	**Difficult,** suitable for experienced DIY mechanic	**Very difficult,** suitable for expert DIY or professional

1 General information

These models feature an all-steel welded construction, where the floorpan and body components are welded together and attached to separate front and rear subframe assemblies. Certain components are particularly vulnerable to accident damage, and can be unbolted and repaired or renewed. Among these parts are the body mouldings, bumpers, bonnet, doors, tailgate, and all glass.

Only general body maintenance procedures and body panel repair procedures within the scope of the do-it-yourselfer are included in this Chapter.

2 Bodywork and underframe - maintenance

The general condition of a vehicle's bodywork is the one thing that significantly affects its value. Maintenance is easy, but needs to be regular. Neglect, particularly after minor damage, can lead quickly to further deterioration and costly repair bills. It is important also to keep watch on those parts of the vehicle not immediately visible, for instance the underside, inside all the wheel arches, and the lower part of the engine compartment.

The basic maintenance routine for the bodywork is washing - preferably with a lot of water, from a hose. This will remove all the loose solids which may have stuck to the vehicle. It is important to flush these off in such a way as to prevent grit from scratching the finish. The wheel arches and underframe need washing in the same way, to remove any accumulated mud, which will retain moisture and tend to encourage rust. Paradoxically enough, the best time to clean the underframe and wheel arches is in wet weather, when the mud is thoroughly wet and soft. In very wet weather, the underframe is usually cleaned of large accumulations automatically, and this is a good time for inspection.

Periodically, except on vehicles with a wax-based underbody protective coating, it is a good idea to have the whole of the underframe of the vehicle steam-cleaned, engine compartment included, so that a thorough inspection can be carried out to see what minor repairs and renovations are necessary. Steam-cleaning is available at many garages, and is necessary for the removal of the accumulation of oily grime, which sometimes is allowed to become thick in certain areas. If steam-cleaning facilities are not available, there are some excellent grease solvents available which can be brush-applied; the dirt can then be simply hosed off. Note that these methods should not be used on vehicles with wax-based underbody protective coating, or the coating will be removed. Such vehicles should be inspected annually, preferably just prior to Winter, when the underbody should be washed down, and any damage to the wax coating repaired. Ideally, a completely fresh coat should be applied. It would also be worth considering the use of such wax-based protection for injection into door panels, sills, box sections, etc, as an additional safeguard against rust damage, where such protection is not provided by the vehicle manufacturer.

After washing paintwork, wipe off with a chamois leather to give an unspotted clear finish. A coat of clear protective wax polish will give added protection against chemical pollutants in the air. If the paintwork sheen has dulled or oxidised, use a cleaner/polisher combination to restore the brilliance of the shine. This requires a little effort, but such dulling is usually caused because regular washing has been neglected. Care needs to be taken with metallic paintwork, as special non-abrasive cleaner/polisher is required to avoid damage to the finish. Always check that the door and ventilator opening drain holes and pipes are completely clear, so that water can be drained out. Brightwork should be treated in the same way as paintwork. Windscreens and windows can be kept clear of the smeary film which often appears, by the use of proprietary glass cleaner. Never use any form of wax or other body or chromium polish on glass.

11

3 Interior trim - maintenance

Interior trim panels can be kept clean by wiping with a damp cloth. If they do become stained (which can be more apparent on light-coloured trim), use a little liquid detergent and a soft nail brush to scour the grime out of the grain of the material. Do not forget to keep the headlining clean in the same way. After cleaning, application of a high-quality rubber and vinyl protector will help prevent oxidation and cracks. The protector can also be applied to weatherstrips, vacuum lines and rubber hoses, which often fail as a result of chemical degradation, and to the tyres.

4 Upholstery and carpets - maintenance

Mats and carpets should be brushed or vacuum-cleaned regularly, to keep them free of grit. If they are badly stained, remove them from the vehicle for scrubbing or sponging, and make quite sure they are dry before refitting. Seats and interior trim panels can be kept clean by wiping with a damp cloth. If they do become stained (which can be more apparent on light-coloured upholstery), use a little liquid detergent and a soft nail brush to scour the grime out of the grain of the material. Do not forget to keep the headlining clean in the same way as the upholstery. When using liquid cleaners inside the vehicle, do not over-wet the surfaces being cleaned. Excessive damp could get into the seams and padded interior, causing stains, offensive odours or even rot.

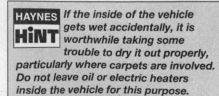
HAYNES HINT *If the inside of the vehicle gets wet accidentally, it is worthwhile taking some trouble to dry it out properly, particularly where carpets are involved. Do not leave oil or electric heaters inside the vehicle for this purpose.*

5 Bodywork repair - minor damage

Note: *For more detailed information about bodywork repair, Haynes Publishing produce a book by Lindsay Porter called "The Car Bodywork Repair Manual". This incorporates information on such aspects as rust treatment, painting and glass-fibre repairs, as well as details on more ambitious repairs involving welding and panel beating.*

Repairs of minor scratches in bodywork

If the scratch is very superficial, and does not penetrate to the metal of the bodywork, repair is very simple. Lightly rub the area of the scratch with a paintwork renovator, or a very fine cutting paste, to remove loose paint from the scratch, and to clear the surrounding bodywork of wax polish. Rinse the area with clean water.

Apply touch-up paint to the scratch using a fine paint brush; continue to apply fine layers of paint until the surface of the paint in the scratch is level with the surrounding paintwork. Allow the new paint at least two weeks to harden, then blend it into the surrounding paintwork by rubbing the scratch area with a paintwork renovator or a very fine cutting paste. Finally, apply wax polish.

Where the scratch has penetrated right through to the metal of the bodywork, causing the metal to rust, a different repair technique is required. Remove any loose rust from the bottom of the scratch with a penknife, then apply rust-inhibiting paint to prevent the formation of rust in the future. Using a rubber or nylon applicator, fill the scratch with bodystopper paste. If required, this paste can be mixed with cellulose thinners to provide a very thin paste which is ideal for filling narrow scratches. Before the stopper-paste in the scratch hardens, wrap a piece of smooth cotton rag around the top of a finger. Dip the finger in cellulose thinners, and quickly sweep it across the surface of the stopper-paste in the scratch; this will ensure that the surface of the stopper-paste is slightly hollowed. The scratch can now be painted over as described earlier in this Section.

Repairs of dents in bodywork

When deep denting of the vehicle's bodywork has taken place, the first task is to pull the dent out, until the affected bodywork almost attains its original shape. There is little point in trying to restore the original shape completely, as the metal in the damaged area will have stretched on impact, and cannot be reshaped fully to its original contour. It is better to bring the level of the dent up to a point which is about 3 mm below the level of the surrounding bodywork. In cases where the dent is very shallow anyway, it is not worth trying to pull it out at all. If the underside of the dent is accessible, it can be hammered out gently from behind, using a mallet with a wooden or plastic head. Whilst doing this, hold a suitable block of wood firmly against the outside of the panel, to absorb the impact from the hammer blows and thus prevent a large area of the bodywork from being "belled-out".

Should the dent be in a section of the bodywork which has a double skin, or some other factor making it inaccessible from behind, a different technique is called for. Drill several small holes through the metal inside the area - particularly in the deeper section. Then screw long self-tapping screws into the holes, just sufficiently for them to gain a good purchase in the metal. Now the dent can be pulled out by pulling on the protruding heads of the screws with a pair of pliers.

The next stage of the repair is the removal of the paint from the damaged area, and from an inch or so of the surrounding "sound" bodywork. This is accomplished most easily by using a wire brush or abrasive pad on a power drill, although it can be done just as effectively by hand, using sheets of abrasive paper. To complete the preparation for filling, score the surface of the bare metal with a screwdriver or the tang of a file, or alternatively, drill small holes in the affected area. This will provide a really good "key" for the filler paste.

To complete the repair, see the Section on filling and respraying.

Repairs of rust holes or gashes in bodywork

Remove all paint from the affected area, and from an inch or so of the surrounding "sound" bodywork, using an abrasive pad or a wire brush on a power drill. If these are not available, a few sheets of abrasive paper will do the job most effectively. With the paint removed, you will be able to judge the severity of the corrosion, and therefore decide whether to renew the whole panel (if this is possible) or to repair the affected area. New body panels are not as expensive as most people think, and it is often quicker and more satisfactory to fit a new panel than to attempt to repair large areas of corrosion.

Remove all fittings from the affected area, except those which will act as a guide to the original shape of the damaged bodywork (eg headlight shells etc). Then, using tin snips or a hacksaw blade, remove all loose metal and any other metal badly affected by corrosion. Hammer the edges of the hole inwards, in order to create a slight depression for the filler paste.

Wire-brush the affected area to remove the powdery rust from the surface of the remaining metal. Paint the affected area with rust-inhibiting paint, if the back of the rusted area is accessible, treat this also.

Before filling can take place, it will be necessary to block the hole in some way. This can be achieved by the use of aluminium or plastic mesh, or aluminium tape.

Aluminium or plastic mesh, or glass-fibre matting, is probably the best material to use for a large hole. Cut a piece to the approximate size and shape of the hole to be filled, then position it in the hole so that its edges are below the level of the surrounding bodywork. It can be retained in position by several blobs of filler paste around its periphery.

Aluminium tape should be used for small or very narrow holes. Pull a piece off the roll, trim it to the approximate size and shape required, then pull off the backing paper (if used) and stick the tape over the hole; it can be overlapped if the thickness of one piece is insufficient. Burnish down the edges of the tape with the handle of a screwdriver or similar, to ensure that the tape is securely attached to the metal underneath.

Bodywork repairs - filling and respraying

Before using this Section, see the Sections on dent, deep scratch, rust holes and gash repairs.

Many types of bodyfiller are available, but generally speaking, those proprietary kits which contain a tin of filler paste and a tube of resin hardener are best for this type of repair. A wide, flexible plastic or nylon applicator will be found invaluable for imparting a smooth and well-contoured finish to the surface of the filler.

Mix up a little filler on a clean piece of card or board - measure the hardener carefully (follow the maker's instructions on the pack), otherwise the filler will set too rapidly or too slowly. Using the applicator, apply the filler paste to the prepared area; draw the applicator across the surface of the filler to achieve the correct contour and to level the surface. As soon as a contour that approximates to the correct one is achieved, stop working the paste - if you carry on too long, the paste will become sticky and begin to "pick-up" on the applicator. Continue to add thin layers of filler paste at 20-minute intervals, until the level of the filler is just proud of the surrounding bodywork.

Once the filler has hardened, the excess can be removed using a metal plane or file. From then on, progressively-finer grades of abrasive paper should be used, starting with a 40-grade production paper, and finishing with a 400-grade wet-and-dry paper. Always wrap the abrasive paper around a flat rubber, cork, or wooden block - otherwise the surface of the filler will not be completely flat. During the smoothing of the filler surface, the wet-and-dry paper should be periodically rinsed in water. This will ensure that a very smooth finish is imparted to the filler at the final stage.

At this stage, the "dent" should be surrounded by a ring of bare metal, which in turn should be encircled by the finely "feathered" edge of the good paintwork. Rinse the repair area with clean water, until all of the dust produced by the rubbing-down operation has gone.

Spray the whole area with a light coat of primer - this will show up any imperfections in the surface of the filler. Repair these imperfections with fresh filler paste or bodystopper, and once more smooth the surface with abrasive paper. Repeat this spray-and-repair procedure until you are satisfied that the surface of the filler, and the feathered edge of the paintwork, are perfect. Clean the repair area with clean water, and allow to dry fully.

 If bodystopper is used, it can be mixed with cellulose thinners to form a really thin paste which is ideal for filling small holes

The repair area is now ready for final spraying. Paint spraying must be carried out in a warm, dry, windless and dust-free atmosphere. This condition can be created artificially if you have access to a large indoor working area, but if you are forced to work in the open, you will have to pick your day very carefully. If you are working indoors, dousing the floor in the work area with water will help to settle the dust which would otherwise be in the atmosphere. If the repair area is confined to one body panel, mask off the surrounding panels; this will help to minimise the effects of a slight mis-match in paint colours. Bodywork fittings (eg chrome strips, door handles etc) will also need to be masked off. Use genuine masking tape, and several thicknesses of newspaper, for the masking operations.

Before commencing to spray, agitate the aerosol can thoroughly, then spray a test area (an old tin, or similar) until the technique is mastered. Cover the repair area with a thick coat of primer; the thickness should be built up using several thin layers of paint, rather than one thick one. Using 400-grade wet-and-dry paper, rub down the surface of the primer until it is really smooth. While doing this, the work area should be thoroughly doused with water, and the wet-and-dry paper periodically rinsed in water. Allow to dry before spraying on more paint.

Spray on the top coat, again building up the thickness by using several thin layers of paint. Start spraying at one edge of the repair area, and then, using a side-to-side motion, work until the whole repair area and about 2 inches of the surrounding original paintwork is covered. Remove all masking material 10 to 15 minutes after spraying on the final coat of paint.

Allow the new paint at least two weeks to harden, then, using a paintwork renovator, or a very fine cutting paste, blend the edges of the paint into the existing paintwork. Finally, apply wax polish.

Plastic components

With the use of more and more plastic body components by the vehicle manufacturers (eg bumpers. spoilers, and in some cases major body panels), rectification of more serious damage to such items has become a matter of either entrusting repair work to a specialist in this field, or renewing complete components. Repair of such damage by the DIY owner is not really feasible, owing to the cost of the equipment and materials required for effecting such repairs. The basic technique involves making a groove along the line of the crack in the plastic, using a rotary burr in a power drill. The damaged part is then welded

back together, using a hot-air gun to heat up and fuse a plastic filler rod into the groove. Any excess plastic is then removed, and the area rubbed down to a smooth finish. It is important that a filler rod of the correct plastic is used, as body components can be made of a variety of different types (eg polycarbonate, ABS, polypropylene).

Damage of a less serious nature (abrasions, minor cracks etc) can be repaired by the DIY owner using a two-part epoxy filler repair material. Once mixed in equal proportions, this is used in similar fashion to the bodywork filler used on metal panels. The filler is usually cured in twenty to thirty minutes, ready for sanding and painting.

If the owner is renewing a complete component himself, or if he has repaired it with epoxy filler, he will be left with the problem of finding a suitable paint for finishing which is compatible with the type of plastic used. At one time, the use of a universal paint was not possible, owing to the complex range of plastics encountered in body component applications. Standard paints, generally speaking, will not bond to plastic or rubber satisfactorily. However, it is now possible to obtain a plastic body parts finishing kit which consists of a pre-primer treatment, a primer and coloured top coat. Full instructions are normally supplied with a kit, but basically, the method of use is to first apply the pre-primer to the component concerned, and allow it to dry for up to 30 minutes. Then the primer is applied, and left to dry for about an hour before finally applying the special-coloured top coat. The result is a correctly-coloured component, where the paint will flex with the plastic or rubber, a property that standard paint does not normally possess.

6 Bodywork repair - major damage

1 Major damage must be repaired by a qualified bodywork repair specialist, or preferably by a BMW dealer. Specialised equipment is required to do the job properly.
2 If the damage is extensive, the bodyshell must be checked for proper alignment, or the vehicle's handling characteristics may be adversely affected and other components may wear at an accelerated rate.
3 Due to the fact that all of the major body components (bonnet, wings, etc.) are separate units, any seriously damaged components should be replaced with new ones rather than repaired.

 Sometimes bodywork components can be found in a scrapyard that specialises in used vehicle components, often at a considerable saving over the cost of new parts.

11

9.1 Open the bonnet and remove the grille retaining clips (arrowed)

9.2a The centre grille is held in place by two screws (arrowed)

9.2b Side grille screw locations (arrowed)

7 Hinges and locks - maintenance

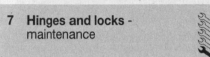

Every six months or so, the hinges and lock assemblies on the doors, bonnet and the boot lid/tailgate should be given a few drops of light oil or lock lubricant. The door or tailgate lock strikers should also be lubricated with a thin coat of grease, to reduce wear and ensure free movement.

8 Fixed glass - renewal

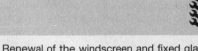

Renewal of the windscreen and fixed glass requires the use of special fast-setting adhesive materials, and some specialised tools and techniques. These operations should be left to a dealer service department or windscreen specialist.

9 Radiator grille - removal and refitting

3-Series

1 Detach the clips along the top of the grille (see illustration).

9.14 Remove the screws and pull the side grille assembly straight out

2 Remove the screws, and lift the centre and side grilles out (see illustrations).
3 Refitting is the reverse of removal.

5-Series

E28 ("old-shape") models

6 Remove the screws, and detach the centre and side grille pieces.
7 Refitting is the reverse of removal.

E34 ("new-shape") models

Centre grille
8 Remove the screws and detach the headlight covers in the engine compartment for access.
9 Remove the screw, and lift out the plastic cover behind the centre grille for access to the clips.
10 From the engine compartment, reach under the headlight housings and detach the clips retaining the centre grille valances, then push the grille forwards (see illustration).
11 Use a screwdriver to depress the clips, detach the grille assembly and remove it by pulling it straight out.
12 Refit the centre grille by placing it in position and pushing it straight back until it clips into place.
Side grille
13 Remove the centre grille.
14 Remove the screws, and lift the side grille assembly out (see illustration).
15 Refitting is the reverse of removal.

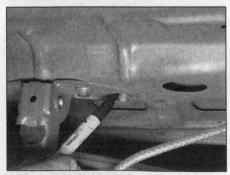

10.1 Use paint or a marking pen to mark on the hinge plate around the bolt heads - mark around the entire hinge plate, if desired, before adjusting the bonnet

10 Bonnet - removal, refitting and adjustment

Note: *The bonnet is heavy and somewhat awkward to remove and refit - at least two people should perform this procedure.*

Removal and refitting

3-Series models

1 Open the bonnet. Scribe or draw alignment marks around the bolt heads to ensure proper alignment on refitting (see illustration).
2 Disconnect the earth cable and windscreen washer hose from the bonnet.
3 Detach the bonnet hinge rod clip and

9.10 Detach the centre grille valance by reaching under each headlight and pressing on the release lever

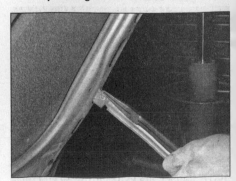

10.3a Use needle-nose pliers to pull off the hinge pin clip . . .

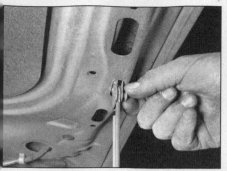

10.3b . . . and pull the hinge pin out while supporting the bonnet

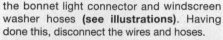

10.8a Use a small screwdriver to prise out the clip pin, then . . .

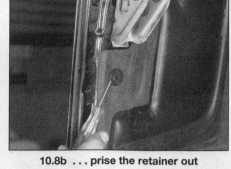

10.8b . . . prise the retainer out

remove the pin (see illustrations). Be sure to support the bonnet while doing this.
4 Have an assistant hold onto the bonnet on one side while you hold the other side.
5 Remove the bonnet-to-hinge assembly bolts on your side of the bonnet, then hold your side of the bonnet while your assistant removes the bonnet-to-hinge bolts on the other side.
6 Remove the bonnet. Place it somewhere safe where it will not be knocked over, with rags to protect the paintwork where it rests on the ground or against a wall.
7 Refitting is the reverse of removal.

5-Series models

8 Open the bonnet. On some later models, it may be necessary to prise out the plastic clips and remove the insulation pad for access to

the bonnet light connector and windscreen washer hoses (see illustrations). Having done this, disconnect the wires and hoses.
9 Detach the clips and withdraw the bonnet support pins (see illustration).
10 Remove the pins from the hinges (see illustration).
11 Have an assistant hold onto the bonnet on one side while you hold the other side.
12 Remove the bonnet-to-hinge through-bolt on your side of the bonnet, then hold your side of the bonnet while your assistant removes the through-bolt on the other side (see illustration).
13 Remove the bonnet. Place it somewhere safe where it will not be knocked over, with rags to protect the paintwork where it rests on the ground or against a wall.
14 Refitting is the reverse of the removal.

Adjustment

15 The bonnet can be adjusted to obtain a flush fit between the bonnet and wings after loosening the bonnet hinge bolts. On some 5-Series models, it will be necessary to remove the side grille sections for access to the hinge bolts.
16 Move the bonnet from side to side, or front to rear, until the bonnet is properly aligned with the wings at the front. Tighten the bolts securely.
17 The rear height of the bonnet can be adjusted by loosening the bolts, and raising or lowering the catch (see illustration). After adjustment, tighten the bolts securely.
18 Side-to-side adjustment of the bonnet can be made by loosening the roller guide bolt nuts, and moving the guide position until it slides into the catch properly (see illustration).

10.9 Pull off the clip with needle-nose pliers

10.10 Support the bonnet and withdraw the pin

10.12 Unscrew the hinge through-bolts (arrowed)

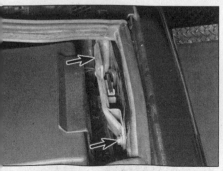

10.17 Loosen the bolts (arrowed) and raise or lower the catch to adjust the bonnet height

10.18 Loosen the bolts (A) and adjust the roller guide from side to side until it engages securely in the catch

10.19 Screw the bonnet stops in or out after making other adjustments

11

12.3 On models without electric windows, prise off the window regulator handle trim piece for access to the retaining screw

19 After adjustment, screw the stop pads in or out to support the bonnet in its new position (see illustration).

20 The bonnet mechanism should be lubricated periodically with grease, to prevent sticking or jamming.

11 Bumpers - removal and refitting

Removal

1 Detach the bumper cover (if applicable) and where necessary the front spoiler.

2 Disconnect any wiring or other components that would interfere with bumper removal.

3 Support the bumper with a jack or axle stand. Alternatively, have an assistant support the bumper as the bolts are removed.

4 Remove the retaining bolts and detach the bumper.

Refitting

5 Refitting is a reversal of removal. Tighten the retaining bolts securely, then refit the bumper cover and any other components that were removed.

12 Door trim panel - removal and refitting

⚠ **Caution: If the radio in your vehicle is equipped with an anti-theft system, make sure you have the correct activation code before disconnecting the battery, Refer to the information on page 0-7 at the front of this manual before detaching the cable.**

Note: If, after connecting the battery, the wrong language appears on the instrument panel display, refer to page 0-7 for the language resetting procedure.

Removal

1 Disconnect the battery negative cable.

2 Remove all door trim panel retaining screws and door pull/armrest assemblies.

13.4 Detach the circlip (arrowed) from the tapered end of the pin

3 On models with manual (non-electric) windows, remove the window regulator handle (see illustration). On models with electric windows, prise off the control switch assembly and unplug it.

4 Disengage the trim panel-to-door retaining clips. Work around the outer edge until the panel is free.

5 Once all of the clips are disengaged, detach the trim panel, unplug any electrical connectors, and remove the trim panel from the vehicle.

6 For access to the inner door, carefully peel back the plastic water shield.

Refitting

7 Prior to refitting the door trim panel, be sure to renew any clips in the panel which may have come out (or got broken) during the removal procedure.

8 Plug in the electrical connectors (where applicable) and place the panel in position in the door. Press the door panel into place until the clips are seated, then refit the armrest/door pulls. Refit the window regulator handle, where applicable.

13 Door - removal, refitting and adjustment

Removal

1 Remove the door trim panel (see Section 12). Disconnect any electrical connectors, and

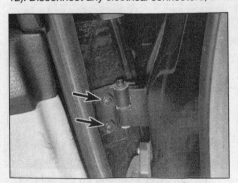

13.5 Remove the nuts (arrowed) and detach the door from the hinges

push them through the door opening so they won't interfere with door removal.

2 Place a trolley jack or axle stand under the door, or have an assistant on hand to support it when the hinge bolts are removed. **Note:** *If a jack or axle stand is used, place a rag between it and the door, to protect the door's painted surfaces.*

3 Scribe or mark around the door hinges.

4 Disconnect the door check strap by prising the circlip out of the end of the pin, then slide the pin out (see illustration). A roll pin is fitted to some models; this is removed by driving it out with a pin punch.

5 Remove the hinge-to-door nuts, and carefully lift off the door (see illustration).

Refitting and adjustment

6 Refitting is the reverse of removal.

7 Following refitting of the door, check the alignment and adjust it if necessary as follows:

a) *Up-and-down and fore-and-aft adjustments are made by loosening the hinge-to-body nuts and moving the door as necessary.*

b) *The door lock striker can also be adjusted both up and down and sideways, to provide positive engagement with the lock mechanism. This is done by loosening the mounting bolts and moving the striker as necessary (see illustration).*

14 Boot lid/tailgate - removal, refitting and adjustment

Boot lid

1 Open the boot lid, and cover the edges of the boot compartment with pads or cloths to protect the painted surfaces when the lid is removed.

2 Disconnect any cables or electrical connectors attached to the boot lid that would interfere with removal.

3 Make alignment marks around the hinge bolts (see illustration).

4 Have an assistant support the lid, then remove the lid-to-hinge bolts on both sides and lift it off.

13.7 The door lock striker position can be adjusted after loosening the screws (arrowed)

14.3 Mark around the hinge bolts so you can refit the boot lid in its original location - unscrew or loosen the boot lid-to-hinge bolts to remove or adjust it

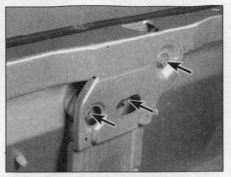

14.7a Loosen the lock bolts (arrowed) and move the lock to adjust the boot lid closing position

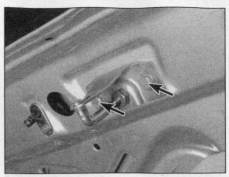

14.7b Adjust the boot lid lock striker after loosening the bolts (arrowed)

5 Refitting is the reverse of removal. Align the lid-to-hinge bolts with the marks made during removal.
6 After refitting, close the lid and make sure it's in proper alignment with the surrounding panels. Fore-and-aft and side-to-side adjustments are controlled by the position of the hinge bolts in the slots. To make an adjustment, loosen the hinge bolts, reposition the lid, and retighten the bolts.
7 The height of the lid in relation to the surrounding body panels when closed can be changed by loosening the lock and/or striker bolts, repositioning the striker and/or lock, and tightening the bolts **(see illustrations)**.

⚠️ *Caution: If the radio in your vehicle is equipped with an anti-theft system, make sure you have the correct activation code before disconnecting the battery, Refer to the information on page 0-7 at the front of this manual before detaching the cable.*
Note: *If, after connecting the battery, the wrong language appears on the instrument panel display, refer to page 0-7 for the language resetting procedure.*

Tailgate

8 Disconnect the battery negative cable.
9 Open the tailgate and cover the rear edge of the roof with pads or cloths to protect the painted surfaces when the tailgate is

removed. On 5-Series models, the window may be removed separately by disconnecting the wiring and unscrewing the mounting screws - have an assistant hold the window while the screws are being loosened **(see illustration)**.
10 Remove the trim from the inside of the tailgate. Also where necessary on 5-Series models, remove the edge covers for access to the strut mountings.
11 Disconnect the wiring loom and the washer tubing. On some models, it will be necessary to pull the wiring loom out of the rear pillar and then disconnect the plug **(see illustration)**.
12 While an assistant holds the tailgate open,

disconnect the struts on both sides by unscrewing the mounting screws. Where applicable, pull out the retaining pin or spring clip, and remove the strut from the ball **(see illustrations)**.
13 Mark the position of the hinge arms on the tailgate with a pencil.
14 Unscrew the bolts and withdraw the tailgate from the hinge arms. On 5-Series models, it will be necessary to use an Allen key or bit **(see illustration)**.
15 Refitting is the reverse of removal, but make sure that the previously-made marks are correctly aligned. Check that the tailgate closes centrally between the rear pillars and enters the lock correctly.

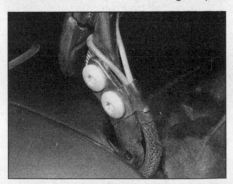

14.9 Tailgate window mounting screws (5-Series)

14.11 Removing the wiring from the rear pillar (5-Series)

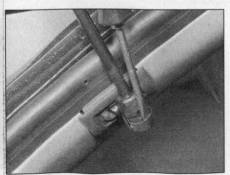

14.12a Removing the tailgate strut spring clip (3-Series)

14.12b Strut mounting on the tailgate (5-Series)

14.12c Removing the retaining pin to disconnect the bottom of the tailgate support strut (5-Series)

11

14.14 Unscrewing the hinge mounting bolts (5-Series)

15 Latch, lock cylinder and handles - removal, refitting and adjustment

1 Remove the trim panel(s) and, on the door, the plastic shield (see Section 12).

Latch

2 Disconnect the operating rods from the latch **(see illustration)**.
3 Remove the latch retaining screws.
4 Detach the latch assembly and withdraw it.
5 Refitting is the reverse of removal.

Lock cylinder

6 Detach the linkage.
7 Use a screwdriver to slide the retaining clip off, and withdraw the lock cylinder.
8 Refitting is the reverse of removal.

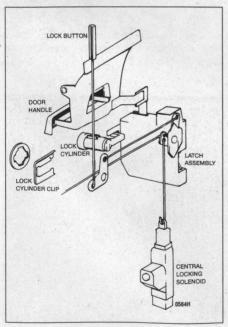

15.2 Typical door latch, lock cylinder and handle details

Interior handle

9 Disconnect the operating rod from the handle.
10 Remove the retaining screws and lift the handle from the door.
11 Refitting is the reverse of removal.

Exterior handle

12 Lift up the handle for access, remove the two retaining screws, then detach the handle from the door.
13 Refitting is the reverse of removal.

16 Door window glass - removal and refitting

Caution: If the radio in your vehicle is equipped with an anti-theft system, make sure you have the correct activation code before disconnecting the battery. Refer to the information on page 0-7 at the front of this manual before detaching the cable.
Note: *If, after connecting the battery, the wrong language appears on the instrument panel display, refer to page 0-7 for the language resetting procedure.*

1 Disconnect the battery negative cable.
2 Remove the door trim panel and the plastic water shield (see Section 12).
3 Prise the door inner and outer weatherstrips from the door.

Front door

4 Raise the window so that the mounting bolts can be reached through the access hole. If electric windows are fitted, temporarily reconnect the battery cable to accomplish this.
5 Support the glass, and remove the retaining bolts securing the glass to the regulator.
6 Lift the window glass up and out of the door window slot, then tilt it and remove it from the door.
7 Refitting is the reverse of removal.

Rear door

8 Carry out the operations described in paragraphs 1 to 5.

3-Series models

9 Disengage the glass from the front guide roller, and prise out the rubber window guides.
10 Remove the door handle screws, and allow the handle assembly to hang out of the way.
11 Remove the rear window frame bolts, push the frame into the door, and remove the window glass.
12 Refitting is the reverse of removal.

5-Series models

13 Loosen the rear window guide mounting bolt.

14 Detach the glass from the front guide roller, disengage the glass from the guide rails, then slide the glass to the rear and remove by lifting from above.
15 The fixed glass can be removed by removing the guide rail bolts, then pulling the rail down to the rear and detaching the glass.
16 Refitting is the reverse of removal. The rear window glass can be adjusted by loosening the adjustment bolts, then raising the glass to within one inch of the top of the door opening. Adjust the glass-to-opening gap evenly, then tighten the bolts securely.

17 Door window regulator - removal and refitting

Removal

1 Remove the door window glass (Section 16).
2 Remove the securing bolts or nuts, and lift the window regulator assembly out of the door (withdraw the regulator mechanism through the access hole). On models with electric windows, unplug the electrical connector.

Refitting

3 Refitting is the reverse of removal.

18 Exterior mirror - removal and refitting

Removal

1 If it is required to renew the mirror glass only, insert a small screwdriver through the hole in the bottom of the exterior mirror, and carefully lever clockwise the plastic holder on the rear of the glass (ie move the bottom of the screwdriver to the right). This will release the glass, which can then be withdrawn. If electric mirrors are fitted, it will be necessary to disconnect the wiring before completely removing the glass.
2 To remove the complete mirror, prise off the cover panel (and/or the tweeter speaker, where applicable).
3 Unplug the electrical connector.
4 Remove the retaining screws and lift the mirror off

Refitting

5 Refitting is the reverse of removal.

19.3 Use a Phillips screwdriver to remove the upper column shroud screws

19.4 The lower screws are located under the tilt lever (where fitted)

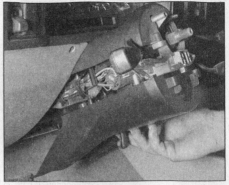

19.5a Pull the tilt lever down (where fitted), and lower the shroud from the steering column

19 Steering column shrouds - removal and refitting

⚠️ **Caution: If the radio in your vehicle is equipped with an anti-theft system, make sure you have the correct activation code before disconnecting the battery, Refer to the information on page 0-7 at the front of this manual before detaching the cable.**
Note: *If, after connecting the battery, the wrong language appears on the instrument panel display, refer to page 0-7 for the language resetting procedure.*

Removal

1 Disconnect the battery negative cable.
2 Remove the steering wheel (Chapter 10).
3 Remove the upper shroud screws (see illustration).
4 Remove the two screws from the underside of the column (see illustration).
5 Detach the lower shroud, then lift the upper half off the column (see illustrations).

Refitting

6 Refitting is the reverse of removal.

20 Seats - removal and refitting

Front seat

1 Remove the four bolts securing the seat track to the floorpan, and lift the seat from the vehicle (see illustration). On some models, it will be necessary to disconnect the seat heating wiring; it may also be necessary to detach the seat belt from the seat.
2 Refitting is the reverse of removal. Tighten the retaining bolts securely.

Rear seat cushion

3 If applicable, first remove the two retaining bolts. Grasp the front of the cushion (Saloon/Convertible models) or the rear of the cushion (Touring/Estate models) securely, and pull up sharply (see illustration).
4 Refitting is the reverse of the removal.

19.5b Rotate the upper shroud up and off the steering column

21 Seat belt check

1 Check the seat belts, buckles, lock plates and guide loops for obvious damage and signs of wear.

20.1 The front seats are held in place by bolts (arrowed)

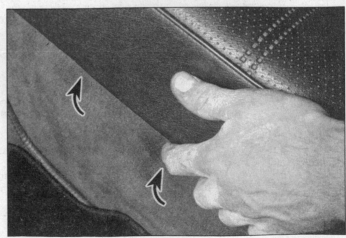

20.3 Grasp the seat at the front edge and pull up sharply (Saloon/Convertible models)

11

22.2 Removing the handbrake lever gaiter

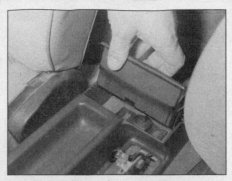

22.3a Lift out the rear ashtray . . .

22.3b . . . and unscrew the large plastic nut

2 Where applicable, check that the seat belt reminder light comes on when the ignition key is turned to the Run or Start position.
3 The seat belts are designed to lock up during a sudden stop or impact, yet allow free movement during normal driving. Check that the retractors return the belt against your chest while driving and rewind the belt fully when the buckle is unlocked.
4 If any of the above checks reveal problems with the seat belt system, renew parts as necessary.
5 Belts which have been subject to impact loads must be renewed.

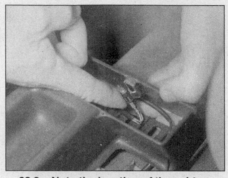

22.3c Note the location of the ashtray illumination bulb . . .

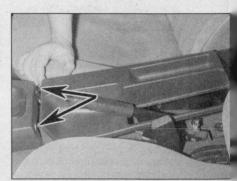

22.3d . . . then remove the console rear section over the handbrake lever - note the two front locating tabs (arrowed)

22 Centre console - removal and refitting

⚠ *Caution: If the radio in your vehicle is equipped with an anti-theft system, make sure you have the correct activation code before disconnecting the battery.*

Note: *If, after connecting the battery, the wrong language appears on the instrument panel display, refer to page 0-7 for the language resetting procedure.*

3-series

Removal

1 Disconnect the battery negative terminal. The battery is located either in the engine compartment, under the rear seat (pull the seat squab upwards for access), or in the luggage compartment.
2 Carefully pull up the gaiter around the handbrake lever, and slide it off the handbrake lever **(see illustration)**.
3 Lift out the console rear ashtray for access

to the large plastic nut beneath. Unscrew the nut, then lift away the console rear section, disengaging the two front locating tabs and disconnecting the ashtray illumination bulb as the console is removed. Note the location of the bulb for reassembly **(see illustrations)**.
4 On manual transmission models, pull the gear lever knob upwards off the lever. Reaching in from the rear of the console front section, unclip the gear lever gaiter **(see illustrations)**. Pull the gaiter upwards over the top of the gear lever.

22.4a Pull off the gear lever knob . . .

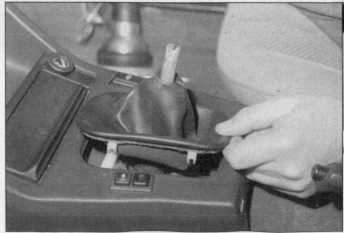

22.4b . . . then unclip and remove the gear lever gaiter

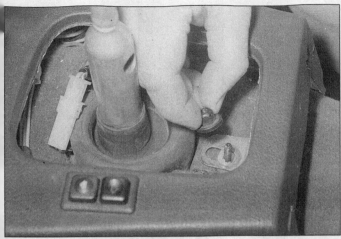

22.6a Unscrew and remove the plastic nut from the floor stud behind the gear/selector lever . . .

22.6b . . . and the screw on the left-hand side below the heater panel

22.7a Turn the plastic fasteners through 90° . . .

22.7b . . . and lower the driver's side trim panel

5 On automatic transmission models, undo the Allen screw in the front of the selector lever handle, and pull the handle upwards off the selector lever.

6 Unscrew and remove the plastic nut behind the gear/selector lever, and the screw below the heater control panel on the left-hand side **(see illustrations)**.

7 Lower or remove the driver's side under-dash trim panel by turning the plastic fasteners through 90° **(see illustrations)**. If the panel is being removed, disconnect the wiring plugs from the headlight beam adjuster, where applicable.

8 Working in the driver's footwell, release the front of the centre console by turning the

plastic fastener through 90° **(see illustration)**.

9 Lift the console front section at the rear, to disengage the mounting bracket from the floor stud behind the gear/selector lever.

10 Disconnect the wiring plugs from the window switches and cigarette lighter, as applicable, and remove the cigarette lighter illumination bulb **(see illustrations)**. Note the

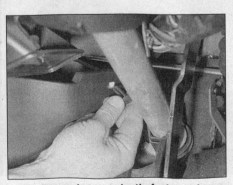

22.8 Removing the plastic fastener from the front of the centre console

22.10a Remove the cigarette lighter illumination bulb . . .

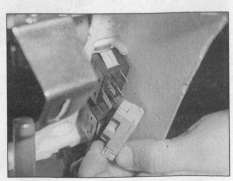

22.10b . . . and disconnect the switch wiring plugs

11

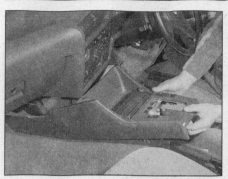

22.11 Removing the centre console front section from the car

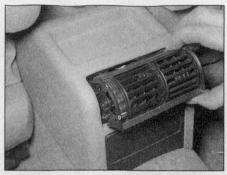

22.14a Removing the rear passenger ventilation grille housing from the centre console

22.14b Removing the console rear section rear securing screws

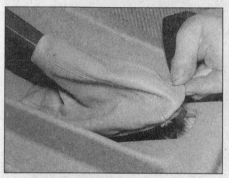

22.15a Pulling the handbrake lever gaiter from the centre console

22.15b Removing the console rear section retaining screw from in front of the handbrake lever

22.16a Prise out the trim cap . . .

locations and correct fitted positions of all plugs and the bulb, for use on reassembly.
11 Lift the console front section out rearwards over the gear/selector lever, and remove it from the car **(see illustration)**.

Refitting
12 Refitting is a reversal of removal, noting the following points:
a) *As the console sections are refitted, make sure that no wiring becomes trapped.*
b) *When refitting the console rear section, engage the front locating tabs in the slots provided in the console front section.*

c) *Reconnect the battery negative lead, then check the operation of all switches and accessories on completion.*

5-series
Removal
13 Disconnect the battery negative terminal. The battery is located either in the engine compartment, under the rear seat (pull the seat squab upwards for access), or in the luggage compartment.
14 Lift out the rear oddments tray or rear passenger ventilation grille housing, as

applicable, from the rear of the console. Remove the two screws at the rear securing the console rear section to the vehicle floor **(see illustrations)**.
15 Carefully pull up the gaiter around the handbrake lever, and turn it inside-out. Remove the screw down in front of the handbrake lever **(see illustrations)**.
16 At the front of the oddments tray next to the handbrake lever, prise out the trim cap (where fitted) and remove the screw **(see illustrations)**.
17 Lift up the console rear section and carefully withdraw it over the handbrake lever

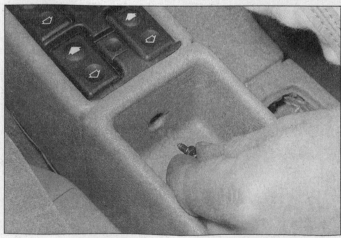

22.16b . . . and remove the screw in the front of the oddments tray

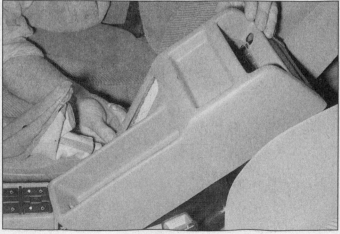

22.17 Lift up the console rear section and remove it over the handbrake lever

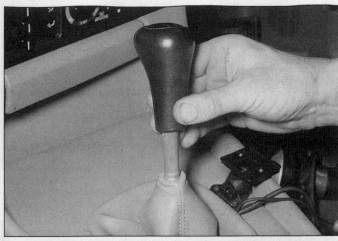

22.18a Pull the gear lever knob upwards off the gear lever

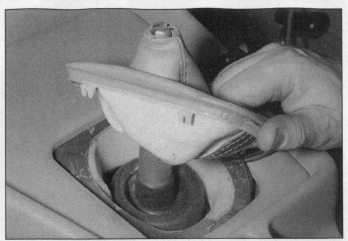

22.18b Unclip and lift off the gear lever gaiter

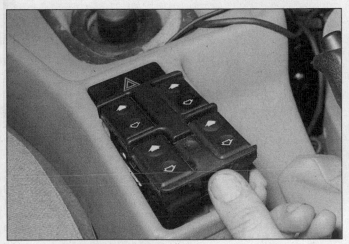

22.21a Push out the window switch panel . . .

22.21b . . . and disconnect the multi-plug(s)

(see illustration). Feed the handbrake gaiter through the console, and remove the console rear section from the car.

18 On manual transmission models, pull the gear lever knob upwards off the lever. Unclip and pull up the gear lever gaiter over the top of the gear lever **(see illustrations).**

19 On automatic transmission models, undo the Allen screw in the front of the selector

lever knob, and pull the knob upwards off the selector lever.

20 The trim panel around the base of the gear/selector lever can now be unclipped and lifted out over the gear/selector lever. This was only found to be necessary on automatic transmission models.

21 Reaching in from the rear of the console, push the electric window switch panel upwards and out of the console. Depress the

retaining tabs either side, and release the multi-plug(s) **(see illustrations).** Remove the switch assembly from the car.

22 Similarly, push out the hazard warning light switch, disconnect the multi-plug, and remove the switch **(see illustrations).**

23 Open the ashtray, then press the retaining catch underneath the ashtray upwards, and remove the ashtray from the front console **(see illustration).**

22.22a Press out the hazard warning light switch . . .

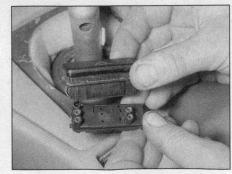

22.22b . . . and disconnect the wiring plug

22.23 Removing the ashtray

11

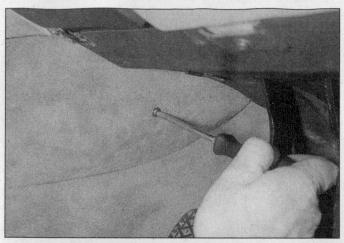

22.24a Remove the securing screw . . .

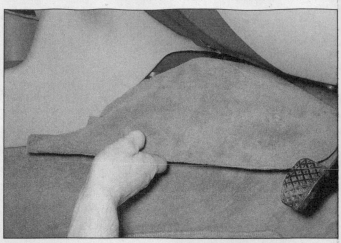

22.24b . . . and remove the carpeted trim panel

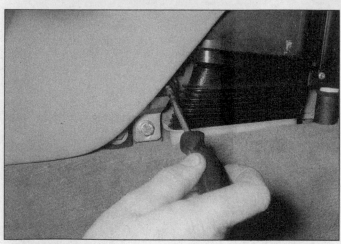

22.25 Removing a front console-to-mounting bracket screw

22.26 Removing the console retaining screw from the glovebox aperture

24 Working in the front footwells, remove one screw and detach the carpeted trim panel either side of the front console (see illustrations).

25 Removing the carpeted trim panels exposes a cross-head screw securing the front console to the floor mounting bracket. Remove the screw each side, and recover the washer (see illustration).

26 Open the glovebox, and remove the screw at the top right-hand corner of the glovebox aperture which secures the top of the console to the facia panel (see illustration).

27 Returning to the driver's side of the car, prise off the trim cap immediately below the instrument panel and remove the screw underneath (see illustration). On certain models, it will also be necessary to remove another screw securing the console to the driver's side lower facia trim panel.

28 Using a small flat-bladed screwdriver, carefully prise off the trim caps either side of the heater/ventilation control panel, for access to the securing screws beneath (see illustration). Take care not to mark the surrounding facia as this is done.

29 Removing the two screws either side of the heater/ventilation control panel will cause the panel to drop down, so be ready to support the panel as the last screw is removed (see

22.27 Prise off the trim cap and remove the screw below the instrument panel

22.28 Prise off the trim caps at either end of the heater control panel

22.29 Removing the heater control panel securing screws

22.30 Removing the plastic nut from the rear of the console

22.31 Pulling the front console rearwards to disengage the front clips from the facia trim

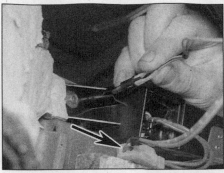

22.32 Pulling out the illumination bulbholder - also note the cigarette lighter wiring plug (arrowed)

illustration). Once the front console has been released from the screws, the screws can temporarily be refitted so that the heater control panel is supported.

30 Unscrew and remove the plastic nut in front of the handbrake lever **(see illustration)**, and lift the console retaining bracket lug up over the stud.

31 It should now be possible to withdraw the front console by pulling it rearwards from the facia **(see illustration)**. The console is secured to the facia trim panels either side by two plastic clips which slide apart. It may be

necessary to have an assistant hold the facia trim in place while the console is pulled rearwards, to release these clips.

32 As the console is removed, pull out the heater control panel illumination bulbholder, noting its fitted location. Also disconnect the wiring plug from the rear of the cigarette lighter **(see illustration)**.

33 Manoeuvre the front console out of position, and remove it from the car.

Refitting

34 Refitting is a reversal of removal, noting the following points:

a) Remember to refit the heater control panel illumination bulbholder and cigarette lighter wiring plug.

b) When initially offering the front console into position, take care to align the two plastic clips either side, so that they slide together correctly.

c) As the console sections are refitted, make sure that no wiring or cables become trapped.

d) Reconnect the battery negative lead, then check the operation of all switches and controls on completion.

11

Notes

Chapter 12 Body electrical systems

Contents

Degrees of difficulty

Easy, suitable for novice with little experience | **Fairly easy,** suitable for beginner with some experience | **Fairly difficult,** suitable for competent DIY mechanic 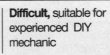 | **Difficult,** suitable for experienced DIY mechanic | **Very difficult,** suitable for expert DIY or professional

1 General information

The chassis electrical system of this vehicle is of 12-volt, negative earth type. Power for the lights and all electrical accessories is supplied by a lead/acid-type battery, which is charged by the alternator.

This Chapter covers repair and service procedures for various chassis (non-engine related) electrical components. For information regarding the engine electrical system components (battery, alternator, distributor and starter motor), see Chapter 5.

 Warning: To prevent electrical short-circuits, fires and injury, always disconnect the battery negative terminal before checking, repairing or renewing electrical components.

 Caution: If the radio in your vehicle is equipped with an anti-theft system, make sure you have the correct activation code before disconnecting the battery, Refer to the information on page 0-7 at the front of this manual before detaching the cable.
Note: If, after connecting the battery, the wrong language appears on the instrument panel display, refer to page 0-7 for the language resetting procedure.

2 Electrical system fault finding - general information

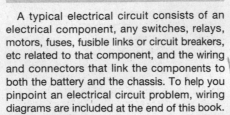

A typical electrical circuit consists of an electrical component, any switches, relays, motors, fuses, fusible links or circuit breakers, etc related to that component, and the wiring and connectors that link the components to both the battery and the chassis. To help you pinpoint an electrical circuit problem, wiring diagrams are included at the end of this book.

Before tackling any troublesome electrical circuit, first study the appropriate wiring diagrams to get a complete understanding of what makes up that individual circuit. Troublespots, for instance, can often be isolated by noting if other components related to that circuit are routed through the same fuse and earth connections.

Electrical problems usually stem from simple causes such as loose or corroded connectors, a blown fuse, a melted fusible link, or a bad relay. Inspect all fuses, wires and connectors in a problem circuit first.

The basic tools needed include a circuit tester, a high-impedance digital voltmeter, a continuity tester and a jumper wire with an in-line circuit breaker for bypassing electrical components. Before attempting to locate or define a problem with electrical test instruments, use the wiring diagrams to decide where to make the necessary connections.

Voltage checks

Perform a voltage check first when a circuit is not functioning properly. Connect one lead of a circuit tester to either the negative battery terminal or a known good earth.

Connect the other lead to a connector in the circuit being tested, preferably nearest to the battery or fuse. If the bulb of the tester lights up, voltage is present, which means that the part of the circuit between the connector and the battery is problem-free. Continue checking the rest of the circuit in the same fashion.

When you reach a point at which no voltage is present, the problem lies between that point and the last test point with voltage. Most of the time, problems can be traced to a loose connection. **Note:** Keep in mind that some circuits receive voltage only when the ignition key is turned to a certain position.

Electrical fault diagnosis is simple if you keep in mind that all electrical circuits are basically electricity running from the battery, through the wires, switches, relays, fuses and fusible links to each electrical component (light bulb, motor, etc) and then to earth, from where it is passed back to the battery. Any electrical problem is an interruption in the flow of electricity to and from the battery.

12

Finding a short-circuit

One method of finding a short-circuit is to remove the fuse and connect a test light or voltmeter in its place. There should be no voltage present in the circuit. Move the electrical connectors from side-to-side while watching the test light. If the bulb goes on, there is a short to earth somewhere in that area, probably where the insulation has been rubbed through. The same test can be performed on each component in a circuit, even a switch.

Earth check

Perform a earth check to see whether a component is properly earthed (passing current back via the vehicle body). Disconnect the battery, and connect one lead of a self-powered test light (often known as a continuity tester) to a known good earth. Connect the other lead to the wire or earth connection being tested. The bulb should light, indicating a good earth connection. If not, dismantle the connection, and clean all relevant parts thoroughly. When re-making the connection, use serrated (shakeproof) washers if possible, and tighten all bolts, etc, securely.

 Caution: If the radio in your vehicle is equipped with an anti-theft system, make sure you have the correct activation code *before disconnecting the battery. Refer to the information on page 0-7 at the front of this manual before detaching the cable.* **Note:** *If, after connecting the battery, the wrong language appears on the instrument panel display, refer to page 0-7 for the language resetting procedure.*

Continuity check

A continuity check determines if there are any breaks in a circuit - if it is conducting electricity properly. With the circuit off (no power in the circuit), a self-powered continuity tester can be used to check the circuit. Connect the test leads to both ends of the circuit, and if the test light comes on, the circuit is passing current properly. If the light doesn't come on, there is a break somewhere in the circuit. The same procedure can be used to test a switch, by connecting the continuity tester to the power-in and power-out sides of the switch. With the switch turned on, the test light should come on.

Finding an open-circuit

When diagnosing for possible open-circuits, it is often difficult to locate them by sight, because oxidation or terminal misalignment are hidden by the connectors. Intermittent problems are often caused by oxidised or loose connections. Merely wiggling an electrical connector may correct the open-circuit condition, albeit temporarily. Dismantle the connector, and spray with a water-dispersant aerosol. On simpler connectors, it may be possible to carefully

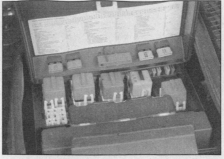

3.1 The fusebox is located in the engine compartment under a cover - the box also includes several relays

bend the connector pins inside, to improve the metal-to-metal contact - don't damage the connector in the process, however.

3 Fuses - general information

The electrical circuits of the vehicle are protected by a combination of fuses and circuit breakers. The fusebox is located in the left corner of the engine compartment (see illustration). On some later models, it is located under the rear seat cushion.

Each of the fuses is designed to protect a specific circuit, and on some models, the various circuits are identified on the fuse panel itself. See page 12•9 for typical fuse applications.

Miniaturised fuses are employed in the fuseboxes. These compact fuses, with blade terminal design, allow fingertip removal and renewal. If an electrical component fails, always check the fuse first. A blown fuse is easily identified through the clear plastic body. Visually inspect the element for evidence of damage. If a continuity check is called for, the blade terminal tips are exposed in the fuse body.

Be sure to renew blown fuses with the correct type. Fuses of different ratings are physically interchangeable, but only fuses of the proper rating should be used. Replacing a fuse with one of a higher or lower value than specified is not recommended. Each electrical circuit needs a specific amount of protection. The amperage value of each fuse is moulded into the fuse body.

If the new fuse immediately fails, don't renew it again until the cause of the problem is isolated and corrected. In most cases, the cause will be a short-circuit in the wiring caused by a broken or deteriorated wire.

4 Relays - general information

Several electrical accessories in the vehicle use relays to transmit the electrical signal to the component. If the relay is defective, that

4.2 Engine compartment relays

component will not operate properly. Relays are electrically-operated switches, which are often used in circuits drawing high levels of current, or where more complex switching arrangements are required.

The various relays are grouped together for convenience in several locations under the dash and in the engine compartment **(see accompanying illustration and illustration 3.1)**.

If a faulty relay is suspected, it can be removed and tested by a dealer or qualified automotive electrician. No overhaul is possible. Like fuses, defective relays must be replaced with the correct type; some relays look identical, but perform very different functions.

5 Direction indicator/hazard warning flasher unit - check and renewal

 Warning: Some later models are equipped with an airbag or Supplemental Restraint System (SRS). To avoid possible damage to this system, the manufacturer recommends that, on airbag-equipped models, the following procedure should be left to a dealer service department, or other specialist, because of the special tools and techniques required. There is a risk of injury if the airbag is accidentally triggered.

1 The direction indicator/hazard flasher unit is a small canister- or box-shaped unit located in the wiring harness on or near the steering column. Access is gained by removing the steering column shrouds (see illustration).

2 When the flasher unit is functioning properly, a regular clicking noise can be heard from it when the indicators or hazard flashers are switched on. If the direction indicators fail on one side or the other, and the flasher unit does not make its characteristic clicking sound, a faulty direction indicator bulb is indicated.

3 If both direction indicators fail to blink, the problem may be due to a blown fuse, a faulty flasher unit, a broken switch or a loose or open connection. If a quick check of the fusebox

5.1 The direction indicator/hazard warning flasher unit is located on the steering column on most models - squeeze the tabs to detach it

indicates that the direction indicator and/or hazard fuse has blown, check the wiring for a short-circuit before fitting a new fuse.

4 Make sure that the new unit is identical to the original. Compare the old one to the new one before fitting it.

5 Refitting is the reverse of removal.

6 Steering column switches - removal and refitting

Warning: Some later models are equipped with an airbag or Supplemental Restraint System (SRS). To avoid possible damage to this system, the manufacturer recommends that, on airbag-equipped models, the following procedure should be left to a dealer service department, or other specialist, because of the special tools and techniques required. There is a risk of injury if the airbag is accidentally triggered.

Caution: If the radio in your vehicle is equipped with an anti-theft system, make sure you have the correct activation code before disconnecting the battery, Refer to the information on page 0-7 at the front of this manual before detaching the cable.
Note: *If, after connecting the battery, the wrong language appears on the instrument panel display, refer to page 0-7 for the language resetting procedure.*

1 Disconnect the battery negative cable, remove the steering wheel (see Chapter 10) and steering column shrouds (see Chapter 11).

Direction indicator/headlight switch

2 Where necessary, remove the switch mounting screws. Depress the tabs and pull the switch out of the steering column mounting **(see illustration)**.
3 Trace the switch wires down the steering column to the electrical connector, and unplug them **(see illustration)**.
4 Refitting is the reverse of removal.

6.2 Squeeze the tabs to release the switch from the mounting

Wiper/washer switch

5 Where necessary, remove the switch mounting screws.
6 Depress the release clip, and detach the switch from the steering column mounting **(see illustration)**. Trace the switch wiring down the steering column to the electrical connector, and unplug it.
7 Refitting is the reverse of removal.

Cruise control switch

8 Remove the wiper/washer switch.
9 Where necessary, remove the switch mounting screw. Squeeze the release tabs, and withdraw the switch from the mounting **(see illustration)**.
10 Disconnect the switch electrical connector from the harness at the base of the steering column.
11 Refitting is the reverse of removal.

7 Ignition switch - removal and refitting

Warning: Some later models are equipped with an airbag or Supplemental Restraint System (SRS). To avoid possible damage to this system, the manufacturer recommends that, on airbag-equipped models, the following procedure should be left to a dealer service department, or other specialist, because of the special

6.6 Squeeze the wiper/washer switch tabs and pull it directly out of the mounting

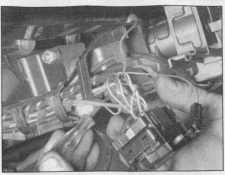

6.3 Follow the wiring down the steering column to the connector

tools and techniques required. There is a risk of injury if the airbag is accidentally triggered.

Caution: If the radio in your vehicle is equipped with an anti-theft system, make sure you have the correct activation code before disconnecting the battery, Refer to the information on page 0-7 at the front of this manual before detaching the cable.
Note: *If, after connecting the battery, the wrong language appears on the instrument panel display, refer to page 0-7 for the language resetting procedure.*

Removal

1 Disconnect the battery negative cable.
2 Remove the steering wheel (see Chapter 10).
3 Remove the steering column shrouds (see Chapter 11).
4 Where necessary, remove the direction indicator/headlight control switch (see Section 6).
5 Detach the clips by inserting a small screwdriver into the openings on the sides while pulling out on the switch **(see illustration)**.
6 Unplug the electrical connector from the harness at the base of the steering column, and remove the switch.

Refitting

7 Refitting is the reverse of removal.

6.9 Cruise control switch removal

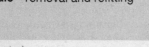

7.5 Insert a screwdriver into the openings (arrowed) on each side of the switch to release the clip while pulling out

8 Radio - removal and refitting

⚠️ **Caution: If the radio in your vehicle is equipped with an anti-theft system, make sure you have the correct activation code** *before disconnecting the battery, Refer to the information on page 0-7 at the front of this manual before detaching the cable.*
Note: *If, after connecting the battery, the wrong language appears on the instrument panel display, refer to page 0-7 for the language resetting procedure.*

Removal

1 Disconnect the battery negative cable.
2 The radios on most models are held in place by internal clips which are usually located at the sides or corners of the unit faceplate. Removal requires a special tool which is inserted into the holes to release the clips so the radio can be pulled out. These tools can be fabricated from heavy wire, or are available from your dealer or a car audio specialist. On anti-theft radios, the clips are moved in and out by internal screws which require another type of tool. Insert the tool into the holes until the clips release, then withdraw the radio from the dash panel. Disconnect the wiring from the radio and remove it.

3 On some models, the radio is held in place by screws located beneath the faceplate. The control knobs must be pulled off before the faceplate can be withdrawn.

Refitting

4 Refitting is the reverse of removal.

9 Aerial - removal and refitting

⚠️ **Caution: If the radio in your vehicle is equipped with an anti-theft system, make sure you have the correct activation code** *before disconnecting the battery, Refer to the information on page 0-7 at the front of this manual before detaching the cable.*
Note: *If, after connecting the battery, the wrong language appears on the instrument panel display, refer to page 0-7 for the language resetting procedure.*

Removal

1 Disconnect the battery negative cable.
2 Use circlip pliers to unscrew the aerial mounting nut.
3 Open the boot lid/tailgate and remove the left side trim panel. On some models, the jack and tail light cluster cover will have to be removed first.
4 Unplug the aerial power and radio lead connectors (as applicable), remove the retaining bolts, and remove the aerial and motor assembly.

Refitting

5 Refitting is the reverse of removal.

10 Instrument cluster - removal and refitting

⚠️ **Caution: The instrument cluster and components are very susceptible to damage from static electricity. Make sure you are earthed and have discharged**

any static electricity (by touching an object such as a metal water pipe) before touching the cluster or components.
⚠️ **Caution: If the radio in your vehicle is equipped with an anti-theft system, make sure you have the correct activation code** *before disconnecting the battery, Refer to the information on page 0-7 at the front of this manual before detaching the cable.*
Note: *If, after connecting the battery, the wrong language appears on the instrument panel display, refer to page 0-7 for the language resetting procedure.*

Removal

1 Disconnect the battery negative cable.
2 Remove the steering column shrouds as described in Chapter 11. As necessary, remove the lower trim panel by turning the fasteners through 90°, then remove the trim below the instrument cluster by unscrewing the retaining nuts from behind.
3 Remove the screws holding the cluster to the facia **(see illustration)**. Note the location of the lower screws to ensure they are refitted in the same place. On 3-Series models, the length of the two lower inner screws must not exceed 9.5 mm.
4 Tilt the top of the cluster back, reach behind it and detach the electrical connectors by pressing on the levers, then lift the cluster out of the facia opening **(see illustration)**.
5 For access to the cluster components, release the catches or remove the screws, and separate the two halves **(see illustration)**.

Refitting

6 Refitting is the reverse of removal.

11 Service Indicator (SI) board - general information

All models that have service indicator lights are equipped with a Service Indicator (SI) board located in the instrument cluster. This board turns the lights on at the proper mileage intervals. The lights can only be turned off using a special tool which plugs into the engine check connector (see Chapter 1). The

10.3 Use a Phillips screwdriver to remove the instrument cluster retaining screws

10.4 Push on the levers to detach the cluster electrical connectors

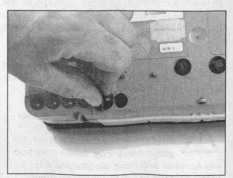

10.5 Turn the plastic knobs to release the back of the cluster (some models use screws)

11.2 These batteries (arrowed) power the Service Indicator (SI) board

12.8 Removing the headlight rear outer cover (3-Series shown)

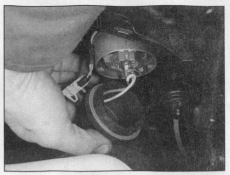

12.9 Twist and release the headlight inner cover

SI board is a self-contained computer which includes a chip and batteries.

The rechargeable SI board nickel cadmium (nicad) batteries maintain power to the computer memory in the event of a power drop (such as during starting) or complete power loss (such as a dead or disconnected battery) **(see illustration)**. This assures power so the computer can continue to keep track of mileage and turn the lights on at the proper interval.

The batteries have a life of approximately six years, at which time they must be replaced with new ones. Also, since they are recharged by the engine charging system, they can run down prematurely if power is cut off for some reason (such as a blown fuse, a fault in the wiring, or extended storage of the vehicle). Excessive heat or cold can also shorten battery life, with heat the greatest enemy. Extreme heat can cause the batteries to actually split open, allowing acid to drip into the instrument cluster.

Several instruments controlled by the SI board can be affected by low or discharged batteries. Symptoms of low or dead SI board batteries can include inconsistent tachometer and temperature gauge readings, background radio noise, and the inability to turn the service lights off with the special tool.

Although only complete SI boards are available from the manufacturer, batteries are available separately from aftermarket sources. While it is possible for the home mechanic to renew the batteries, they are soldered to the board, so unless you are skilled at this and have the proper tools, this job should be left to an experienced electronics technician. Considerable savings can be realised by removing the instrument cluster (see Section 10) and taking it to an electronics specialist.

⚠ *Caution: the instrument cluster and components are very susceptible to damage from static electricity. Make sure you are earthed and have discharged any static electricity (by touching an object such as a metal water pipe) before touching the cluster components.*

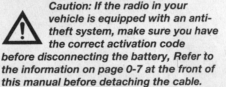

12 Headlights - bulb renewal

⚠ *Caution: If the radio in your vehicle is equipped with an anti-theft system, make sure you have the correct activation code before disconnecting the battery, Refer to the information on page 0-7 at the front of this manual before detaching the cable.*
Note: *If, after connecting the battery, the wrong language appears on the instrument panel display, refer to page 0-7 for the language resetting procedure.*

1 Disconnect the battery negative cable.

Sealed-beam type

2 Remove the grille (see Chapter 11).
3 Remove the headlight retainer screws, taking care not to disturb the adjustment screws.
4 Remove the retainer and pull the headlight out enough to allow the connector to be unplugged.
5 Remove the headlight.
6 To refit the headlight, plug the connector in, place the headlight in position, and refit the retainer and screws. Tighten the screws securely.

7 Refit the grille. Connect the battery negative cable.

Halogen bulb type

⚠ *Warning: Halogen gas-filled bulbs are under pressure, and may shatter if the surface is scratched or the bulb is dropped. Wear eye protection, and handle the bulbs carefully, grasping only the base whenever possible. Do not touch the surface of the bulb with your fingers, because the oil from your skin could cause it to overheat and fail prematurely.*

HAYNES HiNT *If you do touch the headlamp bulb surface, clean it with methylated spirit.*

8 From behind the headlight assembly, remove the outer cover **(see illustration)**.
9 Twist and release the inner cover from the rear of the headlight **(see illustration)**.
10 Disconnect the wire from the rear of the headlight bulb **(see illustration)**.
11 Release the clips, and withdraw the bulb from the headlight unit **(see illustration)**.
12 Fit the new bulb using a reversal of the removal procedure. Make sure that the clips engage the bulb correctly.
13 Connect the battery negative cable.

12.10 Disconnecting the wire from the rear of the headlight bulb

12.11 Removing the headlight bulb (do not touch the surface of the bulb with your fingers)

12

13 Headlights - adjustment

Note: *The headlights must be aimed correctly. If adjusted incorrectly, they could momentarily blind the driver of an oncoming vehicle and cause a serious accident, or seriously reduce your ability to see the road. The headlights should be checked for proper aim every 12 months (as is done during the MOT test), and any time a new headlight is fitted or front-end body work is performed. It should be emphasised that the following procedure will only provide a temporary setting until the headlights can be adjusted by a properly-equipped garage.*

1 Each headlight has two adjusting screws, one controlling up-and-down movement and one controlling left-and-right movement **(see illustration)**. It may be necessary to remove the grille (see Chapter 11) for access to these screws.

2 There are several methods of adjusting the headlights. The simplest method requires a blank wall (or garage door) 25 feet in front of the vehicle, and a level floor.

3 Position masking tape vertically on the wall, to mark the vehicle centreline and the centreline of both headlights. **Note:** *It may be easier to position the tape on the wall with the vehicle parked only a few inches away, and then move the vehicle back the required distance when all marks have been made.*

4 Make a horizontal line on the wall to mark the centreline of all headlights.

5 Move the vehicle back so that it is 25 feet away from the marked wall (keep the front end of the vehicle square to the wall). Adjustment should be made with the vehicle sitting level, the fuel tank half-full, and with no unusually heavy loads in the vehicle.

6 Switch on the dipped beam. The bright spots on the wall should be two inches below the horizontal line, and two inches to the left of the headlight vertical lines. Adjustment is made by turning the adjusting screw to raise or lower the beam. The other adjusting screw

13.1 The headlight adjustment screws (arrowed) are accessible from the back of the headlight on 3-Series models

should be used in the same manner to move the beam left or right.

7 With main beam on, the bright spots on the wall should be exactly on the vertical lines, and just below the horizontal line. **Note:** *It may not be possible to position the headlight aim exactly for both main and dipped beams. If a compromise must be made, keep in mind that the dipped beam is most used, and will have the greatest effect on driver safety.*

8 Have the headlights adjusted by a dealer service department or qualified garage at the earliest opportunity.

14 Headlight housing - removal and refitting

⚠️ **Caution: If the radio in your vehicle is equipped with an anti-theft system, make sure you have the correct activation code before disconnecting the battery, Refer to the information on page 0-7 at the front of this manual before detaching the cable.**
Note: *If, after connecting the battery, the wrong language appears on the instrument panel display, refer to page 0-7 for the language resetting procedure.*

Removal

1 Disconnect the battery negative cable.

14.4 Remove the screws (arrowed) and detach the headlight housing

2 Remove the side grille (see Chapter 11), then remove the rear cover(s) where necessary.

3 Unplug the headlight (sealed beam-type) or remove the bulb (halogen bulb-type).

4 Remove the screws and detach the housing **(see illustration)**.

Refitting

5 Refitting is the reverse of removal.

15 Bulb renewal

1 The lenses of many lights are held in place by screws, which makes it a simple procedure to gain access to the bulbs.

2 On some lights, the lenses are held in place by clips. The lenses can be removed by using a small screwdriver to prise them off.

3 Several bulbs are mounted in self-earthing holders, and are removed by pushing in and turning them anti-clockwise **(see illustration)**. The bulbs can then be removed **(see illustrations)**.

4 The tail lights on 3-Series models are accessible after removing the housing, then removing the bulbs **(see illustrations)**.

5 To gain access to the facia lights, the instrument cluster will have to be removed first **(see illustration)**.

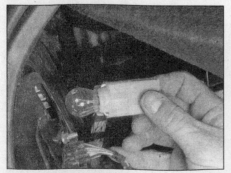

15.3a The tail light bulbs on later 5-Series models are in self-earthing holders which can be simply pulled out of the housing - the bulb is then removed from the holder

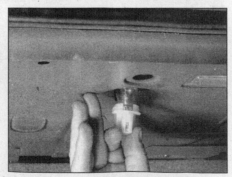

15.3b On models with high-mounted centre brake lights, the self-earthing holder is accessible from the luggage area - pull the holder out . . .

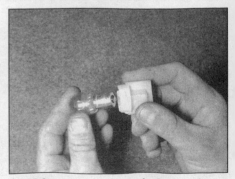

15.3c . . . then pull the bulb from the holder

15.4a On 3-Series models, the entire tail light housing assembly is self-earthing through the mounting screw - loosen the plastic screw and pull the housing back . . .

15.4b . . . then remove the bulb from the housing

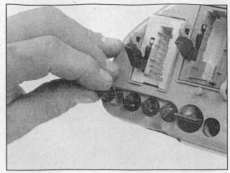

15.5 After removing the instrument cluster (see Section 10), turn the bulbholder anti-clockwise to remove the bulb

16 Windscreen/tailgate wiper motor - removal and refitting

Caution: If the radio in your vehicle is equipped with an anti-theft system, make sure you have the correct activation code before disconnecting the battery, Refer to the information on page 0-7 at the front of this manual before detaching the cable.
Note: *If, after connecting the battery, the wrong language appears on the instrument panel display, refer to page 0-7 for the language resetting procedure.*

1 Disconnect the battery negative cable.

Windscreen wiper motor

2 Remove the covers and nuts, then detach the wiper arms **(see illustrations)**.
3 Prise out the retaining clips and detach the cowl grille for access to the wiper assembly.
4 Remove the screws or nuts and detach the wiper cover located on the engine compartment bulkhead.
5 Unplug the electrical connector and detach the wiper linkage.
6 Mark the relationship of the wiper shaft to the linkage. Detach the wiper link from the motor shaft by prising carefully with a screwdriver.
7 Remove the three retaining bolts and remove the wiper motor from the vehicle.
8 Refitting is the reverse of removal. When fitting the motor, if necessary plug in the

connector and run the motor briefly until it is in the "neutral" (wipers parked) position.

Tailgate wiper motor

9 On 3-Series models, remove the cover and nut, then detach the wiper arm **(see illustration)**. On 5-Series models, open the rear window away from the tailgate.

10 As applicable, remove the trim panel(s), then disconnect the washer tube and the wiring plug.

11 Unscrew the mounting nuts and withdraw the wiper motor **(see illustrations)**. On 5-Series models, the wiper blade and pivot mechanism may be removed from the rear window if necessary after removing the trim panels **(see illustration)**.

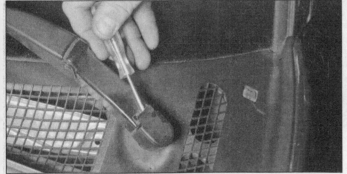

16.2a Use a small screwdriver to detach the wiper arm nut cover, or swivel the cover up

16.2b After removing the nut, use a magnet to lift out the metal washer

16.9 Removing the tailgate wiper arm nut (3-Series)

16.11a Removing the tailgate wiper motor (3-Series)

16.11b Tailgate wiper motor (5-Series)

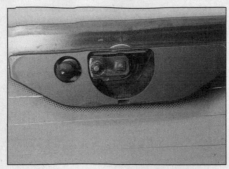

16.11c Wiper blade and pivot mechanism on the rear window (5-Series)

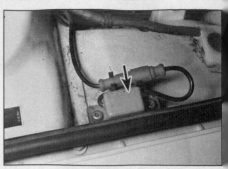

18.3 The SRS system crash sensors (arrowed) are located in the engine compartment - check the wiring regularly for damage

12 Refitting is a reversal of removal. When fitting the motor, if necessary plug in the connector and run the motor briefly until it is in the "neutral" (wiper parked) position.

17 Heated rear window - check and repair

1 The heated rear window consists of a number of horizontal elements on the glass surface.
2 Small breaks in the element can be repaired without removing the rear window.

Check

3 Switch on the ignition and the heated rear window.
4 Place the positive lead of a voltmeter to the heater element nearest to the incoming power source.
5 Wrap a piece of aluminium foil around the negative lead of the voltmeter on the positive side of the suspected broken element, and slide it slowly towards the negative side. Watch the voltmeter needle - when it moves from zero, you have located the break.

Repair

6 Repair the break in the line using a repair kit recommended specifically for this purpose, such as BMW repair kit No. 81 22 9 (or equivalent). Included in this kit is plastic conductive epoxy. The following paragraphs give general instructions for this type of repair; follow the instructions supplied with the repair kit if they are different.
7 Prior to repairing a break, switch off the circuit and allow it to cool down for a few minutes.
8 Lightly buff the element area with fine steel wool, then clean it thoroughly.
9 Use masking tape to mask off the area of repair, leaving a slit to which the epoxy can be applied.
10 Mix the epoxy thoroughly, according to the instructions on the package.
11 Apply the epoxy material to the slit in the masking tape, overlapping the undamaged area about 20 mm on each end.

12 Allow the repair to cure for 24 hours before removing the tape and using the heated rear window.

18 Supplemental Restraint System (SRS) - general information

Later models are equipped with a Supplemental Restraint System (SRS), incorporating an airbag. This system is designed to protect the driver from serious injury in the event of a head-on or frontal collision. It consists of an airbag module in the centre of the steering wheel, two crash sensors mounted on the front inner wing panels, and a crash safety switch located inside the passenger compartment.

The airbag module contains a housing incorporating the airbag and the inflator units. The inflator assembly is mounted on the back of the housing over a hole through which gas is expelled, inflating the bag almost instantaneously when an electrical signal is sent from the system. This signal is carried by a wire which is specially wound with several turns, so the signal will be transmitted regardless of the steering wheel position.

The SRS system has three sensors: two at the front, mounted on the inner wing panels (see illustration), and a safety switch located inside the passenger compartment. The crash sensors are basically pressure-sensitive switches, which complete an electrical circuit during an impact of sufficient force. The electrical signal from the crash sensors is sent to a third sensor, which then completes the circuit and inflates the airbag.

The module containing the safety switch monitors the system operation. It checks the system every time the vehicle is started, causing the AIRBAG warning light to come on, then go out if the system is operating correctly. If there is a fault in the system, the light will stay on. If the AIRBAG warning light does stay on, or if it comes on while driving, take the vehicle to your dealer immediately.

19 Cruise control system - description and check

The cruise control system maintains vehicle speed using a vacuum-actuated servo motor located in the engine compartment, which is connected to the throttle linkage by a cable. The system consists of the servo motor, clutch switch, brake switch, control switches, a relay, and associated vacuum hoses.

Because of the complexity of the cruise control system, repair should be left to a dealer service department. However, it is possible for the home mechanic to make simple checks of the wiring and vacuum connections for minor faults which can be easily repaired. These include:
a) Inspect the cruise control actuating switches for broken wires and loose connections.
b) Check the cruise control fuse.
c) The cruise control system is operated by vacuum, so it's critical that all vacuum switches, hoses and connections are secure. Check the hoses in the engine compartment for loose connections, cracks, or obvious vacuum leaks.

20 Central locking system - description and check

The central door locking system operates the door lock actuators mounted in each door. The system consists of the switches, actuators and associated wiring. Diagnosis is limited to simple checks of the wiring connections and actuators for minor faults which can be easily repaired. These include:
a) Check the system fuse and/or circuit breaker (where applicable).
b) Check the switch wires for damage and loose connections. Check the switches for continuity.
c) Remove the door trim panel(s), and check the actuator wiring connections to see if they're loose or damaged. Inspect the actuator rods to make sure they aren't

bent or damaged. The actuator can be checked by applying battery power momentarily. A discernible click indicates that the solenoid is operating properly.

21 Electric window system - description and check

The electric window system operates the electric motors mounted in the doors which lower and raise the windows. The system consists of the control switches, the motors, window mechanisms (regulators) and

associated wiring. Removal of the motors and regulators is described in Chapter 11.

Diagnosis is usually limited to simple checks of the wiring connections and motors for minor faults which can be easily repaired. These include:

a) *Check the electric window switches for broken wires and loose connections.*
b) *Check the electric window fuse/and or circuit breaker (where applicable).*
c) *Remove the door trim panel(s) and check the electric window motor wires to see if they're loose or damaged. Inspect the window mechanisms for damage which could cause binding.*

22 Wiring diagrams - general information

Since it isn't possible to include all wiring diagrams for every model year covered by this manual, the following diagrams are those that are typical and most commonly needed.

Prior to checking any circuit, check the fuses and circuit breakers to make sure they're in good condition. Make sure the battery is fully charged and check the cable connections (see Chapter 1). Make sure all connectors are clean, with no broken or loose terminals.

Colour codes

BK Black	GE Yellow	GY Grey	R Red	SW Black	VI Violet	WS White
BL Blue	GN Green	OR Orange	RS Pink	TN Tan	W White	Y Yellow
BR Brown	GR Green or Grey	PK Pink	RT Red	V Violet		

Typical fuse application

Fuse	Rated (Amps)	Circuit protected
1	7.5	Left high beam headlight (relay K3)
2	7.5	Right high beam headlight (relay K3)
3	15	Auxiliary fan, 91°C (relay K1)
4	15	Flashing turn indicators
5	30	Wash-wipe, headlight cleaning and intensive cleaning systems (relay K10)
6	7.5	Brake lights (15A if additional brake lights are fitted), automatic cruise control, map reading lights
7	15	Horn (relay K2)
8	30	Heated rear window
9	15	Engine electrical system (carburettor engine), selector lever position indicator for automatic transmission
10	7.5	Instruments, on-board computer, reversing lights, service indicator
11	15	Fuel pump, fuel supply pump
12	7.5	Radio, check control and instruments
13	7.5	Left low beam headlight (relay K4)
14	7.5	Right low beam headlight (relay K4)
15	7.5	Rear fog lights (relay K4, switching off when high headlight beams are selected: relay K9)
16	15	Seat heating (relay K5)
17	30	Sliding roof (relay K5), electric window lifts
18	30	Auxiliary fan, 99°C (relay K6)
19	7.5	Mirror control, mirror heating (relay K7)
20	30	Heater blower, air conditioning (relay K7)
21	7.5	Interior, glove box and luggage compartment lights, hand lamp, clock, radio memory, on-board computer
22	7.5	Left side, rear and parking lights
23	7.5	Right side, rear and parking lights, number plate lights, instrument lighting
24	15	Hazard warning flashers
25	30	Not in use
26	30	Not in use
27	30	Central locking system, door lock heating, on-board computer, horn, sound system
28	30	Cigarette lighter, motor-driven radio aerial, independent fuel-burning heater
29	7.5	Left fog light (relay K8)
30	7.5	Right fog light (relay K8)

12

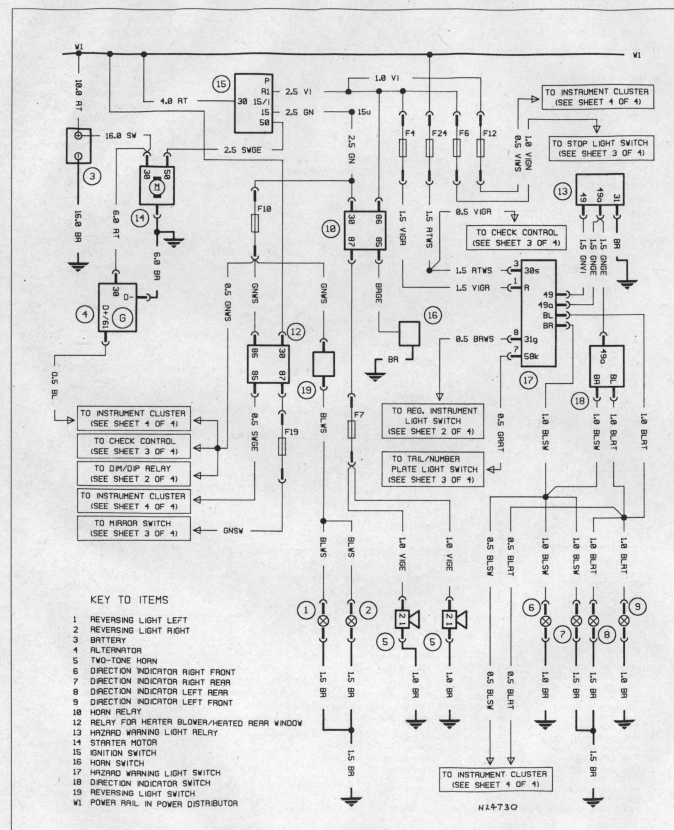

Typical starting, charging, horn, hazard flasher and direction indicators (1 of 4)

KEY TO ITEMS

1 REVERSING LIGHT LEFT
2 REVERSING LIGHT RIGHT
3 BATTERY
4 ALTERNATOR
5 TWO-TONE HORN
6 DIRECTION INDICATOR RIGHT FRONT
7 DIRECTION INDICATOR RIGHT REAR
8 DIRECTION INDICATOR LEFT REAR
9 DIRECTION INDICATOR LEFT FRONT
10 HORN RELAY
12 RELAY FOR HEATER BLOWER/HEATED REAR WINDOW
13 HAZARD WARNING LIGHT RELAY
14 STARTER MOTOR
15 IGNITION SWITCH
16 HORN SWITCH
17 HAZARD WARNING LIGHT SWITCH
18 DIRECTION INDICATOR SWITCH
19 REVERSING LIGHT SWITCH
W1 POWER RAIL IN POWER DISTRIBUTOR

H2473Q

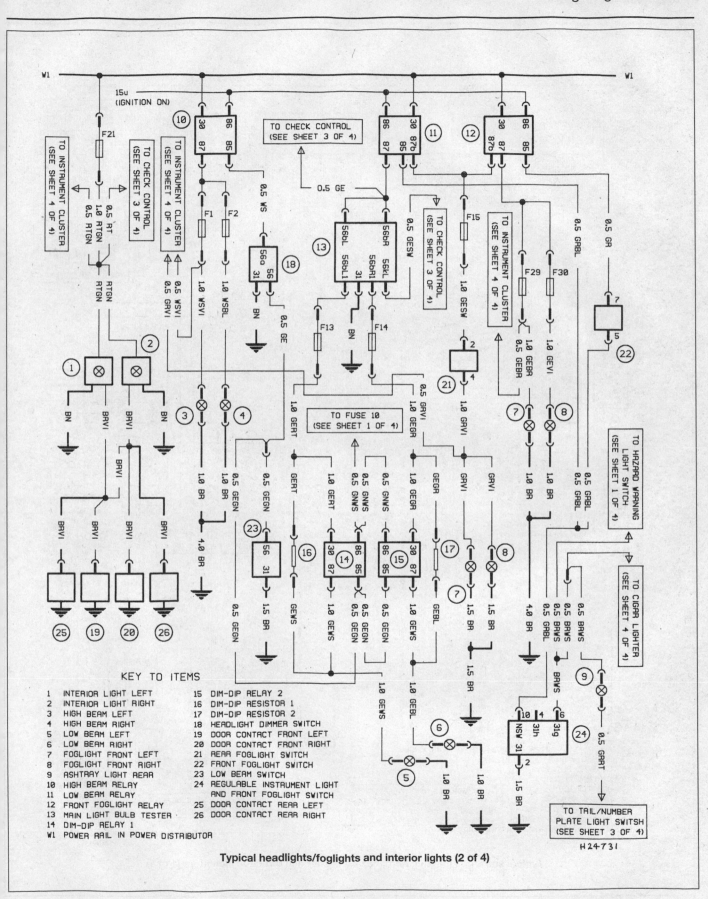

KEY TO ITEMS

1   INTERIOR LIGHT LEFT
2   INTERIOR LIGHT RIGHT
3   HIGH BEAM LEFT
4   HIGH BEAM RIGHT
5   LOW BEAM LEFT
6   LOW BEAM RIGHT
7   FOGLIGHT FRONT LEFT
8   FOGLIGHT FRONT RIGHT
9   ASHTRAY LIGHT REAR
10 HIGH BEAM RELAY
11 LOW BEAM RELAY
12 FRONT FOGLIGHT RELAY
13 MAIN LIGHT BULB TESTER
14 DIM-DIP RELAY 1
W1 POWER RAIL IN POWER DISTRIBUTOR

15 DIM-DIP RELAY 2
16 DIM-DIP RESISTOR 1
17 DIM-DIP RESISTOR 2
18 HEADLIGHT DIMMER SWITCH
19 DOOR CONTACT FRONT LEFT
20 DOOR CONTACT FRONT RIGHT
21 REAR FOGLIGHT SWITCH
22 FRONT FOGLIGHT SWITCH
23 LOW BEAM SWITCH
24 REGULABLE INSTRUMENT LIGHT
     AND FRONT FOGLIGHT SWITCH
25 DOOR CONTACT REAR LEFT
26 DOOR CONTACT REAR RIGHT

Typical headlights/foglights and interior lights (2 of 4)

H24731

12

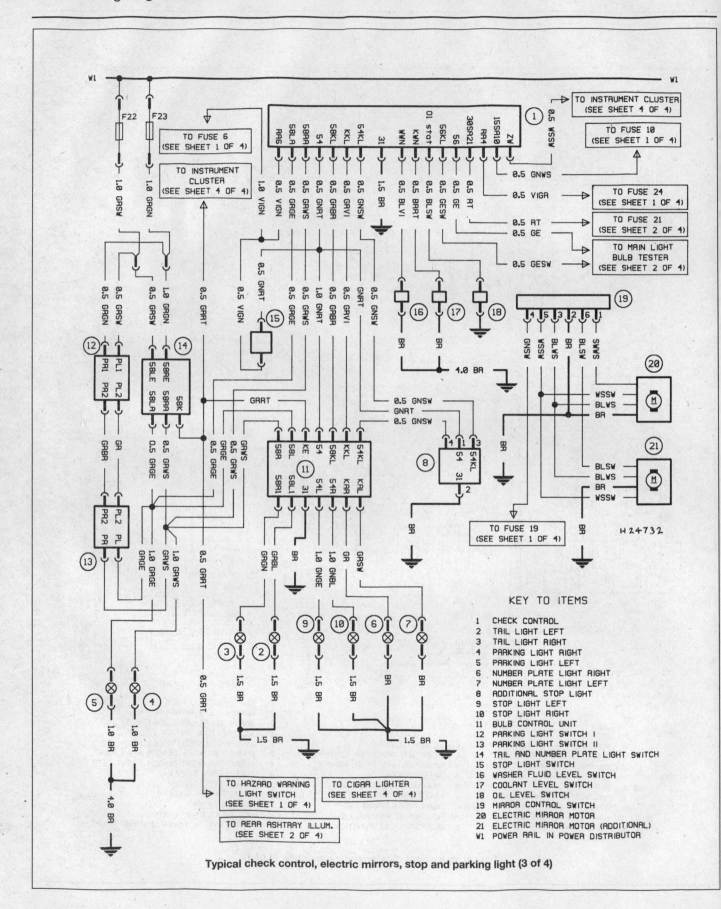

Typical check control, electric mirrors, stop and parking light (3 of 4)

KEY TO ITEMS

1 CHECK CONTROL
2 TAIL LIGHT LEFT
3 TAIL LIGHT RIGHT
4 PARKING LIGHT RIGHT
5 PARKING LIGHT LEFT
6 NUMBER PLATE LIGHT RIGHT
7 NUMBER PLATE LIGHT LEFT
8 ADDITIONAL STOP LIGHT
9 STOP LIGHT LEFT
10 STOP LIGHT RIGHT
11 BULB CONTROL UNIT
12 PARKING LIGHT SWITCH I
13 PARKING LIGHT SWITCH II
14 TAIL AND NUMBER PLATE LIGHT SWITCH
15 STOP LIGHT SWITCH
16 WASHER FLUID LEVEL SWITCH
17 COOLANT LEVEL SWITCH
18 OIL LEVEL SWITCH
19 MIRROR CONTROL SWITCH
20 ELECTRIC MIRROR MOTOR
21 ELECTRIC MIRROR MOTOR (ADDITIONAL)
W1 POWER RAIL IN POWER DISTRIBUTOR

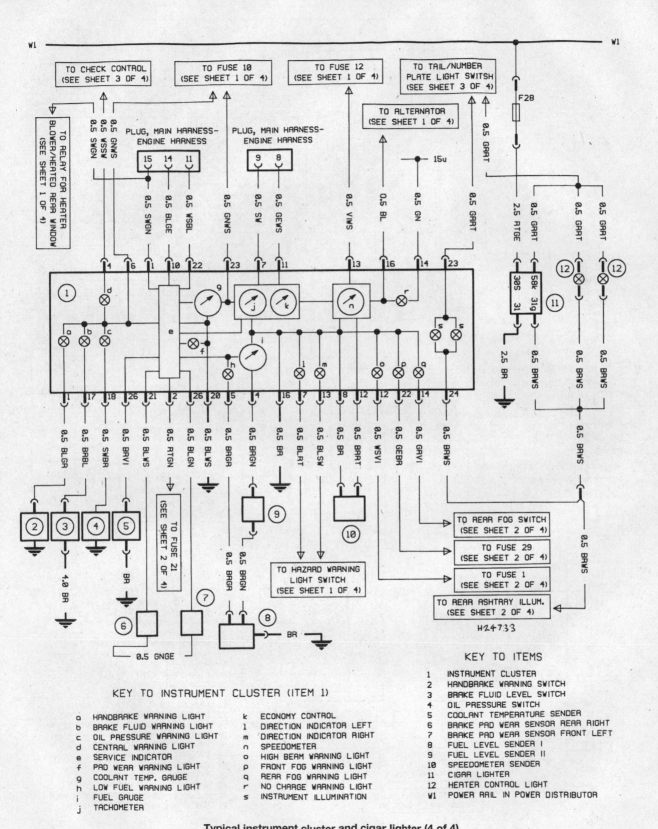

Typical instrument cluster and cigar lighter (4 of 4)

KEY TO INSTRUMENT CLUSTER (ITEM 1)

a HANDBRAKE WARNING LIGHT
b BRAKE FLUID WARNING LIGHT
c OIL PRESSURE WARNING LIGHT
d CENTRAL WARNING LIGHT
e SERVICE INDICATOR
f PAD WEAR WARNING LIGHT
g COOLANT TEMP. GAUGE
h LOW FUEL WARNING LIGHT
i FUEL GAUGE
j TACHOMETER

k ECONOMY CONTROL
l DIRECTION INDICATOR LEFT
m DIRECTION INDICATOR RIGHT
n SPEEDOMETER
o HIGH BEAM WARNING LIGHT
p FRONT FOG WARNING LIGHT
q REAR FOG WARNING LIGHT
r NO CHARGE WARNING LIGHT
s INSTRUMENT ILLUMINATION

KEY TO ITEMS

1 INSTRUMENT CLUSTER
2 HANDBRAKE WARNING SWITCH
3 BRAKE FLUID LEVEL SWITCH
4 OIL PRESSURE SWITCH
5 COOLANT TEMPERATURE SENDER
6 BRAKE PAD WEAR SENSOR REAR RIGHT
7 BRAKE PAD WEAR SENSOR FRONT LEFT
8 FUEL LEVEL SENDER I
9 FUEL LEVEL SENDER II
10 SPEEDOMETER SENDER
11 CIGAR LIGHTER
12 HEATER CONTROL LIGHT
W1 POWER RAIL IN POWER DISTRIBUTOR

12

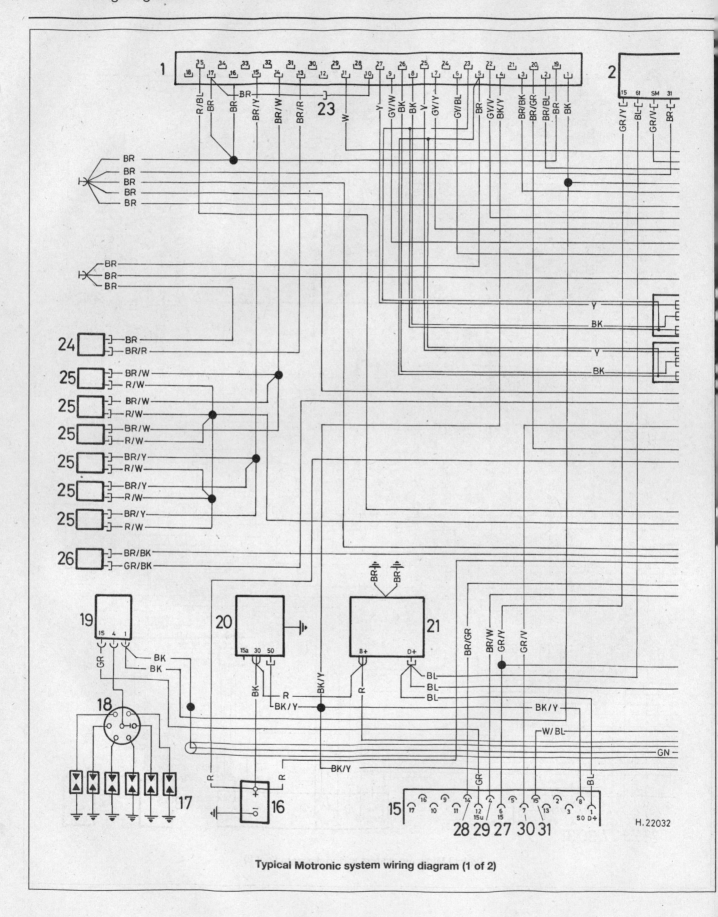

Typical Motronic system wiring diagram (1 of 2)

H.22032

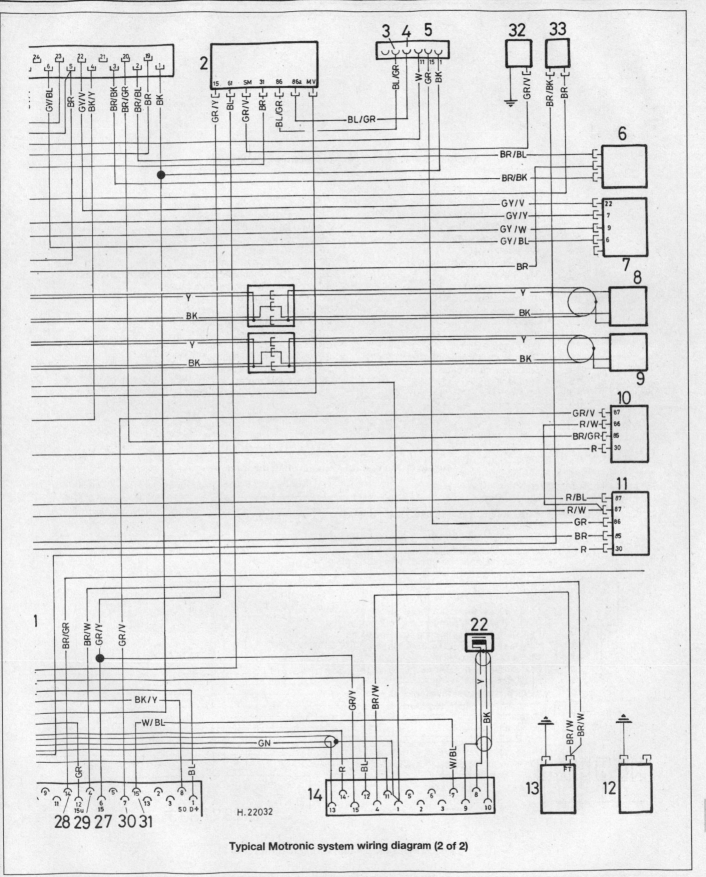

H.22032

Typical Motronic system wiring diagram (2 of 2)

12

Key to Motronic engine control system wiring diagram

No	Description	No	Description
1	Electronic Control Unit (ECU)	18	Distributor
2	Speed control relay	19	Ignition coil
3	Temperature switch	20	Starter
4	Air conditioner	21	Alternator
5	Car wire harness connection	22	Position transmitter
6	Throttle switch	23	Plug disconnected for automatic transmission
7	Airflow sensor	24	Coolant temperature sensor
8	Speed sensor	25	Fuel injector
9	Reference mark sensor	26	Solenoid
10	Relay 1	27	Electric power distributor
11	Relay 2	28	Oil pressure
12	Oil pressure switch	29	Temperature gauge
13	Temperature transmitter	30	Electric fuel pump
14	Diagnosis connection	31	Service indicator
15	Engine plug	32	Drive motor
16	Battery	33	Temperature switch
17	Spark plugs		

Key to cruise control system wiring diagram

No	Description
1	Plug connection – centre section to instrument cluster (26-pin)
2	Steering column switch
3	Instrument cluster
4	Plug connection – range indicator
5	Range indicator D
6	Range indicator N
7	Range indicator R
8	Plug connection – speedometer outlet
9	Connection – instrument cluster (2-pin)
10	Plug connection – steering column switch
11	Plug connection – special equipment
12	Steering column switch
13	Plug connection – rear section to centre section (29-pin)
14	Stoplight switch
15	Plug connection – drive motor
16	Connection – clutch switch to bridge
17	Stoplight left
18	Stoplight right
19	Electronic control – cruise control
20	Drive motor – cruise control
21	Bridge (only for automatic transmission)
22	Clutch switch

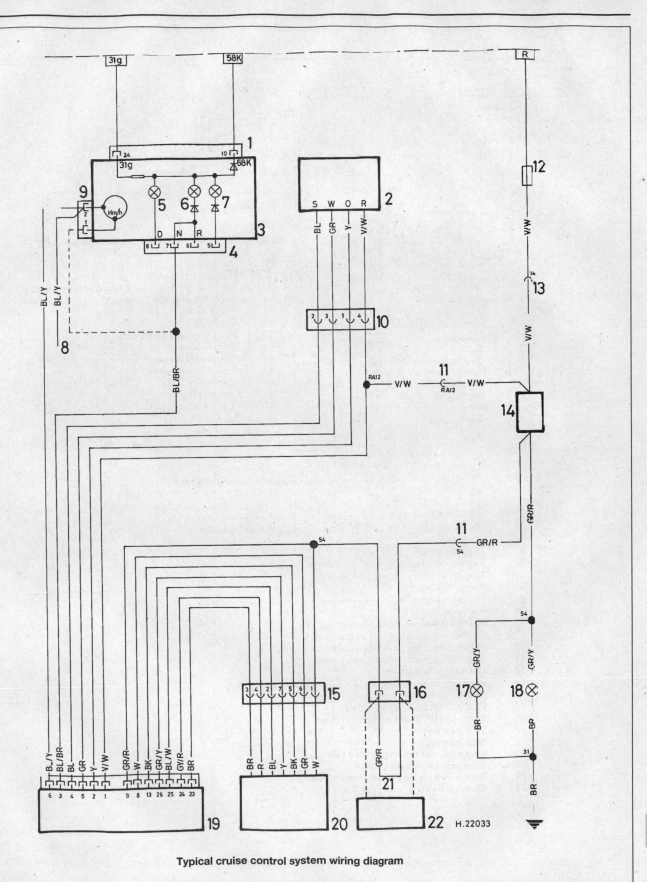

Typical cruise control system wiring diagram

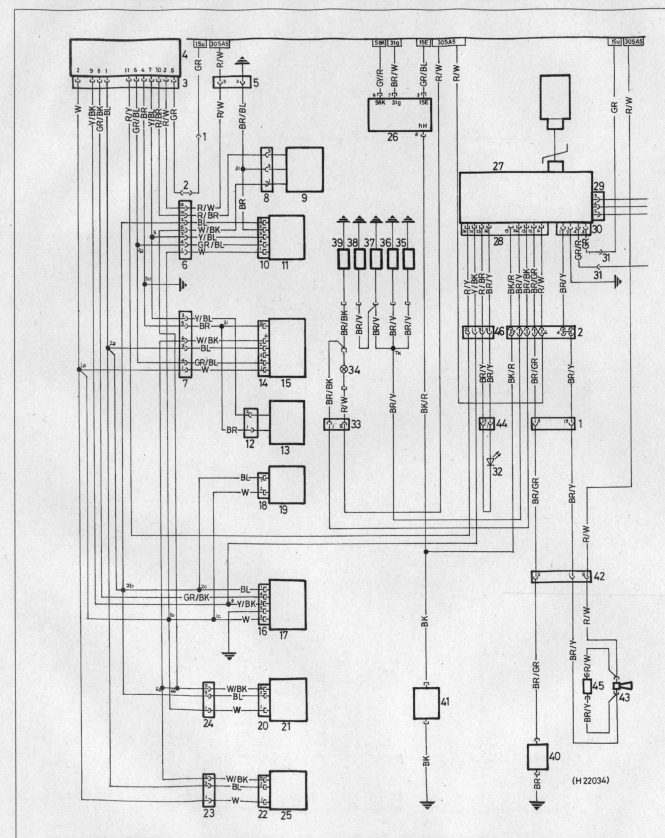

Typical wiring diagram for the central locking, burglar alarm, on-board computer, additional heater and digital clock (1 of 2)

(H 22034)

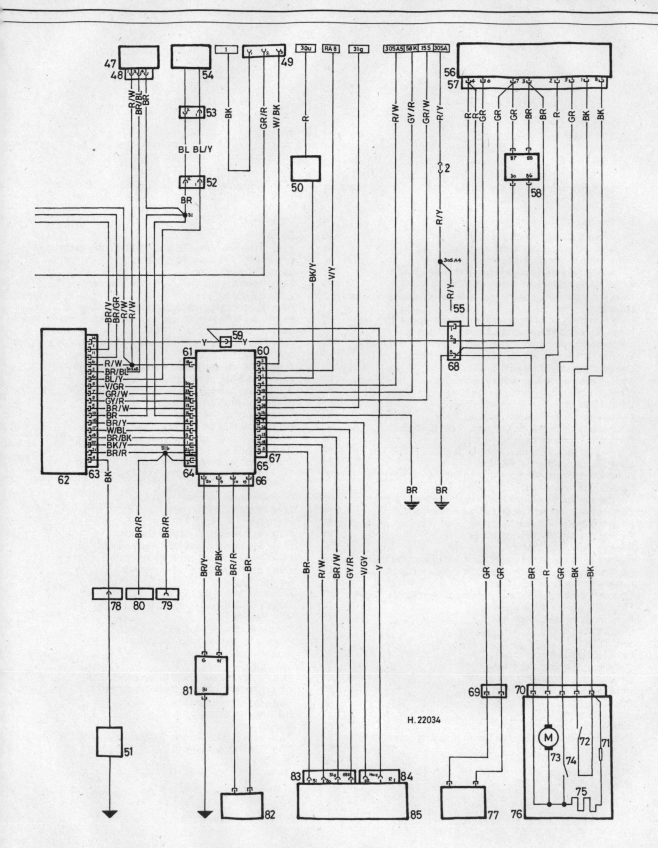

H.22034

Typical wiring diagram for the central locking, burglar alarm, on-board computer, additional heater and digital clock (2 of 2)

12

Key to wiring diagram for the central locking, burglar alarm, on-board computer, additional heater and digital clock

No	Description
1	Plug – rear section to centre section
2	Connection for special equipment plug
3	Connection for central lock control unit
4	Central lock electronic control unit (A pillar end plate)
5	Plug – driver's door wire to rear section
6	Plug – central lock connecting wire to driver's door wire (13-pin)
7	Plug – central lock connecting wire to passenger's door wire
8	Plug – driver's door central lock wire to switch
9	Central lock switch/unblocking arrest (driver's door, on lock)
10	Connection for central lock motor to driver's door (6-pin)
11	Central lock motor – driver's door
12	Plug – passenger's door wire to microswitch
13	Microswitch (passenger's door, on lock)
14	Central lock motor – passenger's door
15	Central lock motor – passenger's door
16	Connection for central lock motor to boot lid (6-pin)
17	Central lock motor – boot lid
18	Connection for central lock motor to fuel filler flap (6-pin)
19	Central lock motor – fuel filler flap
20	Connection for central lock motor to left rear door (6-pin)
21	Central lock motor – left rear door
22	Connection for central lock motor to right door (6-pin)
23	Plug – central lock connecting wire to right rear door (7-pin)
24	Plug – central lock connecting wire to left rear door (7-pin)
25	Central lock motor – right rear door
26	Rear window heater switch
27	Burglar alarm electronic control unit (left of steering column)
28	Connection for burglar alarm electronic control unit I (26-pin)
29	Connection for relay box (4-pin)
30	Connection for burglar alarm electronic control unit II (4-pin)
31	Plug 150 (in main wire harness)
32	Light diode for burglar alarm
33	Plug for boot light
34	Boot light
35	Door contact switch front left
36	Door contact switch front right
37	Door contact switch rear left
38	Door contact switch rear right
39	Boot lid contact
40	Bonnet contact
41	Rear window heater
42	Plug – centre section to wire for on-board computer/burglar alarm
43	Horn
44	Plug for light diode
45	Diode
46	Plug – burglar alarm wire to central lock connecting wire
47	Chime (left of steering column)
48	Connection for chime
49	Plug – centre section to LE-Jetronic wire harness
50	Ignition switch
51	Remote control switch for on-board computer
52	Plug – on-board computer to outside temperature sensor wire
53	Plug – outside temperature sensor wire to outside temperature sensor
54	Outside temperature sensor (lower front panel)
55	Plug – extra heater wire to automatic aerial
56	Parked car heating electronic control unit (on parked car heater underneath right seat)
57	Connection for electronic control unit
58	Relay for parked car heater (on heater)
59	Plug – on-board computer wire to extra heater wire
60	Plug – centre section to instrument cluster
61	Connection for instrument cluster
62	On-board computer electronic control unit (right of instrument cluster)
63	Connection for on-board computer
64	Connection for instrument cluster II
65	Instrument cluster
66	Plug – rear section to instrument cluster
67	Plug – digital clock wire to instrument cluster
68	Plug – extra wire to heater wire
69	Plug – heater wire to fuel pump wire
70	Connection for heater
71	Ballast resistor in heater
72	Thermoswitch (parked car heater)
73	Heater motor
74	Overheating switch (parked car heater)
75	Heater plug for parked car heater
76	Heater
77	Fuel pump
78	Plug – on-board computer to remote control
79	Plug – speed dependent loudness control
80	Plug – wire for cruise control
81	Fuel level transmitter
82	Speed transmitter
83	Plug – digital clock wire to digital clock (4-pin)
84	Plug – digital clock wire to digital clock (2-pin)
85	Digital clock

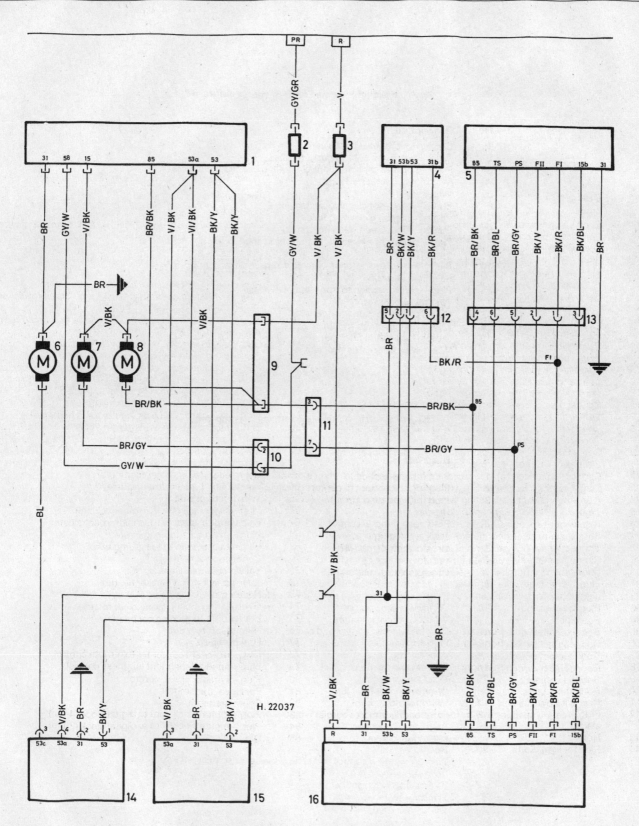

H.22037

Typical headlight washer system wiring diagram

Key to headlight washer system wiring diagram

No	Description
1	Control unit for headlight cleaners (on fluid reservoir)
2	Fuse – overnight, tail and parking lights
3	Fuse – horns, wash/wipe control unit and headlight cleaners
4	Motor – windscreen wipers
5	Wiper switch
6	Pump – headlight cleaning system
7	Pump – intensive cleaning fluid
8	Pump – windscreen washing system
9	Plug – headlight cleaner wire to front section I (washer fluid pump)
10	Plug – Headlight cleaner wire to front section II (plug for headlight cleaners)
11	Plug – centre section to front section (7-pin)
12	Plug for wiper motor
13	Plug – centre section to wiper switch
14	Motor – windscreen wipers
15	Motor – left headlight wiper
16	Wash/wipe interval control unit

Key to electric window system wiring diagram

No	Description
1	Plug for rear section to driver's door (6-pin)
2	Plug for rear section to center section (27-pin)
3	Plug for window control and central lock wire to driver's door (13-pin)
4	Plug for window control and central lock wire to special equipment plug
5	Window switch rear left
6	Window switch rear left
7	Window switch rear right
8	Plug for left rear door wire to window motor rear left
9	Plug for right door wire to window motor rear right
10	Window motor rear left
11	Window motor rear right
12	Plug for window control and central lock wire to left rear door
13	Plug for window control and central lock wire to right rear door (7-pin)
14	Power safety switch
15	Child safety switch
16	Window motor front left
17	Window motor front right
18	Plug for driver's door wire to window motor front left
19	Plug for passenger's door wire to window motor of passenger's door
20	Relay
21	Plug for window control and central lock wire to passenger's door (13-pin)
22	Window switch front left
23	Window switch rear right
24	Window switch front right

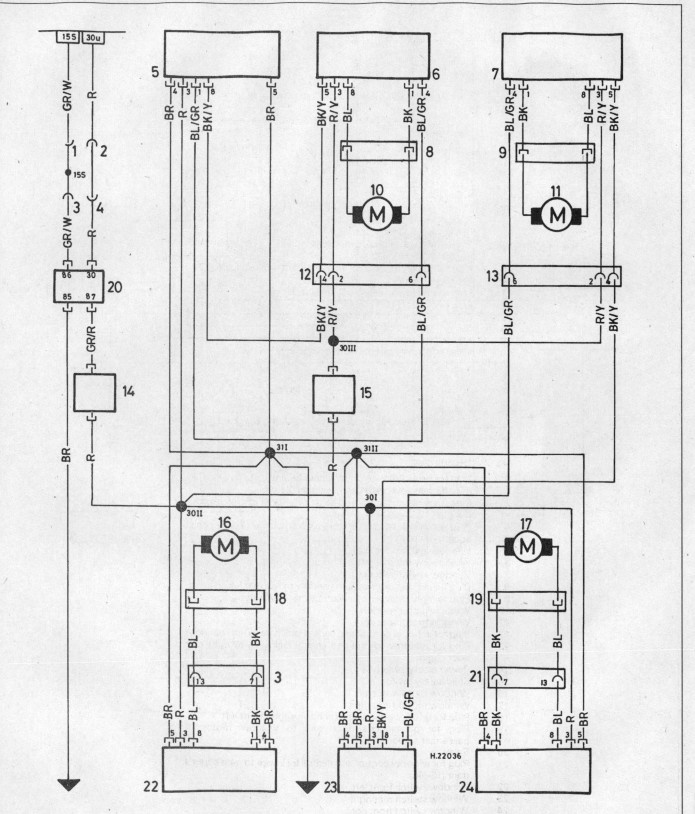

Typical electric window system wiring diagram

H.22036

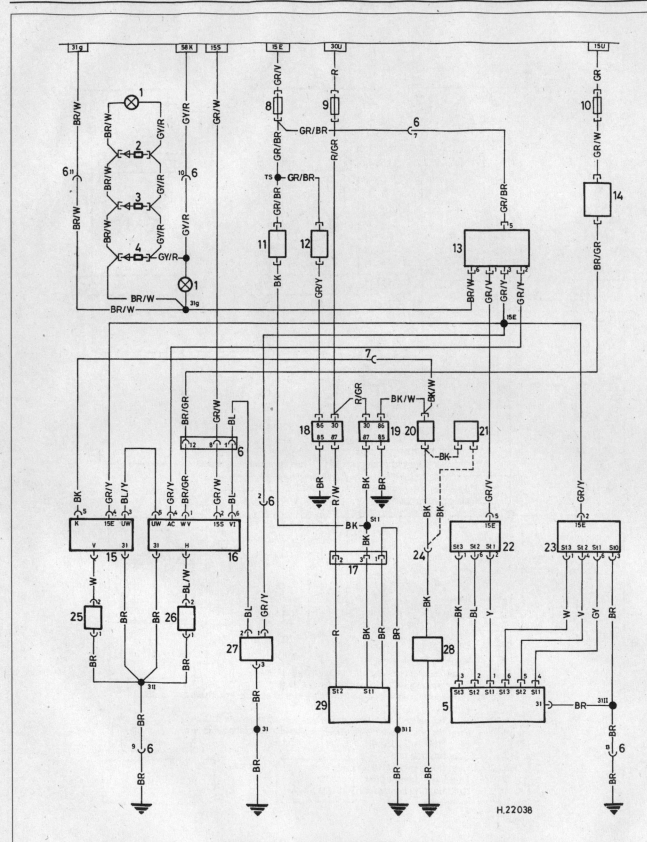

Typical heating and air conditioning system wiring diagram

H.22038

No	Description
1	Light for heater controls
2	Light diode III
3	Light diode II
4	Light diode I
5	Switch – heater/evaporator blower
6	Plug – heater control wire harness to centre wire harness (13-pin)
7	Plug – front wire harness section to heater controls
8	Fuse – heater blower
9	Fuse – extra fan stage II
10	Fuse – ind. lamp, reversing lights, tachometer and mirrors (power distributor)
11	Temperature switch 91°C – stage I
12	Temperature switch 99°C – stage II
13	Switch – air conditioner
14	Water valve
15	Evaporator temperature regulator
16	Air conditioner control unit (heater controls)
17	Plug – extra fan motor (on extra fan motor)
18	Relay – extra fan stage II (on power distributor)
19	Relay – extra fan stage I (on power distributor)
20	Switch – high pressure pressostat (drier)
21	Switch – temperature 110°C (only for 524 td)
22	Motor – heater blower
23	Motor – evaporator blower
24	Plug – high pressure pressostat to electromagnetic coupling
25	Evaporator temperature sensor (in evaporator)
26	Heater temperature sensor (in heater)
27	Inside temperature sensor (lower trim panel left)
28	Electromagnetic coupling for compressor
29	Motor – extra fan

Key to wiring diagram for heated seats

No	Description
1	Heating – passenger's seat
2	Seat heating connection – passenger's side
3	Seat heating switch – passenger's side
4	Plug for heated seat wire (driver's side) to special equipment plug (58K)
5	Plug for heated seat wire (driver's side) to passenger's side
6	Plug for heated seat wire (driver's side) to special equipment plug (15E and 30SA4)
7	Seat heating relay
8	Seat heating switch – driver's side
9	Heating – driver's seat
10	Seat heating connection – driver's side

12

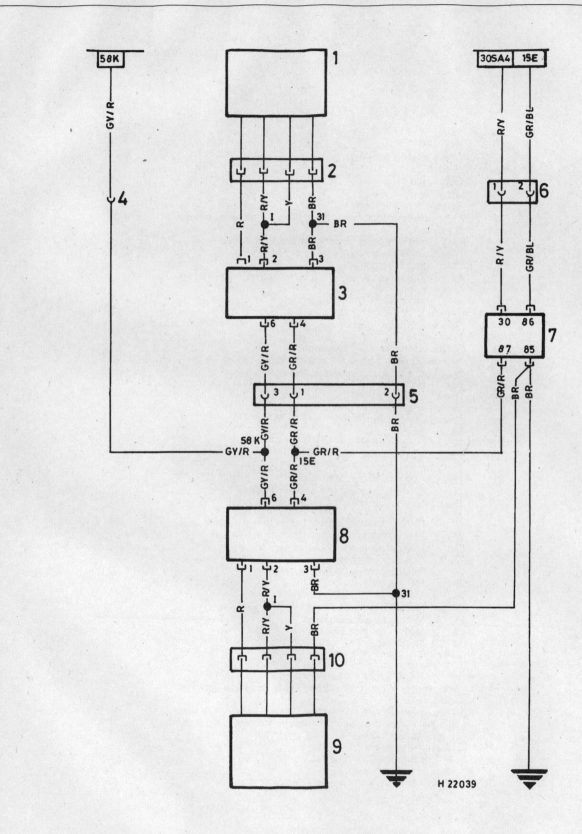

H 22039

Typical heated seats wiring diagram

Key to wiring diagram for memory power seats

No	Description
1	Plug connection for special equipment plug
2	Plug connection of wire for passenger's seat
3	Plug connection of wire for seat control with memory
4	Connection of wire for seat control with memory
5	Seat control switch
6	Backrest
7	Slide
8	Headrest
9	Height front
10	Height rear
11	Plug connection for seat backrest/slide control
12	Plug connection for seat headrest control
13	Plug connection for seat height control
14	Electronic control unit (underneath seat)
15	Plug connection of wire for seat control with memory
16	Plug connection of wire for seat with memory
17	Plug connection for seat control drive
18	Plug connection for memory switch
19	Plug connection for slide potentiometer
20	Plug connection for front height potentiometer
21	Plug connection for rear height potentiometer
22	Plug connection for headrest motor
23	Plug connection for backrest potentiometer
24	Plug connection for backrest motor
25	Memory switch
26	Motor – seat backrest control
27	Motor – headrest control
28	Motor – height control rear
29	Motor – height control front
30	Motor – slide

12

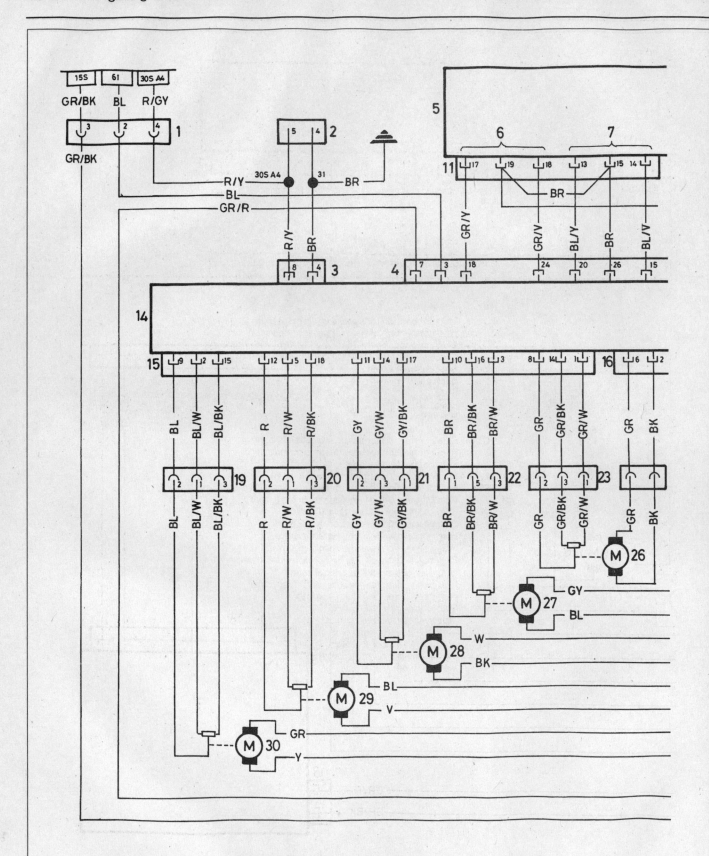

Typical wiring diagram for power seats with memory (1 of 2)

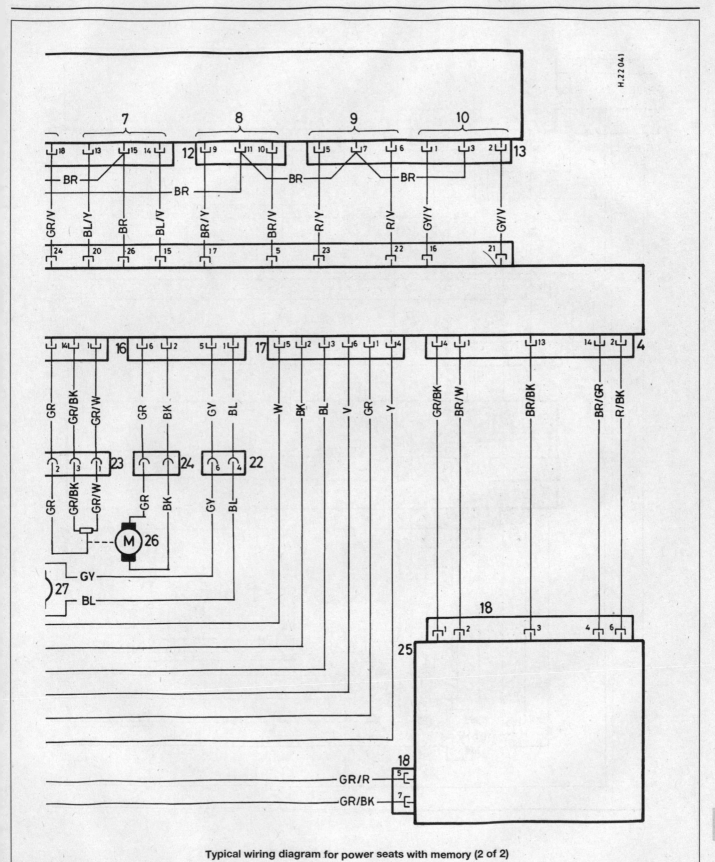

Typical wiring diagram for power seats with memory (2 of 2)

12

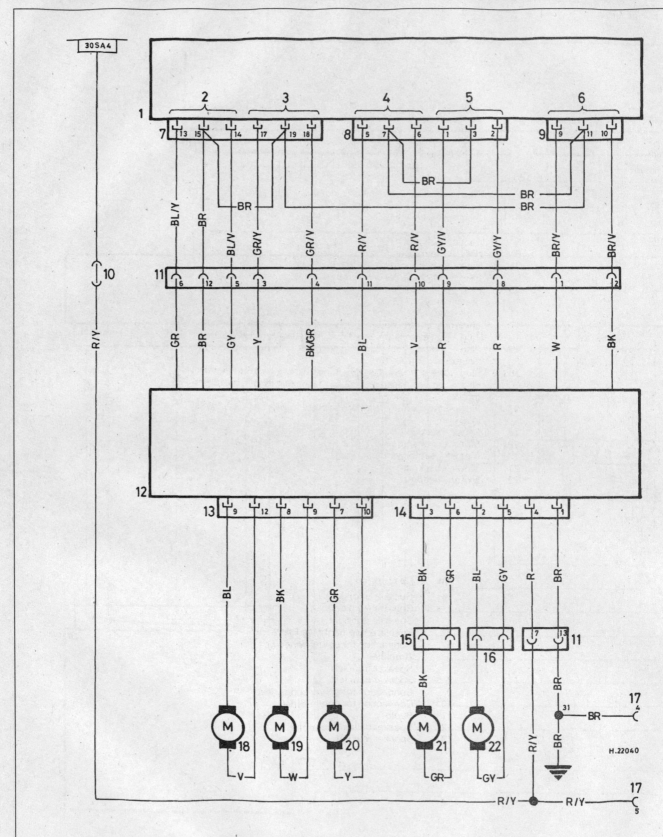

Typical wiring diagram for power seats without memory

Key to wiring diagram for power seats without memory

No	Description
1	Plug connection with special equipment plug
2	Backrest
3	Seat forward/backward
4	Headrest
5	Seat up/down front
6	Seat up/down rear
7	Plug – switch for backrest/seat control
8	Plug – switch for headrest control
9	Plug – switch for front/rear seat up/down control
10	Switch for power seats
11	Plug – power seat wire to power seat electronic control unit
12	Electronic control unit for power seats (below seats)
13	Plug – power seat drive to power seat electronic control unit
14	Plug – power backrest and headrest wire to power seat electronic control unit
15	Plug – power backrest and headrest wire to backrest motor
16	Plug – power backrest and headrest wire to the headrest motor
17	Plug – power seat wire on driver's side to wire on passenger's side
18	Motor – seat up/down front
19	Motor – seat up/down rear
20	Motor – seat forward/backward
21	Motor – backrest
22	Motor – headrest

No	Description
1	Speaker door right
2	Speaker front right
3	Speaker rear right
4	Special equipment plug RA12
5	Connection for power windows
6	Amplifier
7	Speaker front left
8	Speaker door left
9	Connection for power supply lead
10	Connection for power aerial
11	Radio
12	Speaker balance control
13	Speaker rear left

12

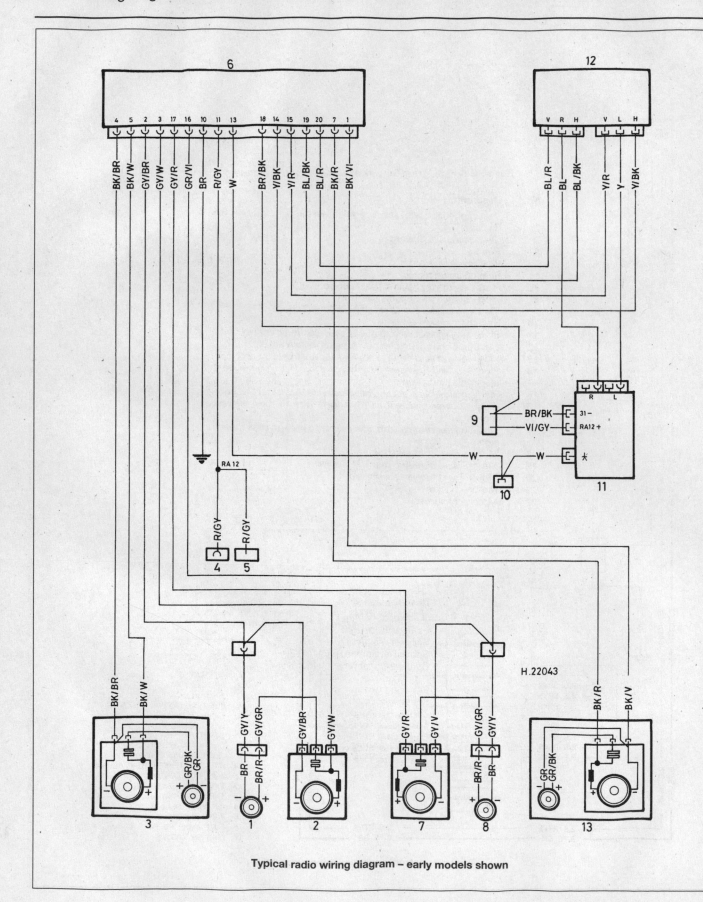

Typical radio wiring diagram – early models shown

H.22043

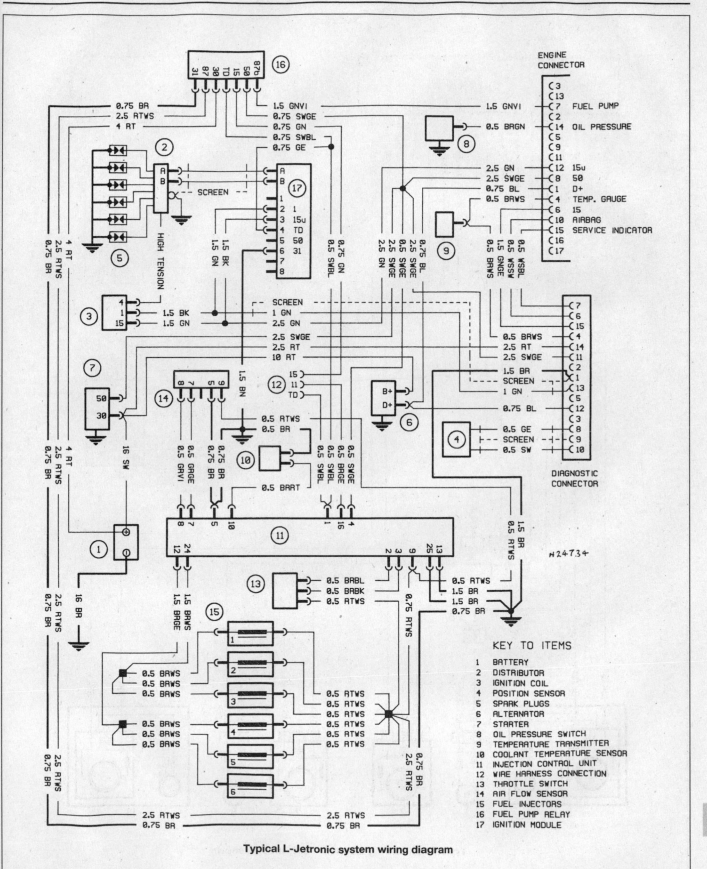

Typical L-Jetronic system wiring diagram

KEY TO ITEMS

1 BATTERY
2 DISTRIBUTOR
3 IGNITION COIL
4 POSITION SENSOR
5 SPARK PLUGS
6 ALTERNATOR
7 STARTER
8 OIL PRESSURE SWITCH
9 TEMPERATURE TRANSMITTER
10 COOLANT TEMPERATURE SENSOR
11 INJECTION CONTROL UNIT
12 WIRE HARNESS CONNECTION
13 THROTTLE SWITCH
14 AIR FLOW SENSOR
15 FUEL INJECTORS
16 FUEL PUMP RELAY
17 IGNITION MODULE

12

Notes

This is a guide to getting your vehicle through the MOT test. Obviously it will not be possible to examine the vehicle to the same standard as the professional MOT tester. However, working through the following checks will enable you to identify any problem areas before submitting the vehicle for the test.

Where a testable component is in borderline condition, the tester has discretion in deciding whether to pass or fail it. The basis of such discretion is whether the tester would be happy for a close relative or friend to use the vehicle with the component in that condition. If the vehicle presented is clean and evidently well cared for, the tester may be more inclined to pass a borderline component than if the vehicle is scruffy and apparently neglected.

It has only been possible to summarise the test requirements here, based on the regulations in force at the time of printing. Test standards are becoming increasingly stringent, although there are some exemptions for older vehicles. For full details obtain a copy of the Haynes publication Pass the MOT! (available from stockists of Haynes manuals).

An assistant will be needed to help carry out some of these checks.

The checks have been sub-divided into four categories, as follows:

1 Checks carried out **FROM THE DRIVER'S SEAT**

2 Checks carried out **WITH THE VEHICLE ON THE GROUND**

3 Checks carried out **WITH THE VEHICLE RAISED AND THE WHEELS FREE TO TURN**

4 Checks carried out on **YOUR VEHICLE'S EXHAUST EMISSION SYSTEM**

---

1 Checks carried out **FROM THE DRIVER'S SEAT**

Handbrake

☐ Test the operation of the handbrake. Excessive travel (too many clicks) indicates incorrect brake or cable adjustment.
☐ Check that the handbrake cannot be released by tapping the lever sideways. Check the security of the lever mountings.

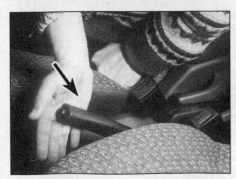

Footbrake

☐ Depress the brake pedal and check that it does not creep down to the floor, indicating a master cylinder fault. Release the pedal, wait a few seconds, then depress it again. If the pedal travels nearly to the floor before firm resistance is felt, brake adjustment or repair is necessary. If the pedal feels spongy, there is air in the hydraulic system which must be removed by bleeding.

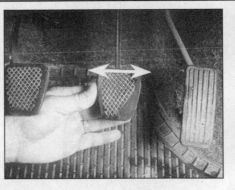

☐ Check that the brake pedal is secure and in good condition. Check also for signs of fluid leaks on the pedal, floor or carpets, which would indicate failed seals in the brake master cylinder.
☐ Check the servo unit (when applicable) by operating the brake pedal several times, then keeping the pedal depressed and starting the engine. As the engine starts, the pedal will move down slightly. If not, the vacuum hose or the servo itself may be faulty.

Steering wheel and column

☐ Examine the steering wheel for fractures or looseness of the hub, spokes or rim.
☐ Move the steering wheel from side to side and then up and down. Check that the steering wheel is not loose on the column, indicating wear or a loose retaining nut. Continue moving the steering wheel as before, but also turn it slightly from left to right.
☐ Check that the steering wheel is not loose on the column, and that there is no abnormal

movement of the steering wheel, indicating wear in the column support bearings or couplings.

Windscreen and mirrors

☐ The windscreen must be free of cracks or other significant damage within the driver's field of view. (Small stone chips are acceptable.) Rear view mirrors must be secure, intact, and capable of being adjusted.

290mm

Seat belts and seats

Note: *The following checks are applicable to all seat belts, front and rear.*

☐ Examine the webbing of all the belts (including rear belts if fitted) for cuts, serious fraying or deterioration. Fasten and unfasten each belt to check the buckles. If applicable, check the retracting mechanism. Check the security of all seat belt mountings accessible from inside the vehicle.

☐ The front seats themselves must be securely attached and the backrests must lock in the upright position.

Doors

☐ Both front doors must be able to be opened and closed from outside and inside, and must latch securely when closed.

2 Checks carried out WITH THE VEHICLE ON THE GROUND

Vehicle identification

☐ Number plates must be in good condition, secure and legible, with letters and numbers correctly spaced – spacing at (A) should be twice that at (B).

☐ The VIN plate and/or homologation plate must be legible.

Electrical equipment

☐ Switch on the ignition and check the operation of the horn.

☐ Check the windscreen washers and wipers, examining the wiper blades; renew damaged or perished blades. Also check the operation of the stop-lights.

☐ Check the operation of the sidelights and number plate lights. The lenses and reflectors must be secure, clean and undamaged.

☐ Check the operation and alignment of the headlights. The headlight reflectors must not be tarnished and the lenses must be undamaged.

☐ Switch on the ignition and check the operation of the direction indicators (including the instrument panel tell-tale) and the hazard warning lights. Operation of the sidelights and stop-lights must not affect the indicators - if it does, the cause is usually a bad earth at the rear light cluster.

☐ Check the operation of the rear foglight(s), including the warning light on the instrument panel or in the switch.

Footbrake

☐ Examine the master cylinder, brake pipes and servo unit for leaks, loose mountings, corrosion or other damage.

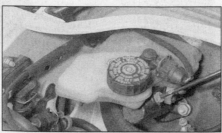

☐ The fluid reservoir must be secure and the fluid level must be between the upper (A) and lower (B) markings.

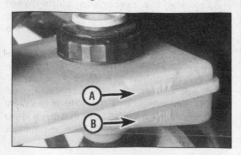

☐ Inspect both front brake flexible hoses for cracks or deterioration of the rubber. Turn the steering from lock to lock, and ensure that the hoses do not contact the wheel, tyre, or any part of the steering or suspension mechanism. With the brake pedal firmly depressed, check the hoses for bulges or leaks under pressure.

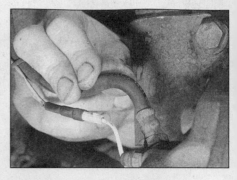

Steering and suspension

☐ Have your assistant turn the steering wheel from side to side slightly, up to the point where the steering gear just begins to transmit this movement to the roadwheels. Check for excessive free play between the steering wheel and the steering gear, indicating wear or insecurity of the steering column joints, the column-to-steering gear coupling, or the steering gear itself.

☐ Have your assistant turn the steering wheel more vigorously in each direction, so that the roadwheels just begin to turn. As this is done, examine all the steering joints, linkages, fittings and attachments. Renew any component that shows signs of wear or damage. On vehicles with power steering, check the security and condition of the steering pump, drivebelt and hoses.

☐ Check that the vehicle is standing level, and at approximately the correct ride height.

Shock absorbers

☐ Depress each corner of the vehicle in turn, then release it. The vehicle should rise and then settle in its normal position. If the vehicle continues to rise and fall, the shock absorber is defective. A shock absorber which has seized will also cause the vehicle to fail.

Exhaust system

☐ Start the engine. With your assistant holding a rag over the tailpipe, check the entire system for leaks. Repair or renew leaking sections.

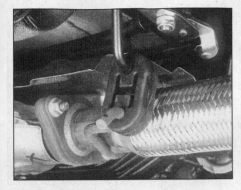

3 Checks carried out
WITH THE VEHICLE RAISED AND THE WHEELS FREE TO TURN

Jack up the front and rear of the vehicle, and securely support it on axle stands. Position the stands clear of the suspension assemblies. Ensure that the wheels are clear of the ground and that the steering can be turned from lock to lock.

Steering mechanism

☐ Have your assistant turn the steering from lock to lock. Check that the steering turns smoothly, and that no part of the steering mechanism, including a wheel or tyre, fouls any brake hose or pipe or any part of the body structure.

☐ Examine the steering rack rubber gaiters for damage or insecurity of the retaining clips. If power steering is fitted, check for signs of damage or leakage of the fluid hoses, pipes or connections. Also check for excessive stiffness or binding of the steering, a missing split pin or locking device, or severe corrosion of the body structure within 30 cm of any steering component attachment point.

Front and rear suspension and wheel bearings

☐ Starting at the front right-hand side, grasp the roadwheel at the 3 o'clock and 9 o'clock positions and shake it vigorously. Check for free play or insecurity at the wheel bearings, suspension balljoints, or suspension mountings, pivots and attachments.

☐ Now grasp the wheel at the 12 o'clock and 6 o'clock positions and repeat the previous inspection. Spin the wheel, and check for roughness or tightness of the front wheel bearing.

☐ If excess free play is suspected at a component pivot point, this can be confirmed by using a large screwdriver or similar tool and levering between the mounting and the component attachment. This will confirm whether the wear is in the pivot bush, its retaining bolt, or in the mounting itself (the bolt holes can often become elongated).

☐ Carry out all the above checks at the other front wheel, and then at both rear wheels.

Springs and shock absorbers

☐ Examine the suspension struts (when applicable) for serious fluid leakage, corrosion, or damage to the casing. Also check the security of the mounting points.

☐ If coil springs are fitted, check that the spring ends locate in their seats, and that the spring is not corroded, cracked or broken.

☐ If leaf springs are fitted, check that all leaves are intact, that the axle is securely attached to each spring, and that there is no deterioration of the spring eye mountings, bushes, and shackles.

☐ The same general checks apply to vehicles fitted with other suspension types, such as torsion bars, hydraulic displacer units, etc. Ensure that all mountings and attachments are secure, that there are no signs of excessive wear, corrosion or damage, and (on hydraulic types) that there are no fluid leaks or damaged pipes.

☐ Inspect the shock absorbers for signs of serious fluid leakage. Check for wear of the mounting bushes or attachments, or damage to the body of the unit.

Driveshafts (fwd vehicles only)

☐ Rotate each front wheel in turn and inspect the constant velocity joint gaiters for splits or damage. Also check that each driveshaft is straight and undamaged.

Braking system

☐ If possible without dismantling, check brake pad wear and disc condition. Ensure that the friction lining material has not worn excessively, (A) and that the discs are not fractured, pitted, scored or badly worn (B).

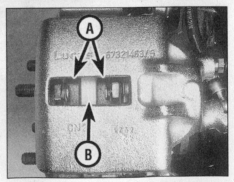

☐ Examine all the rigid brake pipes underneath the vehicle, and the flexible hose(s) at the rear. Look for corrosion, chafing or insecurity of the pipes, and for signs of bulging under pressure, chafing, splits or deterioration of the flexible hoses.

☐ Look for signs of fluid leaks at the brake calipers or on the brake backplates. Repair or renew leaking components.

☐ Slowly spin each wheel, while your assistant depresses and releases the footbrake. Ensure that each brake is operating and does not bind when the pedal is released.

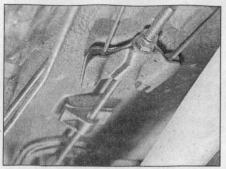

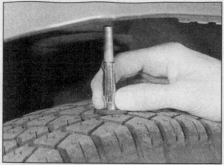

☐ Examine the handbrake mechanism, checking for frayed or broken cables, excessive corrosion, or wear or insecurity of the linkage. Check that the mechanism works on each relevant wheel, and releases fully, without binding.

☐ It is not possible to test brake efficiency without special equipment, but a road test can be carried out later to check that the vehicle pulls up in a straight line.

Fuel and exhaust systems

☐ Inspect the fuel tank (including the filler cap), fuel pipes, hoses and unions. All components must be secure and free from leaks.

☐ Examine the exhaust system over its entire length, checking for any damaged, broken or missing mountings, security of the retaining clamps and rust or corrosion.

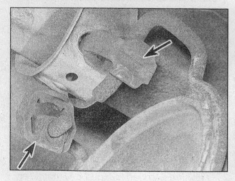

Wheels and tyres

☐ Examine the sidewalls and tread area of each tyre in turn. Check for cuts, tears, lumps, bulges, separation of the tread, and exposure of the ply or cord due to wear or damage. Check that the tyre bead is correctly seated on the wheel rim, that the valve is sound and

properly seated, and that the wheel is not distorted or damaged.

☐ Check that the tyres are of the correct size for the vehicle, that they are of the same size and type on each axle, and that the pressures are correct.

☐ Check the tyre tread depth. The legal minimum at the time of writing is 1.6 mm over at least three-quarters of the tread width. Abnormal tread wear may indicate incorrect front wheel alignment.

Body corrosion

☐ Check the condition of the entire vehicle structure for signs of corrosion in load-bearing areas. (These include chassis box sections, side sills, cross-members, pillars, and all suspension, steering, braking system and seat belt mountings and anchorages.) Any corrosion which has seriously reduced the thickness of a load-bearing area is likely to cause the vehicle to fail. In this case professional repairs are likely to be needed.

☐ Damage or corrosion which causes sharp or otherwise dangerous edges to be exposed will also cause the vehicle to fail.

4 Checks carried out on YOUR VEHICLE'S EXHAUST EMISSION SYSTEM

Petrol models

☐ Have the engine at normal operating temperature, and make sure that it is in good tune (ignition system in good order, air filter element clean, etc).

☐ Before any measurements are carried out, raise the engine speed to around 2500 rpm, and hold it at this speed for 20 seconds. Allow

the engine speed to return to idle, and watch for smoke emissions from the exhaust tailpipe. If the idle speed is obviously much too high, or if dense blue or clearly-visible black smoke comes from the tailpipe for more than 5 seconds, the vehicle will fail. As a rule of thumb, blue smoke signifies oil being burnt (engine wear) while black smoke signifies unburnt fuel (dirty air cleaner element, or other carburettor or fuel system fault).

☐ An exhaust gas analyser capable of measuring carbon monoxide (CO) and hydrocarbons (HC) is now needed. If such an instrument cannot be hired or borrowed, a local garage may agree to perform the check for a small fee.

CO emissions (mixture)

☐ At the time of writing, the maximum CO level at idle is 3.5% for vehicles first used after August 1986 and 4.5% for older vehicles. From January 1996 a much tighter limit (around 0.5%) applies to catalyst-equipped vehicles first used from August 1992. If the CO level cannot be reduced far enough to pass the test (and the fuel and ignition systems are otherwise in good condition) then the carburettor is badly worn, or there is some problem in the fuel injection system or catalytic converter (as applicable).

HC emissions

☐ With the CO emissions within limits, HC emissions must be no more than 1200 ppm (parts per million). If the vehicle fails this test at idle, it can be re-tested at around 2000 rpm; if the HC level is then 1200 ppm or less, this counts as a pass.

☐ Excessive HC emissions can be caused by oil being burnt, but they are more likely to be due to unburnt fuel.

Diesel models

☐ The only emission test applicable to Diesel engines is the measuring of exhaust smoke density. The test involves accelerating the engine several times to its maximum unloaded speed.

Note: *It is of the utmost importance that the engine timing belt is in good condition before the test is carried out.*

☐ Excessive smoke can be caused by a dirty air cleaner element. Otherwise, professional advice may be needed to find the cause.

Introduction

A selection of good tools is a fundamental requirement for anyone contemplating the maintenance and repair of a motor vehicle. For the owner who does not possess any, their purchase will prove a considerable expense, offsetting some of the savings made by doing-it-yourself. However, provided that the tools purchased meet the relevant national safety standards and are of good quality, they will last for many years and prove an extremely worthwhile investment.

To help the average owner to decide which tools are needed to carry out the various tasks detailed in this manual, we have compiled three lists of tools under the following headings: *Maintenance and minor repair, Repair and overhaul*, and *Special*. Newcomers to practical mechanics should start off with the *Maintenance and minor repair* tool kit, and confine themselves to the simpler jobs around the vehicle. Then, as confidence and experience grow, more difficult tasks can be undertaken, with extra tools being purchased as, and when, they are needed. In this way, a *Maintenance and minor repair* tool kit can be built up into a *Repair and overhaul* tool kit over a considerable period of time, without any major cash outlays. The experienced do-it-yourselfer will have a tool kit good enough for most repair and overhaul procedures, and will add tools from the *Special* category when it is felt that the expense is justified by the amount of use to which these tools will be put.

Maintenance and minor repair tool kit

The tools given in this list should be considered as a minimum requirement if routine maintenance, servicing and minor repair operations are to be undertaken. We recommend the purchase of combination spanners (ring one end, open-ended the other); although more expensive than open-ended ones, they do give the advantages of both types of spanner.

☐ *Combination spanners:*
  Metric - 8, 9, 10, 11, 12, 13, 14, 15, 16, 17, 19, 21, 22, 24 & 26 mm
☐ *Adjustable spanner - 35 mm jaw (approx)*
☐ *Transmission drain plug key (Allen type)*
☐ *Set of feeler gauges*
☐ *Spark plug spanner (with rubber insert)*
☐ *Spark plug gap adjustment tool*
☐ *Brake bleed nipple spanner*
☐ *Screwdrivers:*
  Flat blade - approx 100 mm long x 6 mm dia
  Cross blade - approx 100 mm long x 6 mm dia
☐ *Combination pliers*
☐ *Hacksaw (junior)*
☐ *Tyre pump*
☐ *Tyre pressure gauge*
☐ *Oil can*
☐ *Oil filter removal tool*
☐ *Fine emery cloth*
☐ *Wire brush (small)*
☐ *Funnel (medium size)*

Repair and overhaul tool kit

These tools are virtually essential for anyone undertaking any major repairs to a motor vehicle, and are additional to those given in the *Maintenance and minor repair* list. Included in this list is a comprehensive set of sockets. Although these are expensive, they will be found invaluable as they are so versatile - particularly if various drives are included in the set. We recommend the half-inch square-drive type, as this can be used with most proprietary torque wrenches. If you cannot afford a socket set, even bought piecemeal, then inexpensive tubular box spanners are a useful alternative.

The tools in this list will occasionally need to be supplemented by tools from the *Special* list:

☐ *Sockets (or box spanners) to cover range in previous list*
☐ *Reversible ratchet drive (for use with sockets) (see illustration)*
☐ *Extension piece, 250 mm (for use with sockets)*
☐ *Universal joint (for use with sockets)*
☐ *Torque wrench (for use with sockets)*
☐ *Self-locking grips*
☐ *Ball pein hammer*
☐ *Soft-faced mallet (plastic/aluminium or rubber)*
☐ *Screwdrivers:*
  Flat blade - long & sturdy, short (chubby), and narrow (electrician's) types
  Cross blade - Long & sturdy, and short (chubby) types
☐ *Pliers:*
  Long-nosed
  Side cutters (electrician's)
  Circlip (internal and external)
☐ *Cold chisel - 25 mm*
☐ *Scriber*
☐ *Scraper*
☐ *Centre-punch*
☐ *Pin punch*
☐ *Hacksaw*
☐ *Brake hose clamp*
☐ *Brake/clutch bleeding kit*
☐ *Selection of twist drills*

☐ *Steel rule/straight-edge*
☐ *Allen keys (inc. splined/Torx type) (see illustrations)*
☐ *Selection of files*
☐ *Wire brush*
☐ *Axle stands*
☐ *Jack (strong trolley or hydraulic type)*
☐ *Light with extension lead*

Special tools

The tools in this list are those which are not used regularly, are expensive to buy, or which need to be used in accordance with their manufacturers' instructions. Unless relatively difficult mechanical jobs are undertaken frequently, it will not be economic to buy many of these tools. Where this is the case, you could consider clubbing together with friends (or joining a motorists' club) to make a joint purchase, or borrowing the tools against a deposit from a local garage or tool hire specialist. It is worth noting that many of the larger DIY superstores now carry a large range of special tools for hire at modest rates.

The following list contains only those tools and instruments freely available to the public, and not those special tools produced by the vehicle manufacturer specifically for its dealer network. You will find occasional references to these manufacturers' special tools in the text of this manual. Generally, an alternative method of doing the job without the vehicle manufacturers' special tool is given. However, sometimes there is no alternative to using them. Where this is the case and the relevant tool cannot be bought or borrowed, you will have to entrust the work to a franchised garage.

☐ *Valve spring compressor (see illustration)*
☐ *Valve grinding tool*
☐ *Piston ring compressor (see illustration)*
☐ *Piston ring removal/installation tool (see illustration)*
☐ *Cylinder bore hone (see illustration)*
☐ *Balljoint separator*
☐ *Coil spring compressors (where applicable)*
☐ *Two/three-legged hub and bearing puller (see illustration)*

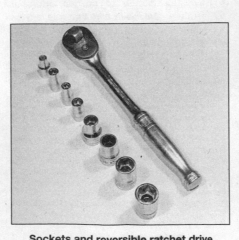

Sockets and reversible ratchet drive

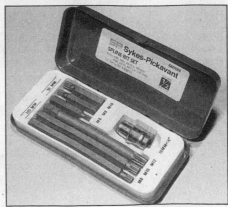

Spline bit set

Tools and Working Facilities

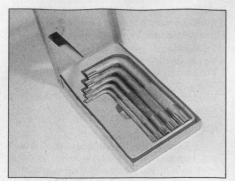

Spline key set

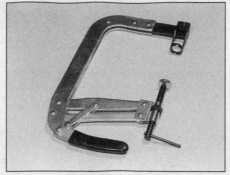

Valve spring compressor

Piston ring compressor

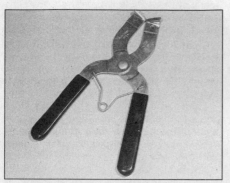

Piston ring removal/installation tool

Cylinder bore hone

Three-legged hub and bearing puller

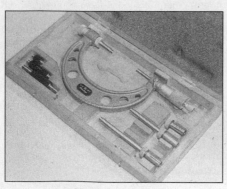

Micrometer set

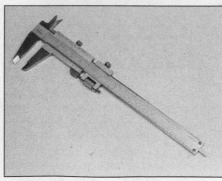

Vernier calipers

Dial test indicator and magnetic stand

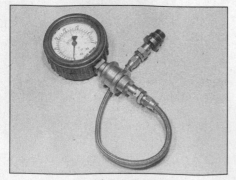

Compression testing gauge

Clutch plate alignment set

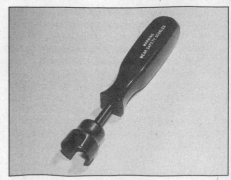

Brake shoe steady spring cup removal tool

- ☐ Impact screwdriver
- ☐ Micrometer and/or vernier calipers **(see illustrations)**
- ☐ Dial gauge **(see illustration)**
- ☐ Universal electrical multi-meter
- ☐ Cylinder compression gauge **(see illustration)**
- ☐ Clutch plate alignment set **(see illustration)**
- ☐ Brake shoe steady spring cup removal tool **(see illustration)**
- ☐ Bush and bearing removal/installation set **(see illustration)**
- ☐ Stud extractors **(see illustration)**
- ☐ Tap and die set **(see illustration)**
- ☐ Lifting tackle
- ☐ Trolley jack

Buying tools

For practically all tools, a tool factor is the best source, since he will have a very comprehensive range compared with the average garage or accessory shop. Having said that, accessory shops often offer excellent quality tools at discount prices, so it pays to shop around.

Remember, you don't have to buy the most expensive items on the shelf, but it is always advisable to steer clear of the very cheap tools. There are plenty of good tools around at reasonable prices, but always aim to purchase items which meet the relevant national safety standards. If in doubt, ask the proprietor or manager of the shop for advice before making a purchase.

Care and maintenance of tools

Having purchased a reasonable tool kit, it is necessary to keep the tools in a clean and serviceable condition. After use, always wipe off any dirt, grease and metal particles using a clean, dry cloth, before putting the tools away. Never leave them lying around after they have been used. A simple tool rack on the garage or workshop wall for items such as screwdrivers and pliers is a good idea. Store all normal spanners and sockets in a metal box. Any measuring instruments, gauges, meters, etc, must be carefully stored where they cannot be damaged or become rusty.

Take a little care when tools are used. Hammer heads inevitably become marked, and screwdrivers lose the keen edge on their blades from time to time. A little timely attention with emery cloth or a file will soon restore items like this to a good serviceable finish.

Working facilities

Not to be forgotten when discussing tools is the workshop itself. If anything more than routine maintenance is to be carried out, some form of suitable working area becomes essential.

It is appreciated that many an owner-mechanic is forced by circumstances to remove an engine or similar item without the benefit of a garage or workshop. Having done this, any repairs should always be done under the cover of a roof.

Wherever possible, any dismantling should be done on a clean, flat workbench or table at a suitable working height.

Any workbench needs a vice; one with a jaw opening of 100 mm is suitable for most jobs. As mentioned previously, some clean dry storage space is also required for tools, as well as for any lubricants, cleaning fluids, touch-up paints and so on, which become necessary.

Another item which may be required, and which has a much more general usage, is an electric drill with a chuck capacity of at least 8 mm. This, together with a good range of twist drills, is virtually essential for fitting accessories.

Last, but not least, always keep a supply of old newspapers and clean, lint-free rags available, and try to keep any working area as clean as possible.

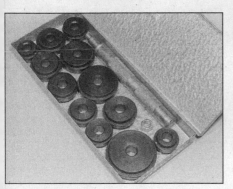

Bush and bearing removal/installation set

Stud extractor set

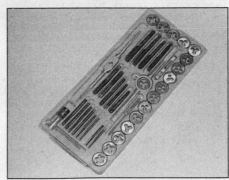

Tap and die set

Whenever servicing, repair or overhaul work is carried out on the car or its components, observe the following procedures and instructions. This will assist in carrying out the operation efficiently and to a professional standard of workmanship.

Joint mating faces and gaskets

When separating components at their mating faces, never insert screwdrivers or similar implements into the joint between the faces in order to prise them apart. This can cause severe damage which results in oil leaks, coolant leaks, etc upon reassembly. Separation is usually achieved by tapping along the joint with a soft-faced hammer in order to break the seal. However, note that this method may not be suitable where dowels are used for component location.

Where a gasket is used between the mating faces of two components, a new one must be fitted on reassembly; fit it dry unless otherwise stated in the repair procedure. Make sure that the mating faces are clean and dry, with all traces of old gasket removed. When cleaning a joint face, use a tool which is unlikely to score or damage the face, and remove any burrs or nicks with an oilstone or fine file.

Make sure that tapped holes are cleaned with a pipe cleaner, and keep them free of jointing compound, if this is being used, unless specifically instructed otherwise.

Ensure that all orifices, channels or pipes are clear, and blow through them, preferably using compressed air.

Oil seals

Oil seals can be removed by levering them out with a wide flat-bladed screwdriver or similar implement. Alternatively, a number of self-tapping screws may be screwed into the seal, and these used as a purchase for pliers or some similar device in order to pull the seal free.

Whenever an oil seal is removed from its working location, either individually or as part of an assembly, it should be renewed.

The very fine sealing lip of the seal is easily damaged, and will not seal if the surface it contacts is not completely clean and free from scratches, nicks or grooves. If the original sealing surface of the component cannot be restored, and the manufacturer has not made provision for slight relocation of the seal relative to the sealing surface, the component should be renewed.

Protect the lips of the seal from any surface which may damage them in the course of fitting. Use tape or a conical sleeve where possible. Lubricate the seal lips with oil before fitting and, on dual-lipped seals, fill the space between the lips with grease.

Unless otherwise stated, oil seals must be fitted with their sealing lips toward the lubricant to be sealed.

Use a tubular drift or block of wood of the appropriate size to install the seal and, if the seal housing is shouldered, drive the seal down to the shoulder. If the seal housing is unshouldered, the seal should be fitted with its face flush with the housing top face (unless otherwise instructed).

Screw threads and fastenings

Seized nuts, bolts and screws are quite a common occurrence where corrosion has set in, and the use of penetrating oil or releasing fluid will often overcome this problem if the offending item is soaked for a while before attempting to release it. The use of an impact driver may also provide a means of releasing such stubborn fastening devices, when used in conjunction with the appropriate screwdriver bit or socket. If none of these methods works, it may be necessary to resort to the careful application of heat, or the use of a hacksaw or nut splitter device.

Studs are usually removed by locking two nuts together on the threaded part, and then using a spanner on the lower nut to unscrew the stud. Studs or bolts which have broken off below the surface of the component in which they are mounted can sometimes be removed using a stud extractor. Always ensure that a blind tapped hole is completely free from oil, grease, water or other fluid before installing the bolt or stud. Failure to do this could cause the housing to crack due to the hydraulic action of the bolt or stud as it is screwed in.

When tightening a castellated nut to accept a split pin, tighten the nut to the specified torque, where applicable, and then tighten further to the next split pin hole. Never slacken the nut to align the split pin hole, unless stated in the repair procedure.

When checking or retightening a nut or bolt to a specified torque setting, slacken the nut or bolt by a quarter of a turn, and then retighten to the specified setting. However, this should not be attempted where angular tightening has been used.

For some screw fastenings, notably cylinder head bolts or nuts, torque wrench settings are no longer specified for the latter stages of tightening, "angle-tightening" being called up instead. Typically, a fairly low torque wrench setting will be applied to the bolts/nuts in the correct sequence, followed by one or more stages of tightening through specified angles.

Locknuts, locktabs and washers

Any fastening which will rotate against a component or housing during tightening should always have a washer between it and the relevant component or housing.

Spring or split washers should always be renewed when they are used to lock a critical component such as a big-end bearing retaining bolt or nut. Locktabs which are folded over to retain a nut or bolt should always be renewed.

Self-locking nuts can be re-used in non-critical areas, providing resistance can be felt when the locking portion passes over the bolt or stud thread. However, it should be noted that self-locking stiffnuts tend to lose their effectiveness after long periods of use, and should then be renewed as a matter of course.

Split pins must always be replaced with new ones of the correct size for the hole.

When thread-locking compound is found on the threads of a fastener which is to be re-used, it should be cleaned off with a wire brush and solvent, and fresh compound applied on reassembly.

Special tools

Some repair procedures in this manual entail the use of special tools such as a press, two or three-legged pullers, spring compressors, etc. Wherever possible, suitable readily-available alternatives to the manufacturer's special tools are described, and are shown in use. In some instances, where no alternative is possible, it has been necessary to resort to the use of a manufacturer's tool, and this has been done for reasons of safety as well as the efficient completion of the repair operation. Unless you are highly-skilled and have a thorough understanding of the procedures described, never attempt to bypass the use of any special tool when the procedure described specifies its use. Not only is there a very great risk of personal injury, but expensive damage could be caused to the components involved.

Environmental considerations

When disposing of used engine oil, brake fluid, antifreeze, etc, give due consideration to any detrimental environmental effects. Do not, for instance, pour any of the above liquids down drains into the general sewage system, or onto the ground to soak away. Many local council refuse tips provide a facility for waste oil disposal, as do some garages. If none of these facilities are available, consult your local Environmental Health Department, or the National Rivers Authority, for further advice.

With the universal tightening-up of legislation regarding the emission of environmentally-harmful substances from motor vehicles, most vehicles have tamperproof devices fitted to the main adjustment points of the fuel system. These devices are primarily designed to prevent unqualified persons from adjusting the fuel/air mixture, with the chance of a consequent increase in toxic emissions. If such devices are found during servicing or overhaul, they should, wherever possible, be renewed or refitted in accordance with the manufacturer's requirements or current legislation.

OIL CARE
FOLLOW THE CODE

OIL BANK LINE
0800 66 33 66

Note: It is antisocial and illegal to dump oil down the drain. To find the location of your local oil recycling bank, call this number free.

Engine

- [ ] Engine will not rotate when attempting to start
- [ ] Engine rotates, but will not start
- [ ] Engine hard to start when cold
- [ ] Engine hard to start when hot
- [ ] Starter motor noisy or excessively-rough in engagement
- [ ] Engine starts, but stops immediately
- [ ] Oil puddle under engine
- [ ] Engine idles erratically
- [ ] Engine misses at idle speed
- [ ] Engine misses throughout driving speed range
- [ ] Engine misfires on acceleration
- [ ] Engine surges while holding accelerator steady
- [ ] Engine stalls
- [ ] Engine lacks power
- [ ] Engine backfires
- [ ] Pinking or knocking engine sounds when accelerating or driving uphill
- [ ] Engine runs with oil pressure light on
- [ ] Engine runs-on after switching off

Engine electrical system

- [ ] Battery will not hold charge
- [ ] Ignition (no-charge) warning light fails to go out
- [ ] Ignition (no-charge) warning light fails to come on when key is turned

Fuel system

- [ ] Excessive fuel consumption
- [ ] Fuel leakage and/or fuel odour

Cooling system

- [ ] Overheating
- [ ] Overcooling
- [ ] External coolant leakage
- [ ] Internal coolant leakage
- [ ] Coolant loss
- [ ] Poor coolant circulation

Clutch

- [ ] Pedal travels to floor - no pressure or very little resistance
- [ ] Fluid in area of master cylinder dust cover and on pedal
- [ ] Fluid on slave cylinder
- [ ] Pedal feels "spongy" when depressed
- [ ] Unable to select gears
- [ ] Clutch slips (engine speed increases with no increase in vehicle speed)
- [ ] Grabbing (chattering) as clutch is engaged
- [ ] Noise in clutch area
- [ ] Clutch pedal stays on floor
- [ ] High pedal effort

Manual transmission

- [ ] Vibration
- [ ] Noisy in neutral with engine running
- [ ] Noisy in one particular gear
- [ ] Noisy in all gears
- [ ] Slips out of gear
- [ ] Leaks lubricant

Automatic transmission

- [ ] Fluid leakage
- [ ] Transmission fluid brown, or has a burned smell
- [ ] General shift mechanism problems
- [ ] Transmission will not kickdown with accelerator pedal pressed to the floor
- [ ] Engine will start in gears other than Park or Neutral
- [ ] Transmission slips, shifts roughly, is noisy, or has no drive in forward or reverse gears

Brakes

- [ ] Vehicle pulls to one side during braking
- [ ] Noise (high-pitched squeal) when the brakes are applied
- [ ] Brake vibration (pedal pulsates)
- [ ] Excessive pedal effort required to stop vehicle
- [ ] Excessive brake pedal travel
- [ ] Dragging brakes
- [ ] Grabbing or uneven braking action
- [ ] Brake pedal feels "spongy" when depressed
- [ ] Brake pedal travels to the floor with little resistance
- [ ] Handbrake does not hold

Suspension and steering

- [ ] Vehicle pulls to one side
- [ ] Abnormal or excessive tyre wear
- [ ] Wheel makes a "thumping" noise
- [ ] Shimmy, shake or vibration
- [ ] High steering effort
- [ ] Poor steering self-centring
- [ ] Abnormal noise at the front end
- [ ] Wandering or poor steering stability
- [ ] Erratic steering when braking
- [ ] Excessive pitching and/or rolling around corners or during braking
- [ ] Suspension bottoms
- [ ] Unevenly-worn tyres
- [ ] Excessive tyre wear on outside edge
- [ ] Excessive tyre wear on inside edge
- [ ] Tyre tread worn in one place
- [ ] Excessive play or looseness in steering system
- [ ] Rattling or clicking noise in steering gear

This Section provides an easy-reference guide to the more common problems which may occur during the operation of your vehicle. These problems and their possible causes are grouped under headings denoting various components or systems, such as Engine, Cooling system, etc. They also refer you to the Chapter and/or Section which deals with the problem.

Remember that successful fault diagnosis is not a mysterious black art practised only by professional mechanics. It is simply the result of the right knowledge combined with an intelligent, systematic approach to the problem. Always work by a process of elimination, starting with the simplest solution and working through to the most complex - and never overlook the obvious. Anyone can run the fuel tank dry or leave the lights on overnight, so don't assume that you are exempt from such oversights.

Finally, always establish a clear idea of why a problem has occurred, and take steps to ensure that it doesn't happen again. If the electrical system fails because of a poor connection, check all other connections in the system to make sure that they don't fail as well. If a particular fuse continues to blow, find out why - don't just renew one fuse after another. Remember, failure of a small component can often be indicative of potential failure or incorrect functioning of a more important component or system.

Engine

Engine will not rotate when attempting to start

☐ Battery terminal connections loose or corroded (Chapter 1).
☐ Battery discharged or faulty (Chapter 1).
☐ Automatic transmission not completely engaged in Park (Chapter 7B) or (on models with a clutch switch) clutch not completely depressed (Chapter 8).
☐ Broken, loose or disconnected wiring in the starting circuit (Chapters 5 and 12).
☐ Starter motor pinion jammed in flywheel ring gear (Chapter 5).
☐ Starter solenoid faulty (Chapter 5).
☐ Starter motor faulty (Chapter 5).
☐ Ignition switch faulty (Chapter 12).
☐ Starter pinion or flywheel teeth worn or broken (Chapter 5).
☐ Engine internal problem (Chapter 2B).

Engine rotates, but will not start

☐ Fuel tank empty.
☐ Battery discharged (engine rotates slowly) (Chapter 5).
☐ Battery terminal connections loose or corroded (Chapter 1).
☐ Leaking fuel injector(s), faulty fuel pump, pressure regulator, etc (Chapter 4).
☐ Fuel not reaching fuel injection system or carburettor (Chapter 4).
☐ Ignition components damp or damaged (Chapter 5).
☐ Fuel injector stuck open (Chapter 4).
☐ Worn, faulty or incorrectly-gapped spark plugs (Chapter 1).
☐ Broken, loose or disconnected wiring in the starting circuit (Chapter 5).
☐ Loose distributor mounting bolts causing ignition timing to wander (Chapters 1 and 5).
☐ Broken, loose or disconnected wires at the ignition coil, or faulty coil (Chapter 5).

Engine hard to start when cold

☐ Battery discharged (Chapter 1).
☐ Fuel system malfunctioning (Chapter 4).
☐ Injector(s) leaking or carburettor automatic choke faulty (Chapter 4).
☐ Distributor rotor carbon-tracked (Chapter 5).

Engine hard to start when hot

☐ Air filter element clogged (Chapter 1).
☐ Fuel not reaching the fuel injection system or carburettor (Chapter 4).
☐ Corroded battery connections, especially earth (negative) connection (Chapter 1).

Starter motor noisy or excessively-rough in engagement

☐ Pinion or flywheel gear teeth worn or broken (Chapter 5).
☐ Starter motor mounting bolts loose or missing (Chapter 5).

Engine starts, but stops immediately

☐ Loose or faulty electrical connections at distributor, coil or alternator (Chapter 5).
☐ Insufficient fuel reaching the fuel injector(s) or carburettor (Chapters 1 and 4).
☐ Damaged fuel injection system speed sensors (Chapter 5).
☐ Faulty fuel injection relays (Chapter 5).

Oil puddle under engine

☐ Oil sump gasket and/or sump drain plug seal leaking (Chapter 2).
☐ Oil pressure sender unit leaking (Chapter 2).
☐ Valve cover gaskets leaking (Chapter 2).
☐ Engine oil seals leaking (Chapter 2).

Engine idles erratically

☐ Vacuum leakage (Chapter 4).
☐ Air filter element clogged (Chapter 1).
☐ Fuel pump not delivering sufficient fuel to the fuel injection system or carburettor (Chapter 4).
☐ Leaking head gasket (Chapter 2).
☐ Timing belt/chain and/or sprockets worn (Chapter 2).
☐ Camshaft lobes worn (Chapter 2).
☐ Faulty charcoal canister, where fitted (Chapter 6).

Engine misses at idle speed

- [ ] Spark plugs worn or incorrectly-gapped (Chapter 1).
- [ ] Faulty spark plug HT leads (Chapter 1).
- [ ] Vacuum leaks (Chapter 1).
- [ ] Incorrect ignition timing (Chapter 5).
- [ ] Uneven or low compression (Chapter 2).
- [ ] Faulty charcoal canister, where fitted (Chapter 6).

Engine misses throughout driving speed range

- [ ] Fuel filter clogged and/or impurities in the fuel system (Chapter 1).
- [ ] Low fuel output at the injectors, or partially-blocked carburettor jets (Chapter 4).
- [ ] Faulty or incorrectly-gapped spark plugs (Chapter 1).
- [ ] Incorrect ignition timing (Chapter 5).
- [ ] Cracked distributor cap, disconnected distributor HT leads, or damaged distributor components (Chapter 1).
- [ ] Faulty spark plug HT leads (Chapter 1).
- [ ] Faulty emission system components (Chapter 6).
- [ ] Low or uneven cylinder compression pressures (Chapter 2).
- [ ] Weak or faulty ignition system (Chapter 5).
- [ ] Vacuum leak in fuel injection system, intake manifold or vacuum hoses (Chapter 4).

Engine misfires on acceleration

- [ ] Spark plugs fouled (Chapter 1).
- [ ] Fuel injection system or carburettor malfunctioning (Chapter 4).
- [ ] Fuel filter clogged (Chapters 1 and 4).
- [ ] Incorrect ignition timing (Chapter 5).
- [ ] Intake manifold air leak (Chapter 4).

Engine surges while holding accelerator steady

- [ ] Intake air leak (Chapter 4).
- [ ] Fuel pump faulty (Chapter 4).
- [ ] Loose fuel injector harness connections (Chapters 4 and 6).
- [ ] Defective ECU (Chapter 5).

Engine lacks power

- [ ] Incorrect ignition timing (Chapter 5).
- [ ] Excessive play in distributor shaft (Chapter 5).
- [ ] Worn rotor, distributor cap or HT leads (Chapters 1 and 5).
- [ ] Faulty or incorrectly-gapped spark plugs (Chapter 1).
- [ ] Fuel injection system or carburettor malfunctioning (Chapter 4).
- [ ] Faulty coil (Chapter 5).
- [ ] Brakes binding (Chapter 1).
- [ ] Automatic transmission fluid level incorrect (Chapter 1).
- [ ] Clutch slipping (Chapter 8).
- [ ] Fuel filter clogged and/or impurities in the fuel system (Chapter 1).
- [ ] Emission control system not functioning properly (Chapter 6).
- [ ] Low or uneven cylinder compression pressures (Chapter 2).

Engine stalls

- [ ] Idle speed incorrect (Chapter 1).
- [ ] Fuel filter clogged and/or water and impurities in the fuel system (Chapter 1).
- [ ] Distributor components damp or damaged (Chapter 5).
- [ ] Faulty emissions system components (Chapter 6).
- [ ] Faulty or incorrectly-gapped spark plugs (Chapter 1).
- [ ] Faulty spark plug HT leads (Chapter 1).
- [ ] Vacuum leak in the fuel injection system, intake manifold or vacuum hoses (Chapter 4).

Engine backfires

- [ ] Emissions system not functioning properly (Chapter 6).
- [ ] Ignition timing incorrect (Chapter 5).
- [ ] Faulty secondary ignition system (cracked spark plug insulator, faulty plug HT leads, distributor cap and/or rotor) (Chapters 1 and 5).
- [ ] Fuel injection system or carburettor malfunctioning (Chapter 4).
- [ ] Vacuum leak at fuel injector(s), intake manifold or vacuum hoses (Chapter 4).
- [ ] Valve clearances incorrect (Chapter 1), or valve(s) sticking or damaged (Chapter 2).

Pinking or knocking engine sounds when accelerating or driving uphill

- [ ] Incorrect grade of fuel.
- [ ] Ignition timing incorrect (Chapter 5).
- [ ] Fuel injection system or carburettor in need of adjustment (Chapter 4).
- [ ] Damaged spark plugs or HT leads, or incorrect type fitted (Chapter 1).
- [ ] Worn or damaged distributor components (Chapter 5).
- [ ] Faulty emission system (Chapter 6).
- [ ] Vacuum leak (Chapter 4).

Engine runs with oil pressure light on

⚠️ **Caution: Stop the engine immediately if the oil pressure light comes on and establish the cause. Running the engine while the oil pressure is low can cause severe damage.**

- [ ] Low oil level (Chapter 1).
- [ ] Idle speed too low (Chapter 1).
- [ ] Short-circuit in wiring (Chapter 12).
- [ ] Faulty oil pressure sender unit (Chapter 2).
- [ ] Worn engine bearings and/or oil pump (Chapter 2).

Engine runs-on after switching off

- [ ] Idle speed too high (Chapter 1).
- [ ] Excessive engine operating temperature (Chapter 3).
- [ ] Incorrect fuel octane grade.
- [ ] Spark plugs defective or incorrect grade (Chapter 1).

Engine electrical system

Battery will not hold charge

- [ ] Alternator drivebelt defective or not adjusted properly (Chapter 1).
- [ ] Electrolyte level low (Chapter 1).
- [ ] Battery terminals loose or corroded (Chapter 1).
- [ ] Alternator not charging properly (Chapter 5).
- [ ] Loose, broken or faulty wiring in the charging circuit (Chapter 5).
- [ ] Short in vehicle wiring (Chapters 5 and 12).
- [ ] Internally-defective battery (Chapters 1 and 5).
- [ ] Ignition (no-charge) warning light bulb blown - on some early models (Chapter 5)

Ignition (no-charge) warning light fails to go out

- [ ] Faulty alternator or charging circuit (Chapter 5).
- [ ] Alternator drivebelt defective or out of adjustment (Chapter 1).
- [ ] Alternator voltage regulator inoperative (Chapter 5).

Ignition (no-charge) warning light fails to come on when key is turned

- [ ] Warning light bulb defective (Chapter 12).
- [ ] Fault in the printed circuit, wiring or bulbholder (Chapter 12).

Fuel system

Excessive fuel consumption

- [ ] Dirty or clogged air filter element (Chapter 1).
- [ ] Ignition timing incorrect (Chapter 5).
- [ ] Emissions system not functioning properly (Chapter 6).
- [ ] Fuel injection internal parts or carburettor jets excessively worn or damaged (Chapter 4).
- [ ] Low tyre pressure or incorrect tyre size (Chapter 1).
- [ ] Unsympathetic driving style, or unfavourable conditions.

Fuel leakage and/or fuel odour

⚠️ **Warning: Don't drive the vehicle if a fuel leak is suspected. Leaking fuel in the engine compartment could catch fire.**

- [ ] Leak in a fuel feed or vent line (Chapter 4).
- [ ] Tank overfilled.
- [ ] Fuel injector or carburettor parts excessively worn, or fuel system gaskets leaking (Chapter 4).

Cooling system

Overheating

- [ ] Insufficient coolant in system (Chapter 1).
- [ ] Water pump drivebelt defective or out of adjustment (Chapter 1).
- [ ] Radiator matrix blocked, or grille restricted (Chapter 3).
- [ ] Thermostat faulty (Chapter 3).
- [ ] Radiator cap not maintaining proper pressure (Chapter 3).
- [ ] Ignition timing incorrect (Chapter 5).

Overcooling

- [ ] Faulty thermostat (Chapter 3).

External coolant leakage

- [ ] Deteriorated/damaged hoses; loose clamps (Chapters 1 and 3).
- [ ] Water pump seal defective (Chapters 1 and 3).
- [ ] Leakage from radiator matrix, heater matrix or header tank (Chapter 3).
- [ ] Radiator/engine block drain plugs or water jacket core plugs leaking (Chapters 2 and 3).

Internal coolant leakage

- [ ] Leaking cylinder head gasket (Chapter 2).
- [ ] Cracked cylinder bore or cylinder head (Chapter 2).

Coolant loss

- [ ] Too much coolant in system (Chapter 1).
- [ ] Coolant boiling away because of overheating (see above).
- [ ] Internal or external leakage (see above).
- [ ] Faulty radiator cap (Chapter 3).

Poor coolant circulation

- [ ] Inoperative water pump (Chapter 3).
- [ ] Restriction in cooling system (Chapters 1 and 3).
- [ ] Water pump drivebelt defective/out of adjustment (Chapter 1).
- [ ] Thermostat sticking (Chapter 3).

Clutch

Pedal travels to floor - no pressure or very little resistance

- [ ] Master or slave cylinder faulty (Chapter 8).
- [ ] Fluid line burst or leaking (Chapter 8).
- [ ] Connections leaking (Chapter 8).
- [ ] No fluid in reservoir (Chapter 1).
- [ ] If fluid is present in master cylinder dust cover, master cylinder rear seal has failed (Chapter 8).
- [ ] Broken release bearing or fork (Chapter 8).

Fluid in area of master cylinder dust cover, and on pedal

- [ ] Rear seal failure in master cylinder (Chapter 8).

Fluid on slave cylinder

- [ ] Slave cylinder plunger seal faulty (Chapter 8).

Pedal feels "spongy" when depressed

- [ ] Air in system (Chapter 8).

Unable to select gears

- [ ] Faulty transmission (Chapter 7).
- [ ] Faulty clutch plate (Chapter 8).
- [ ] Fork and bearing not assembled properly (Chapter 8).
- [ ] Faulty pressure plate (Chapter 8).
- [ ] Pressure plate-to-flywheel bolts loose (Chapter 8).

Clutch slips (engine speed increases with no increase in vehicle speed)

- [ ] Clutch plate worn (Chapter 8).
- [ ] Clutch plate is oil-soaked by leaking rear main seal (Chapter 8).
- [ ] Warped pressure plate or flywheel (Chapter 8).
- [ ] Weak diaphragm spring (Chapter 8).
- [ ] Clutch plate overheated.

Grabbing (chattering) as clutch is engaged

- [ ] Oil on clutch plate lining, burned or glazed facings (Chapter 8).
- [ ] Worn or loose engine or transmission mountings (Chapters 2 and 7A).
- [ ] Worn splines on clutch plate hub (Chapter 8).
- [ ] Warped pressure plate or flywheel (Chapter 8).

Noise in clutch area

- [ ] Fork improperly fitted (Chapter 8).
- [ ] Faulty release bearing (Chapter 8).

Clutch pedal stays on floor

- [ ] Fork binding in housing (Chapter 8).
- [ ] Broken release bearing or fork (Chapter 8).

High pedal effort

- [ ] Fork binding in housing (Chapter 8).
- [ ] Pressure plate faulty (Chapter 8).
- [ ] Incorrect-size master or slave cylinder fitted (Chapter 8).

Manual transmission

Vibration

- ☐ Damaged propeller shaft (Chapter 8).
- ☐ Out-of-round tyres (Chapter 1).
- ☐ Tyre out-of-balance (Chapters 1 and 10).
- ☐ Worn propeller shaft universal joint (Chapter 8).

Noisy in neutral with engine running

- ☐ Worn clutch release bearing (Chapter 8).
- ☐ Worn transmission input shaft bearing (Chapter 7A).

Noisy in one particular gear

- ☐ Damaged or worn constant-mesh gears.
- ☐ Damaged or worn synchronisers.

Noisy in all gears

- ☐ Insufficient lubricant (Chapter 1).
- ☐ Damaged or worn bearings.
- ☐ Worn or damaged input gear shaft and/or output gear shaft.

Slips out of gear

- ☐ Worn or incorrectly-adjusted linkage (Chapter 7A).
- ☐ Transmission-to-engine mounting bolts loose (Chapter 7A).
- ☐ Shift linkage binding (Chapter 7A).
- ☐ Worn shift fork (Chapter 7A).

Leaks lubricant

- ☐ Excessive amount of lubricant in transmission (Chapters 1 and 7A).
- ☐ Loose or broken input shaft bearing retainer (Chapter 7A).
- ☐ Input shaft bearing retainer O-ring and/or lip seal damaged (Chapter 7A).

Automatic transmission

Note: *Due to the complexity of the automatic transmission, it is difficult for the home mechanic to properly diagnose and service this unit. For problems other than the following, the vehicle should be taken to a dealer or transmission specialist.*

Fluid leakage

- ☐ Automatic transmission fluid is a deep red colour. Fluid leaks should not be confused with engine oil, which can easily be blown by airflow onto the transmission.
- ☐ To pinpoint a leak, first remove all built-up dirt and grime from the transmission housing with degreasing agents and/or by steam-cleaning. Then drive the vehicle at low speed, so airflow will not blow the leak far from its source. Raise the vehicle and determine where the leak is coming from. Common areas of leakage are:
  a) *Transmission sump (Chapters 1 and 7B)*
  b) *Filler pipe (Chapter 7B)*
  c) *Transmission fluid cooler lines (Chapter 7B)*
  d) *Speedometer sensor (Chapter 7B)*

Transmission fluid brown, or has a burned smell

- ☐ Transmission fluid burned; fluid should be changed. May indicate transmission internal fault (Chapters 1 and 7B).

Transmission will not kickdown with accelerator pedal pressed to the floor

- ☐ Kickdown cable out of adjustment (Chapter 7B).

General shift mechanism problems

- ☐ Chapter 7B deals with checking and adjusting the shift linkage on automatic transmissions. Common problems which may be attributed to poorly-adjusted linkage are:
  a) *Engine starting in gears other than Park or Neutral.*
  b) *Indicator on selector lever pointing to a gear other than the one actually being used.*
  c) *Vehicle moves when in Park.*
- ☐ Refer to Chapter 7B for the shift linkage adjustment procedure.

Engine will start in gears other than Park or Neutral

- ☐ Inhibitor switch malfunctioning (Chapter 7B).

Transmission slips, shifts roughly, is noisy, or has no drive in forward or reverse gears

- ☐ There are many probable causes for the above problems, but the home mechanic should be concerned with only one possibility - fluid level. Before taking the vehicle to an automatic transmission specialist, check the level and condition of the fluid as described in Chapter 1. Correct the fluid level as necessary, or change the fluid if needed. If the problem persists, have a professional diagnose the probable cause.

Brakes

Note: *Before assuming that a brake problem exists, make sure that:*
a) *The tyres are in good condition and properly inflated (Chapter 1).*
b) *The wheel alignment (tracking) is correct (Chapter 10).*
c) *The vehicle is not loaded with weight in an unequal manner.*

Vehicle pulls to one side during braking

- [ ] Incorrect tyre pressures (Chapter 1).
- [ ] Wheel alignment (tracking) incorrect (Chapter 10)
- [ ] Unmatched tyres on same axle.
- [ ] Restricted brake lines or hoses (Chapter 9).
- [ ] Malfunctioning caliper assembly (Chapter 9).
- [ ] Loose suspension parts (Chapter 10).
- [ ] Loose calipers (Chapter 9).

Noise (high-pitched squeal) when the brakes are applied

- [ ] Front and/or rear disc brake pads worn out. The noise comes from the wear sensor rubbing against the disc. Renew the pads immediately (Chapter 9).

Brake vibration (pedal pulsates)

Note: *If the vehicle has ABS, it is normal for the brake pedal to pulsate when the system is working.*
- [ ] Excessive lateral disc run-out (Chapter 9).
- [ ] Parallelism not within specifications (Chapter 9).
- [ ] Uneven pad wear - caused by caliper not sliding, due to improper clearance or dirt (Chapter 9).
- [ ] Defective disc (Chapter 9).

Excessive brake pedal travel

- [ ] Partial brake system failure (Chapter 9).
- [ ] Insufficient fluid in master cylinder (Chapters 1 and 9).
- [ ] Air trapped in system (Chapters 1 and 9).

Excessive pedal effort required to stop vehicle

- [ ] Malfunctioning brake servo unit (Chapter 9).
- [ ] Partial system failure (Chapter 9).
- [ ] Excessively-worn pads or shoes (Chapter 9).
- [ ] Caliper piston stuck or sluggish (Chapter 9).
- [ ] Brake pads contaminated with oil or grease (Chapter 9).
- [ ] New pads fitted and not yet seated. It will take a while for the new material to seat against the disc.

Dragging brakes

- [ ] Master cylinder pistons not returning correctly (Chapter 9).
- [ ] Restricted brakes lines or hoses (Chapters 1 and 9).
- [ ] Incorrect handbrake adjustment (Chapter 9).
- [ ] Rear drum brake self-adjuster mechanism faulty (when applicable) (Chapter 9).

Grabbing or uneven braking action

- [ ] Malfunction of brake servo unit (Chapter 9).
- [ ] Binding brake pedal mechanism (Chapter 9).

Brake pedal feels "spongy" when depressed

- [ ] Air in hydraulic lines (Chapter 9).
- [ ] Master cylinder mounting bolts loose (Chapter 9).
- [ ] Master cylinder defective (Chapter 9).

Brake pedal travels to the floor with little resistance

- [ ] Little or no fluid in the master cylinder reservoir, caused by leaking caliper piston(s), loose, damaged or disconnected brake lines (Chapter 9).

Handbrake does not hold

- [ ] Handbrake linkage incorrectly adjusted (Chapter 9).
- [ ] Handbrake shoe linings worn out or contaminated (Chapter 9).

Suspension and steering

Note: *Before assuming that a problem exists, check the following items:*
a) *Tyre pressures and tyre condition (also check for out-of-round or out-of-balance tyres, and bent wheel rims).*
b) *Steering universal joints from the column to the steering gear (for play or wear).*
c) *Front and rear suspension, and the rack-and-pinion assembly (for loose or damaged parts).*
d) *Wheel bearings (wheel wobble or roughness when spun).*

Vehicle pulls to one side
☐ Mismatched or uneven tyres (Chapter 10).
☐ Broken or sagging springs (Chapter 10).
☐ Front wheel or rear wheel alignment incorrect (Chapter 10).
☐ Front brake problem (Chapter 9).

Abnormal or excessive tyre wear
☐ Front wheel or rear wheel alignment incorrect (Chapter 10).
☐ Sagging or broken springs (Chapter 10).
☐ Tyre out of balance (Chapter 10).
☐ Worn shock absorber (Chapter 10).
☐ Overloaded vehicle or unsympathetic driving style.
☐ Tyres not rotated regularly.

Wheel makes a "thumping" noise
☐ Blister or bump on tyre (Chapter 10).
☐ Faulty shock absorber action (Chapter 10).
☐ Wheel bolts loose.

Shimmy, shake or vibration
☐ Tyre or wheel out of balance or out of round (Chapter 10).
☐ Loose, worn or incorrectly-adjusted wheel bearings (Chapter 1).
☐ Worn tie-rod ends (Chapter 10).
☐ Worn balljoints (Chapter 10).
☐ Excessive wheel run-out (Chapter 10).
☐ Blister or bump on tyre (Chapter 10).
☐ Wheel bolts loose.

High steering effort
☐ Lack of lubrication at balljoints, tie-rod ends and steering gear (Chapter 1).
☐ Incorrect front wheel alignment (Chapter 10).
☐ Low tyre pressure(s) (Chapter 1).
☐ Power steering fluid low, or steering pump drivebelt slipping, where applicable (Chapter 10)

Poor steering self-centring
☐ Lack of lubrication at balljoints and tie-rod ends (Chapter 1).
☐ Binding in balljoints (Chapter 10).
☐ Binding in steering column (Chapter 10).
☐ Lack of lubricant in steering gear (Chapter 10).
☐ Inaccurate front wheel alignment (Chapter 10).

Abnormal noise at the front end
☐ Lack of lubrication at balljoints and tie-rod ends (Chapter 1).
☐ Damaged shock absorber mounting (Chapter 10).
☐ Worn control arm bushings or tie-rod ends (Chapter 10).
☐ Loose anti-roll bar (Chapter 10).
☐ Loose wheel bolts.
☐ Loose suspension mounting bolts (Chapter 10).

Wandering or poor steering stability
☐ Mismatched or uneven tyres (Chapter 10).
☐ Lack of lubrication at balljoints and tie-rod ends (Chapter 1).
☐ Worn shock absorbers (Chapter 10).
☐ Loose anti-roll bar (Chapter 10).
☐ Broken or sagging springs (Chapter 10).
☐ Front or rear wheel alignment incorrect (Chapter 10).

Erratic steering when braking
☐ Wheel bearings worn (Chapter 1).
☐ Broken or sagging springs (Chapter 10).
☐ Leaking wheel cylinder (rear drum brake models) or caliper (Chapter 9).
☐ Warped discs (Chapter 9).

Excessive pitching and/or rolling around corners or during braking
☐ Loose anti-roll bar (Chapter 10).
☐ Worn shock absorbers or mountings (Chapter 10).
☐ Broken or sagging springs (Chapter 10).
☐ Overloaded vehicle.

Suspension bottoms
☐ Overloaded vehicle.
☐ Worn shock absorbers (Chapter 10).
☐ Broken or sagging springs, or incorrect springs fitted (Chapter 10).

Unevenly-worn tyres
☐ Front wheel or rear wheel alignment incorrect (Chapter 10).
☐ Worn shock absorbers (Chapter 10).
☐ Wheel bearings worn (Chapter 10).
☐ Excessive tyre or wheel run-out (Chapter 10).
☐ Worn balljoints (Chapter 10).

Excessive tyre wear on outside edge
☐ Tyre pressures incorrect (Chapter 1).
☐ Excessive cornering speed.
☐ Wheel alignment incorrect (excessive toe-in) (Chapter 10).
☐ Suspension components damaged (Chapter 10).

Excessive tyre wear on inside edge
☐ Tyre pressures incorrect (Chapter 1).
☐ Wheel alignment incorrect (excessive toe-out) (Chapter 10).
☐ Loose or damaged steering components (Chapter 10).

Tyre tread worn in one place
☐ Tyres out of balance.
☐ Damaged or buckled wheel. Inspect and renew if necessary.
☐ Defective tyre (Chapter 1).

Excessive play or looseness in steering system
☐ Wheel bearing(s) worn (Chapter 10.
☐ Tie-rod end loose or worn (Chapter 10).
☐ Steering gear mountings loose (Chapter 10).

Rattling or clicking noise in steering gear
☐ Insufficient or incorrect lubricant in rack-and-pinion assembly (Chapter 10).
☐ Steering gear mountings loose (Chapter 10).

Notes

Length (distance)

Inches (in)	25.4	= Millimetres (mm)	x 0.0394	= Inches (in)
Feet (ft)	0.305	= Metres (m)	x 3.281	= Feet (ft)
Miles	1.609	= Kilometres (km)	x 0.621	= Miles

Volume (capacity)

Cubic inches (cu in; in³)	x 16.387	= Cubic centimetres (cc; cm³)	x 0.061	= Cubic inches (cu in; in³)
Imperial pints (Imp pt)	x 0.568	= Litres (l)	x 1.76	= Imperial pints (Imp pt)
Imperial quarts (Imp qt)	x 1.137	= Litres (l)	x 0.88	= Imperial quarts (Imp qt)
Imperial quarts (Imp qt)	x 1.201	= US quarts (US qt)	x 0.833	= Imperial quarts (Imp qt)
US quarts (US qt)	x 0.946	= Litres (l)	x 1.057	= US quarts (US qt)
Imperial gallons (Imp gal)	x 4.546	= Litres (l)	x 0.22	= Imperial gallons (Imp gal)
Imperial gallons (Imp gal)	x 1.201	= US gallons (US gal)	x 0.833	= Imperial gallons (Imp gal)
US gallons (US gal)	x 3.785	= Litres (l)	x 0.264	= US gallons (US gal)

Mass (weight)

Ounces (oz)	x 28.35	= Grams (g)	x 0.035	= Ounces (oz)
Pounds (lb)	x 0.454	= Kilograms (kg)	x 2.205	= Pounds (lb)

Force

Ounces-force (ozf; oz)	x 0.278	= Newtons (N)	x 3.6	= Ounces-force (ozf; oz)
Pounds-force (lbf; lb)	x 4.448	= Newtons (N)	x 0.225	= Pounds-force (lbf; lb)
Newtons (N)	x 0.1	= Kilograms-force (kgf; kg)	x 9.81	= Newtons (N)

Pressure

Pounds-force per square inch (psi; lbf/in²; lb/in²)	x 0.070	= Kilograms-force per square centimetre (kgf/cm²; kg/cm²)	x 14.223	= Pounds-force per square inch (psi; lbf/in²; lb/in²)
Pounds-force per square inch (psi; lbf/in²; lb/in²)	x 0.068	= Atmospheres (atm)	x 14.696	= Pounds-force per square inch (psi; lbf/in²; lb/in²)
Pounds-force per square inch (psi; lbf/in²; lb/in²)	x 0.069	= Bars	x 14.5	= Pounds-force per square inch (psi; lbf/in²; lb/in²)
Pounds-force per square inch (psi; lbf/in²; lb/in²)	x 6.895	= Kilopascals (kPa)	x 0.145	= Pounds-force per square inch (psi; lbf/in²; lb/in²)
Kilopascals (kPa)	x 0.01	= Kilograms-force per square centimetre (kgf/cm²; kg/cm²)	x 98.1	= Kilopascals (kPa)
Millibar (mbar)	x 100	= Pascals (Pa)	x 0.01	= Millibar (mbar)
Millibar (mbar)	x 0.0145	= Pounds-force per square inch (psi; lbf/in²; lb/in²)	x 68.947	= Millibar (mbar)
Millibar (mbar)	x 0.75	= Millimetres of mercury (mmHg)	x 1.333	= Millibar (mbar)
Millibar (mbar)	x 0.401	= Inches of water (inH₂O)	x 2.491	= Millibar (mbar)
Millimetres of mercury (mmHg)	x 0.535	= Inches of water (inH₂O)	x 1.868	= Millimetres of mercury (mmHg)
Inches of water (inH₂O)	x 0.036	= Pounds-force per square inch (psi; lbf/in²; lb/in²)	x 27.68	= Inches of water (inH₂O)

Torque (moment of force)

Pounds-force inches (lbf in; lb in)	x 1.152	= Kilograms-force centimetre (kgf cm; kg cm)	x 0.868	= Pounds-force inches (lbf in; lb in)
Pounds-force inches (lbf in; lb in)	x 0.113	= Newton metres (Nm)	x 8.85	= Pounds-force inches (lbf in; lb in)
Pounds-force inches (lbf in; lb in)	x 0.083	= Pounds-force feet (lbf ft; lb ft)	x 12	= Pounds-force inches (lbf in; lb in)
Pounds-force feet (lbf ft; lb ft)	x 0.138	= Kilograms-force metres (kgf m; kg m)	x 7.233	= Pounds-force feet (lbf ft; lb ft)
Pounds-force feet (lbf ft; lb ft)	x 1.356	= Newton metres (Nm)	x 0.738	= Pounds-force feet (lbf ft; lb ft)
Newton metres (Nm)	x 0.102	= Kilograms-force metres (kgf m; kg m)	x 9.804	= Newton metres (Nm)

Power

Horsepower (hp)	x 745.7	= Watts (W)	x 0.0013	= Horsepower (hp)

Velocity (speed)

Miles per hour (miles/hr; mph)	x 1.609	= Kilometres per hour (km/hr; kph)	x 0.621	= Miles per hour (miles/hr; mph)

Fuel consumption*

Miles per gallon (mpg)	x 0.354	= Kilometres per litre (km/l)	x 2.825	= Miles per gallon (mpg)

* It is common practice to convert from miles per gallon (mpg) to litres/100 kilometres (l/100km), where mpg x l/100 km = 282

Temperature

Degrees Fahrenheit = (°C x 1.8) + 32

Degrees Celsius (Degrees Centigrade; °C) = (°F - 32) x 0.56

A number of automotive chemicals and lubricants are available for use during vehicle maintenance and repair. They include a wide variety of products ranging from cleaning solvents and degreasers to lubricants and protective sprays for rubber, plastic and vinyl.

Cleaners

Carburettor cleaner and choke cleaner is a strong solvent for gum, varnish and carbon. Most carburettor cleaners leave a dry-type lubricant film which will not harden or gum up. Because of this film, it is not recommended for use on electrical components.

Brake system cleaner is used to remove grease and brake fluid from the brake system, where clean surfaces are absolutely necessary. It leaves no residue, and often eliminates brake squeal caused by contaminants.

Electrical cleaner removes oxidation, corrosion and carbon deposits from electrical contacts, restoring full current flow. It can also be used to clean spark plugs, carburettor jets, voltage regulators and other parts where an oil-free surface is desired.

Moisture dispersants remove water and moisture from electrical components such as alternators, voltage regulators, electrical connectors and fuse blocks. They are non-conductive and non-corrosive.

Degreasers are heavy-duty solvents used to remove grease from the outside of the engine and from chassis components. They can be sprayed or brushed on, and are usually rinsed off with water.

Lubricants

Engine oil is the lubricant formulated for use in engines. It normally contains a wide variety of additives to prevent corrosion and reduce foaming and wear. Engine oil comes in various weights (viscosity ratings) from 5 to 60. The recommended weight of the oil depends on the season, temperature and the demands on the engine. Light oil is used in cold climates and under light load conditions. Heavy oil is used in hot climates, and where high loads are encountered. Multi-viscosity (multigrade) oils are designed to have characteristics of both light and heavy oils, and are available in a number of weights from 5W-20 to 20W-50.

Gear oil is designed to be used in differentials, manual transmissions and other areas where high-temperature lubrication is required.

Chassis and wheel bearing grease is a heavy grease used where increased loads and friction are encountered, such as for wheel bearings, balljoints, tie-rod ends and universal joints.

High-temperature wheel bearing grease is designed to withstand the extreme temperatures encountered by wheel bearings in disc brake-equipped vehicles. It usually contains molybdenum disulphide (moly), which is a dry-type lubricant.

White grease is a heavy grease for metal-to-metal applications where water is a problem. White grease stays soft at both low and high temperatures, and will not wash off or dilute in the presence of water.

Assembly lube is a special extreme-pressure lubricant, usually containing moly, used to lubricate high-load parts (such as main and rod bearings and cam lobes) for initial start-up of a new engine. The assembly lube lubricates the parts without being squeezed out or washed away until the engine oiling system begins to function.

Silicone lubricants are used to protect rubber, plastic, vinyl and nylon parts.

Graphite lubricants are used where oils cannot be used due to contamination problems, such as in locks. The dry graphite will lubricate metal parts while remaining uncontaminated by dirt, water, oil or acids. It is electrically conductive, and will not foul electrical contacts in locks such as the ignition switch.

Penetrating oils loosen and lubricate frozen, rusted and corroded fasteners and prevent future rusting or freezing.

Heat-sink grease is a special electrically non-conductive grease that is used for mounting electronic ignition modules where it is essential that heat is transferred away from the module.

Sealants

RTV sealant is one of the most widely-used gasket compounds. Made from silicone, RTV is air-curing; it seals, bonds, waterproofs, fills surface irregularities, remains flexible, doesn't shrink, is relatively easy to remove, and is used as a supplementary sealer with almost all low- and medium-temperature gaskets.

Anaerobic sealant is much like RTV in that it can be used either to seal gaskets or to form gaskets by itself. It remains flexible, is solvent-resistant, and fills surface imperfections. The difference between an anaerobic sealant and an RTV-type sealant is in the curing. RTV cures when exposed to air, while an anaerobic sealant cures only in the absence of air. This means that an anaerobic sealant cures only after the assembly of parts, sealing them together.

Thread and pipe sealant is used for sealing hydraulic and pneumatic fittings and vacuum lines. It is usually made from a Teflon compound, and comes in a spray, a paint-on liquid and as a wrap-around tape.

Chemicals

Anti-seize compound prevents seizing, chafing, cold welding, rust and corrosion in fasteners. High-temperature anti-seize, usually made with copper and graphite lubricants, is used for exhaust system and exhaust manifold bolts.

Anaerobic locking compounds are used to keep fasteners from vibrating or working loose, and cure only after installation, in the absence of air. Medium-strength locking compound is used for small nuts, bolts and screws that may be removed later. High-strength locking compound is for large nuts, bolts and studs which aren't removed on a regular basis.

Oil additives range from viscosity index improvers to chemical treatments that claim to reduce internal engine friction. It should be noted that most oil manufacturers caution against using additives with their oils.

Fuel additives perform several functions, depending on their chemical make-up. They usually contain solvents that help dissolve gum and varnish that build up on carburettor, fuel injection and intake parts. They also serve to break down carbon deposits that form on the inside surfaces of the combustion chambers. Some additives contain upper cylinder lubricants for valves and piston rings, and others contain chemicals to remove condensation from the fuel tank.

Miscellaneous

Brake fluid is specially-formulated hydraulic fluid that can withstand the heat and pressure encountered in brake systems. It is poisonous and inflammable. Care must be taken so this fluid does not come in contact with painted surfaces or plastics. An opened container should always be resealed, to prevent contamination by water or dirt. Brake fluid absorbs moisture from the air, if left in an unsealed container.

Weatherstrip adhesive is used to bond weatherstripping around doors, windows and boot lids. It is sometimes used to attach trim pieces.

Underseal is a petroleum-based, tar-like substance that is designed to protect metal surfaces on the underside of the vehicle from corrosion. It also acts as a sound-deadening agent by insulating the bottom of the vehicle.

Waxes and polishes are used to help protect painted and plated surfaces from the weather. Different types of paint may require the use of different types of wax and polish. Some polishes utilise a chemical or abrasive cleaner to help remove the top layer of oxidised (dull) paint on older vehicles. In recent years, many non-wax polishes containing a wide variety of chemicals such as polymers and silicones have been introduced. These non-wax polishes are usually easier to apply, and last longer than conventional waxes and polishes.

Buying spare parts

Spare parts are available from many sources; for example, BMW garages, other garages and accessory shops, and motor factors. Our advice regarding spare part sources is as follows.

Officially-appointed BMW garages - This is the best source for parts which are peculiar to your vehicle, and which are not generally available (eg complete cylinder heads, internal transmission components, badges, interior trim etc). It is also the only place at which you should buy parts if the vehicle is still under warranty. To be sure of obtaining the correct parts, it will be necessary to give the storeman the full Vehicle Identification Number, and if possible, to take the old parts along for positive identification. Many parts are available under a factory exchange scheme - any parts returned should always be clean. It obviously makes good sense to go straight to the specialists on your vehicle for this type of part, as they are best equipped to supply you.

Other garages and accessory shops - These are often very good places to buy materials and components needed for the maintenance of your vehicle (eg oil filters, spark plugs, bulbs, drivebelts, oils and greases, touch-up paint, filler paste, etc). They also sell general accessories, usually have convenient opening hours, charge lower prices, and can often be found not far from home.

Motor factors - Good factors will stock all the more important components which wear out comparatively quickly (eg exhaust systems, brake pads, seals and hydraulic parts, clutch components, bearing shells, pistons, valves etc). Motor factors will often provide new or reconditioned components on a part-exchange basis - this can save a considerable amount of money.

Vehicle identification numbers

Modifications are a continuing and unpublicised process in vehicle manufacture, quite apart from major model changes. Spare parts manuals and lists are compiled upon a numerical basis, the appropriate identification number or code being essential to correct identification of the component concerned.

When ordering spare parts, always give as much information as possible. Quote the vehicle model, year of manufacture, Vehicle Identification Number and engine numbers, as appropriate.

The *Vehicle Identification Number (VIN)* is located on the right-hand front wheel arch next to the front suspension strut upper mounting, on the driver's door, and on a plate on top of the facia, just inside the windscreen **(see illustrations).**

The *engine number* is stamped on a machined face on the left-hand side of the cylinder block, near the base of the oil level dipstick tube.

The *body number* is located on the seam between the left-hand front wing and inner panel.

The VIN (arrowed) is stamped on the bulkhead

The VIN is also present on the edge of the driver's door

A

ABS (Anti-lock brake system) A system, usually electronically controlled, that senses incipient wheel lockup during braking and relieves hydraulic pressure at wheels that are about to skid.

Air bag An inflatable bag hidden in the steering wheel (driver's side) or the dash or glovebox (passenger side). In a head-on collision, the bags inflate, preventing the driver and front passenger from being thrown forward into the steering wheel or windscreen.

Air cleaner A metal or plastic housing, containing a filter element, which removes dust and dirt from the air being drawn into the engine.

Air filter element The actual filter in an air cleaner system, usually manufactured from pleated paper and requiring renewal at regular intervals.

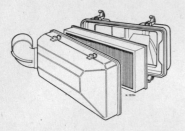

Air filter

Allen key A hexagonal wrench which fits into a recessed hexagonal hole.

Alligator clip A long-nosed spring-loaded metal clip with meshing teeth. Used to make temporary electrical connections.

Alternator A component in the electrical system which converts mechanical energy from a drivebelt into electrical energy to charge the battery and to operate the starting system, ignition system and electrical accessories.

Alternator (exploded view)

Ampere (amp) A unit of measurement for the flow of electric current. One amp is the amount of current produced by one volt acting through a resistance of one ohm.

Anaerobic sealer A substance used to prevent bolts and screws from loosening. Anaerobic means that it does not require oxygen for activation. The Loctite brand is widely used.

Antifreeze A substance (usually ethylene glycol) mixed with water, and added to a vehicle's cooling system, to prevent freezing of the coolant in winter. Antifreeze also contains chemicals to inhibit corrosion and the formation of rust and other deposits that would tend to clog the radiator and coolant passages and reduce cooling efficiency.

Anti-seize compound A coating that reduces the risk of seizing on fasteners that are subjected to high temperatures, such as exhaust manifold bolts and nuts.

Anti-seize compound

Asbestos A natural fibrous mineral with great heat resistance, commonly used in the composition of brake friction materials. Asbestos is a health hazard and the dust created by brake systems should never be inhaled or ingested.

Axle A shaft on which a wheel revolves, or which revolves with a wheel. Also, a solid beam that connects the two wheels at one end of the vehicle. An axle which also transmits power to the wheels is known as a live axle.

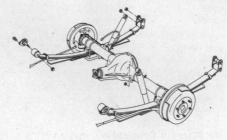

Axle assembly

Axleshaft A single rotating shaft, on either side of the differential, which delivers power from the final drive assembly to the drive wheels. Also called a driveshaft or a halfshaft.

B

Ball bearing An anti-friction bearing consisting of a hardened inner and outer race with hardened steel balls between two races.

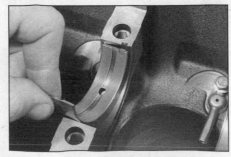

Bearing

Bearing The curved surface on a shaft or in a bore, or the part assembled into either, that permits relative motion between them with minimum wear and friction.

Big-end bearing The bearing in the end of the connecting rod that's attached to the crankshaft.

Bleed nipple A valve on a brake wheel cylinder, caliper or other hydraulic component that is opened to purge the hydraulic system of air. Also called a bleed screw.

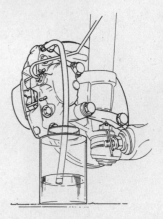

Brake bleeding

Brake bleeding Procedure for removing air from lines of a hydraulic brake system.

Brake disc The component of a disc brake that rotates with the wheels.

Brake drum The component of a drum brake that rotates with the wheels.

Brake linings The friction material which contacts the brake disc or drum to retard the vehicle's speed. The linings are bonded or riveted to the brake pads or shoes.

Brake pads The replaceable friction pads that pinch the brake disc when the brakes are applied. Brake pads consist of a friction material bonded or riveted to a rigid backing plate.

Brake shoe The crescent-shaped carrier to which the brake linings are mounted and which forces the lining against the rotating drum during braking.

Braking systems For more information on braking systems, consult the *Haynes Automotive Brake Manual*.

Breaker bar A long socket wrench handle providing greater leverage.

Bulkhead The insulated partition between the engine and the passenger compartment.

C

Caliper The non-rotating part of a disc-brake assembly that straddles the disc and carries the brake pads. The caliper also contains the hydraulic components that cause the pads to pinch the disc when the brakes are applied. A caliper is also a measuring tool that can be set to measure inside or outside dimensions of an object.

Camshaft A rotating shaft on which a series of cam lobes operate the valve mechanisms. The camshaft may be driven by gears, by sprockets and chain or by sprockets and a belt.

Canister A container in an evaporative emission control system; contains activated charcoal granules to trap vapours from the fuel system.

Canister

Carburettor A device which mixes fuel with air in the proper proportions to provide a desired power output from a spark ignition internal combustion engine.

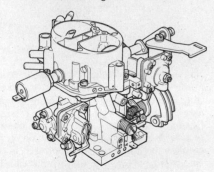

Carburettor

Castellated Resembling the parapets along the top of a castle wall. For example, a castellated balljoint stud nut.

Castellated nut

Castor In wheel alignment, the backward or forward tilt of the steering axis. Castor is positive when the steering axis is inclined rearward at the top.

Catalytic converter A silencer-like device in the exhaust system which converts certain pollutants in the exhaust gases into less harmful substances.

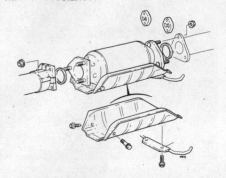

Catalytic converter

Circlip A ring-shaped clip used to prevent endwise movement of cylindrical parts and shafts. An internal circlip is installed in a groove in a housing; an external circlip fits into a groove on the outside of a cylindrical piece such as a shaft.

Clearance The amount of space between two parts. For example, between a piston and a cylinder, between a bearing and a journal, etc.

Coil spring A spiral of elastic steel found in various sizes throughout a vehicle, for example as a springing medium in the suspension and in the valve train.

Compression Reduction in volume, and increase in pressure and temperature, of a gas, caused by squeezing it into a smaller space.

Compression ratio The relationship between cylinder volume when the piston is at top dead centre and cylinder volume when the piston is at bottom dead centre.

Constant velocity (CV) joint A type of universal joint that cancels out vibrations caused by driving power being transmitted through an angle.

Core plug A disc or cup-shaped metal device inserted in a hole in a casting through which core was removed when the casting was formed. Also known as a freeze plug or expansion plug.

Crankcase The lower part of the engine block in which the crankshaft rotates.

Crankshaft The main rotating member, or shaft, running the length of the crankcase, with offset "throws" to which the connecting rods are attached.

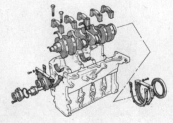

Crankshaft assembly

Crocodile clip See Alligator clip

D

Diagnostic code Code numbers obtained by accessing the diagnostic mode of an engine management computer. This code can be used to determine the area in the system where a malfunction may be located.

Disc brake A brake design incorporating a rotating disc onto which brake pads are squeezed. The resulting friction converts the energy of a moving vehicle into heat.

Double-overhead cam (DOHC) An engine that uses two overhead camshafts, usually one for the intake valves and one for the exhaust valves.

Drivebelt(s) The belt(s) used to drive accessories such as the alternator, water pump, power steering pump, air conditioning compressor, etc. off the crankshaft pulley.

Accessory drivebelts

Driveshaft Any shaft used to transmit motion. Commonly used when referring to the axleshafts on a front wheel drive vehicle.

Driveshaft

Drum brake A type of brake using a drum-shaped metal cylinder attached to the inner surface of the wheel. When the brake pedal is pressed, curved brake shoes with friction linings press against the inside of the drum to slow or stop the vehicle.

Drum brake assembly

E

EGR valve A valve used to introduce exhaust gases into the intake air stream.

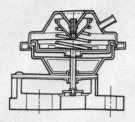

EGR valve

Electronic control unit (ECU) A computer which controls (for instance) ignition and fuel injection systems, or an anti-lock braking system. For more information refer to the *Haynes Automotive Electrical and Electronic Systems Manual.*

Electronic Fuel Injection (EFI) A computer controlled fuel system that distributes fuel through an injector located in each intake port of the engine.

Emergency brake A braking system, independent of the main hydraulic system, that can be used to slow or stop the vehicle if the primary brakes fail, or to hold the vehicle stationary even though the brake pedal isn't depressed. It usually consists of a hand lever that actuates either front or rear brakes mechanically through a series of cables and linkages. Also known as a handbrake or parking brake.

Endfloat The amount of lengthwise movement between two parts. As applied to a crankshaft, the distance that the crankshaft can move forward and back in the cylinder block.

Engine management system (EMS) A computer controlled system which manages the fuel injection and the ignition systems in an integrated fashion.

Exhaust manifold A part with several passages through which exhaust gases leave the engine combustion chambers and enter the exhaust pipe.

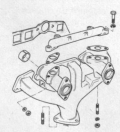

Exhaust manifold

F

Fan clutch A viscous (fluid) drive coupling device which permits variable engine fan speeds in relation to engine speeds.

Feeler blade A thin strip or blade of hardened steel, ground to an exact thickness, used to check or measure clearances between parts.

Feeler blade

Firing order The order in which the engine cylinders fire, or deliver their power strokes, beginning with the number one cylinder.

Flywheel A heavy spinning wheel in which energy is absorbed and stored by means of momentum. On cars, the flywheel is attached to the crankshaft to smooth out firing impulses.

Free play The amount of travel before any action takes place. The "looseness" in a linkage, or an assembly of parts, between the initial application of force and actual movement. For example, the distance the brake pedal moves before the pistons in the master cylinder are actuated.

Fuse An electrical device which protects a circuit against accidental overload. The typical fuse contains a soft piece of metal which is calibrated to melt at a predetermined current flow (expressed as amps) and break the circuit.

Fusible link A circuit protection device consisting of a conductor surrounded by heat-resistant insulation. The conductor is smaller than the wire it protects, so it acts as the weakest link in the circuit. Unlike a blown fuse, a failed fusible link must frequently be cut from the wire for replacement.

G

Gap The distance the spark must travel in jumping from the centre electrode to the side

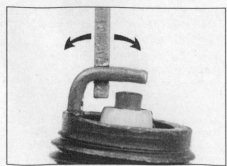

Adjusting spark plug gap

electrode in a spark plug. Also refers to the spacing between the points in a contact breaker assembly in a conventional points-type ignition, or to the distance between the reluctor or rotor and the pickup coil in an electronic ignition.

Gasket Any thin, soft material - usually cork, cardboard, asbestos or soft metal - installed between two metal surfaces to ensure a good seal. For instance, the cylinder head gasket seals the joint between the block and the cylinder head.

Gasket

Gauge An instrument panel display used to monitor engine conditions. A gauge with a movable pointer on a dial or a fixed scale is an analogue gauge. A gauge with a numerical readout is called a digital gauge.

H

Halfshaft A rotating shaft that transmits power from the final drive unit to a drive wheel, usually when referring to a live rear axle.

Harmonic balancer A device designed to reduce torsion or twisting vibration in the crankshaft. May be incorporated in the crankshaft pulley. Also known as a vibration damper.

Hone An abrasive tool for correcting small irregularities or differences in diameter in an engine cylinder, brake cylinder, etc.

Hydraulic tappet A tappet that utilises hydraulic pressure from the engine's lubrication system to maintain zero clearance (constant contact with both camshaft and valve stem). Automatically adjusts to variation in valve stem length. Hydraulic tappets also reduce valve noise.

I

Ignition timing The moment at which the spark plug fires, usually expressed in the number of crankshaft degrees before the piston reaches the top of its stroke.

Inlet manifold A tube or housing with passages through which flows the air-fuel mixture (carburettor vehicles and vehicles with throttle body injection) or air only (port fuel-injected vehicles) to the port openings in the cylinder head.

J

Jump start Starting the engine of a vehicle with a discharged or weak battery by attaching jump leads from the weak battery to a charged or helper battery.

L

Load Sensing Proportioning Valve (LSPV) A brake hydraulic system control valve that works like a proportioning valve, but also takes into consideration the amount of weight carried by the rear axle.

Locknut A nut used to lock an adjustment nut, or other threaded component, in place. For example, a locknut is employed to keep the adjusting nut on the rocker arm in position.

Lockwasher A form of washer designed to prevent an attaching nut from working loose.

M

MacPherson strut A type of front suspension system devised by Earle MacPherson at Ford of England. In its original form, a simple lateral link with the anti-roll bar creates the lower control arm. A long strut - an integral coil spring and shock absorber - is mounted between the body and the steering knuckle. Many modern so-called MacPherson strut systems use a conventional lower A-arm and don't rely on the anti-roll bar for location.

Multimeter An electrical test instrument with the capability to measure voltage, current and resistance.

N

NOx Oxides of Nitrogen. A common toxic pollutant emitted by petrol and diesel engines at higher temperatures.

O

Ohm The unit of electrical resistance. One volt applied to a resistance of one ohm will produce a current of one amp.

Ohmmeter An instrument for measuring electrical resistance.

O-ring A type of sealing ring made of a special rubber-like material; in use, the O-ring is compressed into a groove to provide the sealing action.

O-ring

Overhead cam (ohc) engine An engine with the camshaft(s) located on top of the cylinder head(s).

Overhead valve (ohv) engine An engine with the valves located in the cylinder head, but with the camshaft located in the engine block.

Oxygen sensor A device installed in the engine exhaust manifold, which senses the oxygen content in the exhaust and converts this information into an electric current. Also called a Lambda sensor.

P

Phillips screw A type of screw head having a cross instead of a slot for a corresponding type of screwdriver.

Plastigage A thin strip of plastic thread; available in different sizes, used for measuring clearances. For example, a strip of Plastigage is laid across a bearing journal. The parts are assembled and dismantled; the width of the crushed strip indicates the clearance between journal and bearing.

Plastigage

Propeller shaft The long hollow tube with universal joints at both ends that carries power from the transmission to the differential on front-engined rear wheel drive vehicles.

Proportioning valve A hydraulic control valve which limits the amount of pressure to the rear brakes during panic stops to prevent wheel lock-up.

R

Rack-and-pinion steering A steering system with a pinion gear on the end of the steering shaft that mates with a rack (think of a geared wheel opened up and laid flat). When the steering wheel is turned, the pinion turns, moving the rack to the left or right. This movement is transmitted through the track rods to the steering arms at the wheels.

Radiator A liquid-to-air heat transfer device designed to reduce the temperature of the coolant in an internal combustion engine cooling system.

Refrigerant Any substance used as a heat transfer agent in an air-conditioning system. R-12 has been the principle refrigerant for many years; recently, however, manufacturers have begun using R-134a, a non-CFC substance that is considered less harmful to the ozone in the upper atmosphere.

Rocker arm A lever arm that rocks on a shaft or pivots on a stud. In an overhead valve engine, the rocker arm converts the upward movement of the pushrod into a downward movement to open a valve.

Rotor In a distributor, the rotating device inside the cap that connects the centre electrode and the outer terminals as it turns, distributing the high voltage from the coil secondary winding to the proper spark plug. Also, that part of an alternator which rotates inside the stator. Also, the rotating assembly of a turbocharger, including the compressor wheel, shaft and turbine wheel.

Runout The amount of wobble (in-and-out movement) of a gear or wheel as it's rotated. The amount a shaft rotates "out-of-true." The out-of-round condition of a rotating part.

S

Sealant A liquid or paste used to prevent leakage at a joint. Sometimes used in conjunction with a gasket.

Sealed beam lamp An older headlight design which integrates the reflector, lens and filaments into a hermetically-sealed one-piece unit. When a filament burns out or the lens cracks, the entire unit is simply replaced.

Serpentine drivebelt A single, long, wide accessory drivebelt that's used on some newer vehicles to drive all the accessories, instead of a series of smaller, shorter belts. Serpentine drivebelts are usually tensioned by an automatic tensioner.

Serpentine drivebelt

Shim Thin spacer, commonly used to adjust the clearance or relative positions between two parts. For example, shims inserted into or under bucket tappets control valve clearances. Clearance is adjusted by changing the thickness of the shim.

Slide hammer A special puller that screws into or hooks onto a component such as a shaft or bearing; a heavy sliding handle on the shaft bottoms against the end of the shaft to knock the component free.

Sprocket A tooth or projection on the periphery of a wheel, shaped to engage with a chain or drivebelt. Commonly used to refer to the sprocket wheel itself.

Starter inhibitor switch On vehicles with an

automatic transmission, a switch that prevents starting if the vehicle is not in Neutral or Park.

Strut See MacPherson strut.

T

Tappet A cylindrical component which transmits motion from the cam to the valve stem, either directly or via a pushrod and rocker arm. Also called a cam follower.

Thermostat A heat-controlled valve that regulates the flow of coolant between the cylinder block and the radiator, so maintaining optimum engine operating temperature. A thermostat is also used in some air cleaners in which the temperature is regulated.

Thrust bearing The bearing in the clutch assembly that is moved in to the release levers by clutch pedal action to disengage the clutch. Also referred to as a release bearing.

Timing belt A toothed belt which drives the camshaft. Serious engine damage may result if it breaks in service.

Timing chain A chain which drives the camshaft.

Toe-in The amount the front wheels are closer together at the front than at the rear. On rear wheel drive vehicles, a slight amount of toe-in is usually specified to keep the front wheels running parallel on the road by offsetting other forces that tend to spread the wheels apart.

Toe-out The amount the front wheels are closer together at the rear than at the front. On front wheel drive vehicles, a slight amount of toe-out is usually specified.

Tools For full information on choosing and using tools, refer to the *Haynes Automotive Tools Manual*.

Tracer A stripe of a second colour applied to a wire insulator to distinguish that wire from another one with the same colour insulator.

Tune-up A process of accurate and careful adjustments and parts replacement to obtain the best possible engine performance.

Turbocharger A centrifugal device, driven by exhaust gases, that pressurises the intake air. Normally used to increase the power output from a given engine displacement, but can also be used primarily to reduce exhaust emissions (as on VW's "Umwelt" Diesel engine).

U

Universal joint or U-joint A double-pivoted connection for transmitting power from a driving to a driven shaft through an angle. A U-joint consists of two Y-shaped yokes and a cross-shaped member called the spider.

V

Valve A device through which the flow of liquid, gas, vacuum, or loose material in bulk may be started, stopped, or regulated by a movable part that opens, shuts, or partially obstructs one or more ports or passageways. A valve is also the movable part of such a device.

Valve clearance The clearance between the valve tip (the end of the valve stem) and the rocker arm or tappet. The valve clearance is measured when the valve is closed.

Vernier caliper A precision measuring instrument that measures inside and outside dimensions. Not quite as accurate as a micrometer, but more convenient.

Viscosity The thickness of a liquid or its resistance to flow.

Volt A unit for expressing electrical "pressure" in a circuit. One volt that will produce a current of one ampere through a resistance of one ohm.

W

Welding Various processes used to join metal items by heating the areas to be joined to a molten state and fusing them together. For more information refer to the *Haynes Automotive Welding Manual*.

Wiring diagram A drawing portraying the components and wires in a vehicle's electrical system, using standardised symbols. For more information refer to the *Haynes Automotive Electrical and Electronic Systems Manual*.

Note: *References throughout this index relate to Chapter•page number*

C

Cables - 4•9, 5•2, 7B•3, 9•12
Calipers - 9•4
Cam followers - 2B•11
Camshaft - 2A•12, 2B•11
Carburettor - 4•10, 4•11
Carpets - 11•2
Catalytic converter - 4•20, 6•6
Central locking - 12•8
Centre console - 11•9
Charging - 1•17, 5•9
Chemicals - REF•18
Choke - 4•13
Clutch and driveline - 8•1 *et seq*
Clutch fault finding - REF•12
Clutch fluid - 1•3, 1•9
CO level adjustment - 1•15, REF•4
Coil - 5•5
Coil springs - 10•7, 10•9
Cold start injectors - 4•17, 4•18
Compression check - 2B•4
Compressor - 3•14
Condenser - 3•14
Connecting rods - 2B•12, 2B•16, 2B•21
Constant velocity (CV) joint - 8•2, 8•8, 8•9
Continuity check - 12•2
Control arm - 10•4, 10•5
Conversion factors - REF•17
Coolant - 1•3, 1•8
Coolant pump - 3•5
Coolant temperature sender unit - 3•6
Coolant temperature sensor - 6•2
Cooling fan - 3•4
Cooling, heating and air conditioning systems - 1•21, 1•24, 3•1 *et seq*
Cooling system fault finding - REF•12
Crankshaft - 2A•12, 2A•13, 2A•19, 2B•13, 2B•17, 2B•19, 2B•20
Cruise control - 12•3, 12•8
Crushing - 0•5
Cushion - 11•9
CV joints - 8•2, 8•8, 8•9
Cylinder head - 2A•13, 2B•7, 2B•10, 2B•12
Cylinder honing - 2B•15

D

Dents in bodywork - 11•2
Differential (final drive) - 8•2, 8•10, 8•11
Differential oil - 1•3, 1•19, 1•26
Direction indicators - 12•2, 12•3
Discs - 1•22, 9•5
Distributor - 1•18, 5•4
Door - 11•6, 11•8, REF•2
Drivebelts - 1•14
Driveplate - 2A•18
Driveshafts - 1•22, 8•2, 8•9
Drums - 1•23

E

Earth check - 12•2
Electric fan - 3•4
Electric shock - 0•5
Electric windows - 12•9

Electrical equipment - REF•2
Electrical system fault finding - 12•1
Electronic control system - 4•3, 4•14
Electronic control unit (ECU) - 6•1
Engine fault finding - REF•10
Engine tune-up - 1•7
Engine electrical systems - 5•1 *et seq*
Engine electrical systems fault finding - REF•11
Engine management and emission control systems - 6•1 *et seq*
Engine oil - 1•3, 1•7, 1•11
Environmental considerations - REF•8
Evaporative emissions control (EVAP) system - 1•26, 6•5
Evaporator - 3•15
Exhaust emission checks - REF•4
Exhaust manifold - 2A•6
Exhaust system - 1•21, 4•20, REF•3

F

Fan - 3•4, 3•5
Fault finding - REF•9 *et seq*
Fault finding - automatic transmission - 7B•2, REF•13
Fault finding - braking system - REF•14
Fault finding - clutch - REF•12
Fault finding - cooling system - REF•12
Fault finding - electrical system - 12•1, REF•11
Fault finding - engine - REF•10
Fault finding - fuel system - 4•21, REF•12
Fault finding - manual transmission - REF•13
Fault finding - suspension and steering - REF•15
Filling - 11•3
Final drive - 8•2, 8•10, 8•11
Final drive oil - 1•3, 1•19, 1•26
Fire - 0•5
Flexible coupling - 8•7
Fluid level checks - 1•7
Fluid seals - 7B•5
Flywheel - 2A•18
Fuel and exhaust systems - 1•20, 4•1 *et seq*, REF•4
Fuel system fault finding - REF•12
Fuel filter - 1•25
Fuel hoses - 1•14
Fuel injection system - 4•3, 4•14
Fuel injection system - fault finding - 4•21
Fuel injectors - 4•18
Fuel level sender unit - 4•5, 4•6
Fuel lines and fittings - 4•7
Fuel pressure - 4•3
Fuel pressure regulator - 4•16
Fuel pump - 4•3, 4•4, 4•5
Fuel tank - 4•7, 4•8
Fume or gas intoxication - 0•5
Fuses - 12•2, 12•9

G

Gaiters - 1•22, 8•9, 10•13
Gashes in bodywork - 11•2
Gaskets - REF•8
Gear lever - 7A•1
Gearbox - See *Manual transmission*
Gearbox oil - 1•3, 1•19, 1•25
General engine overhaul procedures - 2B•1 *et seq*
Glass - 11•4, 11•8
Glossary of technical terms - REF•20
Grille - 11•4

Haynes Manuals – The Complete List

Title	Book No.
ALFA ROMEO	
Alfa Romeo Alfasud/Sprint (74 - 88) up to F	0292
Alfa Romeo Alfetta (73 - 87) up to E	0531
AUDI	
Audi 80 (72 - Feb 79) up to T	0207
Audi 80, 90 (79 - Oct 86) up to D & Coupe (81 - Nov 88) up to F	0605
Audi 80, 90 (Oct 86 - 90) D to H & Coupe (Nov 88 - 90) F to H	1491
Audi 100 (Oct 82 - 90) up to H & 200 (Feb 84 - Oct 89) A to G	0907
Audi 100 & A6 Petrol & Diesel (May 91 - May 97) H to P	3504
Audi A4 (95 - Feb 00) M to V	3575
AUSTIN	
Austin A35 & A40 (56 - 67) *	0118
Austin Allegro 1100, 1300, 1.0, 1.1 & 1.3 (73 - 82)*	0164
Austin Healey 100/6 & 3000 (56 - 68) *	0049
Austin/MG/Rover Maestro 1.3 & 1.6 (83 - May 95) up to M	0922
Austin/MG Metro (80 - May 90) up to G	0718
Austin/Rover Montego 1.3 & 1.6 (84 - 94) A to L	1066
Austin/MG/Rover Montego 2.0 (84 - 95) A to M	1067
Mini (59 - 69) up to H	0527
Mini (69 - Oct 96) up to P	0646
Austin/Rover 2.0 litre Diesel Engine (86 - 93) C to L	1857
BEDFORD	
Bedford CF (69 - 87) up to E	0163
Bedford/Vauxhall Rascal & Suzuki Supercarry (86 - Oct 94) C to M	3015
BMW	
BMW 1500, 1502, 1600, 1602, 2000 & 2002 (59 - 77)*	0240
BMW 316, 320 & 320i (4-cyl) (75 - Feb 83) up to Y	0276
BMW 320, 320i, 323i & 325i (6-cyl) (Oct 77 - Sept 87) up to E	0815
BMW 3-Series (Apr 91 - 96) H to N	3210
BMW 3- & 5-Series (sohc) (81 - 91) up to J	1948
BMW 520i & 525e (Oct 81 - June 88) up to E	1560
BMW 525, 528 & 528i (73 - Sept 81) up to X	0632
CITROËN	
Citroën 2CV, Ami & Dyane (67 - 90) up to H	0196
Citroën AX Petrol & Diesel (87 - 97) D to P	3014
Citroën BX (83 - 94) A to L	0908
Citroën C15 Van Petrol & Diesel (89 - Oct 98) F to S	3509
Citroën CX (75 - 88) up to F	0528
Citroën Saxo Petrol & Diesel (96 - 01) N to X	3506
Citroën Visa (79 - 88) up to F	0620
Citroën Xantia Petrol & Diesel (93 - 98) K to S	3082
Citroën XM Petrol & Diesel (89 - 00) G to X	3451
Citroën Xsara Petrol & Diesel (97 - Sept 00) R to W	3751
Citroën ZX Diesel (91 - 98) J to S	1922
Citroën ZX Petrol (91 - 98) H to S	1881
Citroën 1.7 & 1.9 litre Diesel Engine (84 - 96) A to N	1379
FIAT	
Fiat 126 (73 - 87) *	0305
Fiat 500 (57 - 73) up to M	0090
Fiat Bravo & Brava (95 - 00) N to W	3572
Fiat Cinquecento (93 - 98) K to R	3501
Fiat Panda (81 - 95) up to M	0793
Fiat Punto Petrol & Diesel (94 - Oct 99) L to V	3251
Fiat Regata (84 - 88) A to F	1167
Fiat Tipo (88 - 91) E to J	1625
Fiat Uno (83 - 95) up to M	0923
Fiat X1/9 (74 - 89) up to G	0273
FORD	
Ford Anglia (59 - 68) *	0001
Ford Capri II (& III) 1.6 & 2.0 (74 - 87) up to E	0283

Title	Book No.
Ford Capri II (& III) 2.8 & 3.0 (74 - 87) up to E	1309
Ford Cortina Mk III 1300 & 1600 (70 - 76) *	0070
Ford Cortina Mk IV (& V) 1.6 & 2.0 (76 - 83) *	0343
Ford Cortina Mk IV (& V) 2.3 V6 (77 - 83) *	0426
Ford Escort Mk I 1100 & 1300 (68 - 74) *	0171
Ford Escort Mk I Mexico, RS 1600 & RS 2000 (70 - 74)*	0139
Ford Escort Mk II Mexico, RS 1800 & RS 2000 (75 - 80)*	0735
Ford Escort (75 - Aug 80) *	0280
Ford Escort (Sept 80 - Sept 90) up to H	0686
Ford Escort & Orion (Sept 90 - 00) H to X	1737
Ford Fiesta (76 - Aug 83) up to Y	0334
Ford Fiesta (Aug 83 - Feb 89) A to F	1030
Ford Fiesta (Feb 89 - Oct 95) F to N	1595
Ford Fiesta (Oct 95 - 01) N-reg. onwards	3397
Ford Focus (98 - 01) S to Y	3759
Ford Granada (Sept 77 - Feb 85) up to B	0481
Ford Granada & Scorpio (Mar 85 - 94) B to M	1245
Ford Ka (96 - 02) P-reg. onwards	3570
Ford Mondeo Petrol (93 - 99) K to T	1923
Ford Mondeo Diesel (93 - 96) L to N	3465
Ford Orion (83 - Sept 90) up to H	1009
Ford Sierra 4 cyl. (82 - 93) up to K	0903
Ford Sierra V6 (82 - 91) up to J	0904
Ford Transit Petrol (Mk 2) (78 - Jan 86) up to C	0719
Ford Transit Petrol (Mk 3) (Feb 86 - 89) C to G	1468
Ford Transit Diesel (Feb 86 - 99) C to T	3019
Ford 1.6 & 1.8 litre Diesel Engine (84 - 96) A to N	1172
Ford 2.1, 2.3 & 2.5 litre Diesel Engine (77 - 90) up to H	1606
FREIGHT ROVER	
Freight Rover Sherpa (74 - 87) up to E	0463
HILLMAN	
Hillman Avenger (70 - 82) up to Y	0037
Hillman Imp (63 - 76) *	0022
HONDA	
Honda Accord (76 - Feb 84) up to A	0351
Honda Civic (Feb 84 - Oct 87) A to E	1226
Honda Civic (Nov 91 - 96) J to N	3199
HYUNDAI	
Hyundai Pony (85 - 94) C to M	3398
JAGUAR	
Jaguar E Type (61 - 72) up to L	0140
Jaguar MkI & II, 240 & 340 (55 - 69) *	0098
Jaguar XJ6, XJ & Sovereign; Daimler Sovereign (68 - Oct 86) up to D	0242
Jaguar XJ6 & Sovereign (Oct 86 - Sept 94) D to M	3261
Jaguar XJ12, XJS & Sovereign; Daimler Double Six (72 - 88) up to F	0478
JEEP	
Jeep Cherokee Petrol (93 - 96) K to N	1943
LADA	
Lada 1200, 1300, 1500 & 1600 (74 - 91) up to J	0413
Lada Samara (87 - 91) D to J	1610
LAND ROVER	
Land Rover 90, 110 & Defender Diesel (83 - 95) up to N	3017
Land Rover Discovery Petrol & Diesel (89 - 98) G to S	3016
Land Rover Series IIA & III Diesel (58 - 85) up to C	0529
Land Rover Series II, IIA & III Petrol (58 - 85) up to C	0314
MAZDA	
Mazda 323 (Mar 81 - Oct 89) up to G	1608
Mazda 323 (Oct 89 - 98) G to R	3455
Mazda 626 (May 83 - Sept 87) up to E	0929
Mazda B-1600, B-1800 & B-2000 Pick-up (72 - 88) up to F	0267
Mazda RX-7 (79 - 85) *	0460

Title	Book No
MERCEDES-BENZ	
Mercedes-Benz 190, 190E & 190D Petrol & Diesel (83 - 93) A to L	3450
Mercedes-Benz 200, 240, 300 Diesel (Oct 76 - 85) up to C	111
Mercedes-Benz 250 & 280 (68 - 72) up to L	0346
Mercedes-Benz 250 & 280 (123 Series) (Oct 76 - 84) up to B	0677
Mercedes-Benz 124 Series (85 - Aug 93) C to K	3253
Mercedes-Benz C-Class Petrol & Diesel (93 - Aug 00) L to W	3511
MG	
MGA (55 - 62) *	0475
MGB (62 - 80) up to W	0111
MG Midget & AH Sprite (58 - 80) up to W	0265
MITSUBISHI	
Mitsubishi Shogun & L200 Pick-Ups (83 - 94) up to M	1944
MORRIS	
Morris Ital 1.3 (80 - 84) up to B	0705
Morris Minor 1000 (56 - 71) up to K	0024
NISSAN	
Nissan Bluebird (May 84 - Mar 86) A to C	1223
Nissan Bluebird (Mar 86 - 90) C to H	1473
Nissan Cherry (Sept 82 - 86) up to D	1031
Nissan Micra (83 - Jan 93) up to K	0931
Nissan Micra (93 - 99) K to T	3254
Nissan Primera (90 - Aug 99) H to T	1851
Nissan Stanza (82 - 86) up to D	0824
Nissan Sunny (May 82 - Oct 86) up to D	0895
Nissan Sunny (Oct 86 - Mar 91) D to H	1378
Nissan Sunny (Apr 91 - 95) H to N	3219
OPEL	
Opel Ascona & Manta (B Series) (Sept 75 - 88) up to F	0316
Opel Ascona (81 - 88) (Not available in UK see Vauxhall Cavalier 0812)	3215
Opel Astra (Oct 91 - Feb 98) (Not available in UK see Vauxhall Astra 1832)	3156
Opel Astra & Zafira Diesel (Feb 98 - Sept 00) (See Astra & Zafira Diesel Book No. 3797)	
Opel Astra & Zafira Petrol (Feb 98 - Sept 00) (See Vauxhall/Opel Astra & Zafira Petrol Book No. 3758)	
Opel Calibra (90 - 98) (See Vauxhall/Opel Calibra Book No. 3502)	
Opel Corsa (83 - Mar 93) (Not available in UK see Vauxhall Nova 0909)	3160
Opel Corsa (Mar 93 - 97) (Not available in UK see Vauxhall Corsa 1985)	3159
Opel Frontera Petrol & Diesel (91 - 98) (See Vauxhall/Opel Frontera Book No. 3454)	
Opel Kadett (Nov 79 - Oct 84) up to B	0634
Opel Kadett (Oct 84 - Oct 91) (Not available in UK see Vauxhall Astra & Belmont 1136)	3196
Opel Omega & Senator (86 - 94) (Not available in UK see Vauxhall Carlton & Senator 1469)	3157
Opel Omega (94 - 99) (See Vauxhall/Opel Omega Book No. 3510)	
Opel Rekord (Feb 78 - Oct 86) up to D	0543
Opel Vectra (Oct 88 - Oct 95) (Not available in UK see Vauxhall Cavalier 1570)	3158
Opel Vectra Petrol & Diesel (95 - 98) (Not available in UK see Vauxhall Vectra 3396)	3523
PEUGEOT	
Peugeot 106 Petrol & Diesel (91 - 01) J to X	1882
Peugeot 205 Petrol (83 - 97) A to P	0932
Peugeot 206 Petrol and Diesel (98 - 01) S to X	3757
Peugeot 305 (78 - 89) up to G	0538

* Classic reprint

Title	Book No.
Peugeot 306 Petrol & Diesel (93 - 99) K to T	3073
Peugeot 309 (86 - 93) C to K	1266
Peugeot 405 Petrol (88 - 97) E to P	1559
Peugeot 405 Diesel (88 - 97) E to P	3198
Peugeot 406 Petrol & Diesel (96 - 97) N to R	3394
Peugeot 505 (79 - 89) up to G	0762
Peugeot 1.7/1.8 & 1.9 litre Diesel Engine (82 - 96) up to N	0950
Peugeot 2.0, 2.1, 2.3 & 2.5 litre Diesel Engines (74 - 90) up to H	1607

PORSCHE
Title	Book No.
Porsche 911 (65 - 85) up to C	0264
Porsche 924 & 924 Turbo (76 - 85) up to C	0397

PROTON
Title	Book No.
Proton (89 - 97) F to P	3255

RANGE ROVER
Title	Book No.
Range Rover V8 (70 - Oct 92) up to K	0606

RELIANT
Title	Book No.
Reliant Robin & Kitten (73 - 83) up to A	0436

RENAULT
Title	Book No.
Renault 4 (61 - 86) *	0072
Renault 5 (Feb 85 - 96) B to N	1219
Renault 9 & 11 (82 - 89) up to F	0822
Renault 18 (79 - 86) up to D	0598
Renault 19 Petrol (89 - 94) F to M	1646
Renault 19 Diesel (89 - 96) F to N	1946
Renault 21 (86 - 94) C to M	1397
Renault 25 (84 - 92) B to K	1228
Renault Clio Petrol (91 - May 98) H to R	1853
Renault Clio Diesel (91 - June 96) H to N	3031
Renault Clio Petrol & Diesel (May 98 - May 01) R to Y	3906
Renault Espace Petrol & Diesel (85 - 96) C to N	3197
Renault Fuego (80 - 86) *	0764
Renault Laguna Petrol & Diesel (94 - 00) L to W	3252
Renault Mégane & Scénic Petrol & Diesel (96 - 98) N to R	3395
Renault Mégane & Scénic (Apr 99 - 02) T-reg onwards	3916

ROVER
Title	Book No.
Rover 213 & 216 (84 - 89) A to G	1116
Rover 214 & 414 (89 - 96) G to N	1689
Rover 216 & 416 (89 - 96) G to N	1830
Rover 211, 214, 216, 218 & 220 Petrol & Diesel (Dec 95 - 98) N to R	3399
Rover 414, 416 & 420 Petrol & Diesel (May 95 - 98) M to R	3453
Rover 618, 620 & 623 (93 - 97) K to P	3257
Rover 820, 825 & 827 (86 - 95) D to N	1380
Rover 3500 (76 - 87) up to E	0365
Rover Metro, 111 & 114 (May 90 - 98) G to S	1711

SAAB
Title	Book No.
Saab 90, 99 & 900 (79 - Oct 93) up to L	0765
Saab 95 & 96 (66 - 76) *	0198
Saab 99 (69 - 79) *	0247
Saab 900 (Oct 93 - 98) L to R	3512
Saab 9000 (4-cyl) (85 - 98) C to S	1686

SEAT
Title	Book No.
Seat Ibiza & Cordoba Petrol & Diesel (Oct 93 - Oct 99) L to V	3571
Seat Ibiza & Malaga (85 - 92) B to K	1609

SKODA
Title	Book No.
Skoda Estelle (77 - 89) up to G	0604
Skoda Favorit (89 - 96) F to N	1801
Skoda Felicia Petrol & Diesel (95 - 01) M to X	3505

SUBARU
Title	Book No.
Subaru 1600 & 1800 (Nov 79 - 90) up to H	0995

SUNBEAM
Title	Book No.
Sunbeam Alpine, Rapier & H120 (67 - 76) *	0051

SUZUKI
Title	Book No.
Suzuki SJ Series, Samurai & Vitara (4-cyl) (82 - 97) up to P	1942
Suzuki Supercarry & Bedford/Vauxhall Rascal (86 - Oct 94) C to M	3015

TALBOT
Title	Book No.
Talbot Alpine, Solara, Minx & Rapier (75 - 86) up to D	0337
Talbot Horizon (78 - 86) up to D	0473
Talbot Samba (82 - 86) up to D	0823

TOYOTA
Title	Book No.
Toyota Carina E (May 92 - 97) J to P	3256
Toyota Corolla (Sept 83 - Sept 87) A to E	1024
Toyota Corolla (80 - 85) up to C	0683
Toyota Corolla (Sept 87 - Aug 92) E to K	1683
Toyota Corolla (Aug 92 - 97) K to P	3259
Toyota Hi-Ace & Hi-Lux (69 - Oct 83) up to A	0304

TRIUMPH
Title	Book No.
Triumph Acclaim (81 - 84) *	0792
Triumph GT6 & Vitesse (62 - 74) *	0112
Triumph Herald (59 - 71) *	0010
Triumph Spitfire (62 - 81) up to X	0113
Triumph Stag (70 - 78) up to T	0441
Triumph TR2, TR3, TR3A, TR4 & TR4A (52 - 67)*	0028
Triumph TR5 & 6 (67 - 75) *	0031
Triumph TR7 (75 - 82) *	0322

VAUXHALL
Title	Book No.
Vauxhall Astra (80 - Oct 84) up to B	0635
Vauxhall Astra & Belmont (Oct 84 - Oct 91) B to J	1136
Vauxhall Astra (Oct 91 - Feb 98) J to R	1832
Vauxhall/Opel Astra & Zafira Diesel (Feb 98 - Sept 00) R to W	3797
Vauxhall/Opel Astra & Zafira Petrol (Feb 98 - Sept 00) R to W	3758
Vauxhall/Opel Calibra (90 - 98) G to S	3502
Vauxhall Carlton (Oct 78 - Oct 86) up to D	0480
Vauxhall Carlton & Senator (Nov 86 - 94) D to L	1469
Vauxhall Cavalier 1300 (77 - July 81) *	0461
Vauxhall Cavalier 1600, 1900 & 2000 (75 - July 81) up to W	0315
Vauxhall Cavalier (81 - Oct 88) up to F	0812
Vauxhall Cavalier (Oct 88 - 95) F to N	1570
Vauxhall Chevette (75 - 84) up to B	0285
Vauxhall Corsa (Mar 93 - 97) K to R	1985
Vauxhall/Opel Corsa (Apr 97 - Oct 00) P to X	3921
Vauxhall/Opel Frontera Petrol & Diesel (91 - Sept 98) J to S	3454
Vauxhall Nova (83 - 93) up to K	0909
Vauxhall/Opel Omega (94 - 99) L to T	3510
Vauxhall Vectra Petrol & Diesel (95 - 98) N to R	3396
Vauxhall/Opel 1.5, 1.6 & 1.7 litre Diesel Engine (82 - 96) up to N	1222

VOLKSWAGEN
Title	Book No.
Volkswagen 411 & 412 (68 - 75) *	0091
Volkswagen Beetle 1200 (54 - 77) up to S	0036
Volkswagen Beetle 1300 & 1500 (65 - 75) up to P	0039
Volkswagen Beetle 1302 & 1302S (70 - 72) up to L	0110
Volkswagen Beetle 1303, 1303S & GT (72 - 75) up to P	0159
Volkswagen Beetle Petrol & Diesel (Apr 99 - 01) T reg onwards	3798
Volkswagen Golf & Bora Petrol & Diesel (April 98 - 00) R to X	3727

Title	Book No.
Volkswagen Golf & Jetta Mk 1 1.1 & 1.3 (74 - 84) up to A	0716
Volkswagen Golf, Jetta & Scirocco Mk 1 1.5, 1.6 & 1.8 (74 - 84) up to A	0726
Volkswagen Golf & Jetta Mk 1 Diesel (78 - 84) up to A	0451
Volkswagen Golf & Jetta Mk 2 (Mar 84 - Feb 92) A to J	1081
Volkswagen Golf & Vento Petrol & Diesel (Feb 92 - 96) J to N	3097
Volkswagen LT vans & light trucks (76 - 87) up to E	0637
Volkswagen Passat & Santana (Sept 81 - May 88) up to E	0814
Volkswagen Passat Petrol & Diesel (May 88 - 96) E to P	3498
Volkswagen Passat 4-cyl Petrol & Diesel (Dec 96 - Nov 00) P to X	3917
Volkswagen Polo & Derby (76 - Jan 82) up to X	0335
Volkswagen Polo (82 - Oct 90) up to H	0813
Volkswagen Polo (Nov 90 - Aug 94) H to L	3245
Volkswagen Polo Hatchback Petrol & Diesel (94 - 99) M to S	3500
Volkswagen Scirocco (82 - 90) up to H	1224
Volkswagen Transporter 1600 (68 - 79) up to V	0082
Volkswagen Transporter 1700, 1800 & 2000 (72 - 79) up to V	0226
Volkswagen Transporter (air-cooled) (79 - 82) up to Y	0638
Volkswagen Transporter (water-cooled) (82 - 90) up to H	3452
Volkswagen Type 3 (63 - 73) *	0084

VOLVO
Title	Book No.
Volvo 120 & 130 Series (& P1800) (61 - 73) *	0203
Volvo 142, 144 & 145 (66 - 74) up to N	0129
Volvo 240 Series (74 - 93) up to K	0270
Volvo 262, 264 & 260/265 (75 - 85) *	0400
Volvo 340, 343, 345 & 360 (76 - 91) up to J	0715
Volvo 440, 460 & 480 (87 - 97) D to P	1691
Volvo 740 & 760 (82 - 91) up to J	1258
Volvo 850 (92 - 96) J to P	3260
Volvo 940 (90 - 96) H to N	3249
Volvo S40 & V40 (96 - 99) N to V	3569
Volvo S70, V70 & C70 (96 - 99) P to V	3573

AUTOMOTIVE TECHBOOKS
Title	Book No.
Automotive Air Conditioning Systems	3740
Automotive Brake Manual	3050
Automotive Carburettor Manual	3288
Automotive Diagnostic Fault Codes Manual	3472
Automotive Diesel Engine Service Guide	3286
Automotive Electrical and Electronic Systems Manual	3049
Automotive Engine Management and Fuel Injection Systems Manual	3344
Automotive Gearbox Overhaul Manual	3473
Automotive Service Summaries Manual	3475
Automotive Timing Belts Manual – Austin/Rover	3549
Automotive Timing Belts Manual – Ford	3474
Automotive Timing Belts Manual – Peugeot/Citroën	3568
Automotive Timing Belts Manual – Vauxhall/Opel	3577
Automotive Welding Manual	3053
In-Car Entertainment Manual (3rd Edition)	3363

* Classic reprint

CL13.4/02

Preserving Our Motoring Heritage

< The Model J Duesenberg Derham Tourster. Only eight of these magnificent cars were ever built – this is the only example to be found outside the United States of America

Almost every car you've ever loved, loathed or desired is gathered under one roof at the Haynes Motor Museum. Over 300 immaculately presented cars and motorbikes represent every aspect of our motoring heritage, from elegant reminders of bygone days, such as the superb Model J Duesenberg to curiosities like the bug-eyed BMW Isetta. There are also many old friends and flames. Perhaps you remember the 1959 Ford Popular that you did your courting in? The magnificent 'Red Collection' is a spectacle of classic sports cars including AC, Alfa Romeo, Austin Healey, Ferrari, Lamborghini, Maserati, MG, Riley, Porsche and Triumph.

A Perfect Day Out

Each and every vehicle at the Haynes Motor Museum has played its part in the history and culture of Motoring. Today, they make a wonderful spectacle and a great day out for all the family. Bring the kids, bring Mum and Dad, but above all bring your camera to capture those golden memories for ever. You will also find an impressive array of motoring memorabilia, a comfortable 70 seat video cinema and one of the most extensive transport book shops in Britain. The Pit Stop Cafe serves everything from a cup of tea to wholesome, home-made meals or, if you prefer, you can enjoy the large picnic area nestled in the beautiful rural surroundings of Somerset.

> John Haynes O.B.E., Founder and Chairman of the museum at the wheel of a Haynes Light 12.

< Graham Hill's Lola Cosworth Formula 1 car next to a 1934 Riley Sports.

The Museum is situated on the A359 Yeovil to Frome road at Sparkford, just off the A303 in Somerset. It is about 40 miles south of Bristol, and 25 minutes drive from the M5 intersection at Taunton.
Open 9.30am - 5.30pm (10.00am - 4.00pm Winter) 7 days a week, *except Christmas Day, Boxing Day and New Years Day*
Special rates available for schools, coach parties and outings Charitable Trust No. 292048